Less managing. More teaching. Greater learning.

 INSTRUCTORS...

Would you like your **students** to show up for class more **prepared**? *(Let's face it, class is much more fun if everyone is engaged and prepared...)*

Want ready-made application-level **interactive assignments,** student progress reporting, and auto-assignment grading? *(Less time grading means more time teaching...)*

Want an **instant view of student or class performance** relative to learning objectives? *(No more wondering if students understand...)*

Need to **collect data and generate reports** required for administration or accreditation? *(Say goodbye to manually tracking student learning outcomes...)*

Want to **record and post your lectures** for students to view online?

 With **McGraw-Hill's** *Connect® Plus Organizational Behavior,*

INSTRUCTORS GET:

- Interactive Applications – **book-specific interactive assignments** that require students to APPLY what they've learned.

- Simple **assignment management,** allowing you to spend more time teaching.

- **Auto-graded** assignments, quizzes, and tests.

- **Detailed Visual Reporting** where student and section results can be viewed and analyzed.

- Sophisticated **online testing** capability.

- A **filtering and reporting** function that allows you to easily assign and report on materials that are correlated to accreditation standards, learning outcomes, and Bloom's taxonomy.

- An easy-to-use **lecture capture** tool.

Want an online, **searchable version** of your textbook?

Wish your textbook could be **available online** while you're doing your assignments?

 ### *Connect® Plus Organizational Behavior* eBook

If you choose to use *Connect® Plus Organizational Behavior*, you have an affordable and searchable online version of your book integrated with your other online tools.

Connect® Plus Organizational Behavior eBook offers features like:

- Topic search
- Direct links from assignments
- Adjustable text size
- Jump to page number
- Print by section

 Want to get more **value** from your textbook purchase?

Think learning management should be a bit more **interesting**?

 ### Check out the STUDENT RESOURCES section under the *Connect®* Library tab.

Here you'll find a wealth of resources designed to help you achieve your goals in the course. You'll find things like **quizzes, PowerPoints, and Internet activities** to help you study. Every student has different needs, so explore the STUDENT RESOURCES to find the materials best suited to you.

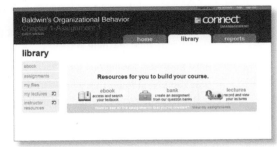

MANAGING ORGANIZATIONAL BEHAVIOR

What Great Managers Know and Do

SECOND EDITION

Timothy T. Baldwin
Indiana University

William H. Bommer
California State University, Fresno

Robert S. Rubin
DePaul University

MANAGING ORGANIZATIONAL BEHAVIOR: WHAT GREAT MANAGERS KNOW AND DO

Published by McGraw-Hill/Irwin, a business unit of The McGraw-Hill Companies, Inc., 1221 Avenue of the Americas, New York, NY, 10020. Copyright © 2013, 2008 by The McGraw-Hill Companies, Inc. All rights reserved. Printed in the United States of America. No part of this publication may be reproduced or distributed in any form or by any means, or stored in a database or retrieval system, without the prior written consent of The McGraw-Hill Companies, Inc., including, but not limited to, in any network or other electronic storage or transmission, or broadcast for distance learning.

Some ancillaries, including electronic and print components, may not be available to customers outside the United States.

This book is printed on acid-free paper.

7 8 9 10 11 12 QVS 22 21 20 19 18

ISBN 978-0-07-353040-6
MHID 0-07-353040-9

Vice president and editor-in-chief: *Brent Gordon*
Editorial director: *Paul Ducham*
Executive editor: *John Weimeister*
Executive director of development: *Ann Torbert*
Development editor: *Jane Beck*
Editorial coordinator: *Heather Darr*
Vice president and director of marketing: *Robin J. Zwettler*
Marketing director: *Amee Mosley*
Senior marketing manager: *Michelle Heaster*
Vice president of editing, design, and production: *Sesha Bolisetty*
Senior project manager: *Diane L. Nowaczyk*
Buyer II: *Debra R. Sylvester*
Senior designer: *Mary Kazak Sander*
Senior photo research coordinator: *Jeremy Cheshareck*
Photo researcher: *Ira C. Roberts*
Lead media project manager: *Daryl Horrocks*
Media project manager: *Suresh Babu, Hurix Systems Pvt. Ltd.*
Cover and interior design: *Kay Lieberherr*
Cover image: *Jan Greune/Getty Images*
Typeface: *10/12 New Aster LT Std*
Compositor: *Laserwords Private Limited*
Printer: *LSC Communications*

Library of Congress Cataloging-in-Publication Data

Baldwin, Timothy T.
    Managing organizational behavior : what great managers know and do / Timothy T. Baldwin, William H. Bommer, Robert S. Rubin. — 2nd ed.
        p. cm.
    Rev. ed. of: Developing management skills : what great managers know and do / Timothy T. Baldwin, William H. Bommer, Robert S. Rubin. 2008
    Includes index.
    ISBN-13: 978-0-07-353040-6 (alk. paper)
    ISBN-10: 0-07-353040-9 (alk. paper)
    1. Management—Study and teaching. 2. Organizational behavior. 3. Executive ability.
I. Bommer, William. II. Rubin, Robert S. III. Baldwin, Timothy T. Developing management skills. IV. Title.
HD30.4.B355 2013
658.4'07124—dc23

2011040779

www.mhhe.com

To JoEllen—25 years together and I can't imagine the journey without you.
—*Tim Baldwin*

To the kids—always a test of my management skills.
—*Bill Bommer*

To Leah—the glue that holds us all together.
—*Bob Rubin*

TIMOTHY (Tim) T. BALDWIN is the Eveleigh Professor of Business Leadership at the Indiana University Kelley School of Business. Professor Baldwin holds a PhD in organizational behavior and an MBA from Michigan State University. He has published his research work in leading academic and professional outlets, including the *Academy of Management Journal, Journal of Applied Psychology, Personnel Psychology, Journal of Management, Leadership Quarterly*, and *Academy of Management Learning & Education*. He has won several national research awards including eight Best Paper Awards from the Management Education & Development division of the Academy of Management. He has twice been the recipient of the Richard A. Swanson Excellence in Research Award presented by the American Society for Training & Development (ASTD). He is the co-author of *Improving Transfer Systems in Organizations* (Jossey-Bass: 2003) and his current research interests include leadership development and organizational training effectiveness.

In his time at Indiana University, Tim has been recognized frequently for teaching excellence, winning eight MBA Teaching Awards, the Eli Lilly Alumni Teaching Award, the FACET All-University Teaching Award, and the Dow Innovation in Teaching Fellowship. He is a proud member of the Organizational Behavior Teaching Society (OBTS) and a passionate supporter of the mission of that organization to improve teaching effectiveness in our discipline.

Tim's background includes consultation with Cummins Engine, Eli Lilly, FedEx, Ingersoll Rand, Whirlpool, and a variety of other organizations in both the public and private sectors. He has also designed and delivered numerous executive education seminars in the U.S. and abroad, including the Kelley School's Asia-Pacific Management Development program. He serves on the Board of Directors of Cripe Architects & Engineers, Inc., a professional services firm based in Indianapolis.

Tim is married with one son, one dog, one cat, and until recently, one gerbil (a sad story, and the cat is implicated). His interests include coaching youth sports, golf, basketball, gardening, and a little amateur magic.

WILLIAM (Bill) H. BOMMER earned his master's degree in organizational development from Bowling Green State University, and his PhD in organizational behavior from Indiana University. He is currently a professor of management in the Craig School of Business at California State University, Fresno. Prior to his move to California, Bill served as faculty at Bowling Green State University, Southern Illinois University at Edwardsville, Georgia State University, and Cleveland State University.

Bill has published widely in the management area in journals including the *Academy of Management Journal, Academy of Management Learning & Education, Leadership Quarterly, Organizational Behavior and Human Decision Processes, Personnel Psychology, Journal of Applied Psychology, Journal of Management, Journal of Vocational Behavior*, and *Organization Science*. His current research interests include transformational leadership, organizational and personal change, and the linkage between attitudes and behavior.

Prior to entering academia, Bill worked as a financial analyst and as a group process consultant in private industry. Bill has remained active in his business relationships and has designed and led numerous executive education programs over the last 15 years. In support of his research interests, he has served as a trainer and consultant to a large number of manufacturing companies across the United States and has had a long-term relationship with the Centers for Disease Control. In this capacity, Bill has designed corporate universities for his clients. Bill is also managing partner of Collegiate Assessment Partners (CAPs), a company that builds management skills assessment tools and consults with university business schools in support of their learning objectives and their compliance with accreditation standards. When not involved with teaching, researching, or consulting, Bill enjoys traveling, hiking, eating, and cycling.

Robert (Bob) S. Rubin is an associate professor of management in the Kellstadt Graduate School of Business at DePaul University. He received his BA in psychology from Indiana University, his MA in industrial-organizational psychology from Southern Illinois University at Edwardsville, and his PhD in organizational psychology from Saint Louis University.

Bob specializes in human resource management and organizational behavior at DePaul, where he is an avid and award-winning teacher committed to advancing the field of management education. He has been nationally recognized for his dedication to management andragogy and scholarship, including multiple Best Paper Awards from the Management Education Division of the Academy of Management. His research interest centers on individual differences and their role in effective leadership and management development and includes forays into aspects of transformational leadership, managerial assessment and development, academic assessment centers, and emotions at work. Bob has published his work in leading academic journals such as *Academy of Management Journal, Journal of Applied Psychology, Personnel Psychology, Journal of Management, Academy of Management Learning & Education, The Leadership Quarterly, Journal of Organizational Behavior,* and *Journal of Management Education.* Currently, Bob is an editorial board member of three journals, the *Academy of Management Learning & Education, Journal of Organizational Behavior,* and *Leadership and Organizational Studies.*

In addition to his academic work, Bob has been an active human resources and organization development consultant to a variety of industries including biotechnology, health care, dentistry, and transportation. His consulting work has spanned employee selection, management assessment, and development. Bob also frequently serves as a coach for purposes of management skill development. When he's not engaged in managing his more senior textbook co-authors (Note: He had a full head of hair prior to beginning this book project), Bob enjoys playing music, traveling, hiking, and wrestling with his three kids.

"The great thing about having a PhD is when people do not understand you, they think it's them."

—Henry Kissinger

A Different Kind of Textbook—Because Teaching and Learning OB Are *Hard Enough!*

Contemporary students put extraordinary demands on OB instructors and textbooks alike. On one hand, students immersed in quantitative courses such as finance and accounting and other business disciplines are often quick to dismiss OB/management courses as "soft" or "elementary" or "common sense"—so there is a pressing need for relevance and richness. On the other hand, modern technology and short attention spans have created an aversion to the theoretical grounding and evidence-based education necessary to build true understanding and applicable skills.

Thoughtful **OB** and management instructors are therefore often torn between opting for a traditional descriptive text, strong on concepts and definitions, but with little application focus, or choosing a more popular-press reading, strong on war-story anecdotes and prescriptions (often more popular with students), but short on theory and evidence.

Recognizing this tension in our own **OB** classrooms, we set out to create a book (and ancillary package) with an express mission of **balance.** To work for us, the book would have to be one that students would find engaging but also would have the coverage, rigor, and evidence base demanded of professional **OB** and management instructors. So this text is evidence-based but targeted to application. It covers traditional **OB** topics but in a decision-oriented, not just descriptive, way. It embraces the best **OB** models and evidence but engages students in how to use those models to improve their skill-sets and more successfully navigate organizational life. Just as the book's title conveys, it is about both *knowing* and *doing*. It is expressly designed to reconcile student demands for relevance and application with instructor interests in rigor, evidence, and appropriate coverage of the discipline. We know firsthand that teaching **OB** today is akin to straddling a glacier crevasse and this book is designed in that spirit.

Put another way, we saw our charge as creating a book that would inform, illuminate, and inspire. We wanted to *inform* students of the best and most current knowledge about organizational behavior and its application to management contexts. We wanted to *illuminate* those concepts with the most vivid and memorable examples and illustrations. And we wanted to *inspire* learners by capturing and conveying the challenge and excitement and even playfulness involved in managing and working with people. To do that, we found it appropriate to diverge from conventional textbooks in several significant ways, and we briefly highlight those choices in the following.

"Ideal management education should reorient its priorities and focus on skill training. A great deal is known about inculcating such skills, but the knowledge does not typically make its way into the business curriculum."

—Henry Mintzberg, McGill University

Skills and Decisions vs. Concepts and Description

For whatever reason, almost every leading OB textbook today still has a decidedly *descriptive* orientation. For example, team effectiveness may *sound* like a very applied topic. Yet most textbook chapters so titled deal exclusively with the different types of teams, comparisons of individual and team decision making, theories of team development and conflict, and so on. In most cases, the information is accurate, but it leaves students marginally prepared to work effectively in a team.

Similarly, chapters on motivation and leadership often trace the history of research and theory in those areas but end up not directly addressing the skills and behaviors a student needs to actually motivate others or lead a group or a change project. Our goal in this text was to get beyond description to skill development and decisions, that is, not just what defines a good group, but how one might make a group function better. Our goal was to translate from description to decisions—from OB *concepts* to organizational and managerial *action*.

Student-Centric Evidence and Learning vs. Comprehensive Body of Knowledge

In recent years, we have come to understand much more about how students actually consume textbook material. As a result, we approached the process of writing this book in a different way than perhaps a traditional textbook might be written. For example, in selecting the content for each chapter in this book, we purposively did *not* start by spreading out all of the existing textbooks and looking at all the accumulated knowledge about that topic. Rather, we began with the key questions, problems, and challenges people face in, say, managing time, communicating a persuasive message, overcoming resistance to change, or dealing with a problem team member, and then turned to the existing literature to build chapters around those problems.

Indeed, as we wrote each chapter, we adopted a position akin to editors of *Consumer Reports* magazine. That is, we tried to test assumptions about what students *really read and consume,* and what instructors *really use* from a textbook. And we asked ourselves: What do *we* want to use? What material connects with students? What are the best readings and exercises? What material do we rarely or never use? We call this *student-centric* material.

The Russian author Tolstoy once insightfully noted that *"all happy families resemble each other, but each unhappy family is unhappy in its own way."* Similarly, we would contend that all effective managers resemble one another, but poor ones are ineffective in their own unique ways. And the first phase of competence is how readily and skillfully novices can respond to routine situations, not simply their ability to handle unusual ones. So we should strive less for comprehensiveness and more on achieving fundamental skills and knowledge that can help aspiring managers operate in the most core and recurring situations commonly faced (e.g., our Manage *What?* scenarios that frame each chapter are designed to do just that). Our goal was to include the material and evidence, and *only* that material and evidence, that might be labeled "mission critical." The book is relatively short in order to do important things well, rather than attempt to superficially cover the waterfront.

We hasten to add, however, that to suggest that students today want nothing to do with research, or want their texts "dumbed down," is both inaccurate and condescending. Indeed, our experience is that students *do* want to know the origins of what they are being taught—provided the research helps bring concepts to life. For example, a fascinating recent study found that monkeys will turn down very desirable food if they know that *other* fellow monkeys are getting even more desirable food. In our view, this is a terrific illustration of the intense power of equity perceptions, and something that is likely to stick with students in their study of motivational concepts.

Hearing the Voice of the Student vs. Pushing the Discipline

We like to think that our "partners" in writing this book were the many students and practicing managers who have been in our courses, completed our surveys, and shared with us the ideas, tools, quotations, and "little gems" that helped them develop and refine their own skills. Indeed, over the last few years we have asked our students to interview practicing managers and to find out how those managers would evaluate the organizational behavior and management courses they took in college. In doing so, the managers frequently pointed out that courses focused a lot of attention on theories and concepts but, in their view, focused too little on relevant prescriptive principles and *skills*. They were challenged most by the "people problems" in their work, and yet felt their management education had not emphasized, or adequately prepared them for, that component of their job. So in writing this text, we tried to consistently take into account what those who ultimately must go and practice management most need to know.

Finally, in the course of writing this book we were often asked how our book would differ from popular-press books. In responding to that we are always quick to clarify that we certainly do not consider "popular" to be synonymous with *bad*. Indeed, there are some wonderful and useful popular works that we draw from in this book. We do, however, think the distinction between this book and many of the popular-press books on similar topics is pronounced and critically important. In our view, any book targeted to students in a university context must provide exposure to the "whys," that is, the conceptual foundation of skills. We think this book's defining value is its practicality and usefulness, but we contend that this is so *because* it is based on good theory and research, not because we *avoided* the important conceptual grounding.

The OB Teaching Challenge: Aiming for Balance

We believe that inculcating OB/management skills is perhaps the greatest challenge in business education today—and it is time to more directly and intentionally take on that challenge. Few people question the analytic capability of today's graduating students—but the jury is still out on their interpersonal and leadership competence. We think a skills-based, decision-oriented approach, manifest in this text, is critical to addressing that challenge. In sum, working and managing effectively in organizations today is an act of supreme balance—and our hope is that we have created a textbook that is true to that charge.

Features of the Book

Manage *What?*

One of our favorite teaching colleagues is an accounting professor who enjoys pointing out to us that, while every organization has accounting, information systems, and marketing departments, he has *never* heard of a corporation that has a management department. He further chides us that having a degree in management invites the question, *"Management of what?"* In reality, he is a passionate advocate for improving the management skills of his accounting students and even pushed us to write this text. But his observation raises an important issue.

One of the legitimate criticisms of OB and management courses and textbooks, even those with a stated skills focus, is that they tend to be rather abstract about what is really being managed. There is often a curious lack of focus on the specifics of what managers are challenged to do, and on how great professionals might respond to those challenges.

With that in mind, we decided to open each chapter with a section we call Manage *What?* The Manage *What?* feature consists of several fundamental and specific questions or challenges related to the skill focus of that chapter. For example, in the chapter on *team effectiveness,* one scenario poses a challenge regarding how to deal with members who are not pulling their weight. In the *motivation* chapter, one of the scenarios addresses how to diagnose and deal with a person who shows little desire to do better work, and so on. So that students can conduct a "skills check," we have also included selected critiques or debriefings of how a skilled manager might have proceeded on the Manage *What?* scenarios. We have intentionally, however, not included all of the debriefs at the end of the chapters. Some of the debriefs are only available in the instructor's manual so that those critiques can be distributed to students at any point— or sometimes as the key when we use the Manage *What?* scenarios as exam questions.

Taken together, the Manage *What?* scenarios comprise a set of the most fundamental of management skills. They are hardly comprehensive—there is clearly much more to learn about management (and in the book) than how to handle just those scenarios—but the set is a concrete start toward isolating the mainstream and recurring things that great managers do well.

Our accounting professor friend likes to heighten student interest by pointing out how his course material is good preparation to become a CPA (certified public accountant). We would contend that an understanding and mastery of the Manage *What?* scenarios would likewise constitute a good step toward becoming a hypothetical CPM or "certified people manager." No such certification actually exists, but we have sought to include the recurring skills we would expect someone to demonstrate to be certified as a great manager if there were such a reputable credential. Those skills are the focus of the Manage *What?* scenarios.

Management Live

We doubt there is an OB/management instructor alive who would deny the critical importance of illustration and examples in helping students develop the skills of great managers. So, in addition to liberally using examples in the text itself, we also have created a separate feature designed to highlight the most vivid and engaging illustrations, stories, and short cases we could find. We call the section Management Live to capture the spirit of those illustrations, which is expressly to enliven the text and bring to life the concepts in ways meaningful and memorable to learners.

"Example is not the main thing in influencing others. It is the only thing."

—Albert Schweitzer

Learning theorists have begun using the term "stickiness" to describe learning stimuli that ultimately stay with learners, and that very much captures the spirit of this feature of the book. Our experience is that our students often recall specific cases and examples long after they have forgotten lectures and text. So our goal was to infuse each chapter with Management Live examples that catch attention, strike the imagination, and really do "stick" with students as examples and guides.

Manager's Tool Kits

An irrefutable aspect of applying skills is to have a good set of tools. In our executive education work, we have been struck by how much participants appreciate "takeaways" like self-assessments, good forms, quick checklists, and so on. Although we have never been particularly focused on such takeaways for our degree students, it occurred to us that such tools would be useful for *anyone* trying to improve his or her management skills. Indeed, a fundamental supposition of the evidence-based management movement is that once evidence is well established, it should be codified into practice through the use of checklists or other decision supports. In this spirit, we therefore embed several Manager's Tool Kits into each chapter. For example, the *performance management* chapter has Manager's Tool Kits for choosing the right performance evaluation method, analyzing a performance problem, and terminating or reassigning an employee. The *motivation* chapter has a quick guide to rewarding effectively, the *conflict* chapter includes a checklist for effective mediation, and so on. The Manager's Tool Kits are presented in a way that students can copy and actually make use of them now or in the future. Taken collectively, the Manager's Tool Kits comprise something of a management skills manual. We make no claims that these are original or novel or provocative or anything fancy at all. However, they are the things that make their way onto managers' office doors, desktop frames, purse cards, and so on.

Contemporary Cases

Contemporary OB teaching is hard because students often think that OB teaching is *not* contemporary. That is unfortunate because many of the most progressive and "hottest" companies today are, in fact, wonderful exemplars of the best of OB practice. For example, Google's recent investigation into what makes a great boss at the firm turned up a list of characteristics that have been validated for years by OB researchers. Zappos' 10 cultural commandments read like a synthesis of OB research on high-performance cultures. Facebook, Microsoft, and leading hospitality firms do *not* rely on low-validity unstructured interviews and subjective selection practices favored by too many organizations. Rather, they employ the most valid of selection procedures supported by decades of rigorous research.

It was these observations that prompted us in this edition of our text to open each chapter with a case that would satisfy our students' craving for examples that are (a) *authentic*—what they like to call "real world," and (b) *current and relevant*. We expressly sought firms that would strike their imagination, and our goal was to show a clear linkage between what they are reading in the text and the application of those concepts in the most progressive and admired of today's organizations. So we have endeavored to include cases that have that character at the end of each of our chapters. A master list of the contemporary cases is shown below:

Chapter 1 – eHarmony
Chapter 2 – CIGNA
Chapter 3 – Threadless and ChallengePost
Chapter 4 – TRUTHY
Chapter 5 – Tableau
Chapter 6 – Ritz-Carlton
Chapter 7 – The Dallas Mavericks
Chapter 8 – Klout
Chapter 9 – Google
Chapter 10 – Team Concepts
Chapter 11 – The NFL Players Association
Chapter 12 – Google, Microsoft, Southwest Airlines, and Doubletree Hotels
Chapter 13 – Zappos
Chapter 14 – The Indiana Bureau of Motor Vehicles

Ancillaries

It is hardly provocative to suggest that the ways students learn today have changed rather dramatically from a generation ago. Just as iPods have changed the way music is delivered and consumed, so too has the Internet, wireless technology, and portable video capability transformed the way learners consume education. Moreover, learning researchers have long recognized that students have different learning styles: some favoring reading and reflection, and others engaged more by visual depictions and hands-on experience.

The instructional implication is that the most successful courses will be those that expose learners to *multiple* educational stimuli. With that in mind, we have supplemented this text with a set of supporting resources designed to facilitate the learning of management skills in multiple ways. Central to these support materials are the Online Learning Center (OLC) at **www.mhhe.com/baldwin2e** and McGraw-Hill *Connect Organizational Behavior.*

In summary, we have tried to translate our own experiences in the classroom into a package of learning stimuli that will both appeal to and challenge students of organizational behavior and management. Although sometimes characterized as being elementary or commonsensical, great management is neither common nor easy, and the existence of so many ineffective managers and toxic organizations attests to that. We firmly believe that many aspects of management can be learned, but it takes a focus on skills and a more concerted effort to bring those skills to life than many of our traditional learning materials provide. Our hope is that this text and set of ancillaries will be useful in that regard—but we consider it all a work in progress. We actively invite your input as we all try to foster better-managed organizations and healthy and engaging places to work.

"Happiness is coming to class and seeing the video projector set up."
—Charlie Brown

McGraw-Hill *Connect®* Organizational Behavior

Less Managing. More Teaching. Greater Learning.

McGraw-Hill *Connect Organizational Behavior* is an online assignment and assessment solution that connects students with the tools and resources they'll need to achieve success. McGraw-Hill *Connect Organizational Behavior* helps prepare students for their future by enabling faster learning, more efficient studying, and higher retention of knowledge.

McGraw-Hill *Connect Organizational Behavior* Features

Connect Organizational Behavior offers a number of powerful tools and features to make managing assignments easier, so faculty can spend more time teaching. With *Connect Organizational Behavior,* students can engage with their coursework anytime and anywhere, making the learning process more accessible and efficient. *Connect Organizational Behavior* offers you the features described next.

Simple Assignment Management

With *Connect Organizational Behavior,* creating assignments is easier than ever, so you can spend more time teaching and less time managing. The assignment management function enables you to:

- Create and deliver assignments easily with selectable end-of-chapter questions and test bank items.

- Streamline lesson planning, student progress reporting, and assignment grading to make classroom management more efficient than ever.
- Go paperless with the ebook and online submission and grading of student assignments.

Smart Grading

When it comes to studying, time is precious. *Connect Organizational Behavior* helps students learn more efficiently by providing feedback and practice material when they need it, where they need it. When it comes to teaching, your time also is precious. The grading function enables you to:

- Have assignments scored automatically, giving students immediate feedback on their work and side-by-side comparisons with the correct answers.
- Access and review each response; manually change grades or leave comments for students to review.
- Reinforce classroom concepts with practice tests and instant quizzes.

Instructor Library

The *Connect Organizational Behavior* Instructor Library is your repository for additional resources to improve student engagement in and out of class. You can select and use any asset that enhances your lecture. The *Connect Organizational Behavior* Instructor Library includes:

- Instructor's manual
- PowerPoint slides
- Test bank
- The *Connect Organizational Behavior* ebook

Student Study Center

The *Connect Organizational Behavior* Student Study Center is the place for students to access additional resources. The Student Study Center:

- Offers students quick access to lectures, practice materials, ebooks, and more.
- Provides instant practice material and study questions; easily accessible on the go.
- Gives students access to the Personalized Learning Plan described next.

Student Progress Tracking

Connect Organizational Behavior keeps instructors informed about how each student, section, and class is performing, allowing for more productive use of lecture and office hours. The progress-tracking function enables you to:

- View scored work immediately and track individual or group performance with assignment and grade reports.
- Access an instant view of student or class performance relative to learning objectives.
- Collect data and generate reports required by many accreditation organizations, such as AACSB.

Lecture Capture

Increase the attention paid to lecture discussions by decreasing the attention paid to note-taking. For an additional charge, Lecture Capture offers new ways for students to focus on the in-class discussion, knowing they can revisit important topics later. Lecture Capture enables you to:

- Record and distribute your lecture with a click of a button.
- Record and index PowerPoint presentations and anything shown on your computer so it is easily searchable, frame by frame.
- Offer access to lectures anytime and anywhere by computer, iPod, or mobile device.
- Increase intent listening and class participation by easing students' concerns about note-taking. Lecture Capture will make it more likely you will see students' faces, not the tops of their heads.

McGraw-Hill *Connect Plus*® *Organizational Behavior*

McGraw-Hill reinvents the textbook learning experience for the modern student with *Connect **Plus** Organizational Behavior*. A seamless integration of an ebook and *Connect Organizational Behavior, Connect **Plus** Organizational Behavior* provides all of the *Connect Organizational Behavior* features, plus the following:

- An integrated ebook, allowing for anytime, anywhere access to the textbook.
- Dynamic links between the problems or questions you assign to your students and the location in the ebook where that problem or question is covered.
- A powerful search function to pinpoint and connect key concepts in a snap.

In short, *Connect Organizational Behavior* offers you and your students powerful tools and features that optimize your time and energies, enabling you to focus on course content, teaching, and student learning. *Connect Organizational Behavior* also offers a wealth of content resources for both instructors and students. This state-of-the-art, thoroughly tested system supports you in preparing students for the world that awaits.

For more information about *Connect*, go to **www.mcgrawhillconnect.com,** or contact your local McGraw-Hill sales representative.

Tegrity Campus: Lectures 24/7

Tegrity Campus is a service that makes class time available 24/7 by automatically capturing every lecture in a searchable format for students to review when they study and complete assignments. With a simple one-click start-and-stop process, you capture all computer screens and corresponding audio. Students can replay any part of any class with easy-to-use browser-based viewing on a PC or Mac.

Educators know that the more students can see, hear, and experience class resources, the better they learn. In fact, studies prove it. With Tegrity Campus, students quickly recall key moments by using Tegrity Campus's unique search feature. This search helps students efficiently find what they need, when they need it, across an entire semester of class recordings. Help turn all your students' study time into learning moments immediately supported by your lecture.

To learn more about Tegrity, watch a two-minute Flash demo at **http://tegrity campus.mhhe.com.**

Assurance of Learning Ready

Many educational institutions today are focused on the notion of *assurance of learning,* an important element of some accreditation standards. *Managing Organizational Behavior: What Great Managers Know and Do,* Second Edition, is designed specifically to support your assurance of learning initiatives with a simple yet powerful solution.

Each test bank question for *Managing Organizational Behavior: What Great Managers Know and Do,* Second Edition, maps to a specific chapter learning outcome/objective listed in the text. You can use our test bank software, EZ Test and EZ Test Online, or *Connect Organizational Behavior* to easily query for learning outcomes/objectives that directly relate to the learning objectives for your course. You can then use the reporting features of EZ Test to aggregate student results in a similar fashion, making the collection and presentation of assurance of learning data simple and easy.

AACSB Statement

The McGraw-Hill Companies is a proud corporate member of AACSB International. Understanding the importance and value of AACSB accreditation, *Managing Organizational Behavior: What Great Managers Know and Do,* Second Edition, recognizes the curricula guidelines detailed in the AACSB standards for business accreditation by connecting selected questions in the test bank to the six general-knowledge and skill guidelines in the AACSB standards.

The statements contained in *Managing Organizational Behavior: What Great Managers Know and Do,* Second Edition, are provided only as a guide for the users of this textbook. The AACSB leaves content coverage and assessment within the purview of individual schools, the mission of the school, and the faculty. While *Managing Organizational Behavior: What Great Managers Know and Do,* Second Edition, and the teaching package make no claim of any specific AACSB qualification or evaluation, we have within *Managing Organizational Behavior: What Great Managers Know and Do,* Second Edition, labeled selected questions according to the six general-knowledge and skills areas.

McGraw-Hill Customer Care Contact Information

At McGraw-Hill, we understand that getting the most from new technology can be challenging. That's why our services don't stop after you purchase our products. You can e-mail our Product Specialists 24 hours a day to get product-training online. Or you can search our knowledge bank of Frequently Asked Questions on our support website. For Customer Support, call **800-331-5094,** e-mail **hmsupport@mcgraw-hill.com,** or visit **www.mhhe.com/support.** One of our Technical Support Analysts will be able to assist you in a timely fashion.

McGraw-Hill Higher Education and Blackboard Have Teamed Up. What Does This Mean for You?

1. **Your life, simplified.** Now you and your students can access McGraw-Hill's *Connect* and Create™ right from within your Blackboard course—all with one single sign-on. Say goodbye to the days of logging in to multiple applications.

2. **Deep integration of content and tools.** Not only do you get single sign-on with *Connect* and Create™; you also get a deep integration of McGraw-Hill content and content engines right in Blackboard. Whether you're choosing a book for your course or building *Connect* assignments, all the tools you need are right where you want them—inside of Blackboard.

3. **Seamless gradebooks.** Are you tired of keeping multiple gradebooks and manually synchronizing grades into Blackboard? We thought so. When a student completes an integrated *Connect* assignment, the grade for that assignment automatically (and instantly) feeds your Blackboard grade center.

4. **A solution for everyone.** Whether your institution is already using Blackboard or you just want to try Blackboard on your own, we have a solution for you. McGraw-Hill and Blackboard can now offer you easy access to industry-leading technology and content, whether your campus hosts it, or we do. Be sure to ask your local McGraw-Hill representative for details.

Changes from the First Edition

The response to our first edition was immensely gratifying, as OB and management instructors seem to be gravitating toward a more skills-oriented and decision-making approach. Among the most favored elements of the original edition was our overt recognition of the knowing–doing gap and the features that engaged students to think about personal and managerial action rather than just the learning of descriptive concepts.

We also received many useful ideas for enhancing the text and have tried to incorporate those ideas into this new edition. Among the most significant changes, this new edition includes:

- ***Broader coverage to better fit OB courses.*** While many of our adoptions *were* for OB courses, and all three authors use the book in such courses at their respective institutions (Indiana University, California State University–Fresno, and DePaul University) feedback suggested that some instructors, who otherwise were attracted to the skills-oriented approach, did not find the book quite broad enough for their OB course. In response, we restructured the text by adding some significant content and brand-new chapters, resulting in a text that more fully reflects the scope and evidence base of organizational behavior. Naturally, we changed the title to reflect this substantial restructuring.

  Note that there was no divergence from our skills-orientation or our focus on personal and managerial action. Indeed, we retained the subtitle

(What Great Managers Know and Do) and intentionally included some content that has *not* typically been part of most traditional OB books (for example, performance management, selecting and retaining talent, change management, and so on), because the evidence is clear that these areas are *essential* to effective management and therefore critical in exposing students to what great managers *really* know and do. Importantly, these topics are all discussed from a *manager's* perspective and should not interfere with or detract from other functional courses such as human resource management, but rather reinforce the close ties between organizational behavior and human resource management in actual practice. In short, our aim was to make the book better-suited to fit the content and structure of a typical OB course. And while not for everyone, we do think the text is a great option for those instructors who feel drawn to take a more skills-based and decision-oriented approach to their OB or management skills course

- *Knowing and Doing Objectives.* As our subtitle suggests, great management is about both knowing and doing, and so we now overtly include *both* knowing and doing learning objectives at the outset of each chapter. Instructors (and administrators) have told us that this feature is very useful for those schools concerned with assurance of learning (AACSB), alignment of curriculum to objectives, and related issues that are so ubiquitous in business schools.

- *Addition of Contemporary Cases and Discussion Questions* (with debriefs for instructors). We consistently hear from our students—and now from fellow instructors using the book—that contemporary students want more cases and examples of OB ideas in practice. So we heeded that call by adding two cases to every chapter—most of them drawn from progressive contemporary firms that best capture student interest. We also include accompanying discussion questions that challenge students to wrestle with ideas from the book using context from the most exciting and interesting contemporary firms.

- *Embedded Manager's Tool Kits.* Staying true to our focus on knowing and doing, the new edition integrates the Manager's Tool Kits (which used to appear at the end of the chapter) directly into the chapter text. We think this embedding makes the popular book feature more user-friendly and, most importantly, facilitates more efficient transition from knowledge to action.

- *More Manage What? Challenges—and New Debriefs.* Any student of math knows how important "problem sets" are in facilitating the transition from knowing principles to solving actual problems correctly. Moreover, it is *really* wonderful to have the *answers* to those problem sets in the back of the book. We think OB learning is analogous. So we have added more of our popular Manage *What?* challenges that appear at the opening to every chapter. Moreover, in this edition we have also added answers so that students can compare their responses to expert commentary on how to address the challenge. On the advice of our book adopters, however, the debrief to at least one such challenge in each chapter is still provided only to instructors so it can be used as an evaluation tool if an instructor so chooses.

- *Enhanced Ancillaries and Video Supplements.* In today's contemporary classroom, it takes more than a textbook to bring a class to life. So the book comes complete with an entirely new set of ancillaries, including McGraw-Hill's innovative *Connect* program.

WALKTHROUGH

An Applied Text for an Applied Topic

In a world full of challenging analytic courses such as finance, accounting, and computer science, students are often quick to dismiss OB/management courses as "soft" or "common sense" or "just theory." Unfortunately, many existing textbooks serve only to support those misconceptions. Teaching and learning organizational behavior and management are hard enough—your textbook shouldn't make it harder.

So, unlike other textbooks today, *Managing Organizational Behavior: What Great Managers Know and Do*, Second Edition, is written with a style and purpose to fit the demands of contemporary students and instructors. While including full coverage of the most important OB models and evidence, the book's distinct value is its focus on the *skills and decisions* required to function effectively as a manager (or individual contributor) in today's organizations. Unlike traditional texts, the authors draw from the best OB theory and models to describe how to develop the right mix of skills—and how those skills can be implemented in contemporary contexts. The distinctive features of the text include the following.

Addresses the Knowing–Doing Gap

The most formidable challenge to OB learning is not knowing but *doing*—and this book is expressly focused on facilitating the transition from knowing principles to solving actual problems. Put another way, when it comes to behaving effectively in organizations, there is no knowledge advantage without an *action* advantage.

As the text subtitle *(What Great Managers Know and Do)* suggests, the authors engage students to think specifically about personal and managerial action rather than just learning descriptive concepts. Toward that end, every chapter opens with a section called *Manage What?* which consists of several fundamental and specific challenges related to the topical focus of the chapter. These scenarios are great for class discussions or written assignments and focus on recurring skills that are fundamental to any manager's success. Moreover, at the end of each chapter are debriefs or "answers" to those challenges that describe how skilled professionals would best respond.

MANAGE *WHAT?*

1. Making a Difficult Ethical Choice

You have worked for your boss for five years, and he has become a trusted mentor for you in the firm. Indeed, there is no one in the firm toward whom you feel more respect or loyalty. You just met with him and, due to an unforeseen market downturn, he let you know of a proposed layoff that will affect one of the three people who report to you (Joe). Because the decision has not been announced, and it will surely send shockwaves through the firm, he asked that you absolutely not tell any of your subordinates. In fact, concerned the information might get prematurely leaked, he even says, "It is critically important that no one know. Can I count on you?" You agreed emphatically that he could. Unfortunately, that evening you see Joe, who coaches a little league team with you. He tells you he and his wife have been accepted into an adoption process for a new child and he wanted to share his joy with you. He also has heard rumors of a layoff and says, sort of jokingly, "I am not going to be laid off, am I? We could never afford to take care of a new child without my income."

What should you do? Is this an ethical issue? You are forced to choose between loyalty and your expressed promise on one hand, and your sense of caring and honesty toward Joe (and his potential new child) on the other. What factors will you consider in your decision? On what basis would you justify the ethics of your decision?

2. You Be the Ethicist

Author Randy Cohen serves as The Ethicist for *The New York Times Sunday Magazine*. He frequently poses ethical dilemmas to his readers and an adapted set of those (and similar themes) are listed next. Respond to each of the following scenarios, being sure to identify the ethical frame (utilitarian, universalism, or virtuous person) you are using as the rationale for your response.

a. Is it ethical to buy a sweater to use for a family picture and then return it for a refund?

b. Is it ethical to download a song from the Internet without paying for it given that (a) you would not have downloaded it if you had to pay, (b) you have no money and the artist and record label (or Apple, Inc.) are beyond wealthy, (c) you are actually promoting the artist by listening to and sharing your impressions with others.

c. How much is a cat worth? Your affectionate and obedient cat needs a procedure that will cost a few hundred dollars. Your instinct is to pay for what she needs, but you can't help thinking it's wrong. Wouldn't the cash be better spent on sick humans?

d. Can you ethically round off your 2.958 GPA to 3.0 when using it on your resumé?

e. Is it OK to take those hotel shampoos and soaps and give them to homeless shelters?

f. Should you tell on someone you observe researching bomb-making on the Internet? Or on a friend having a too-friendly dinner with a woman who is not his wife?

g. Is it ethical to buy cheap seats to a baseball game you know will be sparsely attended and then sneak down and sit in the expensive seats? Similarly, is it ethical to grab open first-class seats (once everyone is on board and in their purchased seats) when you only paid for coach?

h. Is it ethical for a homeless mother to steal a loaf of bread to feed her starving child?

i. If you scored the wrong answer on a test, and the instructor marked it correct and you very honestly let him know, is it ethical for the instructor to let you keep the points and reward your honesty?

3. Creating a Culture That People View as Fair

You are a relatively new manager and times are tough at your firm. You know you are going to have to make some really tough decisions regarding promotions, job assignments, bonuses, and even who gets laid off and who stays. When you took your new management position two years ago, the firm was booming, and with ample resources to work with you thought to yourself that you would just give everyone the same rewards and schedules and anything you controlled and that would solve the problem. But now resources are scarce and you are worried that if people view your decisions as unfair you will run the risk of destroying your positive culture and even losing key people. If your goal is to create a fair workplace that is also a productive one, what should you do? What types of standards would you put in place and then how would you decide "who gets what"?

4. Being a Responsible Whistle-Blower

As a manager in your firm, you have become disturbed with some of the claims that are being made (by people in your marketing and sales group) about some of your products. Although you often work with that department, you are employed in a different function and not sure if you should "stick your nose" into that area. Moreover, although you feel something of an ethical obligation to ensure that no customers are harmed by false information, you also are very concerned that blowing the whistle in this case could prompt serious repercussions and potentially be detrimental to your career, cause the loss of trust and friends in the firm, and even impact your family.

Provides *Contemporary* Cases and Examples

One of the most frustrating student perceptions is that organizational behavior is irrelevant or old-fashioned. That is unfortunate because many of the most progressive and "hottest" companies today are, in fact, wonderful exemplars of the best of OB and management practice. So every chapter in this text opens with a case that will satisfy students' craving for examples that are (a) authentic—what they like to call "real world" and (b) current and relevant. The profiled firms (e.g., Google, Zappos, and eHarmony) are readily visible to students, strike their imagination, and show a clear linkage between what they are reading in their text and the application of those concepts in the most progressive and admired of modern organizations.

Written to Be "Sticky"

Another persistent student criticism of organizational behavior coursework is that it is too abstract or even "boring"—and given the nature of many existing texts, it is not hard to see how students might reach that conclusion. The spirit of this book was to infuse each chapter with examples that catch attention, strike imagination, and really do "stick" with students as examples and guides. Such examples are sprinkled liberally within the text, but there are also separate boxes labeled "Management Live" that highlight the most vivid and engaging illustrations, stories, and short cases that bring to life the concepts in ways meaningful and memorable to learners.

⇄ MANAGEMENT LIVE 1.2

The Best Places to Work Are Also the Best-Performing Companies

Independent financial analysts have studied the financial performance of the "100 Best" companies beginning with the publication of the book *The 100 Best Companies to Work for in America* (by Robert Levering and Milton Moskowitz, 1994), and have accompanied that with each of the "100 Best Companies" lists from *Fortune* since that list's inception in 1998. Using various profitability indicators, these data illustrate the extent to which the publicly traded 100 Best Companies consistently outperform major stock indices over the 10-year periods preceding the publication of the 100 Best lists. It is notable that those companies selected for the 100 Best list generally spend far more on employee benefits and services than their counterparts—that is, it is often *expensive* to be a best place to work. However, the data clearly support that the expense is worthwhile because people ultimately engage more fully, work productively, and lift company performance.

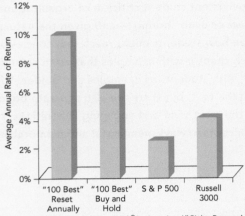

100 Best Companies to Work For vs. Overall Stock Market 1998–2010

Includes Pragmatic Tool Kits

An irrefutable aspect of applying skills is to have a good set of *tools*. Most executive education seminars and corporate training programs are known for providing participants with such tools for better conducting their work. Yet, while common-place in many business educational settings, for some reason the notion of tools and tool kits has not made its way into traditional college texts. This book rectifies that omission by embedding very practical "how to" tool kits in each chapter. These tool kits offer tangible takeaways for students through self-assessments, forms, and quick checklists.

MANAGER'S TOOL KIT

Tool Kit 1.2   Personal Quality Checklist[43]

Building on the principles of organizational quality improvement efforts, Bernie Sergesteketter and Harry Roberts have devised a tool for self-management called the personal quality checklist (PQC). Using their approach, you define desirable standards of personal behavior and performance and then keep track of failures or "defects" to meet those standards. The specific steps to the approach are:

1. **Draw up a checklist of standards.** This is the hardest part. Two samples are included at the end of this Tool Kit as illustrations (one by a practicing manager and one from a college student). Each standard should have a clear relationship to a "customer" either in the workplace or in your family or circle of friends. Each standard has to be unambiguously defined so you can recognize and tally a defect when it occurs. Thus, "get in shape" is not a good standard. A better standard would be to "break a sweat every day."

   There are two broad types of standards: (1) waste reducers/time savers (for example, be on time to class or group meetings), and (2) activity expanders (call parents at least once a week, get résumé completed). If you include all activity expanders on your list, be sure you have enough waste reducers and time savers to create free time for them.

2. **Tally your daily defects.** Defects should be tallied by days but can ultimately be aggregated by weeks or months. One intriguing strategy is to let others help you keep score. For example, if a checklist standard is to talk to your spouse only in respectful tones, or spend at least a half hour with your daughter each day, then your spouse or daughter may well be the best tally keeper for those standards.

3. **Review your tallies and action plan.** Some people find the word "defect" objectionable, but it is key to the system. First, it is easy to recognize and tally. Moreover, defects can become your friends because they suggest opportunities for improvement. Why did it occur? How can it be prevented? The whys lead to hows and suggest possible routes toward improvement.

Do not put faith in trying harder; you probably already are trying hard. Rather, figure out a different way to reach your objective. As the adage goes, rather than trying to be a better caterpillar, become a butterfly.

As a general rule you should stick with 10 or fewer standards, or the process becomes unwieldy and unfocused. Of course, your checklist standards will only be a small fraction of your activities. Your first PQC should focus on a few things you currently do that, if improved, could increase your customer satisfaction. Once you determine that you have those standards under control and customer satisfaction is high, then you can ask your colleagues and family for help in raising the bar and adding new standards. The approach is deceptively simple but powerful. Sergesteketter and Roberts report on a wide variety of successes by managers and executives from leading firms who have enjoyed success with the personal quality checklist approach. Draw up your own checklist and give it a try!

Sample Manager PQC

- On time for meetings
- Never need a haircut
- Answer phone in two rings
- No more than one project on desk at time
- Shoes always shined
- Weight below 190 pounds
- Exercise at least three times a week

Responsive to Management Education Critics

Few people question the analytic capability of today's graduating students—but the jury is still out on their managerial and interpersonal competence. Critics of business education are increasingly focusing on the development of OB/management skills as perhaps the greatest gap and challenge today—and it is time to more directly and intentionally take on that criticism and challenge. Although sometimes characterized as being elementary or common sense, great management is neither common nor easy, and the existence of so many ineffective managers and toxic organizations attests to that.

With those criticisms very much in mind, the overriding goal of this text is to help instructors inform, illuminate, and inspire. *Inform* students of the best and most solid and current evidence in organizational behavior and its application to management contexts—never "dumbing it down" or neglecting key theory or models. *Illuminate* those concepts with the most vivid and "sticky" examples and illustrations—not the tired old examples (often from dated manufacturing contexts) that have too often defined OB instruction in the past. And *inspire* learners by capturing and conveying the challenge and excitement and even playfulness involved in managing and working with people— not simply describing the concepts of the field.

We hope you will join in the crusade to redefine OB teaching and try to foster better-managed organizations and healthy and engaging places to work.

Heard from Past Adopters

"This text has proven ideal for my intro organizational behavior course. It blends sound theory and evidence—which I think is critical—with a practical skills orientation, engaging writing style, and contemporary flavor that my students really enjoy."

—Brian Blume, University of Michigan–Flint

"[This text provides an] even mix of concept, examples, and application/action. . . . In academic circles from years past, authors seemed to believe the more theory and cases, the better. But today, it is about telling them what they need to know, showing them how to do it, and then letting them experience the material. Students will like the text. This text, as indicated, covers everything, but it is application-based. [It has] enough theory and concept to move you forward, but [it is a] clear application so that you can move forward sooner."

—Stephen Peters, Clarkson College

"The focus of this text is exactly what I've been looking for. . . . It is more comprehensive, includes relevant research evidence for its propositions and the theories explained, and includes a truly relevant set of experiential exercises and examples."

—Deborah Erdos Knapp, PhD, Kent State University

Heard from the Workplace

One of the biggest challenges instructors face in teaching OB and management is helping students understand the importance of *starting now* to develop their managerial skills. Students are rightly focused on their first role after college—often analyst or individual contributor jobs that do not entail people management responsibility. But the misnomer is that OB and management skills are not important *right away*. As some recent graduates eloquently attest in their own words below, the reality is that, regardless of industry or job, managerial skills are a critical differentiator in the marketplace and are important very early in careers.

"I am now regularly trusted to manage teams of new hires joining us out of college and it happened so much earlier in my career than I ever expected. Having good management skills—so that you can lead your team to a common goal, teach them the skills they need to achieve success, and correct them when they veer astray—is just as important as your analytic competence. Once you build a high-performing team, their success makes you more valuable, and this will be evident to your own managers."

—Mason Duke, Private Equity Management

"Understanding how managers motivate and effectively utilize their subordinates is absolutely crucial for a new hire analyst. There are often situations in the workplace where your supervisor does not necessarily have your best interests in mind. This lack of support is not always malicious but can be driven by numerous factors, including competing priorities, upward pressure, or large spans of control. In these situations, understanding how to manage upwards is a powerful skill that can help you meet your professional objectives."

—Ricky P. Singh, Financial Services Industry

"The managerial skills that I learned in my behavioral management class have helped to catapult me into a position where I continue to grow and lead, where I am also the youngest in my group. I have been able to provide an open mind, solid work ethic, and great cost benefit analysis skills that put me in a different league. I have been able to show to my co-workers that leadership isn't always tied directly to age and experience."

—Megan Mennel, Real Estate Industry

"I work in a service industry where our assets are the people working for us; therefore managing them and motivating each of the team members individually is key to our success. A critical part of my job is to ensure that I inspire my team to grow and become future leaders of our business, thereby always focusing on a succession plan. This ensures that our business doesn't stagnate and continues to be a solid going concern."

—Shradha Adnani, Media Industry

Enhanced Ancillary Package

In today's contemporary classroom, it takes more than a textbook to bring a class to life. So the book comes complete with an entirely new set of ancillary resources designed for students and instructors—including McGraw Hill's innovative *Connect* program. Seamlessly integrated within the book's pedagogy, the OLC at **www.mhhe.com/baldwin2e** serves as a resource for both instructors and students. Instructors will find the following resources for each chapter in a password-protected location on the OLC:

- Comprehensive instructor's manual that contains chapter summaries, lecture outlines, suggested solutions to exercises in the text, and teaching notes to help instructors utilize the Management Live, Manager's Tool Kit, and Manage *What?* materials in each chapter.
- PowerPoint presentations that outline the key points, learning objectives, and exhibits in each chapter; the PPTs may be customized for each instructor's needs.
- Test banks that challenge students' application of the concepts covered in the text through multiple-choice, true-false, short-answer, and essay questions; each test bank question is tagged according to learning objective, Bloom's Taxonomy, AACSB guidelines, and level of difficulty.
- Interactive components in the form of the Asset Gallery (Manager's Hot-Seat videos, Self-Assessments, and Test Your Knowledge exercises) and suggested videos to accompany each chapter.

Students can refer to the OLC for chapter reviews, self-grading quizzes, and select premium content.

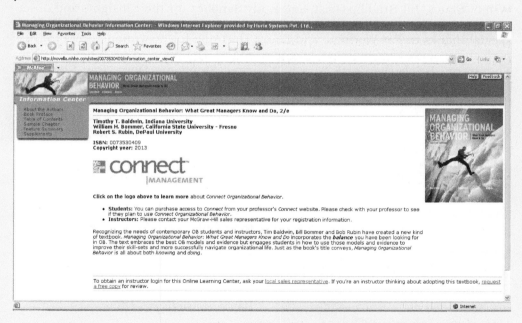

Ask your local McGraw-Hill sales representative how to gain access to the Asset Gallery and Premium Content for your course.

ACKNOWLEDGMENTS

No set of authors ever really endeavors to write a book by themselves, and we are grateful to so many people who have had a hand in helping this text come to life. Among those we would particularly like to recognize are Halden Williams and Corey Gallon, two young consulting stars at PricewaterhouseCoopers (Corey has since taken a promotion elsewhere) for their immense help in uncovering contemporary business cases that demonstrate how the concepts in the book are being used by progressive organizations worldwide. We are also indebted to Bob Marx of the University of Massachusetts and Mark Wellman at the University of Maryland for their excellent recommendations of cases, videos, and materials. Both Bob and Mark are widely acclaimed master teachers and we are fortunate to have their contributions to our text package.

All of our institutions are special places and we are indebted to many colleagues who have directly or indirectly contributed to this project. At Kelley, special thanks to Steve Whiting, Brian Blume (now at University of Michigan –Flint) and Jason Pierce who have all used the first edition of this book in their own classes and subsequently provided insights and feedback that have been instrumental in this new edition. Tim Baldwin would also like to acknowledge Al Oak, Fred Green, Denny Southerland, Bruce Breeden, and his many other great friends and colleagues at Cripe Architects and Engineers. He treasures that association, and many lessons from his connection there are incorporated into this text.

At Fresno State, special thanks to Jim Schmidtke, Brian Lyons (now at Wright State), Jill Bradley-Geist, and Rudy Sanchez for their insights and observations that have improved various aspects of the second edition. At DePaul, special thanks to Pat Werhane and Laura Hartman for providing access to their perfected course materials on business ethics. Thanks also to colleagues Ken Thompson, Erich Dierdorff, Alyssa Westring, Stephanie Dorn, Ray Coye, and Patricia Spencer for their many hall conversations that helped to inform the development of this book.

We are all indebted to John Weimeister, Jane Beck, Diane Nowaczyk, Anke Weeks, and Michelle Heaster of McGraw-Hill, who have supported this project with zeal and who love the author team more than ice cream.

A hearty thanks to you all!

We also gratefully acknowledge a sterling set of reviewers who include:

Valerie Atherley
Suffolk University

Forrest Aven
University of Houston, Downtown

Erica Berte
Indiana University–Purdue University, Columbus Center

Scott Bryant
Montana State University

Marian Crawford
University of Arkansas, Little Rock

George De Feis
Iona College

Beverly Dennis
Alaska Pacific University

Megan Endres
Eastern Michigan University

Mamdouh Farid
Hofstra University

Ann Fischer
University of Pennsylvania

Allen Frazier
Harding University

Mahmoud Gaballa
Mansfield University

Javier Garza
Cerritos College

Michele Gee
University of Wisconsin, Parkside

Barry Gold
Pace University, NYC

Joan Hartley
Portland Community College

Merrily Joy Hoffman
San Jacinto College Central

Melissa Houlette
College of Mt. Saint Joseph

John Humphreys
Texas A&M University, Commerce

Sharron Hunter-Rainey
North Carolina Central University

Uma Iyer
Austin Peay State University

John Jemison
Southwestern Assemblies of God University

Sirkwoo Jin
Merrimack College

Camille Johnson
San Jose State University

Paul Johnson
Western Carolina University

Dorothy Kirkman
University of Houston, Clear Lake

Mary Beth Klinger
College of Southern Maryland

Jack Kondrasuk
University of Portland

Arlene Kreinik
Western Connecticut State University

Don Larsen
Montana State University, Billings

Marc Lavine
University of Massachusetts, Boston

Lee Lee
Central Connecticut State University

David Maddox
Regis University

Kimberly Melinsky
College of St. Rose

Frances McDonald
Nova Community College, Annandale

Christine Miller
Tennessee Tech University

Tracy Miller
University of Dayton

Leann Mischel
Susquehanna University

Rakesh Mittal
New Mexico State University, Las Cruces

Lam Dang Nguyen
Palm Beach State College

David Nino
University of Houston, Downtown

Gianna Phillips
Golden Gate University

Emily Porschitz
Keene State College

Rosemarie Reynolds
Embry Riddle Aero University, Daytona Beach

DeShawn Robinson-Chew
Nova Community College, Woodbridge

Nancy Rossiter
Jacksonville University

Golnaz Sadri
California State University

Christy Shell
Houston Community College, Northwest College

Art Shriberg
Xavier University

Paula Silva
California State University, Fullerton

C. Mike Smith
Roanoke College

George Smith
Albright College

Chester Spell
Rutgers University, Camden

Shane Spiller
Western Kentucky University

Gil Taran
Carnegie Mellon University

Pat Thompson
Virginia Commonwealth University

Neil Tocher
Idaho State University

Tyra Townsend
University of Pittsburgh

William Turnley
Kansas State University

Anthony Urban
Rutgers University, Camden

Alix Valenti
University of Houston, Clear Lake

John Watt
University of Central Arkansas

Barbara Wech
University of Alabama, Birmingham

Joann White
Jackson State University

Robert Yamaguchi
Fullerton College

John Yudelson
California State University, Channel Islands

BRIEF CONTENTS

CONTENTS

PART ONE   PERSONAL SKILLS

CHAPTER 1 Organizational Behavior and Your Personal Effectiveness

CHAPTER 2 Managing Stress and Time

CHAPTER 3 Solving Problems

CHAPTER 4 Making Ethical Decisions

PART TWO   INTERPERSONAL SKILLS

CHAPTER 5 Communication

CHAPTER 6 Motivating Others

CHAPTER 7 Managing Employee Performance

CHAPTER 8 Using Power and Influence

CHAPTER 9 Leading Others

PART THREE   GROUP AND ORGANIZATIONAL SKILLS

CHAPTER 10 Team Effectiveness

CHAPTER 11 Resolving Conflict Through Negotiation and Mediation

CHAPTER 12 Recruiting, Selecting, and Retaining Talent

CHAPTER 13 Culture and Diversity

CHAPTER 14 Making Change

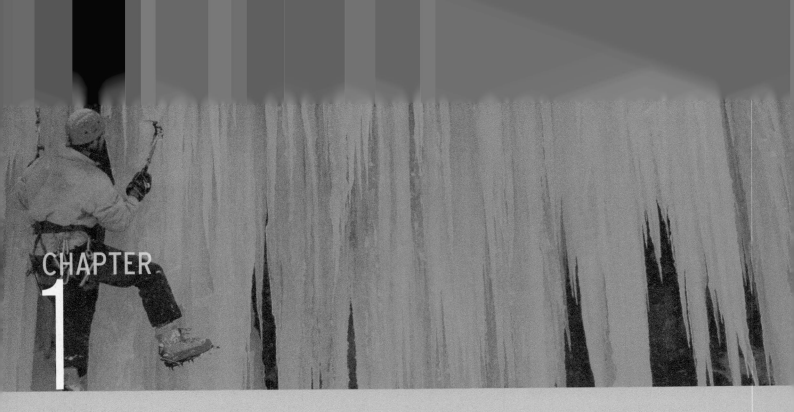

Organizational Behavior and Your Personal Effectiveness

OBJECTIVES

KNOWING　　　　　　　　**DOING**

After reading this chapter, you should be able to:

"If you want to be a great manager, the most fundamental lesson is that it starts with you. Know yourself. Listen to feedback. Build on your strengths. Do what you say you will do. Build a network of support. Be positive. If we can find people who do those things well, they tend ultimately to be successful managers."

—Al Oak, Chief Executive Officer, Cripe Architects & Engineers

KO 1-1　Describe the importance of people skills for achieving business success.

KO 1-2　Describe what is meant by evidence-based management.

KO 1-3　Define organizational behavior.

KO 1-4　Explain the role of organizational behavior and evidence-based management in effective management.

KO 1-5　Explain the steps involved in making a personal change.

KO 1-6　Describe the importance of self-awareness in becoming an effective manager.

DO 1-1　Develop a strong argument for the importance of people-skill development.

DO 1-2　Persuade a colleague to utilize evidence-based methods in management interventions.

DO 1-3　Apply evidence-based methods of self-management to make a personal improvement.

DO 1-4　Solicit high-quality feedback consistently with others.

DO 1-5　Demonstrate self-awareness by accurately describing your strengths and developmental needs.

Case: eHarmony

Founded in 1998 by Dr. Neil Warren and his son-in-law, Greg Forgatch, eHarmony was targeted to a segment of the e-dating market that had not been well served: singles seeking serious and sustainable relationships. That is, unlike other e-dating sites emerging at the time, the key selling point of eHarmony was matching people on the basis of *long-term* compatibility.

In an effort to create such long-lasting matches, Warren and his team felt they had to get much more information on singles than had been typically solicited by matchmaking services. Toward that end, before the launch of their website, they surveyed over 2,000 couples in an effort to discern the most critical personal information required to successfully match people for the long term. The result was the creation of the eHarmony Relationship Questionnaire, which had to be filled out by anyone who wanted to become an eHarmony member. Although originally much longer, today the questionnaire is 258 questions and takes about 45 minutes to complete.

Dr. Warren claims that the length of the questionnaire and the involvement required is an important part of the process because, since it is so time-consuming to sign up, eHarmony people self-select. This means that only those willing to go through the extensive process are ultimately included on the site. As Dr. Warren notes, "There is a shared sense of investment to be part of eHarmony. A full completion of the questionnaire says in effect, 'I'm really serious about this . . .'"

Today, eHarmony is millions of members strong and claims tens of thousands of successful matches. TV commercials regularly trumpet the success of their system and the many wonderful long-term matches and marriages that have resulted.

1. Relative to other matchmaking services, why has eHarmony been so successful?

2. What is it about the eHarmony approach that seems to promote long-term matches? Why is self-awareness so important here?

3. What are the most important things you would want to know about a potential partner? If you were to see two eHarmony profiles, what would be the most important aspects of a match? For example, would you look solely for shared interests and preferences?

4. List a few questions that you think might be on the eHarmony relationship questionnaire.

5. If you were to become an eHarmony member, would you be fully honest, or put a positive spin on your profile? Similarly, would you post a "touched up" picture? In that regard, critique the following post with respect to the individual's and eHarmony's goals: "Bald, short, fat, and ugly male, 53, seeks short-sighted woman with tremendous sexual appetite."

6. Pretend you are to match two members of your class team. Gather some information, hypothetically make the match, and then reflect on how you went about the matchmaking process.

1. Making the Business Case for People Management Skills

You have been asked to serve on a committee at your firm and make recommendations for cutting costs in response to a weak economy and a downturn in revenue. The very first meeting is kicked off by your company president who goes around to each committee member with the goal of identifying any "untouchables"—that is, those areas that committee members feel should be off limits to cuts or at least targeted as a last resort. Unfortunately, you are seated at the immediate right of your president and he asks you to go first. You take the opportunity to suggest that the firm should do nothing that would detract from the quality of people management you have or erode the people-oriented culture. You even quote from your long-lost organizational behavior textbook (burned in a weenie roast celebration years ago) that "*few things matter more to the success of a firm than the way people feel about how they are managed.*" The president seems to accept this.

But the VP of Research and Technology is so angry he is about to burst a blood vessel. He rises and in an angry tone says, "With all due respect, I have to say that all this stuff about the importance of people management strikes me as non-sense. I have nothing against our management development efforts, but if you give me the same amount of money for new technology and research funding, I will turn it into far more of a benefit for this firm than we will get from trying to improve our managerial performance. In fact, I have two specific problems: (1) I see no connection between the quality of our people management and important outcomes that relate to our "bottom line," and (2) good people management is so fuzzy that there really is no way to determine who is doing a good job and who is not, anyway."

The president nods. "Hmm, he may have a point." He then looks at you and says, "I suspect you disagree. So go ahead and make a business case for me as to why we *should* devote significant resources to building better people management and a people-oriented culture. But I don't want any soft 'touchy-feely' babble. Be specific and use examples."

2. Using OB Evidence Instead of Just Intuition

You have heard so many stories of bad managers and read so many accounts of poor decisions that you are determined to be more "evidence-based" in your own organizational career. But why are more decisions not made on good research evidence? How do you go about finding more evidence? Where would you find such evidence, and how might you apply it to commonly faced managerial situations such as how to set appropriate goals, motivate high effort, or build strong employee commitment and a high-performance culture?

3. Making a Personal Improvement

You have been in your first job for two years and are itching to get promoted as quickly as possible. In your last performance review, however, your boss identified time management as a weakness. You have never felt that your time management was superb, but you did not know that weakness might affect your career advancement. In any case, you are now committed to improving your management of time. However, realizing that old habits die hard and that accomplishing personal change is very difficult, you know you will have to do more than just "hope" to change.

So how would you proceed to improve yourself? What would you do first? What strategies would give you the best chance of actually improving your time management skills significantly?

4. Describing Yourself and Your Style: Expanding Your Self-Awareness

"Tell us about yourself" is the first query in your introductory meeting with the four people who will be reporting to you in your new managerial job. You naturally struggle with where to start. You have been a great individual contributor for four years, but everyone has told you that managing people is a very different responsibility. And the thing that really scares you is you have heard sarcastic joking around the firm about a colleague who got promoted to manager and how with that promotion the firm "lost its best analyst and found its worst manager."

So what should you tell the group about yourself and how you will manage? What would be most relevant and useful? Based on your own self-assessment, what particular characteristics would you highlight? What should you be doing to know yourself even better so you can answer this question more confidently in the future? What would it be like to be managed by you?

Introduction

If you're like most students who are new to management courses, you're probably preparing to be totally *underwhelmed* and perhaps a little skeptical about what this text and course have to offer. Our experience tells us that you probably come to this course with at least one of the following concerns (or perhaps complaints). First, you may be concerned about the overall usefulness of the knowledge contained within this text. In fact, you may have heard from others that your management course will be nothing more than common sense, bloated theory, and will be essentially a "blow off." Even if you haven't heard such things about this course, you might feel that at the end of the day management can't be taught. Unlike say, accounting, where there are clearly specified rules and principles to follow, you may believe that management isn't something that can be taught in a course, much less from a textbook. Second, as you look out at the decades of organizational work life ahead of you, management may seem so very unimportant compared to functional areas like finance, marketing, and accounting. These functions, after all, represent the major departments or units in organizations and they house critical jobs—the very jobs recruiters are posting to fill. Third, you may feel that your career is going to be one that is built on your technical expertise and managing others is simply not something you want to do or will ever do. As such, you might feel like this course is just one more in a long line of required educational obligations on the road to getting your degree. You are not alone if you have such concerns and we are not surprised—we face such skepticism prior to every course we teach. Indeed it was our sense that organizational behavior and management courses are undervalued by business students (at every level)—relative to the importance of those topics for success in the real world—that stoked our passion for a new kind of textbook. Specifically, the idea for this book was born out of three important observations we shared from our collective experience of teaching organizational behavior and management courses to college students and practicing managers.

1. ***Managing people is a distinct and critically important skill set.*** Our most influential business leaders have always recognized that management and *people skills*—not just financial and technical knowledge—are critically important to the success of individuals and organizations. Yet, as we will discuss shortly, such skills often do not get the educational attention they warrant.

2. ***Evidence for the importance of management may be less accessible to you, but is nonetheless abundant and clear.*** The research evidence is overwhelmingly clear that the possession of management skills creates a competitive advantage for individuals and organizations. Although management skills appear on the surface to be relatively straightforward, the chief complaint of most senior leaders is that they can't find enough competent people-managers.

3. ***Most OB and management textbooks do not focus on developing the most critical management skills.*** Sadly, most existing books and courses on managing organizational behavior are not well suited to helping students develop and refine the skills they really need to become great managers. Most textbooks are accurate, informative, and descriptive but lack a decision- or action-oriented approach that allows for real skill development.

With those observations in mind, we insisted that the focus of this book be on the *application* of organizational behavior evidence to the skills required to be a great manager and organizational contributor. That is, we do not want you to just *know* and understand a book full of ideas—we want you to be able to *do* something with that knowledge.

A simple philosophy that permeates this book is that organizations succeed through people. If there is one ultimate truth of organizational life it is this: Organizations big and small, public or private, for profit and not, only succeed when

"Take away my people, but leave my factory, and soon grass will grow on the factory floor. Take away my factory, but leave my people, and soon we will have a new and better factory."
—Andrew Carnegie

"I will pay more for the ability to handle people than for any other talent under the sun."
—John D. Rockefeller

Practice this!
Go to www.baldwin2e.com

their people succeed. A great product doesn't market itself—great marketing people do. A new accounting practice doesn't implement itself—outstanding accountants do. An organization doesn't simply grow sales—salespeople increase their productivity. And yet despite this simple principle, a recipe for how to get people to succeed (and thus organizations) remains incredibly elusive. To be certain, there is not one formula or playbook that leads people to be successful in organizations. But the best chance organizations have for creating successful people is by finding and nurturing great managers. The most successful organizations are those with work environments that are personally fulfilling, rewarding, and challenging. And the single most important factor in creating such successful environments is great managers.

Of course not all managers are very good, or for that matter even competent. Indeed, we laugh at the clueless antics of managers in comic strips like Dilbert, movies like *Office Space,* and television shows like *The Office.* In these examples, and perhaps from your own personal experiences with bad bosses, we see the impact on people and firms when managers act in dysfunctional ways. In real life, however, such managers have a toxic effect on the people they manage, as well as their own careers, and it's far from a laughing matter. In the following sections, we will talk about what managers do to be successful and how organizational behavior knowledge is a contributing factor.

KO **1-1**

DO **1-1**

Practice this!
Go to www.baldwin2e.com

Success Through People Management

The hero or heroine in this text is that of a manager. You might find that to be a bit odd given most peoples' reaction to the word "manager." For decades, the term "management" has had a decidedly negative connotation. Consider the following account by Professor Denise Rousseau, former President of the Academy of Management:[1]

> Management was a nasty word in my blue collar childhood, where everyone in the family was affected by how the company my father worked for managed its employees. When the supervisor frequently called my father to ask him to put in more overtime in an already long work week, all of us kids got used to covering for him. If the phone rang when my father was home, he'd have us answer it. We all knew what to say if it was the company calling: "Dad's not here." The idea of just telling the supervisor that he didn't want to work never occurred to my father, or anyone else in the family. The threat of disciplinary action or job loss loomed large, reinforced by dinnertime stories about a boss's abusive behavior or some inexplicable company action.

The term "manager" can evoke notions of a person who is power hungry and incompetent and can't do "real" work themselves. This reputation of managers as people who abuse and exploit their subordinates and care only about their own personal success and advancement has been reinforced over the decades by real anecdotes of bad bosses.[2] These negative connotations of managers are unfortunate because volumes of research studies and organizational examples have shown that when managers get it right, employees, organizations, customers, and the managers themselves all win. For example, meta-analytic studies (that is, the syntheses of many studies) have demonstrated that the financial performance of organizations is positively associated with management practices like selective hiring, succession planning, reward systems, performance management, and training and development.[3] Other research indicates that managers are a key component in reducing high employee-related costs, such as turnover and counterproductive behaviors (for example, theft and the abuse of resources), as well as increasing employee and team performance, cooperative behaviors, commitment, and employee satisfaction.[4] Still other studies have shown that personal career outcomes, such as speed of progression and leadership effectiveness, stem from competent and supportive management.[5] Finally, it is also clear that *poor* management practices (see the section "Management Live 1.1"), such as abusive supervision and harassment, have substantial harmful effects on individuals and their organizations, resulting in counterproductive behavior, low performance, and psychological stress, as well as career derailment and financial loss.[6]

Management skills are also the key elements in what makes for healthy and desirable workplaces. Indeed, the Great Place To Work Institute (GPTWI), which conducts the research on the nation's best employers for *Fortune* magazine's "100 Best Companies to Work for in America" annual article, has found that the single most important element of every great workplace is the trust between employees and management.[7] Such trust stems from the managers' skill level in those organizations. GPTWI research has found that workplaces with great managers receive more qualified job applications for open positions, experience less turnover, have lower health care costs, enjoy higher levels of customer satisfaction, and induce greater customer loyalty.

While you may not be familiar with the research evidence, we hope none of it comes as a huge shock to you. Anyone would rather have a good manager than an incompetent one. You probably know of someone who is technically or analytically skilled but has few "people skills," or is de-motivating, or cannot "get along well with others." Few of us would refute that it takes a competent manager to lead groups who go the extra mile required to achieve highly satisfied customers, and so on.

But, having taught OB and management courses for many years, what we find is not typically intuitive to most aspiring managers is that good management is so essential to good *business*. Management is often characterized as being elementary or "just common sense," but great management is neither common nor easy, and the existence of so many ineffective managers and toxic organizations attests to that. Indeed, as important as they may be, management skills have proven stubbornly hard to develop; thus making great managers and management rare commodities. Some estimates indicate that nearly 50 percent of

⤢ MANAGEMENT LIVE 1.1

What Is the Real Cost of a Bad Manager?

A recent advance in research on learning and education is known as *value-added* analysis. It uses standardized test scores to look at how much the academic performance of students in a given teacher's classroom changes between the beginning and end of the year.[8] Accumulating evidence suggests that students of a very bad teacher will learn, on average, half a year's worth of material in one school year. On the other hand, the students in the class of a very good teacher will learn a year and a half's worth of material—and the cost to the school district of those two teachers is (usually) roughly the same. Moreover, while the United States currently is behind many developed nations in student test performance, researchers have estimated that the gap could be closed simply by replacing the bottom 6 to 10 percent of teachers with others of just *average* quality.[9]

We believe that this same type of value-added approach and mindset is long overdue in management education—and the urgency is great. Given the dismal scores found in recent research on applied management knowledge (see "Management Live 1.3"), imagine the productivity lost and the number of people who have spent time working for an incompetent manager. What truly is the cost of a bad manager? More importantly, what is the *value* of competent ones? The accumulating evidence reveals that organizations can no longer afford to neglect the development of their managers—the costs are simply too high.

people moved into management roles essentially fail.[10] In other rather depressing surveys, over half of employees have reported they were less than satisfied with their current manager and many noted that the worst aspect of their job was their immediate boss.[11] Some even rated their manager as "remarkably bad." The same skills that will advance your career also happen to be the skills that make an organization a great place to work. And the best places to work also happen to be the highest-performing firms. That's the good news. The bad news is that the reason management skills create a competitive advantage for people and organizations is because they are hard to master and are therefore still quite uncommon.

⇄ MANAGEMENT LIVE 1.2

The Best Places to Work Are Also the Best-Performing Companies

Independent financial analysts have studied the financial performance of the "100 Best" companies beginning with the publication of the book *The 100 Best Companies to Work for in America* (by Robert Levering and Milton Moskowitz, 1994), and have accompanied that with each of the "100 Best Companies" lists from *Fortune* since that list's inception in 1998. Using various profitability indicators, these data illustrate the extent to which the publicly traded 100 Best Companies consistently outperform major stock indices over the 10-year periods preceding the publication of the 100 Best lists. It is notable that those companies selected for the 100 Best list generally spend far more on employee benefits and services than their counterparts—that is, it is often *expensive* to be a best place to work. However, the data clearly support that the expense is worthwhile because people ultimately engage more fully, work productively, and lift company performance.

100 Best Companies to Work For vs. Overall Stock Market 1998–2010

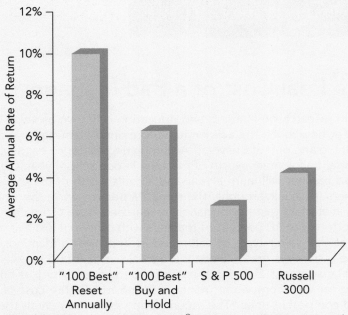

TABLE 1.1 Managerial Realities

Managerial Reality 1: *Management is the process of getting things done through others.* This means that your primary role as a manager is to manage other people. Sometimes organizations lose sight of this and ask managers to engage in substantial technical work leaving little room for this primary people-management role. This is, by and large, a costly mistake.

Managerial Reality 2: *Managers get rewarded for what their employees do, not for what managers do.* In other words, your success as a manager occurs only when others succeed. The extent to which you can make others successful in their jobs will determine how successful you are as a manager.

Managerial Reality 3: *People join organizations but they leave managers.* Managers play such an important role in peoples' work life that it is almost trite to suggest that when people leave organizations they do so, in part, because their manager has failed them, failed to find ways to challenge them, promote them, reward them, and provide good opportunities.

Managerial Reality 4: *People generally manage the way they themselves have been managed.* As we discuss later in the chapter, we learn by watching. If you have had great bosses in your previous work experience, you should be excited about your prospects to be an effective manager. If on the other hand, your managerial models have been largely ineffective, you will likely have to work extra hard to break away from their methods.

Managerial Reality 5: *People problems are far more complex than any other organizational problem.* When asked what keeps managers awake at night, the response is rarely, "We don't know how to market a product well" or "I'm not sure how we'll integrate our software system with the old legacy system." Rather, the response is almost always about *people*, "Jim is a great performer, but he's a lousy teammate," "Marsha's husband is sick, so she's taking six weeks off. How will I get others to take on her work?" and so forth.

The Central Role of Management in Organizations

One of the reasons that good management is so hard is that few managers, particularly aspiring ones, are forced to confront the realities of management early enough to understand them. In Table 1.1 we outline these primary managerial realities.

Managing people is indeed complex work requiring a wide variety of competencies. These competencies can generally be sorted into one of three broad categories: conceptual, technical/administrative, and interpersonal.[12]

Conceptual Competencies.   Managerial work requires that managers collect and analyze an enormous amount of information. Such information is used to diagnose problems, formulate plans, integrate ideas, and examine effectiveness of current practices.

Technical/Administrative Competencies.   Effective management requires that managers be well equipped to understand the functions of business such as accounting, operations, and marketing. Importantly, managers must use their technical/administrative expertise to coordinate activities.

Interpersonal Competencies.   Managers are required to interact with, influence, and lead others. To do so, managers must possess competencies that allow them to negotiate conflict, communicate, motivate, and develop other people—competencies that require managers to manage relationships with others.

According to the results of a recent large-scale study of 52 managerial occupations in the U.S. labor force, all managers' jobs, regardless of occupation (for example, financial manager, funeral director, CEO, and so on), require proficiency in these three categories of competencies to be successful. That is not to say that managerial jobs do not differ in their skill requirements; they do. In particular, managerial roles differ substantially in the type of technical expertise required for a given role. For example, although all managers must coordinate activities among employees, sales managers are not coordinating the same activities as production managers. So by and large, managerial work, regardless of the occupation, is more the same than it is different. This is generally good news as the skills discussed in this book are largely applicable to any managerial role you will ever fill. It is certainly true that you will need to gain expertise in the technical skills associated with the particular occupational role you assume, but the skills presented throughout this book will support your success in that role by helping build your conceptual and interpersonal managerial competencies. Further, although such competencies are essential for those wanting to be great managers, our experience is that these competencies are also critical to those wanting virtually any type of career that involves substantial interaction with people (for instance, nurse, sales representative, engineer). Moreover, while such competencies are certainly necessary for *future* success, we would also contend they should have an impact on your performance *right now*. Decision making, teamwork, conflict management, and others are fundamental to most any line of work.

Playing for Keeps: Getting Serious About OB Right Now

One of the problems we face as management educators is, quite frankly, trying to help our students understand the importance of starting now to develop their managerial skills. The reason for this is twofold. First, students are rightly focused on their first role after college which is not likely to entail full-blown management responsibility. Thus, it's hard to capture students' attention when recruiters are on campus seeking applicants for individual contributor roles such as a staff accountant, marketing specialist, or financial analyst position. Second, we find that students simply aren't aware of how competitive managerial skills will make them in the marketplace and how absolutely detrimental the lack of such skills will be to their early careers and beyond. In order to explain this second point more fully, we need to take a quick detour and look at a few important studies about managerial skills and success on the job.

All managers deploy their skills to manage six key general work activities at work, which are as follows:[13] (1) *managing human capital* (for example, staffing, motivating, leading, performance management, and so on); (2) *managing tools and technology* (for example, production, operations, information technology); (3) *managing decision-making processes* (for example, gathering information, analyzing data, conducting research); (4) *managing administrative activities* (for example, budgeting, financial management and control); (5) *managing strategy/innovation* (for example, future planning, product development, strategic decisions); and (6) *managing the task environment* (for example, public relations, marketing).

Which of these six activities do you think are most critical or important to a manager's success? In a recent study utilizing U.S. Department of Labor data from 8,633 managers across all managerial occupations, professors Erich Dierdorff, Robert Rubin, and Fredrick Morgeson found that while all six activities are seen as important, *managing human capital* and *managing decision-making processes* were rated by managers as being significantly more important than the rest. This means that to be successful in a managerial role you will need to pay particularly close attention to how to manage people and gather and analyze information that will enable effective decision making.

In another study, researchers from the Center for Creative leadership tracked young professionals who were viewed by their organizations as having high potential to reach the executive ranks in Fortune 500 organizations.[14] The study followed these professionals over a 20-year period and sought to understand why some of them (all of whom were seen initially as having great potential) did not make it to the top echelon of their organization. The results generated five major themes for why these managers were "derailed" or fell off the track leading to the top: (1) failure to *meet their business objectives* over time; they simply were not consistent about reaching their goals; (2) they showed an *inability to build and lead a team* as they progressed in the organization; (3) they exhibited an *inability to develop, change, and adapt* with the changing times; (4) despite moving into broad management roles, they retained a *narrow functional/technical orientation;* and (5) they displayed consistent *problems with interpersonal relationships.* Thus, the findings of this study demonstrate that the rise to the top of a Fortune 500 organization certainly involves getting results, but to do so professionals rely heavily on their ability to manage relationships with others.

So it's clear from these two powerful studies that interpersonal skills, so-called "people skills," must be mastered to achieve long-term success in managerial roles. Why then aren't students knocking down the doors of management professors and enrolling in elective courses where these skills are learned, as opposed to taking yet another finance class? Maybe it's that recruiters simply don't care about skills involved with managing people and thus students don't pursue it because there's no immediate payoff. The evidence suggests just the opposite, however. In a study of 1,300 recruiters, these recruiters rated interpersonal skills, leadership, communication and adaptability as the *most desirable* yet *scarcest* skills present in today's graduates. These recruiters claim that the possession of such skills is rare among graduates and that recruiters routinely struggle to find these skills in the marketplace of talent.

We have observed that students often think that they can pick up these managerial skills at some later time or that perhaps they'll learn them on the job. Once again, the evidence doesn't support such a conclusion. In one study, MBA alumni cohorts spanning a five-year period were asked how often they used various skills and what skill areas they felt needed additional training. The results of that

FIGURE 1.1
MBA Skills Acquisition
in School and Skills
Use After Graduation:
A Gap Analysis

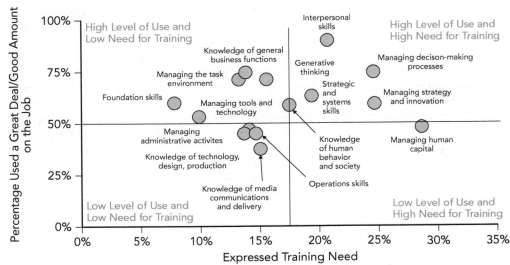

From 2008 MBA Alumni Perspectives Survey (Survey Report). GMAC®, GMAT® Graduate Management Admission Council® and Graduate Management Admission Test® are registered trademarks of the Graduate Management Admission Council in the United States and other countries.

study revealed a significant skills gap between what is currently being covered in MBA programs and what people report that they ultimately need when they get on the job. That result is illustrated in Figure 1.1 in the upper-right quadrant, which represents the skills MBA alumni reported using most *and* most in need of additional training. These findings held true regardless of the functional areas in which these MBA alumni were working, including marketing/sales, operations/logistics, consulting, general management, finance/accounting, human resources, and information technology/management information systems. Thus, even after completing an MBA, alumni report needing considerably more development of their interpersonal, decision-making, generative-thinking (creativity), and managing human capital skills.

The bottom line is that *now* is the time to get serious about management skills. If you want to be both competitive in the marketplace and effective on the job, you must start to master managerial skills today. Importantly, mastering managerial skills should never be to the exclusion of mastering discipline-based technical skills. To be certain, you must become an expert at something. Organizations won't promote people to sales management positions who are not competent salespersons themselves, nor will they promote a staff accountant to an accounting manager role if the person is not a capable accountant. So do not misunderstand: Technical, financial, strategic, and operational skills are of course important elements in job success and career advancement. But a steadily increasing body of research is showing that what ultimately distinguishes the good from the great achievers is the development and refinement of their *management* skills. Thus, the general rule of thumb is as follows: On average, great technical skills get you noticed in organizations and great management skills get you promoted. If you're playing for keeps, now is the time to invest.

KO **1-2**

DO **1-2**

Becoming a Great People-Manager

If managers and good management matter so much, you might wonder why more attention isn't given to such skills and why good management seems more like the exception rather than the rule. Although there are numerous and systemic explanations to these questions, one critical explanation is that learning about managing organizational behavior is fraught with traps and distractions.

For example, although there are hundreds of books on leadership, there are probably less than ten built on a solid foundation of evidence that might be applicable across managerial situations. The problem is, as you stare at the long list of books on Amazon.com, how do you decide which ones to read because they will be helpful and which ones to reject as nothing more than a "good read"? Learning about management first requires a critical understanding about what constitutes strong evidence for a given managerial practice. Every consultant, newspaper article, or book on the topic of management uses the phrase "research shows." Yet, determining the usefulness of such "research" is one of the most vexing problems facing managers today.

Let's say you've injured your back somehow and you go to a doctor who examines you. She proceeds to write you a prescription about which you ask a very reasonable question, "What is this that you're prescribing?" She says, "Oh, it's a great drug that everybody has been using lately." To which you reply, "Well, what does it do?" "It reduces swelling and spasms in muscle tissues." "Got it," you remark, "so my problem is muscle spasms?" "Not sure," the doctor replies, "but it worked for the last guy who was in here for pain in his ankle." A bit befuddled now, you ask, "Well, has the drug been tested on people with back pain?" She responds, "Not specifically, but I've had two patients who responded well to it for back pain—I think it should work for you."

Before you're half-way out the door, you are hopefully looking for a new doctor and you're certainly not taking this drug. It just doesn't pass the logic smell test. In this case, you should want to know that the doctor has correctly diagnosed your injury, that the drug being prescribed is designed specifically to treat your injury, and that the drug has been tested and studied in large populations to understand its effectiveness and potential side-effects. Put simply, you should be looking for better evidence.

Unfortunately, this little vignette illustrates how we too often go about applying management concepts. First, like the doctor, we are drawn to solutions to problems that we have heard others say do "work." Yet such evidence is usually built on rather limited data or information, or more commonly on **half-truths**—practices or concepts that may be true some of the time in some instances. Second, we tend to apply solutions broadly, regardless of whether it will specifically address the underlying problem. Third, in the absence of credible information or evidence, we make the assumption that the doctor (or another perceived expert) knows best, even if the recommendations don't stand up to simple logic.

Evidence-based management (EBM) refers to translating principles based on the best available scientific evidence into organizational practices and "making decisions through the conscientious, explicit, and judicious" use of such evidence. More specifically, evidence-based management includes the following five key practices:[15]

1. **Learning about cause and effect connections.** If you've ever pondered whether employee job satisfaction is related to employee turnover, you're engaging in a fundamental EBM practice of trying to understand the relationships among important organizational factors. Like doctors who attempt to link certain life-style choices (for example, a high-fat diet) to health outcomes (for example, heart disease), management researchers study relationships over time and in different settings in order to draw conclusions about effective management practices.

2. **Isolating variations that affect desired outcomes.** It's not enough to know that low job satisfaction may increase employee turnover. In order to practice EBM, one must also attempt to understand the specific conditions under which such a relationship might be strengthened or weakened. For example, while job dissatisfaction, on average, may be

associated with increased employee turnover, in economically depressed times, such a relationship may be considerably weakened.

3. **Reducing the overuse, underuse, and misuse of specific practices.** If the best available evidence suggests that graphology (handwriting analysis), for example, is not a good predictor of who will make a good manager, EBM suggests that it is our obligation to discontinue the use of such a practice in selecting our management talent. If, on the other hand, evidence is clear that cognitive ability tests are useful, we ought to seek ways to increase the use of cognitive ability testing. To be clear, sometimes practices are useful for one situation, but not for another. Thus, EBM holds that effective managers use practices only as solutions to the problems for which they were developed.

4. **Building decision supports to promote practices that evidence validates.** Once it is known that certain practices work more often than not under certain conditions, EBM suggests that managers institutionalize such practices through the use of tools (or "Tool Kits" as we do throughout the book) to help keep managerial behavior consistent with the evidence.

5. **Creating a culture of evidence-based decision making and research participation.** When managers take an evidence-based approach, they also contribute to an organization that values and encourages active participation in the evidence-based process. For example, in many manufacturing environments, teams of employees meet weekly to discuss quality control issues. These teams are actively engaged in developing research questions, collecting data, analyzing data and making decisions consistent with the evidence they discover.

KO 1-3   So where is the research evidence that can serve as the foundation of effective management practices? In short, organizational behavior is the primary field of study that contributes to the foundation of evidence from which to formulate evidence-based management practices. Specifically, **organizational behavior (OB)** is a social science that attempts to describe, explain, and predict human behavior in an organizational context. As such, organizational behavior scientists are dedicated to studying and ultimately prescribing how individuals, groups, and organizations can be most effective. The key to this definition is that OB represents the study of people in an *organizational context*. In other words, the study of OB is concerned with how to achieve important organizational outcomes such as profitability, productivity, and performance, as well as individual outcomes like employee turnover, commitment, satisfaction, and safety. Organizational behavior certainly does not describe all research on organizations. Indeed, substantial contributions to the study of organizational behavior come from other core social sciences such as sociology, psychology, anthropology, and political science. However, much of what translates into effective managerial practice will be found in the research domain of OB.

Learning About Organizational Behavior Is Hard

Unfortunately, EBM of organizational behavior is not widely practiced. This is not because people believe it's a bad idea, but rather multiple impediments exist that simply make it difficult. One of the key reasons EBM is not widely practiced is that learning about organizational behavior is not straightforward. Indeed, to become a great manager you will have to learn to become something of a "bullfighter," able to sort out the many myths and misconceptions frequently espoused about what is and is not effective management. Managing organizational behavior absolutely requires you get beyond just reading and study. To really learn and master skills, you will have to actively engage in practice and actually *experience* those skills in your life and work. Certainly, mastering management skills is difficult and the process of learning them can be more challenging than you ever may have imagined. Three key learning challenges are likely to arise that include, but are not limited to: (1) learning how to evaluate and use evidence to make decisions; (2) learning how to use management frameworks; and (3) learning how to overcome the knowing-doing gap so prevalent in management development. We briefly discuss these next.

Evaluating and Using Evidence

KO 1-4

Mark Twain once quipped that there are three types of lies: lies, damn lies, and statistics. This aptly describes the dilemma new managers face as they contemplate their most important people-related decisions: namely, differentiating between facts and fictions, especially those cloaked as "research." The biggest impediment here, however, may not be other people, but rather our own experience. That's right. It's your own experience that may get in the way of you becoming a great people-manager. One reason for this is that our experience in the world tends to be heavily influenced by our belief system and how we view world events.[16]

That is, your beliefs about the world—or rather what you *want* to believe—may often stand in the way of you applying the best available evidence. For example, most people assume that ibuprofen (used in Advil, Motrin, and other products) is highly effective in reducing pain. Yet, a large study found that the relationship between ibuprofen and pain reduction is incredibly low—almost so low as to have little effect on *most* people (unless of course your pain is associated with inflammation where ibuprofen is most effective). Similarly, most people assume that psychotherapy (that is, psychological counseling) is essentially an ineffective treatment for depression.[17] Here again, our beliefs are not accurate because substantial research shows that psychotherapy can greatly improve peoples' well-being. And for most people who have never been in psychotherapy, the way they learn about psychotherapy is through television, movies, and stories. Few competent psychotherapists would agree, however, that movies like *Anger Management, What About Bob?*, or TV shows like *The Sopranos* accurately depict the psychotherapeutic process.

For an example closer to home, we routinely ask our students how important grades are to their success on the job. The answer from most is, "not at all." In other words, students tend to believe that grade point average (GPA) is simply an academic indicator and irrelevant. Yet, recent evidence based on 71 studies suggests that undergraduate GPA is highly correlated with performance on the job in the first year post-college and remains a good predictor of job performance through five years post-college. Graduate school GPA (for example, an MBA) is even more highly correlated with job performance post-graduate school.[18] Even after we present this evidence, students remain in disbelief. "How can this be?" they say. "My brother had a very low GPA in college and is now a star salesperson for an awesome company." Unfortunately, this sort of conclusion based solely on a very small sample and personal experience (what we call a *hasty generalization* in Chapter 4) does not lead to the right conclusion. If you care about your future job performance, the right conclusion based on the evidence is that you should put forth great effort in school. GPA captures a high degree of motivation and knowledge accumulation, both of which are immediately important on the job.

The point is that throughout your career in organizations, you will be confronted with information and observations and existing practices, and not all of it will be good or even accurate. In many cases, our experience in the world often gets in the way of being able to make this determination because we take for granted relationships we believe exist despite the evidence. It is for this reason that every chapter in this text begins with a discussion on the prevailing myths or conventional wisdom about the topic, with the explicit idea of exposing our "taken for granted" view of the world.

One easy way to begin to understand the usefulness of evidence is to make a distinction between Big E evidence and little e evidence. **Big E evidence** refers to generalizable knowledge regarding cause and effect connections derived from scientific methods. Big E evidence is based upon years of studies, across many different types of samples or contexts, with many different types of jobs, people, and organizations. Most importantly, Big E evidence represents a form of research which is *systematic*—meaning that it is planned and methodical and avoids drawing conclusions simply on the basis of opinion or anecdote. Such evidence is often summarized in large scientific literature reviews or empirical summaries known as meta-analyses or "studies of studies." Goal setting (see Chapter 7), for instance, is one such idea that has substantial Big E evidence support. Decades of research supports the idea that setting specific and challenging goals increases employee performance, and this finding is highly generalizable (applies broadly to most any situation). By and large, when managing organizational behavior, Big E evidence is likely to be the best source for informing practices since it is drawn from years of study across large populations under varying circumstances. Like our doctor example, this is the type of information you want when asking, "Will this management practice work in my office?"

In contrast, **little e evidence** represents local or organizational specific data collection efforts to inform a specific decision. Popular quality improvement processes such as Six Sigma provide little e evidence, important information that helps the organization but may not generalize or translate into other arenas or other organizations. Examples abound of organizations that failed by trying to apply a practice that while wildly successful in another organization didn't take hold in their own. Thus, while little e evidence may improve decision making in any organization, we must be careful not to apply it broadly.

Learning and Using Evidence-Based Frameworks

It is often said that the absence of evidence is not evidence of its absence. In other words, not every problem you will encounter has been studied with such depth that it constitutes Big E or even little e evidence. In such cases, we encourage you to begin by seeking evidence-based *frameworks* that rely on logic and well-developed theory. It may strike you as unusual that, in a skills-oriented book, we do not shy away from discussions of research evidence and theories. In fact, we *sought out* every good research study we could find. That may seem like a direct contradiction of a skills-based approach, but actually it is central to it. Many students these days are unfortunately led to believe that theoretical means irrelevant or not practical or just simply boring. But in reality, to paraphrase the great sociologist Kurt Lewin, nothing is as practical as a good theory. Our goal is to have a practical skills development text based in the best and most recent theory and research. Short of that, any material becomes just someone's opinion or cannot rightly be generalized to other situations.

Studies in many fields have explored how experts go about attacking particular challenges or problems in practice. What those studies have generally found is that such experts internalize their own "theories in use" or what we call frameworks. That is, they do not have a rote way to act in every situation. However, they do habitually evoke ways of framing problems and considering options. So a great deal of our focus in designing this book was to include frameworks that are conceptually sound but also practical in application. Those frameworks can help you diagnose situations and proceed more thoughtfully. Hopefully, the frameworks will stick with you and help you know where to start, what information to get, and what not to do as you face new and different situations.

Yet sometimes even the most nicely crafted framework is baseless with respect to evidence, and recent research suggests that even when well-intentioned managers seek evidence and frameworks to inform their practice, they face enormous amounts of misinformation—some of which is potentially harmful. For example, researcher Sara Rynes and colleagues examined five years of popular business magazine articles for their representation of three critical managerial topics, namely, (1) personality in the workplace, (2) intelligence, and (3) use of goals.[19] Their results were shocking. Across five years, less than 1 percent of the 537 articles in their sample addressed these topics. More importantly, when they did address them, the authors in those articles did so in ways that disguised the topic so as to appear novel or cutting-edge. Further, few of the articles that addressed the important topics relied on any empirical evidence to substantiate their points. As Rynes and colleagues remarked, their findings showed the overwhelming tendency to:

> . . . focus on claims and testimonials from individuals that were unsupported by any references to empirical evidence. In the absence of such evidence, readers are left completely to their own devices in choosing how to decide among competing claims. Evidence suggests that under such circumstances, people are likely to choose the claims that most closely conform with their prior beliefs. As a result, the odds that anyone will actually learn something new or change his or her behavior as a result of reading such periodicals would seem to be quite small.

If you're surprised by this, keep in mind that those in the business of selling magazines likely feel that discussing issues from an evidence-based perspective doesn't give an article the feeling of freshness or innovation. This pattern of misinformation or lack of attention to the evidence is not unique to business magazines but rather it's endemic to business book publishing in general, where advice is dispensed based upon anecdotal evidence. This general practice led Ed Lawler, a well-respected organizational scholar, to comment:

> A great deal that passes as "best practice" in [management] most likely is not. In some cases, there simply is no evidence to support what is thought to be best practice. In other cases, there is evidence to support that what are thought to be best practices are, in fact, inferior practices. In short, most organizations do not practice evidence-based [management]. As a result, they often underperform with respect to their major stakeholders: employees, investors and the community.

Thus, when someone says "research shows" or the "evidence is clear," great managers know to dig a little deeper to understand the quality of that evidence. At the end of the day, anecdotes and previous experience may be all that is available to help inform decisions, but in far too many cases anecdotes are used where a rich scientific literature exists to help make better decisions.

Overcoming the Knowing-Doing Gap

For most management skills, the conceptual rules are relatively easy to know and understand. Most 12-year-olds could be taught to pass a test on the general rules or guidelines of the skills that comprise great management. The real challenge is to actually execute them. For example, listing the rules of effective behavior in a team is relatively easy. However, actually joining a team in a competitive business situation and contributing in a way that adds real value to that team is an entirely different matter. Similarly, the fundamental elements of models of motivation are elementary. But trying to create a culture that motivates peoples' best efforts is extraordinarily complex.

We chose the subtitle of this book—*What Great Managers Know and Do*—because it takes both knowledge ("know *that*") and application practice ("know *how*") to master a skill. Successful application of management skills is more than just following a cookbook list of sequential behaviors and is much more complicated than developing skills such as those associated with a trade (say, welding) or a sport (hitting a golf ball). That is because management skills (1) are linked to a more complex knowledge base than other types of skills and (2) are inherently connected to interaction with other (frequently unpredictable) people. A standardized approach to welding or hitting golf balls or baking a cake may be feasible, but a standardized approach to managing human beings is not possible.[20]

Nonetheless, one of the most encouraging elements of management skills is that they *can* be improved—we have seen it happen countless times. You do not, however, master the skills simply via hope, intuition, or common sense. Rather, it requires conscious persistent effort and practice. At the same time, practice without the necessary conceptual foundation is misguided and ignores the need for flexibility and adaptation to different situations. In short, any serious attempt to develop management skills must involve a dose of both conceptual learning and behavioral practice. It requires intentional study and a skill-oriented and problem-based approach.[21]

So one of the key questions that students studying organizational behavior must confront is whether or not investing time, money, energy, or any other resource in developing the skills associated with good management is really worth the effort. You might rightly ask yourself, "Given my limited resources, would I be better off perfecting my coding skills or should I invest in learning how to run a team?" "Should I take an extra finance course in preparation for the CFP exam or should I spend time running a club?" The answer quite simply is, "yes." Yes, you should hone your technical skills, and yes, you should start now (while the stakes are rather low) to seek every opportunity to practice managing organizational behavior. In the remaining sections of this chapter, we discuss the process of learning how to learn about yourself and managing organizational behavior.

↹ MANAGEMENT LIVE 1.3

Knowing vs. Doing: The Disturbing State of Applied Management Effectiveness[22]

A wealth of anecdotal data suggests that, despite sufficient book knowledge of what constitutes effective management practice, managers may often lack the ability to apply that knowledge in *context*—and a recent comprehensive research report supports those suspicions. The authors used a management assessment known as the MSAT (Management Skills Assessment Test) to measure the applied management capability of over 20,000 managers, or aspiring managers, over the past 25 years. The MSAT consists of eight common fundamental management scenarios (for example, delegating jobs, dealing with a low-performing employee, managing conflict) presented on the Internet. For each of the eight items in the MSAT, candidates must respond by (1) identifying the important issues, (2) describing the actions they would take to be most effective, and (3) actually taking those actions (writing memos, follow-up notes, and so on) where appropriate. That means that they have to be able to execute the action and also know *when to* do so and *why* they chose to do so—all without any cues or prompts.

The results leave little question that there is, in fact, a substantive knowing-doing gap in management practice. More specifically, despite relatively high scores on cognitive aptitude and multiple-choice tests of management principles, the MSAT test-takers generally failed to reach even the midpoint scores of the assessed items. There was considerable variance and some candidates scored very high, but the disturbingly low level of the average scores points to the critical importance of a focus on skill application and decision making in management education—and the pressing need to get beyond just the conceptual knowledge of principles.

Learning and Personal Improvement

Personal Effectiveness: The Foundation of Great Management

Effective management starts from the inside. Indeed, when people are asked to describe great managers, it is remarkable how often they give personal, rather than interpersonal or organizational, descriptions. Put simply, those who can manage themselves are much more likely to be effective managers of others. Personal effectiveness is the foundation of great management, and the skills presented in the following chapters all stem from a base of personal excellence. Although many elements comprise personal effectiveness, our focus is on *actionable* knowledge and behaviors—things you can actively learn and do to improve your personal competence. No one is born a great manager, or becomes one overnight. So the most fundamental aspect of personal competence is to know yourself and to have a clear understanding of how you learn new skills and motivate yourself to improve your capability.

We start with models of learning and self-management. Great management is often as much about not acting on misconceptions, and avoiding what not to do, as it is about expertly pursuing a course of action.[23] With that in mind, the Myths 1.1 box contains five of the more persistent myths of personal effectiveness.

KO **1-5**

DO **1-3**

Hope is not a personal improvement strategy.

—Anonymous

Practice this!
Go to www.baldwin2e.com

?¿ MYTHS 1.1   Myths of Personal Effectiveness

- *Management learning comes with age and experience.* Unfortunately, that simply is not true. Learning is hard work and comes from a conscious and persistent desire to attend to effective models, learn and retain what they do, and practice new behaviors consistently.

- *We know ourselves.* In fact, a number of revealing research studies have shown that the gap between how we perceive ourselves and how others perceive us is often significant. These gaps, many of which we are blind to, frequently lead to management problems or failure.[24] True self-awareness is the foundation of personal effectiveness.

- *Growth opportunities lie solely in our weaknesses.* We succeed because of what we do well. However, it is common to become so focused on improving our weak areas and gaps that we neglect our strengths. Personal development of new skills is important, but you should also spend time clarifying what it is you do well and then try to position yourself in situations where you can leverage your strengths to excel.

- *Personal development is all just about positive thinking.* With the appeal of popular books like *The Secret*, people may believe that being optimistic is all there is to development. Just wish it and it will become true! While an optimistic outlook does have a number of benefits, you will not become a skilled manager by just wishing it. Becoming a skilled manager takes practice, dedication, and rational optimism.

- *It's not me, it's them!* If you learn one management "truth" it should be this: You can never fully control the behavior of others, but you *do* have control over your own behavior. The best way to change others is to first change *yourself.*

Learning How to Learn

The will to win is vastly overrated as a means of doing so. What is more important is the will to practice and the means to execute.

—Bob Knight, Basketball Hall of Fame Coach

FIGURE 1.2
Social Learning Theory

Personal factors include a person's internal mental processes such as motivation, attention, self-regulation, and self-efficacy. *Behavior* is the person's response or action. *Environment* includes the physical and social environment surrounding an individual. It includes reinforcement and punishment contingencies and models.

Much has been written about the high failure rates of people trying to learn and change. For example, a tiny percentage of people actually keep their New Year's resolutions. The vast majority of people who set out to "get in shape" are back to being overweight in a couple of months. Most of those who say, "This is the year I am going to get organized," find that it ultimately was, in fact, not the year. The problem with most personal improvement attempts is they are mostly wishful thinking with far too little understanding of how personal improvement really happens. That is, most everyone *hopes* to improve, or *wishes* they could enhance their effectiveness. However, far too few actually know and discipline themselves to do what is necessary to learn new skills.

The most powerful and useful framework for thinking about personal improvement in management skills comes from the work of Albert Bandura, and his **social learning theory**.[25] Bandura's theory suggests that the learning of any new behavior is the result of three main factors—the person, the environment, and the behavior—and they all influence each other. Behavior is not simply the result of the environment and the person, just as the environment is not simply the result of the person and the behavior. This mutual influence is referred to as **reciprocal determinism** and is at the root of social learning theory. This is because the environment provides important models of behavior from which we learn. A model of social learning theory can be seen in Figure 1.2.

Personal factors include a person's internal mental processes such as motivation, attention, self-regulation, and self-efficacy. *Behavior* is the person's response or action. *Environment* includes the physical and social environment surrounding an individual. It includes reinforcement and punishment contingencies and models.

Although this concept may sound a little abstract, the principles of social learning theory are exceptionally practical and have been applied to help foster personal change in a wide variety of settings including but not limited to counseling, acting, addictive behaviors, and athletics. One reason social learning has been so influential is because it refutes widely held notions that people only learn through their own personal experience of rewards and consequences. For example, traditional conceptions of learning suggest you would learn that a stove burns you only by *actually touching* that stove yourself. Bandura suggests that, in fact, most learning is actually done through observation and **modeling** of the behaviors of others. That is, most people learn the stove burns by watching the behavior of others (perhaps seeing them burned or actively avoiding it). This simple phenomenon helps explains why so many people who work for ineffective managers often become poor managers themselves; we often manage the way in which we were managed.

In theory, there is no difference between theory and practice. But, in practice, there is.

—Jan L. A. van de Snepscheut

A second reason social learning notions are particularly appropriate for management skills is because there is such a big disconnect between knowing and doing. For most management skills, the conceptual rules are relatively easy to know and understand. Most teenagers could be taught to pass a test on the general rules or guidelines of the skills that comprise great management. But the real challenge is to actually execute them.

Fortunately, one of the most encouraging elements of management skills is that it is possible to improve your execution of such skills—but not simply via intuition or common sense. Rather, improvement requires conscious persistent effort and practice. Bandura outlines four critical components required to learn through observation, and these are the key building blocks of the most successful management training methods used in organizations today.[26] These components are attention, retention, reproduction, and motivation.

↹ MANAGEMENT LIVE 1.4

Where Does Talent Really Come From?

Some fascinating findings are emerging from a group of researchers trying to answer an important and age-old question: When someone is very good at doing something, what is it that actually makes him or her good? This stream of research work, led by Anders Ericsson, Conradi Eminent Scholar and Professor of Psychology at Florida State University, is collectively known as the Expert Performance Movement. Ericsson's first experiment, nearly 30 years ago, involved memory—training a person to hear and then repeat a random series of numbers.

Ericsson's study refuted the commonly held notion that cognitive skills, particularly those like memory, are mostly genetically determined (for example, "He was born with a photographic memory"). As he notes, "With the first subject, after about 20 hours of training, his digit span had risen from 7 to 20. He just kept improving, and after about 200 hours of training he had risen to over 80 numbers."

Based on that and later research showing memory is *not* genetically determined, Ericsson concludes that the act of memorizing is more a function of dedicated commitment and practice than a genetic gift. In other words, whatever innate differences two people may exhibit in their abilities, those differences are overwhelmed by how well each person has engaged in *deliberate practice*. Deliberate practice is not just simply repeating a task—playing a C-minor scale 100 times, for instance, or hitting tennis serves until your shoulder pops out of its socket. Rather, it involves setting specific goals, obtaining immediate feedback, and concentrating as much on technique as on outcome.

Ericsson and his colleagues have since taken to studying expert performers in a wide range of pursuits, including soccer, golf, surgery, piano playing, Scrabble, writing, chess, software design, stock picking, and darts. Based on that work, they made the startling assertion that the trait we commonly call talent is important but generally *overrated*.

Ericsson's research further suggests that when it comes to choosing a life path, you should do what you love—because if you don't love it, you are unlikely to work hard enough to get very good. Most people naturally don't like to do things they aren't "good" at doing. So they often give up, telling themselves they simply don't possess the talent for math or skiing or the violin. But what they really lack is the desire to be good and to undertake the deliberate practice that would make them better.

Source: Adapted from Dubner, S. J., and S. D. Levitt. (2006, May 7). "A Star Is Made." *New York Times Magazine*, p. 24.

Attention.   Not too surprisingly, if you want to learn anything, you have to pay specific **attention.** Thus, the first challenge of learning is to focus. Anything that puts a damper on attention will decrease your learning comprehension. If you are unfocused, nervous, or distracted by other things, you will not learn as well. Thus, a critical step in learning new skills is to find the right models and devote undivided attention to them. If you do not make what you want to learn a top priority and give the subject ample attention, you are unlikely to succeed.

In addition, it is critical you isolate as specifically as possible the behaviors you hope to learn. This approach may seem like common sense, but it is frequently violated. Many try to learn too much or change too many things at once. An example from basketball would be to repeatedly watch a successful player's form while shooting foul shots rather than trying to learn to shoot foul shots from watching an entire basketball game. In a management context, it would be better to isolate the nonverbal motions of an effective speaker than to attempt to emulate the speakers in a debate.

Retention.   You must be able to understand and remember what you have observed. Coding what we observe into words, labels, or images results in better retention than simply observing. If you can relate your observations to a theory or framework, and understand *why* what you observed was effective or ineffective, you have a better chance of retrieving it when you need it. This is where the study of written models and frameworks can be most useful. That is, just observing an effective speech, decision process, or team meeting is a good start. But real learning—the kind you can ultimately transfer to your own situations—comes from understanding the underlying principles that made the behaviors effective and being able to recall and translate those principles when appropriate.

Reproduction.   Perhaps the most critical contribution of social learning theory to developing management skills is it highlights the importance of practice, or actual demonstration, of a skill. That is, you cannot learn management by just observing, reading, or understanding the concept. Rather, you have to translate the images or descriptions into actual behavior. Research shows that our abilities improve even when we just imagine ourselves performing![27] Many athletes, for example, imagine their performance in their mind's eye prior to actually competing. However, the more we can actually reproduce the skill we aim to learn, in the actual context where the skill will be applied, the more likely we are to add that skill to our repertoire.

Another critical point with respect to reproduction is that the saying "Practice makes perfect" is only a half-truth. "Practice with *feedback* makes perfect" or at least enables people to learn. Feedback is essential for learning or developing any kind of skill. This is one of the reasons why video games are so satisfying for people to play. They provide an opportunity to reproduce the behavior (that is, play the game) with immediate feedback (your score).

Motivation.   Finally, even with careful attention, retention, reproduction, and feedback, you still won't successfully acquire a new skill unless you are motivated to persist and stay with it. Without some conscious reason to keep up the effort required to learn a new skill, or change a habit, you are doomed to fail. Your motivation may derive from past reinforcement, promised reinforcements (incentives) that you can imagine, or vicarious reinforcement—seeing and recalling the models you observe being reinforced. Of course, you may also use punishments for *failure* to achieve your learning goals. However, Bandura has found that punishment does not work as well as reinforcement and, in fact, has a tendency to backfire on us.

The way to get started is to quit talking and begin doing.
—Walt Disney

Bandura's principles may seem intuitive to most of us, but observational learning is neither easy nor self-evident. If it were easy to just observe and mimic the effective behavior of others, many more people would be successful in improving themselves. Rather, it takes disciplined self-management to apply the principles Bandura has proposed. In Table 1.2, we present a common example of breakdowns in learning, using the example of improving interviewing skills.

A Model of Self-Management

Nothing will work unless you do.
—Maya Angelou

Using Bandura's work as a base, Charles Manz and his colleagues have created a simple and practical framework for self-management.[28] They define **self-management** as a process of modifying our own behavior by systematically altering how we arrange different cues in our world, how we think about what we hope to change, and how we attach behavioral consequences to our actions. The framework takes into account that personal change is rarely a discrete, single event but rather a process with multiple influences. The underlying theme is that we all have the ability to change our immediate worlds in ways that will help us learn new things and behave in desirable ways.

TABLE 1.2 What's Keeping Max from Learning to Interview Better?

Max, who is soon graduating from college, has a strong record of achievement (high grades and a good extracurricular profile) but is struggling with the recruiting process. After several interviews, he has failed to make it to the next round a single time, and feeling discouraged, he has asked some of his interviewers for comments. The three who were willing to respond all essentially said he did not "interview well." As a result, Max hopes to improve his interviewing skills. Overlaying the principles of social learning and self-management can help illuminate Max's challenge and common traps that occur.

Attention. Max needs to address at least two issues to be consistent with effective social learning. First, he needs to set aside time to practice his interviewing skills in the midst of many competing time demands. He is likely to feel his classes, part-time job, and social life take precedence and thus may well not devote enough time to improving his interviewing skills—a classic case where hoping will supersede a real learning strategy.

Second, Max needs to understand more specifically what he is doing or *not doing* in his interviews that is leading to poor outcomes. Without some specific understanding of his weaknesses (and relative strengths), he is destined to flounder in trying to determine how to improve. Unfortunately, that information may well be hard to come by in this case and he may need some mock interviews to tease it out.

Retention. Max needs to build an understanding of what makes for an impressive interview performance. Learning how to illustrate his background and accomplishments using the STAR model outlined in Chapter 12 would likely be a good step.

Max would also benefit from observing models with *recognizable excellence* in what he is trying to improve. In these cases, we often see people make the mistake of attempting to learn from friends or relying on anecdotal evidence from well-intentioned, but non-expert, sources.

Reproduction. Max needs practice accompanied by feedback on that practice. Practice should be treated like an actual interview. The more elements Max can re-create, the better his learning will be. A great deal of time needs to be dedicated to rehearsal, feedback, and more rehearsal. Mock interviews would seem to be essential here but are often awkward or difficult to arrange and therefore are not utilized.

Motivation. Max needs to decide how important improving his interview skills is to him and if he is willing to dedicate the time to changing. He needs the discipline to avoid taking shortcuts and saying "good enough" to really make a long-term lasting change. He should find ways to reinforce himself for devoting the time and should certainly celebrate any success on the interview front.

The self-management framework provides a means of avoiding some of the most common "hope vs. action" traps and of putting Bandura's principles into practice. It includes strategies we directly impose on ourselves to influence our own behavior and those whereby we attempt to alter our external world to help affect our behavioral change. While Manz and colleagues have presented their model in a variety of ways and with different labels (for example, self-management, self-leadership, super leadership),[29] we have condensed it here to the five essential elements most effective in facilitating personal improvement (see Tool Kit 1.1).

Note that this self-management framework has been successfully applied in many different contexts, including drug therapy, weight loss, health care, theater, and athletics. For example, all successful golf training is based on the elements of this framework. As you progress further in this book, you will see that

Tool Kit 1.1   Five Behavior-Focused Strategies to Improve Self-Management[30]

1. **Self-Observation/Exploration:** Observe and collect information about the specific behaviors you have targeted for change.
2. **Self-Set Goals:** Determine what more effective behavior is (often by observing effective models) and set specific goals for your own behaviors.
3. **Management of Cues:** Organize your work environment to assist you in performing the behaviors you want to change.
4. **Positive Self-Talk and Rehearsal:** Go over the behavior in your head and imagine its successful application. Actually practice the new behavior at available opportunities and seek feedback.
5. **Self-Reward and Punishment:** Provide yourself with personally valued rewards that are linked to performing desirable behaviors or with punishments linked to undesirable behaviors.

the effective behaviors of self-management are also entirely consistent with what great managers do when it comes to coaching and motivating *others*. This should not be surprising because, as we noted earlier, effective people-managers are first successful in managing themselves.

Self-Observation/Exploration

Not everything that is faced can be changed, but nothing can be changed until it is faced.

— James Baldwin

You can't induce or recognize a change in behavior until you have some information about what you currently are doing. **Self-observation** involves determining when, why, and under what conditions you currently use certain behaviors. For example, if your personal improvement challenge is to improve your grades via more focused study time, it is important to ask when and where you find you study best now. How many hours are you currently devoting to each subject? Which courses are you doing the best in? And so on.

Self-observations provide the building blocks for managing ourselves. The best self-observation strategies involve actually recording your observations and keeping close tabs on your behavior, both before you begin changes and after. This recording can be as simple as counting how many minutes you are late to meetings or can be more complex diaries of your behavior. Learning a new skill or habit often requires that we also change or *unlearn* other dysfunctional habits, adding significantly to the challenge.

If you're not making mistakes, then you're not doing anything. I'm positive that a doer makes mistakes.

— John Wooden

In that vein, a critical aspect of self-observation is to learn from mistakes or failed efforts. While we all have a tendency to be defensive, look to blame others, or ignore failure, viewing mistakes as learning opportunities builds a foundation for further learning. Mistakes can prompt us to look inward and evaluate our limitations and shortcomings. Mistakes are only problems if you repeat them or do not learn from them. Indeed, if you are not making mistakes, it is worth asking whether you are stretching yourself in your job and taking any developmental risks. Great managers make a lot of mistakes, but those mistakes are seen as "productive failures" and are rarely made twice.[31]

Self-Set Improvement Goals

The first task of setting goals is to determine what your desired outcome or effective behaviors look like. The best goals often derive from attention to effective models. Some of the things that influence our attention involve characteristics of the model or learning stimuli. As a result, we are more likely to adopt a modeled behavior if the model is similar to the observer (more like us), has admired status, and if the behavior has functional value (gets us something we want). Thus, if the model is attractive or prestigious or appears to be particularly competent, we pay more attention.

An example of this can be seen in thinking about how to effectively study for a class. One tactic for this challenge would be to observe the study habits of highly successful students to see if you might emulate some of their behaviors. Self-set goals need to address long-range pursuits and short-run objectives along the way. The shorter-range goals should be consistent with the long-range goals for maximum consistency. The process takes effort, and although our goals are likely to change, it is important we try to have current goals for our immediate efforts. Goal setting is so fundamental to great management that we reinforce it throughout this book.

Studies have shown that goal setting works because:

1. In committing to a goal, a person devotes attention toward goal-relevant activities and away from goal-irrelevant activities.
2. Goals energize people. Challenging goals lead to higher effort than easy goals.
3. Goals affect persistence. High goals prolong effort, and tight deadlines lead to more rapid work pace than loose deadlines.
4. Goals motivate people to use their knowledge to help them attain the goal and to discover the knowledge needed to obtain it.[32]

The best goals are characterized by the acronym **SMART,** which represents specific, measurable, attainable, relevant, and time-bound. SMART goals make for smarter learners.[33]

Management of Cues

Taking your lead from your self-observations and goals, you can begin to modify your environment. The objective is to organize your world to assist you in performing the behaviors you want to change. For example, if you are trying to quit smoking and improve your health, put away the ashtrays, drink tea instead of coffee, and take the ice cream out of the freezer and replace it with low-fat substitutes. If you are trying to study more on Thursday nights, get out of the apartment when everyone is heading to social engagements (and enticing you to come along), and go to the library or some quiet spot.

A related strategy is to create reminders and attention focusers you will notice and act on. A sticky note on the refrigerator reminding you of your weight loss goal, or a screensaver or text message to yourself about a forthcoming test, can provide a cue that will help you focus on an important improvement objective.

Positive Self-Talk and Rehearsal

Positive self-talk and rehearsal are applications of the social learning principle of *reproduction.* Search for opportunities to practice new behavior in the most realistic situations you can find. Basketball players know that just shooting 100 free throws will not simulate the pressure of shooting one at the end of a close game. So the best shooters find ways to practice under conditions that mirror those pressurized conditions (for example, team running for missed free throws, everyone lined up around the key trying to distract the shooter, simulated crowd noise). Some people treat their jobs as games (like salespeople) by trying out new techniques and seeing how well they work. Whatever the context, you must practice and rehearse any new skill for it to ultimately become part of your repertoire.

"One must learn by doing the thing, for though you think you know it, you have no certainty until you try."

—Sophocles

Further, the use of **positive self-talk** is extremely important. If you have ever repeatedly said to yourself, "I know I can do this," before attempting a difficult task, you were practicing a proven technique of self-management. The idea is to create a frame of mind that energizes your self-confidence and gets you beyond self-defeating and negative feelings that can accompany learning difficult tasks. Just as managers and coaches work on team morale and motivation, individuals can affect their behavior by getting "pumped up" and self-motivated.

Self-Reward and Punishment

Although no manager would deny the importance of **reward** and **punishment** for influencing employee behavior, the concept is strangely neglected when we think of ourselves. The truth is we can profoundly induce our actions by rewarding ourselves for desirable behavior. For example, "I will go out to dinner on Saturday night if I accomplish my goal. I will do paperwork instead if I do not." You simply arrange to reward yourself when you adhere to your plan and possibly punish yourself when you do not.

Generally speaking, it is better to use self-reward than self-punishment. Celebrate your victories and don't dwell on your failures. A great deal of learning research has found that punishment does not work as well as reinforcement.[34] However, there may be times when the most powerful or immediate incentive for you may be a punishment, and in such cases it may make an appropriate disincentive. Do not, however, punish yourself for slips or lapses. Changing habits and learning new things is never a straight path, and as the Tool Kit on relapse prevention at the end of this chapter illustrates, expecting and preparing for those inevitable lapses will be more fruitful.[35]

Putting It All into Practice

The self-management model represents the best methodology currently available for facilitating personal improvement. The basic notions are simple. To really get beyond mere hope and make a sustainable personal improvement requires you to:

1. Understand your current behavior and desired future behavior.
2. Set SMART goals for your change.
3. Arrange your world so it focuses your attention and reminds you of your improvement plan and goals.
4. Stay positive and rehearse the desired behaviors at every opportunity.
5. Create your own rewards for accomplishing your targets.

Since many of us already use some of these strategies, and they seem simple enough, why are most people not more effective at self-management? It is mostly because we often use them either ineffectively or inconsistently. That is, the piecemeal use of these strategies tends to make them relatively ineffective. Thinking through your own experiences, consider how often you see (or practice) one of these strategies in isolation, but how rarely you see them together.

For instance, many people have started down a path of weight loss by setting a goal and monitoring their eating behavior—a good start. But more often than not, they do not consistently manage their cues, practice new habits of grocery shopping and ordering while dining out, or create reinforcements powerful enough to sustain their efforts. So they start well, with much hope, but do not have the strategies in place to persist until they have succeeded. Engaging in one strategy, while not engaging in the others, is much like ordering a Diet Coke to go with a big greasy cheeseburger and super-sized fries. It may be better than having a milk shake, but it is really not helping someone lose weight.

We suspect that much here has validated what you already knew and are doing to some extent. Hopefully, though, it can make it easier to more systematically go about learning and managing yourself in an increasingly complex world.

Building Self-Awareness

Self-Awareness: The Key to Successful Learning and Growth

KO **1-6**

DO **1-4**

DO **1-5**

Practice this!
Go to www.baldwin2e.com

Success in the new economy comes to those who know themselves—their strengths, their values, and how they best perform.

—Peter Drucker

The models of learning and self-management described earlier point to the critical importance of self-awareness. Self-awareness is mission critical for those attempting to accelerate their managerial learning and to become more personally effective. The best managers not only consistently seek feedback to know themselves better and what areas they need to improve, but also isolate their personal strengths and preferences so they can best position themselves for success. Self-awareness is essential to learning and growth in a management role because it forms the basis by which we learn about ourselves and how we differ from others.

Individual Differences and Their Importance

There is perhaps no more obvious yet curiously neglected truth than "people are different." Recognizing our own differences is important because they impact how we react and behave in different situations.

Every popular magazine these days seems to include some sort of self-assessment of an intriguing individual difference. Headlines claim you can learn some hidden truth about yourself by answering a few questions and then scoring yourself with the provided scoring guide. Magazines like *Cosmopolitan*, *GQ*, and *Vogue* regularly have some sort of "self-assessment" that sounds like it will be helpful, but they are rarely what they appear to be. But since your "cool quotient," "hottie index," or "marriage potential" are not of great concern in managerial environments (at least hopefully not), what, specifically, should the self-aware manager know?

Of course, people differ in an infinite number of ways. From a managerial performance perspective, however, the two important categories of difference are (1) ability and (2) personality (which includes values and motives).[36] **Ability** can be simply defined as what a person is capable of doing.[37] This "capacity to do" leads some people to be able to dunk a basketball, calculate complex math in their heads, or interpret abstract patterns very quickly. Abilities come in many dimensions and include **cognitive ability,** physical ability, and emotional ability (now often referred to as **emotional intelligence** and an area of study in which there's been a recent explosion of interest).

Personality represents the pattern of relatively enduring ways in which a person thinks, acts, and behaves.[38] Personality is determined both by nature (genetics) and nurture (situational factors) and tends to represent our "dominant" or "natural" behavior. While it may be appealing to think about it in these terms, there is not a "good" or "bad" personality profile. Although some personality characteristics have been associated more frequently with some occupations and interests, no personality combination limits you from types of occupations you might enjoy or determines your destiny.

How you behave at any given time is an interaction of your personality and your environment. This interaction accounts for why we often behave differently at home than we might at work or school. For example, your dominant personality trait may be one of **introversion,** yet in order to perform well on your job you have to "turn it on" to talk with clients and customers—that is, demonstrate **extraversion.** Sometimes the situation or environment has much more to do with how we behave than does our personality. It is a fundamental error to assume that behavior is solely a function of one's personality since the environment will always play a role as well.

Assessment of managerial ability and personality has become increasingly popular in both organizational and educational contexts. It can be intriguing, even fun, to see where we stand on different scales (for example, who would not be curious about your own "love quotient"?), and some form of assessment is essential if we are to clarify our own abilities, personality traits, values, and preferences. However, our experience suggests assessments are most useful when an individual has a defined *need to know.* Put another way, the most fruitful assessment process is ideally a research project where *you* are the focus of the research.

With that in mind, we sought to identify the set of fundamental personal questions most important to managerial and interpersonal self-awareness, and to identify assessment tools that can help you begin your personal inquiry into those questions. We boldly call our seven elements of self-awareness the Essential Managerial Assessment Profile. Other aspects of self-awareness (for example, learning style, tolerance of ambiguity, conflict style, leadership behavior) are relevant and important, and we include measures of some in your instructor's supplemental materials. If you become more self-aware on these seven aspects in an informed and thoughtful way, you will have a firm baseline of self-knowledge.

All facts are friendly.

—Unknown

Ultimately, we want you to be able to answer the question "Tell me about yourself" in a way that will have meaning and relevance to those you might work with or manage. The goal is not simply to describe your favorite characteristics, but to know how your abilities and personality may impact your behavior and performance. Table 1.3 categorizes and defines the seven dimensions, identifies leading assessment tools associated with each dimension, and briefly highlights the positive implications of higher self-knowledge on each dimension. Today, there are many online resources for taking self-assessments and getting feedback and developmental recommendations. The appendix to this text and your instructor should help you identify appropriate self-assessments for your personal performance.

Important Self-Awareness Issues

As you embark on a journey toward greater self-awareness, you should also take into account several important points regarding the interpretation of assessments. First, assessment results are simply feedback. As we've stated before, these results are not the absolute or final truth, nor do they dictate your destiny. Abilities (sometimes called talents) are only valuable when they are applied and manifested as skills or behaviors. The world is full of high-ability folks who do not succeed; athletic coaches often refer to such people as "wasted talent." Similarly, just *having* certain personality characteristics is less important than how you attempt to put yourself in positions where those traits are most valued and rewarded.

Second, as we noted earlier, literally thousands of self-assessments exist but many have questionable legitimacy. So look for measures that have an established norm base (significant data reporting from prior assessments) and have stood the test of time. The example assessments included in your essentials profile are all well established with a base of research evidence related to their outcomes and relevance for managerial contexts.

Third, preferences are choices we make about how we perceive the world and function best in it. Some of these "choices" are not necessarily conscious ones but rather modes of behaving that seem most natural for us. If you've ever done any acting, you know that attempting to "be someone you're not" is not easy and

TABLE 1.3 The Essential Managerial Assessment Profile

Self-Awareness Dimension	Ability, Personality, or Preference?	Example Assessment Tool	Implication
Cognitive Ability (critical and analytical thinking)	**Ability** to recognize quantitative and verbal patterns quickly and accurately. Includes the ability to acquire knowledge.	• Watson-Glaser Critical Thinking Test • Wonderlic Personnel Test	Is cognitive ability a strength or an area to supplement with the help of others? What types of jobs and industries suit my analytical ability?
Emotional Intelligence	**Ability** to accurately recognize and understand emotions in others and self and to use emotional information productively.	• MSCEIT	Do I understand and use emotion to make effective decisions? Can I relate to people well because I appropriately read their emotional states?
Cultural Intelligence	**Ability** to function effectively in the context of differences.	• Cultural Quotient Scale (CQS)	Am I aware of important cultural differences? Do I understand and act in ways that will value those differences and create stronger relationships?
Personality Traits	Primary **personality** characteristics that remain relatively stable over one's life.	• Big Five Inventory	What are my dominant personality traits? How do I maximize my fit to best utilize my personality?
Personality Preferences (temperament)	**Preference** for direction of energy, decision making, information acquisition, and orientation to the outer world.	• Myers-Briggs Type Indicator	How do I like to work with others and process information? What do I look for in others to complement my preferences? How will I best interact in different team combinations?
Personal Values	**Preference** for desirable ends or goals and the process for attaining them.	• Rokeach Values Checklist • Hogan MPV Scale	What do I value most and seek in others? What will I not bend or compromise on? What to me is non-negotiable?
Career Orientation	**Preference** for particular types of work environments and occupations.	• Holland Occupational Preference Scale	What occupational elements are most important to me? With what types of people will I thrive?

requires a great degree of attention, direction, and energy. Our personal characteristics such as core values, interpersonal preferences, and career orientations are those with which we feel most comfortable and natural. You can choose to behave outside your preferences, but it will require a significantly higher level of your conscious energy to do so.

Finally, we always recommend you look for patterns and consistency across your assessments. When you find consistency, it is evidence of a more dominant trait or preference. Inconsistency suggests a less-defined characteristic. Perhaps most importantly, you should always interpret your self-assessments in the context of other feedback you've received and not dwell on assessed weaknesses or limitations. We elaborate on those two issues next.

Involve Others: Seek Regular Feedback

Although the evidence is compelling that feedback-seeking behavior and increases in self-awareness are associated with positive outcomes like job satisfaction and performance,[39] many young managers do not actively pursue greater self-awareness. Why is that so?

A useful analogy for this curious reluctance can be found in the field of medicine. Many illnesses could be cured and diseases halted, if only people were not afraid to get a checkup—but they are often too scared to find out if anything is wrong. The same holds for seeking interpersonal and management feedback. We all want to protect, maintain, and enhance our self-concepts and the impressions we think others hold of us. And we often have fears and inadequacies (for example, I hate speaking to groups; I can't handle conflict; I look awkward on camera) that we would prefer not to focus on or reveal even to ourselves.

We would rather be ruined by praise than saved by critique.
—Norman Vincent Peale

Reliable knowledge about ourselves can help us gain insights into what areas we want to change and improve, and even more importantly, the strengths we should aim to utilize more in our work and relationships. Always keep in mind your perception of yourself is likely to differ from others',[40] and some folks we typically turn to (for instance, our mothers) are not always likely to be entirely truthful with us.

Simply put, the major obstacle to seeking feedback is fear. So the first and most important step toward developing self-awareness is a willingness to put aside that natural fear and push beyond our comfort zone in learning things about ourselves. However, a critically important point is that it is virtually impossible to dramatically increase self-awareness unless we interact with and disclose ourselves to others. That is, while self-assessments are a good first step, no amount of self-examination is enough to really know yourself. You can analyze yourself for weeks, or meditate for months, and you will not fully know yourself, any more than you can tickle yourself or smell your own breath.

The reason it is so important to get beyond yourself is that we are just not very good judges of our own behavior and ability. There are many ways in which other people know us better than we know ourselves, particularly when it comes to how adept we are in our relationships. **Multisource feedback** (that is, feedback provided by many sources other than yourself, such as a boss, co-worker, customer, and subordinate) enhances self-knowledge and consequently improves managerial behavior.[41] In fact, research has found that higher levels of agreement between managerial "self" and "other" behavioral ratings are associated with managerial effectiveness and performance.[42]

In short, the ideal evaluation relies not on any one source but on multiple perspectives. These may include self-reports as well as peer, boss, and subordinate feedback. Feedback from multiple sources can be a powerful source of data for highlighting your strengths and targeting the competencies that need to improve. Multiple perspectives on yourself are extremely powerful ways to build self-awareness and get you ready to embark on personal improvement.

MANAGER'S TOOL KIT

Tool Kit 1.2 Personal Quality Checklist[43]

Building on the principles of organizational quality improvement efforts, Bernie Sergesteketter and Harry Roberts have devised a tool for self-management called the personal quality checklist (PQC). Using their approach, you define desirable standards of personal behavior and performance and then keep track of failures or "defects" to meet those standards. The specific steps to the approach are:

1. **Draw up a checklist of standards.** This is the hardest part. Two samples are included at the end of this Tool Kit as illustrations (one by a practicing manager and one from a college student). Each standard should have a clear relationship to a "customer" either in the workplace or in your family or circle of friends. Each standard has to be unambiguously defined so you can recognize and tally a defect when it occurs. Thus, "get in shape" is not a good standard. A better standard would be to "break a sweat every day."

    There are two broad types of standards: (1) waste reducers/time savers (for example, be on time to class or group meetings), and (2) activity expanders (call parents at least once a week, get résumé completed). If you include all activity expanders on your list, be sure you have enough waste reducers and time savers to create free time for them.

2. **Tally your daily defects.** Defects should be tallied by days but can ultimately be aggregated by weeks or months. One intriguing strategy is to let others help you keep score. For example, if a checklist standard is to talk to your spouse only in respectful tones, or spend at least a half hour with your daughter each day, then your spouse or daughter may well be the best tally keeper for those standards.

3. **Review your tallies and action plan.** Some people find the word "defect" objectionable, but it is key to the system. First, it is easy to recognize and tally. Moreover, defects can become your friends because they suggest opportunities for improvement. Why did it occur? How can it be prevented? The whys lead to hows and suggest possible routes toward improvement.

Do not put faith in trying harder; you probably already are trying hard. Rather, figure out a different way to reach your objective. As the adage goes, rather than trying to be a better caterpillar, become a butterfly.

As a general rule you should stick with 10 or fewer standards, or the process becomes unwieldy and unfocused. Of course, your checklist standards will only be a small fraction of your activities. Your first PQC should focus on a few things you currently do that, if improved, could increase your customer satisfaction. Once you determine that you have those standards under control and customer satisfaction is high, then you can ask your colleagues and family for help in raising the bar and adding new standards. The approach is deceptively simple but powerful. Sergesteketter and Roberts report on a wide variety of successes by managers and executives from leading firms who have enjoyed success with the personal quality checklist approach. Draw up your own checklist and give it a try!

Sample Manager PQC

- On time for meetings
- Never need a haircut
- Answer phone in two rings
- No more than one project on desk at time
- Shoes always shined
- Weight below 190 pounds
- Exercise at least three times a week

Sample College Student PQC

- No more than 10 hours of TV viewing a week
- Use stairs instead of elevator for four floors or less
- Follow up job contacts within 24 hours
- Stick to one subject when studying, do not hop around
- In bed before midnight on all school nights
- Pay bills on time
- Make a to-do list for the next day before turning in

Focus on Strengths, Not Just Weaknesses

Too many people overvalue what they are not and undervalue what they are.

—Malcolm Forbes

Getting assessment feedback can be humbling, and sometimes even discouraging, so it is particularly important to not focus on just the gaps or weaknesses in your profile. Of course, some focus on weak areas is often appropriate, but it is all too easy to become obsessed with the negative feedback. Indeed, some recent authors have made the case that a "deficit reduction" or problem-fixing approach may actually hinder personal effectiveness.[44] Rather, they contend individuals are better served by recognizing and building on their strengths and *managing*, rather than obsessively trying to improve, their weaknesses.

Managing a weakness means taking ownership of it and acknowledging it both as a weakness and as part of you. Rather than trying to make it a strength, aim to find ways to minimize its impact on you. Such strategies can include doing it as little as possible, engaging others for whom the characteristic is a strength, and developing and using support systems and tools to compensate (for example, become a zealot for a practical time management system if managing time is a weakness for you). The key point, and the one that is often the most productive, is placing your focus on your strengths and those things you can realistically change.

⇄ MANAGEMENT LIVE 1.5

Identifying and Crafting Your Own Personal Brand

Back in 1997, Tom Peters wrote an article in *Fast Company* titled "The Brand Called You." In the article, he said:

> It's time for me—and you—to take a lesson from the big brands, a lesson that's true for anyone who is interested in what it takes to stand out and prosper in the new world of work. Regardless of age, regardless of position, regardless of the business we happen to be in, all of us need to understand the importance of branding. We are CEOs of our own companies, Me, Inc. To be in business today, our most important job is to be head marketer for the brand called You. It's that simple—and that hard. And that is inescapable.

Since that time, the emergence of social media on the Internet has made Mr. Peters' call to action even more relevant and created a whole industry of personal branding consultants, speakers, and authors. While you may not yet be consciously creating an online presence, you may be surprised to find out what's already out there on Facebook, Twitter, blogs, or in myriad other places. Many experts agree that online branding is not just for celebrities (although certain celebrities seem to have practically invented the entire idea). In fact, as part of your efforts to enhance your own personal effectiveness, we challenge you to conduct the following personal-branding exercises.

1. Identify an individual who currently holds a position that you think you would aspire to in 5 or 10 years. This could be a person in your current organization or employed elsewhere. Search the Web for information on this person and write a brief summary of that person's "brand," as expressed in the information you find on the Web.

2. Search and summarize what is on the Internet today about you. You might start with Google and also check out Technorati for blogs and social media sites. Are there persons with the same name as you that come up in these searches? Would others be able to distinguish between you and those people with the same name?

3. If you were to get serious about building an online brand presence, what would you do? What brand would you hope to convey and why? What, if any, social media sites would you use? Would you develop a blog, and if so, what topics would you address and discuss?

4. How would you monitor your personal brand on the Web? Would any measures or sources of information be most useful?

> CASE CONCLUDED

The eHarmony Personality Profile questionnaire includes 258 questions that assess three primary personal characteristics: personality, values, and interests. Specific areas assessed include personal lifestyle preferences, communication style, family background, birth order, energy level, intelligence, spirituality, special interests, and future aspirations. eHarmony developed the Personality Profile by first generating a voluminous set of items asking people to report on most anything imaginable. They then had different people look at the items and pare them down, followed by small focus groups, and then larger groups to get some initial estimates of relevance and reliability.

Beyond completion of the questionnaire, eHarmony also requires members to proceed through what they call "guided communication." Guided communication was created because the company suspected that, if left on their own, people would gravitate to the most superficial questions, like sports or activities, but *not* to those issues that eHarmony had determined were most important to sustainable long-term relationships.

Guided communication leads potential couples through a formal process before ever allowing them to communicate directly, and the process is comprised of three distinct activities. First, each member of the pair is asked to choose five easy-to-answer questions from a list provided by eHarmony—and then send their responses to the other member.

Questions such as "If you were taken by your date to a party where you knew no one, how would you respond?" would be followed by multiple-choice answers, like (a) Stay close to my date, letting him/her introduce me; (b) Find a quiet spot and relax alone; (c) Strike out on my own and make friends; or (d) Ask my date if I could skip the event.

Once both parties answer, they move on to the next stage, where they are asked to exchange their personal list of "must haves" and "can't stands." In the final stage, the potential pair are asked to exchange three open-ended questions to allow for more detailed descriptions of respective values. eHarmony provides some sample questions, such as "What person in your life has been most inspirational and why?" or "Tell me about your closest friend. How long have you known them, and what do you like best about them?" But members can also write in their own questions.

Once this exchange is successfully completed, the two parties can move into "open communication." During open communication, the pair can send e-mails to each other, exchange photos, and prepare for their first meeting. A potential couple could then decide when, where, and how to meet in the offline world if they wanted to pursue a relationship. Moreover, at any point in the process, either party can "close" the match and cease any further contact. Given the number of opportunities to drop out, only 20 to 30 percent of matches ended up in open communication.

(continued)

> CASE CONCLUDED *(continued)*

The result is that when people do meet in person to pursue the relationship they already have a collective history and many starting points for discussion. Indeed, eHarmony claims that, by the time people actually meet, it will feel like they already know each other quite well. And it seems to work. The company estimates that, on average, a successful subscriber takes four to six months to get matched to someone they will eventually marry and the company boasts of tens of thousands of happy marriages.

Questions

1. Do you see any parallels to the process eHarmony promotes that might be relevant for managing people or selecting teams or job choice?

2. Would you be concerned about people reporting things about themselves that were not true?
3. eHarmony contends that "opposites attract and then attack." Explain this and support or refute the statement.
4. Note that all personal information revealed on eHarmony is *self*-reported. What are the pros and cons of self-reported information as a means of self-assessment?
5. Assume you had been through the eHarmony guided communication process and no dates emerged from your exchanges; how would you proceed? Should you address your weaknesses or build on your strengths, or both?

Concluding Note

It is easier to act yourself into a better way of feeling than to feel yourself into a better way of acting.

—O. H. Mowrer

As we noted earlier, although sometimes characterized as being elementary or simply common sense, great management is neither common nor easy, and the existence of so many ineffective managers and toxic organizations attests to that.

Much of management deals with managing other people, but the subject of this opening chapter is about managing oneself. The most personally effective managers are those who are active learners, who know themselves and their strengths and weaknesses, and who act professionally in a way that develops and nurtures strong relationships. You will undoubtedly find it difficult to apply these principles all the time. But a large part of management is by example; managers who are not personally effective set the wrong example. Personal effectiveness is perhaps more a self-discipline than a complex learning task and is a lifetime endeavor. Great management starts with your personal effectiveness. Make it your first priority!

KEY TERMS

ability 27
attention 21
Big E evidence 16
cognitive ability 27
conceptual competencies 10
emotional intelligence 27
evidence-based management 13
extraversion 28
half-truths 13
interpersonal competencies 10

introversion 28
little e evidence 16
modeling 20
motivation 22
multisource feedback 30
organizational behavior (OB) 14
personality 27
positive self-talk 26
punishment 26

reciprocal determinism 20
reproduction 22
reward 26
self-management 22
self-observation 24
SMART goals 25
social learning theory 20
technical/administrative competencies 10

Adam Bryant conducted and condensed this interview. A longer version is at

www.nytimes.com/2009/08/02/business/02corner.html. Published: August 1, 2009.

John T. Chambers, chairman and C.E.O. of Cisco Systems, has learned that big setbacks make great companies and great leaders.

CASE
In a Near-Death Event, a Corporate Rite of Passage

Q. What are the most important leadership lessons you've learned?
A. People think of us as a product of our successes. I'd actually argue that we're a product of the challenges we faced in life. And how we handled those challenges probably had more to do with what we accomplish in life.

I had an issue with dyslexia before they understood what dyslexia was. One of my teachers, Mrs. Anderson, taught me to look at it like a curve-ball. The ball breaks the same way every time. Once you get used to it, you can handle it pretty well.

So I went from almost being embarrassed reading in front of a class—you lose your place, and I read right to left—to the point where I knew I could overcome challenges. I think it also taught me sensitivity toward others.

I learned another lesson from Jack Welch. It was in 1998, and at that time we were one of the most valuable companies in the world. I said, "Jack, what does it take to have a great company?" And he said, "It takes major setbacks and overcoming those."

I hesitated for a minute, and I said, "Well, we did that in '93 and then we did it again in '97 with the Asian financial crisis." And he said, "No, John. I mean a near-death experience." I didn't understand exactly what he meant.

Then, in 2001, we had a near-death experience. We went from the most valuable company in the world to a company where they questioned the leadership. And in 2003, he called me up and said, "John, you now have a great company." I said, "Jack, it doesn't feel like it." But he was right.

Q. How has your leadership style evolved over time?
A. I'm a command-and-control person. I like being able to say turn right, and we truly have 67,000 people turn right. But that's the style of the past. Today's world requires a different leadership style—more collaboration and teamwork, including using Web 2.0 technologies. If you had told me I'd be video blogging and blogging, I would have said, no way. And yet our 20-somethings in the company really pushed me to use that more.

Q. Did you need to be pushed?
A. I thought I was very leading-edge in terms of how I communicated. My team just kept pushing, and I finally said, "Why do you want me to do this?" And they said: "John, if you don't do it our company won't learn how to do this. It won't be built into our DNA for the way we interface with customers, our employees. The top has to walk the talk." I was expecting text blogging and we did video blogging.

The first one was a little bit uncomfortable, because it's very unprofessional. You just basically put a camera there, and you go. By the second one, I realized this was going to transform communications—not just for the C.E.O., but it would change how we do business.

Q. You mentioned Jack Welch. Who else do you rely on for advice?
A. My wife. She has a way of picking me up when I get knocked on my tail. But also if I get a little bit overconfident, she brings me back to earth.

The other day, I was practicing a concept with her and saying, "You know, there are two major mistakes that I make and Cisco makes repeatedly." She looked at me and she said, "Only two?" My mistakes are always around moving too slow, or moving too fast without process behind it. And it's something that, if we're not careful, we'll repeat again and again.

Q. How do you hire?
A. First thing I want to ask you about: tell me about your results. I

(continued)

(continued)

never get hard work confused with success. So I'd walk you through the successes, and what did you do right. I'd also ask you to tell me about your failures. And that's something people make a tremendous mistake on. First, all of us have had mistakes and failures. And it's surprising how many people say, "Well, I can't think of one." That immediately loses credibility. It's the ability to be very candid on what mistakes they've made, and then the question is, what would you do differently this time?

Then I ask them who are the best people you recruited and developed, and where are they today? Third, I try to figure out if they're really oriented around the customer. Are they driven by the customer, or is the customer just somebody who gets in the way?

And I look at their communication skills, and one of the largest parts of communications is . . . what?

Q. Listening?
A. You betcha. Seeing how they listen, and are they willing to challenge you? And then I look at their knowledge in industry segments, especially the area I'm interested in.

Q. What's changed in the last few years?
A. Big time, the importance of collaboration. Big time, people who have teamwork skills, and their use of technology. If they're not collaborative, if they aren't naturally inclined toward collaboration and teamwork, if they are uncomfortable with using technology to make that happen both within Cisco and in their own life, they're probably not going to fit in here.

Discussion Questions

1. What two major lessons would you take from John Chambers and his background and career at Cisco? What surprised you about his background and perspectives?
2. How would Mr. Chambers contend that you treat setbacks and failures? Should you talk about them in a job interview?
3. What does Mr. Chambers think are the biggest changes in the workforce today? What implications does that have for your personal development and career success?
4. Invite a leading manager in your area to be interviewed. Ask similar questions that were asked of Mr. Chambers and compare and contrast the responses.

Adapted and excerpted from "In a Near-Death Event, A Corporate Rite of Passage," Adam Bryant, *The New York Times,* August 1, 2009.

SELECT MANAGE WHAT? DEBRIEFS

Making the Business Case for People Management Skills: Debrief

The overall theme of your response should be that there are very strong and documented relationships between people management quality and important firm variables like turnover, applicant attraction, citizenship behavior, performance, and productivity. The Great Places to Work institute has even found relationships between lower health care costs and safety records and customer satisfaction.

Perhaps most impressively, there is a very strong relationship between people management satisfaction and *financial performance.* For example, the charts in the text show that if you invested in just the 100 Best Places to Work in America—rated such in large part because of the quality of their people management practices—you would get a financial return of better than twice the standard market indices over the same period. That is particularly powerful data because people management practices (for example, training, family-friendly benefits, perks like subsidized vacations, sabbaticals, meals, and so on) are quite expensive and might be thought to therefore *lower* the net financial performance of firms that spend in those ways. But, in fact, those firms still dramatically *outperform* the market—simply because they attract, retain, and motivate the best people to do the best work.

With respect to how we know who the good managers are, employee ratings (360 feedback and other sources) that look at employee satisfaction (not just happiness) with their supervision are pretty good indicators. A critical point is that it is ratings of *immediate managers*—not some general index of culture or management or leadership—that makes all the difference. So if a manager's direct reports say that he/she sets clear expectations, supports their work, provides regular feedback, respects them as human beings, communicates important information to them, and distributes rewards fairly, it is safe to say that they are providing the type of people management that will yield positive outcomes for the firm.

One other potentially powerful point is that, with no other information to the contrary, we can probably assume that this firm is *average* in its people management performance. If so, that means that probably 50 percent of people in the firm are currently less than satisfied with their current manager, and probably less than 25 percent of managers engage in the people management basics at least once a week.

So, the overall point is that money spent on people management development (for example, the selection of managers, management development, mentoring, rewards geared to the success and development of others, and so on) would be well directed and, if well spent, would certainly have the potential for impact on a par with investments in product development, technology, and so on. The quote in the book, "Nothing is more important in the life of a firm than the way people feel about how they are managed," is an apt synthesis of all this.

Using OB Evidence Instead of Just Intuition: Debrief

A good goal for every organizational decision, and certainly for managers, is to try to be more evidence-based in your decisions. That is, your ultimate objective should be to find ways to make the right decision more often than not. One way to do this is to adopt an *"evidence-based decision making" (EBM) approach,* as discussed in this chapter. This form of decision making rejects using gut feeling and relying on past limited personal experience and instead is based on seeking available evidence.

Perhaps the major obstacle to EBM is that in many organizations it often runs counter to the way things are currently done. A great deal that passes as "best practice" most likely is not. In some cases, there simply is no evidence to support what is thought to be best practice. In other cases, there is evidence to support that what are thought to be best practices are, in fact, inferior practices. In short, most organizations do not practice evidence-based management. As a result, they often underperform with respect to their major stakeholders: employees, investors, and the community.

Although there are many specifics and nuances to becoming more evidence-based in your decision style, three strategies are particularly important: (1) Do not jump to conclusions—seek and ask for evidence; (2) know the different types of evidence; (3) evaluate your decisions.

Do not jump to conclusions. Perhaps the biggest, and most elusive, element in using EBM is to be able to mitigate the natural human tendency to rely on first instincts and our own experience or a compelling testimonial, and instead to actually seek evidence. Thus, when someone says "research shows" or the "evidence is clear," great managers know to dig a little deeper to seek out that evidence. At the end of the day, anecdotes and previous experience may be all that is available to help inform decisions, but in far too many cases anecdotes are used where a rich scientific literature exists to help make better decisions. This text, for example, relies heavily on the scientific base of knowledge that exists in organizational behavior.

Understand the different types of evidence. One easy way to understand the usefulness of evidence is to make a distinction between Big E evidence and little e evidence. *Big E evidence* refers to generalizable knowledge regarding cause and effect connections derived from scientific methods. Big E evidence is based upon years of studies, across many different types of samples or contexts with many different types of jobs, people, and organizations. Most importantly, Big E evidence represents a form of research that is *systematic*—meaning that it is planned and methodical and avoids drawing conclusions simply on the basis of opinion or anecdote. Such evidence is often summarized in large scientific literature reviews or empirical summaries known as meta-analyses or "studies of studies." Big E evidence is likely to be the best source for informing practices since it is drawn from years of study across large populations under varying circumstances.

In contrast, *little e evidence* represents local or organizational specific data collection efforts to inform a specific decision. Popular quality improvement processes such as Six Sigma provide little e evidence, important information that helps the organization but that may not generalize or translate into other arenas or other

(continued)

(continued)

organizations. Examples abound of organizations that failed by trying to apply a practice that while wildly successful in another organization didn't take hold in their own. Thus, while little e evidence may improve decision making in any organization, we must be careful not to apply it broadly.

Evaluate your decisions and create a culture of EBM. No true EBM can exist without some systematic evaluation of decisions. That is, once decisions are made, how did it go? What worked and didn't work? What additional evidence will we have to inform future decisions? When managers take an evidence-based approach, they contribute to an organization that values and encourages active participation in the evidence-based process.

Describing Yourself and Your Style: Expanding Your Self-Awareness: Debrief

There are, of course, an almost infinite number of things you could talk about (education, past jobs, hobbies, and so on) in responding to the question "Tell us about yourself." As a result, rambling and unfocused responses to that question are all too common. The key is to try and focus on those elements of your personality, background, and experience that would be *directly relevant* to your role as a manager.

A good place to start would be to engage in multiple self-assessments (such as those presented in Table 1.3). Having completed these types of assessments, you should be able to talk in an informed way about your critical-thinking capacity, your personality characteristics and preferences, what you value most, your emotional and cultural competence, and/or your career orientation.

It is important to note here that there really is no one preferred managerial profile—and that is not just sugar-coated "nice talk." Most personal profiles can be adapted in ways to be successful in most situations, but to do so it *is* critical that you are fully aware of your personal profile—and very few young managers rarely are. Moreover, you need to be able to translate your profile into an understanding of the implications (both strengths and potential liabilities) of that profile for success in a particular managerial role. For example, if your personality is especially extroverted, you may excel in stimulating ideas and dealing with people, but are challenged in listening to others and paying attention to details. If you value collective behavior and cooperation, you may wish to seek contexts where such values are embraced and rewarded relative to solely individual outcomes. If your analytical ability is below average, you may wish to leverage other strengths and partner with colleagues who have more refined analysis skills to complement your profile. Reflect on the type of situations where you have been most successful and be aware of when and how you have been able to adapt your personal style to be effective in different situations.

Most importantly, you should feel no compulsion to suggest that you are something you are *not*—indeed that is a recipe for managerial failure. Rather, you want to accurately convey who you are and then determine how best to leverage your strengths and mitigate your weaknesses to excel in any given situation. And always start by focusing on your strengths—research has shown that it is both easier and far more productive to leverage your strengths than to try to "fix" your weaknesses.

Finally, although a self-assessed profile gives you a means of framing your different personal characteristics and orientations in a logical and focused way, such self-assessments are only one "lens" on yourself. It is also important to include actual examples of how you have behaved in ways that are consistent with your profile, as well as external feedback from sources *outside yourself*. That is, your credibility is enhanced if you can provide external validation of your self-assessment, and examples of how you have, say, shown conscientiousness in an actual work situation, or found ways to complement your strengths (and compensate for weaknesses) with the differing strengths of others, or clarified your preferences in ways that facilitated the accomplishment of a team goal. Ideally, you will be able to create your own personal story that conveys who you are in an informed way that paints a picture of a manager we would want to be led by.

Managing Stress and Time

OBJECTIVES

KNOWING   DOING

After reading this chapter, you should be able to:

KO 2-1 Describe the personal and organizational consequences of excessive stress.

KO 2-2 Describe the most common causes of stress in work contexts.

KO 2-3 Describe supporting evidence for effective stress management interventions.

KO 2-4 Explain the fundamentals of effective time management.

KO 2-5 Describe the characteristics of workplace cultures that reduce stress while retaining high performance and productivity.

DO 2-1 Diagnose your own sources of stress.

DO 2-2 Demonstrate effective strategies to manage your own workplace stress.

DO 2-3 Advise a colleague about how to manage stress using evidence-based recommendations.

DO 2-4 Apply research-supported strategies for minimizing choking in a pressure situation.

DO 2-5 Apply fundamental time management strategies to your work or school life.

DO 2-6 Advocate for development of workplace characteristics that create high-performance, low-stress work environments.

"Stress primarily comes from not taking action over something that you can have some control over. So if I find that some particular thing is causing me to have stress, that's a warning flag for me. What it means is there's something that I haven't completely identified that is bothering me, and I haven't yet taken any action on it."

—Jeff Bezos, CEO, Amazon

Case: CIGNA

Most competitive business organizations have taken the approach that work is inevitably stressful and that managing stress is up to each individual employee—*not* the company. However, one progressive firm that has taken a more responsive approach to managing its employees' stress is CIGNA. CIGNA is a global health care insurance organization, based in Philadelphia, Pennsylvania, that has over 30,000 employees. The company has concluded that the stressors facing their workforce today are greater than ever before. Among the growing sources of stress are increased hours necessitated by tight economic times and leaner staffs, new technologies that keep the job in front of people 24/7, and "survivor guilt" that workers feel when their co-workers lose their jobs.

Instead of expecting its workers to soldier on despite unsettling feelings and situations, CIGNA devotes considerable time and resources to help its employees resolve their stress. The assistance is available via CIGNA's pioneering Employee Assistance Program (EAP), which provides counseling for a wide range of personal and work-related stressors. CIGNA even offers its EAP services to some of its *client companies* as part of its health benefits plan.

1. Is personal stress really a company's business? Shouldn't personal issues be kept private and dealt with by each individual employee?

2. What are the most damaging contemporary causes of stress? Is stress more or different today than ever before? Does technology and rapid change make our workplaces more or differently stressful?

3. How do stress-related issues potentially reduce an individual's performance in a firm?

4. What potential *business performance* metrics (for example, productivity, cost reduction, customer service) might be affected by effective stress management strategies or interventions?

1. Getting a Priority Done Under Stress

You have been in a management role for two years and find yourself absolutely overwhelmed. While you feel as if you are working hard most every hour of the day, you are frustrated with your inability to get all your priority work done. You have begun to work much longer hours and are experiencing a great deal of stress and a loss of balance in your life. There are so many distractions during the day that you generally find it difficult to get started on bigger projects. Now you have a really important project due and have already missed one deadline. You feel guilty about missing that deadline, but you feel so tired and stressed that you aren't sure how you're going to keep from slipping further behind in your most important work.

How would you define the problem here? How might you deal with the many time robbers and distractions that keep you from working on the big project? What specific strategies might you use? What should you do right away?

2. Overcoming the Two Biggest Time Management Traps

Effective time management is among the most pronounced cases of a knowing-doing gap. That is, most everyone has a pretty good idea what they *should* do—but most of us just can't muster the discipline to actually do it. Simply stated, the two biggest time management traps are (1) failure to prioritize—that is, research shows that we often procrastinate and put off working on our major priorities in favor of more easily accomplished chores with lower priorities; and (2) we do not devote our peak productivity times to our most important tasks (for example, responding to our e-mail first thing in the morning).

Given that you want to be an effective manager of your time, identify three proven strategies, feasible for you, that will help you avoid the two time management traps that haunt so many.

3. Minimizing Your Chances of Choking in a Pressure Situation

You are under consideration for the biggest job of your life. You just found out that you have made it to the final three candidates and will be asked to come to the company headquarters where you will be evaluated in a panel interview (multiple interviewers shooting questions at you), a half-hour presentation, and a leaderless group discussion where company executives will observe your performance.

Like any normal person, the opportunity excites you—you want it so much—but the process scares you to death and you are fearful that you will choke and lose your chance. The cold reality is that many people, even superstar athletes, choke in the situations that matter most—so your fear is hardly unwarranted or irrational. You talked with your father and he said, "Hey, don't worry about it, just go and do your best," but that was not very satisfying and does little to calm your nerves. So what should you do to prepare? What type of preparations and strategies give you the best chance of avoiding choking?

4. Making Changes in a Workplace to Lower Stress and Enhance (Not Lower) Productivity

The president of your company just appointed you to a task force that he says is a high priority in the company. In kicking off the first meeting, he notes that he is concerned that ". . . stress has gotten out of hand in our workplace. Economic times are hard and our revenue streams are at risk, but we cannot be so worried about our bottom line that we stress-out our people to the point of exhaustion and sickness. My understanding is that lower stress can save us in health care costs, keep absenteeism and turnover low, and even raise productivity if we do it right. I want to have a generally healthier and lower-stress place to work. I hear Google has foosball tables in their headquarters and their people just love them—should we get a few of those or stuff like that? . . ."

Given that your president is truly serious about creating a lower-stress workplace culture, what feasibly could be done? What features of the workplace have been linked to lower stress, and is there any evidence they could be implemented without a huge investment and without lowering productivity?

Introduction

The demands of work are ever-increasing, and organizations are expecting people will do more and more with less and less. A recent survey of American workers found almost 80 percent of employees felt the previous year was their most stressful year ever at work.[1] At one point or another, all of us have experienced stress. Some of you may very well be feeling it right now. Stress is a common feature of modern life; indeed, it is so well known to many of us that it seems almost unnecessary to define what stress is exactly. It is, however, helpful to know how scientists and researchers have defined stress so that we have a common language to use throughout this chapter. **Stress** is the physiological and psychological states of arousal (for example, rapid heartbeat, loss of sleep, anxiety) activated when we encounter a stressor. Think about a time you have experienced stress. Almost always, it was because you were uncertain about something you really cared about: You weren't sure you could finish an important project on time, you worried whether you had the ability to handle an assignment, or perhaps you were overwhelmed with the prospect of competing with someone you perceived as more skilled or competent.

Strains are defined as outcomes of stress. Often, strains are more long-term consequences of chronic stress that have not been alleviated by some means. If you are a sufferer of tension headaches, low back pain, depression, or fatigue, your woes could possibly be caused by unmanaged stress. While some people used to scoff at stress as being something that is trivial and "all in your head," a massive amount of research suggests otherwise. The evidence is clear that sustained stress plays a role in strains, ranging from heart disease to cancer, and can weaken the body's immune function so that it is less capable of fighting off illness and disease. Moreover, stress and the accompanying strains can take a huge toll on an organization's productivity and performance.

Stress is often misunderstood, and some of the most persistent misconceptions are presented in the Myths 2.1 box below.

Practice this!
Go to www.baldwin2e.com

?¿ MYTHS 2.1 Myths of Stress and Time Management

- *Stress is a personal, non-work issue and should not be a concern in a work organization.* This myth prevails all too often and leads to nonsense like "stress is all in your head" and "people should deal with personal issues on their own time." The reality is that stress generates enormous costs for organizations and should be a priority consideration for anyone working or managing.

- *All stress is bad.* In fact, all stress is not bad and some level of stress is necessary for performance—and has even been shown to be positively related to good mental health. Too much stress, however, is extraordinarily damaging to both people and organizations.

- *A stressor is a stressor.* One of the most important lessons of stress management is that stress is personal on several levels. Most obviously, what stresses one person may not stress another. In addition, the best coping strategies should be customized to an individual context and time. The best stress management strategy for a soldier about to enter a battle is generally very different than a parent caring for a terminally-ill child, or a manager with too many competing priorities.

- *Only novices choke.* Research on professional soccer players and golfers reveals that even their performance declines dramatically as the pressure and consequence of failure increases. Choking stems from pressure situations and mental overload, and even people we recognize as superstars often choke under pressure.

- *Good time management means being an efficient workaholic.* Just the opposite is true. The best time managers work smarter, rather than harder, and focus their energy on true priorities.

Personal and Organizational Consequences of Stress

Stress has many detrimental consequences and can inhibit effective listening, decision making, planning, and the generation of new ideas. For example, several research studies have shown that managers experiencing high stress are more likely to selectively perceive information, fixate on single solutions to problems, revert to old habits to cope with current situations, show less creativity, and overestimate how fast time is passing.[2]

In addition to the direct effects on work performance, people who incur long-term stress are also much more likely to develop physical and mental problems. Medical researchers estimate that between 50 and 70 percent of disease and illness are in part due to long-term stress. Common stress-related physical problems include heart disease, stroke, cancer, diabetes, and lung disease. Stress-related psychological problems include sleep dysfunction, sexual dysfunction, depression, and problems with interpersonal relationships. The evidence is clear that a high degree of sustained stress makes our immune systems less effective at fighting illness.

Clearly, if stress goes on unmanaged, there are consequences for an individual's health and well-being. However, there are also consequences that extend beyond the individual and impact relationships, work, and society. From a managerial perspective, the costs of job stress and strain are great, with estimates ranging as high as $300 billion annually in the U.S. alone.[3] Researchers have linked stress to a variety of workplace outcomes and have found that stress has a detrimental effect in terms of reducing people's commitment to their organization and increasing absenteeism and turnover intentions.[4]

Some Stress Is Good

At the same time, although stress is thought of as a negative or unpleasant state, some level of stress is essential to high performance. The father of stress research, Hans Selye, called this **eustress,** which he defined as a controlled or productive stress.[5] It is eustress (pronounced "u-stress") that gives us our competitive edge. Without any sense of pressure and arousal, many of us would have no reason to get out of bed in the morning; thus eustress represents that ideal amount of arousal.

Increasingly, researchers are probing the upside of stress. Some now believe that short-term boosts of stress can strengthen the immune system and protect against some diseases like Alzheimer's by keeping the brain cells working at peak capacity. People who experience moderate levels of stress before surgery have a better recovery than those with high or low levels. Other research has found that stress can help prevent breast cancer because it suppresses the production of estrogen, and children of mothers who had higher levels of the stress hormone cortisol during pregnancy were developmentally ahead of those of women with lower levels.[6] In organizations, it is well known that sales representatives often respond to quotas, and customer service people often work hardest to mollify angry customers—revealing that stress can and does facilitate higher performance and productivity.

So, the paradox of stress is that too much will kill performance, but so will too little (see Figure 2.1)! Each person has an optimal point at which stress helps improve performance by motivating and grabbing their attention as if to say, "Don't take this for granted, it's important." So the challenge is not to eliminate stress, but to understand how it arises and to manage it in a way that does not derail our life and work. Great managers are aware of different sources of stress and seek ways to proactively manage it to avoid its harmful effects.

We hire for skills but then the whole person shows up.
—Unknown

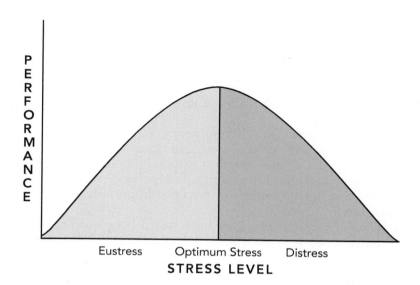

FIGURE 2.1
The Stress/Performance
Curve

Stress Is Personal: Individual Differences and Their Relationship to Stress

Have you ever wondered why it is some people under stress can still function and move forward while others sit depressed, withdrawn, or become physically sick? Given that so many stressors are inevitable and beyond our control, the most critical lesson of stress management is not to aim to eliminate all stresses in your life, but rather to build your resiliency and personal systems (for example, time management) to cope with the stress you will face. The fact is that events by themselves do not cause stress; it is how we experience events, and how resilient we are, that determines how stress affects us.

Imagine that you are about to give a speech in front of an auditorium of hundreds of people. How would you feel? Exhilarated? Terrified? Bored? How about instead of a speech you were about to go skydiving? Can you think of any activities or things that you find particularly stressful that are not stressful (or perhaps are even *enjoyable*) to other people? Those who study stress have made the same observation and have proposed a theory, known as **transactional theory,** which suggests that the negative effects of stress on a person are a function of the *interaction* between the person and their environment.[7] They specify several major components to the stress process: First, when people encounter something potentially stressful in the environment, they go through primary appraisal where they evaluate the potential stressor with respect to its potential impact on them. It is possible that different people will recognize the same situation in different ways.

One person may view a trip to the dentist as threatening while another person may have no problem with the dentist but may instead be fearful of being in confined spaces like in an elevator. If the stimulus is not deemed threatening to the person in question, he or she simply goes on with life as normal. However, if the stimulus is perceived as a threat during primary appraisal, the person will engage in secondary appraisal, which is the individual's assessment of what he or she can do in response to the threat. The individual can engage in coping, which can include cognitive and behavioral responses to the stressor. Coping strategies, which we will be discussing in greater detail later in the chapter, vary by person and also by the type of stressor. Some people have certain coping strategies they frequently turn to—for example, avoiding problems or seeking help from other

It is not falling in the water that makes you drown. It is what you do once you're in there.

—Anonymous

people. Different stressors also call for different coping strategies. Sometimes we can avoid the stressor altogether by changing the environment. For example, people who are afraid of heights can often avoid situations with this stressor. In contrast, people who are afraid of crowds might not be able to avoid large groups of people indefinitely. Instead, these individuals might try to use rationalization to remind themselves that their fears are unwarranted or may try relaxation or deep-breathing exercises.

In addition to the idea that different people have different ideas of what is or is not a stressor, researchers have identified certain personality variables that affect people's appraisal of and reaction to potential stressors. That is, differences in personality can impact how someone experiences and copes with stress, and we describe and illustrate three of the most important of these personality characteristics next.

Type A behavior pattern. You may have heard people describe themselves as being "Type A"—you may even have described yourself this way. The term has been around since the 1950s when first identified and reported by medical doctors Friedman and Rosenbaum.[8] Being cardiologists, Friedman and Rosenbaum were particularly interested in the relationship between cardiovascular disease and people's personality. They described a cluster of characteristics and

MANAGER'S TOOL KIT

Tool Kit 2.1   Type A Personality Assessment

Read the following questions and then put an X next to the items with which you agree.

1. _____ I never seem to have enough time to accomplish my goals.
2. _____ I don't understand people who become so impatient in traffic that they start honking.
3. _____ I frankly don't care whether I do or do not make it into the top 10 percent.
4. _____ I find it difficult and useless to confide in someone.
5. _____ A driver's license should be more difficult to get in order to avoid having all those idiots on the road.
6. _____ It doesn't bother me if I cannot finish what I planned for the day.
7. _____ I often choose to spend time with my friends or family, even though I have something important to do.
8. _____ I am hardly ever satisfied with my achievements.
9. _____ I get no particular pleasure out of acquiring things.
10. _____ It is easy for me to express my feelings.
11. _____ People who don't know what they want get on my nerves.
12. _____ I think that hobbies such as fishing or bowling are just a waste of time.
13. _____ When I finish my task, I feel good about myself.
14. _____ I function best under stress or pressure.
15. _____ Talking about emotions is a sign of weakness and can be used by others to get at you.
16. _____ It doesn't matter whether my family is financially secure. The important thing is to be together.
17. _____ If everybody did their job properly, my life would be much easier.

To calculate your score, count the number of X's that were next to numbers 1, 4, 5, 8, 11, 12, 13, 14, 15, 17.

Scores of 0–3 suggest a strong Type B, 14–17 suggest a strong Type A, and scores of 4–13 suggest a mixed Type A/B profile.

behaviors that included time urgency, hostility, ambitiousness, impatience, and perfectionism. Specifically, they described people with a **Type A behavior pattern** as "individuals who are engaged in a relatively chronic struggle to obtain an unlimited number of poorly defined things from their environment in the shortest period of time and, if necessary, against the opposing effects of other things or persons in this same environment."[9] In their rush to achieve success and conquer their environments, Type A individuals (see Tool Kit 2.1 for a quick measure of your behavior type) are likely to do everything quickly from talking to walking to eating to driving. Because achievement is typically very important to them, Type A individuals usually like to have control over their environments and sometimes dislike working in teams or with other people.[10]

Although initially thought to be related to coronary heart disease, current research shows that it is one specific aspect of the Type A behavior pattern—hostility—that is most predictive of one's health. For example, a recent study found that together with job demands, trait hostility predicted individuals' health care usage.[11]

Locus of control. Do you believe that the stars are responsible for your fate and that whatever your horoscope reads is what you are destined for that day? Or do you think you are in control of your day and your ultimate fate? If you answered yes to the latter question, you are likely someone with an internal locus of control and you can be pleased by the knowledge that you are likely more resilient to stressors and stress than are people who answered yes to the first question. **Locus of control** is the extent to which we believe we control our own environments and lives. Having an internal locus of control means that you believe you have control over your environment, whereas having an external locus of control means you think sources outside yourself (for example, luck or fate) are generally responsible for your environment. In general, having an internal locus of control is more beneficial with regard to job performance and stress because people with such a mindset are more likely to take positive actions to address stressors because they believe that their actions will be effective.[12] Tool Kit 2.2 provides you with a brief locus of control diagnosis.

However, an extremely strong internal locus of control is not always beneficial. After all, we cannot control every situation in our lives, and to think that we can is not healthy. For example, during Hurricane Katrina, many people who could have evacuated decided not to, perhaps because they felt immune to the storm and capable of taking care of the situation themselves. Many of those people ended up having to be rescued by emergency workers and some even died. Research indicates that people who demand an extreme amount of control, even in situations where they *can't* have control, suffer in terms of increased stress and physiological reactivity.[13,14]

Self-efficacy. If the train from the popular children's book *The Little Blue Engine That Could* was given a personality test, that little train would probably score highly on **self-efficacy,** which is a personal assessment of "how well one can execute courses of action required to deal with prospective situations."[15] An abundance of research demonstrates the positive effects of self-efficacy. People who believe they can accomplish something have higher motivation and are more likely to persist in the face of obstacles. Because they think they can succeed, they engage in the behaviors necessary to succeed, and are in fact more likely than people with low self-efficacy to succeed at their jobs and tasks.[16] In contrast, a lack of self-efficacy has been speculated to relate to the stress process because people low in self-efficacy believe they do not have the resources available to cope with stressors. As an example, one study found that self-efficacy played a role in whether or not salespeople experienced symptoms of burnout.[17]

It's not the load that breaks you down. It's the way you carry it.
—Legendary singer and actress, Lena Horne

⚒ MANAGER'S TOOL KIT

Tool Kit 2.2   Locus of Control

Put an X next to the response in each pair with which you agree more.

_____ People's misfortunes result from the mistakes they make.
_____ Many of the unhappy things in people's lives are partly due to bad luck.

_____ In the long run, people get the respect they deserve in this world.
_____ Unfortunately, an individual's worth often passes unrecognized no matter how hard he tries.

_____ Capable people who fail to became leaders have not taken advantage of their opportunities.
_____ Without the right breaks, one cannot be an effective leader.

_____ People who can't get others to like them don't understand how to get along with others.
_____ No matter how hard you try, some people just don't like you.

_____ In the case of the well-prepared student, there is rarely, if ever, such a thing as an unfair test.
_____ Many times exam questions tend to be so unrelated to course work that studying is really useless.

_____ Becoming a success is a matter of hard work; luck has little or nothing to do with it.
_____ Getting a good job depends mainly on being in the right place at the right time.

_____ The average citizen can have an influence in government decisions.
_____ This world is run by the few people in power, and there is not much the little guy can do about it.

_____ In my case, getting what I want has little or nothing to do with luck.
_____ Many times we might just as well decide what to do by flipping a coin.

_____ What happens to me is my own doing.
_____ Sometimes I feel that I don't have enough control over the direction my life is taking.

To calculate your score, count the number of Xs associated with the first (or top) choice in each pair. This is your score. Scores of 7–9 indicate a highly internal locus of control, while scores of 0–3 indicate a highly external locus of control. Scores from 4–6 indicate a middle of the road score.

KO **2-2**   ## Common Sources and Causes of Stress

DO **2-1**   ### Traumatic Events vs. Daily Hassles

Everyone encounters a variety of stressors, and they can derive from many sources. Stress may stem from interpersonal relationships such as conflict with co-workers or subordinates, ambiguity regarding one's role, or feelings of inequity or poor communication with others. It may also stem from conditions in the working environment such as changes in responsibility, reduction in company resources, or pay cuts. It might come from personal issues such as a divorce, potential lawsuit, or the death of a family member. And it may emerge from the pressure of too little time to handle the workload, scheduling conflicts, and deadlines.

Stress is the trash of modern life—we all generate it but if you don't dispose of it properly, it will pile up and overtake your life.

—Terri Guillemets

One important research finding related to the sources of stress is that people tend to *overestimate* how much large events in their lives contribute to their stress level and grossly *underestimate* the effects of "daily hassles."[18] Certainly, major life event stressors such as moving, a new job, or the death of a loved one can take a toll on an individual. Yet these stressors are often accepted as traumatic in people's lives and thus organizations often make accommodations for them.

On the other hand, the stressful effects of daily hassles are typically discounted. Daily hassles are annoying events that occur during the workday that make accomplishing work more difficult. Take, for example, the all-too-common event of a computer crash, and losing all access to e-mail and work files. For many of us, daily hassles also include unexpected walk-ins who want to "shoot the bull," phone calls or e-mails from bosses or colleagues who need immediate responses, and other urgent meetings or requests.

Research has shown that these daily hassles are more likely associated with reported stress than more major life events. Indeed, some research has found that daily hassles are the most significant influence on mood, fatigue, and perceived workload.[19] Put simply, the more you must deal with daily hassles, the more stressed out you are likely to be. Trying to overcome the unexpected unplanned obstacles of daily hassles is often what really wears you down. Conversely, daily uplifts or unexpected positive outcomes can have the opposite impact and can recharge an individual.

Role Conflict and Ambiguity

All of us play multiple roles in our lives. For example, your boss may also be a mother and a dance instructor. Your colleague runs the local chapter of Habitat for Humanity and cares for his aging uncle. Think of all the roles you play in your life. The potential list might be quite lengthy: employee, manager, volunteer, mentor, parent, sibling, daughter/son, neighbor, and so on. **Role theory** is a perspective to understanding stress that focuses on the roles we play in our lives. When we don't know how to fill a role or what we are supposed to do in it, we experience **role ambiguity.** Role ambiguity can occur at work if employees are not given clear job descriptions or managers do not communicate performance expectations and feedback. Role ambiguity is stressful for employees because if they don't know what they are supposed to be doing, they can't very well do a good job at it.

In addition to role ambiguity, another potential problem addressed by role theory is **role conflict,** which occurs when our multiple roles conflict with each other. At work, role conflict might occur for employees answering to two managers who have different expectations. Such arrangements are common in matrix organizations in which employees often report to both their department manager and the project manager. While such arrangements certainly have their benefits, they can also cause problems if the managers have conflicting expectations. If employees fulfilling their department roles are simultaneously unable to fulfill their roles on their project team, you can understand why they might feel stressed: They are in a no-win position because they can't successfully succeed in both roles at once.

Another common role conflict that causes stress has to do with the roles people play inside and outside of work. **Work–family conflict** is "a form of inter-role conflict in which the role pressures from the work and family domains are incompatible in some respect."[20] **Work interferences with family (WIF)** occur when in fulfilling their work roles, people are unable to fulfill their family roles in the way that they want. For example, if a manager must travel for work on the same weekend that his or her child is performing in a sports event, that person's work is interfering with the family role. **Family interferences with work (FIW)** are experienced when in fulfilling a family role, a work role is neglected.

Practice this!
Go to www.baldwin2e.com

Practice this!
Go to www.baldwin2e.com

For example, if someone is going through a divorce or is taking care of an ailing family member, it is likely that this stress will impact his or her work role. Whether the person is physically or simply mentally absent from work, family obligations can prevent a person from performing at 100 percent capacity in the workplace.

Research on role theory has shown that both role ambiguity and role conflict are significantly related to a number of negative outcomes: lower job satisfaction, reduced commitment to one's organization, higher anxiety, and increased turnover intentions.[21] In addition to those findings, research focusing more specifically on work–family conflict has shown that people reporting more extreme WIF and FIW are at increased risk for substance abuse, anxiety disorders, emotional exhaustion, and reduced job performance. In fact, a recent meta-analysis of work–family conflict found that a person's job satisfaction is significantly related to his or her reports of family factors like stress, conflict, and support.[22]

Exhaustion of Resources and Burnout

We only have so much we can give to others in terms of our time, energy, money, and other resources. A model known as **conservation of resources (COR)** suggests that stress results from three possible threats to our resources: (1) the threat of losing a personal resource; (2) the actual net loss of a personal resource; or (3) the lack of resource gain following the investment of our personal energy and resources.[23]

For example, when organizations experience mass layoffs, the remaining employees (the "layoff survivors") are often expected to pick up the slack. They must devote more time and energy, and usually they do not receive additional resources for doing so. These time and emotional pressures, not to mention the threat of the loss of their own job in future layoffs, can lead to severe stress. As another example, counselors, social workers, nurses, and other people who work in the "helping professions" often experience stress as a result of constantly giving their energy and time to take care of others. Indeed workers in these types of professions may be particularly susceptible to a severe state of stress called "burnout." **Burnout** refers to "a syndrome of emotional exhaustion, depersonalization, and reduced personal accomplishment that employees may experience after prolonged stress that has exceeded their resources to address."[24]

A number of specific emotional components are associated with burnout. **Emotional exhaustion** is the state of feeling psychologically "drained" or "used up" by the job. For example, a counselor experiencing emotional exhaustion might feel like he has lost the ability to feel the emotions necessary to perform his work. **Depersonalization** is associated with feeling cynical, psychologically detached, and indifferent to one's work. **Reduced personal accomplishment** is the feeling that one's work doesn't really matter. A manager experiencing reduced personal accomplishment might feel that she can't get positive results out of her employees no matter how hard she tries. She may feel personally ineffective and powerless in her work.

Originally, burnout was conceptualized as something that happened to employees in the helping professions. However, we now know that people in any work can experience burnout if they feel that their resources are depleted. Other research shows that certain kinds of people might be more prone to burnout than others. Age is one of the strongest demographic predictors of burnout with younger employees experiencing significantly greater burnout than older employees.[25] However, because younger workers also tend to have less experience, status, and income on the job, it is difficult to determine whether it is in fact age or these other factors that primarily contribute to burnout. Although burnout was originally presumed to affect more women than men, research does not confirm this assumption. The only gender differences seem to be that men experience more cynicism (depersonalization) symptoms, while women experience slightly more emotional exhaustion symptoms.[26] Some studies show a positive correlation between education and burnout, perhaps because people with more education have jobs that demand more out of them. With regard to marital status, married employees show less burnout than do single employees, perhaps because they have more support.[27]

The time to relax is when you don't have time for it.

—Sydney J. Harris

Emotional Labor

Imagine that you are having a very bad day. You have gotten into an argument with a family member, your car had a flat tire on the way to work, and you have a pounding headache. At work you have a very important meeting with clients who are upset about their account with the company and they start shouting at you. What do you do? If you're like most people, you do your best to remain professional and pleasant even though you actually feel miserable and angry. There is a name for what you're doing and it is called "emotional labor." **Emotional labor** is the process of regulating both feelings and expressions for the benefit of organizational goals.[28] The term was originally coined by a researcher who was observing the phenomenon in flight attendants.[29] Like burnout, emotional labor is likely to be common in the helping professions, but it has been reported by many workers, including supermarket cashiers, Disneyland ride operators, and salon employees. In many of these jobs, part of the job is acting a certain way even if you don't feel like doing so. Expanding on this notion of "acting" on the job, an important distinction can be made between employees engaging in "surface acting" and those engaging in "deep acting." **Surface acting** is "managing observable expressions," such as maintaining a pleasant facial expression and vocal tone. **Deep acting** is the actual management of feelings, or actually trying to feel a certain way that is consistent with the emotions that are supposed to be expressed.[30] Comparing surface to deep acting, the former is like "faking" your emotions while the latter is trying to manage your emotions so you don't really need to fake your expressions.

Obviously, organizations want their employees to act in ways consistent with the organization's goals. However, managers should be aware that emotional labor can be taxing on employees, particularly employees who are not well suited to that type of work. Some research has found that emotional labor is stressful and can lead to burnout, job dissatisfaction, and increased intentions to quit one's job.[31] With regard to preventing or alleviating the problems associated with emotional labor, managers have several strategies available to them. For jobs that require a great deal of emotional labor (for example, bill collectors or flight attendants), managers may want to focus their recruitment and selection techniques on identifying people who are good at managing their emotions and have a natural disposition that suits the job.[32] Beyond selecting the right people for the job, there may be additional benefits to training employees on how to deal with and manage their emotions. Social support and positive group cohesion in the workplace can also be beneficial, as can giving employees *some* latitude over the emotions they can express.[33] For example, instead of subscribing to an unwavering belief that "the customer is always right," employees likely would benefit from some degree of latitude—for example, being allowed to refuse service to a particularly rude or aggressive customer.

Tension is who you think you should be. Relaxation is who you are.

—Chinese Proverb

High Demands and Low Control

Another well-documented source of stress and strain occurs when people are experiencing both high work demands *and* low control over the task.[34] This source of stress has been labeled the "demand-control model" and the basic notion is that the combination of excessive demands *and* low decision latitude (rather than just one in isolation) leads to stress. **Demands** include the physical, intellectual, and emotional requirements of a job. **Control** is the amount of personal discretion and autonomy the person has in doing the job. Some jobs are inherently more stressful than others if they require great demands but afford the employees little control. For example, nurses, food service employees, and customer service representatives often have great demands put on them in terms of time, emotional labor, and physical labor. However, they do not typically have much say in how they do their job, instead being required to follow strict guidelines or procedures. In contrast, jobs like managers, journalists, and engineers may also have great demands placed on them, but are often granted significantly more control.

Research studies of the demand-control model have shown some support. For example, one study found that people reporting high demands but low control in their jobs and lives were at significantly higher risk of illness than other people in the study.[35] A group of researchers found that high demands and low control predicted high systolic blood pressure and lower job satisfaction.[36] In a five-year longitudinal study, nurses with the highest reported demands and lowest reported control were sick more often and had higher health care expenditures than other nurses in the sample.[37]

Some research suggests that social support can buffer the negative effects of high demand and low control.[38] Other studies, however, are not as optimistic that social support can reduce the stress associated with high demands and low control.[39] In spite of the mixed findings, social support from peers and managers rarely has a *negative* impact on employees! Thus, offering social support to employees experiencing high demands and low control can be a relatively easy and inexpensive means of possibly alleviating stress and strain for those around you.

Stress management starts with identifying the sources of stress in your life. This isn't as easy as it sounds. Your true sources of stress aren't always obvious, and it's all too easy to overlook your own stress-inducing thoughts, feelings, and behaviors. Sure, you may know that you're constantly worried about work deadlines. But maybe it's your procrastination, rather than the actual job demands, that leads to deadline stress. To identify your true sources of stress, look closely at your habits, attitude, and excuses:

- Do you explain away stress as temporary ("I just have a million things going on right now") even though you can't remember the last time you took a breather?
- Do you define stress as an integral part of your work or home life ("Things are always crazy around here") or as a part of your personality ("I have a lot of nervous energy, that's all")?
- Do you blame your stress on other people or outside events, or view it as entirely normal and unexceptional?

Until you accept responsibility for the role you play in creating or maintaining it, your stress level will remain outside your control. Tool Kit 2.3 is a good way to begin your journey to better stress management.

```
⚒ MANAGER'S TOOL KIT
```

Tool Kit 2.3 **What Are the Sources of YOUR Stress: Starting a Stress Journal**

A stress journal can help you identify the regular stressors in your life and the way you deal with them. Each time you feel stressed, keep track of it in your journal. As you keep a daily log, you will begin to see patterns and common themes. Write down:

- What caused your stress (make a guess if you're unsure)
- How you felt, both physically and emotionally
- How you acted in response
- What you did to make yourself feel better

Next, think about the ways you currently manage and cope with stress in your life. Your stress journal can help you identify them. Are your coping strategies healthy or unhealthy, helpful or unproductive? Unfortunately, many people cope with stress in ways that compound the problem.

For example, the following strategies may temporarily reduce stress, but they cause more damage in the long run:

- Smoking
- Drinking too much
- Overeating or undereating
- Zoning out for hours in front of the TV or computer
- Withdrawing from friends, family, and activities

- Using pills, alcohol, or drugs to relax
- Sleeping too much
- Procrastinating
- Filling up every minute of the day to avoid facing problems
- Taking out your stress on others (lashing out, angry outbursts, physical violence)

Your ultimate goal is to replace unhealthy strategies with those that have been proven to help prevent and cope with stress—but you cannot do that until you are clear on where your stress comes from and what you currently do to cope.

Stress Management Strategies

KO **2-3**

The Importance of Matching Strategies with Causes

DO **2-2**

DO **2-3**

DO **2-4**

It may seem that there's nothing you can do about your stress level. The job or school requirements aren't going to go away, there will never be more hours in the day for all your commitments, and your career or family responsibilities will always be demanding. But you have a lot more control than you might think. In fact, the simple realization that you're in control of your life is the foundation of stress management.

Managing stress is all about taking charge: taking charge of your thoughts, your emotions, your schedule, your environment, and the way you deal with problems. The ultimate goal is a balanced life, with time for work, relationships, relaxation, and fun—plus the resilience to hold up under pressure and meet

The biggest difference between an experienced speaker and an inexperienced speaker is when an experienced speaker is scared to death, he knows it is normal.

—Mark Twain

challenges head on. Moreover, a critical point that is too often overlooked or just ignored in stress management seminars and books is that no strategy works for all people all the time. Different situations call for different responses. For example, it makes little sense to tell combat soldiers about the advantages of avoiding too much cholesterol or salt in their diets. Similarly, it would be pointless to tell an overwhelmed single parent of four about the stress-reduction advantages of getting a hobby.

Different timing and preferences also call for different stress management strategies. Before a big test, studying hard may be the best way to relieve stress. If necessary, you can tell yourself later that one bad grade won't ruin your life. Exercise can be a great stress reducer, but only if you *like* exercise. If you happen to hate working out, you'll feel stressed out every time you enter the gym. Likewise, experts are always telling stressed-out people to seek social support, something that has been shown in many circumstances to be a proven stress reliever—but *not always.* A bad marriage is much worse than not being married, and nobody needs to build a friendship network with people who will just criticize everything you do.

The simple but powerful point is that the strategies identified and described in the following section are not universally effective nor will they be useful in every situation with every person. Rather, they are strategies for which there is evidence of success in reducing stress and its consequences under certain circumstances. There are many healthy ways to manage and cope with stress, but they all require change. You can either change the situation (prevention) or change your reaction (coping). Prevention strategies are aimed at removing or altering the stressors in your environment. Thus, they are "first line" defenses in that they are aimed at stopping stress before it starts. For example, role ambiguity, one of the stressors identified in role theory, might be reduced by giving employees clear job descriptions, goals, and feedback on goal progress. Excessive work and time demands are frequently cited as stressors and might be lessened with technologies that take some of the burden off the employees.

Practice this!
Go to www.baldwin2e.com

Of course, primary prevention strategies are not always practical because it is not possible to remove every stressor from the work environment or our lives. For example, consider an employee who has experienced the death of a close family member. As the employee's manager, you obviously cannot "undo" this death or remove it as a stressor. Or as another example, consider the problems associated with a bad economy where a business must choose between a number of bad options: layoffs, increased work for current employees, pay cuts, or business closure. In such cases, coping strategies are required.

Coping strategies are aimed at helping people cope and minimizing the negative impact once stress has been experienced. Sometimes coping interventions are known as "band-aid" approaches because they don't really prevent the stressor (the "cut") but hopefully minimize the damage.[40] There are many secondary interventions available, including exercise, meditation, relaxation techniques, social support, time management training, and communication or relationship-building training. Again, no single method works for everyone or in every situation, so experiment with different techniques and strategies. Focus on what fits your situation and the nature of the stress that you (or those working with you) are facing.

Prevention Strategies

Enhancing Control and Predictability

Stress turns out to be much less stressful if you think there's something constructive you can do about it.[41] This makes intuitive sense. If you're trying to sleep at night and there's a barking dog nearby with owners who are not home, you'll experience a lot less stress if you know you can reduce the noise by closing the window or if you have some way to contact the owner. If the dog is so loud that closing the window doesn't reduce the noise much, or if you don't know the owners or have a way of getting in touch with them, the barking is much more stressful. If someone's laid off, they're in much better psychological shape if they have the sense that they'll get another job soon when they go looking. If a person sinks into hopelessness and inaction, they suffer a much greater toll in mind and body.

Indeed, researchers have found that the most important variable among types of stress is an individual's sense of control in a given situation.[42] The least harmful stress scenario is one in which an individual has a sufficient degree of control or some idea of predictability. Put simply, predictable pain is less stressful because individuals know when to relax (gaining relief from pain as well as protecting themselves from its damaging effects). But when individuals have no warning of pain, they are in a state of constant stress. A common example from business organizations is the difference between the stress experienced by top executives who are in control of their fate and their middle-level managers who are not. The former can pick and choose when to enter or engage a stressful situation or problem, but the latter have no control or any ability to predict when such a situation will arise and are constantly on alert or in a state of anxiety.

Although it is not always possible or desirable to reduce the demands and increase the control of a job, managers might benefit from thinking through such possibilities. Especially if managers must place increased demands on employees, for example, during times of layoffs, it may be helpful to give employees more control over how they meet those demands. Using the example of a layoff, when layoff survivors are expected to take on additional workloads, managers might consider allowing for flexible work arrangements that allow them to work some of the time from home.

Predictability figures into the stress equation in one more way. If we know enough about the stressor to judge just how dangerous it is, it's a lot less stressful than if we can't tell. It's easier if we know the barking dog is safely behind a fence than if we're afraid the dog's waiting for us outside or is strong enough to break in through the window.

Novelty, the opposite of predictability, can be stressful in itself. An interesting study of people who lived through the bombing of London during World War II demonstrates this in graphic terms. At the beginning of the bombing, central London was hit every night, whereas in the suburbs the bombing was more intermittent and unpredictable. Suburbanites living through this experience had a significantly greater incidence of stomach problems than those living in the more regularly bombed urban core. By the third month of the bombing, after everyone had had a chance to get used to it, rates dropped back to near-normal.[43]

Social Connectedness

It's no surprise to anyone living with high stress levels that having someone there to share the experience is one of the best stress-relievers. Put simply, stress (or more importantly, stress relief) loves company.[44] Robert Sapolsky, author of the landmark work on stress and its effects, *Why Zebras Don't Get Ulcers*, spent much of his life researching the coping behavior of baboons. Highly intelligent and social, these higher primates serve well in many ways as models for human behavior.

Baboons typically live in groups of 50–150 and structure their societies hierarchically. Alpha males are the dominant baboons in their tribe. Sapolsky has identified two distinct styles of alpha-male baboons—the competitor and the cooperator:

- The competitor climbs to the top and stays on top (while he can) by being the baddest baboon in the tribe. He intimidates, he beats up the opposition, he takes no prisoners.
- The cooperator builds alliances and relationships, spends more time playing with young baboons and grooming younger females in a non-sexual manner.

Guess which one has higher stress levels and a shorter life? That wasn't too hard. The competitor, reminiscent in many ways of classic human Type A behavior, always has to watch his back. The cooperator tends to live a lot longer, aging much more gracefully.[45]

Many studies in humans are consistent with the baboon findings and show that stress is much less damaging if we have social support and can interact well with others.[46] People with larger and more varied social networks tend to have better well-being. There are many types of support that other people can offer us in times of need to help us deal with the stressors in our lives. Sapolsky identified several different kinds of support that include instrumental, emotional, informational, and appraisal. **Instrumental support** is support that is tangible and practical in nature and is a direct means of helping someone. For example, imagine you are experiencing stress because you want to leave work on time to get to an important family event but you need to finish a work project before you leave. Now imagine that your very compassionate co-worker offers to stay late and finish the work so you can attend the family function. In this example, your kind co-worker is offering instrumental support.

Emotional support includes sympathy, listening, and caring for others. If you lost your job or you are going through a divorce and a friend listens to your troubles and tells you that he cares, that person is offering emotional support. Now imagine that you have a particularly touchy human resources issue with an employee and you aren't sure how to handle it. If you have a friend who is a human resource specialist or an employment lawyer, that friend may offer you **informational support,** or information that helps you solve the problem. Another type of support is **appraisal support,** which is feedback that builds your self-esteem. If you just botched a big presentation at work, and a co-worker listens to you and reassures you that it wasn't so bad and that normally you give fantastic presentations, this person is giving you appraisal support.

One of the most arresting examples of the power of connectedness (and the lack thereof) comes from King Frederick II of Sicily, a 14th-century monarch who was prone to dramatic experiments.[47] The king wanted to discover the "natural" language of humans—in other words, what they would speak if they never heard any words from their parents (Latin seemed like a strong possibility). The king "acquired" a group of infants and instructed his servants to feed the children but not hold them, play with them, and above all, speak with them. The children all died before the experiment got very far. At any age, loneliness and isolation are some of the biggest stressors of all and social connectedness is therefore a key element in stress reduction.

Avoiding Choking

One of the most painful consequences of stress is what is commonly known as "**choking**" which is defined as performance decrements under pressure circumstances. Choking got its name because a person frayed by pressure might as well not have oxygen. What makes choking so fascinating is that it happens to all of us—from superstar athletes to high-school test-takers—and it is among the most dreaded fears of human beings.

Preventing Choking

Fortunately, scientists have begun to uncover the causes of choking and some preventative strategies. The sequence of events typically goes like this: When people get nervous about performing, they become self-conscious. They start to fixate on themselves, trying to make sure that they don't make any mistakes. This can be lethal for a performer. The soccer player misses the penalty kick by a mile. The golfer lightly taps his putt and comes up way short. The test-taker suddenly cannot remember how to do the simplest math calculation. In effect, performers are incapacitated by their own thoughts and self-destruct.

The existing research suggests that there are two antidotes for choking that have shown promise: pressure practice and focused automated behavior. A good example of pressure practice comes from the work of a researcher named Raoul Oudejans who studies many kinds of high-pressure situations, with a particular focus on police officers. Oudejans found that training to shoot a handgun under stress helps to prevent police officers from missing an important target when it counts.[48] More specifically, Oudejans asked a group of police officers to practice shooting first at an opponent who was putting the pressure on by actually firing back—not with real bullets, but with colored soap cartridges. He then asked these same police officers to take shots at cardboard targets (the kind you see cops practicing on in the movies). After the shooting practice, Raoul split his police officers into two groups. Half of the officers practiced firing at the live opponent and the other half only practiced shooting at the cardboard targets. Then, everyone came back together and took some final shots—first at the live opponents and then at the stationary cutouts.

During the initial shooting practice, all of the officers missed more shots when firing at a live opponent compared with firing at the sedentary cardboard targets. Not so surprising. This was true after training as well, but only for those officers whose practice had been limited to the cardboard cutouts. For those officers who practiced shooting at an opponent, after training they were just as good shots when aiming at the live individuals as they were when aiming at the stationary cutouts. The opportunity to "practice under the gun" of an opponent, so to speak, helped to develop the police officers' shots for more real-life stressful shooting situations.

You might wonder if this type of "pressure practice" is really effective, given that the stress simulated in training is not nearly as overwhelming as that of a real high-stakes performance. Just think about the pressures a police officer faces when forced to shoot at someone who is firing back with *real bullets* rather than soap cartridges, or the pressure a professional soccer player feels when he is about to take a decisive penalty kick in the World Cup finals, or even the pressure a high-school senior feels as she sits down to take the SAT that will make or break her college dreams. Can you even begin to mimic the types of stressors that come into play in actual high-stakes situations? The answer is, yes, because even practicing under mild levels of stress can prevent people from falling victim to the dreaded choke when high levels of stress come around.

The evidence is clear that regardless of whether you are shooting at someone on the battlefield, shooting hoops in basketball, or sitting for the SAT, you can benefit from mild stress training.[49] When people practice in a casual environment with nothing on the line and are then put under stress to perform well, they often choke under the pressure. But if people practice shooting a gun or shooting hoops or even problem solving on the fly with some mild stressors to begin with (say, a small amount of money for good performance or a few people watching a dress rehearsal), their performance doesn't suffer when the big pressures come around. Even if you are not an athlete or ever in the position of saving lives or performing heroic feats, you too can benefit by closing the performance gap between practice and high-stakes performance situations. The next time you are preparing for a big presentation, don't rehearse alone. Instead, pull aside a co-worker whose opinion you value to hear your speech. The nervousness you feel with your co-worker staring at you might be just what allows you to shrug off the added pressure that will inevitably occur in the real do-or-die business meeting. Simulating low levels of stress helps prevent cracking under increased pressure, because people who practice this way learn to stay calm in the face of whatever comes their way.

You play like you practice.
—Vince Lombardi,
legendary football coach

A second line of research on choking illuminates another antidote. Sian Beilock, a professor of psychology at the University of Chicago, has spent much time studying golfing—a common arena for choking.[50] When people are learning how to putt, it can seem very daunting. Golfers need to assess the lay of the green, calculate the line of the ball, and get a feel for the grain of the turf. Then they have to monitor their putting motion and make sure they hit the ball with a smooth straight stroke. For an inexperienced player, a golf putt can seem unbearably hard, like a life-sized trigonometry problem. Interestingly, Beilock has shown that novices hit better putts when they consciously reflect on their actions. The more time they spend thinking about the putt, the more likely they are to make it. By concentrating on their game, by paying attention to the mechanics of their stroke, they can avoid beginner's mistakes.

A little experience, however, changes everything. After golfers have learned how to putt—once they have memorized the necessary movements—analyzing the stroke is a waste of time. In fact, Beilock's data demonstrate the benefits of relying on the automatic brain when playing a familiar sport. She found that when experienced golfers are forced to think about their putts, they hit *significantly worse* shots. When you are at a high level, your skills become somewhat automated and that is a good thing with regard to choking. That is, you don't want to pay attention to every step in what you're doing. When you do, the part of your brain that monitors your behavior starts to interfere with actions that are normally made without thinking. You begin second-guessing skills that you have refined through years of practice and the worst part about choking is that it tends to spiral. The failures build upon each other, so a stressful situation is made more stressful.

For example, in studies of soccer penalty kicks, researchers found that in the highest-pressure situation, the kickers tended to fixate on the goalie, looking at him earlier in the kicking process and keeping their eyes on him longer. As a result, they subsequently tended to kick their shots toward him more often as well, making their shots easier to block. The tendency of people under stress to focus on the threat to the exclusion of all else is a well-established process called "cognitive narrowing." A driver who is trying to avoid a ditch, for instance, might become so fixated on it that she drives right into it.

It turns out that the best strategy for soccer penalty-kick takers is to pick a spot in the goal net and practice hitting that spot relentlessly, always totally ignoring the goalkeeper in the process. Training in this strategy is likely to build on the tight coordination between eye movements and subsequent actions, making for more accurate shooting. In other words, the way to avoid choking is to devise a strategy and then train, train, train. Well-learned behaviors hold up better under stress than those that haven't been fully transferred to procedural memory. If you want to do something well under intense pressure, make sure you can do it *automatically*—thereby avoiding the critical element of choking—which is thinking too much.

MANAGEMENT LIVE 2.1

Choking Under Stress: It Even Happens to Superstars

Consider the following statistics, reported recently by researchers in Norway:

Professional soccer players in penalty kick shootouts score at a rate of 92 percent when the score is tied and a goal ensures their side an immediate win. But when they need to score to tie the shootout, with a miss meaning defeat, the success rate drops to 60 percent.

Geir Jordet, a professor at the Norwegian School of Sport Sciences in Oslo, has analyzed shootouts with fervor. Jordet also found that shooting percentages tend to drop with each successive kick—86.6 percent for the first shooter, 81.7 for the second, 79.3 for the third, and so on. According to Jordet, his data starkly demonstrate the impact of pressure and stress.[51]

Penalty kicks, in theory, represent a relatively simple task for a professional player: score against only the goalkeeper from 12 yards, and do it at your own pace. And yet the shootout has become a confounding stumbling block, one that regularly has leading stars self-destructing in front of international audiences.

The choking effect is hardly limited to soccer. Chuck Knoblauch, for instance, was one of major league baseball's finest infielders. But in 1999, playing for the New York Yankees as a second baseman, he developed the "yips" and started making inaccurate throws to first base. (This involves throwing the ball less than 20 feet—it's the shortest throw in the game.) Although Knoblauch had been playing in the position for more than two decades, his throws were now sailing into the stands—even injuring fans on occasion. Paradoxically, it was the easy throws that had become the most difficult, simple tosses that allowed him time to think. This strange psychological lapse would ultimately end his career.

Coping Strategies

Psychological Hardiness

The fact is people who have their stress levels under control still experience an equal share of bad events and daily hassles in their lives. They face the same pressures and adversities as everyone else. Yet some people do have a mental resiliency or *hardiness* that helps them cope with stress. During the breakup of AT&T in the 1980s, researchers explored what distinguished those managers who were most susceptible to physical and emotional illness from those who demonstrated **psychological hardiness,**[52] the ability to remain psychologically stable and healthy in the face of significant stress. Other studies of successful coping have been conducted in a variety of demanding settings, including businesses, battlefields, schools, and medical clinics.[53] That research has helped identify four recurring factors that distinguish those with psychological hardiness: physical fitness, commitment, control, and challenge.

Physical Fitness. It may seem a bit far afield for a management book to discuss physical fitness, but fitness boosts mental performance and is critical to coping with stress.[54] Indeed, hundreds of studies demonstrate that exercise can reduce the negative physical and psychological consequences of stress. For example, a meta-analysis of fitness studies demonstrated that exercise can alleviate clinical depression and is just as effective at doing so as more traditional strategies like therapy, behavioral intervention, and social contact.[55] More specifically, one study of college professors found that those most physically active processed data faster and experienced slower age-related decline in information processing.[56] In another study, commercial real estate brokers who participated in an

Physical fitness is the basis for all other forms of excellence.

— John F. Kennedy

aerobics training program (walking or running once a day, three times a week, for 12 weeks) earned larger commissions than brokers who did not participate.[57]

People who are fit are also less likely to suffer from illnesses exacerbated by obesity and more likely to possess higher levels of energy and become more resilient to depression, tension, and stress. The resiliency allows you to fend off those uncontrollable stressors and deal more productively with daily hassles. In an aptly named book, *Fit to Lead*, Christopher Neck and his colleagues outline three essential elements of fitness: body fitness, nutritional fitness, and mental fitness (that is, psychological hardiness).[58] While it is beyond our scope to go into specifics of fitness and nutritional programs, we simply underscore their importance to stress management because they are directly related to psychological hardiness.

In a study of managers in an extremely stressful transition, it was found that those with the highest psychological hardiness engaged in significantly more regular physical exercise.[59] Unfortunately, a common stress-induced trap is to believe we are too busy to exercise and maintain our physical condition. That thinking produces a negative cycle that further reduces our physical capacity to deal with stress at the very times we need it most. The importance of physical hardiness is further illustrated in Management Live 2.2.

Exercise can be beneficial in many forms, such as yoga and lifting weights, and aerobic exercise like running, biking, swimming, or dancing. Organizations can encourage employees to seek the benefits of exercise by offering onsite gyms or discounted gym memberships. Some companies have done creative competitions or activities like having employees log their exercise time to receive prizes for various levels of activity. Or, after the popularity of shows like *The Biggest Loser*, some companies have even started friendly competitions for employees to get healthy, lose weight, and exercise.

Commitment.   Commitment refers to persevering or sticking it out through a hard time. Being committed to an outcome keeps us going even in the midst of setbacks, obstacles, and discouraging news. Being committed to a goal helps us overcome occasional losses of motivation and remain steadfast in our efforts. Commitment can also refer to a sense of connection beyond a single domain.

For example, in the AT&T study, while the hardy managers were clearly invested in the company's reorganization, they were not restricted to interest in their work life. They had a broader life and were nurtured by their commitment to family, friends, religious practice, recreation, and hobbies. Recall the earlier discussion of the research that has shown that social support (friends, family,

⇄ MANAGEMENT LIVE 2.2

Executive Fitness and Performance[60]

Research has demonstrated that physical fitness is associated with managerial performance. Fit managers have more energy and experience more positive moods and well-being. In addition, fit managers are more likely than unfit managers to have lower anxiety, tension, and stress. A large percentage of disease in the United States stems from, or is exacerbated by, stress. Obviously, the sicker one is, the less likely he or she is able to perform at peak levels. A survey of 3,000 companies revealed many leading executives understand the role that diet and exercise play in their performance as those from a range of different firms reported running five miles a day, lifting weights for 30 minutes, or jogging along airport roads between flights. Managers serious about their performance know exercise and diet are key to enhancing their ability to stave off work stress and stay productive under pressure.

and others who will say to you, "You can do this" or "We believe in you") is important in buffering the effects of stress. Social support can help you put your stressors in perspective.

When under intense stress, we naturally withdraw from the world and concentrate exclusively on solving the problem causing the stress. Sometimes that reaction is useful and appropriate, but, more often, asking for help from our network of family and friends is crucially important to coping with stress. Commitments that extend beyond our work world are an especially good remedy for stress.

(Control.) The third element of hardiness is perceived control. In a tough situation, hardy individuals do not become overwhelmed or helpless. Instead, they strive to gain control of what they can by going into action. While acknowledging that many aspects of a crisis situation cannot be controlled, they also understand that, by intentionally holding a positive, optimistic, hopeful outlook, they can determine their reaction to any predicament. If we approach life and its inherent stressors with this optimistic attitude, we're much more likely to deal easily with stressful situations than if we're convinced that what happens to us is outside our control and nothing we do affects our outcomes.

Only optimists get things done.
—Ralph Waldo Emerson

One stress-management strategy closely aligned with control is that of seeking **small wins.** Large projects can be inordinately stressful, and many people facing a daunting task will avoid it as long as possible, thereby only increasing their stress. However, if you break a large task into smaller chunks, with action steps, you'll find you can get early wins. Small but meaningful milestones can give us confidence and insight to know "we can do it." So celebrate and reward yourself each time you get a small win in whatever way reinforces your behavior best.

Celebrate any progress. Don't wait to get perfect.
—Ann McGee Cooper

Challenge. Finally, psychologically hardy individuals see problems as challenges rather than as threats. This difference is important because, rather than being overwhelmed and seeking to retreat, these individuals get busy looking for solutions. Seeing a problem as a challenge mobilizes our resources to deal with it and encourages us to pursue the possibilities of a successful outcome. Quickly dealing with feelings of loss, while not harboring false hopes and illusions about the future, enables us to explore new options. Hardy people view change as a stepping stone, not a stumbling block.

The key point of emphasis here is that psychological hardiness is less about the actual stressors faced and more about how we *frame* our response to those stressors. From a stress management standpoint, that is encouraging. We can never eliminate stressors, but if we can find ways to help cope with the inevitable stressors we will face, then we can more effectively manage stress in our lives.

If people concentrated on the really important things in life, there'd be a shortage of fishing poles.
—Chuck Lawler

Outlets for Relief/Dealing with Stress in the Moment

While much of the previous discussion has been focused on planned stress reduction and longer-term strategies, we are often in situations where we must be able to deal with stress in the moment. Hardy and resilient individuals do not panic, withdraw, or flounder, but rather rely on several techniques for dealing with their stressors. That is, they are more skilled in relaxing their mind and body, taking a timeout, and knowing how to "repair" their mood. The following are examples of techniques you can use to deal with stress in the moment.

Muscle Relaxation.   Sometimes stress is so great that a timeout is needed. Muscle relaxation only takes a few minutes, but can help relieve stress immediately. Simply tense and then release muscle groups, starting with your feet and working your way up your body (legs, torso, arms, neck). Roll your head and shrug your shoulders.

❙ Deep Breathing. ❙ This simple exercise can make a difference in short-term stress relief. First, take in a deep breath and hold it for about five seconds. Then breathe out slowly (that's important) until you have completely exhaled, trying to extend the length of the out-breath a little bit longer each time. Repeat this about 5 to 10 times.

Mood Repair.   Research demonstrates that people in positive mood states are more resilient to stress.[61] Moreover, it has been found that you can curb or "repair" your negative moods by understanding what triggers your positive moods.[62] For some, it's a piece of chocolate or a latte; for others it may be listening to a piece of music, talking on the phone with a friend, or visualizing a scenario that gives them pleasure (their "happy place"). Learn what puts you in a positive mood and use it when you're in a stressed or negative frame of mind.

KO **2-4**
DO **2-5**

Time Management Fundamentals

One of the most important ways of coping with stress is through effective time management. By managing time better, most of us can prevent many of the problems that stress causes by not putting ourselves in stressful situations in the first place. The inability to manage time is among the greatest sources of stress and can doom the most talented, motivated, and conscientious of people. While most everyone would agree that time management and organization are among the most critical elements of personal effectiveness, a person trying to enhance his or her time management is often told to exercise willpower, try harder, resist temptation, or seek divine guidance. Although well intentioned, this advice offers little in terms of actionable strategies or skills to help an individual undertake the process of development. Remember, it's the execution of time management skills that remains your biggest challenge. So learn the fundamentals of time management, but remember that it is the discipline to apply them that is your ultimate objective.

Today, there are thousands of books on time management and a staggering number of training programs and "systems" on the market. Close inspection of this bewildering volume of material, however, reveals a few simple but powerful principles. In the following, we discuss and illustrate four principles that, although called by various names, are consistently present in the research and writing of time management experts.

If you are not sure why you are doing something, you can never do enough of it.

—David Allen

First Be Effective, Then Be Efficient

Managing time with an effectiveness approach means you actually pay attention to your goals and regularly revisit what is important to you—and avoid just diligently working on whatever comes up or is urgent or in front of you. As management guru Peter Drucker has famously noted, *doing the right things* should come before *doing things right*.

Start with Written Goals

Most people have an intuitive sense that goals are an important organizing mechanism. Stephen Covey, author of *The 7 Habits of Highly Effective People*, calls this "starting with the end in mind." The notion is simple. A set of long-term lifetime goals can help you discover what you really want to do, help motivate you to do it, and give meaning to the way you spend your time. It can help you feel in control of your destiny and provide a measuring stick to gauge your success. Written goals can help you choose and decide among many different aspects of your life.

A goal unwritten is only a dream.
— Anonymous

For some reason, however, a surprisingly small percentage of people actually write down, review, and or update their short- or long-term goals. This is unfortunate because studies have shown that those with written goals actually achieve higher levels of success. There is nothing mystical about writing personal goals, and though perhaps not explicitly aware of it, you have probably been thinking about your lifetime goals almost as long as you have been alive. However, thinking about your goals is quite different from writing them down. Unwritten goals often remain vague or utopian dreams such as "get a great job" or "become wealthy." Writing down goals tends to make them more concrete and specific and helps you probe beneath the surface. So always start with goals and revisit them regularly. And don't limit them to financial or career progression goals. What personal, social, or spiritual aspirations do you have?

Follow the 80/20 Rule

Often referred to as Pareto's Law, the **80/20 rule** holds that only 20 percent of the work produces 80 percent of the value, 80 percent of sales come from 20 percent of customers, 80 percent of file usage is in 20 percent of the files, and so on. Sometimes that ratio may be a little more, and sometimes a little less, but the rule generally holds true. In the context of time management, then, if all tasks on a list were arranged in order of value, 80 percent of the value would come from 20 percent of the tasks, while the remaining 20 percent of the value would come from 80 percent of the tasks. Therefore, it is important to analyze which tasks make up the most important 20 percent and spend the bulk of your time on those.

Practice this!
Go to www.baldwin2e.com

Use the Time Management Matrix

Expanding on the 80/20 principle, several time management experts have pointed out the usefulness of a "time management matrix," in which your activities can be categorized in terms of their relative importance and urgency (Table 2.1).[63]

TABLE 2.1   Time Management Matrix

	Urgent	Not Urgent
Important	**QUADRANT I** • Crises • Pressing problems • Deadline-driven projects	**QUADRANT II** • Prevention • Relationship building • Recognizing new opportunities • Planning
Not Important	**QUADRANT III** • Interruptions • Some calls • Some mail • Some reports • Some meetings	**QUADRANT IV** • Trivia • Busy work • Some mail • Some phone calls • Time wasters

Important activities are those that are tied to your goals and produce a desired result. They accomplish a valued end or achieve a meaningful purpose. Urgent activities are those that demand immediate attention. They are associated with a need expressed by someone else or relate to an uncomfortable problem or situation that requires a solution as soon as possible.

Of course, one of the most difficult decisions you must make is determining what is important and what is urgent. There are no easy rules, and life's events and demands do not come with "important" or "urgent" tags. In fact, every problem or time demand is likely important to someone. However, if you let others determine what is and is not important, then you certainly will never effectively manage your time. Perhaps the most important objective is to manage your time in a way that reduces the number of things you do on an urgent basis and allows you to devote your attention to those things of true importance to your life and work.

Just DON'T Do It: Learn to Say No

One of the most powerful words in your time management vocabulary should be the word *no*. In fact, a good axiom for your time management improvement might well be a reversal of Nike's popular *Just do it!* slogan to *Just don't do it!* Of course, that approach is a lot easier to talk about than to actually use when we are confronted with demands or attractive offers from others. Many of us have an inherent desire to please and fear we may miss out on some opportunity. However, as noted earlier, effective time management is largely learning to devote yourself fully to your most important tasks. That means what you choose *not* to do can be as important as what you do. So learn how to say no. Three effective ways to say no are:

- "I'm sorry. That's not a priority for me right now."
- "I have made so many commitments to others; it would be unfair to them and you if I took on anything more at this point."
- "No."

For more specific time management suggestions, please read Management Live 2.3.

⇄ MANAGEMENT LIVE 2.3

Never Check E-Mail in the Morning—and Other Surprising Time-Savers[64]

Don't look at e-mail first thing.   Instead, use the morning to focus on your most important tasks. Most people's minds are sharpest in the morning, and completing important responsibilities before lunch creates a sense of relief and accomplishment that can carry you through the afternoon. If the first thing you do in the morning is check your e-mail, then there are any number of ways that you'll be diverted from your critical tasks to deal with all the little things your inbox has for you. E-mail creates a false sense of accomplishment for people because in the span of an hour or so you're likely to deal with a large number of different issues (likely half of them are personal) and so you feel like you've accomplished quite a bit, but now that it's almost time for lunch you really haven't done much at all. You feel like you have been working very hard but you probably haven't done anything that is a priority on your to-do list.

Avoid the urge to multitask.   When many things need to get done, it's tempting to try to do them all at once. But multitasking isn't the secret to productivity—it's a sure way to be inefficient. Recent evidence suggests that it takes the brain longer to recognize and process each item it is working on when multitasking than when it is focused on a single job. Other studies have found that work quality suffers when we try to multitask.[65] To get many things done, either in the office or at home, do just one thing at a time. If another obligation crops up or an unrelated idea pops into your head, pause from your current task only long enough to enter it in your planner.

Shorten your workday.   If 10 hours isn't enough, try nine and a half. Losing 30 minutes of work time each day makes you organize your time better. No longer will you tolerate interruptions . . . make personal phone calls from the office . . . or chat around the water cooler. Your pace will pick up, your focus will sharpen, and you'll soon find you're getting more done despite the shorter workday. You have freed up two and a half hours for yourself each week. This works just as well outside the workplace. Allot fewer hours for chores and projects, and you're more likely to buckle down and get them done.

Take a break.   Hard workers often feel that they don't have time to take a break. Recharging your batteries isn't wasted time—it keeps you running. Escape from your workday life for at least 30 minutes each day or a few hours each week. Use this escape time to do whatever it is that most effectively transports you away mentally from your daily responsibilities. That might be reading a novel, exercising at the gym, or listening to music. These escapes keep your mind sharp and your energy level high. If you just can't find the time, add the escape more formally to your schedule. If your escape is exercise, plan a game of tennis or golf with a friend—the friend will be counting on you, so it will be tough for you to back out. If your escape is music, buy season tickets to a local concert series—you're more likely to attend if you have already purchased the tickets.

Don't do chores when big deadlines loom.   Faced with a big important task and several small, easy, but less vital chores, many people start by tackling the chores. Knocking these off provides a sense that progress has been made, and it clears the tables to focus on the big responsibility—but it is still a poor strategy.

Always tackle the most important job first, though it might be the most difficult and time-consuming.   In the corporate world, the most important task usually is the one that will generate or save the most money for the company. If you put off this crucial task, unforeseen complications or new assignments might prevent you from getting the important tasks done at all.

Plan the Work, Then Work the Plan

Make Good Lists for Effective Prioritization

The time management matrix is essentially about prioritization, and virtually every time management expert focuses on the importance of prioritizing and scheduling, usually in the form of a daily or weekly "to-do" list, a "next-action" listing, or a defect tally checklist. The basics of good lists are simple: create and review them every day, ideally at the same consistent time; keep them visible; and use them as a guide to action (see Tool Kit 2.4 for how to make effective "to-do" lists). One of the important rules is to keep all of your to-do items on a master list, rather than jotting them down on miscellaneous scraps of paper or typing them indiscriminately in a cell phone or iPad. You may want to keep your list in a separate planner or in your phone or computer.

Perhaps the more difficult challenge is to determine what goes on the list and how to prioritize it. David Allen, author of the bestseller *Getting Things Done*, argues that what he calls "collection" is the foundation of productive time

MANAGER'S TOOL KIT

Tool Kit 2.4   Making Effective To-Do Lists[66]

Making effective to-do lists saves time, energy, stress, and even gas. A good list lets you forget—once you have a written reminder, your mind is free to concentrate on other things. A to-do list even helps you meet your goals. Whether you're a legal pad, iPhone, or back-of-the-phone-bill type, pick a system that works—and write it down!

Have **one master list—in one place.** Pull those scraps out of your pockets, purse, and glove compartment, and gather them in one place.

- **Investigate the many electronic options** for list makers. Your PDA is a great repository for all of your lists, including movies to rent, gifts to buy, and important contacts who expect a call that day.

- **Categorize your to-dos,** keeping like items together such as calls to make, things to buy, and errands to run. Other categories might include gifts, projects, contacts, and goals.

- **Prioritize the items** on your list to stay focused on what's critical. Revisit your to-do list regularly to reassess and reprioritize as situations change, and to check off completed items.

- **Break it down.** Then break it down some more. Don't confuse to-dos with goals or projects. A to-do is a single, specific action that will move a project toward completion. It's just one step. For example, "Plan the committee lunch" is a project. "E-mail Karen to get catering contact" is a to-do. In this case, the action of e-mailing Karen is a simple, two-minute undertaking—something small and innocuous that you can do without thinking. The lunch plans won't be complete after you've finished this to-do, but you'll be much closer than you were while you were ignoring the "Plan the committee lunch" project. After it's done, add the next step to your list. Breaking down your task to the smallest possible action forces you to think through each step up front. With the thinking out of the way, it's easy to dash off that e-mail, make that call, or file that report, and move your work along with much less resistance.

- **Use specific action verbs and include as many details as you'll need.** You're overdue for a cleaning, but the "Make a dentist appointment" to-do just hasn't gotten done. When you write that task down, use an actionable verb (call? e-mail?) and include whatever details your future self needs to check it off. "Call Dr. M. at 555-4567 for a cleaning any time before 11AM on Jan 17, 18, or 19" is a specific detailed to-do. Now that's something you can get done while you're stuck in traffic with a cell phone.

Your to-do list is your way of assigning tasks to yourself, so be as helpful to yourself as you would to a personal assistant. Make your to-dos small and specific to set yourself up for that glorious moment when you can cross them off the list as DONE.

management.[67] He suggests that you need to collect everything that commands your attention and do so in some place other than in your head. Contrary to some traditional time management advice, you do not want things on the top of your mind, unless you are working on them. Some people, students in particular, often try to just keep their to-do list in their heads. That rarely works well. Effective time managers collect and organize their tasks where they can be reviewed and serve as a reminder, so they do not have to be stored in their minds.

Once you've collected your to-do list, most experts recommend you review not just routine items but everything that has a high priority today or might not get done without special attention. Alan Lakein further suggests you use what he calls the **ABC method:** assigning an A to a high-priority item, a B to an item of medium priority, and a C to low-priority items. To use the ABC system effectively, you should ensure you are incorporating not just short-term but long-term items, derived from your lifetime goals. Most importantly, always start with As, not with Cs, even when you have just a few minutes of free time. The essence of effective time management is to direct your efforts to high priorities. That is easily stated but exceedingly hard to do.[68] For a good example of the importance of having a good list, see Management Live 2.4.

Ask "What's the Next Action?"

The most critical question for any to-do item you have collected is: What is the next action? Consideration of that step is one of the most powerful mindsets of effective time management. Many people think they have determined the next action when they write it down or note something like "set meeting." But in this instance, "set meeting" is not the next action because it does not describe a physical behavior. What is the first step to actually setting a meeting? It could be making a phone call or sending an e-mail, but to whom? Decide. If you don't know, you simply postpone the decision and create inefficiency in your process because you will have to revisit the issue and will have it hanging over you.

Know Yourself and Your Time Use

Consistent with the earlier section on self-awareness, a principle that is included in almost every good time management discussion is that you have to know yourself and your style. While we would not recommend you monitor *every* minute of your time, some documented record of how you currently spend your time is certainly a useful exercise. One good strategy is to record your time selectively, keeping track of particular problem items you feel are consuming an inordinate amount of time.

Each of us has both external and internal prime time. Internal prime time is that time of the day when we typically work best—morning, afternoon, or evening. External prime time is the best time to attend to other people—those you have to deal with in classes, at work, or at home.

Internal prime time is the time when you concentrate best. If you had to pick the two hours of the day when you think most clearly, which would you pick? The two hours you select are probably your internal prime time and you should aim to save all your internal prime time for prime high-priority projects.

Interestingly, studies have shown that most business people pick the first couple hours at work as their internal prime time, yet this is usually the time they read the newspaper, answer routine mail, get yesterday's unanswered e-mails and voicemails, and talk to colleagues and employees. It would be much better to save such routine tasks for non-prime hours.

Fight Procrastination

The secret of getting ahead is getting started. The secret of getting started is breaking your complex overwhelming tasks into small manageable tasks, and then starting on the first one.

—Mark Twain

It is hardly provocative to point out that procrastination is a major stumbling block everyone faces in trying to achieve both long- and short-term goals. Procrastination is that familiar situation when you have written down and prioritized a critical A task and just can't seem to get started on it. Instead, we may resort to doing a bunch of C priority tasks, like straightening the desk, checking our e-mail, or reading a magazine, to avoid focusing on the A task.

One strategy to address this common human scenario is what Alan Lakein calls the **Swiss Cheese Method.**[69] The Swiss Cheese Method refers to poking small holes in the A project and those holes are what Lakein calls instant tasks. An instant task requires five minutes or less of your time and makes some sort of hole in your high-priority task. So in the 10 minutes before you head off to class, you have time for two instant tasks. To find out what they should be, (1) make a list of possible instant tasks and (2) set priorities. The only rule for generating instant tasks is that they can be started quickly and easily and are in some way connected to your overwhelming A project. Perhaps the nicest thing about the Swiss Cheese Method is it does not really matter what instant tasks you ultimately select. How much of a contribution a particular instant task will make to getting your A project done is far less important than to do something, anything, on that project. Whatever you choose, at least you will have begun.

The Two-Minute Rule

One of the great shared traditions of many families with young children is "the five-second rule." The five-second rule holds that if a piece of food accidentally ends up on the ground it can still be eaten safely, provided it was retrieved in less than five seconds. While the five-second rule is actually nonsense,[70] the two-minute rule is a functional and rational approach to time management. The two-minute rule suggests that any time demand that will take less than two minutes should be done *now*. The logic is that it will take more time to categorize and return to it than it will to simply do it immediately. In other words, it is right at the efficiency cutoff. If the thing to be done is not important, throw it away. If you are going to do it sometime, do it now. Getting in the habit of following the two-minute rule can be magic in helping you avoid procrastination. Do it now if you are ever going to do it at all. For specific guidance on being more efficient, see Tool Kit 2.5.

⇆ MANAGEMENT LIVE 2.4

Is This Advice Worth $250,000.00?[71]

Charles Schwab was appointed in 1903 to run Bethlehem Steel, which became the largest independent steel producer in the field. One day, Schwab was approached by a man named Ivy Lee, an efficiency consultant. Unlike most modern consultants, Lee agreed to work for nothing if his techniques did not pay off. After a few days, Lee left without payment. He asked Schwab to give his technique 90 days and send whatever amount his advice had been worth. In three months, Schwab generously sent $35,000.00—or the modern-day equivalent of roughly $250,000.00.

What was the advice Schwab felt was so valuable? Lee said, for each day, write down six things you must accomplish. Then do those six things in order of priority. Work on the first until it's finished, then the second, and so on. If you don't complete the list, don't worry; you finished the most important tasks. Make a list, prioritize, and do it. That's $250,000.00 worth of advice.

Tool Kit 2.5   Getting Yourself Organized: A Quick Primer

Most people struggle with personal organization because of one of three things: technical limitations (like inadequate storage space), external limitations (like working conditions), and psychological obstacles (like anxiety over changing your routine). If your limitations are technical, the best approach is usually to minimize as much as possible—get rid of stuff you don't use, for starters. If external elements are limiting things, look for options to reduce your workload for a bit so you can get organized, as this will enable you to tackle more work efficiently. If the limitations are psychological, throw yourself into focusing on something else and let organization just be something that's assistance, not a primary focus.

To get started, ask yourself these five questions about the area you wish to organize:

What's working?

What's not working?

What items are most essential to you?

Why do you want to get organized?

What is causing the problems?

For your paper and e-mail, use the TRAF system[72]

- **Toss:** Open your mail over the wastebasket, tossing as you go. This goes symbolically for your e-mail as well: Use the Delete button in the same way you would dispose of paper. For those items you are unsure about, it is generally preferable to bite the bullet and throw them away or delete.

- **Refer:** Create individual "referral folders" for the handful of classes or projects you deal with most frequently. Make those folders especially accessible. For your personal affairs, create a "personal" file.

- **Act:** A key obstacle to good organization is to push aside a piece of paper or quickly blow by an e-mail thinking, this isn't pressing, I will just look at it tomorrow. A good rule is to take some action, however small, on every paper or e-mail touched. Remember the two-minute rule—if it is worth doing and can be done in two minutes or less, go ahead and do it now.

- **File:** A good filing system can be a gift to yourself and your future. Start now and get in the habit of maintaining such a system. Three important rules are (1) opt for a few big files instead of many little ones, (2) name your files using general recognizable labels (for example, job search) and store them alphabetically, and (3) make a point to mark the files you use. After a year, throw out or store in a remote place any file you did not use in that year. This is hard to do but key to good organization.

Workplace Cultures That Foster High Performance with Lower Stress

KO **2-5**

DO **2-6**

Global business and its inherent hyper competition have made organizations potentially more stressful than ever before. The most successful organizations, however, are those that have been able to maintain their competitive edge while maintaining a lower-stress environment. Regardless of the stress management strategies chosen, supervisor support has been shown to decrease job stress and increase performance. People who feel supported are also more likely to take actions that are favorable to the organization and that go beyond assigned responsibilities. The perception that the organization is supportive, respectful, and caring about its members can have a significant impact on helping people

connect

Practice this!
Go to www.baldwin2e.com

meet stressful demands. Other organizational characteristics that have been associated with high performance and lower stress include the following (with action strategies included for each):

Frequent and Open Communication

- Share information with employees to reduce uncertainty about their jobs and futures.
- Clearly define employees' roles and responsibilities.
- Make communication friendly and efficient, not mean-spirited or petty.

Employee Participation

- Give workers opportunities to participate in decisions that affect their jobs.
- Consult employees about scheduling and work rules.
- Be sure the workload is suitable to employees' abilities and resources; avoid unrealistic deadlines.
- Show that individual workers are valued.

Incentives for Work–Life Balance

- Praise good work performance verbally and institutionally.

Practice this!
Go to www.baldwin2e.com

> CASE CONCLUDED

So how exactly does CIGNA's EAP work? Here are the mechanics: Employees as well as their family members can use up to five EAP counseling visits for any particular issue (for example, survivor guilt, substance abuse, smoking cessation, family turmoil, or a number of other personal problems). Employees can speak with counselors to alleviate their despair and stress, reawake their sense of purpose, and revive personal enthusiasm for their work.

In addition, employees can avail themselves of any special CIGNA-sponsored seminars, such as "*Employees in Crisis: How Personal Finance Can Impact Job Performance*" and "*Working Through Difficult Times.*" The latter is especially popular. Says Marilyn Paluba, director of health programs at CIGNA, "We find that 8 percent to 10 percent of employees are dealing with this problem."

Of course, CIGNA is a for-profit business and, while widely appreciated by employees, the EAP is quite costly and not a cost shared by most competitors. So how does the firm justify the expenditures? "Our stress reduction programs are certainly not altruistic or just about making people feel better," says Mary Bianchi, EAP program manager at CIGNA. "People tell us the EAP has made them more productive at work, and allows them to actively do something rather than just sit and worry about their problems. They say: 'My family is healthier, and I'm not taking time off to deal with my problem.'"

Even more objectively, CIGNA has seen a 5 percent reduction in its medical costs which they attribute directly to their EAP. And at a company the size of CIGNA, that amounts to very big savings and a substantive contribution to their business outcomes.

Beyond the financial benefits, the overt attempt by CIGNA to acknowledge and address issues that are generally not openly discussed has led to a healthier workplace. No matter how workers and managers choose to use the EAP, Marilyn Paluba says, the results can be summed up simply: "People say they have better control over their lives."

Questions

1. As a manager, what are your options when you see stress taking its toll on people? What are the most progressive firms (and managers) doing to manage stress and increase productivity?

2. Is there really a *business case* for stress reduction? Can't high stress be a good thing and a powerful driver for high-performance firms?

3. Don't tough-minded managers and coaches say "Drive out the weak and the strong survive"? What, if anything, is misguided about that philosophy?

4. EAPs like those of CIGNA are *reactive*. How might a firm or manager be proactive in trying to *prevent* rather than simply treat stress?

- Provide opportunities for career development.
- Promote an "entrepreneurial" work climate that gives employees more control over their work.

Cultivate a Friendly Social Climate

- Provide opportunities for social interaction among employees.
- Establish a zero-tolerance policy for harassment.
- Make management actions consistent with organizational values.

Concluding Note

Stress robs people of their health and organizations of productivity so it is a critical topic for students of organizational behavior and management. Effective stress control is largely a function of your physical hardiness, your psychological hardiness, and your management of time. Learning the behaviors that contribute to each of those three can yield big payoffs in your productivity and health.

KEY TERMS

ABC method 67	emotional labor 51	role theory 49
appraisal support 56	emotional support 56	self-efficacy 47
burnout 50	eustress 44	small wins 61
choking 56	family interference with work (FIW) 49	strains 43
conservation of resources (COR) 50	informational support 56	stress 43
control 52	instrumental support 56	surface acting 51
deep acting 51	locus of control 47	Swiss Cheese Method 68
demands 52	psychological hardiness 59	transactional theory 45
depersonalization 50	reduced personal accomplishment 50	Type A behavior pattern 47
80/20 rule 63	role ambiguity 49	work–family conflict 49
emotional exhaustion 50	role conflict 49	work interference with family (WIF) 49

Adapted from divinecaroline. com and 100 Best Companies to Work For.

Going to work each day for some people is a joy, believe it or not. While a large portion of Americans dread crawling out of bed in the morning and going through the daily grind en route to a paycheck, some people are happy to do it. Working for a company that allows you to enjoy your work is a

CASE
Creating a Low-Stress Happy Workplace: SAS, Google, and Other Companies That Take It Seriously

blessing, and a few companies do it better than most of their peers. Six of the most dedicated to creating

low-stress, people-first workplaces are briefly described next.

(continued)

(continued)

SAS

SAS is a North Carolina software company specializing in *business* analytics. It also specializes in making employees happy. The first perk of being an SAS employee was free M&M's. Now there's a country club, onsite daycare, onsite doctors and nurses, a 35-hour work week, live piano music during lunch, a 50,000-square-foot fitness center, swimming pools, no dress code, a masseur, onsite car detailing, and more. If you need assistance in adopting a child or finding a college for your child or a nursing home for a parent, they have people to help you with that, too.

Google

With Google's success has come the opportunity to treat its lucky employees like few other companies can. Employees at Google enjoy a great benefits package that includes affordable medical coverage, company-matched 401(k) plans, maternity and paternity leave, as well as a lot of *unique* workplace extras. Within the offices of Google, employees can see the in-house dentist or doctor, get a massage, or do yoga. Snacks are also available to those who want them throughout the day and there are outdoor activities such as a running trail when fresh air seems like the best environment for a meeting.

Genentech

San Francisco biotech giant "DNA by the Bay," as employees affectionately call it, is the absolute paragon of perk-laden employers. What sets them apart? Onsite daycare not just for the kids, but pets, too. Doggie daycare and optional bargain pet insurance are offered as well. Add to that six-week paid sabbaticals to prevent burnout, a free shuttle service that garners employees a four-dollar daily credit, a drop-off laundry service, and seasonal produce stands in company cafeterias. Jealous yet?

Patagonia

For employees at Patagonia, the Ventura, California–based outdoor clothing and equipment company, "surf's up" is more than a marketing ploy. Daily surf reports are posted at the reception desk and particularly outstanding swells generate a companywide loudspeaker announcement. Running out to catch a few waves during the workday is an accepted practice and a way to keep employees from burning out. Surfing not your thing? Company bikes are waiting outside, as are volleyball courts. Want a more reflective break? Head back inside for the onsite yoga.

eBay

Is the daily grind putting your stress meter in the red? That's not a problem for workers at the online auctioneer's two San Jose, California, campuses. eBay sets aside ergonomic meditation and prayer rooms decorated in relaxation-inducing colors and replete with pillows and comfy mats so employees can take a load off.

Accenture

Sometimes, the best job is the one that lets you not come to the office at all. At Accenture, the global consulting and tech firm, the work day begins wherever you might be or want to be—a full 92 percent of employees telecommute. Staffers get reimbursed for home-office setups and are required to work just one hour a week to get health insurance. And it's family friendly. New moms get eight paid post-delivery weeks off; dads get one.

Discussion Questions

1. What is the motivation for these firms to invest so much in employee perks?

2. Is the low-stress happy worker a more productive worker?

3. The six companies described certainly appear to be good companies to *work for*—but would you want to *invest* in such firms? Explain.

4. Does it have to be expensive to create an enjoyable, low-stress workplace? In what ways might a lower-stress organizational environment be created without significant financial cost?

5. SAS and Google are facing increasing competition in their markets. Do you suspect this means their employee perks will eventually decrease?

SELECT *MANAGE WHAT?* **DEBRIEFS**

Getting a Priority Done Under Stress: Debrief

Prioritization is a challenge faced daily by managers at all levels, and the addition of stress (for example, a looming deadline, a demanding boss or customer, distracting personal issues) makes this a particularly challenging skill. The central point is that the addition of stress does not change the fundamental personal strategies that will be effective, but rather simply heightens their importance.

The most general prescription is to ensure that you are as physically hardy as you can be. While it is tempting to neglect exercise and sleep and good nutrition because you are "too busy," the reality is that stressful times are when those elements are most essential. Research has shown that those who are able to maintain healthy habits when under pressure are more likely to stay productive and avoid the ravages of stress. You want to be as "fit to lead" as you can be, so either stay with or establish routines of good health and nutrition.

More specifically, to accomplish a priority in the face of stress, you will want to direct your focus on the most recurring lessons of good time management. Three of those lessons would seem to be most pertinent in this case: (1) a focus (even obsession) with written goals; (2) good lists and action steps tied to those goals; (3) an awareness and management of your internal and external prime times.

Goals.   The first step is to ensure you are crystal clear about what your actual priorities are and how you will determine if you have accomplished (or ideally exceeded) them. Put simply, ask yourself: What is the priority and why is it a priority? (Is it goal-related?) Among all that you have to do, is this truly among the top priority? (Related to your most important goals?) Assuming that it is, then make sure you have the ultimate goal you are seeking written down.

Lists and action steps.   Collect everything you need to do on one master list and then cut it into small pieces and get to work. Use the "Swiss Cheese Method," which simply means poking small holes in your priority project by doing small tasks. Small tasks require five minutes or less of your time and make some sort of hole in your high-priority task. Use your to-do list like a daily map and get obsessive about making progress on it every day. Your momentum will typically carry you if you can get yourself to truly drive your activity off a set of goals and a living to-do list.

Your prime times.   Each of us has both external and internal prime time. Internal prime time is that time of the day when we typically work best—morning, afternoon, or evening. External prime time is the best time to attend to other people—those you have to deal with in classes, work, or at home. Internal prime time is the time when you concentrate best. If you had to pick the two hours of the day when you think most clearly, which would you pick? The two hours you select are probably your internal prime time and you should aim to save all of that time for high-priority projects.

Interestingly, studies have shown that most business people pick the first couple of hours at work as their internal prime time, yet this is usually the time they read the newspaper, answer routine mail, review yesterday's unanswered e-mails, and talk to colleagues and associates. It would be much better to save such routine tasks for non-prime hours. Students often schedule their classes during their internal prime time when it would be better used for study and the completion of deliverables.

Overcoming the Two Biggest Time Management Traps: Debrief

As noted in the Manage *What?* scenario, the two biggest time management traps are (1) a failure to prioritize and thus we procrastinate on our major tasks, and (2) not devoting our peak productivity times to our most important tasks. Perhaps the more difficult challenge is to first get clear on what your personal priorities really are. To do that, collect everything that commands your attention and do so in some place other than in your head. Contrary to some traditional time management advice, you do not want things at the forefront of your mind unless you are working on them. Some people, students in particular, often try to just keep their to-do list in their heads. That rarely works well. Effective time managers collect and organize their tasks where they can be reviewed and serve as a reminder. This way the tasks do not have to be stored in their heads.

(continued)

(continued)

Once you've collected your to-do list, most experts recommend you review not just routine items but everything that has a high priority today or might not get done without special attention. One straightforward way to do that is to use the ABC method: assigning an A to a high-priority item, a B to an item of medium priority, and a C to low-priority items. To use the ABC system effectively, you should ensure you are incorporating not just short-term but long-term items, derived from your lifetime goals. Most importantly, always start with A items, not with C items, even when you have just a few minutes of free time. So, for example, don't look at e-mail first thing in the morning. Instead, use the morning to focus on your most important tasks. One specific strategy to avoid procrastination is what is known as the Swiss Cheese Method.

Making Changes in a Workplace to Lower Stress and Enhance (Not Lower) Productivity: Debrief

Your president is right to believe that the most successful organizations are those that have been able to maintain their competitive edge while maintaining a lower-stress environment. However, he would be wrong if he thought it was just foosball tables, or fancy free lunches, or casual dress codes that create such environments. In some cases, those elements might be part of the mix but there are a set of more general cultural factors that have been repeatedly linked to both employee commitment and high organizational performance.

First, supervisor support has been shown to decrease job stress and increase performance. People who feel supported are also more likely to take actions that are favorable to the organization and that go beyond assigned responsibilities. The perception that the organization is supportive, respectful, and caring about its members can also have significant impact on helping people meet the demands of job stress. Other organizational characteristics that have been associated with high performance and lower stress include (a) frequent and open communication, (b) employee participation in decision making, (c) incentives for work–life balance, and (d) an actively promoted social climate. Put simply, the healthiest and highest-performing workplaces are those where people feel "in the know" and are asked for input on key decisions that affect them. Moreover, they are places where there is overt recognition of the importance of employee health and balance, and an encouragement of personal relationships and connecting with fellow employees, as well as complete intolerance of harassment and discrimination.

So your advice to your boss should be to worry less about using Google's foosball tables and well-publicized perks, and more on the ways in which the company involves associates in decision making and promoting a social climate of cooperation and innovation.

Solving Problems

OBJECTIVES

KNOWING   DOING

After reading this chapter, you should be able to:

"The great thing about fact-based decisions is that they overrule the hierarchy. The most junior person in the company can win an argument with the most senior person with regard to a fact-based decision. For intuitive decisions, on the other hand, you have to rely on experienced executives who've honed their instincts."

—Jeff Bezos, CEO, Amazon

KO 3-1 Define intuition and its role in solving problems.

KO 3-2 Recognize judgment traps that hinder the decision-making process.

KO 3-3 Describe the key steps in the PADIL framework for making a good decision.

KO 3-4 Identify evidence-based methods for increasing the quantity of solution alternatives.

DO 3-1 Implement techniques to minimize or avoid decision-making biases.

DO 3-2 Solve a problem using the PADIL framework.

DO 3-3 Apply a stakeholder analysis to a problem.

DO 3-4 Use decision tools to narrow a set of problem alternatives.

Case: Two Contemporary Companies' Use of Crowdsourcing: Threadless and ChallengePost

The renowned American physicist Linus Pauling once observed that "the best way to have a *good* idea is to have *lots* of ideas." And the growing popularity of a strategy known as crowdsourcing is very much in that spirit. Crowdsourcing is defined as the act of outsourcing tasks, traditionally performed by an employee or contractor, to an undefined large group of people or community (a "crowd"), through an open call made possible by the wide and instantaneous reach of the Internet.

Jeff Howe, one of the first authors to employ the term, contends that crowdsourcing works because open calls to a large undefined group of people ultimately attract those who are the most motivated and able to offer relevant and fresh ideas. In the following, we highlight two contemporary companies that are creatively employing crowdsourcing to address some of their most important objectives.

Threadless is an online apparel store co-founded in 2000 by Jake Nickell and Jacob DeHart. The founders started with just $1,000 in seed money that they had won in an Internet T-shirt design contest. The company has now grown to be a multimillion-dollar enterprise and is revolutionizing the process of product design.

While most design shops employ high-priced talent to create their product lines, Threadless uses the crowdsourcing concept to execute an entirely different approach. More specifically, the firm invites anyone interested in being part of the Threadless community to submit T-shirt designs online—afterward, the designs are put to a public vote. A small percentage of submitted designs are selected for printing and then sold through their online store. Creators of the winning designs receive only a small cash prize and some store credit. In the open-source community, a Threadless T-shirt or design is considered to be crowdsourced because the designer and the company retain all rights to the design.

On average, around 1,500 designs compete in any given week. Designers upload their T-shirt designs to the website, where visitors and members of the community score them on a scale of 0 to 5. Each week, the staff selects about 10 designs. Not surprisingly, the printed T-shirts tend to sell well because they have already been proven popular via the design process. Threadless shirts are run in limited batches and when shirts are sold out, customers can request a reprint. However, reprinting occurs only when there is enough demand, and the decision to reprint is ultimately up to the company.

The Threadless experience amounts to something of a revolution in product design models and cost efficiency. It is an intriguing example of the power of crowdsourcing.

1. Why is Threadless so successful? What competitive advantages do they have over comparable design firms using traditional strategies for product design?

2. What is the logic of crowdsourcing and why has it caught on in so many areas and for so many applications?

3. What are some potential traps and limitations of crowdsourcing efforts?

4. Identify at least two other businesses, or business functions, that you think could achieve breakthrough gains via the use of crowdsourcing.

IN TODAY'S WORLD, WHY SOLVE YOUR PROBLEMS ALONE?

1. Defining and Structuring a Vague Problem

The third-quarter quality figures for the customer call center you manage have been posted. Although your numbers look good, you quickly notice that, compared to other call centers in the company, your ratings for customer service are below average. Given that part of your bonus is tied to these figures, you are obviously concerned and very motivated to fix the problem. You call your counterparts in other call centers to see what they've been doing recently and to generate some ideas that might influence customer service. One manager said she instituted a new game called "Answer the Call for Baseball," where the top 10 customer service representatives get to take off work for a midday baseball game. Another manager in a successful call center has increased his monitoring of reps on the phone and is intervening immediately when a rep doesn't perform well. A third manager hasn't done much of anything innovative and said, "I guess my customers are easier to handle than yours." You sit back in your chair, perplexed to say the least.

What is the problem here? What other information would be useful? How would you begin to improve your customer service quality rating? Is the problem definitely with your reps, or could it be something else?

2. Avoiding Common Decision Errors

Putting your answers in the grid that follows, respond with your first instinct to each of the following six items. Also include your level of confidence in each of the responses you provide.

A. Which is the more likely cause of death in the United States: being hit by a falling airplane part or being attacked by a shark?

B. Take just five seconds for each mathematical string and estimate the multiplicative product of $8 \times 7 \times 6 \times 5 \times 4 \times 3 \times 2 \times 1$, and then $1 \times 2 \times 3 \times 4 \times 5 \times 6 \times 7 \times 8$.

C. You have been carefully monitoring two slot machines in a Las Vegas casino. One has paid off twice in the last hour. The other has not paid off. You are now ready to play yourself. Which one of those machines would give you the best chance of winning?

D. Suppose each of the following cards has a number on one side and a letter on the other, and someone tells you: "If a card has a vowel on one side, then it has an even number on the other side." Which card(s) would you need to turn over in order to decide whether the person is lying?

- Card 1: E
- Card 2: K
- Card 3: 4
- Card 4: 7

E. Which city is located farther north, New York, NY, or Rome, Italy?

F. Six months ago, you sank the last $5,000 of your student loan money into the purchase of a stock that was highly recommended to you by a trusted family friend. As of today, the stock has already dropped 20 percent and is now worth just $4,000. You are nervously ready to sell, but you simply cannot afford to lose that $1,000 (plus commission costs) and still pay for school next year. Would you sell?

How confident are you in each of your decisions to these problems? Do you suspect there might be inaccurate biases or judgment errors in any of your decisions? Are there any keys or cues you can look for to avoid falling prey to the most common and insidious judgment errors and decision traps?

Problem	Record Your Answer	Confidence Level How confident are you that your answer is correct, on a scale from 1 (not at all) to 100 (totally)?
A		
B		
C		
D		
E		
F		

3. Excelling in a Case Interview

Recognizing the importance of problem-solving skills, many organizations now use case interviews to evaluate candidates for jobs. Assume you are in an interview and have been presented with the following case problem: "Your firm is a U.S.-based manufacturer of natural, health food products and is considering growing the business by entering the huge and expanding Chinese market. Should it?" How would you respond? How would you go about analyzing the opportunity? What questions would you ask? How might you structure your answer to best demonstrate problem-solving skills?

4. Learning from Past Decisions

You belong to a local service club and have been asked to serve a three-year term as chair of the club's annual fund-raiser. However, the club has decided to scrap their traditional fund-raiser and "start a new chapter" with you as the leader. This means that many, many decisions have to be made and you have very little past history or precedent to go on. In an effort to manage expectations (and not let them get too high), you tell the club that "this year is a pilot and we will learn from it and certainly have greater success in the next two years."

How do great managers ensure that such learning really occurs? What questions will you ask and what types of information will you collect? What mistakes are typically made that get in the way of such learning from experience?

Introduction

If you are like most people, you make about 100 decisions a day. Some are easy decisions (for example, what to eat for breakfast), while others are more difficult (how to allocate your work time). Every day, management life brings new decisions to be made and problems to be solved. Many managers report truly loving the problem-solving aspect of the job—ever-changing, always interesting—while others frequently cite problem solving as among the most challenging and difficult aspects of management life. Deciding on courses of action, especially when other people are involved, is what keeps managers awake at night. Unfortunately, examples in today's organizations of poor problem solving are all too common. The good news is that much is known about solving problems and avoiding decision traps. This chapter is devoted to these very important skills.

The Challenge of Problem Solving

Of the skills covered in this book, problem solving may well be the most complex—and one of the most important to your day-to-day work life. By definition, a "problem" does not have a clear solution; otherwise it wouldn't be considered a problem. Given the complexity inherent in most problems, it is probably not surprising that problem solving is typically found to be among the most deficient skills in assessments of young managers. Some research even suggests as high as 50 percent of managerial decisions made in organizations either fail or are suboptimal.[1] With odds like that, it might seem that flipping a coin would save the time and effort involved. The reality, however, is we can achieve a much higher decision success rate—but only if we consistently adhere to methods of solving problems that have a demonstrated record of success.

Most problem-solving frameworks are simple in form and concept, but the trap is assuming simple understanding can substitute for the discipline of execution. Moreover, perhaps more than any other skill, effective problem solving and decision making are in large part a function of what traps to avoid and what

"When you confront a problem, you begin to solve it."

—Rudy Giuliani

?¿ MYTHS 3.1   Problem-Solving Myths

- *Taking action is better than standing by.* When faced with a problem, we want to act; it makes us feel like we're accomplishing something. But taking action isn't always better. Sometimes a poorly conceived cure can be much worse than the disease. Many problems managers face *today* come directly from *yesterday's* solutions. The "do nothing" option is too often ignored or neglected and should be at least recognized as an option in almost all problem-solving situations.

- *Trust your gut.* Of course, sometimes your "gut" is right. But unless you've tracked your gut decisions to know your success rate, your gut probably won't be very helpful. Experience can play an important role in problem solving, but requires knowledge of previous results to evaluate its effectiveness. In organizational situations, intuition is vastly overrated as a source of decision success.

- *I know when I'm making a poor decision.* In truth, few people can know this without training and practice. Researchers have discovered a phenomenon known as the bias blind spot. Even when people are good at spotting decision traps and logical fallacies in the decisions of *others,* they often fail miserably in spotting the same fallacies in their *own* decisions.

- *Dividing an elephant in half produces two small elephants.* In reality, few complex problems lend themselves to easy solutions or effective knee-jerk compromises. Effective problem solving focuses on facts and recognizes that problems are rarely as they appear. Most are symptoms of more complex issues and require a holistic approach to solve effectively.

not to do. The following section outlines some of the most common traps to good decisions and why smart people can often make such bad choices. We then describe a framework to help overcome biases and approach problem solving in an effective way.

KO **3-1**

KO **3-2**

DO **3-1**

"I'm guilty of doing too much, and I'm guilty of not seeing my mistakes coming. What I'm not guilty of is making the same mistake twice."

—Michael Dell

Why Smart People Make Bad Decisions

As we noted in the introduction, research on decision making suggests bad decisions happen about as frequently as good ones. Very smart, well-intentioned managers make many of these flawed decisions. In fact, very smart people often make very bad decisions because several insidious judgment traps exist that have been found to hamper the decision making of the best of us. Decision making is another area where true expertise involves knowing the traps that so frequently hinder sound judgment.

Intuition

Talking glowingly about the importance and value of "going with your gut" or of using your intuition to guide decisions is popular these days. In fact, a survey of executives in Fortune 1,000 firms found that 45 percent relied upon "their gut" more often than facts and figures when running their businesses.[2] However, evidence is mixed regarding how useful intuition is in solving problems. Despite the courageous tone often characterizing descriptions of making decisions from the gut, we can't recommend relying solely on your intuition in problem solving. That doesn't mean you should totally discount intuition, but just that you should

⇄ MANAGEMENT LIVE 3.1

The "First Instinct" Fallacy

One great example of how conventional intuitive wisdom can be wrong involves the question of whether to change answers in the course of taking a test. Most of us have probably been told something on the order of "When taking a multiple-choice test, always trust your first instinct." It usually includes a rationale such as "If you are not fully certain of an answer, do not change it because your first instinct was probably right."

While that may sound reasonable enough, a recent meta-analysis (33 studies in all, representing over 70 years of research) found that going with your first instinct is actually likely to be a *poor* choice. In one study,[3] researchers examined midterm exam answer sheets (or Scantrons) of over 1,500 students taking the same course. They noted each instance in which students changed an initial response to an alternative response by examining erasure marks made on the Scantron sheets. If the saying about trusting your first instinct is true, then students hoping for the right answer should stick with their first response. Yet the results showed that over *half the time* a student changed an initial response, the student benefited!

Student Response Changes and Results

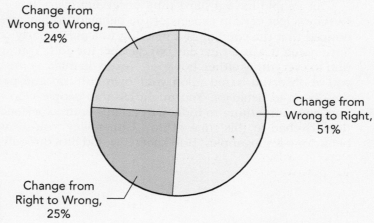

Change from Wrong to Wrong, 24%

Change from Wrong to Right, 51%

Change from Right to Wrong, 25%

The researchers found that students dread the notion of potentially changing a right answer to a wrong one. Thus, they become paralyzed and place more stock in their first instinct than they should. This first instinct, which is hard to detect in ourselves, drives our behavior and often leads to poorer decisions.

bear in mind most people have a difficult time applying their intuition *systematically* to solve problems.

In its simplest form, our **intuition** represents a collection of what we've learned about the world, *without knowing we actually learned it.*[4] Intuition can be useful if we track what we have learned and under what circumstances that learning led to success so we can replicate it in the future. Moreover, some research shows intuition is important in automatic processes such as social interactions or driving a car—things we do without thinking about them.

However, knowing without understanding becomes problematic in decision making. For example, unconscious biases we bring to bear on situations commonly influence our intuition. Such biases help explain the long-standing phenomenon of the disproportionately large number of men being selected to

"My life is the complete opposite of everything I want it to be. Every instinct I have in every aspect of life, be it something to wear, something to eat . . . It's all been wrong."

—George Costanza, character from the TV sitcom *Seinfeld*

professional orchestras. Orchestra directors traditionally held auditions face-to-face and apparently held an unconscious bias in favor of men.[5] When the auditions were held blindly (with a screen separating the judges and the musician), women were selected at a much higher rate than before.

The Ladder of Inference

Practice this!
Go to www.baldwin2e.com

To show how our intuition operates and can lead to mistakes, it's useful to consider what has been termed the **ladder of inference.**[6] Inference is drawing a conclusion about something we don't know based on things we do know. We make inferences multiple times a day to try to make sense of our world. The problem is we don't realize we're making such inferences. Why? The process happens so quickly and effortlessly we almost never devote cognitive energy to it. The ladder of inference (Figure 3.1) is an analogy that illustrates just how this process of making inferences occurs.

At the very bottom of the ladder, we observe or experience what people say and do. This information is objective in the sense that the behavior doesn't change from person to person. For example, say your teammate Bob is 45 minutes late for a team meeting. You would all observe that fact—that he is indeed 45 minutes late. There is no disputing that.

Yet people have a hard time observing every possible aspect of situations, so they select certain aspects of the behavior to pay attention to. You may have noticed that the content of a meeting was particularly controversial; others may have noted it was a nice day out, perfect for golf. You probably didn't pay attention to everything either, however. Next, you make some assumptions about what you've observed based upon your own cultural and personal experiences with the observed behavior. You might assume people who don't show up for meetings have something to hide. Or perhaps your experience tells you traffic is particularly bad at this time of day. Either way, you draw conclusions about the behavior—for example, "Bob knew it would be a difficult meeting and opted out."

FIGURE 3.1
The Ladder of Inference

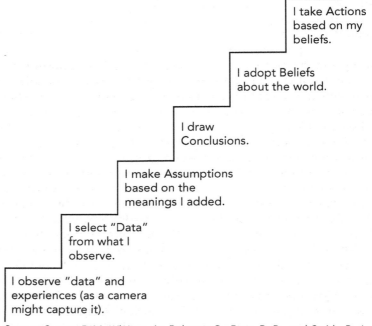

Source: Senge, P. M., Kleiner, A., Roberts, C., Ross, R. B., and Smith, B. J. (1994). *The fifth discipline fieldbook*. New York: Doubleday.

FIGURE 3.2
The Ladder
of Inference Example

Bob is unreliable.
We shouldn't include
him anymore. (Action)

Bob probably can't
deal with tough issues.
(Adopted Belief)

Bob *knew* it was
going to be a rough
meeting and came
late on purpose.
(Assumption —
Personal Meaning)

The meeting started
at 4:00 p.m. and Bob
arrived at 4:45 p.m. —
and didn't say why.
(Objective Data)

At this point, you have adopted a belief about how the world works: "Some people skip meetings when they anticipate controversy." Those adopted beliefs then influence how you see future events and the actions you take. You might then believe, "Bob can't deal with tough issues," and take action that says, "We shouldn't include Bob in our meetings going forward" (see Figure 3.2).

Well, the truth is Bob was just at the wrong location. Let's not let Bob off the hook for that move, but should we take the action of not including him on the team? Solving problems requires heightened awareness to our limited human abilities to consider all alternatives simultaneously. Solving problems also requires we not jump to inappropriate conclusions and that we keep an open mind about people, problems, and situations.

When we analyze people's ladders of inference, a highly destructive error becomes readily apparent. The error deals with the process of attributing causes to events—that is, explaining why things occurred. This error is so important to understanding human behavior it has been termed **fundamental attribution error.** The essence of the fundamental attribution error is people tend to over-attribute behavior to internal rather than external causes. Thus, when determining the cause of another person's behavior, you are more likely to consider factors related to the person's disposition (personality, ethnicity, gender, and so on) than to her particular situation (weather, lighting, traffic, and so on).

Perhaps more insidious is the **self-serving bias,** where we attribute personal *successes* to internal causes and personal *failures* to external causes. For example, let's say you got an A on your last test. To what would you likely attribute your success? Hard work, excellent study habits, natural intellect? But what if you failed the test miserably? To what would you likely attribute your failure? Tricky questions, perhaps a confusing professor, or the sniffling of students with colds during the test. The self-serving bias helps us maintain a comfortable positive image about ourselves. Unfortunately, that image is often built on false information.

This process plays out in problem solving every day. "Why is our customer service so poor? Must be those customer service agents; they're incompetent." Or "How are we ever going to compete in this market? Get more talented people in the organization." If you are going to solve problems well, you need to expand your thinking about the causes of events and others' behaviors.

"If there is such a thing as a basic human quality, self-deception is it."
—Colin Turnbull

"Informed decision-making comes from a long tradition of guessing and then blaming others for inadequate results."
—Scott Adams, creator of the "Dilbert" cartoon strip

Six Ways People Exercise Poor Judgment Without Knowing It[7]

We've tried to show that people are just not very good at consistently drawing appropriate or accurate conclusions from intuition.[8] We now discuss ways in which people, using their gut instinct and "experience," exercise poor judgment. Our hope is you will (1) recognize quickly how easy it is to make simple mistakes by using intuition alone, (2) learn to spot the most common decision-making biases, and (3) discover simple methods for combating these biases in judgment.

Judgment Error 1: Availability

The following are eight corporations (divided into two groups) that were highly ranked in the Fortune 500 according to total sales volume in 2009.

> **Group A includes:** Apple, Coca-Cola, McDonald's, Nike
>
> **Group B includes:** Japan Post Holdings, Dexia Group, Gazprom, Pemex

Which group of four companies (A or B) had the larger total sales volume in 2009? If you answered Group A, pat yourself on the back, as you're not alone. You're wrong, but not alone! In fact, Group B's sales were approximately six times that of Group A. Further, every company in Group B had sales higher than all of Group A combined. Let's try another one. Which of the following causes more deaths per year in the United States, suicide or homicide? Most people believe homicides cause more deaths, but in fact suicides lead to more deaths by a ratio of 2 to 1.

These two simple problems represent what's known as the **availability bias.** This bias clouds our judgment because things more readily available to us (that is, those more easily brought to mind) are likely to be interpreted as more frequent or important. There are many stories in the news about homicides, few about suicides. The companies in Group A are household names, but not as large as the lesser-known companies in Group B. When solving a problem, we often choose solutions we've heard about. We feel more comfortable with them and assume that if we've heard about them, they'll work. Marketing firms know this well, which explains why they want their products on the tip of your tongue.

Judgment Error 2: Representativeness

Let's say we told you the best student in our MBA class this past term writes poetry and is rather shy and quite introspective. What was the student's undergraduate major—fine arts or business? Which type of job is the student likely to accept—management of the arts or management consulting? When asked these questions, most students suggest the student's major must have been fine arts and that the student will likely take a job in managing the arts. These conclusions completely ignore, however, that the majority of MBA students hold undergraduate degrees in business and that many more MBAs take jobs in management consulting firms than they do in arts management. In other words, people ignore the "base rate" or the frequency of which people belong to certain groups or categories. The easily made mistake—**representative bias**—is that people pay more attention to descriptors they believe to be more *representative* of the person's career choice than the key base rate information that leads to the better choice.

Another classic example of the representative bias comes in the form of people's misconceptions about chance. For example, people assume that, when a sequence appears nonrandom, it must be nonrandom.[9] If you won the lottery, would you play different numbers? If you flipped a coin and it was heads nine times in a row, are you due for a tails on the tenth toss? Of course not, but this bias is applied with great regularity. So much so, it has been termed the "gambler's fallacy," in which people truly believe that each coin flip or pull of the slot machine is somehow connected to previous actions. The coin, the slot machine, and so on, have no memory, yet it is common to assume the probabilities of future outcomes must somehow increase or decrease to offset or "compensate for" earlier outcomes. If you have ever played roulette, the posting of previous winning numbers is designed to trick you into making this error. Another great example of this is the "hot hand" in basketball that we discuss in Management Live 3.2. Even highly paid, experienced coaches make some very poor decisions based on this very seductive fallacy.

Another special case of the representative bias is what is known as the **hasty generalization fallacy.** For a variety of reasons, people often draw inappropriate general conclusions from specific cases because they do not realize (or they think *you* don't realize) their specific example is not necessarily so in all, or even most, cases. Consider the guy who argues against motorcycle helmet legislation because he has ridden for 25 years without a helmet and has never been hurt. That may well be true, but so what? One helmet-less rider's personal experience in no way refutes the notion that it is safer to ride with a helmet. Similarly, it is not uncommon to hear someone assert, "I do not agree with all the fuss over cholesterol. My grandfather lived to 95, and he ate bacon and eggs every morning."

The hasty generalization fallacy occurs because we tend to operate by what has been called the law of small numbers—that is, we are willing to leap to general conclusions after seeing only one or two examples. In fact, we are particularly

⇄ MANAGEMENT LIVE 3.2

The Hot Hand

Imagine that your favorite team is in the NCAA championship basketball game. There are three seconds left on the clock and your team is down by one. The coach is huddled with his players designing the final play. But everyone knows who's getting the ball—the player with the "hot hand," the one who has made his last six shots. He's on fire! Anyone who has played sports long enough believes in the phenomenon of the streak and the hot hand. Unfortunately, it simply isn't true.

Researchers analyzed the shooting patterns of the Boston Celtics and Philadelphia 76ers in the mid-1980s.[10] They found prior shot performance did not influence or change the likelihood of success on later shot performance. That is, if you make your first three shots, you're no more likely to make the fourth than you were the first three. This is a classic representative bias regarding chance and doesn't only occur in sports but biases decisions in many contexts including where and when to invest money.

PHILADELPHIA 76ERS

Probability of Next Shot Being a Hit After . . .	
Three Straight Hits	.46
Two Straight Hits	.50
One Hit	.51
One Miss	.54
Two Misses	.53
Three Misses	.56

prone to make this thinking error because we tend to personalize all experience (we assume our experience is everyone else's) or even misinterpret our experience ("That's the way the world is—I have seen it with my own two eyes").

Judgment Error 3: Anchoring and Adjustment

Consider an experiment in which students were asked to add 400 to the last three numbers of their student ID and write it down. They then were asked to use this number to estimate when Attila the Hun invaded Europe into regions of France—that is, whether that event happened before or after the date created by the ID number). The results showed the following:

If ID number "date" was between:	Average response was:
400–700	676 CE
701–1000	738 CE
1001–1200	848 CE
1201–1400	759 CE

Students tended to use their initial value as a starting point and adjusted their estimates around that starting value. But remember, this initial value was based on their ID numbers, not any historically relevant data! (By the way, the correct answer is 451 CE.) Research shows we often provide estimates based on the initial starting estimate. Even when people are told the initial estimate is random, their adjusted estimates remain close to the initial estimate or *anchor*.[11] This pattern of **anchoring and adjustment** is quite prevalent. That is, different starting points lead to different end results. Consider the following scenario:

> A newly hired teacher for a large private high school has five years of experience and solid qualifications. When asked to estimate the starting salary for this employee, one friend (who knows very little about the profession) guessed an annual salary of $31,000. What is your estimate?

If you're like most people, your answer will be affected by the friend's initial estimate. In studies using similar scenarios, when the friend's estimate was much higher, say $70,000, subsequent estimates were much higher. This is the case even when the scenario states that the friend knows very little about the profession!

The common mishaps resulting from this bias abound. Think about the last time you negotiated for anything. Who threw out the first number? That figure served as a starting point for the negotiation, regardless of whether it was a reasonable figure or based on anything objective.

Judgment Error 4: Confirmation

Participants were asked in a research study to think about this series of numbers: 2, 4, 6. This series conforms to a particular rule. Students were asked to identify the rule and, to do so, were allowed to propose a new sequence of numbers they believed conformed to the rule to test whether their rule was correct. After this period of experimentation, the students were asked to identify the rule. Common responses were:

- Numbers that increase by two.
- The difference between the first two numbers is equivalent to the difference between the last two.

Practice this!
Go to www.baldwin2e.com

The rule used in the experiment was actually *any three ascending numbers.* Few students actually identified this rule because the solution requires students to collect disconfirming, rather than confirming, information. In other words, the **confirmation bias** represents people's tendency to collect evidence that supports rather than negates our intuition before deciding. When students found a rule that seemed to work, they were done searching. In solving problems, one of the most insidious traps is gathering data that seek to confirm our ideas and exclude data that might disconfirm them.

Judgment Error 5: Overconfidence

Consider the following quotes:

Heavier-than-air flying machines are impossible. —Lord Kelvin, president of the British Royal Society, 1895.

I think there is a world market for about five computers. —Thomas J. Watson, chairman of IBM, 1943.

We don't like their sound, and guitar music is on the way out. —Decca Recording Co. rejecting The Beatles.

Now consider these facts:[12]

- 81 percent of surveyed new business owners thought their business had at least a 70 percent chance of success, but only 39 percent thought that most businesses like theirs would succeed.

- 80 percent of students believed they were in the top 30 percent of safe drivers.

- A survey asked 829,000 high school students to rate their own ability to "get along with others," and less than 1 percent rated themselves as below average. Further, 60 percent rated themselves in the top 10 percent, and 25 percent rated themselves in the top 1 percent.

What do all of these things have in common? They are indicative of peoples' overconfidence in their abilities and underconfidence in others'. Often termed the Lake Wobegon Effect (after the radio show in which the imaginary town boasts all of its children are above average), this **overconfidence bias** leads us to believe we possess some unique trait or ability that allows us to defy odds, whereas others simply don't have such a trait or ability. An example of the overconfidence bias in action can be seen in investor behavior in the late 1990s. Because of a boom in technology stocks, even novice investors experienced huge growth in their portfolios. As technology stocks kept going up, many investors believed that their success was due to their stock-picking ability rather than unsustainable growth in one sector of the economy. The result for many was huge losses. This same process occurred in the recent real estate bubble of 2007. Lenders and buyers were overly confident that prices would keep going up and the subsequent drop in housing values left both banks and borrowers with huge losses.

In an eye-opening study about the role of overconfidence in decision making, researchers examined who could predict stock performance better, laypeople (in this case, students) or stock market professionals (that is, portfolio managers, analysts, brokers, and investment counselors).[13] The two groups were asked to forecast the best performing stocks out of a pair in 30 days with only the name of the company, industry, and monthly percent price change for each stock for the previous 12 months. In addition to trying to pick the winning stock, the two groups were asked to rate how confident they felt about their predictions. The results showed that the students picked the best-performing stock 52 percent of the time, while the stock market professionals were only 40 percent accurate. That's correct,

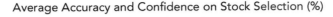

Average Accuracy and Confidence on Stock Selection (%)

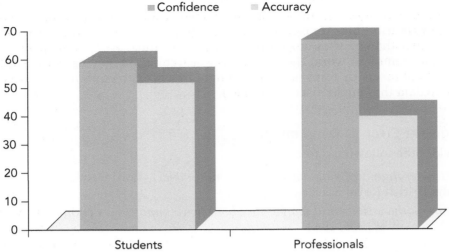

Source: Tomgren and Montgomery (2004).

the stock market professionals performed significantly worse than would be expected by chance alone! Yet these very same professionals indicated that they were, on average, 67 percent confident about their picks, while students indicated being only 59 percent confident about their choices. It turns out that students, like most laypeople, simply relied on past performance in making their predictions. Yet stock market professionals indicated that they relied mostly on their judgment and experience, believing that they possessed knowledge that could defy the outcomes that were reasonably suggested by chance and prior stock performance.

Being confident is a great thing: It allows people to approach difficult situations with courage and determination. Unfortunately, most of us are overconfident and we greatly overestimate the true probability of success. Research has shown there is virtually no relationship between one's confidence level about being right and actually being right. That is, people (think consultants, experts, advisers) often exude confidence about their opinions, but confidence doesn't make them any more accurate. The good news is some research shows that, when given feedback about being overconfident or asking people to explain their estimates, people reduce their subsequent estimates to be more realistic.

Judgment Error 6: Escalation of Commitment

"When you discover you are riding a dead horse, the best strategy is to dismount . . . do not buy a stronger whip, declare that the horse is better, faster or cheaper dead, or harness several other dead horses together for increased speed."

—Judge Thomas Penfield Jackson

"If at first you don't succeed, try again. Then quit. There's no use being a damn fool about it."

—W. C. Fields

You just replaced the entire exhaust system on your somewhat rusty 1996 Volvo sedan, for $850. Two days later, you hear a clanking sound and take your Volvo directly to the mechanic. She tells you your Volvo will need a new clutch and major engine overhaul—at a cost of $1,400. Most people in this situation would spring for the repairs on the car, believing they have already spent $850. Yet the money already spent is irrelevant to the cost of the new repairs. This phenomenon is known as **escalation of commitment.** The idea is simple: People are likely to continue to invest additional resources (time, money, and so on) in failing courses of action even though no foreseeable payoff is evident. The phrase "throwing good money after bad" is the essence of escalation of commitment.

Escalation is prevalent for several reasons. First, we don't want to admit that our solution may not have been the right one, so we stay the course. Second, we don't want to appear inconsistent or irrational, so we continue to hope for the best even though data simply don't justify such a response. Third, in organizations, not continuing could be seen as giving up rather than fighting onward—and nobody likes a quitter.

Overcoming Judgment Biases

Unfortunately, there are no simple or surefire ways to always avoid common decision biases. Such biases remain exceedingly hard to avoid even when we are acutely aware of what they are and how often they occur. Consider the case of Jeffrey Z. Rubin, who was among the most notable scholars in the study of escalation before his death in 1995.[14] Professor Rubin was killed in a climbing accident when he continued to climb after his climbing partner turned back due to adverse weather conditions. Make no mistake, the biases are insidious and hardest to detect in our *own* decision making. Nonetheless, useful tactics exist: (1) confidence estimates, (2) trial-and-error calibration, and (3) healthy skepticism.

"Good judgment comes from experience. Experience comes from bad judgment."

—Walter Wriston

Confidence Estimates

Since we tend toward overconfidence in our decision making, one way to curb that bias is to attach an estimate of confidence to beliefs held by ourselves and others. For example, say you want to improve the on-time delivery problem of your pizza delivery drivers. You ask one driver, "How many on-time deliveries can you make per night?" Your driver says 18. Okay, fair enough. But how confident is your driver? When asked, she (You were thinking it was a man, weren't you? Pesky biases!) claims about an 80 percent confidence level. Well, now it seems 18 isn't really a good estimate after all. In fact, a more accurate and useable estimate would be 14 to 22 on-time deliveries per night. Now you have a more realistic estimate of what your driver can reasonably accomplish.

Most experts agree reliance on "single-point" estimates is dangerous—they just don't provide enough information. So using confidence estimations to build "confidence ranges" can move you away from single-point estimations. As psychologist Scott Plous notes, the best method is simply to stop yourself or others and ask, "What is the chance that this judgment is wrong?"[15]

Trial-and-Error Calibration

One familiar, but underutilized, method for improving problem solving is through trial and error. That is, if you want to improve your success rate and reduce failure *tomorrow*, you must learn from your successes and failures *today*. To illustrate, most people are surprised to learn weather forecasters are incredibly accurate. In fact, when an experienced weather person predicts a 40 percent chance of rain, it rains 39 percent of the time!

Compare that accuracy rate to that of physicians. One study in a clinical setting asked physicians to review patients' medical history and conduct a physical examination, afterward predicting the likelihood that a patient had pneumonia.[16] The results make you wish that physicians were more like weather forecasters. That is, when physicians said there was a 65 percent chance of pneumonia, they were accurate only 10 percent of the time. It didn't improve with confidence either. When they predicted an 89 percent chance of pneumonia, they were right just 12 percent of the time (see Figure 3.3). Why are weather forecasters so accurate and physicians less accurate? The answer lies in a key aspect of trial and error, namely, regular feedback and knowledge of results.

Weather forecasters predict rain and in a few hours get the results of their prediction; they get to see immediately weather that confirms or disconfirms their meteorological model. If the model was right, they note what they did; if it was wrong, they examine the data and note the aspects that led to the wrong prediction. This process repeats itself every day as forecasters *calibrate* their predictions with the results. Research supports this calibration process as a way to avoid biases and make better decisions.

FIGURE 3.3
Accuracy of Weather
Forecasters Versus
Physicians

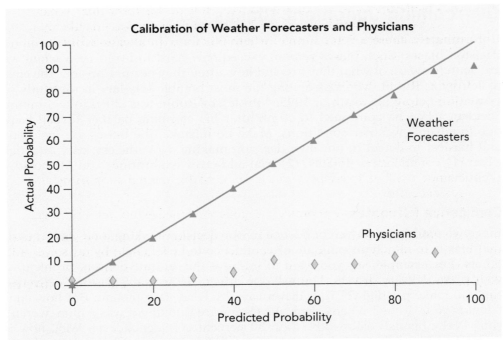

Source: Plous, S. (1993). *The psychology of judgment and decision making.* New York: McGraw-Hill.

Training yourself to use trial-and-error calibration involves a few simple steps. First, with every prediction, record the reasons why you've established the prediction. In several studies, researchers have found that when they make note of the reasons for their decision they do a better job of tracking and learning.[17]

Second, track the results. Consequences are often separated greatly by time; not all of us get the luxury of seeing the immediate results of our forecasts each day. So keep good records of what happened so you have the ability to defend decisions. When others say, "We always lose business when we release a product too soon," you'll be ready with data that might poke holes in such thinking.

Third, study the success *and* failures—you need *both* confirming and disconfirming evidence to truly know. Fourth, remember that chance is not self-correcting. A string of failures does not mean you are "due" for a success or vice versa.

"I've learned that mistakes can often be as good a teacher as success."

—Jack Welch

Healthy Skepticism

Another simple but powerful rule of thumb is to approach all decisions and presented evidence with healthy skepticism. Be prepared to challenge yourself and other "experts" and seek out negative or disconfirming evidence. Here are a few specific questions that reflect a healthy skepticism and can ultimately lead to better decisions:

- What are the strongest arguments against my position? On what basis am I rejecting them? (You may want to write these down.)

- What are the weakest parts of my position? On what basis am I accepting them? Would I find this reasoning convincing if an opponent used it to justify her arguments?

- How will I know if I am wrong? Given that we have a strong tendency toward escalation of commitment and denial, if we can construct in advance a personal definition of failure/error, then we may know when it's time for plan B. Sharing that with someone else is a good way to keep you honest.

- In considering facts, ask questions like: How do we know this? What is the base rate (could something just be random and we mistakenly presume cause)? Percentage of what? What are the available facts?
- Are there more alternatives?

In short, the best defenses for decision biases are:

1. Do not jump to conclusions.
2. Do not assume a relationship is a cause; record and test your decision outcomes.
3. Do not base your conclusion only on your own experience.
4. Do not just look to support your case. Look for the nonsupporting evidence, too.
5. Do not fall prey to overconfidence; get confidence estimates and ranges.

These defenses are simple to know but hard to do. If you find yourself thinking how commonsensical these defenses may seem, you would be wise to recall the remarkable frequency of decision biases even among the brightest of people. Challenge yourself to recognize and steer clear of those biases in your own thinking.

Solving Problems Effectively

In thinking about an effective model for attacking problems, two notes are important to make at the outset. First, as the quote from W. Edwards Deming insightfully conveys, there truly is a difference between good *decisions* and good *outcomes*. That is, you can never fully control the outcomes of your decisions. What you can control is *how* you will decide—and that is the importance of understanding a framework and having the discipline to use it.

Second, there is no such thing as a perfect decision or a perfect decision process. As humans, we will always be subject to **bounded rationality.**[18] Our brains' limitations constrain our thinking and reasoning ability, and, thus, it is impossible to consider simultaneously all information relevant to any decision or problem. Bounded rationality leads managers to engage in what is known as **satisficing** or determining the most acceptable solution to a problem, rather than an optimal one. Nonetheless, adhering to a problem-solving model has been shown to improve decision quality, and a number of proven tools and techniques are worth utilizing in different situations. In the following, we outline a popular model as well as some of the better tools for employing each element of that model. The model consists of five major steps that we abbreviate into the acronym **PADIL** (pronounced "paddle"), or problem, alternatives, decide, implement, learn (see Figure 3.4).

"A good decision cannot guarantee a good outcome. All real decisions are made under uncertainty. A decision is therefore a bet, and evaluating it as good or not must depend on the stakes and the odds, not on the outcome."

—W. Edwards Deming

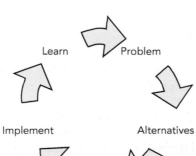

**FIGURE 3.4
The PADIL Problem-Solving Framework**

KO **3-3**

KO **3-4**

DO **3-2**

DO **3-3**

DO **3-4**

"A problem well stated is a problem half solved."

—John Dewey

Practice this!
Go to www.baldwin2e.com

A Problem-Solving Framework: PADIL

Define and Structure the Problem

The first step in any good problem-solving process is to define and structure the problem. Put another way, you want to be sure you are working on the *correct* problem. One common way this seemingly obvious starting point is mishandled is to begin with a *solution,* not the problem. For example, take the common managerial lament: "In my company, there is a serious lack of training." That may potentially be true, but a more appropriate problem-framing process would bring forth the question, "What's the problem that more training would address?" Training is one potential solution to a problem of skill deficiency, but we first need to clarify that skill deficiency is a problem rather than, say, motivation or availability of resources. Moreover, even if skill deficiency is the problem, training is only one possible solution. People can acquire skills through several other means, such as on-the-job practice, experience, and mentoring.

The temptation to jump to a solution is very powerful and leads to what problem-solving expert Ian Mitroff calls "solving the wrong problem precisely."[19] There are several ways in which people solve the wrong problem precisely.

- **Picking the wrong stakeholders.** Solving the wrong problem often occurs because the problem solver fails to include key players. For example, in order to solve a problem on a manufacturing line, including people who actually work on the line to help define the problem would be helpful.

- **Framing the problem too narrowly.** Problems are often larger than they may at first appear. Managers can mistakenly limit that scope early by assuming the problem is narrow. For example, a manager might deal with theft in his department by assuming the problem is unique to his department rather than throughout the organization. Starting with a particular solution in mind is not an effective strategy.

- **Failure to think systemically.** Individuals focus on a particular aspect of the problem, rather than the entire system or interrelated aspects of the problem. Focusing on the system allows for the examination of the real problem or "root cause."

- **Failure to find the facts.** The old adage "First seek to understand" is critical if you are to solve the right problem. There are good and efficient tools for uncovering the facts in any problem situation, rather than making hasty generalizations with untested assumptions and anecdotes.

Assess Key Stakeholders

Few problems in organizations are unique to one person. That is, problems and their proposed solutions likely have far-reaching implications beyond those in your immediate surroundings. For this reason, no problem-solving effort is complete without an understanding of the key stakeholders. A **stakeholder** is literally anyone who has a stake in the problem or solution. Any problem you're trying to solve usually impacts more people than you might initially think. Therefore, one critical piece of problem definition is to conduct a stakeholder analysis, which will help you uncover the various parties involved in a problem and its potential solution. Tool Kit 3.1 describes the specific steps involved in completing such an analysis.

⚒ MANAGER'S TOOL KIT

Tool Kit 3.1   Stakeholder Analysis

Stakeholder analysis is an essential tool for any problem-solving endeavor. It is also a "living" document, meaning that stakeholders require constant attention while solving a problem. Thus, a careful analysis will help you get an understanding of how the decision impacts different groups of people, who has the biggest stake and most power, and which stakeholders are likely to support or resist potential solutions to the problem.

1. **Identify Key Stakeholders.** Create a chart of *primary stakeholders*—individuals or groups that have direct authority or economic influence over the problem—and *secondary stakeholders*—individuals or groups that might be affected indirectly by the problem.

2. **Prioritize Your Stakeholders.** Using a simple 2 × 2 matrix, with the dimensions of Stake and Power, classify (plot) each stakeholder to get a graphic representation of who your most important stakeholders to involve in the process are. For example, those stakeholders who have a high stake and a lot of power or influence should be your top priority. They should be involved in every step of the PADIL process.

3. **Examine Support/Resistance.** Once you've begun defining the problem and generating solutions, it's helpful to determine the degree of support or resistance. Talk to your stakeholders, describe the problem as it has been framed, and talk about potential solutions. Gauge their relative support or resistance for how the problem has been defined and framed.

Stakeholder Analysis					
Stakeholder Name	Strongly Against	Moderately Against	Neutral	Moderately Supportive	Strongly Supportive

⇄ MANAGEMENT LIVE 3.3

Solving the Wrong Problem Precisely[20]

Examples abound of solving the wrong problem precisely. One compelling example is the story of the Make-A-Wish Foundation, a first-rate nonprofit with passion. Its sole mission is to find ways to grant dreams and wishes to terminally ill children. In 1996, the organization made headlines as it attempted to fulfill the wish of a 17-year-old boy named Erik. Erik's dream was to kill a Kodiak bear in the wild and display the skin in front of the fireplace. To fulfill the wish, the foundation enlisted the Safari Club International to purchase all the hunting equipment and make the dream happen. With outstanding coordination, the Safari Club and Make-A-Wish fulfilled Erik's wish. Unfortunately, the decision to grant this wish had some unforeseen consequences, namely, outraging every animal activist group in the country. Newspapers were flooded with bad press about the foundation's inability to make good decisions, tarnishing the group's reputation. The foundation solved the problem of "finding a way to make Erik's wish come true" quite precisely because they viewed the problem simply as "granting the wish." In reality, the problem was much more complex and required a full examination of all those potentially affected by this solution, namely, the key stakeholders.

Determining Whom to Involve

One of the more challenging issues you will face in problem solving is determining who owns a particular problem—that is, who should be primarily accountable for solving the problem. For example, it is common for a manager to mistakenly delegate problems to an employee or team when the manager is actually the most appropriate person to solve the problem. Equally common, managers often attempt to solve a problem on their own when employee input or actual delegation is required.

Although research shows getting others involved in problem solving usually results in better decisions, it does not mean others should always make the final decision. In other words, sometimes a manager just needs input from employees (a voice not a vote) and that is the extent of their involvement. In other cases, delegating the decision to those most closely involved is appropriate. As noted earlier, a common trap is to make a habit of solving employee problems in isolation.

One useful tool for helping gauge the appropriate level of involvement in problem solving is that developed by Victor Vroom and Phillip Yetton.[21] Those authors note that a decision-maker could involve others on a broad continuum ranging from no involvement to full employee delegation. As seen in Figure 3.5, this continuum represents five key participation approaches: decide, consult individually, consult group, facilitate group, delegate to group.

FIGURE 3.5
Vroom and Yetton's Problem-Solving Approaches[22]

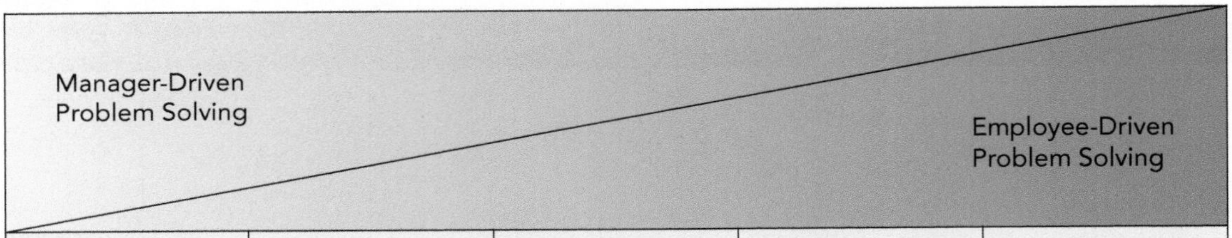

Manager-Driven Problem Solving .... Employee-Driven Problem Solving				
Decide	**Consult Individually**	**Consult Group**	**Facilitate Group**	**Delegate to Group**
Manager makes the decision alone and announces it to employees.	Manager presents the problem to individual employees and uses input to make the decision.	Manager presents the problem to all employees in manager's group and uses group's input to make the decision.	Manager presents the problem to group and acts as a facilitator to help define the problem. Manager acts as a peer on the problem-solving team.	Manager gives problem to employees and permits employees to decide using an appropriate decision-making model. Manager provides necessary resources to ensure the group's success.

Reprinted from *Organizational Dynamics,* Vol. 28, No. 4, by V. H. Vroom, "Leadership and the Decision Making Process," pp. 82–94. Copyright © 1969, with permission from Elsevier.

Thus, you have five approaches for engaging (or disengaging) in the problem-solving process. The model goes one step further, however, in helping you decide which of the five approaches will be most useful given the problem you are facing. The framework identifies seven factors that must be addressed before you decide which approach is best. These factors can be framed as questions to be answered, though not all factors will be present in every problem situation.[23]

- **Decision Significance**—The significance of the decision to the success of the unit/organization.
- **Importance of Commitment**—The importance of employee commitment to the decision.
- **Leader's Expertise**—A manager's knowledge or expertise regarding the problem.
- **Likelihood of Commitment**—The likelihood that employees would commit themselves to a decision made by the manager alone.
- **Group Support**—The degree to which employees support the unit or organization's stake in the problem.
- **Group Expertise**—The degree to which the group of employees has knowledge or expertise regarding the problem.
- **Group Competence**—The employees' abilities to work together in solving the problem.

Using your evaluation of the seven factors in simple high (H) or low (L) terms, you can create a flowchart (see Figure 3.6) that will yield the most effective participation approach. Keep in mind, this is a highly prescriptive approach and certainly cannot take into account every possible scenario. However, Vroom and his colleagues have demonstrated in multiple studies that managers using this method had a success rate of 62 percent versus a 37 percent success rate for managers who did not use the method.[24] Thus, even though it may not take into account every possible factor, it seems to do a good job at capturing the most important factors.

Time-Driven Model

Decision Significance	Importance of Commitment	Leader's Expertise	Likelihood of Commitment	Group Support	Group Expertise	Team Competence	Outcome
H	H	H	H	-	-	-	Decide
			L	H	H	H	Delegate
						L	Consult (Group)
					L	-	Consult (Group)
				L	-	-	Consult (Group)
		L	H	H	H	H	Facilitate
						L	Consult (Individually)
					L	-	Consult (Individually)
				L	-	-	Consult (Individually)
			L	H	H	H	Facilitate
						L	Consult (Group)
					L	-	Consult (Group)
				L	-	-	Consult (Group)
	L	H	-	-	-	-	Decide
		L	-	H	H	H	Facilitate
						L	Consult (Individually)
					L	-	Consult (Individually)
				L	-	-	Consult (Individually)
L	H	-	-	H	-	-	Decide
				L	-	H	Delegate
						L	Facilitate
	L	-	-	-	-	-	Decide

(Problem Statement)

FIGURE 3.6
Vroom Participation Decision Tree

Practice this!
Go to www.baldwin2e.com

"If you're seeking a creative answer to your problem, you must first give sufficient attention to understanding what the problem is."

—Gerard Nierenberg

Framing the Problem Correctly

Before you begin to solve any problem, you must learn to frame the problem correctly. This is the essence of solving the right problem precisely. Strong evidence suggests the way in which a problem is stated determines the quantity and quality of solutions generated.[25] Consider the following problem:

> The parking lot outside an office building is jammed with workers' cars. Management decides to tackle the problem so they convene a committee with instructions to devise different ways to redesign the parking lot to hold more cars. The work group does its job, coming up with six different methods for increasing the lot's capacity.[26]

The problem defined by management in this case is "to redesign the parking lot to hold more cars." Has the real problem been framed correctly? No! Management didn't charge the work group with solving the problem (the jammed parking lot), but rather gave them a solution (redesign the lot) and asked for different methods to implement that solution. Further, the real problem as framed correctly would be, "The parking lot is jammed with cars," and a statement of *why* this is a problem, perhaps "Thus, it can't accommodate all of our employees who drive to work." Framed this way, the work group is free to consider all sorts of potential solutions, which may include expanding the parking lot, but could also include providing benefits for taking public transportation or carpool programs.

Framing problems correctly is difficult since our immediate need is to begin solving the problem. But the way in which a problem is framed can lead to drastically different actions with varied consequences.[27] Consider some research that asked participants either "Do you get headaches *frequently,* and if so, how often?" or "Do you get headaches *occasionally,* and if so, how often?" The words "frequently" versus "occasionally" are the only difference in these statements. In this study, participants asked the first question responded with an average of 2.2 headaches per week (*frequently*), whereas participants asked the second question reported 0.7 headaches per week (*occasionally*). A simple word change in how a problem statement is phrased can lead people to arrive at very different conclusions about the nature of the problem.

When you start to examine problem framing, you will notice the tendency for people to generally frame problems in "either–or" terms. This tendency has been termed the **black or white fallacy,** which assumes our choices are clear and limited to two (it's either black or white), when in reality there may be many other choices (shades of gray). Sometimes people make this mistake unconsciously because it does not occur to them that they have other choices. Other times they do it consciously for manipulative purposes—for example, "If I want you to do A, I can increase your odds of doing it by convincing you your only other alternative is B, which is clearly unacceptable."

Let's look at another example of how framing problems is tricky. In a research study,[28] one group of participants read the following first scenario and another group read the second:

1. The government is preparing to combat a rare disease expected to take 600 lives. Two alternative programs to combat the disease have been proposed, each of which, scientists believe, will have certain consequences. Program A will save 200 people if adopted. Program B has a one-third chance of saving all 600, but a two-thirds chance of saving no one. Which program do you prefer?

2. The government is preparing to combat a rare disease expected to take 600 lives. Two alternative programs to combat the disease have been proposed, each of which, scientists believe, will have certain consequences. Through Program A, 400 people would die if adopted. For Program B, there is a one-third chance that no one would die, but a two-thirds chance that all 600 would die. Which program do you prefer?

MANAGER'S TOOL KIT

Tool Kit 3.2   Methods for Reframing Problems

Here are four simple methods that will help you to view problems differently.

1. **Paraphrase:** Restate in your own words what someone else has stated.
   Initial: How can we reduce our shipping delays?
   Reframe: How can we keep shipping delays from increasing?

2. **180° Turnaround:** Simply turn the problem around.
   Initial: How can we encourage students to study for exams?
   Reframe: How can we discourage students from studying for exams?

3. **Broaden It:** Reframe the problem with a broader frame of reference.
   Initial: Should we expand our product line in China?
   Reframe: How can we achieve increased financial success in China?

4. **Redirect the Problem:** Change the actual focus of the problem.
   Initial: How can we increase our revenue?
   Reframe: How can we decrease our costs?

Both scenarios are exactly the same, that is, they are logically equivalent. In scenario 1, the problem is framed in terms of *lives saved*, whereas in scenario 2 the problem is framed in terms of *lives lost*. This simple change leads participants to avoid risk and heavily endorse program A (72 percent) in the "lives saved" frame and largely seek risk by selecting program B (78 percent) in the "lives lost" frame (see Figure 3.7). Took Kit 3.2 offers some easy methods to examine problem frames in different ways.

Thinking Systemically

No discussion of solving the right problem is complete without a basic understanding of systems and systems thinking. **A system** is a perceived whole whose elements "hang together" because they continually affect each other over time

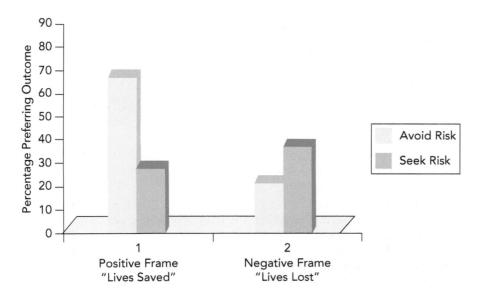

FIGURE 3.7 Framing Effects and Risk

and operate toward a common purpose.[29] The human body is a great example of a system. When you see the doctor because your stomach hurts, the doctor examines other areas of your body and takes your temperature, blood pressure, and pulse. Why is that?

It is because the stomach is part of a larger bodily system. Thus, your doctor is attempting to find the root cause of your stomach problem, which may have nothing to do with your stomach at all, but rather be a problem with your pancreas that contributes to stomach pain or sore back muscles creating pain that feels like it's coming from your stomach. Effective problem solving almost always demands attention to a larger system and uncovering the root cause(s) (for example, the pancreas) whereas simply treating the symptoms (stomach pain) will not solve the problem adequately.

Organizations are elaborate systems and contain thousands of interrelated parts, some of which are more obvious than others. All systems express what is known as **systemic structure** or a pattern of interrelationships among the system components. The challenge is symptoms are always much more visible than their underlying systemic structure. Yet this underlying structure is what holds the promise for real problem solving.

So a systems approach—"How will this change affect other things?"—is critical to being effective. A helpful visual is to think of system structure as being part of an iceberg. Icebergs exist above and below the water, meaning part of the iceberg is quite visible, while another part is completely concealed (see Figure 3.8).

At the tip of the iceberg are events in the system. Turnover has increased, sales are down, or orders are delayed are all examples of events that take place in an organizational system. Problems solved at the event level tend to be short-lived and do nothing to actually address the real problem. For example, if turnover is high, we might institute a new bonus system, hoping to retain employees. But if the real reason turnover is high has nothing to do with the pay system, it is unlikely to work.

Working our way toward the water are patterns of behavior or trends. That means examining the problem by seeking to understand the overall pattern that has persisted over time. For example, as we plot data for turnover, we might find

"The significant problems we face cannot be solved at the same level of thinking we were at when we created them."

—Albert Einstein

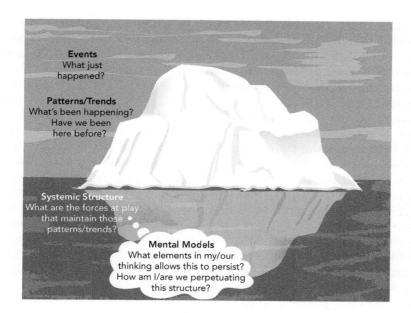

FIGURE 3.8
The Systems-Approach
Iceberg

turnover is always highest in one particular month out of the year when the competition tends to seek new talent. Thinking at the trend level, as opposed to the event level, helps us put the most recent events in context.

Finally, under the water is the systemic structure. The systemic structure represents the most powerful information because it focuses on the actual cause of the patterns of behavior, which then explain the events. If you really want to solve a problem, you must solve the right problem by getting to the systemic structure.

One reason people have trouble thinking systemically is we are taught to view the world in linear, rather than nonlinear terms. Purely linear thinking is a bit of a fallacy in that it rests on the assumption that present trends will continue in the same direction and pace (for example, when you retire, a Toyota Prius will cost $209,000 and a Big Mac $25). Strategy plans often fail because strategists assume the world as we know it will not change much and that current trends are permanent. Perhaps the most common example of linear management thinking is that companies with a hot new product overexpand their capacity only to find themselves out of luck when demand softens.

Let's view another example using the iceberg approach. Suppose a fire breaks out in your area. This is an *event*. If you respond by putting the fire out, you are simply reacting. In other words, you've not done anything that would prevent new fires. If, however, you not only extinguish the fire but study the location of fires in your area, you are paying attention to *patterns*. For example, you might notice certain neighborhoods incur more fires than others. One response would be to adapt to this pattern by adding more fire houses in those areas. What if, however, you examined the *systems*—which might include smoke detector distribution and the building material used—that sustain the pattern's fires? That might lead you to build new fire alarm systems and establish new safety codes. Using this approach, you are getting to the bottom of preventing new fires.[30]

Why do most communities respond to an increase in fires by hiring more fire personnel? The answer is people often solve problems based on faulty thinking and rarely identify the systemic structures at work. To identify these systemic structures requires uncovering one's assumptions (discovering what's below the surface) or our mental models about the systemic structure. **Mental models** are the prevailing assumptions, beliefs, and values that sustain current systems. These habits of thought enable us to ignore valid data, despite the fact that those data are essential to solving the problem. In addition, we protect and preserve these mental models by making them "undiscussable." That is, they become ways of being in organizations. So even if our thinking is faulty, we don't question it or examine it. If you've ever heard, "That's just the way its done," or "We have an understanding about that," that's a clue a mental model may be contributing to the problem.

"He who asks a question may be a fool for five minutes, but he who never asks a question remains a fool forever."

—Tom Connelly

Learning how to bring mental models to the surface or challenge them is important to good problem solving. The best way to learn this skill is by understanding how to ask the right questions about a problem—that is, developing **inquiry skills.** Inquiry skills allow you to examine your own mental models as well as others. For example, let's say you're trying to solve the problem of dropped calls in your customer service center. You seek your employees' opinion by asking the following question: "Why are there so many dropped calls in the service center?" You're likely to get great responses, but how will you know what the real problem is? You won't unless you attempt to find the root cause. That is, when your employees respond with reasons, your response should not be, "OK, thank you," but should be to dig deeper. These question stems can help you dig deeper toward the root cause:

- What leads you to believe that is the case?
- What conditions exist that allow this to occur?
- Can you tell me more?
- What have you seen that may contribute to this problem?
- Can you help me understand your thinking?
- What do we assume to be true?

Inquiry skills are aimed at understanding people's mental models. This includes examining your own mental models, including asking "What is my role in this problem?" and "What about my behavior allows this problem to persist?" You can easily delude yourself into thinking the problem is out there when in fact it may be closer to home than you think!

Tools for Understanding the Problem Scope

"It's not that I'm so smart; it's just that I stay with problems longer."

—Albert Einstein

Some problems have a very well-defined scope, while others are quite broad. Your job is to determine the boundaries of your problem—that is, determining what is truly germane to your problem and what falls outside the realm of the problem. With most problems, potential causes and solutions are infinite. Your job is to narrow the potential causes down and move on to the next step in the PADIL process—*alternatives*. We discuss various tools for helping you understand the problem scope. You can use these tools on your own, but they work best when you have a few key stakeholders working with you. If you engage in these exercises with a team, keep in mind your team members are likely to censor their comments about problems if they think you won't want to hear them. Don't kick off the exercises by offering your opinion first; the group will likely conform to it. Let others go first.

Affinity Diagram.   The affinity (similarity) diagram is an idea generation method that allows you to sort the major aspects of the problem into themes or categories. The categories will help when you begin to gather data about the problem and research alternatives. The following steps outline how to create an affinity diagram.

1. Write the problem statement (one you've framed well) on a flip chart or board. Underneath the problem, write the phrase, "What are the possible causes of it?"

2. Using sticky notes, allow each person to write as many potential causes of the problem as possible, one per sticky note, and place them on the board or flip chart. Do not evaluate the merit of each person's idea.

3. Once all the ideas are posted, begin to look for similarities in the ideas. Group the similar notes together and label them according to the category they represent. For example, "These five seem to deal with our 'Delivery Process' and these three with our 'Customer Service Structure.'" You now have some ideas for where to begin your data collection.

Is/Is Not.   This simple method determines your problem's boundaries by describing aspects that are part of the problem and those that are not. Use the following steps as a guideline.

1. On a piece of paper or flip chart, write the problem statement.

2. Draw a line down the middle. On one side put the word "Is" and on the other the words "Is Not." Down the left-hand side of the paper, write the words "what," "who," "when," and "where."

3. Answer the questions. What *is* the crux of the problem; what *is not* the crux of the problem? Who *is* involved with this problem; who *is not* involved? When *is* the problem a problem; when *is it not* a problem? Where *is* the problem appearing most; where *is it not* appearing most?

Graphic Displays.   Sometimes, a picture is worth a thousand words. Taking what you know about the problem so far and graphing it in some meaningful way can be incredibly helpful. A **histogram** or bar chart allows for the display of data categories (on the X axis) tracked against some important standard (on the Y axis). For example, type of part manufactured (X axis) and the number of parts per type made each hour (Y axis). A scatter plot can also be useful. The scatter plot demonstrates the relationship between two variables. For instance, you might track students' test grades on one axis (Y) and student absences on the other axis (X) to see if there is some type of relationship between test grades and class attendance. For instance, we might expect to find that, as absences decrease, test grades increase.

One of the most powerful graphic displays is known as a behavior-over-time chart, or BOT. In order to create a BOT, you need to have been collecting data for some given time period. Let's say you regularly track customer service behaviors (for example, problems solved in first call, number of calls handled per hour, and so on). As you plot these behaviors over time, you may start to see patterns emerge. For example, you may notice that during two months in the year the call volume skyrockets. As you piece this information together with other data you routinely collect, you also note an increase in employee absenteeism that corresponds with those spikes. Problem-solving experts agree certain patterns that appear in BOTs can help to identify a *systemic* problem, one not likely to respond to a quick fix.[31] These include:

- Increases that level off
- Steeply rising increases
- Steeply falling decreases
- "Boom and bust" cycles (such as up- and downswings)

In Tool Kit 3.3, we offer another graphic display method, known as Pareto graphing, to help identify the most critical components of a problem.

Tool Kit 3.3 Pareto Graphing

Sometimes, in attempting to solve a problem, you can't solve the whole thing, yet solving one component still would make a significant improvement. Applying the Pareto principle, 80 percent of the value to be gained is likely to be accomplished by solving 20 percent of the problem. In other words, some things are just much more important than others. If you could fix the one or two major problem areas, you'd be likely to eradicate over three-quarters of the problem. For that reason, the Pareto principle has become known as the 80/20 rule. Using this principle can help you quickly isolate where you'd like to spend your problem-solving efforts.

For example, professors sometimes receive poorly written student papers. Yet it's often difficult to determine where to spend time helping students improve their writing, particularly when writing is not the course's primary intent. Using the Pareto principle, a professor could quickly isolate the major source of her students' writing problems. While grading an assignment, she could track the following information in all 40 papers she receives: grammar, punctuation, spelling, and typing/computer errors. After compiling the data, she could then create a chart like the following:

Problem	# of Errors	% of Total	Cumulative %
Grammar	47	44	44
Punctuation	28	26	70
Spelling	21	19	89
Typing/Computer	12	11	100
Total	108	100	

Looking at the chart, she would easily see the largest problem by far is grammar. In addition, punctuation causes problems as well. Even if the professor chose only to deal with the grammatical errors of her students, she would drastically improve their writing skills. This is only evident after charting the data.

Generate Creative Alternatives

"The key to having a good idea is to have lots of ideas."

—Linus Pauling

Hopefully, the process of framing the problem will lead you to think about many potential solutions to the problem. Research shows that generating multiple alternatives to problems results in higher-quality solutions. And the key to doing so is finding ways to generate as many creative alternatives as possible. Let's examine the following scenario:

A building manager receives several complaints about the long wait times for the building's elevator. He calls a consultant who recommends three alternatives: (1) build new elevators, (2) space out the elevators between floors, or (3) make the elevators faster. The manager thinks these solutions are good, but costly. The manager then consults a psychologist, who recommends giving people something to do while they wait. The manager installs mirrors by the elevators and the complaints stop.

The alternative proposed by the psychologist was not only cheap but incredibly effective; people simply occupied their time looking at themselves. Would you have thought of that? We certainly didn't and herein lies the quandary: Left to our own thinking, we rarely arrive at truly creative and unique alternatives to problems. Most of the time, our alternative solutions look awfully familiar and offer only slight improvements (What should we do this weekend? Well, what did we do last weekend?). Moreover, we often trust the first solution out of the box.[32] We don't question whether other, perhaps better, solutions exist. Say that a recruiter calls you and offers you a job more attractive than your current one. Would you take the job? Most people will compare their current job with the new offer and arrive at an emphatic "Yes! Where do I sign up?" Yet if you're going to take the step of leaving your current job, why limit yourself to one alternative, the one presented by the recruiter? Wouldn't you want to explore other possible job opportunities that could be even more attractive?[33]

Brainstorming

Another key process issue is idea generation. While it may seem contradictory, good brainstorming sessions are more likely to result from a disciplined protocol (see Management Live 3.4 on IDEO's brainstorming rules). In an effective brainstorming session, the group sits around a table with a flip chart or some way to visibly present the input. The brainstorming facilitator states the problem in a clear manner so all participants understand it. Members then "freewheel" (without limiting themselves) as many alternatives as they can in a given length of time. No criticism is allowed, and all alternatives are recorded for later

⤡ MANAGEMENT LIVE 3.4

Brainstorming at IDEO

The following is a list of brainstorming techniques used by IDEO, a consulting firm noted for its creative ideas and client list of major companies. IDEO staff recommends setting a 20- to 30-minute time limit on your brainstorming and appointing one team member to make sure the team honors these rules:

1. **Defer Judgment.** Don't dismiss any ideas. This will be difficult for a group of analytical types who will instantly want to talk about what is wrong with the idea and why it wouldn't work. But nothing shuts down a brainstorming session like criticism.

2. **Build on the Ideas of Others.** No "buts," only "ands."

3. **Encourage Wild Ideas.** Embrace the most out-of-the-box notions because they can be the key to solutions. Every idea is a good idea. These ideas may not ultimately be adopted, but might trigger other ideas.

4. **Go for Quantity.** Aim for as many new ideas as possible. In a good session, up to 50 ideas are generated in 30 minutes.

5. **Be Visual and Auditory.** Use yellow, red, and blue markers to write on big 30-inch by 25-inch sticky notes that are put on the wall. This is important because reading others' ideas will spur your thinking. As you write your idea, say it out loud for everyone to hear.

6. **Stay Focused on the Topic.** Always keep the discussion on target. Your facilitator will help with this. If there is a question about whether something should be included on the wall, put it up there.

7. **One Conversation at a Time.** No interrupting, no dismissing, no disrespect, and no rudeness.

After the 30-minute brainstorming session, go to the wall and have the team attempt to group the ideas. Precision isn't as important as establishing general categories. Discard identical ideas and pair up ideas that are similar. Next, discuss the ideas the team has come up with, and be sure to discuss what might be interesting about an idea before the team goes into a criticism mode. New ideas may still be popping up. Write down these additional ideas and get them up on the wall. Consider how ideas may be combined to create an even better solution.

The team may then have a long list of ideas and need to narrow them down to a more manageable number for further development. Use a multivote system to narrow the list to three to five items.

discussion and analysis. Judgments of even the most bizarre suggestions are withheld until later because one idea can stimulate others. Disallowing criticism thus encourages group members to "think the unusual."

Brainwriting

Organizations love brainstorming, and the prevailing assumption is it works in generating many creative ideas. So companies all across the country place people in conference rooms and tell them, "Be creative; solve our problems." Unfortunately, recent syntheses of research on brainstorming suggest in some cases brainstorming sessions are rendered ineffective because of problems related to group dynamics in which people aren't able to defer judgment, can be critical of others, and usually don't "let it all hang out" toward solving the problem.[34] Indeed, one meta-analytic study found that involving a team or group of people actually produced far fewer ideas than the same number of individuals generating ideas on their own.

With that in mind, a modest variant of brainstorming called **brainwriting** has emerged as the superior method for generating the highest volume of creative ideas.[35] Using the same rules as brainstorming, brainwriting allows participants time to generate ideas on their own, recording them but not sharing them with the group initially. Then participants in a round-robin format read off their ideas until all alternatives have been presented and people can then build upon them. There are several ways to improve the quantity and quality of the alternatives presented:[36]

- **Diversify Participants.** Make sure the people involved in brainstorming represent diverse perspectives on the topic—your key stakeholders and even some outsiders (customers, suppliers) who aren't familiar with your particular problems. Research shows diverse groups perform better than nondiverse groups on creative problem-solving tasks.[37]

- **Use Metaphors and Analogies.** When a car dealership wanted to increase the number of people walking in the door by creating a more pleasurable shopping experience, they focused on pleasurable things such as food. Using food as a metaphor they agreed that chocolate (smooth, sweet, comforting) made for a good metaphor to focus on delivering services that went smoothly and were sweet and comforting, as opposed to aggressive.[38] The popular potato chips Pringles were the result of an analogical process. The problem was potato chips required too much shelf space, but packing them tightly destroyed them. The manufacturer used the analogy of dried leaves (noting similar properties to potato chips) and showed that when leaves were slightly damp, they could be stacked without losing their shapes, hence Pringles.

- **Performance Standards and Feedback.** Research shows a group of problem solvers can increase the number of ideas generated by setting high performance standards, as long as they are not impossible. In addition, providing feedback on how the brainwriting is going is central. Simply stop every now and then and gauge the number of ideas generated and let people know whether they are ahead or behind the curve.

- **Assume a "Perfect World."** Key to generating really creative alternatives is to encourage people to simply assume there are no constraints to solving a problem. What would you wish for if you could get it? What would a perfect world look like?[39]

Benchmarking

A popular form of generating alternatives known as benchmarking is used in approximately one-quarter of organizational problem-solving scenarios.[40] In **benchmarking,** organizational representatives trying to solve a problem go to visit (either literally or figuratively) other organizations thought to have successfully solved the problem or a similar one. During the visit, problem solvers generate ideas that might work in their own organization. The knee-jerk reaction of most managers is to try to visit others in the same industry that might have some great practices to share. However, benchmarking seems to be most effective for generating ideas when managers visit organizations that specialize in the particular problem area, regardless of the industry. For example, a bank that wants to improve customer service would often benefit more by visiting the Ritz-Carlton or Nordstrom to generate new ideas rather than visiting another financial services organization.

Although benchmarking can be a good starting point and impetus for change, it is hardly a foolproof means of generating alternatives and sometimes even leads to decision failures. For example, problem solvers can be inclined to rush to implement the exact process of the benchmarked company assuming it will work similarly in their organization. It falls short when problem solvers fail to realize their problem is truly different than the one addressed by the benchmark company and that the new solution doesn't quite work in their culture. In addition, people often have strong negative reactions to, and are inclined to resist, ideas not invented in, or derived from, their own organizations.

Once alternatives have been generated, how will you know you've got good ones to choose from? Good alternatives will have the following characteristics:[41]

- **Postponed Evaluation.** The alternatives proposed were all offered without any evaluative components. No one qualified them as "good" or "feasible"; they were simply offered as potential alternatives.
- **Stakeholder Involvement.** The right mix of people had opportunities to look at the problem and offer their take. A well-executed decision will fail if important others don't have input.
- **Organizational Focus.** Great alternatives are consistent with the goals of the organization. Many alternatives may be proposed to fix a problem, but if they violate the organization's values or are inconsistent with its strategic direction, they will likely lead to failure.
- **Time Implications.** The alternatives are not quick fixes or Band-Aids but real solutions. They focus on short- and long-term answers.
- **Effective.** The key litmus test of a good alternative is it addresses the actual problem, not something else or even a tangentially related problem.

Decide on a Solution

After the problem has been defined and the alternatives generated, you'll probably want to collect more information about the alternatives. In fact, no manager worth her salt would ever make a decision without knowing a few key factors, such as (1) How much would implementing the solution cost? (2) Who would be involved? (3) Who would be affected? (4) How much time would it take to implement? Put simply, is the alternative feasible and effective, or can it be done given our resources (or with a reasonable resource stretch) and will it actually solve the problem?

Invariably, managers will use one of two approaches to collect this type of information about their alternatives. Managers under time constraints and pressure to solve a problem will seek out very little information and seek only to confirm what they think they already know about the problem. Other managers, in their desire to reduce the uncertainty associated with a problem, will conduct an endless search for information about each potential alternative, so much so they become paralyzed by the mass of data they accumulate. Neither case is ideal.

"I am quick to admit that I do not have all of the answers. So I am going to listen. But shortly after I listen, the second piece is to pull the trigger. I have all the input, and here is what we are going to do. People need closure on a decision. If you listen and then noodle on it, people get confused, and that's not effective leadership."

—Terry Lundgren, CEO, Federated

Some research now shows great problem solvers know when to say when. One such study found that, as the amount of information available increases, so does one's confidence about one's ability to make the right decision. Unfortunately, decision accuracy does not increase proportional to increases in information or one's confidence (as seen in Figure 3.9).[42]

We've said we'd present a "management truth" when it exists and here is one: *You will always feel like you don't have enough information.* "If only I knew *X*, I would feel better." You can find some comfort in the fact that having "more" information won't improve your chances of making the right decision. Seek out a handful of critically relevant items and then go with them. Otherwise, you will simply delude yourself into thinking that more data will make the decision easier. You will be more familiar with the problem, which makes the problem appear less ambiguous, but in reality the nature of the problem and its potential solutions won't change.

Narrowing Alternatives Tools

One of the most difficult things to do in evaluating alternatives is to narrow your choices. Fortunately, various tools are at your disposal that can help you evaluate the potential of each alternative and quickly narrow them to the few best alternatives. Key to almost all narrowing tools is choosing your criteria carefully. On what basis will you decide which alternative is most attractive? You don't have to identify every single criterion for making the choice, just the big ones.

For example, if you were considering two different job offers, what criteria would be most important? Perhaps salary, work schedule, benefits, and work environment would be the most important. You might deem other criteria like commute time, while important, less critical. Know what criteria are most critical, and then use them to help you narrow the alternatives.

Alternatives Table. The most basic decision tool, then, is to explicitly state the consequences in one table where comparisons can be made easily. Let's continue with our job example.

**FIGURE 3.9
Accuracy, Confidence, and Amount of Information**

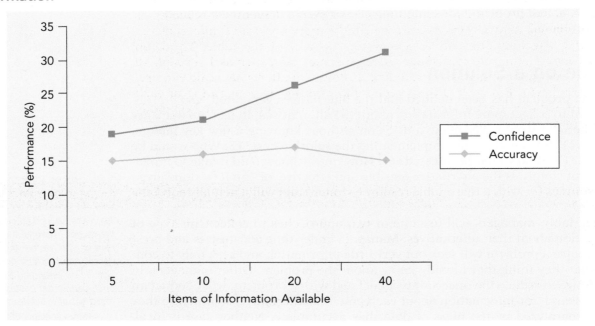

TABLE 3.1 Alternatives Table

Criteria	Alternatives			
	Job 1	Job 2	Job 3	Job 4
Annual Salary	$38,000	$42,000	$41,000	$46,000
Work Schedule	38 hours/week	40 hours/week	50+ hours/week	60+ hours/week
Benefits	Medical, dental, 401(k)	Medical, dental	Medical, company car	Medical, dental, 401(k), concierge service
Work Environment	Cubicle, relaxed	Office, relaxed	Travel, flexible, relaxed	Travel, intense

As can be seen in Table 3.1, we have simply listed our most important decision criteria on the left side of the table and the job alternatives across the top. Then, in simple terms we have listed all the information about each alternative. The beauty of this table is you can quickly see the trade-offs. Job 1 pays less, but it has good benefits and offers a great lifestyle, whereas Job 4 pays more, has good benefits, but work will be your life. You might be inclined to ask, "Why do I need this hokey table; can't I simply do these comparisons in my head?" Here again is where the non-obvious traps of problem solving cause difficulties. According to research, few people can compare even a short list of alternatives in their head effectively[43] and end up focusing or giving too much weight to one particular alternative.

Weighted Ranking. If you've done a great job at generating alternatives and you're facing 25 interesting ideas, you'll probably want to narrow this list rather quickly. Weighted ranking allows you to do this quite nicely. First, in a table, list the criteria down the left side of the first column. Next, compare each criterion with the next and make a tick mark beside the criterion in each pairing you believe to be more important. That is, compare all criteria against each other so you end up with a rank ordering of the most to least important criteria. In other words, count the tick marks next to each criterion and you've got your ranking for your criteria (high numbers are ranked as most important). This captures reality as some criteria will naturally carry more weight (be more important) than others.

Second, list your alternatives across the top row of the table. Third, on each of your criteria, rate every alternative on some scale, such as 1 through 10 where 1 is very poor and 10 is outstanding. It doesn't matter what scale you use, just be consistent. Finally, multiply your rank ordering by your rating of each alternative. Let's look at an example in which you're determining the best mode of transportation for your vacation (Table 3.2).

TABLE 3.2 Weighted Ranking Example

Criteria	Rank Ordering	Train	Car	Plane	Bicycle	Teleportation
Speed	2	$2 \times 6 = 12$	$2 \times 5 = 10$	$2 \times 10 = 20$	$3 \times 2 = 6$	$2 \times 10 = 20$
Safety	2	$2 \times 5 = 10$	$2 \times 3 = 6$	$2 \times 9 = 18$	$2 \times 1 = 2$	$2 \times 1 = 2$
Cost	1	$1 \times 7 = 7$	$1 \times 9 = 9$	$1 \times 5 = 5$	$1 \times 2 = 2$	$1 \times 1 = 1$
Reliability	1	$1 \times 6 = 6$	$1 \times 7 = 7$	$1 \times 6 = 6$	$1 \times 1 = 1$	$1 \times 1 = 1$
	Totals	35	32	49	11	24

As can be seen in Table 3.2, the "airplane" satisfies our decision criteria the best. Interestingly, teleportation is better than riding a bike—at least once it's invented (Beam me to South Beach, Scottie).

Paralyzed by Choices

Organizational systems display what is known as **equifinality,** a condition in which *different* initial conditions lead to *similar* effects. In other words, not all roads lead to Rome, but many do. Sometimes the best way to solve a problem is to select *any one* of your final solutions. It may not be the perfect solution or even the optimal one, but it is likely to jump-start your problem solving. Using this logic, attempt to choose the solution that will provide the greatest payoff (not always financial) or leverage. Remember, systems are comprised of many inter-related parts. Your final solution likely will trigger reactions in the system that provide feedback about whether you're on the right track. That doesn't mean you should just start with any old solution; rather, you can breathe easier knowing that, when you've narrowed your choices to a few strong, well-crafted solutions, you are likely to make an impact.

One important technique to help illuminate trade-offs is known as the **devil's advocate** method, which increases debate and explores a problem from all angles.[44] This method can be accomplished with a group of people or with individuals. Either way, you start by clearly articulating the problem and your favored alternative solution (the one you're "leaning" toward). Assign someone (co-worker, key customer, experienced employee) to play the role of devil's advocate. Your instructions to this person are simple: to challenge the idea, provide a scathing critique of the proposal, poke holes in the logic, and question the assumptions behind it. The devil's advocate will not only help you think through previous blind spots in your solution but will also help you anticipate consequences. Again, no decision will be perfect, but the more problems you can anticipate up front, the better you can prepare as you go forward and implement the decision.

Once you've made your decision, state the solution plainly and succinctly. You should be able to explain the problem and the solution in less than 30 seconds. If you can't, others probably won't understand it either. A simple method for doing this is to follow this template: (1) state the problem, (2) state the assumed reason or cause, (3) state the proposed solution, and (4) describe what the solution will do and for whom. For example:

- **Problem:** Customers are complaining about a long wait time at the elevators.
- **Reason:** The elevators are not significantly slow; customers are just bored waiting.
- **Solution:** Install video screens with CNN and other news channels by elevators.
- **Outcome:** Video screens will preoccupy customers with something other than the elevator, lessen complaints, and increase management's time to devote to other problems. They also have the additional benefit of keeping customers informed about world events!

Make the Decision

The reality is that all decisions require trade-offs. By definition, when you decide on one course of action, you will eliminate others. You can't do everything. You'll likely find that, when you narrow your alternatives down to only a few, each will have pros and cons. One might cost less, but take much longer to implement than another, whereas another alternative may maximize use of funding and time, but is in direct opposition to top management's wishes. Nothing is perfect, but don't panic.

Inherent to all decisions is the issue of risk and perceptions of fairness. Although you can produce elegant mathematical calculations, algorithms, and probability charts for any decision to represent how much risk is involved, there is always an element of personal perception and judgment.[45] Risk usually presents itself in a few different forms, leading people to make different judgments about how much risk is involved.

First, risk presents itself in terms of *dread,* or circumstances in which people feel they have no control or influence. Terrorism is a prime example of such forms of risk. Second, risk often appears as *unknown,* whereby people assume consequences truly are unknown. The risks involved in mapping the human genome, for instance, remain largely unknown at this time. Third, risk presents itself differently depending on the sheer number of people exposed to a given risk. For example, if a single case of a rare disease is found in your town, you are less likely to see it as a high risk compared to an outbreak where 1 in 3 have contracted the disease. Thus, the manner in which risk presents itself leads people to assess their risk exposure quite differently.

In addition, numerous traps are involved in people's assessment of risk. For example, research shows that, all things being equal, people are more likely to view positive outcomes as more probable than negative outcomes. In one study, students on average stated that, compared to their peers, they were 15 percent more likely to have positive life events and 20 percent less likely to experience negative life events. That is, although the "objective" risk generally does not change, we believe that for us nature, risk, or chance behaves differently. What does this mean for you? You should attempt to calculate risks objectively but also recognize others will likely view the numbers and the meaning of the risk differently than you.

Implement

As if making the decision were not difficult enough, you must then implement the solution. This chapter is primarily about solving the problem, meaning determining the most appropriate solution. Executing any change in an organization is itself a complex process, one you will read about more fully in Chapter 10 on implementing change. However, a few points deserve mention here.

First, implementing a solution invariably involves others—your stakeholders. That means before you "just do it" you should revisit your stakeholder analysis and discuss with your key stakeholders the best way to roll out your solution. Second, implementation doesn't have to happen all at once. Sometimes the best way to execute a decision is to attain **small wins.** The concept of small wins is a simple but powerful notion of splitting an implementation plan into many steps. Each step is considered a mini-project, and momentum is gained. In this way, you can demonstrate to others your solution has merit, without dumping the whole solution in their lap at one time.

Third, while implementing a solution, many problem solvers unfortunately find they underestimated the problem's scope or defined the problem incorrectly. Although underestimating is discouraging, nothing is gained by staying the course simply to be perceived as consistent or confident in the solution. In the course of implementation, if you uncover significant information indicating you've solved the wrong problem, stop the implementation. Many managers have been burned by implementing solutions they knew were incorrect but forging ahead even with this knowledge. Retreating so far along in the process will cause pain in the short term, but in the long term you will have acted appropriately.

Learn and Seek Feedback

"Punishing honest mistakes stifles creativity. I want people moving and shaking the earth and they're going to make mistakes."
—Ross Perot

Have you ever made the same mistake twice? Do you remember saying to yourself, "I'll never do that again," and lo and behold, you do it again? Harvard's Chris Argyris observes that everyone fails, but truly successful people view the failure as an opportunity to learn or to have a "productive failure."[46] In addition, he notes that most professionals are defensive of their failures and rarely examine their successes. In that sense, very little learning takes place after implementing a decision that will help a manager repeat the success or avoid the failure of the problem-solving process.

"A man who has committed a mistake and doesn't correct it is committing another mistake."
—Confucius

So the first step in the post-implementation phase of problem solving is to attempt to determine whether the decision was truly successful and continues to be the right solution. That is, the problem should be solved in the way you have defined it. Luckily, because you presumably have already defined success in the early stages of the problem-solving process, you have the basics of what's needed. In the elevator problem, for example, we stated we had hoped our solution would lower customer complaints and increase management's time. Clearly, these measurements are easy to take and should be done periodically to ensure your decision continues to be the right one.

⇄ MANAGEMENT LIVE 3.5

After Action Review (AAR)[47]

One business buzzword—*knowledge management*—has received a lot of recent attention. The basic idea is that organizations and managers tend to repeat poor decisions. Using knowledge management, managers can attempt to build a database of these poor decisions and learn from them so as to not make the same mistakes in the future. This is much easier said than done as politics and turf battles take precedent and managers feel reluctant to take accountability for poor decisions. An outstanding tool known as **after action review** (AAR) has been developed, however, in which the sole purpose is to learn from mistakes and dilute the political atmosphere.

The AAR was created in the military to review the results of a military exercise immediately after the exercise was completed. To do so, the military exposes every aspect of the exercise to a thorough review of what went well and what did not. This includes an examination of everyone's role in the exercises, including the unit's highest leaders. When a private feels his commanding officer failed to provide information in time, for example, the private reports this information as part of the AAR—a rare opportunity to question commanding officers. Tool Kit 3.4 describes a basic AAR plan.

Beyond these primary points of learning, you should also return to your stakeholders once again and collect information about their perceptions of the problem and the solution. We want to know whether or not the final implementation has satisfied stakeholders, but also whether or not the stakeholders were pleased with the process. Did they feel included in the process? Were their voices heard throughout? Completing another brief stockholder analysis is helpful as you look forward to solving other problems in the future. You will know what people like and dislike and the degree to which they wish to be included. In Took Kit 3.4, we offer a basic method for conducting AAR.

MANAGER'S **TOOL KIT**

Tool Kit 3.4   After Action Review

The basic premise of the after action review (AAR) is simple. Each problem-solving effort should be thoroughly reviewed on several factors, including answering these key questions:

- What did we intend to accomplish in solving this problem?
- What was actually realized?
- Is there a gap between what we intended and what actually happened?
- If so, what is causing that gap? Why didn't the solution solve the problem?
- What were the strengths involved in this process, and how can they be repeated in the future?
- What were the weaknesses involved in this process, and how can they be improved or avoided in the future?

The AAR is not simply a postmortem in which positives and negatives are listed; rather, it involves serious conversations with stakeholders about the impact of the solution and an examination of what to do to improve the problem-solving process in the future.

> CASE CONCLUDED

ChallengePost is a privately funded startup firm based in New York City. The company enables individuals and organizations to challenge the public to solve problems and to build communities of people around common goals. ChallengePost contends that challenges are a uniquely powerful source of new ideas and discovery and are effective across a range of problems, from the grandest science and engineering challenges, such as advancing space travel, to more organization-specific goals, such as new software applications or persuasive marketing campaigns. Recent posts at ChallengePost have included making the Edinburgh Festivals even more amazing, developing healthier school lunch programs, and creating more economical home energy use. Public challenges tap the wisdom of the public and enlist talent outside an organization and from other disciplines, often leading to solutions from unexpected sources. One inspiration for ChallengePost was the 1919 challenge issued by New York City hotel owner Raymond Orteig, who offered a $25,000 prize for the first nonstop transatlantic flight between New York and Paris. Charles Lindbergh, who was relatively unknown, won the prize with his famous flight in the *Spirit of St. Louis.* This inspired the Ansari X

PRIZE 80 years later, which offered $10 million for two launches of the first privately funded, reusable spacecraft. More recently, the $1 million Netflix Prize sought software to improve the accuracy of predictions about how much someone will enjoy a movie based on his or her movie preferences and ratings. A multinational team beat out thousands of other teams from over 180 countries to capture the prize.

Compelling challenges lead participants to invest substantial time, and sometimes capital, in developing solutions. The nine teams that competed for the $25,000 Orteig Prize spent $400,000 trying to complete the first transatlantic flight. The $10 million Ansari X PRIZE led to an estimated $100 million investment in spacecraft technology. ChallengePost has powered numerous challenges where the value of submissions created was estimated at 100 to 200 times the prize money. However, challenge participants are motivated not only by prizes, but also by a shared interest in the goal, altruism, the joy of problem solving, and their own competitive spirit.

ChallengePost provides the tools needed to publish a challenge online, promote it, build community around the challenge, and evaluate submissions. The rules for publishing challenges are straightforward

(continued)

CASE CONCLUDED *(continued)*

and include: (1) Challenges must clearly define success. The definition of success must be certifiable by a third party like us or the general public. (2) You must have some skin in the game. Every challenge must be seeded with at least $100. You can use a credit card, and no money will be charged unless the challenge is solved. (3) The challenge must have a deliverable that is viewable by the public. If it's a video, it should be online. If it's software, it should be downloadable. The web platform is geared toward bringing in everyday citizens, not just skilled solvers. This citizen engagement provides the social rewards that are important in recruiting and motivating potential entrants. Once a challenge is created, other people can follow the challenge and join the discussion, or even enter their submission to the challenge.

Questions

1. Given that there is usually no more than a modest (and often no) financial award for personal contributions to a crowdsourced challenge, why are smart and capable "strangers" so willing to contribute?

2. Under what circumstances are crowdsourced solutions likely to be better than individual ones? Where might they be less effective? What accounts for the "wisdom of crowds"?

3. What limitations do you foresee in ChallengePost as a means of solving big challenges?

4. Would you be inclined to post a new business startup idea on ChallengePost? Why or why not?

5. Come up with a challenge the world should know about. That is, working with your class team, identify a big challenge that you think would be well suited to ChallengePost—and one in which you would be very much intrigued by the crowd responses.

Sources: http://en.wikipedia.org/wiki/Threadless and *Challenge Post*, http://challengepost.com/about.

Concluding Note

Problem solving is tough, and good decisions never guarantee good outcomes. Yet, as we have attempted to show throughout this chapter, being conscious of common biases and taking careful consideration of how to go about solving a problem can greatly increase your odds of good outcomes. As the old adage goes, "If all you have is a hammer, everything looks like a nail." We rarely know with certainty the outcome of our decisions. Thus, it's important to have a toolbox of frameworks or ways of thinking about problems that can facilitate clear judgment and maximize to the best of our ability the outcomes of the choices we make.

KEY TERMS

after action review 110
anchoring and adjustment 86
availability bias 84
benchmarking 104
black or white fallacy 96
bounded rationality 91
brainwriting 104
confirmation bias 87
devil's advocate 108

equifinality 108
escalation of commitment 88
fundamental attribution error 83
hasty generalization fallacy 85
histogram 101
inquiry skills 100
intuition 81
ladder of inference 82
mental models 99

overconfidence bias 87
PADIL 91
representative bias 84
satisficing 91
self-serving bias 83
small wins 109
stakeholder 92
system 97
systemic structure 98

When Dr. Ross Fletcher visits patients at the Washington, DC, Veterans' Administration Hospital, he knows he should first cleanse his hands. A quick rub with an alcohol-foam disinfectant can help prevent the spread of bacterial infections. Those kill tens of thousands of hospital patients every year. Most health care providers know they should follow the hand-cleansing procedure, but they don't always do it. Fletcher says the VA decided to change that. "When we first started this program, we noticed that about 40 percent of the time hand cleansing occurred satisfactorily. More recently, it's been more well into the 80 percent range and we hope to get it close to 100 percent, so that any patient requiring hand cleansing will have that happen. What we've noticed in addition is that using the alcohol foam cleansing agent, we've been able to further reduce, over just simple hand washing, the incidence of very serious antibiotic resistant infections."

The VA managed to double the rate of hand cleansing in the simplest of ways—for instance, by putting disinfectant dispensers on the walls of patients' rooms. It's a small change that saves both money and lives, and it's just the sort of measure called for in a blockbuster report by the Institute of Medicine. Titled "To Err Is Human," the report estimated that avoidable errors in U.S. hospitals were killing 44,000 to 98,000 Americans a year. They were injuring thousands more. The report

> > **CASE**
> # Using Systems Thinking to Prevent Medical Errors at the VA Hospital[48]

said that was the equivalent of a jumbo jet crashing every day.

If there's good news, say these safety experts, it's that despite the lack of national commitment, some health systems like the VA are taking steps to solve problems. Dr. Jonathan Perlin, who heads the VA health system, acknowledges that was not always the case. "It's fair to say that historically, the VA's reputation was not—was not perfect and we realized we needed to change and what we saw was that we needed to improve safety, improve quality, and improve the compassion with which we delivered care."

Applying Aviation Safety Techniques to Health Care

To lead its own campaign against medical errors, the VA picked physician and former astronaut James Bagian. Among other things, Bagian had helped to investigate space shuttle disasters at NASA. He thought aviation and aerospace had plenty to teach health care. Bagian noted that "an air-mail pilot back in the '30s had a life expectancy on the job of three to four years. And it wasn't until the '50s that aviation really started looking and saying, we can't just keep building more planes when we crash them."

So aviation developed a systems approach to improving safety. That includes an emphasis on teamwork and fixed procedures; those prevent airline crews from making mistakes, or provide a backstop to thwart crashes in the event that errors occur. As Bagian remarked, "It was understanding, we standardize. It's not like everybody has their own little way they want to fly the plane. We said, there are certain ways to do it; that we use checklists for certain things; that, you know, you take away certain latitudes."

Bagian says applying systems-thinking to VA health care started with a similar cultural change. Rather than burying mistakes or punishing people involved in them, the VA had to actively seek them out. Borrowing another leaf from airline safety, VA personnel are now required to report any adverse events through an internal computerized reporting system. They're also required to report so-called "near-misses" or "close calls"—instances when something dangerous almost happens to patients but doesn't.

Dr. Bagian says that "close calls happen anywhere from 10 to 200 times more frequently than the event they're the precursor of.

(continued)

(continued)

So you can think of for every incorrect surgery that's done, there's anywhere from 10 to 200 that almost happened. Why not learn from those?" VA safety experts analyze these reports and then launch a so-called root-cause analysis. That's when a small team is assembled to probe the chain of factors leading up to a given adverse event.

For example, take the problem of operating on the wrong side of the patient's body. It's surprisingly common throughout U.S. hospitals, especially when surgery involves a part that the body has two of, like eyes or kidneys. To avoid wrong-site surgery, a national hospital oversight body, the Joint Commission for Accreditation of Healthcare Organizations, now requires that the correct surgical site be clearly marked. But Bagian says that when VA performed root-cause analysis, it discovered an even bigger problem: "We found that 44 percent of incorrect surgeries—that's what we call them; we don't call them wrong-sited, because that's

not right—44 percent were left/right foul-ups; 36 percent were the wrong patient. The reason they did the wrong knee was they thought I was you."

The solution was to adopt a protocol in which each patient to be operated on first identifies himself by name, birth date, and Social Security number. Bagian says that when these procedures have been followed at the VA, they've drastically reduced wrong-site or wrong-person surgery. The VA is the first large health system in the nation to replace paper charts with this fully electronic record. The VA spent more than a billion dollars developing the record, but it now costs just $78 per patient per year to operate, and Perlin says it produces a huge safety payoff. For example, once a prescription order is checked against the electronic health record, it's routed to the hospital pharmacy, where medication is labeled with the patient's name and a unique bar code. That's an innovation dreamed up by a VA nurse who saw

the bar-coding technology in use at a car rental agency and suggested it could be adapted by the VA.

With the exception of the costly step of converting to electronic health records, most of these changes have come cheaply. They amount to ten cents for every $100 the VA spends on delivering medical care. A new report from the government accountability office, Congress's watchdog arm, gives the VA generally high marks for its safety initiatives.

Discussion Questions

1. Why don't doctors wash their hands with 100 percent compliance?

2. What problem-solving biases are being enacted in hospitals across the country where medical errors persist? How does the VA's approach overcome some of those biases?

3. What did it take to ultimately solve the problem of wrong-sited surgery? Why was marking the side of the surgical site only marginally effective?

SELECT MANAGE *WHAT?* DEBRIEFS

Defining and Structuring a Vague Problem: Debrief

As noted in the text, a problem well framed is half solved and thus this is perhaps the most fundamental of all decision-making skills. Moreover, problem structuring is often characterized by recurring mistakes such as framing the problem too narrowly, picking the wrong stakeholders, failing to think systemically, and too little reliance on facts.

This call center problem seems particularly ripe for those "not to dos," and indeed, several are already happening. So one good way to most effectively define and structure this problem is to consciously invert those common errors into appropriate problem-structuring strategies.

Start by framing the problem(s) broadly. From the limited information provided, it seems as if this problem has already been framed as a customer service representative motivation problem. That may well be some or all of the issue—but you cannot know this yet. It seems entirely plausible that the below-average ratings could also be attributable to the training and ability of your reps, or technology, or call volume, or differences in your customer base, or some external events. Without more data, do not immediately attribute the problem here to the motivation of your reps.

Get all the facts and information you can. The only real data you currently have are that your group's overall customer service ratings are below average in the firm and some anecdotal accounts of what other managers are doing (or not doing) with respect to motivational inducements for their people. Before jumping to solutions, you need to know much more. For example, what is the variance in your ratings (maybe your ratings are generally high but just one or two people are bringing them down) and trends (is your overall average trending down or up or staying constant?), and are there any differences in your employee characteristics or in external variables such as call volume or technology capability or customer pools that might influence ratings?

In pursuit of defining and structuring this problem, it will be key to involve the right people. In this case, you have already talked to other managers (a good start) but it would seem appropriate here to gather information from your representatives and from some select customers as well. There may also be key managers from other functions in the firm who could own and help resolve the problem.

As you can hopefully see, what may seem like a simple little challenge on the surface may well take a fairly comprehensive approach to actually resolve. Effectively defining and structuring the problem at the outset will be key to such resolution.

Avoiding Common Decision Errors: Debrief

a. Are more deaths attributable to sharks or falling airplane parts?

Availability Bias. Most people in this situation say sharks (or at least believe it is sharks but may say airplane parts to avoid being tricked). This is what's known as the availability bias. This bias clouds our judgment because things that are more readily available to us (that is, they can be more easily brought to mind) are likely to be interpreted as more frequent or important. A single shark attack gets extraordinary news coverage, but a falling airplane part might get none. When solving a problem, we often choose solutions we've heard about in the belief that if we've heard about them, they'll work. Marketing firms know this well, which explains why they want their products frequently on your mind.

b. Estimates of the products of two identical number strings are presented in inverted order.

Anchoring and Adjustment Bias. People tend to make far higher estimates with the first set of numbers than the second—though multiplication is reciprocal and thus the correct answer in both cases is 40,320. Research suggests that this occurs because we are prone to bias our estimates in favor of early information or "anchors." That is, different starting points lead to different end results. Once you have 8×7 in your mind and you look at the multiplication to follow, you quickly estimate a much higher number than if you started with 1×2. Be wary of how much initial anchoring can influence your ultimate decisions.

c. Do you stand a better chance of winning with a slot machine that has not paid off recently?

Representativeness Bias. Most people are quick to opt for the machine that has not paid off but the odds of winning are identical. A common bias is to assume that when a sequence appears non-random it must actually be non-random. But if you won the lottery, would you play different numbers? If you flipped a coin 9 times in a row and it was heads, are you due for a tails on the 10th toss? Of course not, but this bias seduces us with great regularity. Representativeness bias has also been termed the "gambler's fallacy" because too many gamblers truly believe that each coin flip, pull of the slot machine, or new deal of the cards is somehow connected to previous actions. The coin, the slot machine, and the deck have no memory, yet it is common to assume that the probabilities of future outcomes must somehow increase or decrease to offset or "compensate for" earlier outcomes.

d. Which card(s) should you turn over to determine the existence of the rule?

Confirmation Bias. Few people typically solve this correctly because it requires the search for disconfirming, rather than confirming, information. The confirmation bias represents the tendency to collect evidence that supports rather than negates our intuition. In solving problems, one of the most insidious traps is the gathering of data that seek to confirm our preconceived notions but to exclude data that might disconfirm them.

(continued)

(continued)

e. Which is farther north, New York or Rome?

Overconfidence Bias. Most people say New York and accompany their response with a very high confidence rating. Indeed, it is not uncommon for people to say they are 100 percent sure that New York is farther north—but it is not. Rome is north of New York (we suspect you still do not believe this—so go look at a globe). Being confident is a great thing—it allows people to approach difficult situations with courage and determination. Unfortunately, most of us are overconfident in our decision-making style. In fact, some research has shown that there is virtually no relationship between one's confidence level about being right and actually being right. That is, people often exude confidence about their opinions—but confidence doesn't make them any more accurate. Seek data whenever possible and do not let overconfidence sabotage your decision effectiveness.

f. Should you sell the stock?

Escalation of Commitment. Most people in this situation will not sell, somehow believing that prior decisions bind them to staying the course even though any prior decisions are essentially irrelevant here—it should be the future gain/loss that is of sole importance. This bias is known as escalation of commitment. This bias reveals that people are likely to continue to invest additional resources (that is, time, money, and so on) in failing courses of action even though no foreseeable payoff is evident. The phrase "throwing good money after bad" is the essence of escalation of commitment. Escalation is prevalent for a number of reasons. First, we don't want to admit that our earlier decisions were not the right ones, so we "stay the course." Second, we don't want to appear inconsistent or "irrational" so we continue to hope for the best even though data simply don't justify such a response. Third, in many situations, changing course might be seen as "giving up" rather than fighting onward—and nobody wants to be a quitter.

Learning from Past Decisions: Debrief

The unfortunate reality is that organizations and managers tend to repeat poor decisions. Everyone fails on occasion, but truly successful people view the failure as an opportunity to learn or to have a "productive failure." In addition, too many of us are defensive of our failures and also fail to closely examine our successes. In such cases, very little learning takes place after implementing a decision that will help a manager repeat the success or avoid the failure of the problem-solving process.

In this case, your goal is to try to be as successful as you can in year one, but given that you have not done this before it is likely it will not be a perfect execution. As noted earlier, the real key, then, is to learn from what happens this year, so you can repeat those things and avoid repeating any mistakes. An outstanding tool for this very purpose is known as an after action review (AAR). The basic premise of AAR is simple. Each problem-solving effort should be thoroughly reviewed by judging several factors, which include answering these key questions:

- What did we intend to accomplish with this initiative? (What were the goals/objectives?)
- What was actually realized?
- Is there a gap between what we intended and what actually happened?
- If so, what is causing that gap? Why didn't the solution solve the problem?
- What were the strengths involved in this process, and how can they be repeated in the future?
- What were the weaknesses involved in this process, and how can they be improved or avoided in the future?

Beyond these primary points of learning, you should also return to your stakeholders once again and collect information about their perceptions of the problem and the solution. We want to know whether or not the final implementation has satisfied stakeholders, but also whether or not the stakeholders were pleased with the process. Did they feel included in the process? Were their voices heard throughout? Completing another brief stockholder analysis is helpful as you look forward to solving other problems in the future. You will know what people like and dislike and the degree to which they wish to be included. In Took Kit 3.4, we offer a basic method for conducting AAR.

The AAR is not simply a postmortem in which positives and negatives are listed; rather, it involves serious conversations with stakeholders about the impact of the solution and an examination of what to do to improve the problem-solving process in the future.

CHAPTER
4

Making Ethical Decisions

OBJECTIVES

KNOWING   DOING

After reading this chapter, you should be able to:

KO 4-1 Recognize the ethical implications of a problem.

KO 4-2 Describe the concept of moral intensity.

KO 4-3 Explain the key differences between ethical perspectives.

KO 4-4 Describe different forms of fairness rules and when to apply them in the workplace.

KO 4-5 Describe and differentiate three types of organizational justice.

DO 4-1 Use decision rules to help you solve right-versus-right problems.

DO 4-2 Interpret what form of moral intensity is influencing a decision.

DO 4-3 Use the ethical decision-making steps to guide an ethical decision.

DO 4-4 Use moral imagination and "quick tests" to make a difficult ethical decision.

DO 4-5 Demonstrate competence in navigating common ethical situations.

Case: Truthy

THE ANTI-SOCIAL SIDE OF SOCIAL MEDIA

< <

Since young voters discovered they could "friend" Barack Obama on Facebook during the 2008 election, social media has become ingrained in the way we think about political campaigns. Many see it as the key to a new type of politics, whereby campaigns and candidates can better engage citizens, facilitate grassroots organizations, and craft legislation with the direct input of a tweeting electorate. The result, optimists argue, will be a sort of "digital democracy," defined by a closer, more coherent relationship between elected officials and their constituents, and where genuine comments and discourse, unfiltered by spin doctors in the national media, can thrive.

But social media, like any tool, can be used to *erode* democratic practices as well. For example, a few days before the special election in Massachusetts to fill the Senate seat formerly held by the late Edward Kennedy, the American Future Fund (AFF) conducted a "Twitter-bomb" campaign against Attorney General Martha Coakley, one of the candidates for the position. The AFF set up nine anonymous Twitter accounts in the early morning hours prior to the election that sent hundreds of tweets to other influential Twitter accounts around the state accusing Martha Coakley of taking money from health insurance lobbyists and providing links to anonymous websites containing further details. This sudden spike in tweeting caused the attacks on Coakley to turn up in Google searches for her name, effectively gaming Google's real-time search functions. The approach is not partisan or limited to particular parties, but it has been employed to some extent by all political groups.

1. Why is social media such a powerful way to engage in ethically questionable behavior?

2. Beyond politics, in what other arenas has social media been used in what you would consider to be unethical ways?

3. Given the Internet is predicated on the notion of open, uncensored, and unfiltered input, how might unethical behavior in social media be managed?

1. Making a Difficult Ethical Choice

You have worked for your boss for five years, and he has become a trusted mentor for you in the firm. Indeed, there is no one in the firm toward whom you feel more respect or loyalty. You just met with him and, due to an unforeseen market downturn, he let you know of a proposed layoff that will affect one of the three people who report to you (Joe). Because the decision has not been announced, and it will surely send shockwaves through the firm, he asked that you absolutely not tell any of your subordinates. In fact, concerned the information might get prematurely leaked, he even says, "It is critically important that no one know. Can I count on you?" You agreed emphatically that he could. Unfortunately, that evening you see Joe, who coaches a little league team with you. He tells you he and his wife have been accepted into an adoption process for a new child and he wanted to share his joy with you. He also has heard rumors of a layoff and says, sort of jokingly, "I am not going to be laid off, am I? We could never afford to take care of a new child without my income."

What should you do? Is this an ethical issue? You are forced to choose between loyalty and your expressed promise on one hand, and your sense of caring and honesty toward Joe (and his potential new child) on the other. What factors will you consider in your decision? On what basis would you justify the ethics of your decision?

2. You Be the Ethicist

Author Randy Cohen serves as The Ethicist for *The New York Times Sunday Magazine*. He frequently poses ethical dilemmas to his readers and an adapted set of those (and similar themes) are listed next. Respond to each of the following scenarios, being sure to identify the ethical frame (utilitarian, universalism, or virtuous person) you are using as the rationale for your response.

   a. Is it ethical to buy a sweater to use for a family picture and then return it for a refund?

   b. Is it ethical to download a song from the Internet without paying for it given that (a) you would not have downloaded it if you had to pay, (b) you have no money and the artist and record label (or Apple, Inc.) are beyond wealthy, (c) you are actually promoting the artist by listening to and sharing your impressions with others.

   c. How much is a cat worth? Your affectionate and obedient cat needs a procedure that will cost a few hundred dollars. Your instinct is to pay for what she needs, but you can't help thinking it's wrong. Wouldn't the cash be better spent on sick humans?

   d. Can you ethically round off your 2.958 GPA to 3.0 when using it on your resumé?

   e. Is it OK to take those hotel shampoos and soaps and give them to homeless shelters?

   f. Should you tell on someone you observe researching bomb-making on the Internet? Or on a friend having a too-friendly dinner with a woman who is not his wife?

   g. Is it ethical to buy cheap seats to a baseball game you know will be sparsely attended and then sneak down and sit in the expensive seats? Similarly, is it ethical to grab open first-class seats (once everyone is on board and in their purchased seats) when you only paid for coach?

   h. Is it ethical for a homeless mother to steal a loaf of bread to feed her starving child?

   i. If you scored the wrong answer on a test, and the instructor marked it correct and you very honestly let him know, is it ethical for the instructor to let you keep the points and reward your honesty?

3. Creating a Culture That People View as Fair

You are a relatively new manager and times are tough at your firm. You know you are going to have to make some really tough decisions regarding promotions, job assignments, bonuses, and even who gets laid off and who stays. When you took your new management position two years ago, the firm was booming, and with ample resources to work with you thought to yourself that you would just give everyone the same rewards and schedules and anything you controlled and that would solve the problem. But now resources are scarce and you are worried that if people view your decisions as unfair you will run the risk of destroying your positive culture and even losing key people. If your goal is to create a fair workplace that is also a productive one, what should you do? What types of standards would you put in place and then how would you decide "who gets what"?

4. Being a Responsible Whistle-Blower

As a manager in your firm, you have become disturbed with some of the claims that are being made (by people in your marketing and sales group) about some of your products. Although you often work with that department, you are employed in a different function and not sure if you should "stick your nose" into that area. Moreover, although you feel something of an ethical obligation to ensure that no customers are harmed by false information, you also are very concerned that blowing the whistle in this case could prompt serious repercussions and potentially be detrimental to your career, cause the loss of trust and friends in the firm, and even impact your family.

Introduction

Most discussions of ethics, particularly directed at young people, have an idealistic tone. For example, it is common to hear platitudes like "Good ethics pays" and "Ethics is good business." Unfortunately (and disturbingly), any casual observer of business these days knows that behaving unethically can "pay off" as well, and ethical behavior can often result in a loss of business or desired outcomes. Further, traditional conceptions of right and wrong are often blurred in organizational life. Consider that a recent survey of 111 executives found that 52 to 90 percent of executives agreed that behaving unethically was appropriate when (1) performance contingencies demand otherwise, (2) it is necessary to get the job done, (3) unfair or overly restrictive performance standards exist, and (4) it would be necessary to avoid negatively affecting the organization.[1] Most frightening was that 56 percent of those surveyed indicated managers who bend rules are more effective than managers who do not. This is hardly encouraging news when many of these same companies are also claiming that they act with the "highest moral standards."

A few other statistics may hit closer to home. In a major study of 6,000 students on 31 campuses in the United States, researchers found the data presented in Figure 4.1.[2]

Roughly two-thirds of students in this research admitted to cheating at least once as an undergraduate. When asked why, students cited pressures and

> "The first of all moral obligations is to think clearly."
>
> —Michael Novak

?¿ MYTHS 4.1 Ethical Decision-Making Myths[3]

- **It's easy to be ethical.** The truth is that it's downright difficult to be ethical. In fact, by definition, merely determining that you are facing an ethical dilemma (that is, the first step in solving it) is a complex process. Ethical dilemmas don't come with flags waving, "Look at me. I'm an ethical issue."

- **Unethical behavior is simply a problem of "bad apples."** Even people that most of us would judge as having strong ethical values make unethical decisions. The truth is that much of our behavior is guided by watching others and simply following their lead. When your boss rounds up his expense reports, you rightfully assume that it's "okay" to do the same for yours. Does this make you a bad apple? No, but your behavior is likely unethical.

- **Ethics can be managed with codes of conduct.** Research shows that formal codes of conduct can have a positive influence on ethical behavior in organizations. Yet, in order for them to have such an effect, they must be part of a larger coordinated part of the organization that supports ethical conduct every day.[4] In other words, if a senior manager is found to be in violation of the code of conduct and he is not punished in accordance with the policy, it sends the very real message that the code of ethics can be practically ignored.

- **People are less ethical than they used to be.** Incidents of unethical behavior haven't changed much for centuries. What has changed is the pace of organizational life and the access to information via technology that has lent a new creativity to acting in unethical ways!

- **Managing ethics is not my problem.** Like it or not, ethical issues are with us every day and each decision you make as a manager holds the potential for ethical issues to arise.

FIGURE 4.1
College Student
Actions

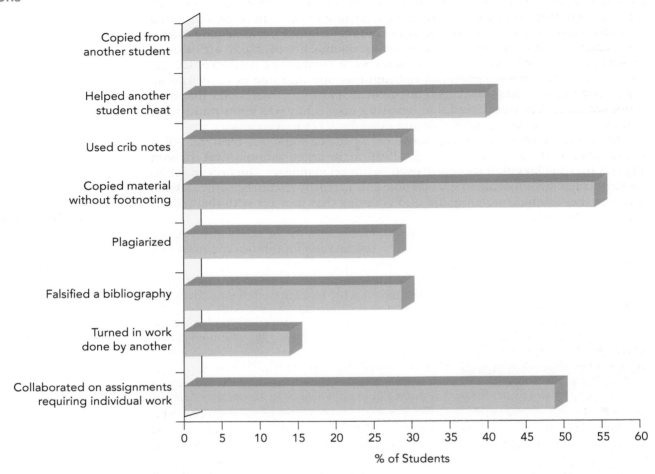

competition related to graduate school admissions. Researchers also collected information about the students' future career choices. The lowest number of admitted cheaters (57 percent) was found in students planning on pursuing education-related professions. The numbers rise from there, including medicine (68 percent admitted cheating), government (66 percent), engineers (71 percent), and future MBAs (76 percent). Students also indicated cheating was a relatively harmless crime. Of course, as ethics author Rushworth Kidder points out, cheating really isn't so harmless:[5]

> You have only to ask who engineered the bridge you are about to cross, or where your doctor got his or her training, to begin questioning whether a widespread propensity for cheating among professionals—and the consequent danger of unleashing into the world a cadre of individuals who don't know what they are doing—is in fact a "victimless crime."

While it may seem that one small act of cheating may not be such a big deal, when you consider the ramifications of a professional culture based on cheating, the act becomes highly objectionable. Think of it this way, if you knew your heart surgeon cheated her way through medical school, would you be eager to let her perform a triple bypass?

The lesson here is that ethics is synonymous with behavior and all behavior has consequences. Although ethical philosophy implies that we must "think before we act," we are not judged on our thinking but on our actual behavior. Even if you have good intentions, nobody will see your intentions, only your behavior and its consequences. Consider the Make-A-Wish foundation's dilemma in letting a terminally ill boy kill a Kodiak bear (see Chapter 3, Management Live 3.3). Management's intentions were beautifully aligned with the organization's values and yet their behavior resulted in a poor outcome. Unfortunately, ethical behavior is almost never simple or easy, and it is often not self-evident (and no shared consensus exists) what the most ethical action is in any given situation. There are no ethical switches that we can turn on or off, and simply stating that "I am an ethical person" provides nothing to substantiate that claim.

While the situation sounds rather bleak when it comes to ethics, there is a great deal of work being done in the field, and some of this work provides us with important guidelines that we can use to guide our behavior. According to the Josephson Institute, a center dedicated to the study and practice of ethics, ethical behavior is multidimensional, and the most ethical people act in ways that reflect ethical commitment, consciousness, and competency.

> "Obviously everyone wants to be successful, but I want to be looked back on as being very innovative, very trusted and ethical and ultimately making a big difference in the world."
>
> —Sergey Brin, Google founder

Ethics: Making the Tough Choices

KO **4-1**

KO **4-2**

DO **4-1**

DO **4-2**

If you choose to strive toward ethical decisions and behavior, it will require your **ethical commitment.** Ethical commitment refers to your level of dedication or desire to do what is right even in the face of potentially harmful personal repercussions. This requires a healthy dose of courage and **integrity** (or the adherence to an ethical code or standard) to make decisions that may be unpopular or go against the prevailing culture. How do you want to live your life? What do you want to be remembered for? What values are worth fighting for? What kind of relationships do you want to have? Do you want to be known as someone who will take a stand for what they believe is right? It has been and always will be quite challenging to be an ethical person. Ethical commitment is about accepting that challenge.

Solving problems ethically also requires an **ethical consciousness** in which you develop an ability to understand the ramifications of choosing less ethical courses of action. Unlike the student who believes that cheating doesn't hurt anyone else, students with an ethical consciousness understand the far-reaching implications of such behavior. Those who are ethically conscious make themselves aware of the implications of their actions and are not oblivious to the many ethical concerns around us.

Finally, a third dimension of ethical behavior is **ethical competency,** which involves a thoughtful consideration of ethics in each stage of the problem-solving process. There are no easy ways to ascertain the most ethical choice in a given situation, but there are very useful models for framing and dissecting ethical dilemmas. Whether defining a problem, generating alternatives, or making a decision, ethically competent people consider such models in their choices.

Recognizing Ethical Issues

Ethics may be defined as "the principles, norms and standards of conduct governing an individual or group."[6] As we noted in the myths of ethical decision making, ethical decisions are far from "easy." Perhaps the most difficult challenge in making ethical decisions is recognizing that one is facing an ethical dilemma in the first place. As researchers Linda Trevino and Mike Brown have noted, the notion that "it's easy to be ethical" presumes that people know when they are facing an ethical dilemma and, with such understanding, make the "right choice."[7] The opposite is almost always true—ethical decisions rarely come with red flags waving that call out to you, "Hey, I'm an ethical issue! Think about me in moral terms!" Consider an employee who is asked to sign a document for her boss. This employee is likely to see this as a simple act that any "good" employee should do. Yet what if this employee failed to recognize this as a request to "forge" legal documents?

Most problems you face do have ethical or moral implications—whether you consider them or not. Some problems, however, seem to be more easily identifiable as having ethical implications—that is, we sense the tension or dilemma immediately. In fact, dilemmas often (not always) present themselves not as "right versus wrong" but as "right versus right" (or perhaps "wrong versus wrong").[8] That is, ethical dilemmas, the really tough choices, often don't involve clearly right and wrong alternatives, but rather two alternatives that may both have merit. Consider tough issues like what to do with differing abilities in youth sports or academics or views on how to spend disposable income.

- It is right to give all little league players equal playing time, and it is also right to field the best team possible.
- It is right to help out a struggling fellow student by letting him see your homework, and it is right to keep your homework proprietary.
- It is right to give money to those living in poverty, and it is right to save money for your family.

These types of dilemmas are what might be termed "right versus right" scenarios and are discussed next.

Right-vs.-Right Scenarios

"Right-versus-right" scenarios are the most perplexing of ethical dilemmas. According to Kidder, these dilemmas can be boiled down to a few major themes. With *truth-versus-loyalty dilemmas,* the struggle is between providing information about some objective truth versus compromising one's loyalty to others. For example, when a patient discloses to a doctor that she is likely to commit suicide, the doctor is ethically obligated to breach patient confidentiality, thus compromising trustworthiness or loyalty in the doctor–patient relationship. Not all truth-versus-loyalty situations are so clear. Managers often face such dilemmas when caught between the confidence of a senior manager ("Don't announce the pay cuts.") and an employee who wants to know particular information ("Will there be layoffs?").

A second major theme is *individual versus community.* The needs of individuals such as confidentiality or privacy often clash with those of the community. Terrorism has brought this dilemma clearly to the forefront with governments attempting to preserve individual rights and needs while also understanding the greater good of the community. Much of the controversy surrounding the conduct of airport security personnel has been related to this very issue.

A third category of dilemmas is *short-term versus long-term,* which involves the clash between living in the present versus thinking about the future. Investing financially for the future, for example, often clashes with enjoying the present. Finally, a fourth theme has to do with *justice versus mercy.* Professors who catch a student cheating face this very problem. On one hand, students who cheat deserve a punishment commensurate with their behavior. On the other hand, students are human and sometimes make bad choices and deserve our compassion to help avoid such mistakes in the future. These themes play out every day. As you explore ethical dilemmas, try to identify the theme at play, and it will help you understand the issues more clearly.

Moral Intensity

As you know by now, human bias often leads to poor judgment. Judging ethical dilemmas is not different. The framing of an ethical dilemma, for example, leads to very different judgments of what to do. For example, to what extent would you agree with the following claim: "People who download music from the Internet without paying for it are unethical." What if we state it slightly differently: "People who *steal* music from the Internet without paying for it are unethical." Is downloading without permission different from stealing without permission? Not really, but people see stealing as clearly wrong and downloading as more acceptable. The way in which we perceive ethical dilemmas depends heavily on the **moral intensity** the issue possesses. That is, something in the context or situation of how an ethical dilemma is perceived leads people to endorse the situation as unethical. Yet the same situation with less intensity would not lead people to see it as unethical. Consider the following scenario known as the Switch Dilemma:

> A trolley is running out of control down a track. In its path are five people who have been tied to the track. Fortunately, you can flip a switch, which will lead the trolley down a different track to safety. Unfortunately, there is a single person tied to that alternative track. Do you flip the switch?"

Now consider a similar scenario known as the Footbridge Dilemma:

> A trolley is hurtling down a track toward five people. You are on a bridge under which it will pass, and you can stop it by dropping a heavy weight in front of it. As it happens, there is a very heavy man next to you—your only way to stop the trolley is to push him over the bridge and onto the track, killing him to save five. Do you push the man?"

The consequence in both these scenarios is the exact same—one person is killed in order to save five others. Yet, in a recent study, researchers found that while some 90 percent of study participants said they would "flip the switch," only 30 percent stated they would "push the man."[9] Despite the consequence that five people would die, the proximity or nearness one had to the heavy man made the decision to kill him seem highly unethical, while flipping a switch felt far removed from killing the person on the track. This is a perfect example of how the intensity of a situation can alter the way people process ethical dilemmas. Researcher Thomas Jones identified six ways in which ethical issues are perceived as more or less intense and therefore as more ethical or unethical.[10]

1. **Magnitude of Consequences.** The sum of the cost-benefit to the object of the action in question. For example, an action that causes the death of a human being is of greater magnitude of consequence than an act that causes a person to suffer a minor injury. This is often how people will judge whether an act was "bad enough" to be considered unethical.

2. **Social Consensus of Evil/Good.** The amount of social agreement toward the action. For example, many believe it far more unethical to bribe a customs official in Texas than a customs official in Mexico. Both involve bribery, but what is considered unethical in one situation may be less so in others.

3. **Probability of Harm/Benefit.** The likelihood that the act in question will actually happen and produce the predicted harm/benefit. For example, selling a gun to a known armed robber has a greater probability of harm than selling a gun to a law-abiding citizen. We immediately underestimate the probability that a law-abiding citizen will do harm and overestimate the probability that the known armed robber won't.

4. **Temporal Immediacy.** The time between the act and the onset of the consequences. For example, reducing the retirement benefits of current retirees has a greater temporal immediacy than reducing the retirement benefits of current employees who are between the ages of 40 and 50. We tend to perceive decisions that affect us today as less ethical, whereas we view decisions in which the consequences are delayed in time as more acceptable since people might have time to recover from the decision.

5. **Proximity.** The feeling of nearness (psychologically or physically) that people have to the object of the action. For example, layoffs in your own work unit have greater issue intensity than layoffs in another part of the company. Layoffs are never easy, but we have less trouble endorsing a layoff as ethical when it doesn't hit as close to home.

6. **Concentration of Effect.** The magnitude of the action on those involved. For example, denying coverage to 10 people with claims of $100,000 each has a greater concentration of effect than denying coverage to 100,000 people with claims of $10 each. No one wants to lose $10, but it's not likely to change your life significantly. On the other hand, losing $100,000 would force many people to make some very tough financial choices. People perceive a highly concentrated effect like this as unethical.

As can be seen from the six issue intensity types just discussed, the very nature of a situation can easily change your perspective on what you judge to be ethical versus unethical.

Ethics and the Law

With centuries of philosophers, religions, and courts of law considering issues of right or wrong, one would think that progressive communities would have figured out ethics by now and that legal standards would encompass the collection of ethical standards. Unfortunately, legal norms and ethical norms are not identical, nor do they always agree. Some ethical requirements, such as treating one's employees fairly, are not legally required, though they may be ethically warranted. Conversely, some actions that can be legally allowed, such as firing an employee for no reason, would fail ethical standards. For this reason, we might consider the law to be a "floor" with respect to ethics, certainly not a ceiling. There are at least five important reasons why the law may not align with ethics in organizations.

First, consider how slowly law often changes. Just because segregation was legal in the first half of the 20th century didn't mean it was the "right" thing to do. Thus, holding that obedience to the law is sufficient to fulfill one's ethical duties raises the question of whether or not the law itself is ethical. Dramatic examples from history, Nazi Germany and apartheid South Africa being the most obvious, demonstrate that one's ethical responsibility may run counter to the law. On a more practical level, this question can have significant implications in a global economy in which businesses operate in countries with legal systems different from their home country. Some countries make child labor or sexual discrimination legal, but businesses that choose to adopt such practices do not escape ethical responsibility for doing so. From an ethical perspective, you do not forgo your ethical responsibilities by a blind obedience to the law.

Second, societies that value individual freedom will be reluctant to legally require more than just an ethical minimum. Such societies will seek legally to prohibit the most serious ethical harm, but they will not legally require acts of charity, common decency, and personal integrity that may otherwise comprise the social fabric of a developed culture. The law can be an efficient mechanism to prevent serious harm, but it is not very effective at promoting "good." Even if it were, the cost in human freedom of legally requiring such things as personal integrity would be too high. Imagine a society that legally required parents to love their children, or even a law prohibiting lying.

Third, on a more practical level, telling business that its ethical responsibilities end with obedience to the law is just inviting more and more legal regulation. Consider the difficulty of trying to create laws to cover each and every possible business challenge; the task would require such specificity that the number of regulated areas would become unmanageable. Additionally, it was the failure of personal ethics among such companies as Enron and WorldCom, after all, which led to the creation of the Sarbanes-Oxley Act and many other legal reforms. If business restricts its ethical responsibilities to obedience to the law, it should not be surprised to find a new wave of government regulations that require what were formerly voluntary actions.

Fourth, the law cannot possibly anticipate every new dilemma facing contemporary business, because so often there may not be a regulation for the particular dilemma confronting a business leader. For example, when workplace e-mail was in its infancy, there were not yet laws regarding who actually owned the e-mail transmissions, the employee or the employer. As a result, one had no choice but to rely on the ethical decision-making processes of those in power to respect the appropriate boundaries of employee privacy while also adequately managing the workplace. When new quandaries arise, one must be able to rely on ethics since the law might not yet—or might never—provide a solution.

Fifth, the perspective that compliance is enough relies on a misleading understanding of law. To say that all a business needs to do is obey the law suggests that laws are clear-cut unambiguous rules that can be easily applied. This rule model of law is very common, but not very accurate. Remember, if the law was clear and unambiguous, there wouldn't be much of a role for lawyers and courts!

KO **4-3**

DO **4-3**

DO **4-4**

Six Steps to Making an Ethical Decision

Many evidence-based frameworks exist to guide you in ethical decision making. As you might imagine, however, there is considerable overlap and consensus about the key elements of the process. In the following, we describe six key steps that reflect these critical elements. In order to help you work through an ethical decision, we refer back to the first Manage *What?* (or the "Joe Case") used throughout this section. If you haven't read this short dilemma, please do so prior to reading this section.[11]

Step 1: Gather the Facts

Before you can apply any ethical framework, you need to gather as many relevant facts in the situation as possible. Sometimes the "cause" of the ethical dilemma you face is simply that your "facts" are incongruent with someone else's "facts." Put simply, what appears to be an ethical dilemma may more aptly be a disagreement or difference in perception about the facts. Thus, it is imperative that you act like a journalist might and start not by drawing conclusions or developing a response, but by understanding the basic facts of a given situation. Who is involved? Is there anyone involved who isn't apparent (in other words, that is operating behind the scenes)? How did this situation come to be? Have I (the organization or others) been in this situation before? Is this situation the consequence of previous decisions? Is this an issue over which I have direct control? These types of questions can help you make sure you're working with a reasonable set of objective facts.

According to business ethicist Laura Hartman, an ethical decision is one that is made with a determination of the facts. As such, Dr. Hartman suggests that "a person who acts in a way that is based upon careful consideration of the facts has acted in a more ethically responsible way than a person who acts without deliberation."[12] Thus, the mere act of getting as much information about the situation before acting is likely to improve your chances of making the right call.

Step 2: Define the Ethical Issues

Once you've got the basic facts of any particular dilemma, the next step is to use those facts to help you sort through the primary ethical issues involved. The challenge here is to withhold our natural tendency to determine a quick or knee-jerk solution based upon the facts we've gathered and expose those facts to a systematic review. Enter ethical theory. Ethical theories are attempts to provide systematic answers to ethical dilemmas by providing rational justification for why we should act or decide a particular way. Ethical theories may be divided into two categories: teleological and deontological.[13] The distinction between the two is that **teleological** theories determine the ethics of an act by looking to the probable outcome or consequences of the decision (the ends), while **deontological** theories determine the ethics of an act by looking to the process of the decision (the means) and are based on concepts of universal principles or rights. In the following, we introduce the primary teleological (that is, utilitarianism) and deontological (or, universalism) theories that can help define ethical issues. Importantly, there is no one best theory. In fact, all perspectives have strengths and weaknesses, which means that we cannot evaluate an ethical dilemma using one perspective, but must subject the facts we collect to multiple perspectives in order to more fully understand our real choices.

Utilitarianism

The theory most representative of the teleological approach is **utilitarianism,** which directs us to make decisions based on the greatest "good" for the greatest number. The origins of this direction come from the description that, as humans, we seek benefits over costs, pleasures over pains, and that this is a good thing to do because pains/harm are "bad." This leads to a normative principle (or a "should") that we ought to create a balance of pleasures over pains, so the highest good is to create the greatest good for the greatest number, or minimally, to reduce harm. The most basic form of utilitarian analysis is cost-benefit analysis where one measures the costs and benefits of a given decision and follows the decision that provides for the greatest overall gain. According to utilitarianism, ethical decisions are therefore determined by their end results. No act is ever right or wrong in all cases in every situation. It will always depend on the end results of that particular decision. For example, lying in a marketing campaign is neither right nor wrong in itself, according to utilitarians. There might be situations in which lying will produce greater overall good than telling the truth (for example, lying about having knowledge of individuals in a witness protection program).

Utilitarianism is the most popular perspective invoked in organizations, usually in the form of a cost-benefit analysis. It's viewed as a strong and powerful theory because it is liberal; it appeals to no authority in resolving differences of opinion—in fact, differences of opinion are irrelevant except for when they create a majority or minority. It is also able to describe much of the process of human decision making, and its process seems "natural" and well suited to many decisions. Further, using a utilitarian approach is quite egalitarian in that no one person's "good" is valued more than another's. Unlike many approaches, utilitarianism is also very easy to apply and helps people focus on the potential outcomes of their decisions.

Yet, while utilitarianism is superficially easy to apply (majority rule, profit/loss statements, and so on), there remain complexities. For instance, if an action would render one person exquisitely happy and three people moderately unhappy, does the happiness of that one outweigh the unhappiness of the three? How do we measure happiness? Further, when the majority rules, who protects the minority? Who ensures that a minority voice is heard (or if it even should be heard), and who ensures that new opinions are expressed so that intellectual growth is possible? One of the more serious shortcomings of the utilitarianism perspective is that some decision-makers may reach different conclusions about what is considered "good."

Practice this!
Go to www.baldwin2e.com

Consider the ethical and political controversy that arose in recent years regarding the treatment of hundreds of prisoners captured during the fighting in Afghanistan and Iraq. The U.S. government argued that these were dangerous individuals who posed a significant threat to the United States and that this threat justified the treatment they received. Government attorneys even argued that because these individuals were not members of the military of a recognized country, they were not protected by international law and prohibitions against torture. Thus, the government argued that they were justified in using severe treatment that bordered on torture to extract information from these prisoners if this information could prevent future attacks on the United States. Yet critics argued that some actions, torture among them, are so unethical that they should never be used, even if the result was lost opportunity to prevent attacks. Many argued that all people, even terrorists, deserve fundamental rights of a trial, legal representation, and due process. Do the ends of preventing attacks on the United States ever, under any circumstances, justify the means of torture? It would appear that a utilitarianism perspective may not help us work through this dilemma very well.

Considering our Manage *What?* scenario regarding how to deal with Joe, a utilitarian is likely to focus on the consequences of telling Joe about the layoff. Although Joe might benefit, on par, a utilitarian would probably find far more harmful consequences in telling Joe the truth. For example, as Joe's manager, you're putting your own job on the line. In addition, telling Joe would likely send reverberations throughout the firm, lowering productivity and causing undue anxiety among employees about who will or will not be out of a job. Further, if the plan doesn't go through, the loss of trust and so forth is likely to be fairly large.

MANAGEMENT LIVE 4.1

The Biology of Ethical Decision Making

For centuries, philosophers have wrestled with how people *should* make a moral decision. New research in the area of neuroscience and biology, however, is now exploring not how people should make such decisions, but rather how people *actually* make ethical decisions. One new area of study is that of behavioral endocrinology, which attempts to link biological bases in human beings to certain forms of decision making. A recent study by Dana Carney and Malia Mason linked testosterone levels to moral judgments.[14] Previous research had suggested that testosterone is associated with diminished sensitivity to emotional signals, which cause people to have empathy or to make choices that would suggest concern for others. First, the researchers measured testosterone levels in 117 graduate students (32 of which were female) by collecting saliva samples from each participant. Next, they asked participants to respond yes or no to the "switch and footbridge" trolley dilemmas discussed previously in this chapter. The researchers found that three types of decision making emerged: (1) *intransigent utilitarians* who always endorsed trading one life to save five (39 participants); (2) *fair-weather utilitarians* who gave a utilitarian response to the switch dilemma but not for the footbridge dilemma (66 participants); and (3) *avoiders*, who refrained from getting involved in either case (12 participants). Figure 4.2 shows the results for these three groups based on the average testosterone levels in the group.

The researchers found that individuals who always endorsed sacrificing one life to save five had significantly higher levels of testosterone. That is, regardless of the situation (flipping a switch or pushing a man on the tracks to stop the trolley) these intransigent utilitarians justify their decisions by the ends (saving lives) over the means. Looking just at the responses to the "push the man" scenario, those willing to push versus not push displayed consistently higher levels of testosterone. Carney and Malia conclude that ". . . high testosterone individuals appear willing to endorse a tough and costly decision, provided it promotes the greater good. . . . A heightened focus on outcomes and disregard for the cost of pursuit may help explain why individuals high in testosterone have more success on Wall Street and in other contexts where success requires insensitivity to some of the more immediate consequences of one's actions."

In all, this study highlights the notion that on top of thinking about ethical decisions, human beings may be predisposed to behave in ways of which they are not entirely aware. This makes exposing dilemmas to multiple ethical lenses even more important so as to ensure that a decision is based on sound logic and judgment and not simply our biological instincts.

FIGURE 4.2
Relation Between the Decision-Making Approach to the Trolley Problem and Testosterone

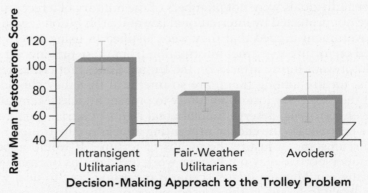

Error bars are 95 percent confidence intervals (CI); intransigent utilitarians are highest on testosterone.

Source: Carney, D. R., and Mason, M. F. (2010). Decision-making and testosterone: When the ends justify the means. *Journal of Experimental Social Psychology, 46*, 668–671.

Universalism

Making decisions based upon the end results certainly should be a part of responsible ethical decision making. However, you might suggest that some decisions should be a matter of principle, not consequences. Yet how do we know which principles we should follow and how do we decide when a principle should trump truly beneficial consequences? Deontological ethical theories help us think about the details of such questions. Decision making within a business context will involve many situations in which one ought to follow legal rules even when the consequences seem undesirable. Other rules come from various institutions in which we participate, or from various roles that we fill in society. A referee in a sporting event has the duty to enforce the rules fairly, even when it would be easier not to do so. Similar rule-based duties follow from our roles as friends (do not gossip about your friends), family members (do your chores at home), students (do not plagiarize), church members (contribute to the church's upkeep), citizens (vote), and good neighbors (do not operate your lawn mower before 8 a.m.). The classic deontological perspective is that of universalism or a consideration of whether a decision would be acceptable if everyone in every situation made the same decision.

This perspective was put forth by German philosopher Immanuel Kant (1724–1804), who believed that the rightness of rules, rather than consequences, is how an ethical dilemma ought to be resolved. Accordingly, the rightness of an act depends little (or, in Kant's view, not at all) on the results of the act. Thus, the student who refuses to cheat on exams is ethical if her or his decision springs from a universal duty, but morally unworthy if the decision is merely one born of self-interest, such as the fear of being caught. To identify these universal duties, Kant developed the **categorical imperative,** the notion that each of us should act on only those principles that she or he would identify as universal laws to be applied to everyone. **Universalism** says that, in reaching a decision, we should consider whether it would be acceptable if everyone in every situation made this same decision—"Act only according to that maxim whereby you can at the same time will that it should become a universal law," writes Kant.

The origins of this principle are based on our sense that—as humans—some things are simply "the right thing to do." Kant suggests that this is uniquely human. So, when we make choices, we do so in terms of that which we can control—and that is the source of morality for Kant. This concept is similar to a parent scolding a child about to steal candy from another child, "How would you feel if everyone stole candy from their friends?" Or it may remind you of the Golden Rule, directing you to treat others only as you would have them treat you. In sum, applying universalism entails two questions: (1) Would it be all right for *everyone* to make the decision you are about to make, and (2) would this decision infringe on any universal rights, such as those that originate in religious doctrine or from other fundamental principles?

Universalism carries with it the strength of reflecting collective logic that is consistent from situation to situation and not based on an arbitrary analysis of impact. Further, Kant contended that above anything else, people ought to respect the dignity of each individual human being, no matter what the consequences. Clearly, this is a much more motivational or inspirational approach than utilitarianism, which can seem "cold" or impersonal. At the same time, finding "universal principles" upon which to base decisions is not easy, particularly when such principles or rights conflict (for example, doing the right thing that results in hurting people, the earth, animals, and so on).

With respect to dealing with Joe, we suspect that a universalist might see the right to information concerning one's self, health, or well-being as a universal right. In this case, the universalist might suggest that it's not the results that matter here but respect for Joe's dignity that is the issue. To knowingly withhold such critical information from Joe would be subversive and violate his basic human rights.

Virtue Ethics

A third perspective is that of virtue ethics—this is neither teleological nor deontological but rather emphasizes the affective side of peoples' character. **Virtue ethics** recognizes that our motivations—our interests, wants, desires—are not the sorts of things we choose anew each morning. Instead, human beings act in and from character. By adulthood, these character traits are typically deeply ingrained and conditioned within us. Virtue ethics can offer us a more fully textured understanding of life within business. Rather than simply describing people as good or bad, right or wrong, an ethics of virtue encourages a fuller description. Faced with a difficult dilemma, we might ask what would a person with integrity do? What would an honest person say? Do I have the courage of my convictions? In other words, you might consider someone you believe to be virtuous and ask yourself what that person would do in this situation.

The major application of virtue ethics comes in the common tension between self-interest and ethical values. For example, should you act in a virtuous way if it is likely to have a negative impact on you (for example, loss of a substantial amount of money or personal reputation)? Virtue ethics suggests that the degree to which we are capable of acting for the well-being of others depends on a variety of factors such as our desires, our beliefs, our dispositions, and our values—in short, it depends on our character. If a person is caring, empathetic, charitable, and sympathetic, then the challenge of self-interest should be less of a factor in his or her decision-making process. Thus, virtue ethics encourages us to think about people who act in ways that embody such character.

Interestingly, scholars have long known that people do in fact differ in their ability to act in ways that might be consistent with a virtuous person. Researcher Lawrence Kohlberg has found that people develop moral reasoning capabilities from childhood through adulthood that have considerable impact on how they view and approach ethical dilemmas. Higher stages of moral reasoning rely on thinking that is not available to people at lower stages, and higher stages are thought to be morally advanced and consistent with principles of ethical theories. According to Kohlberg's research, however, very few adults are able to reach the highest levels of moral reasoning. This suggests that most of us can be striving to develop an approach that is more selfless and caring.[15]

To summarize Step 2, exposing the facts you've gathered to these different ethical lenses is likely to result in different conclusions about the nature of your dilemma. You might be inclined to be satisfied with applying one perspective—this is clearly a recipe that will limit the scope of possible decisions. We encourage you at this stage to "poll the crowd" by asking others how they see the dilemma and determine the perspective they are taking. Table 4.1 summarizes these major ethical perspectives.

Step 3: Identify the Affected Parties, Consequences, and Obligations

Regardless of the ethical perspective you adopt, all ethical decision making involves understanding who might be affected by your decision. This almost always requires you to exercise substantial "perspective-taking" or walking in

TABLE 4.1   Summary of Three Major Ethical Theories

Theory	Primary Focus	Rule	Clues You Are Using This Perspective
Utilitarianism	Pleasure over pain (or benefit over harm).	Do that which produces the greatest good for the greatest number.	• It's wrong to impose personal values on other people. • Results or consequences are all that count.
Universalism	Individual and universal rights.	1. Never treat others as a means to an end. 2. Act only in such a way as it would be all right for all to act (that is, if it were a universal rule). 3. Do not infringe on others' universal rights.	• I believe some principles can't be sacrificed for anything. • Fundamental right and wrong don't change. • The way in which something is done is more important than what is done. • There are certain things I would never consider "right."
Virtue	Character traits that enable ethical behavior.	Actions that enhance human capacities are good; those that deter them are bad.	• People should act in ways meant to better the world. • I will always hold myself to the highest standards or principles.

others' shoes. Start by considering the primary stakeholders in the situation. In Chapter 3, we discussed how to conduct a stakeholder's analysis. The same approach applies here as well.

Primary stakeholders are people who will be *directly* affected by any decision you make. This means that although there are likely many people and institutions that might be ultimately affected, it's best to start with those closest to the decision and work your way out toward secondary stakeholders. In many cases as a manager, you are likely to be a primary stakeholder in many employee-related decisions because your work as a manager is tied so strongly to your employees. Place yourself in each primary stakeholder's position. Imagine how you would feel about any particular decision. If you do this earnestly, you will quickly find that your perspective on the dilemma will change. What if you were Joe the employee? You'd probably want a straight answer from your boss—actually you might *expect* such an answer as consistent with your trusting relationship. What if you were your own boss? You'd want to know that information meant to be confidential is safe with your employees. Importantly, Joe's yet-to-be-adopted child is not a direct stakeholder. It certainly is true that he/she is affected, but it's Joe, you, your employees, and your manager who are most directly affected because any decision serves to constrain future actions of these stakeholders.

Once you feel comfortable that you've identified the affected parties, you next need to consider the consequences of any decision on each of the affected parties. This is a step that is easily "gamed" if you are not careful. Identify what consequences might *reasonably* occur to the affected party and avoid creating scenarios with a low probability of occurrence that serve to confuse the issues more. For example, a reasonable consequence of not telling Joe is that ultimately

Joe will likely know that you had some privileged information that you chose not to share, which could strain your relationship in the future. It is not likely (given what you know about Joe) that Joe will go to the local newspaper and drum up a negative story about you or the organization.

As we've learned already, consequences often have a temporal nature to them. Some consequences will have a strong immediate impact and will dissipate rather quickly. Others may take time but will swell to a large impact in a year or two. Regardless, one must try to sort through the various consequences likely to occur immediately and in the future. Of course, not all consequences are seeable or intended. These unintended consequences are difficult to predict but can turn what is initially seen as the right thing to do into the conclusion that the decision was a complete failure. One area of such consequences might be ones that are largely symbolic in nature. For example, if you terminate an employee who has been underperforming and who is known for complaining a lot about management, this decision is likely to carry a strong symbolic consequence. That is, despite having strong justification for the termination decision, other employees who are not privy to the same performance data as you could easily interpret the decision as one based on the employee's complaining (in other words, "You complain—you're fired").

Finally, you must consider the various obligations you might have to the affected parties. Obligations are requirements or responsibilities one holds based upon his or her role, occupation, or position in life. For example, physicians have an obligation to treat people who have been critically injured regardless of their life circumstances. They therefore have the duty to not withhold treatment based upon their own personal biases or preferences. Although many professions (for example, lawyers, scientists, accountants, psychologists, and others) have extensive ethical guidelines that govern their practice, not all people have such neatly prescribed obligations, which makes assessing one's obligations sometimes difficult. Virtue ethics plays a significant role here. For example, do you believe that Joe's boss has an obligation to tell the truth no matter what? If so, where does such an obligation originate? Certainly a person of great virtue might hold to such a claim, but is self-interest always the wrong choice? This is a difficult process, but it's important to try to tease out what obligations you think govern each affected party.

An easy way to bring all the elements together from Step 4 is presented in Tool Kit 4.1, with the Joe case as a backdrop.

Step 4: Consider Your Integrity

Unfortunately, as with most decision making, people begin the process with a solution in mind and spend time rationalizing why that solution is ethical. In fact, people go to great lengths to justify their predetermined solution to an ethical problem. Here is just a partial list of the most common rationalizations used to justify unethical behavior:

- **If it's legal, it's ethical.** The law stipulates what is minimally acceptable. Thus, the law is the floor for any ethical decision, not the ceiling. The law cannot take into account all the various potential impacts of any decision; ethics does. As a general guideline, we always tell our students that just because it's legal doesn't mean it's ethical.

- **I was only trying to help.** We can rationalize very easily that our behavior was for the good of someone else. So we withhold the truth from people and act as vigilantes, protecting others from information. This

⚒ MANAGER'S TOOL KIT

Tool Kit 4.1 Affected Parties, Consequences, and Obligations

Primary Stakeholders (Affected Parties)	Potential Consequences	Key Obligations	Unknowns
Me	Loss of trust with my boss if I tell Joe; potential harm to my career; loss of friendship with Joe.	To keep my word—to remain trustworthy; to be fair with my employees (not necessarily treat them based on equality); to ensure all employees' rights are protected.	How my own career might be impacted long-term by any decision.
Boss	My boss may be blamed for the information leak; his own career may suffer.	To remain loyal and credible; to encourage my boss to uphold basic employee rights.	What might happen to the boss or group as a result of the decision made.
Employees	The fear of job loss now and in the future; the loss of a liked colleague; the fear of workload increases.	To reduce the potential harmful impact on Joe and the remaining employees; to avoid harm through rumors or by neglecting responsibilities.	Reactions upon hearing that the boss lied or that layoffs are imminent.

type of behavior generally is not helpful to others but really is a means of avoiding difficult or uncomfortable situations.

- **Everyone else does it.** Just because you perceive that others behave unethically in no way transforms it into ethical behavior. Behaving ethically takes courage, and bucking norms is often part of it.

- **It's owed to me.** People often feel that, due to their hard work or frequent patronage or the like, certain rewards are owed them. This may be why office supplies theft, personal copies at work, or Internet abuses on the job are so commonplace—people see it as a right owed to them.

- **As long as I don't gain.** Behaving unethically for the greater good of the organization is no more ethical than stealing food for your family is legal. Personal gain is not the sole metric for determining ethical behavior; the impact of your behavior, regardless of who benefits, has far-reaching implications.

These rationalizations often lead people to move in directions that are away from their better selves. Business ethicist Craig Johnson notes that three factors are involved in disrupting peoples' moral reasoning: insecurities, greed, and ego.[16] First, he suggests that people who have inner doubts are more likely to fall prey to others' persuasive messages regarding certain behavior. Second, in a society that rewards people who take risks, greed is inevitable since many jobs are based upon a "winner takes all" model. Third, as substantial research suggests, people tend to believe they are above average in almost every domain of life, including ethics (see Chapter 3). Such overconfidence unfortunately results in an inflated ego—or a feeling that things will simply work out in your favor. Yet, as ethicist Dennis Moberg sees it:

> . . . not all corporate misdeeds are committed by bad people. In fact, a significant number of unethical acts in business are the likely result of foibles and failings rather than selfishness and greed. Put into certain kinds of situations, good people inadvertently do bad things. . . . We must identify situational factors that keep people from doing their best and eliminate them whenever we can.

Moberg's observations are well established by scholarly evidence on at least three fronts. First, it is well known that human beings follow psychological "scripts" that help us navigate our daily lives. We have scripts for how to order a meal at a restaurant, how to behave in a class, or how to talk to a client. When we encounter these very familiar situations, we go into "autopilot" mode—relying on our script to guide us. Although such scripts help us move through our day with ease, they also serve to block us from hearing, seeing, and sensing important information about the ethicality of the situation. It's not surprising then that ethical violations go entirely unnoticed in an organization—not because people don't care or they are complicit, but because they are blinded by their scripts.

Second, similar to the scripts we have in place, people generally follow others. Although "everyone's doing it" isn't a reason people readily admit as driving their actions, the power of group norms to guide behavior is well documented.[17] Breaking norms is both uncomfortable and impractical for most. This is mostly true because formal and informal rewards are geared toward employees who go along. Further, people do what gets rewarded and avoid behaviors that do not have rewards associated.[18] Rarely are there rewards for breaking norms even if it would be a good thing for the organization. Third, when making decisions at work, personal responsibility is often diffused throughout the group or work unit. In a series of classic studies over many decades, researchers have found that, by and large, individuals are more likely to help those in need when they are alone.[19] In one such study, participants were asked to complete surveys sitting in one of two settings: a room by themselves or in a group with others.[20] In both settings, while completing the surveys, smoke started to billow into the room under a door or through a vent. After a short period of time (four minutes or so) a majority of participants who were alone reported the smoke to the researcher. Yet less than 15 percent of people in the group settings reported the smoke. The lesson here is clear, that people are likely to interpret events as less important or urgent when others are present, thereby lowering their personal accountability for the outcome of such events.

The key point is that it's very easy to say "Act with integrity"; however, myriad human tendencies and external forces stand in the way of our ability to make an ethical decision. So rather than assume that you'll simply be able to do the right thing, you must put in place a system that allows you to continually check your thinking against some more objective criteria. For instance, all great managers ask themselves the following questions before making the tough choice:

1. Is my action legal?
2. Am I behaving fairly?
3. Is my decision in line with my own values?
4. Will others be negatively impacted?

As an important step in the ethical process, employees may be faced with the situation where they find that actions around them violate their own integrity and also harm others in the process. When cases like this occur, **whistle-blowing** is one way of bringing the issue to the attention of people who have the power to make changes. While whistle-blowing should not be considered a first option, in some cases it is the last alternative but one that needs to be exercised. We have provided a basic whistle-blowing model in Tool Kit 4.2.

Step 5: Think Creatively About Actions

In Chapter 3, we discuss ways to broaden solution sets (for example, reframing the problem). Solving ethical problems requires a similar approach. As the term "ethical dilemma" suggests, we typically frame our ethical scenarios in

MANAGER'S TOOL KIT

Tool Kit 4.2   The Last Resort: How to Blow the Whistle on Unethical Behavior[21]

Research has shown that when people do in fact see unethical behavior at work, they aren't necessarily inclined to report it or "blow the whistle." Employees often fear retaliation or simply believe that blowing the whistle will simply be met with an apathetic response by management. Interestingly, however, some research has found that some people simply do not have the confidence on how to best go about blowing the whistle.[22] This Tool Kit was designed to provide a model of when to "blow the whistle" and offer a logical process to guide you through that decision.

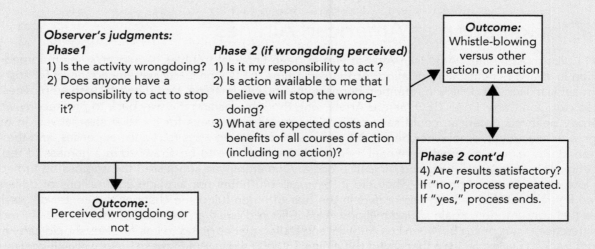

either-or terms. We tell Joe or we don't tell Joe. An easy way around this is to think in terms of the *trilemma*—"a third way forward, a middle ground between two seemingly implacable alternatives."[23] In many cases, the third way is a compromise between two alternatives that are perceived as "lose–lose." With respect to Joe, we might see the trilemma as a decision not about whether we should or shouldn't tell Joe but how best to communicate to Joe that during turbulent times, all employees should have their resumés up to date and be prepared for reorganizations or layoffs. In this sense, we keep our promise to the boss, but send a clear message to Joe that now may not be the best time to go forward with the adoption since his salary is an influential element for his decision.

All of this suggests that to really solve an ethical dilemma creatively, you must learn to improve your **moral imagination.** Moral imagination is the ability to (1) step out of your situation and see the possible ethical problems present, (2) imagine other possibilities and alternatives, and (3) evaluate from an ethical standpoint the new possibilities you have envisioned. In other words, making the tough ethical decision is the same thing as solving a difficult problem. At some point, you must flex your ability to generate truly unique alternatives and offer possibilities beyond a single course of action. Moral imagination is this process as it is applied to solving problems ethically.

If managers making downsizing or layoff decisions use their moral imagination, they would first frame the problem differently. If the problem is framed as "Should we or shouldn't we downsize?" then it will necessarily lead to one of two conclusions. But if the question is "How can we revitalize our financial performance?" then moral imagination is free to run. Sometimes it is truly necessary to reduce the number of people on the payroll, but even then, morally imaginative managers understand there are some creative alternatives, including asking people to make sacrifices in pay and benefits, designing new ways to cut costs, and so on. In other words, there are creative ways to get to the bottom line that don't involve purging an organization of its people. (See Management Live 4.2 for an example of moral imagination.)

MANAGEMENT LIVE 4.2

Moral Imagination at American Airlines[24]

After 9/11, like most airlines, American Airlines was in deep financial troubles. American's union agreed to cut $1.8 billion in salary, benefits, and vacation. At the same time, CEO Don Carty secretly arranged for top executives to receive millions of dollars in retention bonuses. As you can imagine, that didn't fly with employees or the unions, so exit Don Carty. Enter CEO Gerard Arpey, who thought slashing the way back to profitability wouldn't work. Arpey believed American could save millions by asking employees for creative alternatives. In monthly meetings with executives, employees began the process of describing ways to reduce expenses, and the executives listened. For example, engine overhaul mechanics used to have to be strapped in a harness to repair the 11-foot engines, a time-consuming and difficult process. One employee suggested the engines be turned vertical and lowered onto the shop floor. They did it. Savings: 140/hours per airplane and millions of dollars. One employee figured out that seating passengers in the rear of a non-full plane changes the center of gravity and improves fuel consumption, again saving millions. A pilot figured out that, because of the 42 cents or more per gallon difference in gas prices between Los Angeles and Dallas, planes going to Los Angeles should carry enough fuel to get back to Dallas, an idea that saved the airline $50,000 a day. When these ideas were all implemented, it led to a total savings for American of $4 billion annually.

Step 6: Check Your Instincts

When you finally arrive at a solution and select a course of action, you may want to subject your decision to some gut checks that will put your decision into perspective.

- **The Wall Street Journal Test.** Would I stand by my decision if it made the front page of *The Wall Street Journal?* Would I be embarrassed if others knew of the choice I had made?
- **The Platinum Rule Test.** Am I treating others in a way in which they would want to be treated?
- **The Mom Test.** Would I be proud to tell my mother of my decision?
- **The Personal Gain Test.** Is the opportunity to gain personally standing in the way of my thinking? Have I given my personal gain too much weight?
- **The Cost-Benefit Test.** Does my decision benefit some to the detriment of others? Have I considered the true impact on others?

Fairness in the Workplace

When judging the fairness of decisions, three major factors often come into play: economics, equality, and justice.

Economics

Perhaps the most common ethical issues that arise in the economic domain relate to supply and demand. To illustrate, imagine you're in downtown Seattle and it begins to rain heavily. You stop in a store and ask, "How much for that umbrella over there?" The clerk tells you $18. You look at the price tag that says $13 and immediately rebuke the clerk, but he doesn't budge on the price and says take it or leave it. Is it ethical for the clerk to change the price? Economically speaking, the clerk made the right call. The demand is obviously higher for umbrellas when it's raining and, thus, the market will support a higher price—great decision. Yet this practice violates most people's sense of basic fairness. A research study[25] asked participants whether they believed raising the price in such a situation was fair or unfair; 82 percent responded it was unfair.

In this same vein, consider the following two scenarios from a research study:

1. A company is making a small profit. It is located in a community experiencing a recession with substantial unemployment but no inflation. Many workers are anxious to work at the company. The company decides to decrease wages and salaries 7 percent this year.

2. A company is making a small profit. It is located in a community experiencing a recession with substantial unemployment and inflation of 12 percent. Many workers are anxious to work at the company. The company decides to increase wages and salaries 5 percent this year.

In scenario 1, 62 percent of the study's participants believed the organization's behavior was unfair, compared to only 22 percent of participants in scenario 2. Factoring in inflation, the two scenarios provide a net wage and salary of the exact same amount. Yet most people perceive any form of pay cut as unfair, while pay increases are seen as fair, despite the fact that the increase is being outpaced by inflation. These studies make clear that even the most rational, economically based decisions will not be seen universally as fair by stakeholders.

Practice this!
Go to www.baldwin2e.com

Equality

Consider the following scenario. You go out to buy a mattress. You lie on a number of them and decide on the one you want. The price tag says $1,200. You approach the salesperson and say, "I'd like to buy that mattress. I'll give you $800 for it." He counters with $1,150, and you counter with $900. He counters again with $1,100 and you counter with $950. He pauses and says, "Look, it seems to me you want to buy this mattress, and I want to provide you with the best service possible. I assume we're both reasonable people, so why don't we just split the difference with $1,025." Most people see this logic as fair, disregarding the fact that the split agreed upon is totally arbitrary. Had you started with a lower number or countered with lower numbers, and then split, you may have saved yourself a few hundred bucks.

People inherently see anything that seems like a 50-50 split as fair and ethical. Many people have been exploited on these seemingly equality-driven splits. Decisions framed in terms of compromise and "middle ground" usually appeal to peoples' need for equality—that is, to treat everything and everyone as equal. Just remember that equality doesn't necessarily make a decision fair or ethical.

Justice

Consider this situation. Two of your employees are up for a promotion. Ted has been with you five years and is seen by all as your second-in-command. Jim has been with you for about three years but is considered by many employees to be the most talented employee in your group. After an exhaustive process, you end up selecting Ted for the job. Your employees are outraged and confront you. "How could you hire Ted over Jim?" You respond, "He's the right person for the job." They say, "Well how do you know? Ted didn't have to take the tests you gave Jim nor interview with you." Stunned, you respond, "Well, I know Ted very well; I don't know Jim as well." In your eyes, the decision was very easy. Ted's demonstrated track record and loyalty to you won the day. In employees' eyes, Ted was given preferential treatment. At the heart of many issues that concern ethics and fairness are perceptions of justice. Justice perceptions are so important to effective ethical management that we devote the next section to understanding and managing justice perceptions.

KO **4-4**
KO **4-5**

Managing Justice Perceptions

Organizational justice perceptions are simply the beliefs people hold about the fairness of their organization and manager. Justice judgments can be categorized into three forms: *distributive justice* (outcomes), *procedural justice* (process), and *interactional justice* (personal treatment).

Distributive Justice

Distributive justice is perceived when people view fairness of a particular *outcome*. Consider a simple decision to give Tim a bonus and not Bill. As a manager, you no doubt have good logic for such a choice. Yet Bill, who occupies the same job, will likely ask questions about whether or not such a bonus is fairly distributed. More specifically, Bill will likely compare his efforts and results to Tim's. If Bill perceives discrepancies, he is likely to believe that you haven't allocated such resources appropriately. "So what," you might say, "I'm the manager and it's left to my discretion how best to allocate rewards." You are correct; however, even if your intention is good and you believe you've made a solid choice, Bill may still see it as unfair. The problem here is that when Bill believes that you have been distributively unjust, he is likely to lower his performance and withhold extra effort beyond what the job requires. In addition, he's likely to have lower job satisfaction, decreased commitment to the organization, and is far more likely to quit.[26] If Bill is a solid employee (even if he's simply meeting his goals, not exceeding them), the perception Bill holds about your distributive fairness as a manager is going to be costly.

Thus, great managers realize that different situations call for different types of distributive justice. In a reward situation, people are likely to examine the outcome of a decision's impact on *equity*. That is, were the resources distributed with respect to people's contributions rather than favoritism or other preferences? In performance situations, managers should be very clear and transparent with employees regarding how rewards and privileges are obtained and what level of performance is necessary to obtain them. To the extent to which this can be spelled out clearly, the more likely it is that employees are able to accept the distribution of resources and see such decisions as fair.

In some managerial situations, people will evaluate distributive justice based upon *equality*, where resources are distributed so each person gets the same outcome, regardless of their contributions. A classic example of where people invoke equality as a determination for distributive justice is the case of distributing medical benefits. People universally see that all those employed by the organization deserve access to the same health plans, regardless of the job they perform or their contributions to the organization. Likewise, people view access to grievance procedures or necessary physical accommodations as things that should be distributed equally.

Finally, people often evaluate distributive justice based on *need*, or examining whether resources are distributed to the person who needs them the most, as in distributing food to the disadvantaged. Consider the difficult decisions financial aid staff must make in determining how best to allocate scholarships based upon need. Should scholarships go only to those whose income (or parents' income) is below a certain level? What about the student who exceeds the threshold but only because she works two jobs and 50 hours a week versus the student who is not working but has a similar economic status? Considering instances of need in the workplace is littered with landmines and very hotly charged issues. This is perhaps why most managers try to distribute resources based upon equity. Yet we would argue that managers must often consider need to be perceived as fair. What about the small business employee, who just lost a spouse, has no savings and no vacation days left (because she put all of her resources toward taking care of her spouse). Should you give her time off with or without pay? Policy might say you should not pay her; a needs-based distributive justice perspective would probably endorse giving some portion of her time off as paid.

Procedural Justice

Procedural justice occurs when the *process* used to determine the outcome is perceived as fair. Returning to our employees Bill and Tim, Bill might consider his not receiving a raise as unfair if he thinks the process taken to arrive at the decision was somehow skewed. For example, let's say that in determining who would get the bonus, you asked Tim to determine the goals he was to achieve while you personally assigned them to Bill. Bill is likely to see you as being procedurally unfair by not giving him the same voice or say in the process. Several conditions lead people to perceive justice in a process. For example, people want to be able to have a say or voice in any decision that might affect them. People also want to be treated with consistency over time. Further, people want to know

Practice this!
Go to www.baldwin2e.com

that managers and those with power in an organization are suspending their personal biases and relying on objective data to the best possible extent. Finally, procedural justice is perceived when people are presented with a mechanism for correcting perceived errors or poor decisions. For instance, when a student is accused of plagiarizing, it is only procedurally fair he be able to appeal such a claim.

Although as a manager you should strive to establish procedural justice in your day-to-day management processes, it appears that managing perceptions of procedural justice is most important in situations where the favorability of outcomes is poor. For example, in one study, 147 employees were told that they were about to be laid off from their manufacturing jobs.[27] They were surveyed two months after they found out they were told about the layoff, but one month before they actually stopped working. Clearly, no employee is going to view a layoff as a highly positive event. So the researchers instead evaluated employees' perceptions of favorability of the layoff by asking the employees to consider how much other support they had regarding the layoff. For example, they asked about employee perceptions of unemployment insurance, severance pay, company help with finding another job, and so forth. Then the researchers asked employees about their reactions to the organization by asking whether or not they would, despite everything that had happened, be "proud to tell others" they worked there, or if they had little "problem recommending" the organization to a friend or relative.

As can be seen in Figure 4.3, a very interesting relationship emerges. Specifically, when the outcome is seen as highly favorable, employees may hold positive attitudes or reactions toward the organization despite the layoff. That is, when employees believed that the organization was doing all it could to support them through the layoff, they maintained favorable views of the company, regardless of their procedural justice perceptions. However, when employees viewed the outcome favorability as low, reactions to this low favorability were greatly enhanced by perceptions of procedural justice. The message from this study and others like it is clear: Procedural justice matters most in situations of low outcome favorability. When there are going to be large discrepancies in employee outcomes, for example, people will maintain their perceptions of fairness regardless of the outcome for them if procedural justice is maintained. Said differently, for most people, "the means justify the ends," and even if the outcome is unfavorable, people will still react well if the procedure was fair. See Tool Kit 4.3 for ways to strengthen procedural justice perceptions.

FIGURE 4.3
When Does Procedural Justice Matter Most?[28]

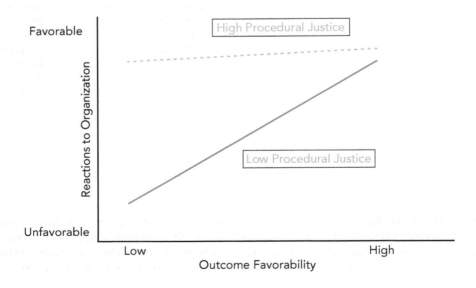

⚒ MANAGER'S TOOL KIT

Tool Kit 4.3 Methods for Increasing Procedural Justice[29]

Action	Description	Positive Example
Allow for participation in decision making.	Give people a voice or a "say" in how decisions that affect them directly are determined.	Allow employees the opportunity to "sign off" on a set of goals for the year and to make revisions when presented with evidence to do so.
Apply rules consistently.	Rule violations are likely to be seen as procedurally unfair if such a violation impacts one person more than another. Remember, sometimes the rule to apply is based on equity. Being consistent doesn't mean being equal, but rather a consistent application of the rule.	Use the same data collection method and standards to evaluate employee performance for the same job.
Create mechanisms for appeals and correct inaccurate information.	Mistakes happen, and when they do, employees want to be able to have a way of appealing such a mistake, or disputing information that is objectively inaccurate.	A manager misses a critical sale by an employee and does not count it toward her overall sales revenue, on which 50 percent of her bonus is based. The manager, however, gives employees the opportunity to petition him in writing if an employee believes that a mistake was made in calculating revenue.
Suppress all personal biases.	Nothing erodes procedural justice faster than a belief that despite clear standards in place, a manager is using personal preferences as a criterion for making decisions.	In order to determine who is nominated for an elite project team working on a high-profile product rollout, a manager uses transparent criteria and makes them public or shares them with a colleague to thwart the presence of personal preferences.

Interactional Justice

Interactional justice is comprised of two important fairness perceptions: interpersonal treatment and informational adequacy. Simply speaking, when a manager is seen as treating others with respect and explaining the rationale behind decisions adequately, she or he is likely to be seen as fair. Interpersonal treatment

MANAGEMENT LIVE 4.3

Downsizing: Competitive Strategy or Decision-Making Malpractice?

Overall, research has found that **downsizing**—terminating large numbers of employees to recapture losses or gain some form of competitive advantage—does not work.[30] That is, it doesn't accomplish what people say it's supposed to accomplish. Companies downsize as the result of a simple economic formula that says there are two ways to profit, one through costs and one through revenues. For most companies, cutting costs seems a heck of a lot easier than increasing revenues, and payroll expenses tend to be a very large expense. So when companies feel the pinch, they start shaving the biggest expense—people. Yet significant research has shown organizations rarely achieve the level of profitability they once had *prior* to downsizing. In fact, successful companies don't cut their way to success but grow their way to financial performance. Further, the research shows that many companies aren't downsizing because they are in real financial straits, but rather are looking for a quick boost in their quarterly earnings and stock price. Armed with this knowledge, would you say downsizing is an ethical choice? Consultants often frame downsizing as a necessary evil or a tough business decision—that is, it is entirely removed from ethics. Downsizing discussions are perfect places to increase your moral imagination. It's fairly clear you won't ever be able to cut your way to organizational growth.

Researcher Wayne Cascio suggests a few key actions to improve the ethicality of downsizing decisions.[31] First he suggests that organizations *be clear about short- and long-term goals.* Ask questions such as, "What do our customers expect from us and how will downsizing help us meet those expectations?" Second, *use downsizing as a last resort only.* Companies often restructure because they see others doing it and assume that their shareholders will expect similar actions. Of course, this frames the dilemma as "downsize or don't compete." When framed in this way, there really isn't a choice is there? The trilemma here is to consider alternative approaches to reducing costs. A reduction in head-count is indeed a very fast way to reduce costs; however, a more creative approach would be to consider actions such as delaying new-hire start dates, reducing perks, revoking job offers, freezing salaries and promotions, and asking all employees to take unpaid vacations over time. Third, make *communication open and honest.* As you already know from the research on procedural and interactional justice, people can handle adversity; they can't handle leaders lying, deceiving, or acting in any way that would undermine their own well-being. Fourth, if layoffs must occur, don't forget to *pay attention to the survivors.* The effects on those who remain after a significant layoff can be just as damaging as the effect on those who left. Cascio notes that most organizations underestimate the emotional damage that survivors suffer, which includes increased stress, burnout, and uncertainty. Survivors will be hypercritical of perceived justice and ask themselves routinely whether it makes sense for them to stay as well. Not surprisingly, a recent study found that for every half of 1 percent reduction in the workforce, an organization can expect another wave of voluntary turnover in the realm of five times the number of employees initially let go. This means that for most organizations, not paying attention to the needs of survivors will continue to be a very costly endeavor.[32]

includes treating people with dignity and value by refraining from improper remarks and establishing a collegial relationship. Informational adequacy is perceived when people believe they have been given the whole story and that managers are not purposely or strategically withholding information that might affect employees. Further, interactional justice is often perceived when people believe that the information used to make a decision was fair.

Consider how you would feel if your boss told you that you and your fellow employees are going to have to take a 20 percent pay cut indefinitely due to the current performance of the company. When you ask your manager why this is happening, she says "This was a corporate decision; I had nothing to do with it," and walks away. Your manager could have easily raised your perceptions of fairness by engaging in a bit of interactional justice. First, she should have stopped and talked with you, knowing full well that a pay cut of any type is not likely to be received positively. In doing so, she would have demonstrated that she respects you as a human being and that you are valued, despite the fact that the company has to take such measures. Second, she should have provided much more information about the pay cut. For instance, she could have explained that the organization looked at future orders or new business trends, coupled with the economy, and decided that it was headed for serious financial problems. Further, she could have added that the decision to cut pay was taken with the intent of not laying off a single employee. These simple steps would likely make a significant difference in your fairness perceptions of your manager.

If you're thinking that interactional justice may just be a little too "soft" or "touchy feely" for you to handle, it's instructive to understand how such fairness perceptions can impact the bottom line. One research study across 97 hotels (over 4,500 employees) showed that employees who felt as if they were unfairly treated were significantly more likely to quit and were associated with lower levels of customer satisfaction.[33] The impact of these two outcomes combined can result in a substantial loss of business and loyalty, particularly in the hospitality industry where competition is fierce (see Management Live 7.3 for another example). The point here is that while managing interactional justice perceptions may seem like soft practice, its negative consequences can hit an organization hard, which has potential harmful effects on your own success as a manager.

⇄ MANAGEMENT LIVE 4.4

The Ethics of Executive Compensation

How much more should the people in the top of an organization earn over the people at the bottom? The question can be approached in many ways. For example, we might take a moralistic approach and argue for certain rights or living wages. We might suggest an answer more consistent with capitalism and survival of the fittest. Or we might examine the business case, which a recent study set out to do. In particular, the study examined the ratios of the top-to-bottom level of pay in organizations and looked at performance metrics for both individuals and organizations. Results showed that, as organizations increase the disparity between the top and bottom, *both* individual and organizational performance decreases. In other words, people at the top *may* perform better, but people at the bottom (of which there are many more, explaining the overall decline in the organization's performance) perform worse.[34] Given these findings, it is difficult to justify the large dispersion between the top and bottom—it just doesn't make good business sense. Yet U.S. corporations are leading the way (almost twice as much) among the most industrialized countries in pay dispersion. A wide disparity in wages from top to bottom can be particularly damaging to the morale of the workforce when senior executive wages are *not* tied to the overall performance of the firm. Further, as executive pay has generally increased over time, consistent with corporate profits, employee pay of the average worker has remained relatively flat. Thus, even when organizations are doing well, the opportunity to reward all individuals for such success is generally missed. You might suggest, however, that since the great recession of 2008 began, organizations have reexamined such policies in light of increasing scrutiny of public corporations and the substantial number of layoffs that have occurred since 2008. Yet, as a recent report details, more than three-quarters of these layoffs took place at just 50 firms: "Of the 50 top corporate layoff leaders, 72 percent ended last year in the black. CEOs at these 50 major firms that have

(continued)

laid off the most workers since the onset of the economic crisis took home nearly $12 million each on average in 2009, 42 percent more than the average compensation that went to S&P 500 CEOs."[35] Whichever lens you might apply to examine this issue, it's clear that excessive CEO pay is difficult to justify from public perception to the organizational bottom line.

Ratio of Average CEO Total Direct Compensation to Average Production Worker Compensation, 1965–2009

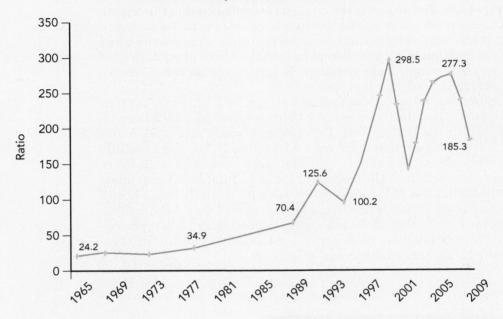

Source: Economic Policy Institute (2011). More compensation heading to the very top. The State of Working America. Washington, D.C.: Economic Policy Institute. August 28, 2011, http://www .stateofworkingamerica.org/articles/view/9

DO **4-5**

Navigating Common Managerial Ethical Situations[36]

Although we'd like to be able to prepare you for every single ethical situation you will face in the workplace, we obviously can't anticipate everything you're likely to face with respect to ethics. There are, however, some very common situations that are managerial lightning rods for ethical traps. These situations include work assignments and opportunities, terminations, performance management, harassment, and work/family issues.

Work Assignments and Opportunities

One of your primary responsibilities as a manager is to coordinate work among your staff. In doing so it is inevitable that some employees will be given assignments that are more preferable. These attractive assignments could be better because they involve nice locations or travel, established customers, or they could represent significantly better success opportunities in the form of achieving results or acquiring new skills. How will you decide who gets these types of assignments? Will you always select your best-performing employee? Is your best employee a good employee because she always gets these assignments? How will others on your staff perceive the decision process you used to make these assignments? The trap here is to assume that people will always see these assignments as equitably distributed, based solely on merit or some standardized process. To the contrary, people are likely to see much of this as based on personal bias and preference for a certain "type" of employee. The key is to remember that management is about getting things done through others. By not distributing such assignments in a more egalitarian fashion, you run the risk of quickly diminishing your staff to a small number of "doers" and a large number of employees who withhold their extra effort.

Performance Evaluation

Performance evaluations represent a minefield of ethical traps. If you really want to encourage unethical behavior, simply focus your performance evaluations on results only. As we describe in depth in Chapter 7, fair performance evaluations take into account the process people use on the way to their results. This is much easier said than done, however. What happens when your best-performing employee happens to be a real jerk? He treats everyone—customers, staff, and you—with utter contempt and disrespect, but for whatever reason is able to get results. It would be easy to simply find a place for him to hide out, thereby ignoring his behavior. To do so will send the clear message to others that you will tolerate counterproductive behavior as long as results are strong. Another trap in performance evaluation is to ignore, or worse, to deny opportunities for employees to have a voice or say in their evaluation process. A large meta-analysis showed that people are far more likely to see their manager as fair and just when they are given opportunities to participate in the evaluation process.[37] In fact, one of the strongest findings of the study was that managers are more likely to be seen as fair when they simply express value in hearing an employee's perspective on his/her performance. Further, the study showed increased fairness perceptions when managers actually implement aspects of the employee's voice in the process, such as taking into account the employee's perspective of a particular performance incident, or adding an additional evaluation criterion the employee deems as important.

Punishment and Discipline

Great managers don't like having to punish or discipline employees. Unfortunately, sometimes employee behavior does require it. The primary circumstances under which punishment or disciplinary action should be used include safety violations that endanger self or others, legal infractions, major policy violations, and counterproductive behavior such as abuse of resources (that is, theft, excesses on an expense account, and so on). The ethical traps here revolve mainly around how punishment is used and the severity of the punishment. Firing an employee for making a clerical error would be met with suspicion and contempt by most employees who might assume you were simply looking for any reason to fire the employee. Of course, such suspicion is likely to promote worry about who might be next and will serve to severely limit creativity out of fear of making mistakes. Perhaps the best way to avoid the ethical trap involved in punishment is twofold. First, make clear to all employees the circumstances under which you will move toward disciplinary action. Give them concrete examples of behavior and the likely corresponding punishment. For instance, "I expect that you will not intentionally fudge your expense reports. If you are found violating this, I will give you a warning and write a disciplinary action in your personnel file. A second infraction will move toward loss of pay and potentially termination."

Second, when an employee does actually engage in punishable behavior, you must then follow through and pursue disciplinary action. One reason for this is that if you say that the behavior is unacceptable and punishable and do not follow through, you will—through your passive acceptance of the behavior—reinforce it. Further, when you punish contingent upon the unethical behavior, you actually reinforce trust with employees. One recent study found that the trust between employee and manager is only diminished when managers punish noncontingently (in other words, the punishment is not tied to any particular violation or behavior).[38] That is, employees like to know the rules of the game and whether you follow through with the punishment you prescribed for the offense. If so, then employees appear to both expect and accept their punishment much more readily than if it seems mostly random. The bottom line on punishment is that it should be used sparingly so that when employed it will serve to send the appropriate message about the repercussions of unethical behavior.

Harassment

Let's say an employee comes to see you in your office and immediately starts complaining about a co-worker who is bullying her and making inappropriate remarks about her physical appearance. What would you say to this employee? What if this employee had a history of being just overly sensitive to many work-related issues? Might you be tempted to ignore her complaints? The minute you ignore such complaints or look to make excuses for her co-worker, you have fallen into a critical ethical trap. Harassment of any kind, including sexual harassment, has the potential to derail even the most successful managers for a number of reasons.

First, under federal law, individual managers can be held liable for their complicity in allowing harassment to occur in their work group. Thus, managers (not just companies) can be sued for compensatory damages. Second, multiple meta-analyses have shown that harassment at work has extremely toxic effects not just for the victim but for those who work with the victim as well. For example, one large-scale study shows that victims of workplace harassment are much more likely to retaliate against the organization in counterproductive behaviors and are more likely to experience burnout, anxiety, depression, and serious illness (both mental and physical).[39] Further, some studies have shown that harassment is associated with decreases in work group productivity.[40] The point here is that regardless of your ethical perspective, harassment is bad for everyone. Clear ethical considerations exist regarding the dignity and rights of human beings (universalism) and clearly the harms outweigh the benefits for organizations (for example, turnover costs, benefit claims, and so on) and for individuals alike. Thus, any competent manager should take *all* complaints of harassment seriously and shouldn't depend solely on his/her human resources department or others to "handle it."

Family and Personal Issues

Consider the scenario involving an employee who consistently leaves work early in order to pick up her kids at a day care center that has strict policies about being on time for pick-up. On the one hand, as a manager you want to be compassionate and want this employee to know that performance is what you care about, not necessarily face-time. On the other hand, this employee's co-workers see it as unfair that just because she has kids in day care, she is allowed to leave early. These types of issues have the potential to bring about ethical dilemmas for managers regarding how to best manage justice in the workplace. What is clear is that the nature and composition of the workforce has changed so drastically that *all* of your employees are likely to feel significant strain in coordinating their work demands with life outside of work. For example, the percentage of dual career couples aged 18–64 increased from 36 percent of the American population in 1970 to 60 percent in 2000. Single-parent households increased from 11 to 24 percent, and over 55 percent of the workforce has elder care responsibilities.[41]

Regardless of the type of family situation, significant numbers of employees struggle on a daily basis to balance their family responsibilities with their jobs. Moreover, this work–family conflict is likely to have a mostly negative influence on employees. For example, research has shown that when work–family conflict is present, people are more likely to burn out on the job, dislike their jobs, look for other work or quit, and likely will experience poorer health such as depression or somatic complaints.[42] Given these potential outcomes, it's in a manager's best interest to care about and actively respond to an employee's work–life conflict issues. Should you always accommodate employee requests as they relate to work–family conflict? The knee-jerk response of most managers is to establish a firm policy about such requests and treat everyone equally. Unfortunately, this is an area where context matters, and to establish a strict policy that is applied blindly to all situations, while simplifying things, is not likely to engender feelings of fairness.

What you *should* do is be transparent with employees about how such decisions are made. First, state your expectations about the requirements of each employee's job. For some jobs, being at work is imperative, in order to maintain availability to customers, for example. Other jobs don't require that work be completed at the place of business. Second, once you've communicated expectations about work time, indicate to employees how you evaluate requests made for accommodation. Some research suggests that increasing flexible work schedules reduces the amount of work–life conflict that employees experience. Yet too much telecommuting (for instance, more than 2.5 days a week) harms relationships with co-workers who may feel like their telecommuting colleague is taking advantage of the situation.[43] Again, it makes little sense to draw up a one-size-fits-all policy. For some employees, working from home more will make sense—for others, it won't. The key is to communicate to the rest of your staff the reasons for different work arrangements and how you arrived at the decision. Third, make it clear to employees that accommodations are not "free passes," only the ability to shift their work arrangements. Thus, you ought to communicate to employees that it is their responsibility for demonstrating the ability to get work done with increased autonomy and that taking advantage of accommodations won't be tolerated.

 CASE CONCLUDED

One outgrowth of the Internet is the use of *memes*, which are viral ideas propagated through the World Wide Web. A meme may take the form of a hyperlink, video, picture, website, or just a word or phrase. Memes may spread from person to person via social networks, blogs, direct e-mail, news sources, or other web-based services. Memes are used legitimately by public relations and marketing professionals as an inexpensive vehicle for viral marketing and for creating "buzz" about a product or service. For example, film studios use Internet memes to create interest in movies that would otherwise not generate positive publicity among critics. The 2006 film *Snakes on a Plane* generated much publicity via this method. Internet memes can evolve and spread extremely rapidly, sometimes reaching worldwide popularity and vanishing within a few days. They are also seen as a way to create an image of cleverness or trendiness.

The rapid growth and impact of memes—particularly dishonest or illicit ones—has caught the attention of researchers and practicing marketers alike. Focused explicitly on the political arena, TRUTHY is a project founded by Filippo Menczer of Indiana University, and is devoted to tracking the spread of memes online. TRUTHY is named after popular TV personality Stephen Colbert and his playful notion of "truthiness," which is a "truth" that a person claims to know intuitively without regard to evidence, logic, intellectual examination, or facts. The TRUTHY team uses an algorithm based on election-specific keywords and

(continued)

> CASE CONCLUDED *(continued)*

mood indicators to follow political misinformation campaigns on Twitter. The TRUTHY team, inspired by the Massachusetts election, decided to track digital campaigns during election years.

"We have a 90 percent success rate at tracking abnormal behavior on social networks, and it happens frequently," says Menczer. "People are being manipulated without realizing it because a dishonest or inaccurate meme can be given instant global popularity by a high search engine ranking, in turn perpetuating a falsehood. If you think about how much putting an ad on TV costs, for the same investment you could pay an army of people to post fake information and promote it through social networks . . .," says Menczer, who, based on his research, anticipates future manipulation of the Twittersphere for political gains. "It's a form of information pollution. Spamming on social networks has very low cost and has the potential to influence a large amount of people . . ."

TRUTHY is one attempt to promote integrity and accountability in the social media sphere, where anonymity is still easy to maintain. "If anything, many of these actions are violations of Twitter terms of service . . . but so what? You can just make another account. There's no accountability," says Menczer. "I think it's scary. It's extremely easy to fabricate news and use these methods to manipulate the Web because people want to believe what they want to believe."

Questions

1. Social media seems like the ultimate open, egalitarian, and democratic phenomenon. But what are some major ethical issues that can arise?

2. What are the ethics of online ratings like Facebook's genesis "facematch," which covertly obtained pictures and then asked observers to directly rate the comparative attractiveness of all the young women at a college?

3. Is it ethical to post a slam with no supporting evidence that is simply your passionate opinion? Conversely, is it ethical to just arbitrarily *remove* a slam from a rating site?

4. If you raised a large amount of money for charity, or got a good candidate elected via social media manipulation, do the ends justify the means?

5. In your opinion, is it ethical to:
   a. Post the statement, "Everybody vote for Kim as our best employee"?
   b. Ask students to rate their college highly because it will enhance the long-term value of their degrees?
   c. Ask employees to vote on which retail branch of their company to keep open?
   d. Post the amount of individual United Way contributions from everyone in your work group?

From Jared Keller, "When Campaigns Manipulate Social Media," *The Atlantic Monthly,* November 10, 2010. Copyright 2010, The Atlantic Media Co. as published in *The Atlantic Monthly.* Distributed by Tribune Media Services.

Concluding Note

Ethical decision making is tough, and being ethical is never easy. The most critical element will always be your personal dedication and the commitment to do what is right. However, because what is right is not always crystal clear, it is important to have a toolbox of frameworks or ways of thinking about ethical dilemmas that can facilitate clear thinking and ultimately ethical choices.

KEY TERMS

categorical imperative 131
deontological 128
distributive justice 140

downsizing 144
ethical commitment 123
ethical competency 123

ethical consciousness 123
ethics 123
integrity 123

> > **CASE**
> **Merck & Co. and River Blindness**[44]

Headquartered in New Jersey, Merck & Co. is one of the largest pharmaceutical companies in the world. In 1978, Merck was about to lose patent protection on its two best-selling prescription drugs. Because of this, Merck poured millions into the research and development of new medications, investing over $1 billion and resulting in the discovery of four potent medications. Although profits were important, the son of the founder of Merck, George W. Merck, said, "We try never to forget that medicine is for people. It is not for the profits. The profits follow, and if we have remembered that, they have never failed to appear. The better we have remembered that, the larger they have been." This philosophy was at the core of Merck & Co.'s value system. Enter "river blindness."

The disease onchocerciasis, known as "river blindness," is caused by parasitic worms that live in small black flies that breed in and about fast-moving rivers in developing countries in the Middle East, Africa, and Latin America. When a person is bitten by a fly, the larvae of the worm can enter the person's body and often grow to two feet long causing horrible growths on an infected person. The most severe problem over time, however, is that the larvae can cause blindness. In the late 1970s, the World Health Organization estimated that more than 300,000 people were blind because of the disease, and another 18 million were infected. In 1978, the disease had no cure and although there were two drugs that could kill the parasite, both had serious, even fatal, side effects. To make matters worse, the flies had built up immunity to the chemical sprays used to try to combat them.

Merck's Ethical Quandary

Since it takes roughly $200 million in research and approximately 12 years to bring the average drug successfully to market, the decision to pursue drug research is complex. Since resources are finite, research dollars are spent on drugs that hold the most promise—that is, in their potential to make money and alleviate human suffering. More complicated is what to do about rare diseases affecting relatively few individuals where the investment is never likely to be recovered. The problem with developing a drug to combat river blindness was not that there weren't enough people to justify the investment, but rather that the disease afflicted individuals in the poorest parts of the world. Thus, those suffering from the disease were not likely to be able to purchase the medication.

In 1978, Merck was testing a drug for animals called "ivermectin" to see if it could effectively kill parasites and worms. During this clinical testing, Merck discovered that the drug killed a parasite in horses that was very similar to the worm that caused river blindness in humans. This, therefore, was Merck's dilemma: company scientists were encouraging the firm to invest further research to determine if the drug could be adapted for safe use with humans.

Discussion Questions

1. Should Merck pursue investment toward curing river blindness? Why or why not?

2. Who are the key stakeholders in this case upon which you might base your decision?

3. What are the potential costs/benefits of this decision?

4. Compare how a strict universalist versus a strict utilitarian might view this dilemma.

SELECT MANAGE WHAT? DEBRIEFS

Making a Difficult Ethical Choice: Debrief

Most ethical choices present themselves not as "right versus wrong" but as "right versus right." That is, the really tough choices don't involve clearly right and wrong alternatives, but rather two alternatives that may both have merit. This situation is one of those and is a case of trust/loyalty versus truth/honesty. On one hand, you have the virtues of trust and promises kept and avoiding unproductive rumor spreading. On the other, you have your loyalty to a friend and the potential well-being of a young child and your own integrity in being honest.

The fact that they arise as ethical dilemmas means there are no simple or storybook answers. And always the most important aspect of ethical behavior is commitment—your personal intention to do what you think is most right. In the absence of that, no amount of behavioral expertise will suffice. However, presuming such commitment, there are a few strategies that have been shown to be helpful in making choices in these situations.

First, try to invoke some moral imagination, which involves avoiding seeing the choice set with just two alternatives (black or white). Although it may initially seem as if there are only two choices, it is often the case that many other creative alternatives can be generated. In this case, for example, you might go back to your boss and tell him your dilemma and see if there are ways you could get the word to your friend without feared consequences.

Second, it may help to consider several other features, including the magnitude of consequences each way, the probability of harm/benefit and temporal immediacy. Put more simply: What will be the comparative harm to each party? What is the likelihood that the act in question will actually happen and that it will produce the predicted harm/benefit? What is the time between the act and the onset of the consequences?

Third, in Tool Kit 4.1, we present a method for deconstructing the potential consequences, key obligations, and unknowns about the ethical dilemma. It is always a good idea to ask at least four questions before deciding on a course of action: (1) Is my action legal? (2) Am I behaving fairly? (3) Is my decision in line with my own values? (4) Will others be negatively impacted? Beyond these key questions, you may want to subject your decision to the following "gut checks" to keep your choice in perspective:

The Wall Street Journal Test—Would I stand by my decision if it made the front page of *The WSJ*? Would I be embarrassed that others knew the choice I made?

The Platinum Rule Test—Am I treating others in a way in which they would want to be treated?

The Mom Test—Would I be proud to tell my mother of my decision?

The Personal Gain Test—Is the opportunity to gain personally standing in the way of my thinking? Have I given my personal gain too much weight?

The Cost/Benefit Test—Does my decision benefit some to the detriment of others? Have I considered the true impact on others?

In the end, it comes down to a deep look inside, and a driving commitment toward making the choice you feel is most appropriate. As you will learn when you ultimately face this type of dilemma for real, ethical decision making is a lot easier to talk about than to do.

You Be the Ethicist: Debrief

Before offering some thoughts on the most ethical responses, two notes are in order. First, as Cohen and many others rightly note, there is not just one set of ethics. Different frames, models, contexts, and even cultures often suggest different responses—so offering "answers" to ethical dilemmas is always dicey and you should be aware of that. In this regard, just because something is against the law (for example, smoking marijuana to alleviate the pain of certain diseases) doesn't make it unethical. The opposite is also true. It is perfectly legal to spend thousands of dollars pampering your pet, but is that "proper" conduct while there's a family living in a station wagon just a few blocks away?

Second, to really address an ethical dilemma creatively, you must learn to improve your *moral imagination*. Moral imagination is the ability to (1) step out of your situation and see the possible ethical problems present,

(2) imagine other possibilities and alternatives, and (3) evaluate from an ethical standpoint the new possibilities you have envisioned. In other words, making the tough ethical decision is the same thing as solving a difficult problem. It is common to think of only two choices, and this is known as the black or white fallacy (the choice is either black or white). Perhaps the single best advice for ethical decision making is to avoid that fallacy and aim to generate other possibilities beyond a single course of action.

a. *Is it ethical to buy a sweater to use for a family picture and then return it for a refund?* In a word, no. It involves intentional misrepresentation and the garment is lessened in value and at risk of wear and damage. It is hard to justify this on any conventional ethical grounds.

b. *Is it ethical to download a song from the Internet without paying for it, given that (a) you would not have downloaded it if you had to pay, (b) you have no money and the artist and record label (or Apple) are beyond wealthy, and (c) you are actually promoting the artist by listening to and sharing your impressions with others.* Again, no, and all the other information is irrelevant in this context. You are in essence taking someone else's work and property for no return. From a utilitarian frame, if everyone did that over time there would be no record business. From a universalism frame, it is stealing. From a virtuous person framework, would you want someone taking your work for nothing?

c. *How much is a cat worth? Your affectionate and obedient cat needs a procedure that will cost a few hundred dollars. Your instinct is to pay for what she needs, but you can't help thinking it's wrong. Wouldn't the cash be better spent on sick humans?* If you pose the question that way—cat care or human care?—most people would say the answer is easy—although most cats would disagree. However, this amounts to a false equivalency. That is, the money you spend at the vet need not reduce what you would donate to help sick people. It could just as easily come from your vacation fund or your coffee money. It would be troubling if you ignored the needs of people around you in order to treat your cat, but not if you merely sacrificed a weekend in Vegas. In short, in so far as you are able, care for your cat and help your fellow humans.

d. *Can you ethically round off your 2.958 GPA to 3.0?* From a universalism frame, probably not—it is misrepresentation, albeit minor. However, given that it is well known that resumés are a personal commercial and the standard convention is to round up from .5 or higher, a virtuous person could sleep well with that adjustment.

e. *Is it OK to steal those hotel shampoos and soaps and give them to homeless shelters?* Here again, framed as "stealing" the shampoos and soaps, most people would say no. However, if you are just using those allocated to your own room, which you ostensibly paid for, then it sounds like a nobler alternative than just popping them in your own cosmetic bag or simply throwing them out.

f. *Should you tell on someone you observe researching bomb-making on the Internet? Or a friend having a too-friendly dinner with a woman who is not his wife.* As discussed in a following scenario in this chapter, when and how to "blow the whistle" is an extraordinarily delicate matter. Generally speaking, unless you have witnessed or suspect real physical damage (for example, child or spousal abuse) or have confirmed a regular pattern of harmful events, it is probably best to opt for the respect of privacy.

g. *Is it ethical to buy cheap seats to a baseball game you know will be sparsely attended and then sneak down and sit in the expensive seats? Similarly, is it ethical to grab open first-class seats (once everyone is on board and in their purchased seats) when you paid only for coach?* This is one that varies across ethical frames. Universalism would dictate that you may not opt for seats of a higher value than what you paid for—that is dishonest and deceives the provider. From a utilitarian framework, it would be problematic if everyone did that and would make for funny seating arrangements. However, provided that you take advantage of no services for which you did not pay (for example, complimentary soft drinks and so on) then it is possible for a virtuous person to frame the move in an ethical way. The seats were unused, no value was extracted, and the team gets fans closer to the action and more supportive. In some ways, it seems petty to deny folks that opportunity. Roughly the same calculus would apply to the first-class seats on an airplane.

h. *Is it ethical for a homeless mother to steal a loaf of bread to feed her starving child?* This is an example where moral imagination comes into play—there must be some way we can arrange it so the young woman does not have to "steal" food for her child. From a universalism framework, human harm trumps dishonesty, so the child's welfare could justify the act.

i. *If you scored the wrong answer on a test, and the instructor marked it correct, and you very honestly let him know, is it ethical for the instructor to let you keep the points and reward your honesty?* The ethical choice here is to lower the grade to what the student actually earned. Some teachers take the contrary position: Their error raised a student's hopes, so the extra points compensate him for his disappointment and reward him for his honesty. That would be fine if he were the only student in the class. However, this benefits one student at the expense of all the others. What's more, the class will resent not only the student who received an unearned credit but also the teacher who

(continued)

(continued)

granted it, undermining the sense of the classroom as a place where justice prevails. In addition, it teaches not the virtue of honesty but its utility: Speak up only when it's to your advantage.

Being a Responsible Whistle-Blower: Debrief

This is one of the most critically important Manage *What?* scenarios because one of the most difficult situations any employee will ever encounter is to see or suspect that colleagues have violated ethical standards. It is easy to find excuses to do nothing, but someone who witnesses misconduct (particularly that with potential for human harm) has an obligation to act. Unfortunately, too few of us actually do. A recent study found that while roughly half of corporate employees witness significant misconduct on the job, over 40 percent never act on their knowledge. The two barriers most frequently cited are the belief that bearing witness will not make a difference and the fear of retaliation.

So should a responsible person blow the whistle when he or she suspects misconduct? It depends on several factors and a would-be whistle-blower should be very thoughtful before proceeding. In the following, we briefly describe a set of considerations and guidelines related to both *whether* to report misconduct and *how* to go about it responsibly once you have deemed it necessary to do so.

1. *Only blow the whistle in good faith.* Good faith whistle-blowers are those who report in good conscience and are not doing it out of some sense of animosity or maliciousness or retaliation. So, first consider your own motives in coming forward with allegations of wrongdoing—if they are not solely related to the misconduct and its implications then stop right there.

2. *Consider alternative explanations (especially that you might be wrong).* All of the following guidelines are based on this one. That is, at every juncture consider seriously the fact that your perceptions of the situation may be mistaken. Actively seek and remain open to information that provides an alternative explanation to your own.

3. *Ask questions before making charges.* Before charging anyone with anything, it is good to pose your concerns as questions, allowing for the fact that you might have misunderstood or misinterpreted the situation. Some common mistakes are the failure to consult with loved ones affected by the decision or to carefully test the water for solidarity and support among peers. Whistle-blowers also often don't give their company a chance to do the right thing before breaking ranks, which can help the company sustain plausible deniability when the case goes to court.

4. *Determine what documentation supports your allegations.* Given the potentially serious personal consequences at risk, you desperately want to avoid a "he said, she said" type of scenario. So the more you can keep the focus on factual matters with documentation, the better off you will be. All too often the personality of the whistle-blower becomes the issue in these matters instead of the factual issues.

5. *Assess your goals.* What are you seeking from this situation? What would it take to make you feel comfortable that it has been adequately resolved? How will you know when you have achieved your goals. Long before you "go public" with allegations, it is critical to know what you personally seek from the situation (see guideline #1). These situations can escalate very quickly and being crystal clear on your own motives can help you navigate the best path.

6. *Seek advice and listen to it.* It is always good to talk confidentially with someone you trust and to help determine how and with whom to proceed. Do not go it alone and (regarding guideline #2 earlier) remain open to other opinions and issues you may have missed or misunderstood.

7. *Understand existing protocol in your organization.* Know before you take any public steps what procedures are typically followed in your firm for this type of charge. If it exists, get a copy of the relevant policies and be sure you know the answer to questions like: Are you required to submit something in writing? Who will be informed of the charges you make? Is confidentiality protected? Will you be kept informed of case progress? And so on. Know the answers to those questions before you ever start to blow the whistle.

It is worth noting that organizations can and do retaliate against whistle-blowers, and so the act should never be taken lightly. However, it is possible to be a responsible whistle-blower and still have a career, but it takes a combination of discipline, openness, good faith, and adherence to the guidelines proposed here.

CHAPTER
5

Communication

After reading this chapter, you should be able to:

"There is no greater differentiator among business people than
the ability to communicate. Most
everyone thinks he or she is a
good communicator, but precious
few really are. If you are truly serious about setting yourself apart,
devote yourself to improving your
ability to communicate, not just
in giving formal presentations but
in working face to face with your
boss, associates and customers."

**—Thomas Lillis, President,
Magellan Business Partners**

KO 5-1 Explain how the curse of knowledge creates a barrier to effective communication.

KO 5-2 Describe the fundamental elements of persuasion.

KO 5-3 Describe the key elements in making a communication "sticky."

KO 5-4 Articulate methods for overcoming common weaknesses in presentations.

KO 5-5 Explain the barriers to active listening.

KO 5-6 Describe the strategies for listening more effectively.

DO 5-1 Create a persuasive message that communicates personal credibility and evidence, while arousing people's emotions.

DO 5-2 Deliver a presentation that incorporates strategy, structure, support, style, and supplements.

DO 5-3 Choose the appropriate media for communication in various speaking circumstances.

DO 5-4 Communicate your wishes using empathy and unambiguous statements.

DO 5-5 Actively listen to gain shared understanding.

Case: Tableau

<< INTERACTIVE PICTURES, NOT WORDS, RULE THE COMMUNICATION WORLD TODAY

With the increased emphasis on data-driven solutions, and with no one having the time to produce time-intensive graphics, today's PowerPoint presentations struggle to engage audiences and communicate information in compelling or efficient ways. Fortunately, a new field known as data visualization is transforming how we see, work, and present data. Tableau Software is one leading data visualization example that has caught fire in leading consulting companies and progressive organizations worldwide.

The company has carved out a particular niche with media organizations, which use Tableau software to enable their readers to play with data in uniquely interactive ways. That is, Tableau does not just "show" the data but allows observers to personally interact with and manipulate the data in ways that enable them to learn what they desire. One impressive recent example is a data visualization on CNN Money, showing where mortgage foreclosures were happening in 2010. Users could drag their mouse over a certain part of the country to view just the data from that area. Further analysis is possible using drag-and-drop controls and the small menu at the bottom of the chart.

The fundamental idea is the customization of data presentations that help observers become more engaged with the information and dive deeper into data if they wish.

1. What makes certain data and information stick with you while most is either ignored or quickly forgotten?

2. What common communication failings does Tableau help overcome? Why do you think it has caught on so quickly and has such passionate users in today's corporate world?

3. Is using a tool like Tableau considerably harder or more complicated than just presenting raw data?

4. What concerns might you have about the effective use of Tableau?

1st Quarter 2010 Foreclosures

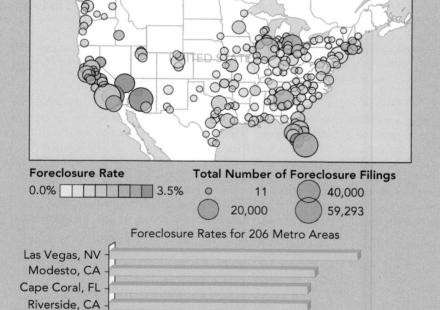

Foreclosure Rate
0.0% [   ] 3.5%

Total Number of Foreclosure Filings
○ 11   ⬤ 40,000
⬤ 20,000   ⬤ 59,293

Foreclosure Rates for 206 Metro Areas

Las Vegas, NV
Modesto, CA
Cape Coral, FL
Riverside, CA
Stockton, CA
Merced, CA
Phoenix, AZ
Vallejo, CA
Bakersfield, CA
Orlando, FL
Miami, FL

0%   1%   2%   3%   4%

Foreclosure Rate

Sources: Map data © OpenStreetMap contributors, CC-BY-SA. Graph data provided by Realty Trac.

157

1. Selling an Idea to Your Boss

You are the assistant manager of a restaurant and believe that the restaurant is long overdue to adopt a more proactive stance with electronic marketing, such as an informative web page, online ordering and reservations, and some limited marketing via Facebook and Groupon. Unfortunately, your boss is a traditionalist and, while progressive in many respects, is a bit "old school" and skeptical on the ultimate usefulness of e-marketing. He not only does not see the potential, but finds such new tools to be "faddish" and superficial. How would you go about selling your boss on your idea? What will it take to get your idea legitimately considered? What common traps just create greater resistance and should be avoided? What mistakes do young people often make in trying to "sell up" in this type of situation?

2. The Elevator Pitch: Making Your Case in a Very Short Time

You manage a team of writers for the local newspaper. Your staff is hard working and very willing to put in long hours to make deadlines, but they have to work with electronic equipment that is outdated and commonly crashes. While you recognize that other departments at the paper do similar work and have similar needs, you feel your team needs a little more than their standard allocation for upgrades in this year's budget. You mention this problem in a meeting with your boss, and she replies, "Well, your timing is perfect. I'm on my way to a budget meeting upstairs on the 18th floor. Why don't you take the elevator with me and give me what I need to present to the budget committee, and I'll see if I can convince them to increase your allocation."

What key strategies should you follow in creating and delivering your pitch? Are there any "must-dos" you should consider if you want to be persuasive? What common mistakes should you try to avoid?

3. Fixing a Typically Bad PowerPoint Presentation

You were asked by your boss to research and prepare a presentation on using social media for internal communications in your firm. You put together what you thought was a solid PowerPoint presentation of the existing data and the important issues for your firm. After a practice run for your boss and a couple of her colleagues, however, they spend 20 minutes giving you frank feedback which included comments like, "Nice slides but it was kind of long and boring," "It was a lot of good bullet points, but didn't have much punch," "It was often hard to see where you were going," and "Forget the jazzy PowerPoint features and just cut to the chase." One even said, "With all due respect, I felt like I was undergoing death by PowerPoint."

How would you proceed in trying to "fix" this presentation? Are there any guidelines you would follow to avoid the kind of comments you evoked in your practice run? Similarly, given that so many presentations end up just as yours has, what are some of the traps that seem to consistently make their way into such presentations, and probably did in yours?

4. Actively Listen to Understand a Problem

You work in the customer service department of a software manufacturer. You have already received a number of complaints regarding a product designed to help young people make their own home video productions. Now you are about to meet with a waiting customer who has had problems trying to use the product with his son. You are a bit annoyed in that you suspect that this guy either does not have the sufficient hardware capacity or is not using the product correctly, which is usually the case.

What traps or barriers could get in the way of really listening to this customer? What type of active listening would be warranted here—what strategies would you use? This could be a good chance to gather information that would be very useful to your marketing group. How do you make sure you engage this customer and truly listen and consider his perspective?

Introduction

It's probably trite, but we'll say it: Communication skills are central to success in every kind of organization. Not surprisingly, those who become successful managers are the people who can best transmit their views, ideas, and enthusiasm to others. This is because good communicators inspire confidence in others and are perceived as having more credible ideas than people with weaker communication skills, whether or not their ideas are actually better.[1] In contrast, more careers are derailed, and managers fired, because of poor communication skills than for lack of any other competency. Surveys of recruiters who hire college graduates repeatedly show that communication skills are the most recurring deficiency in such graduates.[2]

Communication affects almost every aspect of managerial behavior. To motivate, give feedback, work in teams, negotiate, and lead change all require effective communication skills. Research also shows a strong positive link between a leader's communication ability and worker innovativeness.[3] That is, the better a manager communicates with employees, the more likely those people are to come up with new and creative ideas to help the organization. In short, to be an effective manager, you must be an effective communicator.

Unfortunately, many barriers exist to developing superior communication skills. We frequently hear comments like, "It's all common sense; I know how to communicate well" or "Great communication can't be taught; you either have it or you don't," or "With technology today, it's not that important." The truth is that effective communication is hardly elementary or common (and the existence of so many ineffective and fearful communicators attests to that), there are specific and concrete principles and techniques that can certainly be learned and refined, and the importance of communication has never been higher.

So what is communication? Figure 5.1 presents a traditional model of the communication process. While straightforward in appearance, a model of the process is useful in that it highlights that communication success and failure is multidimensional (not just one event or element), and thus dependent on several links in a chain. For example, an intended communication from a source may not be what is ultimately heard by the receiver because of an ill-conceived message, faulty transmission, noise (distractions) in the system, or selective perception on the part of the receiver. The model can be a good starting point in designing a communication strategy or diagnosing the specific cause(s) of a communication breakdown.

Perhaps the most defining feature of communication is *sharing information with other people.* While many textbook discussions of communication focus exclusively on formal presentations and speeches, managers are far more commonly communicating in small meetings with teams or bosses or associates. So in this chapter the focus is not just how to give a good speech but rather the broader concept of sharing information with other people. How do you craft and deliver a persuasive message? What are the elements of a successful presentation? How can you more actively listen and overcome the traps and barriers that get in the way of understanding?

"At its heart, communication is speaking so other people will listen, and listening so other people will speak."

—Anonymous

Practice this!
Go to www.baldwin2e.com

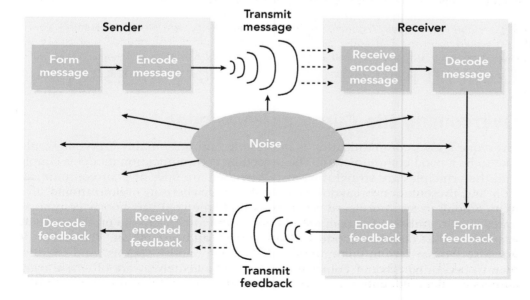

FIGURE 5.1
Model of the Communication Process

As with many management skills, communication is an area associated with a number of misperceptions or myths. We identify a few of the most common of those next.

?¿ MYTHS 5.1   Communication Myths

- **If you have a strong case, everyone will be convinced.** Many attorneys often wish this were true, but they quickly realize people are moved not just by evidence, but by *who* presents that evidence and *how* it is presented. Moreover, a single well-told story or anecdote can often be as effective as a pile of hard evidence.

- **If communicated enough times, your communications are effective.** Too many presentations are boring and miss their mark. Most messages are forgettable and do not stick with the listener. Many of us have a hard time staying focused and presenting the information our boss needs to make a good decision. Indeed, communication is consistently rated as among the biggest management weaknesses in organizations today.

- **Words mean what they mean.** I *love* French toast. I also *love* my spouse. Clearly, words carry different meanings. Ensuring mutual understanding is the primary challenge of communication. Words that mean one thing to you may mean something else to your listener.

- **PowerPoint presentations are always the best way to persuade.** Slides provide continuity and structure to a message, can be changed easily, and can reflect creativity. However, with the now widespread use of PowerPoint and similar software, too many slide shows become one-way information dumps, are scripted and inflexible, and do not connect with the audience's needs. Before choosing PowerPoint (or any other presentation program), be sure it is the best medium for accomplishing your objectives.

- **Being assertive means being a jerk.** Real **assertive communication** is not being hostile or aggressive. When you are assertive, you stand up for your (or someone else's) rights without hurting or diminishing anyone else.

- **Listening is a passive activity.** *Hearing* is a passive activity, but research shows we ultimately fail to listen to the majority of what we hear. Good listening is hard work and an *active*, not a passive, skill.

KO **5-1**

Creating Persuasive and Sticky Messages

KO **5-2**

Overcoming the Curse of Knowledge

KO **5-3**

DO **5-1**

Everyone knows communication is important, and presumably everyone would like to be a good communicator. The preceding communication model is simple and the principles are straightforward. Why then are tales of poor communication and presentation breakdowns virtually everywhere in organizational life? Who among us has not heard complaints that "the goal was poorly communicated," the members of a team are not communicating well, the professor knew his subject but could not communicate it well, and on and on. The reason is because the barriers to communication are many and insidious. And the first step to becoming a better communicator is to be acutely aware of where communication so often fails and to try to avoid such failure in your own contexts.

Imagine that you are telling your boss about a new iPhone app, who you follow on Twitter, and your hope that you will soon surpass 500 Facebook friends. Or perhaps you are an American working in Bangalore and are complaining to your Indian boss about the wisdom of a recent baseball trade. You swing your hands wildly and get quite animated while your boss patiently listens and nods. Later, you overhear him telling another associate that he often has no idea what you are talking about and that you don't seem very smart. You may shake your head, laugh at him, or even consider him to be unbelievably ignorant. From a communication standpoint, however, the real problem is *you*. That is, you just got cursed by your own knowledge.

Similarly, have you ever been in a presentation where the speaker was obviously an expert but she just couldn't convey her ideas to the audience—leaving them confused and uninspired? She too was cursed by her own knowledge. Supremely gifted golfers, baseball hitters, and dancers often make ineffective *coaches*—because their own knowledge and skill makes it so difficult for them to take the perspective of a beginner, leading to frustration on the part of the expert and the beginner alike.

The curse of knowledge is the tendency for an informed knowledgeable person to not be able to communicate that knowledge to others. Put another way, when we know something well it is easy to forget how it feels to *not* know it. Research has shown that we generally overestimate the overlap between our own knowledge base and that of others.[4] A whole host of communication breakdowns stem from the curse of knowledge and it is difficult to avoid. After all, you cannot simply unlearn what you already know. Our knowledge has "cursed" us and it becomes difficult for us to readily re-create our listeners' state of mind. Management Live 5.1 is a powerful illustration of the curse of knowledge and that phenomenon occurs every day across organizations. The tune playing in the message sender's head is one that the recipient simply cannot hear. Fortunately, there are two proven strategies for beating the curse: (1) analyze and know your audience, and (2) transform your messages so they embody the critical elements of persuasion and "stickiness."

Practice this!
Go to www.baldwin2e.com

⇄ MANAGEMENT LIVE 5.1

Tappers and Listeners—The Curse of Knowledge

Stanford University researcher Elizabeth Newton conducted an experiment in which she assigned people to one of two roles: "tappers" or "listeners."[5] Tappers received a list of 25 well-known songs (for example, "Happy Birthday" and "The Star-Spangled Banner"). Each tapper was asked to pick a song and tap out the rhythm by knocking on a table. The listener's job was to guess the song, based on the rhythm being tapped. It turned out that the listener's job was quite difficult. Over the course of Newton's experiment, 120 songs were tapped out. Listeners guessed only *3 out of 120* songs correctly (or 2.5 percent).

What was even more interesting, however, was that before the listeners guessed the name of the song, Newton asked the tappers to *predict* the odds that the listeners *would* guess correctly. They predicted that the listeners would correctly guess 50 percent of the songs. In fact the tappers got their message across 1 time in 40, but they thought they would get their message across 1 time in 2. How can that possibly be? When a tapper taps, she is hearing the song in her head. Go ahead and try it for yourself—tap out "The Star-Spangled Banner." It's impossible to avoid hearing the tune in your head. Meanwhile, the listeners can't hear that tune—all they can hear is a bunch of disconnected taps, like a kind of bizarre Morse code. In the experiment, tappers were frustrated at how hard the listeners seemed to be working to pick up the tune. When a tapper tapped "The Star-Spangled Banner" and the listener enthusiastically guessed "Happy Birthday," the expressions of disbelief on the tapper's face were priceless. This is the curse of knowledge at work.

Audience Analysis

The first and most important rule of effective communication is to analyze your audience. In the discussions that follow regarding what persuades people to act, and what makes a message sticky, you will see time and again that it depends on your audience. And note that we use the term "audience" very broadly here to include, for example, an audience of *one*. So whether it is an auditorium full of people or a meeting with your boss, or a customer or peer, audience analysis is critical and always the first step to achieving successful communication outcomes.

So, what can you learn about the people with whom you will be communicating? What kinds of goals and objectives do they have? What will your audience care most about? The key to persuasion is to develop an argument that speaks to your listeners. They probably don't want to hear about *your* issues or frustrations or problems—remember, this is not to persuade *you*. Your audience will always be more persuaded by issues that directly affect *them*. So, regardless of the situation or limited time you may have to prepare, your first task is to analyze your audience. In formal presentation contexts, it can often be useful to do some audience analysis at the beginning of a presentation by directly asking your audience about their expectations and preferences. For face-to-face meetings, it is always wise to do a little research about the background and interests of your communication recipient. However you choose to conduct your analysis, the fundamental lesson is to align your appeals with the values and beliefs of your audience, to "hit them where they live."

Adam Hanft, a Manhattan-based consultant to small businesses, emphasizes the importance of audience analysis when helping his customers pitch new products. He says: "I once had a client who had spent many years—and many millions of dollars—creating a powerful database of historical financial data. It was a significant achievement, and the company, rightfully proud of having pulled it off, was eager to cast itself as the leading provider of historical data. I reminded the company of an important fact that had gotten lost in the process: Customers do not want data because they are historians. They use it to help predict what's going to happen next. Armed with that insight, the client switched from selling the past to offering the future. Guess which one commands a higher price?"[6]

The Fundamental Elements of Persuasion

As proof of how timeless some of the best practical ideas are, it was the Greek philosopher Aristotle who first articulated the three fundamental elements of persuasion as ethos, pathos, and logos. Unfortunately, although known for centuries, most of us are not nearly as intentional about trying to infuse those three elements into our messages as we should be. The goal of communication is to persuade your audience that your ideas are valid and to act in ways you desire. Whether you are giving direction to your employees, presenting an idea to a client, or creating new marketing copy for your website, ethos, pathos, and logos are the keys to communicating your message and persuading others to do what you want them to do. In the following, we expand on those elements and illustrate with strategies shown to enhance each of them.

Ethos: Building Personal Credibility

Ethos is an appeal to the authority and personal credibility of the speaker. We tend to believe people whom we respect and who we believe understand who we are and what we value. Ethos, then, requires affirmative answers from your audience to questions such as: Does this person really know what she is talking about? Why should I trust what he says? Who is this woman and what does she know about me? What background or experience or credentials does she have to make her believable?

Research has shown that ethos derives largely from your ability to establish a bond or relationship with your audience and how well you establish your credentials. You can enhance ethos by uncovering things you share with your audience and signaling that you are in many ways similar to them or that you at least intimately understand their interests, values, and context. Another way to enhance your ethos is by establishing your authority or expertise. Evidence shows that people believe, and are persuaded by, testimony from someone perceived to be an *expert*. People defer to others' expertise in matters where they either lack sufficient knowledge or background to make an informed decision, or when the issue is simply too complex for them to properly analyze.[7]

To capitalize on this, you might stylistically insert phrases into your message that use "I" or "we." For example, "as an avid video gamer myself" or "in my own experience as a single parent . . .," or "as expert snowboarders for the past decade, we see no reason why . . ." Note that no one will recognize you as an expert simply because you are the one chosen to speak on a particular topic, so you need to go the extra step to prove your knowledge and skills. You don't need to go overboard, toting around diplomas and other hyped credentials—in fact, usually the more subtle and indirect the better. Ideally, you can relate examples of your role in solving previous problems or explain research you have done that led to your conclusion. These personal disclosures should be made early in a presentation so your audience is primed to listen to your ultimate recommendations.[8]

Pathos: Arousing Others' Emotions

Pathos is an appeal to the audience's emotions. Persuasive appeals that tug at your heartstrings, make you laugh, or even scare you are using **pathos** to arouse your emotions. Pathos is often stimulated via a demonstration that something is unfair or unjust. It can be in the form of passionate delivery, a simple claim, or a story. It is important to note that direct appeals to the reader to feel an emotion (for example, "You should be crying now") are rarely effective. Instead, creating an emotion with words usually requires re-creating a scene or event that arouses

"What you do speaks so loudly that I cannot hear what you say."
—Ralph Waldo Emerson

the emotion. Thus, descriptions of painful or pleasant things often work best as natural "triggers" of emotions. For example, since we often feel anger at someone who, we believe, has received benefits without deserving them, a communicator who wants to make us angry will offer a case of someone rewarded unfairly. On the other hand, if we want to invoke pity, we might present an example of a small child who is somehow disadvantaged.

Consistent with our emphasis on audience analysis, pathos is accentuated when speakers use stories and examples that are highly relevant to their audience, appealing to identity and self-interest. This is why the recovering addict plays such an important role in 12-step programs and why stories of religious conversion are so powerful during worship. The audience in these cases is greatly interested in the story, because ultimately the story could be about them (or they can at least see parts of themselves in the story). We also naturally find more persuasive a communicator who flatters us (especially indirectly) instead of insulting us. If, for example, a writer wants a reader to evaluate something negatively, she or he may try to arouse the reader's anger. Or to produce action to benefit someone (for example, to persuade us to make a charitable donation), an arguer may work on our pity.

Logos: Appealing to Logic

"Men decide far more problems by hate, love, lust, rage, sorrow, joy, hope, fear, illusion, or some other inward emotion, than by reality, authority, any legal standard, judicial precedent, or statute."

—Cicero

Finally, a communicator can persuade by appealing to an audience's sense of logos. **Logos** comes from logical arguments, facts, figures, and evidence. Logos is what makes listeners feel like they are making an informed rational choice. As a speaker, you have two avenues to enhance logos. The first is to construct logically sound arguments in support of your position, and the second is to find evidence in support of those claims.

Logical Arguments.   In the most general sense, there are two types of arguments: **inductive** and **deductive**. Induction is moving from the specific to the general, while deduction begins with the general and ends with the specific. Arguments based on experience or observation are best expressed inductively, while arguments based on laws, rules, or widely accepted principles are best expressed deductively. Consider the following example:

> *JoEllen:* I tried a profit-sharing plan for my restaurant managers for two months last year and our restaurant had its best sales performance in both of those months. Paying for performance works!
>
> *Matthew:* That's reinforcement theory—people do what is rewarded. If you reward people for higher performance, you will generally get more of it.

JoEllen is using *inductive reasoning*, arguing from observation. Matthew is using *deductive reasoning*, arguing from the theory of reinforcement. Matthew's argument is clearly from the general (reinforcement theory) to the specific (the higher restaurant sales). JoEllen's argument may be less obviously from the specific (individual instances in which she has observed reinforcement work) to the general (her prediction that a specific action will result in a specific outcome in the future).

In most business and interpersonal relationships, inductive logic is used most often and is the more powerful form of persuasion. Politicians, for example, are quick to isolate individual people who have had some positive or negative experience with a policy as a means of advocating their own stance. That is an inductive approach (in other words, if this person had a good experience, you will; if this person is getting ripped off, so are you). In the classroom, many students prefer to learn inductively (via current cases and real-world examples) rather than deductively via general theories and models. In any case, it is important to recognize whether the form of an argument is inductive or deductive, because each requires different types of support. JoEllen's inductive argument demands support from compelling personal experiences or observations. Matthew's deductive argument should be supported by some accepted law or recognized theory.

Use of Evidence. Beyond the structure of your argument, logos is also enhanced via your effective use of facts and evidence. So a critical question to always ask yourself in building a persuasive case is "What is my evidence?" Evidence can take many forms, of course, but in most contexts at least one form of powerful evidence is financial or performance-oriented—what is commonly called the "business case" for an idea or action. That is, you need to be prepared to get beyond the "feel" or intuitive appeal of a recommendation and be able to argue how it can positively impact the "bottom line" of your audience. In business contexts, compelling evidence might relate to employee or customer attitudes, social responsibility measures, environmental impact or new growth or innovation. Once again, the most important considerations when using evidence are the validity of your data and its relevance to your specific audience.

Remember, although solid evidence is often critical to a persuasive presentation, you don't want to overwhelm your audience with evidence, and remember that logos is not the *only* component of a successful message. What an audience is looking for in a speaker is **prudence,** the practical wisdom to make the right choice at the right time. You show prudence by demonstrating your mastery over the subject matter, not by proving yourself to be the smartest or best-informed person in the room.[9]

A typically asked question concerns which approach is the *most* important among *ethos, pathos,* and *logos.* The answer is twofold: (1) as with almost every communication prescription, it depends on the audience—so analyze your audience and know the type of appeals likely to persuade them; and (2) since all three elements have persuasive potential, a good general presentation strategy is to aim to use *all three elements* as part of your message. Probably the biggest persuasive weakness of many communications is a disproportionate reliance on just one of the elements. For example, pathos can be particularly powerful if used well and delivered with passion but, especially in business contexts, most effective communications do not rely solely on pathos. Similarly, logos can be effective in many contexts but can easily overwhelm and confuse the recipient. So, while incorporating all three elements is not always possible, it is certainly a good starting point for planning persuasive appeals. Ethos, pathos, and logos are also a central part of the specific strategies for making your messages sticky—which we discuss next.

Making Messages Sticky: The SUCCES Model

One of the most exciting and useful contributions to persuasive communication in recent years has been the concept of "stickiness." The term "stickiness" was popularized by Malcolm Gladwell in his book *The Tipping Point*[10] and more fully developed and illustrated by Chip and Dan Heath in their book, *Made to Stick.*[11] The authors set out to better understand a question that lies at the heart of all effective communication: What makes an idea memorable or "sticky"? They conclude that there are six underlying principles of stickiness, represented by the acronym SUCCES. We describe and illustrate each of those principles next.

"When dealing with people, let us remember we are not dealing with creatures of logic. We are dealing with creatures of emotion, creatures bustling with prejudices and motivated by pride and vanity."

—Dale Carnegie

Simple—Find the Core of the Idea

A successful defense lawyer once noted, "If you argue 10 points to a jury, even if each is a really good point, when they get back to the jury room they won't remember *any*." So the first key of sticky messages is to find and express the essential core of our ideas. To strip an idea down to its core, you must be great at exclusion. That is, you will likely need to discard a lot of great insights in order to get the most important insight to really shine and stick. The hard part is weeding out ideas that may be really important but just aren't *the most important*.

The United States Army invokes this idea with what they call Commander's Intent. The idea is to force a commanding officer to always highlight, in advance of the mission, the single most important goal of an operation. The value of the Intent comes from its singularity. Even if everything breaks down and different tactics are required, the troops still always know their number-one priority. Note that finding the core is not the same as *dumbing down* or creating *sound bites*. Saying something short is not the mission. Rather, we want to present ideas that are both simple *and* profound. You can't have five primary advantages, you can't have five "most important goals," and you can't have five Commander's Intents. So always ask yourself, What is my core idea? Management Live 5.2 is a twist on this idea.

Unexpected—Grab Attention with Surprise

A second key element of stickiness is unexpectedness. How do you get an audience to pay attention to your idea and strike their interest? The most basic way is to be unpredictable and break a thinking pattern, or be boldly counterintuitive. Surprise is a proven way to increase alertness and sharpen focus—to grab people's attention. You simply do not want your listeners to be thinking, "I've heard all this before." Rather, you want them thinking, "Really? Wow! Now I'm not sure what to expect." So a key to being unexpected is to determine how to violate, not conform to, people's expectations. So figure out what in your

⇄ MANAGEMENT LIVE 5.2

Getting to the Core: A Six-Word-Long Story?

Legend has it that the famous American writer Ernest Hemingway was having lunch with several other famous writers, claiming he could write a *six-word-long* short story. The other writers dismissed his idea. Hemingway told them to ante up 10 dollars each. If he was wrong, he would match it. If he was right, he would keep the pot. He quickly wrote six words. The words were: "For Sale, Baby Shoes, Never Worn."

Hemingway won the bet: His short story was complete. It had a beginning, a middle, and an end! More than that, think about how much is conveyed in those words and how they prompt curiosity. Was a baby on the way at one point? Was that a life dream? Why sell now? And so on. The lesson is that it is possible to boil down a lot of information into a core—but it is neither easy nor intuitive. Indeed, the irony is that creating meaningful short messages is actually *harder* than crafting longer ones. In fact, a famous quote variously attributed to Mark Twain, Blaise Pascal, T. S. Eliot, and Henry Thoreau famously notes, "If I had more time, I would write you a *shorter* letter."

Building on the spirit of six-word brevity, *Smith Magazine* started a reader contest asking people to tell their own life story in six words.[12] The magazine was flooded with entries including one from a plumber: "Fix a toilet, get paid crap"; a dominatrix, "Woman Seeks Men—High Pain Threshold"; and celebrity chef Mario Batali "Brought it to a boil, often!" Comedian Stephen Colbert offered, "Well, I thought it was funny," and the creator of Wikipedia, Jimmy Wales, submitted: "Yes, you can edit this biography." Whether it is life stories or other persuasive messages, the search for a six-word synthesis can be both fun and useful. So whatever your message, try capturing it in six words. It will help you find the core.

message could be framed as a surprise, or at least counterintuitive, and insert that into your presentation.

Concrete—Illustrate Your Ideas in Ways That Are Tangible and Easy to Grasp

A third characteristic of sticky messages is concreteness. Concrete is memorable, while abstract is not. So look for common, simple, and well-known images and examples to make your points. Where possible, you want to explain your ideas in terms of human actions and sensory information that people can readily relate to and feel. This is one place where far too many business presentations go wrong. Abstract talk of mission statements, synergies, competencies, return on investment, and so on are often ambiguous to the point of being meaningless. In contrast, naturally sticky messages are full of concrete images that most anyone can see and feel—angry customers, a bonus check of $15,000, a surgery patient jogging out of the hospital—because we are wired to remember concrete images. Effective coaches use concrete rather than abstract images to convey what they want from their players (for example, "I want your belly button stuck to his belly button" rather than "We need to play tighter defense"). That is because concreteness also makes it easier for us to coordinate our activities with others, who may interpret abstraction in very different ways. So seek to illustrate your message with clear and concrete examples and images.

Credible—Ensure That People Believe You

The fourth element of stickiness deals with how you get people to see your message as believable. This principle should be familiar—it is further emphasis on the persuasive principle of ethos, discussed earlier. And while the familiar sources of ethos—expertise, honesty, and trustworthiness—are the core of credibility, three other strategies are proven sources of stickiness as well. We discuss each of those three next.

Vivid Details. First, the richer and more vivid you can make your illustrations, the stickier they will be. If you want to raise charitable contributions to a village devastated by a natural disaster, do not just cite general evidence of suffering. Rather, *detail* the deprivation and squalor—one young man is sleeping in feces, a young woman has not had clean water for four days, and so on. If you want to claim that customers really love your corporate brand, get beyond citing survey results and show a picture of a group of bare-chested guys with the company logo *tattooed* on their chests. Studies of jury decisions are particularly compelling in showing that jurors rate arguments illustrated with vivid details significantly more credible than their less detailed counterparts.[13]

Anti-authorities. While we intuitively associate credibility with demonstrated expertise and authority, sometimes it is anti-authorities, or at least people who are not authorities in any conventional sense, who make the most credible sources. For example, a smoker dying of lung cancer can make a powerful and credible voice for *not* smoking. Similarly, a cheater who got caught and dismissed from school can be a strong model for others to avoid that kind of temptation. A car company trying to sell you a car is *not* very credible—they have an obvious agenda. Conversely, your best friend who loves that car model is a *very* credible source. It is her honesty and trustworthiness—not her expert status—that gives her credibility. So be creative in searching for credible support of your messages and recognize that sometimes anti-authorities are even better than authorities.

Testable Credentials.   The idea of testable credentials can be simply translated as "Don't take my word for it; go see for *yourself*." Indeed, while external sources and expert validation have their place, it is personal validation that is often the most powerful source of credibility. Wendy's famous advertising slogan "Where's the Beef?" was an example of testable credentials. In effect, the restaurant chain was saying to customers, "Go get one of our competitor's hamburgers and see if it stacks up to ours." The idea of testable credentials is even what makes eBay work. Think of the feedback rating system for sellers. This is actually a testable credential that shows how that seller has behaved with other buyers. Management Live 5.3 is a particularly poignant and arresting example of how testable credentials can be so sticky.

Emotions—Make Them Care

Here again, we see another one of the principles of persuasion, pathos, as a key to stickiness as well. Put simply, we get people to care about our ideas by getting them to take off their analytical hats and to experience emotions related to our message. We show how our ideas are associated with things that people already care about. We appeal to their self-interest and current identities, but also to the people they would *like* to be.

⇄ MANAGEMENT LIVE 5.3

Risks in Promiscuous Sexual Activity: The Power of Testable Credentials

Each year the National Basketball Association (NBA) faces the challenge of educating incoming NBA rookie players about life in the big leagues—including how to deal with the media, maintain healthy nutritional habits, make sensible investments with their new riches, and the dangers of HIV/AIDS. NBA rookies are young men often under 21 and they are sudden celebrities, with all the adoration that goes with new fame. They have heard about HIV/AIDS their entire lives, so the risk is not that they are unaware of AIDS; the risk is the circumstances of their lives prompt them to drop their guard for a night. Until a few years ago, the NBA would use standard strategies to alert these young men: doctors relaying the effects of the virus; other players who had contracted HIV and would solemnly warn them; and so on. A few years ago, however, the NBA came up with a different approach—one that belongs in the stickiness hall of fame.

A few weeks before the NBA season began, all the rookie players were required to meet in Tarrytown, New York, for a mandatory orientation session. They were essentially locked in a hotel for six days with no phones or laptops, and attended classes on the topics just discussed (for example, media, nutrition, money). Despite the secrecy surrounding the orientation, a group of female fans staked out the location. On the first night of the orientation, they were hanging out in the hotel bar and restaurant, dressed to be noticed. The players were pleased with the attention. There was a lot of flirting and the players made plans to meet up with some of the women later in the orientation. The next morning, the rookies dutifully showed up for their class session. They were surprised to see the female fans in front of the room. The women re-introduced themselves, one by one. "Hi, I'm Sheila and I'm HIV positive." "Hi, I'm Donna and I'm HIV positive." Suddenly the talk about HIV clicked for the rookies. In the past, the NBA had put forth a doctor or veteran player as a credible source to persuade the rookies. But what is more likely to stick with you: hearing about others who got fooled, or being fooled *yourself*? The NBA was using the very sticky power of testable credentials. Search for ways to use that same tactic in your own messages.

Source: Condensed from Heath, C., and Heath, D. (2007). *Made to stick*, pp. 162–163. New York: Random House.

So place an emphasis on benefits and how people will feel if they buy into your message. Research shows that people are more likely to make a charitable gift to a single needy individual than to an entire impoverished region. We are wired to feel things for people, not for abstractions. Sometimes the hard part is finding the right emotion to harness. For instance, it's difficult to get teenagers to quit smoking by scaring them with the consequences of such a habit. It's easier to get them to quit by drawing on their resentment of big tobacco companies. In a related vein, some of the most successful charities now invite participation to honor those loved ones lost to a certain disease—rather than appealing directly to donors for help in preventive research.

In creating a sticky message, the key question is: Will what I am presenting strike an emotional chord? Will people smile, laugh, or become repulsed or frightened? If so, then you're on the right path to creating something that is emotional and ultimately sticky.

"One death is a tragedy; one million is a statistic."

—Joseph Stalin

Stories—Bring Ideas to Life by Showing Not Telling

The final principle of stickiness is to use a story (or stories) to bring your ideas to life. Storytelling is one of the oldest, most powerful modes of communication. Research has found that stories are more convincing to an audience than rational arguments, statistics, or facts.[14] Well-told stories can illustrate almost any business concept: customer service, culture, teamwork, decision making, and leadership are all readily conveyed through stories.

Stories make information more relevant and "richer" to the listener. Those on the receiving end can see themselves in the story and become emotionally charged by the narrative. When listeners begin to ask themselves, "Who do I know like that?" or "When did something like that happen to me?" or "I see how others I admire acted in that situation," then you have them hooked.

Well-crafted stories embody several of the other stickiness principles. That is, stories are almost always *concrete*. Most of them have *emotional* and *unexpected* elements. The hardest part of using stories effectively is making sure they're *simple*—that they reflect your core message. It's not enough to tell a great story; the story has to reflect your agenda. Indeed, while stories can clearly be a key element in making a message sticky, the reality is that they are often poorly crafted and thus fall short of reaching their stickiness potential. Table 5.1 is a summary of the characteristics of a good story.

Delivering Powerful Messages

KO **5-4**

DO **5-2**

The Basics of Effective Presentations

Effective communication depends on two factors: a persuasive and sticky message and a clear and powerful delivery of that message. The most compelling information in the world won't make it through to most of your audience unless you convey it in a compelling way. To grab—and keep—your audience's attention, it is critical to make a powerful connection at the outset. A simple, five-step process can guide you when preparing any persuasive presentation. For simplicity, they are known as the **Five S's,** and are shown in Figure 5.2. The S's are sequential, in that each step builds on the preceding one. The most important key to persuasive communication is good planning. So, as you will see in the following, the first three steps involve preparation, while the fourth and fifth focus on the actual presentation. We shall now discuss each of the steps in more detail.

Practice this!
Go to www.baldwin2e.com

TABLE 5.1   Characteristics of a Good Story[15]

At some level we all know that stories can be powerful communication tools. But we also know that not all stories, or storytellers, are effective. In the following, we highlight a select list of the keys to a good story. Consciously try to use those principles in crafting stories that will help your messages stick.

Good stories make the details count. The great Russian playwright Chekov once said that if there is a gun on the wall in the first act, it has to go off in the third act—why else put it there? In our lives, individual events or details might be random, but in a story, details are selected for a purpose. So include the kind of detail you need in order to tell the story you want to tell and the amount of detail you need—no more and no less.

Good stories are aimed at a particular audience. The teller shapes the tale—but so does the teller's sense of the listener. This is not to say you should tell true stories to some audiences and not to others. It is to say that the kind of story you tell, the degree of disclosure your story aims at, and the degree of detail you need depend on the particular audience you are trying to reach. Students do not tell the same story of their weekend to their parents that they tell to their roommates, though both stories can be true.

Good stories have structure. This is another way of saying that the story should either have a beginning, middle, and end, or else it should reveal a significant pattern. So begin at a point that serves as a beginning, an event that (in your mind) shapes the story to come. And find a place to end that offers at least a degree of clarification for what has preceded it.

Good stories express wishes and fears. Wishes and fears are the moving forces behind all stories: what the characters want and what they fear give the story its emotional power and drive it forward. And because every wish has a corresponding fear (I want to be successful—I fear failure; I want to be loved—I don't want to be alone), good stories acknowledge the force of both emotions.

Good stories establish common ground between teller and listener. Stories connect teller and listener by expressing wishes and fears that the teller and listener share. Sometimes they establish explicitly common ground (the listener is similar to the teller in specific ways) and sometimes they rely on a broader common ground (the teller has wishes and fears and so do the listeners). Establishing common ground is one of the central goals of storytelling.

Good stories "show" rather than "tell." It might at times be necessary for you to point out to your listener what your story is about. But if the listener doesn't get the point without your spelling it out, you haven't told the story well enough; you haven't really drawn on the power of stories. Stories move us more effectively than any other medium precisely by cutting underneath the rational level and working on the level of specifics; the details and events, as they connect and build, cut underneath our rational defenses. You can reject overt messages, but how do you argue with a true story?

Good stories include trouble or its possibility as well as (or instead of) successes. Stories are the central metaphor humans have devised to express the shape and meaning of our lives. Therefore, we expect stories to include trouble, sadness, and failure (or at least the fear of these things), because our lives inevitably include these complexities. If stories avoid complication, we don't believe them.

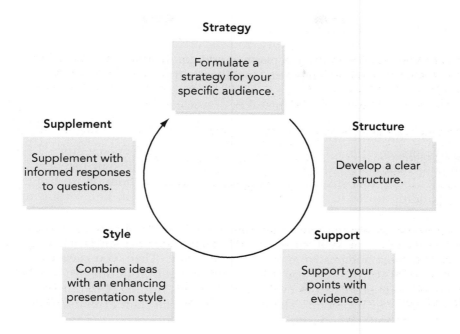

FIGURE 5.2
The Five S's of Delivering
Presentations

Strategy

Think about this scenario for a moment. You are in sales and you need to swap sales calls with someone because you have a bad history with a person who could be a potentially important client for your company. You have two other salespeople with whom you could swap clients: a co-worker whom you do not know very well, but who has a client that would fit your needs well, and your best friend at work who has an acceptable client to trade as well. What will you do?

If you are an effective persuader, you will not likely use the same approach for both sources. Instead, you may focus on the merits of your client and the good of the company when you develop your persuasive message for the co-worker you do not know well. On the other hand, you will likely draw on a more personal appeal when making the pitch to your best friend. You would choose different approaches and arguments because the audiences are different. Similarly, you might even use different language and presentation styles when you interact with your friend versus when you talk with the colleague you know less well.

Consistent with our prior discussion of audience analysis and the elements of persuasion, good planning for a presentation would include consideration of your goal for the presentation, who is your audience, and your general approach for persuading. Recalling our earlier discussions of Commander's Intent and audience analysis, this is where you determine your core idea and what would make your presentation a success in addition to figuring out your listeners' hot buttons.

Structure

Once you have decided on your core ideas and the key "hot buttons" of your audience, a second key element is determining the structure of your presentation. That is, how do you start? How do you sequence your ideas? How will you finish crisply and with a flourish? As noted earlier, research has shown audiences

"Don't take me through the pain of your journey."

—Steve Ballmer, CEO of Microsoft (referring to presentations that focus too much on what the presenters went through to arrive at their recommendations rather than quickly stating and defending those recommendations)

remember material better and respond to it more positively when it is arranged in a logical sequence or tells a story. You can create a story by organizing the elements of your presentation in a planned and compelling way. For a few illustrations of what to avoid when putting together your presentation, see Management Live 5.4.

One of the most common mistakes of novice presenters is to take too long to get to their main point or recommendations. Former McKinsey & Company consultant Barbara Minto has developed a winning strategy for beginning effective presentations in a manner that tells the audience a story.[16] She recommends beginning "with the end in mind" and easing your listeners into the message. Using this strategy, you state your recommendation up front, rather than building up to it. You begin with a statement you know your audience agrees with, such as, "We all know that our company needs to remain profitable." Second is a statement of complication: "However, our profits are higher at some times of the year and then bottom out at other times, making it hard for us to project budgets from quarter to quarter." Then, you state your recommendation: "I want to tell you about a diversification in our product line that can protect our profits from cyclical downturns. Adding X to our product line will alleviate our problem." The rest of the speech then explains why X (your recommendation) is going to resolve the problem you stated (and have other benefits, too!).

There are many ways speeches can be framed. Table 5.2 describes several of the most common strategies for organizing persuasive messages. The most important point is to not "wing it" but rather plan your presentation according to a structure you know can persuade.

MANAGEMENT LIVE 5.4

Presentation War Stories

Peter Shea, a controller for Imperial Chemical Industries, was summoned to his company's headquarters to give a five-minute presentation on his value to the company. He wanted the 18 senior managers to remember him, so he devised a metaphor comparing his factory to a race car, where his job was to keep it running fast. Bad idea. Turns out there were not any racing fans in the group and they just did not understand what he was talking about. The executives cut him off after a few minutes and asked him to leave the room. "I lost it," he cringed. "I wilted and died. Somehow I should have checked to see if it was the kind of audience that would get my analogy."

Dave Jensen of Search Masters International is an executive recruiter in the biotechnology industry. Wanting a memorable beginning for a presentation, he took a joke from a book of speaking tips. Bad idea. "It just died," he reported. "It wasn't very funny. And industrial microbiologists aren't a real loose and funny group to begin with. When you lose something in the first two minutes of a talk, you just can't get it back."

Darryl Gordon, from an advertising agency in La Jolla, California, was invited to demonstrate the power of digital technology to 60 ad agency presidents. He devised a creative computer-based presentation with colorful slides, bright graphics, and lots of sound. Bad idea. He flipped on the power button and nothing happened. It took 15 minutes to load the presentation onto another machine; the first one was ill-equipped to handle a presentation of this size. "Every second of that 15 minutes felt like a lifetime," he recalled. "I'll never forget it."[17]

So what can we learn from these blunders? First, know your audience, and consider their need for information first—and judge your creative ideas using those criteria. Second, unless you are absolutely certain a joke is funny to the type of people in your audience, it is not advisable to use it in your presentation. Third, know your available technology and plan accordingly.

TABLE 5.2 Organizing Strategies for Persuasive Messages

Strategy	Explanation
Chronological	Traces the order of events in a time sequence (such as past, present, future or first step, second step, third step).
Problem-Solution	Describes a problem, and then explains how your proposal solves that problem.
Causal	Develops ideas from cause to effect, or from effect to cause.
Familiarity-Acceptance	Begins with ideas the listener knows or believes, and moves on to new ideas, relating them to the "old" ones.
Inquiry Order	Develops the topic in steps, the same way you acquire information to solve a problem.
Question-Answer	Raises and answers a series of listeners' likely questions.
Elimination	Surveys all available solutions and systematically eliminates each possibility until one remains.

Support

No matter how credible you are, you need to provide some evidence other than your own opinion if you wish to change the "hearts and minds" of an audience. Based on research exploring the use of supporting materials or evidence in speeches, the following patterns emerge as general guidelines:

"Make sure you have finished speaking before your audience has finished listening."

—Dorothy Sarnoff

- If you have moderate credibility, evidence will probably increase your persuasive effectiveness. Speakers with low credibility are almost always seen as more credible when they cite evidence.
- Using evidence is usually better than not using it.
- Evidence can reinforce the long-term effectiveness of persuasion.
- Evidence produces more attitude change when the source and source's qualifications are provided.
- Using irrelevant evidence or poorly qualified sources may provide an effect opposite to what the speaker intends.

There are a wide variety of supporting materials you can use in a persuasive appeal. Some of the most common types are listed in Table 5.3.

TABLE 5.3 Types of Supporting Materials

Type	Explanation
Examples	Specific instances that illustrate the point or clarify the idea.
Statistics	Numbers that express relationships of magnitude, segments, or trends.
Testimony	The opinions or conclusions of others, particularly subject-matter experts.
Stories	Narratives that illustrate a key principle or point, or establish common ground with the audience.

Style

One important research finding is that when your audience has no prior knowledge of you or your reputation, they are likely to determine your credibility partly on the basis of the quality of your delivery. They will use cues such as how you are dressed, how confident you appear, or how professional your visual aids appear to be.[18] So, to be sure you have the maximum possible credibility, you need to make certain the quality of your presentation reflects your expertise.

Do not, however, assume there is a simple "formula" for effective delivery. Rather, the most effective presenters are those who use their natural gestures and style to their best advantage. Trying to mimic the delivery of others is self-defeating: Audiences will detect the unnaturalness of a borrowed technique and conclude you are not being sincere. Delivery is a highly personal matter and there is no one preferred form. Everyone should tailor their speech to their own personal strengths and weaknesses. There are, however, some aspects of delivery that are common to all good speakers.

Show Enthusiasm/Passion.   The most important style factor is to be interested and enthusiastic about your topic. Movement and gestures will come naturally if you genuinely believe what you are saying has value. And if *you* cannot get excited about what you have to say, why should anyone else?

Speak Clearly and Firmly and with Good Pacing.   The speaker's volume must be sufficient for everyone in the room to hear clearly. Nothing damages credibility like a soft-spoken voice, for two reasons: Pragmatically, if I can't hear you, how can I decide whether or not to support your arguments? Plus, speaking with appropriate volume shows confidence in your position. That confidence can—and will—translate into *ethos* for your argument. Moreover, one of the greatest errors made by speakers is speaking so fast that they lose the ability to enunciate properly. Varying the rate at which the words are spoken is an effective technique, but as a rule of thumb, slow is better than fast. Regulating the volume of one's voice is important. Do not speak using a monotone voice. Variations in volume can communicate a great deal of meaning. Think about what a whisper conveys. In contrast, think of a loud shout. Volume and rate of speech are the functional equivalents of italicized or bolded words in a written text.

Make Eye Contact, Smile, and Gesture.   This aspect of delivery is critically important although many speakers fail to make eye contact. In North America, not making eye contact is refusing to engage the audience. Other cultures have different attitudes about eye contact and one should be sensitive to these differences. Second, always stand up straight and smile before you say your first word. Even if your subject matter is serious, a smile will establish a rapport with your audience that can be built upon.

Finally, gestures are very important in maintaining attention but they must be used sparingly and judiciously or else they overwhelm the message's content. To begin with, you may have to force yourself to move and gesture to say it with style. Encourage the action until the style becomes natural and expressive, and you will become a more persuasive and effective speaker. Do be careful about making the same hand gestures over and over again because that can distract your audience.

Avoid Self-Defeating Statements.   Delivering persuasive presentations is tough enough without hurting your own cause through self-defeating behaviors. So avoid statements like *"I am really nervous," "I have a few typos on my slide; please forgive me," "I did not have time to cut this down so I am going to move quickly through a bunch of extra slides,"* or *"I am not sure how to use this* *fancy technology."* Although such comments may be sincerely felt and designed to evoke empathy, all they ultimately do is make you less credible in the eyes of your audience. In fact, rather than empathize, your audience will be inclined to think *"Why are you so nervous—don't you know your stuff?" "Why did you not take the time and preparation to have this better organized?" "Why don't you know how to use the technology?"* And so on.

Supplement

Finally, you will need to be prepared to handle questions after your presentation. Don't make the mistake of thinking your attempt at persuasion ends when your allotted time is done. How you handle the questions and concerns raised by your audience can make or break your persuasive appeal. This is a vulnerable moment, since you are outside the realm of your carefully planned presentation. Still, there are effective ways to prepare for and handle the question-and-answer (Q&A) component of a presentation.

Probably the best tip is to think in advance about the types of objections or questions that your audience might have and come prepared with supplemental slides, or at least have some answers in mind for such questions and issues. Ideally, you will have chosen your most compelling evidence for your actual presentation, but there is never enough time to do it all, so remember to focus on your core idea. It is often wise to hold back some statistics, testimony, or other forms of evidence you have, which can be used to drive home a point or answer a specific question. Having additional supplemental support available adds a strong touch of professionalism and has the added benefit of making you feel confident that you are fully prepared.

When answering questions, paraphrase them back to be sure you understand what the audience member wants to know. Not only does this give you time to think through your response, but it also helps to ensure that you really understand the listener's concerns and are prioritizing them appropriately. After you paraphrase, ask the listener if you have interpreted the question correctly. The added bonus to this technique is that, if you have it right, you have the listener agreeing with you from the start.

Finally, specify when you want the Q&A session. In your introduction, you should state that you'll entertain questions at any time, after each section of the talk, or at the end of the talk. Although taking questions during your presentation can make it longer (and possibly disturb your focus), doing so can also make your talk interactive and more engaging.[19]

> *"Effective management always means asking the right question."*
> —Robert Heller

> *"A recent survey stated that the average person's greatest fear is having to give a speech in public. Somehow this ranked even higher than death which was third on the list. So, you're telling me that at a funeral, most people would rather be the guy in the coffin than have to stand up and give a eulogy."*
> —Jerry Seinfeld

MANAGER'S TOOL KIT

Tool Kit 5.1   The Effective Presentation Checklist

There is a lot to know about persuasive communication and it can rightfully seem overwhelming to try to learn and incorporate it all. Moreover, it is normal to be very nervous prior to a presentation, and that can work against good communication as well. With that in mind, we present the following checklist designed to synthesize the most critical points to consider in preparing to deliver a persuasive presentation. It does not include everything that is important, of course, but if you work through the checklist, our experience is that you will be prepared and confident enough to do your best.

- Answer the question, "Who is this audience and why are they here?"
- Eliminate the extraneous—what is my *core* idea.

(continued)

- Craft your opening and ending.
- Get to your recommendations quickly.
- Intentionally include as many elements of persuasion and stickiness as you can.
- Rehearse, rehearse, rehearse.
- Familiarize yourself with any technology or logistics.
- Predict questions and supplement your materials with backup information to address such questions.
- When the time comes, be enthusiastic and go win the day.

Presenting Plans That Bosses (and Others) Can Approve Of

At many points in your working life, you will be required to present a proposal that someone else needs to approve. To be effective in this endeavor, you need to understand some basic principles about how these decisions are made, and tailor your presentation of a solution appropriately. When you present a proposal, four key components must be included.[20] The elements are usually most effective when presented in the order noted next.

1. *What is the plan?*

Begin with a positive, specific, and future-tense statement of strategy, followed by a list of concrete actions to support the strategy. Think in terms of a statement that the listener can either accept or reject (e.g., "The auto products division will acquire a chain of muffler repair shops").

Why begin with the recommendation? For two reasons. First, in this context, there is no need for a presentation of background or history. The people who are evaluating your proposal already know their history (they lived it) and their goals (they told them to you). They don't need to be reminded of these components. What they are primarily interested in is what you have to offer that is NEW. Second, you get listeners' attention more quickly and effectively when you give them something concrete to evaluate. Why have an audience that is bored with the first part of your presentation? Wow them at the beginning; buildups are unnecessary in business presentations.

2. *Why is the plan recommended?*

Make the plan's rationale clear, rather than forcing listeners to figure this out for themselves by wading through muddled details or unstated operational concerns. Provide synthesized information about markets, competition, costs, and other variables if it is appropriate. Your proposal will only be accepted if the listener remains confident that the opportunity is attractive and that there is a basis for obtaining competitive advantage. Consequently, you must make the rationale for your plan clear.

3. *What important goals will the plan help us achieve?*

The goals are what you expect to have happen if your plan is adopted. You should identify and defend specific goals that could be used to evaluate your plan and determine its ultimate success. While this may make you slightly uncomfortable, it will give your listeners better control over the implementation of your proposal, and make sure the audience's expectations of the project's outcomes are realistic.

4. *How much will the plan cost and what are the risks?*

As the fourth and final step, presenters need to identify the resources necessary to implement the plan. This may take the form of asking for resources for yourself or your work unit if you are presenting a plan to your boss. It is important to give the decision-makers a sense of "costs and benefits" in order to allow them to weigh the merits of your proposal against its potential costs. In other words, having established the plan, its rationale, and its potential benefits/goals, you have to "cut the deal." In order to receive sufficient funds and personnel to implement the project successfully, you have to be successful in this step.

Certainly there is room for variation in this presentation structure. However, a successful proposal will generally include all of these elements—carefully researched, creatively and intelligently presented, and, most important, tailored to the audience you need to persuade. Above all, and we cannot emphasize this enough, you should remain focused on your audience throughout the preparation of your proposal. This isn't about what entertains or sounds good to you, but what your audience cares about. Take to heart the ideas in this chapter about audience analysis and the fundamentals of persuasion and stickiness. Determine what is likely to be most important to this particular listener (or group of listeners) and then focus on that relentlessly.

Effective Use of PowerPoint and Visual Aids

Whether you are presenting an operations budget to the board of directors or doing a sales presentation for an important client, visual support of your message is often essential for success. Certainly some speakers can hold an audience's attention without visual aids, but they are exceptions to the rule. If the audience can't visually relate to what you're saying, they'll tend to shut you out. Visual aids also help your audience track where you are going and feel more comfortable that they understand. They know your presentation has a plan and that you are following it. Graphics also keep people more alert and focused by stimulating their senses.

More pragmatically, visual aids help your audience remember what you said. Of all the information we absorb in a day, less than 20 percent comes from hearing alone. The ability to retain your message has another benefit: Research has shown presentations that use visual aids are significantly more persuasive than those without them.[21] Visual support helps listeners understand abstract concepts, organize complex data, and see connections between topics. Effective visual support also increases audience retention of the material.

With current presentation software and technology, it is now possible to create presentations of far higher cosmetic quality and flashiness than ever before. Unfortunately, too many of today's presentations are famous for overwhelming audiences with boring and confusing material and making audience members want to run from the room. Although it is now popular to demonize PowerPoint for all the horrors perpetrated in its name (for example, "Death by PowerPoint"), we think it is important to clarify that PowerPoint, per se, is not the problem. That is, PowerPoint uses a medium that can be used *effectively*—with effective learning design principles—or *ineffectively*, with ineffective design methods. Either way, the key is the nature of the message and delivery, not the medium on which it is transmitted.

Many opinions and resources are available that delve into the specifics of how to make slides and design graphics—but those are beyond the scope of a management skills text. However, given the importance of visual communication and the time most managers spend either creating or consuming PowerPoint mediated messages, we felt it was important to highlight a few evidence-based principles regarding visual presentations in general. Although there is not yet a rich research literature on PowerPoint, there *is* an extensive literature on how to design effective visual messages. Among the most important lessons are to be clear on your message purpose and to create your visuals based on what is known about how people learn.

Know Your Goal

One of the biggest problems with many PowerPoint presentations is that they suffer from a lack of goal clarity. In this regard, it is worthwhile to distinguish between two possible goals in making a PowerPoint presentation—*information presentation*, in which the goal is simply to package and present information, and *cognitive guidance*, in which the goal is to guide the audience in their processing of presented information. When your goal is information presentation, Power-Point slides can rightly be filled with information that may be hard to quickly interpret or be processed by the audience—and that is okay. Many PowerPoint slide decks today are designed to serve as convenient mediums to package and disburse information. In such cases, you are simply providing information and documentation in PowerPoint form, and persuasion or action is not the priority.

Be Learner-Centered

Unfortunately, however, many of the misuses of PowerPoint occur when the slides are suited to present information when the desired goal is actually cognitive guidance. When the goal is cognitive guidance, you need to design your slides so they are consistent with how people learn. PowerPoint discussions tend to quickly focus on a distinction between a *technology-centered approach* and a *learner-centered approach*. In a technology-centered approach, the focus is on the capabilities of cutting-edge technology. Thus, we would be interested in the effects of the many features of PowerPoint.

In a learner-centered approach, however, the focus is on the way people learn and process information. Thus, we would be interested in finding ways to use the features of PowerPoint to support people's natural ways of learning. Evidence has shown the learner-centered approach to be far more effective in accomplishing presentation goals. Three important features of the human information processing system are particularly relevant for PowerPoint users: dual channels, limited capacity, and active processing. We discuss each of those next.

Dual Channels

First, people have separate information processing channels for visual material and verbal material. So does your presentation take advantage of the dual-channel structure of the human information processing system by presenting complementary material in words and pictures? It is probably a good idea to regularly stray from the PowerPoint default template that suggests "place title here; place bullets here," because that tends to force single-channel learning—when your goal is dual channel.

Presentations do not require a magic number of visual aids. Some talks benefit from extensive visual illustrations, while others may require very little. Let content be your guide. Ask yourself, "Is there something visual I could use to make my point, and in so doing take better advantage of the reality that people learn through dual channels?

Limited Capacity

Second, people can pay attention to only a few pieces of information in each channel at a time. Filling your slides with information will easily overload people's cognitive systems. A good rule of thumb is to put less—not more—on a slide to avoid cognitive overload. Thus, a bar graph should not be presented with three-dimensional bars and lots of cute, but irrelevant, clip art. Moreover, it is more effective to be conversational and *not* put text where you want attention on the graphic. Remember, your audience has a limited capacity. If you want them to read, put text. If you want them to focus on the graphic, leave the text off and simply highlight verbally (and maybe with a few arrows) what you want them to take from the graphic.

Active Processing

People understand presented material best when they attend to the relevant material, organize it into a coherent mental structure, and integrate it with their prior knowledge. So does your presentation promote active cognitive processing by guiding the processes of selecting, organizing, and integrating information? For example, this is where innovative new software programs like Tableau (see chapter-opening case) are so effective in that they allow the users to actively engage and interact with the data. Even in the absence of such innovative technology, there are things you can do to highlight the main ideas that the audience should attend to; an outline can help people organize the material, and concrete examples—perhaps as video clips—can help people relate abstract concepts to their own concrete experience. Most graphical displays are not obvious—even though those who created them may think they are. Does your presentation guide people through your message (with some checkpoints) in ways that prompt them to actively process and follow where you are going?

Choosing Your Communication Medium

DO **5-3**
DO **5-4**

There are many ways you could choose to communicate with someone. Research is clear, however, that some ways clearly are not as effective as others. So when should you rely on face-to-face communication, and when is an e-mail more effective? Will a phone call do, or should you arrange a personal meeting? You should consider two important variables when making such decisions: (1) the information richness of the available communication channels, and (2) the topic's complexity.

Information richness is the potential information-carrying capacity of a communication channel, and the extent to which it facilitates developing a common understanding between people.[22] Media high in information richness can translate more information. In this context, we define information in three ways:

1. **Feedback.** Some ways of communicating offer immediate feedback, while for other channels the rate and amount of available feedback are very low.

2. **Audio/visual.** With visual communication, you have the added benefit of being able to read someone's body language and nonverbal communication. With only audio interaction, you lose this ability.

3. **Personal/impersonal.** Some forms of communication help build relationships between people by encouraging and facilitating personal contact. Other modes are more formal, and the ability to develop relationships outside the topic at hand may be more easily lost.

"This 'telephone' has too many shortcomings to be seriously considered as a means of communication. The device is inherently of no value to us."

—Western Union Internal Memo, 1876

Naturally, face-to-face communication is highest in information richness. First, the participants get the benefit of both visual and audio stimuli. They can read facial expressions, body language, tone of voice, and other nonverbal clues as well as hear the words being spoken. Second, feedback in face-to-face conversations is immediate, both verbally and nonverbally. How many times have you changed tactics in a conversation simply because of the other person's changed facial expression, when she or he hasn't said a word? Face-to-face interaction allows you to clarify things you don't understand immediately and to provide additional support or insight if needed. Finally, conversations are the most intimate type of verbal communication available, and they facilitate relationship development. We learn about someone's sense of humor, interests, and values when we converse, and these allow us to develop trust. It is no mystery why the most important part of the whole eHarmony process (see Chapter 1 case) is the first in-person meeting.

While telephone conversations allow instant access to additional information, they are less information rich than face-to-face conversations. Some nonverbal clues can be gleaned from the tone of the other person's voice, but the person's facial expressions and body language are unclear. Though some information richness is lost, telephone communication has the benefit of being personal and provides the ability to access additional thoughts or information quickly.

Written communication addressed to a specific person is next on the continuum. There is, however, a large drop in information richness between a phone call and an e-mail or note. First, the feedback time is significantly longer with written communication. Since misconceptions often cannot be cleared up as they occur, additional communication is often necessary to clarify intentions and glean additional information. Nonverbal communication is also eliminated from the equation. Although some e-mail users are adept at using **emoticons,** or typewritten faces such as :-), these are not universally accepted. Still, because the message is being sent directly and clearly from one person to another, the communication does have a personal component and can help develop relationships. In fact, the number of people developing friendships online continues to grow.

> *"The real problem is not whether machines think, but whether men do."*
>
> —B. F. Skinner

Finally, formal written communication is essentially one-way. When a memo is sent to a large group of people, usually to outline a new policy or serve as a reminder, there is little opportunity to receive feedback. No audio cues are available, nor is it usually possible for someone to get additional information in a timely way. Because it is not personally addressed, no sense of relationship exists between sender and receiver. As we'll see next, this method of communication may be fine for routine information, but is inappropriate for more complex or personal topics. Table 5.4 provides a quick summary of the varying levels of information richness for different communication channels.

> *"A memorandum is written not to inform the reader but to protect the writer."*
>
> —Dean Acheson

The second aspect to consider when choosing a medium is the complexity of the topic you will be discussing. Low-complexity situations are routine matters where each party has its own ready access to information. On the other hand, high-complexity issues don't happen every day and usually involve several people to adequately address the problem or opportunity. Ideally, the problem's complexity should dictate which communication channel to use. More complex problems need channels that allow for high information richness so that ideas can be more readily exchanged. Routine problems can, on the other hand, be handled through communication channels low in information richness.

Research supports the idea that more complex problems need to be handled in face-to-face meetings. This may explain why, on average, senior level

TABLE 5.4   The Information Richness of Communication Channels[23]

Channel	Feedback Rate	Audio/Visual	Personal/Impersonal	Information Richness
Face-to-face communication	Immediate	Both	Personal	High
Telephone	Fast	Audio	Personal	Moderately high
Personally written missive (i.e., e-mail)	Moderate	No audio or visual	Can be both	Moderately low
Formal letter	Slow	No audio or visual	Impersonal	Low

⇄ MANAGEMENT LIVE 5.5

What Google Can Teach Us About Picking the Right Communication Channel

Note: The following is a blog post from Stew Friedman, Practice Professor at Wharton Business School of the University of Pennsylvania. He is reporting on a trip to Google corporate headquarters (The GooglePlex) for a speaking engagement. His experience is a wonderful example of how important it is to pick the right communication channel.

I had the pleasure of speaking in the Leading@Google series at the company's storied Mountain View campus. It is a remarkable place. Yes, the food is amazing, and it's everywhere (you are always within 100 feet of free, fantastic fare). Yes, the surfaces are ecologically sound and the use of energy is minimal. Yes, the organic culture is reflected in creative work settings and meeting locations, like the five-seated exercise cycle on which people ride and convene simultaneously.

Beautiful and informative electronic displays of information are ubiquitous. Everyone's on email, all the time. So, in this definitely 21st-century work environment, how do you grab employees' attention to entice them to attend a one-hour session with an author talking about his new book? This was the challenge for my hosts and, being creative Googlers, they found a way that cut against the grain, and it worked.

They created small posters on paper and taped them on the glass door entrances to virtually all of the buildings on campus. They used a bit of paper, it's true, because they knew that the medium had to be distinctive. And so it was. We had a great crowd. This was another great example of how Googlers are continually innovating with the use of media, even if it means going back to the future. This episode reinforced a few important lessons for how to choose your medium intelligently:

1. **Know how the people you're trying to reach use various forms of media.** If your kids are texting to converse, and you want to enter the conversation, why bother using email or a phone call?

2. **Experiment with the use of different media to see what works best when.** Is face-to-face as necessary as you think it is? Why not try reducing face-time with some key people in your life (your subordinates, for example) and increasing it with others who might need it more (like your clients and friends)?

3. **When you need to stand out and rise above the din, switch it up.** In today's world there's something special about receiving a personal note or letter, one that displays the distinctive hand of the author. When was the last time you wrote a personal letter?

Condensed from www.totalleadership.com.

executives spend significantly more time in meetings than do middle managers, since senior execs typically deal with the most complex organizational issues.

A couple of other aspects should be considered when choosing a communication channel. First, you should know how comfortable your intended recipient is with the channel you're planning to use. People who are very familiar with e-mail and have been using it for a long time perceive it as a richer communication channel than do those who lack this experience.[24]

Similarly, your relationship with the receiver influences the richness of the communication channel. When people have had significant interaction face to face, they are often able to overcome the limitations of less rich media. In one study, people who had a history of interaction actually did better on a complex decision-making project that they completed over e-mail than teams meeting face to face who had not met before.[25] Again, this makes the value of face-to-face meetings more clear: When people have a chance to get to know one another, they are able to use less rich communication channels more effectively. Tool Kit 5.2 summarizes which medium to choose depending on the situation and results you want.

"It has become appallingly obvious that our technology has exceeded our humanity."

—Albert Einstein

MANAGER'S TOOL KIT

Tool Kit 5.2   Choosing Your Medium: Written vs. Verbal

Put it in writing when . . .	Communicate verbally when . . .
A number of people must receive consistent instructions or information.	You want immediate and direct feedback and input.
You are concerned about legal, regulatory, or other documentation requirements.	You don't want or need a written record of the communication.
You want your position on something to be perceived as formal.	Delivering the message in person will enhance its sense of urgency.
Your recipient has a history of problems with verbal instructions.	Your message may spark an emotional reaction that you need to acknowledge.

About E-Mail

First, some legal issues. The e-mail you write on any computer owned by your employer can be monitored by your employer, and likely is. Most large companies have some sort of monitoring system in place. So, for personal issues, it is a good idea to use a personal (not work) e-mail account and not access that personal e-mail from work.

Second, the messages you send and some of those you receive are routinely saved and stored whenever your employer backs up data. These messages are official documents of the organization, just like memos and other written materials. For example, in the government's antitrust case against Microsoft, e-mail messages sent between the company's executives were subpoenaed and used against the company during the trial.

Third, some pragmatic advice: Even though e-mail communication has become less formal as the medium has become more common, electronic communication still takes place between people who are not physically near one another. Messages can be misinterpreted, jokes taken literally, and succinct and direct messages viewed as abrupt and rude. Before you dash off a quick e-mail, make sure it is complete, clear, and not easily misinterpreted. Above all, be sure it is professional. It's always better to err on the side of professionalism than on the side of casualness.

MANAGER'S TOOL KIT

Tool Kit 5.3   Making E-Mails Reader-Friendly

1. **Beware of confidential subjects.** You can never be sure where your messages will be forwarded, how long they will be kept, or by whom.
2. **Assume high standards.** Many readers are put off by bad writing in any form, including e-mail. Write as well as you can, whenever you can.

3. **Select your readers.** When messaging multiple people, be selective. Send copies only to those who absolutely need to see it.

4. **Don't assume what you see is what they get.** If your readers' systems are different from yours, your line lengths may spill over and cause an annoying text-wrap effect on their screens. To be safe, keep your line lengths to 55 or 60 characters, including spaces. Exaggerate any indentation you use to make sure it "catches" on your readers' screens.

5. **Avoid typing in all capitals.** It's easier to type, but IT SURE LOOKS LIKE SHOUTING, DOESN'T IT? Also, "all cap" writing slows reading by inhibiting recognition of acronyms, proper names, and sentence starts, which all depend on uppercase/lowercase contrasts.

6. **Use informative subject lines.** Readers may screen their e-mails by scanning subject lines, discarding messages that don't seem relevant or clear without reading them. To get your e-mails read, don't use subjects like "Management meeting" or "Project XYZ" if you can use "Request to reschedule meeting" or "How Project XYZ will save $500K this year."

7. **Keep it short.** Try to get your whole message on one screen.

8. **Use emphasis devices.** Even though some e-mail systems don't allow many word-processing options, you can still facilitate reading by using headings, white space, occasional all caps, indents, lists, simulated underlines, and other devices.

9. **Change the subject line of your reply.** Your reply is not the same message as the original e-mail you were sent, is it? So if you can, change the subject line. Reply to "Request to reschedule meeting" with "Meeting rescheduled to May 31," or reply to "How Project XYZ will save $500K this year" with "I'm sold; let's do Project XYZ."

Active Listening

KO **5-5**

KO **5-6**

DO **5-5**

The Paradox and Importance of Active Listening

The paradox is that, despite spending more waking hours listening than doing any other activity, we are typically not very good at it. Listening is a very different process from hearing. **Hearing** refers to the physical reality of receiving sounds; it is a passive act that happens even when we are asleep. **Listening,** on the other hand, is an active process that means a conscious effort to hear and understand. To listen, we must not only hear but also pay attention, understand, and assimilate. **Active listening** involves interaction and good questioning. Listening is a vital yet underestimated part of the communication process. Listening skills can greatly influence the quality of your friendships, the cohesion of your family relationships, and your success as a student and manager. Unfortunately, few people are naturally good listeners. Even at the level of simple information, many people do not listen well. Studies show 75 percent of oral communication is ignored or misunderstood and that very few of us are skilled at listening for the deepest meaning in what people say.[26]

Listening involves caring, hearing, interpreting, evaluating, and responding to oral messages to gain a shared understanding.[27] For managers, listening is how we learn what motivates our associates and what their values and expectations are. Even when managers cannot give employees what they want, employees feel better when they believe their point of view has been heard. Listening to employees is a way of showing support and acceptance, which makes for a more open work climate and higher satisfaction and productivity.[28]

Moreover, managers who listen to employees can learn new ways to approach company problems. Harvard professor Rosabeth Moss Kanter tells of a textile

"My friends listen to what I say, but my parents only hear me talk."

—A teenager's lament

company that for years had a high frequency of yarn breakage. Management considered the breakage an unavoidable business expense until a new manager, who listened to his employees, discovered a worker with an idea on how to modify the machines to greatly reduce the breakage. The new manager was shocked to learn that the man had wondered about the machine modification for *32 years*. "Why didn't you say something before?" the manager asked. The reply: "My supervisor wasn't interested, and I had no one else to tell it to."[29]

On a more personal note, listening is an essential skill for making and keeping good relationships. If you're a good listener, you'll notice others are drawn to you. Friends confide in you and your friendships deepen. Success comes easier because you hear and understand people. You know what they want and what hurts or irritates them, and you can act accordingly. People appreciate you and want you around.

Finally, the success of many leading companies in the Unites States has been attributed to the way in which they listen to their customers. These companies learn valuable information about their products and services, and get suggestions for future offerings. Listening to customers can also increase sales and customer satisfaction. Consider the following example from the training manager at Macy's department store in New York:

> One big difficulty with new, inexperienced sales clerks is that they don't listen. Here's what an inexperienced clerk often does: A customer steps to the counter and says, "I want that blouse on display there. I'd like size 14 with short sleeves." [The clerk] rushes away and brings back a blouse, size 14, but with long sleeves. The customer again explains, "Short sleeves." Back goes the clerk, and again the customer waits. In a store the size of ours, such incidents can run into money. There's useless work for the clerk, unnecessary handling of merchandise and, most important, possibly an irritated customer. That's why in our training we stress, "Listen before you act."[30]

Traps and Barriers to Active Listening

Active listening is a skill that is part what you do right and part what you avoid doing *wrong*. Most people have all the right stuff to listen well and are well intentioned, but have simply acquired bad habits. If you can overcome just some of these habits, you will be a long way toward being a more effective listener.

The Tendency to Evaluate

Humans have a natural urge to evaluate what other people say. If you express confidence that the Chicago Cubs will win baseball's World Series, I will likely respond by agreeing or disagreeing with you, basing my evaluation on my own frame of reference. This tendency to evaluate gets stronger as my emotional stake in the conversation rises. So, if I don't care much about the game of baseball, I may think something like, "Oh, she must be from Chicago." On the other hand, if I am an avid fan of Chicago's other baseball team, the White Sox, I will respond more viscerally— "Are you nuts?" Because I have such a strong emotional stake in my own position, I am less likely to listen to the content of your position. This impulse to use our own perspective to evaluate others' statements effectively blocks good listening.

The key to stopping our tendency to evaluate is to be aware of it. For communication to be most effective, we need to hear other people's statements *from their point of view*. Seeking understanding, rather than evaluating, can lead to fewer emotional and irrational conversations. The next time you find yourself in an argument with someone, try this rule: Before each person talks about her or his perspective, each has to accurately rephrase what the other person has just said, in a manner that shows she or he comprehends. This is communication, or coordination of meaning, at its finest.

"A good listener is not only popular everywhere, but after a while he gets to know something."

—Wilson Mizner

Practice this!
Go to www.baldwin2e.com

"Let go of your attachment to being right, and suddenly your mind is more open. You're able to benefit from the unique viewpoints of others, without being crippled by your own judgment."

—Ralph Marston

Misreading Nonverbal Cues

Nonverbal communication happens all around you. Sometimes it is conscious, as when one person smiles at another in a friendly greeting. Other times it is unconscious, as when someone absentmindedly drums his fingers on a desk. To accurately determine the meaning of a nonverbal message in a business or professional setting, you need to know the sender's personal frame of reference, her cultural background, and the specifics of the situation from her perspective.

Cultural differences can be a big source of misinterpretation (see Figure 5.3). Although research supports the idea that some facial expressions such as laughing, smiling, frowning, and crying are fairly universal,[31] the meaning of many nonverbal messages depends on the culture in which they occur. For example, in the United States embarrassment is normally shown by lowering the head or blushing; in Japan embarrassment is shown by laughter and giggling. Arabs often show embarrassment by sticking out their tongues slightly.[32]

Not surprisingly, many managers use only American norms when interpreting nonverbal communication. For example, in American culture, eye contact

"The most important thing in communication is to hear what isn't being said."

—Peter Drucker, Management Theorist and Presidential Medal of Freedom winner

A-OK Sign

In the United States, this is just a friendly sign for "All right!" or "Good going." In Australia and Islamic countries, it is equivalent to what generations of high school students know as "flipping the bird."

"Hook'em Horns" Sign

This sign encourages University of Texas athletes, and it's a good luck gesture in Brazil and Venezuela. In parts of Africa, it is a curse. In Italy, it is signaling to another that "your spouse is being unfaithful."

"V" for Victory Sign

In many parts of the world, this means "victory" or "peace." In England, if the palm and fingers face inward, it means "Up yours!" especially if executed with an upward jerk of the fingers.

Finger-Beckoning Sign

This sign means "come here" in the United States. In Malaysia, it is used only for calling animals. In Indonesia and Australia, it is used for beckoning "ladies of the night."

"Stop" Sign

In the United States, an upraised hand means "stop." In Singapore and Malaysia, however, it is used to get someone's attention or to ask for permission to speak.

"Good" Sign

In the United States, this means "good job" or "good going," but in most Islamic countries, most of Latin America, and Greece, this is a rude gesture.

FIGURE 5.3
Cultural Misunderstandings in Nonverbal Communication

performs several functions: It shows interest and attention in a speaker, signals someone's willingness to participate and be recognized, and controls the flow of conversation by signaling others that it's okay to talk. However, in some Latin and Asian cultures, eye contact with a superior indicates disrespect.[33]

Here again, awareness is the first step toward improving your ability to understand nonverbal communication. Do not rely solely on your personal lens to view nonverbal behaviors, but instead inquire about the situational and cultural norms that influence others. When you observe nonverbal behaviors, don't jump to conclusions or assume you know what a particular behavior means.

Personal Focus

Many of us either overtly or covertly like to hear ourselves talk and be a significant part of any conversation. This often leads us to focus on what *we* are going to say, rather than paying attention to what others are saying. Several studies have revealed this barrier is particularly common in that most people can remember nearly everything they said in a conversation, but hardly anything about what the other person said. A simple maxim is it is hard to listen to someone else when you are doing the talking.

Thinking Is Faster than Speaking

The human mind is capable of thinking from 400 to 600 words per minute, but the average conversation proceeds at only about 125 words per minute, sometimes slowing to 100 words per minute (particularly if the information is complex).[34] This discrepancy means that the listener has quite a bit of leisure time available while listening. Consequently, listeners often take "side trips" that reduce the amount of things they actually hear. One strategy to help with the thinking versus speaking rate disparity is to try to guess where the speaker is going—either confirming or disconfirming as he gets there. This at least keeps you focused on the conversation at hand and not daydreaming or having your thoughts wander to other concerns.

Selective Perception/Filtering

"No man ever listened himself out of a job."

—Calvin Coolidge

When you **filter,** you listen to some things and not to others. You pay attention only long enough to discern what you predetermined is of interest or what you need. Another way people filter is simply by avoiding hearing certain things—particularly anything threatening, negative, critical, or unpleasant. It's as if the words were never said; you have no memory of them.

One powerful and humorous study related to filtering and selective perception was conducted by Dan Simons of the University of Minnesota.[35] Participants were asked to watch a tape of a basketball game and count the number of passes made by the team in white uniforms. Roughly halfway through the video a man dressed in a gorilla suit runs out on the court, pounds his chest, and stalks off. Approximately one-half of those who watched the video in the study didn't even see the gorilla. Indeed, they expressed shock and surprise when the tape was rerun for them. Apparently, when we are paying very close attention to something in an active way, we can be completely blind to anything else, no matter how odd or exciting it may be. The key to listening is attention, and this study highlights just how dramatic our unintentional blindness can be.

Tendency to Advise

Many of us often substitute advice for listening. That is, we don't have to hear more than a few sentences before we begin searching for the right advice. However, while we are cooking up suggestions and convincing someone to "just try it," we may miss what's most important. That is, we often don't hear the feelings being expressed or recognize that the person may not have been looking for advice. Sometimes people just want to know they've been heard.

Principles of Effective Listening

Of course, just avoiding biases does not constitute truly great active listening. Great listening skill comes from wanting and intending to do so and a mastery of a short set of fundamental behaviors.

Know Your Objective

Not all listening contexts are similar, and thus it is important to first know what your objective is. In some cases, you are trying to empathize with someone; in others you are trying to analyze data or solve problems. How you listen should always be based on what you are trying to achieve. The three types of active listening and associated strategies are summarized in Table 5.5.

Actively Interact

Just being quiet while someone talks is not effective listening. Active listening requires a conscious effort to interact. Reporters often say their jobs require them to be experts for a day depending on their story—one day an expert on public schools and the next an expert in military policy. The truth is that the main expertise of great journalists is asking informed and insightful questions. It's the same for successful listeners. Like a reporter, you can learn to put people at ease and ask questions that engage them and prompt thoughtful responses.

"We have two ears and one mouth so that we can listen twice as much as we speak."

—Epictetus

When asking questions, it is useful to ask "how" and "why" questions that require a certain amount of elaboration, as opposed to questions that can be answered with a simple yes or no. It also can help if you share a little bit about yourself while asking questions. For example, "I have been having a hard time getting customers to buy the extended warranty product. How do you recommend I deal with it?"

TABLE 5.5   Types of Active Listening[36]

Type of Listening	How to Do It
Empathizing. Drawing out the speaker and getting information in a helpful, supportive way.	Empathize with the other person; try to understand not just what the speaker is saying, but the feelings behind the words. You can make the person feel comfortable by maintaining eye contact and minimizing the physical distance between you and the speaker. Pay close attention to what the person is saying, talk very little, and use encouraging nods and words to keep the person talking (such as "Go on" or "I see").
Analyzing. Seeking concrete information and trying to disentangle fact from emotion.	Use analytical questions to discover the reasons behind the speaker's statements, especially if you need to understand a sequence of facts or thoughts. Ask questions carefully, and use the person's responses to help you form your next set of questions. Once you are clear on a key point, write it down and then turn to the next one.
Synthesizing. Guiding the conversation toward a desired objective.	Solicit others' ideas so that you understand potential advantages and disadvantages to your proposal. Keep your mind open and your thoughts unselfish. Focus on the idea and the objective, rather than the personalities involved (including your own).

Other good interactive listening tips include:

- Paraphrase the talker's comments in your own words. This lets the person know you're really understanding what's being said.
- Frequently mirror back to the talker what he's said and your empathy for his position. Let the talker know you recognize his feelings.
- Make supportive comments. Well-placed phrases such as "That's interesting" or "Why do you think that?" not only show the talker that you're focused on the conversation, but encourage him to elaborate on the topics you find personally most interesting or helpful.[37]

Stay Focused

Focus is probably both the most important and most difficult of all listening skills. Listening well requires self-control to not allow your mind to drift into random thoughts. Consider the case of a college lecture. Most students accurately comprehend and retain only about half of what they hear in a 10-minute period.[38] Therefore, students who can stay mentally engaged and focused on

MANAGER'S TOOL KIT

Tool Kit 5.4   Tips for Good Listening

1. **Focus and commit to overcoming bad habits.** Awareness of your own listening deficits is the greatest contributor to improved listening. Some experts claim that 50 percent or more of an average adult's potential improvement in listening can come from realizing he or she has bad listening habits and is capable of listening more effectively.
2. **Look at the person talking.** Looking at the speaker affirms you are interested in what that person is saying. Other good nonverbal behaviors of listeners include unfolding your arms and turning toward the speaker.
3. **Control random thoughts.** Daydreaming and preoccupation with other matters often preclude people from hearing what is being said.
4. **Make supportive comments.** In informal conversations, well-placed exclamations or questions (such as "That's interesting!" or "Why do you think that?") not only show the speaker you're focused on the conversation, but encourage that person to elaborate on the topics you personally find most interesting or helpful.
5. **Find something to get interested in.** Make up your mind at the outset that you're going to find some nugget of valuable information or thought stimulator in what you're about to hear.
6. **Put yourself in the speaker's shoes.** There's nothing like a little empathy to enhance listening. It is often hard to really understand what someone is saying unless you try to see the world from his or her perspective.
7. **Sift and sort.** Mentally consider the words being presented to pull out ideas and feelings that are central to the message. Be sure you're following the main, central ideas rather than merely hearing every word. Don't get sidetracked on irrelevant material.
8. **Rephrase what you're hearing.** In large groups you can do this in your mind, but in conversations it can be very effective to verbally take "reality checks" every once in a while to be sure you're on the same page with the speaker.
9. **Conquer your fear of silence.** For many people, the urge to fill silence with talk is irresistible. Take time to think before answering questions, and make sure you're allowing the other person ample time to do the same.

> CASE CONCLUDED

Concerned that potential users might not be drawn to Tableau out of fear that it would be too complicated or laborious to use, Tableau set as their express goal that anyone who cares about data should be able to work with it. Tableau's primary advantages are (a) it is relatively simple to learn and use and requires no computer programming or sophisticated analytic understanding; (b) it is well suited for use with a full range of new media devices such as iPads and smartphones. According to Tableau's Ellie Fields, "Fast authoring has been a big driver of uptake" and mobile applications are a big opportunity for the firm as well. People are making decisions when out and about, not at their desks. "And when you think pretty data on the Web these days, the iPad is usually front of mind." Tableau is currently developing an iPad app that will allow for touchscreen scrolling through data, pinch down, and more.

Tableau now claims to have tens of thousands of published visualizations and is one of the most visible (pun intended) companies devoted to graphically analyzing and presenting the ever-increasing amount of data in our world.

Questions

1. What is Tableau doing that Excel or PowerPoint cannot?

2. What are the potential traps or limitations of this new technology?

3. How do other new software tools like Prezi and Spotfire compare with and/or complement tools like Tableau and PowerPoint?

4. Partnering with one or more fellow students, create a concept (and use Tableau if you have access) for a visual presentation that will bring a data set to life.

From How One Company Is Taming Big Data with Visualizations by Richard MacManus, **http://www.readwriteweb.com/archives/ taming_big_data_with_visualizations.php.**

listening to their instructors during class stand a much better chance of learning the material presented and accurately applying it in assignments and examinations. One way to increase your focus is to tell yourself at the beginning of a lecture that you're going to find some nugget of valuable information or thought stimulator in what you're about to hear. Think of it as a treasure hunt, a game, or challenge. That's much more fun than being bored, and a better route to good listening.

Concluding Note

In today's wired world, it is easy to be lulled into thinking that oral and written communication skills are no longer so important. Most people today communicate mainly through voicemail, e-mail, and texting and have many relationships with people they have never even laid eyes on. Virtual communication has transformed business, in many cases making it faster, easier, and cheaper to get things done. However, a shift to more virtual media not only does not supplant the need for communication skills but makes such skills even more critical and an even more distinctive personal competency that can set you apart from your peers.

To be effective in almost any job today, you have to communicate well. To be a great manager, you have to communicate *exceptionally* well. Whether it's selling an idea to your boss, making a quick pitch for support on a project or a new initiative, crafting a presentation for a customer, or just trying to listen to your people to fully understand their concerns, management demands communication skill. In short, to be an effective manager, you must be an effective communicator.

KEY TERMS

active listening 183
assertive communication 160
deductive 164
emoticons 180
ethos 162

filter 186
Five S's 169
hearing 183
inductive 164
information richness 179

listening 183
logos 164
pathos 163
prudence 165

< < CASE
Storytelling at Nike and FedEx

One of the most effective ways to arouse pathos in an audience is to tell a story they can relate to or learn from. Corporate executives at Nike and FedEx know this, and use storytelling to fully engage their workers in the company's culture. "Our stories are not about extraordinary business plans or financial manipulations," says Nelson Farris, Nike's director of corporate education and the company's chief storyteller. "They're about getting things done."

Like all great stories, those at Nike offer lessons from which people can learn. For example, employees hear how Bill Bowerman, cofounder of Nike, decided the running team he coached needed better running shoes. So he went out to his workshop and poured rubber into the family waffle iron, and Nike's famous "waffle soled shoe" was born. From this, listeners learn about Nike's support for innovation. Similarly, when they hear about Steve Prefontaine,

one of Bowerman's students who fought to make running a professional sport, they remember Nike's commitment to helping athletes. The company's success in each of these areas is testimony to the power these stories have in shaping employee behavior at Nike.

At FedEx, the stories generally relate to employees who did the extraordinary to meet the company's overnight delivery commitment. For example, one employee rented a helicopter to make a delivery. Another could not access a drop box, so he gathered a group of guys and lifted the entire box into his truck so the package could be extracted and the delivery made on time. Such stories arouse the positive emotions of people and

inspire others to emulate the same level of commitment.

Discussion Questions

1. When you hear the story about the FedEx employee who lifted an entire drop box in order to make an on-time delivery, what does it make you think about FedEx and why?

2. Why is it that good stories carry more "punch" in conveying messages over time?

3. Given that all stories are hardly created equal in their communication and persuasive power (meaning, there are a lot of bad and boring stories), what are some of the recurring elements that make for good and persuasive stories?

Sources: Randsell, E. (2000, January). The Nike story? Just tell it. *Fast Company*, 31, pp. 44–45. Basch, M. D. (2002). *Customer culture: How FedEx and other great companies put the customer first every day*. Upper Saddle River, NJ: Prentice Hall.

SELECT MANAGE *WHAT?* DEBRIEFS

Selling an Idea to Your Boss: Debrief

Naturally, you want to utilize the most persuasive tactics in *any* context, but the tough challenge posed here, and the inevitable resistance from the boss, serve to heighten the importance of having a framework you can turn to quickly and which will help you consider those elements that will matter most in achieving your objectives. Thoughtful and realistic audience analysis and the three elements of persuasion (logos, pathos, and ethos) are the essential tools here.

Always the first thing you need to do to prepare for your "pitch" is analyze your audience. What does your boss care most about? What do you know about his boss and reward structure, and what kinds of goals and objectives does he have? The key to success is to develop an argument that speaks to him—not just you or some notion of what is current or modern or right to do. He probably won't want to hear about your frustration or be moved by your youthful passion alone, but rather will more likely be persuaded by higher customer service or lower costs or enhanced efficiency that comes with these new innovations. In short: How can making these changes make his job easier/better and make him look good as a manager? Moreover, how can you take out some of the threat and fear he may have regarding not being knowledgeable about these new innovations and thus perhaps incapable of getting the most from them or even explaining the expenditures to his boss? The answers to this question become the arguments you present.

As with any time you are trying to persuade, your goal is to try to include at least something that would evoke all three elements of persuasion: logos, pathos, and ethos. The logos could be cost data and some benchmarked projections regarding sales and revenue gains from the new innovations. The pathos could be some critical event at the restaurant (customers lost, spiked costs of advertising, key executive shocked that the restaurant was not already doing some of this stuff, or a recent commercial showing more senior people embracing social media, and so on) that is designed to hit your boss's *emotions* not just his rational and cognitive side (for example, get at the heart—not just the head). The ethos might stem from your own personal experience with the new innovations and perhaps some testimony from others you know regarding the potential. You might also refer to some knowledge or experience you have about the competitive advantage other competing restaurants enjoy that use such tools (remember, you are trying to persuade, so look for every weapon of influence you can find).

You'll also need evidence to support your claims; examples and statistics are likely your easiest source of material in this short time frame. Finally, it will be a good idea to bring along some supporting materials so you have ready access to the information you need to supplement your presentation in the question and answer session.

The two biggest traps here are (a) trying to persuade on the basis of *your* view, perspective, and passion and neglect to fully understand and prioritize your *boss's* perspective (this is akin to the best sales training where you are trained to first understand your client's problem and then aim to solve that problem rather than walk in and try to sell him what you have); and (b) limited tactic persuasion—that is, using only one of the persuasion strategies rather than all three. For example, a single logos strategy here would be to focus only on evidence of social media and e-commerce growth. That might work, of course, but a far better strategy is to also try and hit the heart (pathos) and drive home your personal credibility (ethos).

The importance of managing "up" is sometimes not fully understood by young managers, and yet is critical to effectiveness. This is another case where you have no authority and thus cannot rely on organizational hierarchy or your control of rewards/sanctions to gain you any influence. In fact, any attempts to try to pressure or threaten would be ill-advised and likely career threatening. And once you have presented your recommendation, ask for input. Organizations desperately need people capable of managing up; thus you want to learn what went well, and what did not, and use the opportunity to refine your approach for your next episode.

The Elevator Pitch—Making Your Case in a Very Short Time: Debrief

Here again, you always want to utilize the most persuasive tactics in *any* presentation, but a last-minute scenario and a very short presentation serve to heighten the importance of having a framework you can turn to quickly and that will help you consider those elements that matter most in achieving your objectives. Always the first

(continued)

(continued)

thing you need to do to prepare for your "pitch" is analyze your audience. What does the budget committee care about? What do you know about the people on it, and what kinds of goals and objectives do they have? The key to success is to develop an argument that speaks to your listeners. They probably don't want to hear about your team's frustration with equipment failures. Instead, they will more likely be persuaded by missed deadlines or lower costs or enhanced efficiency that comes with new equipment. In short: How can making this expenditure in the short run make them money in the long run? The answers to this question become the arguments you present.

Then develop a coherent structure for your presentation. One of the simplest, yet most effective, is the problem/solution approach. Here, you would describe the problem in the terms you know will resonate with the budget committee (stories pertaining to missed deliveries, lost revenue, inefficiency, and so on). Then present as coherent and complete a solution as you can. Be specific about the resources you need and how they will solve the problem. You'll also need evidence to support your claims; examples and statistics are likely your easiest source of material in this short time frame.

Next, when crafting your introduction, remember the McKinsey model based on Barbara Minto's work. Begin with a statement about the situation that you know the group agrees with, such as "Budgeting money in the most efficient way possible is important to this company's profitability." Next, discuss the complication, such as "I know the easiest way to allocate funds is on the basis of 'fairness,' but this year that allocation pattern isn't the most efficient choice." Now, your recommendation: "I believe the most efficient and effective use of our limited funds would be to invest in updated equipment for my group." The remainder of your speech is the list of reasons why this will be an effective use of funds.

As you make your pitch, make sure your style is appropriate for this audience. Even if the meeting appears to be informal, it is best to err on the side of formality and professionalism. Finally, it will be a good idea to bring along some supporting materials so you have ready access to the information you need to supplement your presentation in the question-and-answer session.

The big mistakes you should avoid include (a) listing problems first and then your recommendation at the end—you lose your listeners' interest that way; (b) simply listing reasons for your request with no structure or support to your presentation; and (c) looking for sympathy from your audience for your plight. The budget committee might feel badly for you, but they must make decisions based on sound business rationale.

Actively Listening to Understand a Problem: Debrief

The first thing to do in this situation is to get yourself in an active listening *mindset*—sort of like a pre-game pep talk. Particularly in this case, when you are convinced (and maybe right) that you already know the problem and solution, those preconceptions can prevent you from being a good listener. Stress and high emotions have similar detrimental effects on good listening, so getting in the right mindset is even more difficult but crucial in those situations as well.

Active listening is one of those managerial skills that is largely about what *not* to do, so remind yourself of some common bad listening habits you are trying to avoid: premature evaluation and advice; selectively perceiving what is said; and talking too much yourself. Your objective here should be both analyzing (that is, what the problem is and how to fix it) and empathizing (drawing out information in a way that conveys caring and support). So make up your mind that you are going to understand this customer's perspective by the end of the meeting (one useful strategy for focus is to tell yourself that, no matter what, you are going to extract *at least one* new nugget or something you did not know) and consciously tell yourself that your objective is to make him feel heard and respected and to resolve his difficulty with the product—not to be the "expert" or "teacher" here.

More specifically, it might be a good idea to ask the customer to take you through a chronological history of trying to use the product and when it failed. Definitely take notes, but rather than writing down everything you hear, be attentive to nonverbals and aim to focus on his "hot" issues. Mentally sort what is being presented and be sure you're focusing on the main concerns, rather than getting sidetracked with details. Remember the "active" in active listening and be on the ready to inject questions, both to clarify and to give the customer a chance to elaborate and expand on *feelings* as well as technical product issues. So in addition to queries like "What did the screen say?" and "Could you access the setup menu?" it can also be useful to ask "Was that frustrating?" and "What did you do then?" Empathic statements like "I know, that happens to most new users" or "I struggle with that on my own computer" are likely to help the customer feel comfortable and heard.

Perhaps most importantly, to be sure you understand the customer, restate his conversation in your own words, and ask for confirmation that what you heard is correct. That way, you can pinpoint where you have congruence and where you need to probe further to ensure you comprehend and share understanding. Beyond resolving this one issue and keeping this single customer satisfied, information gleaned from this type of meeting could be very useful to your marketing group in selling the advantages, and addressing the most common complaints, typically associated with the product.

CHAPTER 6

Motivating Others

O B J E C T I V E S

KNOWING   DOING

After reading this chapter, you should be able to:

"The one factor that distinguishes a high-performing individual is motivation. Those with high motivation consistently excel and outperform. I will always take a modestly talented person with a driving motivation to succeed over a brilliant person with little hunger in his eye."

—Bill Carpenter, Vice President of Human Resources and Safety, Diamond Chain, Inc.

KO 6-1   Explain the expectancy theory of motivation and its components.

KO 6-2   Articulate the benefits of rewards beyond money.

KO 6-3   Describe five forms of job characteristics.

KO 6-4   Explain how improving job characteristics increases work motivation.

KO 6-5   Explain the conditions under which goal setting is most effective.

KO 6-6   Explain different behavioral strategies available to a manager applying reinforcement theory.

DO 6-1   Diagnose motivational problems.

DO 6-2   Design motivating work by applying the job characteristics model.

DO 6-3   Create a motivational work environment using goal setting and reinforcement theory.

DO 6-4   Use rewards effectively to improve motivation.

< < MOTIVATING ORDINARY PEOPLE TO BEHAVE IN EXTRAORDINARY WAYS

There is a great line from a *Dilbert* cartoon suggesting that you do not need a motivation program to get people to eat a chocolate chip cookie—and Dilbert is right. That is, there is no great magic in motivating highly paid people to do what they love, or to get great athletes to play hard in the championship game. The real test of motivation is getting ordinary people to provide extraordinary performance, and in the absence of any great pay or job excitement. Examples of exactly that phenomenon occur daily at Ritz-Carlton hotels.

Known worldwide for consistently delivering an excellent hotel experience, Ritz-Carlton managers have the difficult challenge of motivating their staff—ordinary people paid a relatively modest wage—to consistently deliver extraordinary levels of customer service. Among the strategies they employ are the following.

Sharing "wow stories." Every day, employees of every department in every Ritz-Carlton hotel around the world gather for a 15-minute staff meeting where they share "wow stories." These are true stories of employee heroics that go above and beyond conventional customer service expectations. In one, a hotel chef in Bali found special eggs and milk for a guest with food allergies in a small grocery store in another country and had them flown to the hotel. In another, a hotel's laundry service failed to remove a stain on a guest's suit before the guest left. The hotel manager flew to the guest's house and personally delivered a reimbursement check for the cost of the suit. Telling stories in these pep talks accomplishes two goals. First, it reinforces the high standards of customer service the hotel strives to provide its guests. But most importantly, it gives employees instant "local fame." Employees want to be recognized in front of their peers, and giving them public recognition is a powerful motivator.

Demonstrating passion. Moods are contagious. Managers who walk around with smiles on their faces and who demonstrate passion for their jobs have an uplifting effect on others. Enthusiasm starts at the top. For example, at a recent staff meeting the supervisor was dressed impeccably in a blue suit, white shirt, purple tie, and shined black shoes. His wardrobe communicated respect for his job and his staff. "Good morning, everyone," he said enthusiastically. The housekeepers returned an energetic greeting. This manager was all smiles and showed respect for his team. He said they returned his commitment through their hard work.

1. Why do employees at Ritz-Carlton, who are not paid significantly more than people at other retail establishments, work so hard to provide remarkable customer service?

2. As a manager, what lessons can you draw from the Ritz-Carlton example regarding how to get people to go the extra mile?

3. Are those that go the extra mile generally paid the highest, and do such firms have the highest labor costs? If it is not just about the money, what is also at stake?

1. Taking Over as Manager: Building a More Motivational Workplace

You have worked as a sales representative for the last three years, and your boss has just quit. You have been asked to take over as manager of your region, and you are going to accept for two reasons. First, you would like to move up and try something different and more challenging. Second, you have been very disappointed with the way your prior manager ran your sales group. He was not a good people manager and he did very little to motivate the sales representatives. More specifically, he let the low performers slide by, while the top performers (which you feel you are) did not seem to be recognized for their contributions. The situation was not horrible; he was not abusive or hostile in any way. But you know the group has some talented people and could do much better—if only they had a motivational spark.

So how would you proceed in this situation? Where would you start? What types of things would you do to enhance motivation? What would be the biggest obstacles to getting this group energized? Would there be any predictable traps to avoid?

2. Dealing with the Unmotivated Person

As a new employee in the accounting department, you are surprised at how few people seem willing to do more than their most basic job duties. To you, it appears ridiculous; you know all of your co-workers have college degrees and several are CPAs. Clearly, they are well paid and have excellent working conditions. When you ask a more senior employee about his apparent lack of motivation, he answers, "Well, the only reward around here for working hard is more work, so if you're smart, you are better off just doing what you are told and flying under the boss's radar. Moreover, all management tries to do is keep us from socializing and being together. I guess they feel like we cannot be trusted to give the company a fair day's work. Just try to have a game of cards at lunch with some buddies and see what management does." How would you diagnose this lack of motivation: Is it the people or the situation? What might be done to increase motivation in this situation?

3. Motivating in an Economic Downturn

You are a successful manager in a leading commercial bank and are attending a meeting with the CEO of your firm. Early in the discussion, he says, "Nobody questions that employees will be happy and motivated in times of prosperity. Employees will freely give their all when they are well treated, appreciated, and compensated with full salaries and nice bonuses. The challenge for us is that we are now under extreme pressure to justify every cost. Although we are still profitable, salaries and bonuses are frozen and there is no way that we can continue to spend as much on our HR programs and benefits."

He then looks at you and asks directly, "So given that we hope to keep morale and motivation high, what do you recommend? Is there anything we can do to enhance motivation and engagement without spending the money we traditionally have?"

4. Motivating People in a Foreign Country

From the day you joined the firm, you have actively sought an international position. Last week you were finally assigned to be an assistant plant manager in an appliance assembly plant in Guangzhou, China. Upon learning that you got the job, your new boss has already sent you an ominous welcoming e-mail that concluded with: "I was great in the states where I knew what people want. In this place I feel like a fish out of water and have no idea what to do. Our productivity and quality is way off the last few months and if I do not get these folks motivated I will probably be out of a job. Can't wait for you to arrive. Happy travels."

How would you proceed? What would you recommend for building motivation in this foreign land and why?

5. Enriching the Boring Job

You share an office suite with four others. The five of you are blessed to work with a secretary who is exceptional at what she does. She handles all clerical requests in the office in a timely manner and with a high level of quality and presents a professional image to all who visit or call in to the office. The only problem is she has just come to you and said her job is boring. As she accurately points out, she is relatively isolated in her work and does the same tasks repeatedly. In addition, she rarely knows whether she is doing a really good job or how she can improve.

What makes a job enriched? What general strategies might make this job more interesting and fulfilling? Are there relatively simple things you could do that might help? What personal and organizational factors need to be considered in deciding whether to significantly change a job description and expectations? What is likely to happen if you do nothing?

Introduction

Not many people would argue with the statement that "motivated people are central to the success of any business." It is reassuring to know, however, that we do not need to rely on "folksy wisdom" or generally accepted statements that have not been subjected to empirical tests. According to the National Benchmarking Study conducted by Dr. Palmer Morrel-Samuels in association with the University of Michigan, employee motivation has been found to be related to four important measures of corporate performance. More specifically, companies with more motivated employees enjoy a stronger return on assets, higher product quality, greater customer satisfaction, and better stock returns than companies with lower levels of employee motivation.

Now that we know "motivation matters," does this mean "case closed" and "mission accomplished"? Far from it! Of course there are piles of books, stacks of research articles, and endless video examples on how to create a motivated workforce. And despite many people having their "five secrets" or "three steps" for building motivated workforces, the reality is that there is no simple formula or easy one-size-fits-all strategies for building motivation. Fortunately, there is a wealth of good theory and evidence that can inform motivational interventions. This evidence suggests that motivation is not just about "morale" or "happiness." There are plenty of happy employees that do not deliver value for their firms. Nor is it just about compensation, perks, and benefits, as important as they may be. Rather, what good theory and models help us understand is how to assess the motivational conditions in any context and to recognize the full range of drivers of motivation at work.

The ultimate goal is to learn how to intelligently assess motivational conditions and then act in ways informed by the best theory and evidence available. Put another way, you want to learn principles that can be *generalized* from situation to situation and that is where good theory and evidence are so important. In this chapter, we attempt to incorporate the best and most useful theories—not for the sake of knowing the theory alone—but in a way that illustrates how they might be applied to enhance motivation at work. In addition to providing guidance as to good examples of theory and research evidence regarding what works in the area of employee motivation, we also provide you with a few persistent myths regarding motivation. Avoiding making the errors described in Myths 6.1 is a good first step.

A recurring question in discussions of motivation is "How do you motivate people?" Although this may intuitively sound like the very question you *want* answered, it is overly simplistic. For example, drawing a parallel to the medical field, an analogous question for physicians would be "How do you heal patients?" Obviously, before doctors are able to make any informed judgment about an appropriate medical treatment, they have to understand their patients' health and treatment history, apparent symptoms, and other specifics of the situation. There is certainly no one best way to heal patients.

Motivation of people is no different. As a result, the question "How do you motivate people?" should rightly be expanded to *"How do you motivate who, to do what, under what circumstances?"* That is, effective motivation strategies always depend on the people involved, their history, and context. While we can learn much from examples where supervisors succeeded using certain motivational tactics (for example, frequent verbal feedback, spot bonuses, enhanced job responsibilities), the recurring trap is to assume what worked in one context with one group of people will work similarly in another. Motivating restaurant servers to "upsell" profitable offerings is very different from trying to motivate

"I consider my ability to arouse enthusiasm among men the greatest asset I possess. The way to develop the best that is in a man is by appreciation and encouragement."

—Charles Schwab

?¿ MYTHS 6.1   Motivation Myths

- *Money is the only effective motivator.* In some situations, money is one of the best methods to motivate people. In others, it is entirely *ineffective.* Most importantly, it is certainly not the *only* motivator. What will motivate always depends on the people and the situation.

- *Everyone is motivated by the same things I am.* Although many people share common needs and desires, different people in different situations are motivated by an extraordinary range of factors, including financial gain, recognition, esteem, personal achievement, desire for equity, need to belong, fear, freedom, involvement, interesting work, and so on. What motivates one may not motivate another, and the same factor that motivates a person in one situation may not motivate that same person in a different situation.

- *Punishment does not motivate.* Although rarely the first choice to influence behavior, punishment, or the threat of it, can be an effective motivator. The problem, however, is that this type of motivation tends to be short term and rarely is associated with getting people to do beyond the minimum. Its appropriateness will depend on the situation. In some cases, it may be the only or most effective consequence available, and thus it is important to learn how to most fairly administer punishment.

- *Low performance is always attributable to low motivation.* Any performance is a function of motivation, ability, and the opportunity to perform. So, although low motivation is a common cause of low performance, it is certainly not the sole cause. Low performers may well lack the ability or the opportunity to achieve high performance.

- *Lack of motivation stems largely from lazy and apathetic people.* That is sometimes the case, of course, but more often it is the *situation* that lacks sufficient incentives to energize people. People labeled as unmotivated in one situation (say their job) are sometimes highly engaged and committed in another case (for example, as a Little League coach). The managerial challenge is to discover what brings out the effort in your people and to influence what you can.

- *Smart people don't need to be motivated.* This is a dangerous myth that can have consequences well beyond what a manager may realize. Because smart people have high ability, their motivation is key to obtaining really high levels of performance. A smart, but unmotivated person may still perform at an acceptable level, but that person is capable of much more and ultimately will probably become disillusioned with the job and leave it—leaving a hole bigger than will be immediately obvious to most managers.

new supervisors to provide regular feedback to their staffs. Similarly, motivating professionals in an accounting firm or law practice can be substantively different than motivating operators on a production line or mechanics on a big production job. Even more so, motivating young Chinese workers in a Shanghai factory is very different from senior engineers in a German chemical firm. The medical school mantra for aspiring doctors is "no treatment without diagnosis" and managers would do well to adopt that same motto.

So ultimately the goal of this chapter is to provide you with the information needed to motivate different types of people, to do different types of things, in different circumstances. While this is a tall order, motivation is central to great management. Before this relatively involved process can be provided, however, some frameworks are needed to help make sense of it all.

The Multidimensional Nature of Performance

A good place to start in our understanding of motivation is with a formula first presented in the 1960s[1] that captures the relationship between motivation, ability, and performance.[2]

$$\text{Performance} = f\,(\text{Motivation} \times \text{Ability} \times \text{Opportunity})$$

According to this simple but useful equation, any performance (job, athletic, music, academic) is a multiplicative function of your ability ("can do"), motivation ("will do"), and opportunity ("get to do"). The multiplicative nature of the equation correctly captures that all three aspects are essential to performance and that one can only modestly compensate for the other.

For example, people who have high motivation and average ability to perform a task can perform at an above-average rate if given the opportunity. However, strong performance is unlikely to be present in the absence of some moderate level of all three factors. No amount of motivation can overcome a complete lack of ability, nor can great ability compensate for a dearth of motivation even when provided multiple opportunities. Thus, if someone is not performing well, a good starting point is to investigate whether the cause of the problem is an issue of motivation, ability, opportunity, or some combination of the three.

Because ability tends to remain relatively stable over time, motivation and opportunity are more subject to managerial influence. That is the good news. The bad news is that motivation derives from multiple sources and can be exceedingly complex to understand and manage. As a result, great managers devote much of their time to trying to discover what motivates their associates and to build work environments that engage those motives.

Framing Motivation Challenges and Ideas: The Expectancy Theory

It is because of the multidimensional and complex nature of motivation that an organizing theory is so important in framing and diagnosing motivational situations. The best available theory of motivation for this type of practical diagnosis is **expectancy theory.** (See Figure 6.1.) Expectancy theory serves as both our starting point for diagnosing and framing motivational challenges and our structure for integrating a variety of other motivational models and concepts.

Expectancy theory is based on three specific employee beliefs:

- Expectancy
- Instrumentality
- Valence

Expectancy is the understanding of what performance is desired and the person's belief that effort will lead to a desired level of performance. Put simply, does the person know what he has to do and will he be able to accomplish the behavior desired? Motivation will decline any time we perceive a low probability of success. For example, few of us would be motivated to study hard for a test if we did not know what material was going to be covered or felt we had no chance of passing. Your resulting expectation would be "Regardless of how hard I study, I'm not likely to perform well." From a managerial perspective, then, expectancy beliefs point to the importance of clarifying goals and expectations, and ensuring that people have confidence that their effort can lead to good performance.

"Never confuse will power with firepower."

—U.S. Marine axiom

". . . Nothing in the world can take the place of motivation. Talent will not; nothing is more common than unsuccessful people with talent. Genius will not; unrewarded genius is almost a proverb. Education will not; the world is full of educated derelicts. Motivation and determination are omnipotent."

—Calvin Coolidge

KO **6-1**

DO **6-1**

FIGURE 6.1
Expectancy Theory

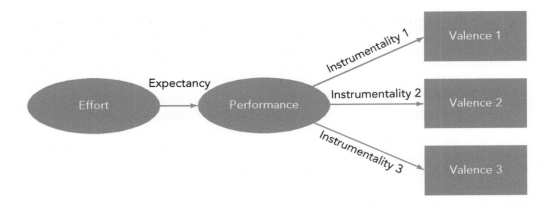

When expectancy is high, the person believes:

- "If I try, I can do it."
- "I have the knowledge, skills, and abilities to get the job done."
- "The goal is reasonable and if I exert myself, I am sure that I can succeed."

In contrast, when expectancy is low, the person may believe:

- "Why bother trying, no one could make that goal."
- "It is not even clear what my goal is, so how can I achieve it?"
- "I don't think Superman could do what is being asked of me."

Instrumentality is the belief that a given level of performance will lead to specific outcomes. Instrumentality perceptions can range from zero—everyone gets the same pay no matter how hard they work and produce—to certain—every time I sell a unit I get a 7 percent commission. Motivation will be high only when people believe that there will be meaningful consequences, positive or negative, from their efforts (or lack thereof). From a managerial perspective, instrumentality beliefs point to the critical importance of *linking rewards directly* to desired performance.

A common example of instrumentality can be seen in the distribution of student grades. If you score a 97 percent on a test, you would normally believe your teacher would assign you an A on that test. However, what would happen if the teacher told you she was giving everyone C's on the test, no matter what score they received? In this case, your instrumentality would be zero because you would not believe your performance (your test percentage) would lead to the expected reward (the A). Your resulting motivation to get a high score would therefore be low.

When instrumentality is high, the person believes:

- "My boss has always followed through on her promises before. I am sure she will this time as well."
- "If I sell 500, I get a $5,000 bonus."

In contrast, when instrumentality is low, the person may believe:

- "They tell us that we will get to take vacation time after this project, but I don't believe it. There is always another project around the corner."
- "I don't count on any promises around here. I've been burned before."

The final component of expectancy theory is **valence,** the value a person places on future outcomes. Valence is another way of saying, "What's in it for me?" Any outcome could be either desirable (for example, a chance to get involved in a project you love or getting a company car) or undesirable (being laid off, being poked repeatedly in the eye with a sharp stick). Much of what we know about motivating people is that different people will place different valences on the same outcome. Just consider the example of a company-provided cell phone. Some people would see this as a great reward and worth a great deal of effort to obtain. Others may view a company-provided phone as a headache and fear a lack of privacy and the rules associated with the phone's use. So from a managerial perspective perhaps the greatest challenge is to find those outcomes that have high valences for your target individuals.

Two important ideas of expectancy theory warrant special emphasis. First, like the ability, motivation, and opportunity equation introduced earlier, the three beliefs of expectancy theory—expectancy, instrumentality, and valence—combine multiplicatively to produce an individual's **motivating force**—symbolically represented as:[3]

> *"Motivation is not something you do to people but something you discover about them."*
>
> —Unknown

$$MF = E \times I \times V$$

Stated simply, high motivation will come only in the case of high levels of *all three* beliefs. Similarly, the absence of any of those three beliefs will render motivation low or zero. Second, always remember that expectancy theory is based on individual beliefs and perceptions, not necessarily on a manager's beliefs or some objective reality. It will not be enough that desirable outcomes are attainable and linked to appropriate behavior. Rather, an individual must *believe* that effort will lead to good performance, *believe* performance will be rewarded, and *believe* the reward to be of high value. In matters of motivation, perception is reality. Contributing to a high level of each of these employee beliefs is a critical component in increasing motivation in the workplace. Some specific skills for effectively using the expectancy approach are provided in Tool Kit 6.1.

Why Capable People Are Not Motivated

Some discussions of motivation focus on "slackers," "deadwood," and other terms to categorize those who seem disinclined to work hard. Of course, there are people who are incapable or lazy and are special motivational challenges.

MANAGER'S TOOL KIT

Tool Kit 6.1 Skills Needed to Improve Motivation Using Expectancy Theory

The following actions are good ways to increase the components of the expectancy formula:

- Select capable and motivated people.
- Provide necessary training.
- Show successful examples.
- Be supportive and available.
- Make the link between performance and outcome extremely clear.
- Follow through quickly.
- Make rewards proportional to effort.
- Reward based on individual preferences.

However, far more common are cases where people have the ability to perform but are not inclined to do so. We have found that one of the most useful ways to begin to diagnose motivational issues is to first think about why capable people might *not* be highly motivated.

To illustrate, consider the case of someone who is not motivated to attend or study hard in a particular college class. An expectancy theory diagnosis would tell us the causes of low motivation likely stem from one or more of three beliefs: (1) the student is unsure about what will lead to high grades or doesn't think her effort will lead to mastering the subject (low expectancy); (2) she doesn't believe the professor will give her a good grade even if she performs well (low instrumentality); or (3) she doesn't value a high grade or fear a low grade in the class (low valence). Additional steps in diagnosing motivational problems can be seen in Tool Kit 6.2.

This diagnosis concisely frames the potential belief pattern of low-motivated students. The motivational challenge for an instructor is to find out which beliefs exist in any particular case and to focus intervention strategies accordingly. Perhaps the biggest trap is to create a motivational strategy geared to beliefs that do not exist. It is always critically important to test your assumptions and uncover the real causes of low motivation. To revisit the parallels from the medical world: "No treatment without diagnosis."

Although expectancy theory is exceptionally useful in framing motivation challenges, it hardly provides all the answers. That is, understanding that high-valence beliefs will be critical to motivate the students in the preceding illustration does not address just what might make different students value attending class if it is not grades. Similarly, recognizing that instrumentality is a key element in motivation does not specify the different types of consequences and how they might best be administered in different academic settings. Likewise, appreciating the importance of clear expectations and confidence does not provide specific guidance on how to enhance expectancy in various contexts.

MANAGER'S TOOL KIT

Tool Kit 6.2   Diagnosing Motivational Problems

Given the complexity of motivational problems, here are some important questions that will help guide you through the diagnostic process.

- Are goals and performance expectations clearly communicated and understood?
- Does the person (or people) in question have the skills, training, and self-confidence needed to perform as asked?
- Is performance rewarded clearly and in a timely fashion? Does the person have strong reason to believe that if the work is performed, the outcome will be delivered?
- Is the outcome important to the person? Do I really know what that person values at this point in time, and how do I know it? Am I offering something that person has told me he or she values?
- Are rewards proportional to effort and administered in a direct and timely way? Have you made sure that the outcomes are proportional to the effort needed?
- Is the job designed to maximize the core job dimensions? What can be done to make the job more motivating?

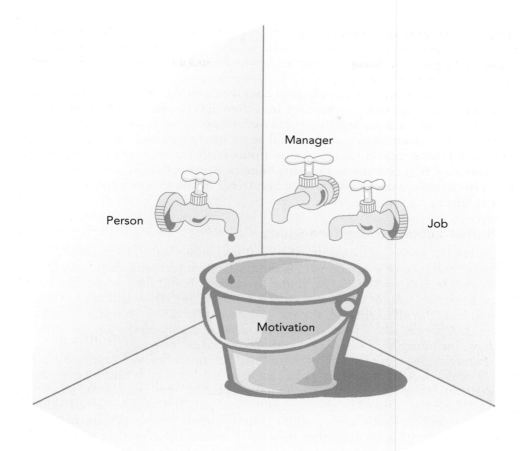

FIGURE 6.2
The Bucket Analogy
of Motivation: Key
Sources

While many discussions of motivation tend to get mired solely in money and financial rewards, the reality is that there are many additional drivers of motivation. Some of those drivers derive from the person, while others are more a function of managerial action or characteristics of the job. In this regard, we like to use a "bucket" analogy of motivation (see Figure 6.2). When a person's bucket is full, she is optimally motivated, and assuming sufficient ability, performance will follow. When a person's bucket is low, greater managerial effort will be required to fill that bucket. As depicted in Figure 6.2, there are three primary faucets or sources available to fill an employee's motivational bucket, each one helping to improve employees' expectancy, instrumentality, and valence beliefs: (1) personal drives, (2) the job or work itself, and (3) managerial actions. Obviously, turning on all of the faucets at once fills an employee's bucket more quickly. But in many cases, such a "flood" of motivation is not necessary. We review and synthesize these major sources of motivation in the following sections.

The Person as a Source of Motivation

KO **6-2**

One source of motivation stems from a person's own motivational drives or needs. Influential theories of human needs include equity theory and David McClelland's model of learned needs.

An Equity Approach to Motivation

Equity refers to workers' perceptions of the fairness of outcomes they receive on the job.[4] These personal equity judgments are based on a social comparison by which people compare what they are getting out of their job (their outcomes) to what they are putting into their job (inputs). Outcomes include things like pay, fringe benefits, increased responsibility, and prestige, while inputs may include hours worked and work quality, as well as education and experience. The ratio of outcomes to inputs is then compared to corresponding ratios of their comparison group. The outcome of this comparison is the basis for beliefs about fairness.[5] See Figure 6.3 for an overall representation of equity theory.

Potential Actions to Restore Equity

When people experience inequity, they will take some action to restore balance. Consider the case of a person who is paid $40,000 a year and then finds out his co-worker is making $48,000 for doing the same job and their respective inputs (education, job tenure, skills, and so on) are the same. How will the lower-paid person react? In all likelihood, the employee will take action to restore a sense of fairness. A person who wishes to restore a sense of equity on the job has multiple options, including both behavioral and perceptual actions.

Behaviorally, workers can increase their outcomes (by, say, requesting a pay raise) or decrease their efforts (take longer lunch breaks, or find ways to avoid work) to balance the equity equation. Perceptually, they may rationalize they weren't working as hard as they thought, thus reducing the perceived value of their own inputs. Further, they might convince themselves that co-workers are actually working harder than they thought. It is difficult to predict exactly how a person will react, but as you can see, few of the choices are really great ones for the person or for the company. Equity perceptions can be surprisingly important in organizations and even nature. Equity is so central an issue that it is even of substantial importance to brown capuchin monkeys! (See Management Live 6.1.)

FIGURE 6.3
The Equity Theory
Diagram

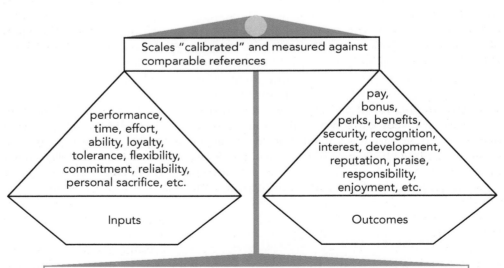

Source: Adapted from Adams (1963).

↤↦ MANAGEMENT LIVE 6.1

Equity Is Also Monkey Business[6]

Even monkeys expect a fair day's pay for a fair day's work. Inspired by a history of work showing that humans inherently reject unfairness, Sarah Brosnan of Emory University wondered whether this was also true for capuchin monkeys. Brosnan designed an experiment that put two capuchin monkeys together where they were trained to exchange a small rock with human handlers to receive a reward—in most cases, a piece of cucumber. Brosnan points out that, while this may sound very simple, "not very many species are willing to relinquish things, especially intentionally."

Partners of monkeys who willingly exchanged received either the exact same reward (a cucumber slice) or a more desirable reward (a grape) for the same work or, in some instances, for doing no work at all. Brosnan observed that those monkeys who saw unfair treatment and failed to benefit from it were ultimately less likely to trade with the handlers in the future. Moreover, the monkeys who had been treated unfairly would often not eat the cucumbers they received and, in other cases, actually threw the cucumbers at the researchers!

While humorous at one level, the results are a powerful confirmation of the influence of equity perceptions. Not only did monkeys expect fair treatment and reject a desirable food item as a result of inequity, but the human desire for equity seems to have a very deep-seeded basis that even occurs in other primates.

Equity Sensitivity

While equity may seem like a relatively objective phenomenon, in truth what different people see as equitable can vary significantly. In fact, an emerging body of research is finding that people differ significantly in what is called **equity sensitivity**.[7] Research has found that those high in equity sensitivity are more outcome-oriented and want more than others for the same level of inputs. Those low in equity sensitivity pay more attention to their inputs and are less sensitive to equity issues. Additional findings suggest people who are high in equity sensitivity place a great deal of importance on **extrinsic outcomes** such as pay, status, and fringe benefits.[8] Employees with low equity sensitivity place more importance on **intrinsic outcomes** such as feelings of personal worth, using one's abilities, and a sense of personal accomplishment. To better understand your own equity sensitivity and that of others, consult Tool Kit 6.3.

"Fairness is what justice really is."
—Potter Stewart

What Managers Need to Do to Maintain Equity

The most important and challenging thing about equity is that we are dealing with both our own perceptions *and* the perceptions of other people, and those may not be the same. As a result, even if you perceive a serious injustice, others may not be aware of it or may consider the inequity trivial. Great managers monitor and constantly use reality checks to gauge associates' perceptions of equity. By asking others about equity issues—"Do you feel that promotion was fair? Why or why not?" or "What types of behaviors should be valued here?"—top managers realize they will be better able to manage equity perceptions and be more aware of treatment that may de-motivate workers.

An understanding of equity theory is why excellent managers *do not* treat or reward all workers the same. That's right—great managers do not treat all people equally but, rather, fairly! Consider this for a minute. If managers provide the same treatment and rewards to everyone, then by definition the managers treat everyone as being "average." What workers would feel like they are being treated

"These men ask for just the same thing—fairness, and fairness only. This, so far as in my power, they, and all others, shall have."

—Abraham Lincoln

MANAGER'S TOOL KIT

Tool Kit 6.3   Equity Sensitivity Measure[9]

In Any Organization I Might Work For:

1. It would be more important for me to:

_____ A. Get from the organization.

_____ B. Give to the organization.

2. It would be more important for me to:

_____ A. Help others.

_____ B. Watch out for my own good.

3. I would be more concerned about:

_____ A. What I received from the organization.

_____ B. What I contributed to the organization.

4. The hard work I would do should:

_____ A. Benefit the organization.

_____ B. Benefit me.

5. My personal philosophy in dealing with the organization would be:

_____ A. If I don't look out for myself, nobody else will.

_____ B. It's better for me to give than to receive.

Scoring. Answering 1A, 2B, 3A, 4B, and 5A all indicate being equity sensitive. 1B, 2A, 3B, 4A, and 5B indicate you are not equity sensitive.

fairly under this system? Poor performers may prefer this system but would have little reason to improve their performance. Average performers would feel equitably treated and likely maintain their level of motivation. High performers would see substantial inequity when everyone is treated equally. As a result, the high performers would be motivated to either reduce their inputs, seek more outcomes (which they will not be able to receive when everyone is rewarded the same), or leave to seek equity elsewhere. If we let a system of *equality* run to its logical conclusion, we will have all low and average performers. Treating everyone the same is not a prescription for great management. In fact, it is a great recipe for mediocrity or worse.

The Platinum Rule

The lasting lesson is that even the best-intentioned managers often confuse the intuitive idea of equality with the real issue at hand—fairness. Therefore, we encourage you to follow this simple rule, often referred to as the **platinum rule** (a variation on the golden rule), which states: "Treat others how *they* wish to be treated." That is, each employee may require a slightly different approach to ensure his or her perceptions of fairness are met, which in the end is entirely appropriate and highly effective to ensure motivation remains high. To further reinforce the idea that different people are motivated differently, a brief synthesis of the work of David McClelland follows.

McClelland's Learned Needs

David C. McClelland found that people would do well to learn the predominant needs in themselves and in others in order to find those roles and situations where success is most likely.[10] McClelland focused specifically on three needs or motives: achievement, affiliation, and power. Although we all have these needs, McClelland noted that people tend to have one need that is most dominant. We can use McClelland's simple framework to provide some structure around the questions of "What do I need from work?" and "What motivates others?" Whether the focus is on you or others, the three basic needs remain the same: the **need for achievement, need for affiliation,** and **need for power** (Figure 6.4).

What Do I Need from Work?

McClelland's research suggests that motivational needs are an important predictor of who will be an effective manager.[11] For example, McClelland argues a high need for affiliation can often be problematic for managers. Since being *liked* is the dominant motive underlying the affiliation-oriented manager's actions, these managers may have difficulty resolving conflicts and be more likely to make exceptions to make people happy. A manager with a dominant need for affiliation may not be inclined to take decisive action when an unpopular course of action is warranted (for example, have people work late to finish an important project).

Further, McClelland argues that, while a high need for power will produce a strong work ethic and commitment to the organization, people possessing this drive may not possess the required flexibility and people-centered skills to be effective in leadership roles. Perhaps most importantly, McClelland argues that people with strong *achievement motivation* make the best leaders, although they can have a tendency to demand too much of their staff in the belief that they are all similarly and highly achievement-focused and results-driven. Maybe not too surprisingly, different personal profiles tend to gravitate toward different jobs. Some examples of these can be seen in Table 6.1.

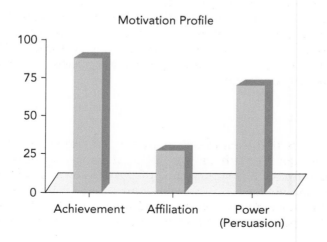

FIGURE 6.4
McClelland's Theory
of Needs

TABLE 6.1   Typical Needs Profiles

Position	Achievement	Affiliation	Power
Sales	Very high	Low	Somewhat high
Entrepreneur	Very high	Very low	Somewhat low
Corporate Manager	Somewhat high	Somewhat low	Very high
Politician	High	Somewhat low	Very high
Support Staff	Somewhat low	Very high	Somewhat low
Information Systems	Very high	Very low	Low

"The difference between a successful person and others is not a lack of strength, not a lack of knowledge, but rather in a lack of will."

—Vincent T. Lombardi

What Motivates Others?   When it comes to addressing the question—"What motivates others?"—McClelland's model provides us with a nice framework for diagnosing basic motivational needs. Of course, the challenge in diagnosing needs is we can't see them. We can only infer them from a person's observable behavior. As a result, great managers pay very close attention to the behavior of people around them. Unfortunately, as Table 6.2 demonstrates, most of us are inaccurate judges of what other people want. The only real way to know is to pay attention and to ask people directly.

In explaining how different needs impact the way people behave, McClelland recounted a story about 450 workers who had been put out of work in Erie, Pennsylvania.[12] Most of the newly unemployed workers stayed at home for a while and then checked with the employment service to see if their old jobs or similar ones were available. But a small minority behaved very differently; the day they were laid off, they started job hunting. They checked both national and local employment offices; they studied the Help Wanted sections of the papers; they checked through their union, their churches, and various fraternal organizations; they looked into training courses to learn a new skill; they even left town to look for work, while the majority when questioned said they would not under

TABLE 6.2   What Do Employees Want?

What Employees Want	Items	What Employers Think Employees Want
1	Interesting work	5
2	Appreciation of work	8
3	Feeling "in on things"	10
4	Job security	2
5	Good wages	1
6	Promotion/growth	3
7	Good working conditions	4
8	Personal loyalty	6
9	Tactful discipline	7
10	Sympathetic help with problems	9

Source: Reprinted from *Business Horizons*, Vol. 30, No. 5, by Kenneth A. Kovach, "What Motivates Employees? Workers and Supervisors Give Different Answers," pp. 58–75. Copyright © 1969, with permission from Elsevier.

any circumstances move away to obtain a job. Obviously, the members of the active minority were differently motivated.

Achievement-motivated people thrive on pursuing and attaining goals. They have a desire to do something better or more efficiently, solve problems, or master complex tasks. They like to be able to control situations. They take moderate, calculated risks. They like to get immediate feedback on how they have done and tend to be preoccupied with a task orientation toward the job to be done. McClelland describes the self-motivated achiever as a person with a tendency to think about ways to accomplish something difficult and significant when he is not being required to think about anything in particular—that is, when he is free to relax and let his or her mind just "idle." The self-motivated achiever tends to set goals and prefers tasks that provide feedback. Achievers strive to reach goals and measure success in terms of what those efforts have accomplished. They learn to set challenging but achievable goals for themselves and for their jobs and, when they achieve them, to set new goals.

Power-motivated individuals see most work situations as an opportunity to influence other people or to take control. Generally, people with strong power motives have the desire to control others, influence their behavior, and be responsible for them. Often these people will volunteer for leadership positions, recommend changes whether or not they are needed, and are very willing to assert themselves when a decision needs to be made. In an organizational sense, the need for power is the need to manage the behavior of others in order to achieve goals. A high need for power does not necessarily imply autocratic, tyrannical behavior, but rather a need to have impact, to be influential, and to be effective in achieving goals. People who spend their time thinking about how to influence others, how to mount arguments, and how to change other people's behavior toward organizational goals are exhibiting a high need for power.

Affiliation-motivated people have the desire to establish and maintain friendly and warm relations with others. Individuals who enjoy helping others, are concerned with the growth and development of subordinates, are fond of spending time in lengthy conversations, and are good listeners tend to have a high need for affiliation. Some people with strong affiliation motives can be distracted from their work, as work can often take a backseat to the social environment. That is, the social environment may not just be viewed as a means of getting work done; it may be viewed as being *more important* than getting work done. They will usually respond to an appeal for cooperation and generally like to be part of a group. They prefer to share in accomplishments rather than to take individual initiative and sole responsibility. They are often presented with opportunities to capitalize on, and take credit for, ideas and actions they conceived and initiated, but generally do not have a high need for recognition for individual achievement and are often quite happy to have their group or department receive the credit.

Applying the Learned Needs in the Workplace

While the research is clear that different people have different needs, the skill challenge for you is how to apply that evidence in the workplace. The idea that people have a dominant need (achievement, affiliation, power) should provide you a starting place by giving you an understanding of what is in each individual's "motivational bucket." For example, people with a high need for achievement are going to start off with their buckets being more full than other people. So your first job with each employee is to get under the surface and determine how much of the bucket needs to be filled or to understand what sources of motivation you will need, because some employees will be starting with practically empty buckets while others will have a good head start on having their buckets full. McClelland, therefore, offers a helpful tool for understanding an important source of motivation—that is, the person as the source of motivation.

"Achievement is largely the product of steadily raising one's levels of aspiration . . . and expectation."
—Jack Nicklaus

"Most people give up just when they're about to achieve success. They quit on the one-yard line. They give up at the last minute of the game, one foot from a winning touchdown."
—Ross Perot

"Power is the ultimate aphrodisiac."
—Henry Kissinger

While equity theory and McClelland's learned needs were covered in detail here, this should not suggest that other motivational scholars and approaches are somehow less important or less "correct." From an applied perspective, however, we consider these two approaches most central. To get a brief summary of a number of other important perspectives and how these frameworks can assist you, look at Table 6.3.

TABLE 6.3   Key Takeaways from Popular Motivation Theories and Writing

Many students of organizational behavior, and prospective or current managers, rightfully find the existing collection of motivational theories and models to be a bit confusing—if not downright bewildering. Moreover, some theories have little actual research support, others fall out of current favor, and others are supplanted because the insights they provided have influenced, and been incorporated by, further generations of management theorists and practitioners.

Nonetheless, our view is that, if a theory has gained popular acclaim, or stood the test of time in textbooks and other sources, it probably has at least a gem or two of an idea that has value. Many such theories do not warrant full coverage or a deep dive into the specifics in a text like this, but we felt it worth synthesizing several of those that frequently make their way into discussions of motivation topics. In that spirit, this table is a brief synthesis of the key takeaways from some of the more popular theories you may have studied or heard of (or will become familiar with in the course of your education and career).

Maslow's Hierarchy of Needs. The same people can be motivated by different needs at different times. In **Maslow's heirarchy of needs,** the most basic needs are breathing, food, water, and shelter and top out with higher human desires such as morality, creativity, spontaneity, and problem solving. The peak of the hierarchy is called self-actualization. Humans are most motivated by higher pursuits and will not stay content for long with work that only fulfills their basic needs. *Research Evidence:* Has been largely discredited through research. Did provide important ideas that were built upon by others (mainly that intrinsic rewards are very important), but specifics were incorrect.

Alderfer's ERG Theory. Alderfer took Maslow's model and tried to align it with research evidence (Maslow's research has not held up well under testing). As a result, Alderfer presented his **ERG theory,** where Maslow's five needs are collapsed into three needs called existence, related, and growth. Alderfer's ERG theory demonstrates that more than one need may motivate at the same time. A lower motivator need not be satisfied before other needs are motivating. As a result, the ERG theory accounts for differences in need preferences between cultures better than Maslow's Needs Hierarchy because the order of needs can be different for different people. This flexibility accounts for a wider range of observed behaviors. For example, it can explain the "struggling musician" who may place growth needs above those of existence. Finally, the ERG theory acknowledges that if a higher-order need is frustrated, an individual may regress to increase the satisfaction of a lower-order need that appears easier to satisfy. This is known as the frustration-regression principle. *Research Evidence:* The structure of the three needs has received support, but measurement issues have prevented some other specific claims from being validated.

McGregor's Theory of X and Y. Douglas McGregor suggested that there are two fundamental approaches to managing people: Theory X and Theory Y. Theory X holds that the average person dislikes work and will avoid it if he/she can; must be forced with the threat of punishment to work toward organizational objectives; prefers to be directed and avoids responsibility; and wants security above all else.

In contrast, Theory Y holds that effort in work is as natural as work and play: people will apply self-control and self-direction in the pursuit of organizational objectives and do so without external control or the threat of punishment. Further, commitment to objectives is a function of rewards associated with their achievement, and people usually accept and often seek responsibility.

McGregor argued that many managers tend toward Theory X, and generally get poor results. Enlightened managers use Theory Y, which produces better performance and results, and allows people to grow and develop. *Research Evidence:* Since the Theory of X and Y is more a typology and has fewer predictions than the other theories, it has not been tested as rigorously.

Herzberg's Two-Factor Theory. The two factors that comprise Herzberg's theory are hygiene and motivation. ***Hygiene factors*** include working conditions, quality of supervision, salary, security, and interpersonal relations. ***Motivation factors,*** such as achievement, recognition, advancement, and growth on the job, are needed in order to motivate an employee into higher performance. Herzberg's most influential idea was that his two sets of factors are *independent* and *not* just two ends of one scale. Thus, it is possible to be satisfied at work even though the working conditions are poor, and it is possible to be relatively content with the latter even though you may not be very motivated to put in any extra effort. Importantly, Herzberg's work focused attention on the work itself, and this was an important precursor to job characteristics theory. *Research Evidence:* Herzberg's findings have been duplicated by some researchers but have been criticized as being "method bound"[13] (in other words, the results only hold up when the research is conducted in a specific manner and are not generally robust).

Deci's Cognitive Evaluation Theory. In a similar vein as Herzberg and Maslow, Edward Deci suggested that there are intrinsic and extrinsic motivators, and one or the other of these may be a more powerful motivator for a given individual. Intrinsically motivated individuals perform for their own achievement and satisfaction. If they come to believe they are doing a job because of the pay or the working conditions or some other extrinsic reason, they begin to lose motivation.

The belief is that the presence of powerful extrinsic motivators can actually *reduce* a person's intrinsic motivation, particularly if the extrinsic motivators are perceived by the person to be controlled by people. In other words, a boss who is always dangling this reward or wielding that stick will turn off intrinsically motivated people. *Research Evidence:* Research has been decidedly mixed, and cognitive evaluation theory has remained relatively controversial since it was introduced.

Daniel Pink's Fundamentals of Drive. Building on the tradition of Maslow, Herzberg, and Deci, Pink boils down motivation into three elements: (1) autonomy, the desire to direct our own lives; (2) mastery, the desire to continually improve at something that matters; and (3) purpose, the desire to do things in service of something larger than ourselves.

Pink warns that traditional carrot-and-stick methods, in which companies use a particular incentive—often money—as a contingent reward for a task, are not only ineffective for motivating employees, but potentially harmful. He offers up his model for corporations that he says will tap into true motivation, yield higher satisfaction among employees, and deliver stronger results. *Research Evidence:* Pink's drive approach is synthesis of other existing research, but it has not been well tested at this point. Considering that it is similar to the job characteristics theory in important ways (and the job characteristics theory has received very strong research support), it likely has significant merit. A weakness may be its equally tight link to cognitive evaluation theory, which may limit some applicability.

Now that we have identified a few important sources of motivation from the "employee bucket," we will shift attention over to the job as a source of motivation.

The Job as a Source of Motivation

KO **6-3**

The Job Characteristics Model

KO **6-4**

We have now seen that how people should be motivated can differ based on the person. Richard Hackman and Greg Oldham have presented an intuitive, practical, and evidence-based model of how motivation can stem from the job or

DO **6-2**

Practice this!
Go to www.baldwin2e.com

work itself.[14] This addresses the second source for filling a person's motivational "bucket." Their **job characteristics model (JCM)** provides a relatively simple yet powerful explanation of why some jobs are more motivating than others and how the motivation potential of a job can be enriched. The model has proven so applicable it is among the most widely referenced frameworks in the management field.

The details of the job characteristics model are important to applying it on the job. As a result, they are presented in some detail next. Even more than the details of the model, it is important to think about the real importance of having people do work that they "love" to do. When people are matched to a job that really "fits" them, most of the problems associated with "unmotivated" or "lazy" people disappear. If people are doing work they love, the job itself becomes the major motivator and fills the motivational bucket up in ways that a manager rarely can. So what we are really in quest of is figuring out the characteristics that make someone love his or her job. Now, it is important to realize that there are some jobs that people are just never going to love (for example, the authors doubt that many people love being sewer inspectors or toll booth workers), but in the vast majority of cases, work can be made significantly better.

The JCM identifies five **core job dimensions**—the vital characteristics of the work itself—and proposes a link between those and the **psychological states** experienced by the worker. In Figure 6.5, the relationship between the core job dimensions, the psychological states they influence, and their subsequent

FIGURE 6.5
The Bucket Analogy of Motivation: Key Sources

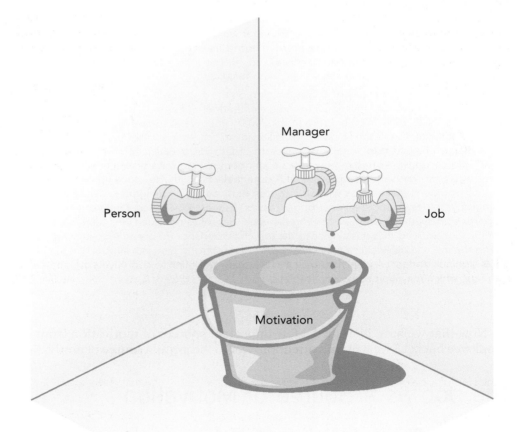

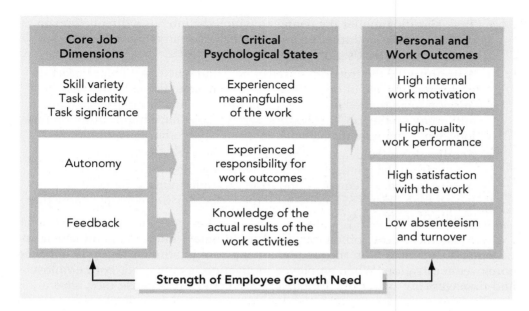

FIGURE 6.6
The Job
Characteristics Model

outcomes is illustrated. As can be seen in Figure 6.6, well-designed work can lead to high-quality work performance, high levels of motivation, low absenteeism and turnover, and increased job satisfaction. See Table 6.4 for some examples of jobs with varying degrees of the core job dimensions.

To further understand the JCM and how it can help isolate desirable motivational perceptions to fill a significant portion of the motivation bucket, we need to further explain the model. People experience a job as more motivating when the job has a high degree of:

- **Skill variety,** or the range in number of skills used to complete the job tasks (conceptual, physical, technical, people skills). Astronauts have a high degree of skill variety stemming from their need to be technically proficient, be in great physical shape, and be good at problem solving.

- **Task identity,** or the degree to which the job requires completion of a whole or identifiable piece of work. Artists enjoy very high task identity because they see their work through from beginning to end.

"When they believe in the company and in what they are doing, employees tend to pitch in and do what it takes to succeed even when it means working longer and harder."

—Roger Ballou, President and CEO, CDI Corp.

TABLE 6.4 Examples of Jobs with Varying Degrees of the Core Job Dimensions

Job Characteristics	"High" Examples	"Low" Examples
Skill Variety	Plant manager, elementary school teacher, astronaut	Data entry clerk, assembly worker, computer programmer
Task Identity	Sales account manager, attorney, artist, carpenter	Insurance underwriter, restaurant host or hostess
Task Significance	Medical doctor, nurse, social worker	Telemarketer, data entry clerk
Autonomy	Self-employed, salesperson, computer programmer	Auditor, police officer, military
Feedback	Telemarketer, medical professional, stand-up comic	Retail sales clerk

- **Task significance,** or the degree to which the job has a direct effect on the work or lives of other people. For instance, surgeons perform a job with very high task significance.
- **Autonomy,** or the freedom to select how and when particular tasks are performed. As one of our colleagues likes to say, "If you have to ask permission to go to the bathroom, it's not likely you will experience high autonomy on the job." Professors, for example, have highly autonomous jobs, while manufacturing workers often have rather low autonomy.
- **Feedback,** or the degree to which individuals receive knowledge of their results from the job itself. Workers with jobs high in feedback normally receive feedback frequently and from multiple sources. Stand-up comics have a high degree of feedback on their job; they immediately know the results of their work.

Because these core job characteristics ultimately influence employee motivation and satisfaction on the job, enhancing core job dimensions will enhance employee motivation. When employee motivation is enhanced, both employees and managers are better off. Employees are better off because they have a job they find more interesting and satisfying. Managers and the organization are better off because high employee motivation is associated with reduced turnover and absenteeism, increased quantity of performance, and improved quality. In addition, maximizing employees' core job dimensions increases their intrinsic motivation and reduces the time a manager spends supervising their work. So enhancing a job really does create a situation where everybody wins.

Using the JCM on the Job

The JCM also provides direct implications for enriching poorly designed or boring jobs. When the JCM was developed in the 1970s, it was primarily used to improve repetitive assembly line work in manufacturing settings. It is important to realize, however, that the JCM is applicable across the entire spectrum of jobs. For example, a recent study[15] used the JCM to redesign jobs of customer service representatives in a technical service call center. Findings indicated the call center workers responded quite well to the job redesign efforts. More specifically, after the intervention, the number of successfully solved problems significantly increased as did the overall customer service score. At the same time, the percentage of repeat calls needed and the percentage of calls escalated to a higher level decreased similarly.

An important part of that job redesign effort was a new process to facilitate learning called the "hot seat." The hot seat was devised to enable specialists to spend a portion of their time off the phones and working on problems on their own without interruption. The specialists worked three days on the phone (in the hot seat) and then two days off the phone working on problems they had been unable to solve. The result was a more in-depth understanding of the problems, problems being solved quicker, and problems being solved right the first time.

The MPS Formula

One feature that makes the JCM so user-friendly is its specification of the five core job dimensions and how they can be combined into an equation calculating the **motivation potential score (MPS)** for any job. The equation is provided in Figure 6.7.

**FIGURE 6.7
The MPS Equation**

$$MPS = \left(\frac{Variety + Identity + Significance}{3} \right) \times Autonomy \times Feedback$$

Within this equation, the properties of multiplication are again very important (as they were in expectancy theory). That is, the absence of any of the core job dimensions is magnified in the model. To improve the motivating potential score of a job then, it is important to consider each of the five elements since a lack of any can be detrimental to the motivating potential. Before we discuss how to increase the core job dimensions, there is an important caveat. If an employee does not have a need for growth, attempts to make a job more motivating will fail. The theory and use of the model is based on the assumption that people want their jobs to be more motivating. This may well be true for many people, but it is important to acknowledge that not all employees would look favorably on interventions to enrich their jobs. More specifically, employees with a low **growth need strength** may be very content to work in a relatively unenriched environment.

JCM Interventions: How to Enrich Boring Work

As noted, in addition to identifying the core dimensions themselves, Hackman and Oldham further outlined a set of interventions shown to influence the MPS. These five interventions provide a blueprint for designing more fulfilling work (see Table 6.5). The first intervention is to *combine tasks*. A combination of tasks

TABLE 6.5   Implementing Concepts for the Job Characteristics Model

Job-Enriching Technique	Enhances . . .
Combine Tasks	Skill variety, task identity, task significance
Form Natural Work Units	Task identity, task significance
Establish Client Relationships	Skill variety, task identity, autonomy, feedback
Vertically Load Jobs	Autonomy, task identity
Open Feedback Channels	Feedback

leads to a more challenging and complex work assignment because it requires people to use a wider variety of skills. Newport Corp. in Irvine, California,[16] emphasizes its training and cross-training programs, which include combining tasks. Newport employees participate and are involved in both classroom and on-the-job training programs to stay current with the latest manufacturing and assembly techniques. The cross-training program adds to the workforce's adaptability and flexibility, allowing for smooth transitions between varied production volumes. A more flexible workforce simultaneously reduces costs and makes jobs more meaningful to the people performing them.

A related strategy is to *form natural work units*. Natural work units are implemented so that task identity and task significance can be increased. This is the basic idea behind the use of the manufacturing cell, instead of straight assembly lines. For years, Volvo has built cars in small groups of employees referred to as cells.[17] These cells are responsible for an entire component of the vehicle, for example, the interior or the engine.

"Most employees have an opportunity to work a rally and do demo rides. They are encouraged to talk to the customers to get a better understanding of their needs and expectations, and how they feel about the product."

—Ron Mundt, Director of Service Support Operations, Harley-Davidson

The third technique for enhancing jobs is to *establish client relationships*. A client relationship involves an ongoing personal relationship between an employee and the client or customer. This relationship can increase autonomy, task identity, skill variety, and feedback. Enhancing jobs in this way has been an important part of the success of Wainwright Industries, St. Peters, Missouri.[18] Wainwright employees serve as customer champions, interfacing with customers and solving problems for them. Any score below 95 percent on a customer satisfaction measure results in a customer champion assembling a cross-functional team, which then develops an action plan within 48 hours. This close personal relationship between employees and customers aids in fast and accurate problem resolution.

The fourth suggestion, vertically load jobs, refers to giving increased authority to workers for making job-related decisions. In reality, *vertical loading* can be thought of as being synonymous with employee empowerment. That is, workers and their bosses share responsibility. As supervisors delegate more authority and responsibility, their subordinates perceive increases in autonomy, accountability, and task identity. At Phelps County Bank in Rolla, Missouri,[19] an extensive training program was set up to give employee owners the motivation and tools to take responsibility for the business. Management established classes in problem solving and financial statement analysis, as well as tutorials where departments exchanged information with each other about their products and services. Employee-owners went through cross-training days where, for example, tellers would inform loan department staff about their roles and responsibilities. As a result of these efforts, employees became more empowered to deal with customer problems on the spot, without having to seek time-consuming approval from management or advice from colleagues.

The last intervention for improving job design is to *open feedback channels*. Feedback is important because workers need to know how well or how poorly they are performing their jobs if improvement is expected. Some jobs are blessed with immediate feedback; for example, a comedian knows within seconds whether or not her material was funny and an Olympic sprinter knows in an instant whether he won or lost a race. For most jobs, however, the problem is receiving too little feedback with few obvious mechanisms available to generate such feedback. When people receive timely and useful feedback, they are best able to adapt their behavior to achieve the highest performance. Karrie Jerman, human resources representative at Colorado Springs, Colorado–based Hamilton Standard Commercial Aircraft, says that 360-degree appraisals (a key tool used to open feedback channels) are imperative. "The thing we gain the most is input from so many people that know the employee's work. Now their peers and customers give feedback," says Jerman. "They feel it's more fair."[20]

Overall, job design interventions have achieved impressive results. Firms that have undergone job redesign efforts typically report higher productivity, higher work quality, improved worker satisfaction, and less absenteeism. Understanding how to create a motivating *job*, not just a motivated *person*, is an important tool in the repertoire of any great manager.

The Manager as a Source of Motivation

KO **6-5**

KO **6-6**

DO **6-3**

DO **6-4**

While many "textbook treatments" to understanding motivation start with managers, we see it as the ending point. This point ties directly into the idea that there cannot be effective treatment without diagnosis. If we are really going to address the questions raised at the beginning of this chapter ("*How do you motivate who, to do what, under what circumstances?*"), we need to view the actions of the manager as coming "last."

We have addressed two parts of our metaphorical bucket, and these ideas have presented us with two major portions of the motivational puzzle. We have seen that some people (people with high needs for achievement) will likely be more motivated to perform in a wide array of settings. We can see that people who have other dominant needs (power or affiliation) will benefit greatly from that which fits their needs well and has a high motivating potential. We can also see that all people need to be treated equitably and that certain people are more sensitive to inequities than are others.

In cases where the bucket is not able to be filled very readily through the job or the person, it will rest upon the manager to provide the bulk of employee motivation (see Figure 6.8). It is not an accident that the previous statement sounds like using the manager as the primary source of motivation is a last resort. In many ways, it should be a last resort, and in many cases it is exactly this environment of last resort that managers are brought into. Consequently, it is also these situations where the actions of the managers are extremely important, because they are faced with a nearly empty bucket and need to get it filled to an adequate level. Going back to the expectancy approach described at the beginning of the chapter provides a good place to look for answers and, again, research has provided us with some useful ones.

Multiple models exist that offer ideas for managers to affect the expectancy and instrumentality beliefs of their people. Perhaps the two most universally recognized, evidence-based, and applicable theories are goal setting and behavior modification.

Goal Setting

Simply stated, the goal-setting effect is that specific, difficult, but attainable goals lead to higher performance than no goals or "do your best" goals. In decades of research, scholars Ed Locke and Gary Latham[21] have convincingly argued and demonstrated with multiple studies that "the beneficial effect of goal setting on task performance is one of the most robust and replicable findings in the psychological literature." Goal setting is the most efficient and effective way to both clearly convey expectations and motivate people to achieve them.

According to Gary Latham,[22] goals work for at least three specific reasons. First, goals direct behavior toward goal-relevant behavior and away from other behaviors. Second, goals energize and increase the persistence of a person. They provide a standard against which people can continually compare their performance, thereby increasing the striving to attain the standard. Third, goals

FIGURE 6.8
The Bucket Analogy of Motivation: Key Sources

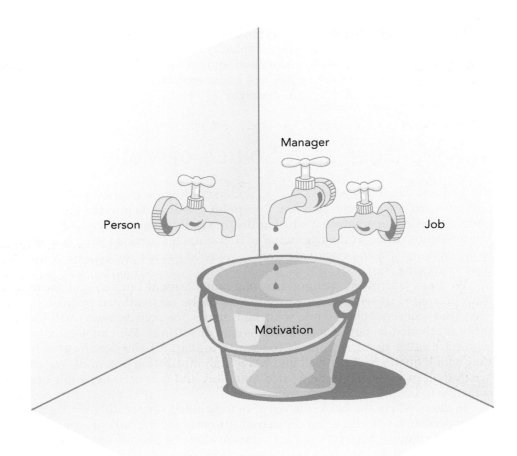

increase the incentive for a person to seek out and use new sources of information to obtain the standard. These three reasons are at work whenever we have a goal and the reasons tend to operate together.

The foundation of many effective motivation programs is proper goal setting.[23] Managers should begin assessing the motivational climate of their work environment by asking themselves, "Do subordinates understand and accept my performance expectations?" Although goal setting works to improve motivation toward accomplishing objectives, great managers know that *not all goals are created equal.* A great deal of research has indicated that some goals are more likely to be accomplished than others—we call these "good goals" versus "bad goals." For some examples of ineffective goals, see Table 6.6. The characteristics of a good goal can be summarized by the acronym **SMART**, or specific, measurable, attainable, relevant, and time-bound.[24] See Chapter 1 for more detail on setting good goals.

Common Goal-Setting Traps

While a robust and powerful motivational technique, goal setting has several limitations and common traps involved in its implementation. For example, setting goals can create ceiling effects, whereby people can reach their goal and then abruptly stop, even though they might be capable of considerably higher performance levels. Thus, goals set too low can actually be harmful. In addition,

TABLE 6.6   Examples of Ineffective Goals

"Try your best."

"Give 110 percent."

"We need to increase our sales."

"Nothing short of a 300 percent improvement will do."

"Let's decrease copier use by 25 percent."

"You need to get 25 new accounts."

"If all goes well, you may be named Employee of the Month."

goals can create the conditions for game-playing and **suboptimization.** That is, in the pursuit of goals, people may ignore other important objectives (not formally covered by goals) and may do things outside the spirit of the goals, even engaging in unethical behavior, to achieve them. This situation is illustrated in Management Live 6.2 about the mortgage crisis.

MANAGEMENT LIVE 6.2

Goals, Rewards, and the Mortgage Crisis

The following is an interview from NPR's *Marketplace* radio program. It does an excellent job of showing the problems inherent in misaligned goals—in this case, a problem that directly contributed to bringing the banking industry perilously close to collapse. The conversation is between Alyssa Katz of NPR and Tess Vigeland, a real estate expert who taught at New York University.

ALYSSA KATZ: During the 2000s, according to their trade group, they [mortgage brokers] sold four out of every five mortgages. Most brokers have relationships with a number of different lenders, and the idea in theory is to have them work with a borrower to find the cheapest loan that's best suited to their needs . . .

VIGELAND: And what do mortgage brokers get out of this transaction?

KATZ: Well, they get fees. And those fees can be paid a couple of ways. One way is cash that the borrower has to put up at closing. But increasingly they can also take what's called a yield spread premium. The borrower can take their compensation by basically arranging to have the borrower pay a higher interest rate than they might otherwise pay. The broker is permitted to take an additional fee for that arrangement, which then profits the broker and the lender. And brokers in the industry more generally defend the practice as a way that a borrower, who can't put cash up front for a broker's fee, can essentially pay it off over time through higher interest rates.

VIGELAND: Now, when someone's bought a house, and they can't even make the first payment, or perhaps they just make one and then no more, that's usually a sign of mortgage fraud. Now we know what happens to the family; they go into foreclosure. What, if anything, has happened to the people who wrote those loans?

KATZ: I mean, nothing. Brokers have—they basically collect their fees immediately, and then the loan is then out of their hands. And if anything happens to the borrower down the road, that is not immediately the broker's responsibility. It's only if that borrower were to sue, and make the case that they were set up with a loan that is illegally made, then the broker could be held accountable. But that is very unlikely that a borrower going into foreclosure is going to do that because they don't have the money to pay a lawyer. That's why they're going into foreclosure.

Further, in many situations, it can be hard to find quantitative metrics for goal setting. For example, consultants may find it quite difficult to derive **SMART** goals since their work is so often tied to helping others or providing them with a service rather than easily quantifiable output. One good strategy in such cases is to identify the internal customers for the job and set goals tied to the satisfaction and needs of those customers. For instance, a secretary could potentially be held accountable for the customer satisfaction (and **SMART** goals set for the target level of overall satisfaction) of the people (customers) in his or her office suite.

Locke and his colleagues[25] have repeatedly found that setting vague goals, such as "Do your best," are actually no better than having no goals at all and are of no real motivational importance. Remember this: Telling a person to "do your best" is equivalent motivationally to giving the person no goals or instructions. Despite this, providing vague goals is exceedingly common in companies today.

A truly specific goal can be seen in use at an Indiana machine shop. In this case, the goal for a lathe operator was to turn 100 feet of a ¾-inch bar into 80 acceptable pieces per hour. That is a goal that certainly meets the standard of being specific!

In addition to setting **SMART** goals, you can increase your chances of success by getting people involved in the goal-setting process. This is because people are also unlikely to accept goals if they do not feel they were part of the goal-setting process.[26] So whenever you can have associates set their own goals or at least have a voice in the process, you are likely to benefit in terms of goal acceptance. Moreover, people are more likely to accept goals that have been declared in public. Those responsible for the treatment of addictive behaviors know this principle well; a tenet of treatment programs is a public statement of the affliction and a plan to treat it. A sense of outside pressure is increased when a goal has been made public, making people feel more bound by these public goals.

There is an important caveat to add about goal setting and it's the main reason why we placed the manager as the source of motivation in the final position. Goal setting has been shown to work across an impressive range of tasks. An area where it is much more difficult to use, however, is in tasks that require significant amounts of creativity. It is not surprising that setting a goal for a person to be creative is not normally effective—it is not something that people can do "on demand." In fact, significant research suggests that goals may actually interfere with creativity for exactly the same reason they work in other cases.[27] As mentioned in the beginning of this section, one of the reasons goals work is because they narrow the focus of the person with the goal and focus his efforts. Oftentimes, this narrowing of focus can lead a person to do things in a very "uncreative manner" due to the outside pressures.

Reinforcement Theory and Behavior Modification

Another major approach for motivating employees that emanates from the supervisor is reinforcement theory. **Reinforcement theory,** or the notion that people are motivated to repeat behavior that gets rewarded, is perhaps one of the oldest and most well supported of all psychological principles.[28] Indeed, it is an undeniable reality of life that people do what is rewarded and avoid what is punished. Would you write a 10-page paper for a class if no grade were attached, but the professor said, "It will be great for your development"? When undesirable behaviors are rewarded and positive behaviors neglected (or sometimes even punished), dysfunctional results occur in organizations. Great managers tie desired behavior to positive behavior and are successful in communicating that linkage to their people.

For students, one close-to-home example of the folly described in Management Live 6.3 is right in our own university settings where learning and skill building

⇄ MANAGEMENT LIVE 6.3

The Folly of Rewarding A, While Hoping for B[29]

One of the truly classic articles in all of the management literature is "On the Folly of Rewarding A, While Hoping for B." The article was written by Steve Kerr, the chief learning officer for Goldman Sachs and formerly in the same position at General Electric. Kerr observed there are countless cases in organizations and society where the folly is present in that we sincerely hope for one thing, but reward another. Notable among his examples is the hope that doctors will make accurate diagnoses, but that the reward system in place disproportionately rewards treating well people as sick, because of more treatment revenue, reduced threat of malpractice, and the appearance of prudent medicine. Another example is the hope that politicians will be open, frank, and honest; however, the existing reward system elects those who do not reveal any potentially divisive beliefs and who get money directed to their constituents. The lesson is to clarify what you really hope for and then dig into your culture to determine if that is truly what is perceived to be rewarded. Kerr has convincingly argued that it too often is not.

are hoped to be the prized behaviors. However, it is hardly provocative to suggest that the indicators we use for learning and knowledge gain—grades—have increasingly become more important than the goals that underlie them. It is now grades, independent of true knowledge or skill, that are often most influential in job placement offices and graduate school admission departments. As a not very surprising result, fraternities and sororities are obsessive about keeping good test files, the Internet has emerged as a source of plagiarized term papers, and cheating is a greater problem than ever in U.S. universities. The point is that if we are going to avoid the folly, we first need to clearly identify the behaviors we want and then find ways to reward those behaviors and only those behaviors. This is exactly what the practice of behavior modification is designed to do.

Based on the basic tenets of reinforcement theory, the managerial practice known as **organizational behavior modification** commonly involves a five-step problem approach to increasing motivation and ultimately performance (Figure 6.9). The five major steps are that (1) performance-related behaviors are identified; (2) the frequency of these behaviors is measured; (3) the contingencies supporting the current behaviors are identified; (4) a behaviorally based intervention strategy is developed and implemented; and (5) the resulting performance-related behaviors are measured.

Examples of Behavior Modification in the Real World

Behavior modification has been used successfully in an extremely wide range of situations. In one of the most famous examples, Emery Air Freight Corp. (which was ultimately bought by UPS) used behavior modification to improve

FIGURE 6.9
The Organizational Behavior Modification Model

The Five Major Steps

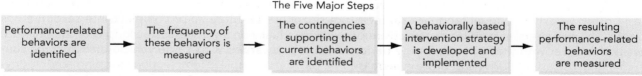

| Performance-related behaviors are identified | → | The frequency of these behaviors is measured | → | The contingencies supporting the current behaviors are identified | → | A behaviorally based intervention strategy is developed and implemented | → | The resulting performance-related behaviors are measured |

Source: Adapted from Luthans, F., and Stajkovic, A. D. (1999). Reinforce for performance: The need to go beyond pay and even rewards. *Academy of Management Executive*, 13, 49–57.

its customer service. Emery had a goal for its customer service department of responding to customer questions within 90 minutes. At first, the employees perceived that they met this goal about 9 times out of 10. In reality, however, Emery Air Freight was only meeting this goal 3 out of 10 times. Under any measure, 30 percent cannot be considered very good! As a result of this poor performance, a behavior modification system was established in which the employees physically recorded how quickly each customer request was answered. The supervisor then gave praise and recognition for high performance. Within one day, performance went from 30 percent to 90 percent goal attainment and stayed between 90 and 95 percent for over three years.[30] This example should give you an idea of just how powerful behavior modification really is!

Some recent examples of the success of behavior modification in handling everyday work issues can be seen in the following examples. A food distribution company implemented a behavior modification program at one of its warehouses. The program reduced order errors by 10 percent, with a cost saving of about $10,000.[31] In the area of safety, recent research estimates suggest money spent on safety-related behavior modification programs can have payoffs of more than 10:1. In other words, for every $1 invested in these programs, more than $10 can be saved due to lower insurance costs, fewer accidents, and reduced worker compensation claims.[32]

To further make the case, behavior modification was recently used in a retail setting to modify the behavior of cashiers in keeping their register drawers balanced. Initially, daily cash shortages averaged $2.27. After the behavior modification program was implemented, average cash shortages were reduced to $0.06 per day.[33] An additional example of a success with pizza delivery drivers can be seen in Management Live 6.4.

Developing and Implementing a Behavioral Strategy

While behavior modification is relatively straightforward, there are some important details specifically related to the fourth step of the process: developing and implementing a behavioral intervention strategy. To effectively develop and implement behavioral modification strategies, it is important to understand some fundamentals of learning and behavioral change. The process of linking

MANAGEMENT LIVE 6.4

Behavior Modification and Pizza Delivery Drivers[34]

When most of us think of safe drivers, pizza delivery drivers aren't at the top of the list. In fact, reckless pizza delivery drivers have been the cause of numerous multimillion-dollar lawsuits and been a serious concern to pizza makers all over the United States. A study conducted by Timothy Ludwig, Jay Biggs, Sandra Wagner, and E. Scott Geller investigated the effects of a safe driving competition utilizing publicly posted individual feedback as the behavioral intervention. Their study looked at the safety behaviors (for example, turn-signal use, safety belt use, and complete stopping at intersections) of 82 pizza deliverers. After getting a baseline measure, pizza deliverers received posted weekly individual feedback on their turn-signal use (at Store A) or complete intersection stops (at Store B). The deliverers' safe driving scores were posted individually on a vertical scale along with their names. Each week the driver with the highest average performance was rewarded with a free vehicle-maintenance coupon. Turn-signal use among drivers at Store A increased 22 percent. Complete intersection stopping among drivers at Store B increased 17 percent. Although the winners of the weekly competitions had the greatest increase in performance, nonwinners also increased their instances of safe driving during the competition.

consequences with voluntary behaviors is referred to as **operant conditioning.** Operant conditioning employs strategies involving the addition or removal of pleasant or aversive consequences. Since there are two actions (addition and removal) and two types of consequences (pleasant and aversive), four different operant conditioning strategies are possible (see Table 6.7).

Positive Reinforcement

As indicated in Table 6.7, **positive reinforcement** occurs when a behavior is linked with a consequence an employee considers pleasant. Examples of positive reinforcement occur all around us every day. A child given a certificate for getting all A's on his report card, an employee given a bonus for meeting a difficult performance goal, and a politician reelected after doing a good job for her constituents are all examples of positive reinforcement. Positive reinforcement should be used whenever the goal is to increase the frequency of a desirable behavior because it modifies behavior in a way that is not viewed as being controlling and because it does not bring about negative side effects. Everybody wins with positive reinforcement. One of the challenges facing many managers, however, is what to provide as a reward. Remember that managers should seek rewards that have value to the employee. This also ties back to the idea of strengthening valence from the beginning of the chapter.

A frequent lament of managers everywhere, public sector or private, is that they have little discretionary power to reward their high performers with more money. Since this is often the case, an important management skill is to be creative in finding reinforcements that are both motivating and cost-effective, especially due to tough economic conditions that impact most organizations. As Management Live 6.5 illustrates, managers have had great success with showing appreciation using some surprisingly simple techniques.

Beyond showing appreciation for good work, it is also a good idea to recognize important milestones and be thoughtful regarding personal issues and crises people face. Purchase a large supply of note cards and get in the habit of sending them for birthdays and promotions or other events. Send flowers with a note for engagements, weddings, or family deaths. People will remember your kindness, probably much longer than you will!

"Simple observation suggests that most of us are trinket freaks—if they represent genuine thanks for a genuine assist."

—Tom Peters

TABLE 6.7   Four Operant Conditioning Strategies

	Consequence Added	Consequence Removed
Pleasant Consequence	**Positive Reinforcement**	**Extinction**
	Increase frequency of a desired behavior	Reduce frequency of an undesired behavior.
	Example: An athletics coach gives hard-working players more playing time to reward their effort.	*Example:* A club president withholds laughter because she is tired of her VP always making jokes.
Aversive Consequence	**Punishment**	**Negative Reinforcement**
	Decrease frequency of an undesired behavior.	Increase frequency of a desired behavior.
	Example: An Army sergeant has a private do 100 push-ups for being late for roll call.	*Example:* Your roommates tell you they will stop nagging you if you do the dishes.

Another good source for creative and cost-effective rewards is a collection of ideas put together by author Bob Nelson, in his book *1001 Ways to Reward Your Employees*.[35] Nelson makes the point that rewards don't need to be expensive to have big impacts. The following list provides a flavor of the types of rewards he suggests:

"There are two things people want more than sex and money . . . recognition and praise."

—Mary Kay Ash

- Write a letter to the employee's family about what his or her efforts mean.
- Arrange for a senior executive to have a recognition lunch with the employee.
- Find out what an employee's hobby is and purchase a small gift related to that hobby.
- Dedicate a prime parking space for the outstanding employee of the month.
- Wash an employee's car in the parking lot during business hours.
- Have a group of managers personally cook lunch for a group of top-performing employees.
- Use outstanding employees in the organization's advertisements.

We need to always remember, however, that different employees will have different valence scores for each of the examples listed. One person might view having lunch with a senior executive as a valued outcome, while another might view it as being worse than a trip to the dentist. See Tool Kit 6.4 for a step-by-step approach to providing effective positive reinforcement.

MANAGEMENT LIVE 6.5

Simple Rewards[36]

For some ideas of how simple rewards can demonstrate appreciation, take a look at the following successful programs from some top U.S. companies.

- **The Spirit of Fred Award.** Walt Disney World in Orlando, Florida, uses this simple recognition program named for an employee named Fred (not too surprisingly!). When Fred got his first salaried position, a few key people taught him the values needed to be successful at Disney. The name Fred became an acronym for Friendly, Resourceful, Enthusiastic, and Dependable. The award has become highly valued within Disney.

- **Thanks a Bunch.** Maritz Performance Improvement Co. in St. Louis, Missouri, has a Thanks a Bunch program in which employees receive a bouquet of flowers in appreciation for special favors or jobs well done. The employee receiving the award then passes the flowers on to someone else who has been helpful, with the idea of seeing how many people can be given the bouquet in a single day. With the flowers, the employees get a written thank-you card. At certain times throughout the year, the cards are entered in a drawing for prizes.

- **The Golden Banana Award.** Years ago, a Hewlett-Packard Co. engineer burst into his manager's office in Palo Alto, California, to announce he had solved an important problem. In response, his manager looked around to find something to reward the employee with and ended up handing the employee a banana from his lunch with the words, "Well done. Congratulations!" The employee was somewhat confused at first, but over the years the Golden Banana Award became a prestigious honor given to inventive Hewlett-Packard employees.

MANAGER'S TOOL KIT

Tool Kit 6.4   Steps to Rewarding Effectively

1. Describe the desirable behavior.
2. Explain the benefits that the desirable behavior is causing.
3. Explain the consequences if the desirable behavior continues.
4. Provide examples and time for questions regarding desired behaviors.
5. Monitor behavior and reward desirable behavior.
6. Follow through with continued rewards should the positive behavior continue.

The work of Richard Easterlin[37] may provide some answers as to why monetary rewards may not always be the most effective reward. His research has to do with how people adapt to having increased amounts of money across their lives. Easterlin, an economist, has found that young adults start out with fairly similar material aspirations. As young adults, he finds that people with more money are happier because they are better able to fulfill their aspirations. In other words, when we all have similar material expectations, people with more money are better able to meet those expectations than people with less money.

As we age, however, getting more money does not cause well-being to increase (for people with low or high incomes) because it generates an equivalent growth in material aspirations. In other words, as you get more money, you have an increased amount of wants. Since happiness is linked to the ratio of what we have versus what we want, this ratio will not tend to change for a person as his or her income goes up. So the more we get, the more we want, and we rarely can close the gap between what we have and what we want.

Extinction

As compared to the relatively straightforward application of positive reinforcement, **extinction** is the most difficult strategy to transfer from the laboratory to the work environment.[38] The technical definition of extinction is a behavior followed by no response. The idea of extinction is that a behavior not followed by any consequence would not likely be repeated again (because it did not bring about any gain for the person performing the behavior). For instance, extinction is normally thought of as a strategy for modifying the behavior of a person who complains about petty issues at work. The idea is that if the supervisor does not respond to petty complaints ("I don't like the color of the walls in the office," "My desk chair has a stain on it," or "Tom's desk is newer than mine"), then the complainer will stop complaining because the complaints do not improve the situation.

However, in real-world situations, people hold expectations about what is likely to follow their actions based upon what they have observed in the past. As a result, what a supervisor intends as a nonresponse is usually interpreted either positively or negatively. Whatever the result, people clearly may interpret a great deal of meaning—quite possibly unintended meaning—from a nonresponse. One good example of extinction working as intended is as a response to a person who

"Poor man wants to be rich, rich man wants to be king. The king ain't satisfied till he rules everything."

—Bruce Springsteen, "Badlands"

makes meetings longer because he's always making jokes. By not laughing at the jokes, co-workers can quickly make the joking stop.

Negative Reinforcement

Like positive reinforcement, **negative reinforcement** is an attempt to increase the frequency of a desirable behavior. Negative reinforcement, however, involves linking desired behaviors with the removal of undesirable consequences, rather than the addition of positive consequences associated with positive reinforcement. For instance, promising a sales representative she can delegate her 10 least favorite accounts if she can increase her sales by 30 percent would be a constructive form of negative reinforcement. It is important to remember the term "negative reinforcement" refers to the act of *removing* an aversive consequence. In general, positive reinforcement is the preferred method to increase the frequency of behavior, but negative reinforcement may serve as an additional tool when a manager is not able to control many desirable positive outcomes but is able to remove negative ones.

When used improperly, negative reinforcement takes the form of "managing by threats." An example of this can be seen when a manager says, "If your numbers don't improve, you'll be fired." When the numbers improve, the person is not fired and the threat is removed. While this may work in the short term, it has harmful side effects and is not recommended as an effective management practice.

⇄ MANAGEMENT LIVE 6.6

Show Me the Money!

In a large meta-analysis, researchers Alexander Stajkovic and Fred Luthans examined 72 studies that used behavior modification principles to increase employee performance. In each of these studies, a particular form of reinforcer was used, including money tied to performance (the employee receives money after reaching a previously set goal), social recognition (the employee receives public praise and honor), and feedback (the employee is told how well he or she is performing the job). The results tell an interesting and important story. As seen in the following figure, all three reinforcers were effective in improving employee performance: money, 21 percent increase; social recognition, 16 percent increase; and feedback, 11 percent increase.

The real lessons from this large study are twofold. First, the largest percentage increase (45 percent) occurred from a combination of providing money, social recognition, and feedback. If you have wondered how great managers use rewards to motivate performance, it seems to be rather straightforward: Frequently tell people how they're doing on the job, recognize their achievements in front of others, and, when possible, reward performance with additional cash.

Second, a frequent complaint of many managers is that they have little power to provide financial rewards, making motivating people impossible. This study clearly demonstrates that by simply providing a little recognition or giving regular feedback, both of which require no financial commitment, managers can significantly increase overall employee performance. In the long run, such increases may ultimately allow a manager increased capacity to provide financial rewards.

Source: Stajkovic, A. D., and Luthans, F. (2003). Behavioral management and task performance in organizations: Conceptual background, meta-analysis, and test of alternative models. *Personnel Psychology*, 56, 155–194.

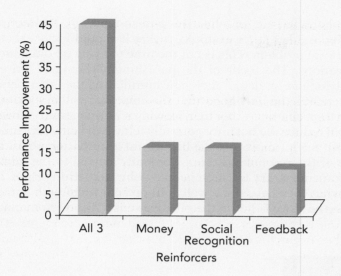

The Effect of Reinforcers on Employee Performance Improvement

Punishment

The final behavioral strategy discussed here is **punishment,** which consists of adding an unpleasant consequence as a response to a person's behavior, with the goal of stopping the behavior from happening in the future. For example, if an employee disregards safety guidelines and acts recklessly on the job, a reprimand would be an appropriate means of trying to reduce this dangerous behavior. Most companies have punishment systems that increase in severity with the number of times the punishment has been administered (called **progressive discipline**). For instance, a first offense may be associated with a verbal warning, whereas a second offense will receive a written warning, and the employee is fired for a third offense.

Although punishment is relatively straightforward, it should be avoided unless it is really needed. Research has suggested that punishment, especially if it is viewed as being unfairly administered, can have negative unintended side effects such as encouraging people to rebel because they feel they are being too tightly controlled.[39] Moreover, there is more useful motivational information in positive reinforcement because it essentially specifies what *to do.* By its very nature, punishment can only specify what *not to do*—of which there may be an infinite number of variations.

Since punishment normally provides people the most trouble, we wanted to provide more guidance on how to effectively discipline. A useful metaphor regarding the application of punishment is that of the "red hot stove." Specifically, that means punishment will be administered most effectively when it has the following four characteristics:

- **Clear Expectations.** The stove is *red hot*—anyone can see and feel that if they touch it they will be burned.
- **Consistent.** Any time anyone touches the stove (commits the behavior) they get burned.
- **Timely.** Anyone who touches the stove gets burned immediately.
- **Powerful.** The stove is *red* hot and leaves a severe and memorable burn. This makes the effect lasting.

"All in all, punishment hardens and renders people more insensible; it concentrates; it increases the feeling of estrangement; it strengthens the power of resistance."

—Friedrich Nietzsche

Another characteristic of effective punishment, in addition to the four described in the red hot stove example, is that it should focus exclusively on the specific behavioral problem. This is not the time to bring up old issues or to make general accusations. The focus of the punishment should be on eliminating a problem behavior, not on demoralizing or humiliating the other person. A behavioral focus increases the likelihood that the employee will associate the negative response with a specific act rather than viewing it as a generalized negative evaluation, which will reduce the hostility normally felt when being reprimanded. Please refer to Tool Kit 6.5 for more specific behavioral information about punishment.

The rules of the red hot stove apply equally as well to the administering of positive reinforcement. Try to catch people doing something right, be specific in telling them what they have done well, and present them with some type of recognition while the stove is hot in the positive sense. Although managers typically

MANAGER'S TOOL KIT

Tool Kit 6.5 **Steps to Effective Punishment**

1. Meet privately. Never punish in public.
2. Describe the undesirable behavior.
3. Explain the problems the undesirable behavior is causing.
4. Allow questions and opportunities for clarification.
5. Explain consequences if the undesirable behavior does not change.
6. Provide examples and time for questions regarding desired behaviors.
7. Monitor behavior, and reward desirable behavior.
8. Follow through with appropriate responses to behavior (an aversive consequence if the behavior has not changed or positive outcomes if the behavior has changed).

have more discomfort and even dread administering punishment, *ineffective positive reinforcement* is often a greater problem because managers are naturally inclined to assume people know they are doing well and to give only global non-specific feedback that has little motivating value (for example, "You are great; I wish I had five more like you").

As is evident from the preceding descriptions, there is a time and place for all four of the behavioral strategies. These strategies can be used either to make unacceptable behaviors acceptable or to transform acceptable behaviors into exceptional ones. They are designed to avoid the harmful effects typically associated with the improper use of discipline as well as to assist with the appropriate use of rewards.

> CASE CONCLUDED

Selling the benefit. In every daily staff meeting, Ritz-Carlton managers reinforce one of 12 service values all employees are expected to embody on the job. Service Value No. 2 is "I am always responsive to the expressed and unexpressed wishes and needs of our guests." The housekeepers were encouraged to discuss how this value applied to their daily tasks.

"What is an expressed wish?" the supervisor asked the group.

"If a guest asks for extra pillows," a woman said.

"That's exactly right," he said. "But it's the unexpressed wishes that create the Ritz-Carlton mystique," he continued, offering the example of a housekeeper who notices a champagne bottle sitting in melted ice and replaces the ice before being asked to do so. The question was then asked: "Why do we do it? Why do we go the extra mile?"

One housekeeper volunteered: "It offers a personal touch that shows we care."

"That's exactly right," another added. "It reflects our commitment to five-star service."

Employees need to understand how their daily actions impact their clients. As shown through Ritz-Carlton, staff meetings help employees make that connection.

Do you think most meetings motivate an organization to exceed expectations? How could meetings be conducted to maximize their impact?

Ask for feedback. Employees are encouraged to speak up during staff meetings. During a housekeeping meeting, the employees were debating the benefit of one cleaner over another. It seemed they preferred the old product over the new one. At first glance, it was a rather mundane discussion except

their supervisor was listening intently, as if the discussion was the most important thing in his life at the moment—nodding, maintaining eye contact, and asking questions. He showed genuine interest in the topic. If it is important to his staff, it is important to him.

Praise effectively. Ritz-Carlton managers don't focus on what employees have done wrong but instead seek to help them improve on a given task. Supervisors use staff meetings to publicly praise employees. Criticism is done in private.

Motivation can and should take place everywhere within an organization. Simon Cooper cannot personally motivate each of his 35,000 employees worldwide, so it's up to his department managers to reinforce the brand and its values through daily interactions with their teams. Are your employees engaged? Are they inspired to follow your vision? Five-star service does not begin with them. It begins with *you*.

Questions

1. What can individual managers do that reflects the same strategies that the most motivating company environments embody?

2. Is there value in selecting people with high motivation potential (see Chapter 12)?

3. Are these techniques limited to the hospitality industry or could they be incorporated into the daily routines of the multitude of organizations that perform business every day.

Concluding Note

Putting It All Together to Increase Motivation

Hopefully, you have seen how the ideas presented can be used to help you "motivate who, to do what, under what circumstances." While this series of questions obviously does not have a short answer that is very satisfying (if it did, we wouldn't have needed an entire chapter to explain it), you should now see the importance of the three techniques for filling the bucket. This metaphor helps us see why it is much easier to motivate certain people rather than others (the motivate *who* question), to do certain things (the issue of creativity comes to mind here and is an important consideration) under certain circumstances (when the person is well matched to a job that is highly motivating according to the job characteristics model).

As you can see, there are clearly multiple ways to "fill up" an employee's motivational bucket. As managers, it is important to be aware of the dominant needs of our people and the various motivators available to us in rewards and the work itself. Motivation theories offer managers many applicable evidence-based tools for creating more energizing workplaces. The challenge is to put them to work in areas that matter. Based on practical experience and the tools and techniques discussed in this chapter, we offer a few critical prescriptions for any manager in almost any situation to ensure high motivation:

1. **Recognize individual differences in motivation.** Few people are motivated by the same things. Use the platinum rule to find out what best motivates each individual, including what type of rewards each employee values most.

2. **Strive for fairness, not equality, in rewards and punishments.** You do not have to give everyone the exact same reward. You *do* need to ensure the rewards you give out are proportional to the performance *and* that they are equitable.

3. **Do everything you can to make the job itself more motivating.** Even in a job that seems boring or difficult to improve, there are usually very concrete ways of implementing the job enrichment interventions to improve the job significantly.

4. **Set good goals.** Always specifically define success. We can't emphasize enough that setting good goals is one of the most efficient ways to increase motivation.

5. **Link rewards and punishments directly to performance.** Make sure the rewards that people receive are based upon their performance.

6. **Give credit where credit is due.** Recognize people publicly for their achievements and don't take credit for your employees' work.

7. **Model the way.** Delegation is an important part of managing. However, nothing is more de-motivating than bosses who ask other people to do things they (the bosses) are not personally willing to do. Model the behavior you want from your people.

KEY TERMS

autonomy 214
core job dimensions 212

equity 204
equity sensitivity 205

ERG theory 210
expectancy 199

< < CASE
Maintaining Employee Motivation

When Gamal Aziz became president of MGM Grand Hotel & Casino in 2001, the huge hotel was doing extremely well—as was Las Vegas. The challenge for Aziz was to take something good and make it even better. Under Aziz, revenue zoomed, and along with the Bellagio, the MGM Grand became one of the most profitable hotels on the Las Vegas strip.

But ask Aziz what was the single most important factor in the jump, and he won't talk about twirling acrobats or signature dishes such as free-range quail stuffed with foie gras. His answer is the employees. Now with times getting tougher in Las Vegas as tourism drops and gambling revenues fall, Aziz says his people have become even more critical to the company's success.

Cost-Cutting Moves

"Employee engagement in times of difficulties and severe economic climate is far more profoundly important now," says Aziz. "Employees are willing to give their all when they are well-treated, appreciated. And the ability to unlock that potential

is a competitive distinction. . . . It's their decisions, their actions, their attitude that really make the difference. Imagine taking 10,000 employees, and each and every one of them wanting to give more. That's really the difference between [us and] a company that has its employees just punching the clock and trying to get through the day."

But Aziz, like all managers, is under pressure to justify every cost. Although his hotel still had high occupancy rates, groups are canceling, and those that do come are spending much less per visit. That's forced Aziz to reduce costs associated with some of these successful programs. He still does regular employee appreciation dinners for top performers, but he's spending about half as much this year as last. He's started recruiting managers from other properties to attend his MGM Grand University as a way

to reduce the costs of training his own top managers. And he's put on hold one program that trains next-generation line managers.

Rank-and-File Insight

Aziz shares with employees the challenges he's facing. Employees, the CEO says, were what got the hotel to the next level, and they are the key to pulling through hard times. "We will get through this, we will survive," says Aziz. "Once we get through this, the employees will be the ones who have gotten us through."

When Aziz arrived in 2001, he quickly sought out rank-and-file insight into the hotel and how it could improve. A survey of the hotel's 10,000 employees made clear that very little was being communicated to the staff about the events going on in the hotel on a daily basis, including such basics

(continued)

(continued)

as who was staying there, and what the hotel had to offer those particular guests. Employees sometimes didn't even know what conventions were at the hotel. That made it difficult for the staff to give the level of service that would affect customer loyalty, return visits, and spending in the hotel.

Aziz came up with a simple fix. There is a short meeting now at the start of every shift in which every employee is given the rundown of what's happening in the hotel that day. It's a simple concept based on meetings that restaurants have long held to get waiters up on the daily specials. But rolled out across 10,000 employees a day, it's a major undertaking.

MGM Programs

The MGM Grand made other moves to help employees grow. In his recent book, *Closing the Engagement Gap*, co-author and Towers Perrin Managing Director Don Lowman highlights many MGM programs, including the MGM Grand University that offers dozens of classes on an invitation-only basis for high achievers. The MGM Grand Leadership Institute is a 24-week program for executives. And REACH! is the hotel's six-month course on basic supervisory skills for ambitious hourly workers. All this investment in the staff, along with recognition dinners and other rewards, has led to more than 90 percent of MGM Grand employees saying they are satisfied with their jobs, and 89 percent saying their work has special meaning. According to the book, 91 percent report they are proud to tell others where they work.

"One of the ways we'll get through this dire economic circumstance we find ourselves in is if leaders set this tone that we're all in this together," says Lowman, who worked with a multitude of companies as a consultant at Towers Perrin and ranks MGM Grand among the best at connecting with employees. "It's very easy to say 'Let's just whack 15 percent of the company.' You can immediately take a lot of costs off your books. But that has a big cost both on the people doing the whacking [and on the company] in the long term, when you'll need those people [you let go] again."

In the book, Lowman sites a finding from the firm's survey of tens of thousands of employees in six countries—including the U.S., China, and India—that the No. 1 thing that engages employees is senior management's interest in their well-being. That trumped career advancement, relationship with one's direct supervisor, and even pay. Visiting the MGM Grand, Lowman says he found evidence of that connection in spades. Aziz was impressive, Lowman says, for his tendency to ask questions and listen to the answers. Engagement starts at the top.

Discussion Questions

1. Using what you learned about rewards, identify some powerful rewards mentioned in the case and explain why they are so powerful.

2. Apply the expectancy theory of motivation to the case and explain what Gamal Aziz is doing well. Now, pick another theory discussed in the chapter and apply it as well. Can multiple theories provide insight about why Aziz is successful?

3. Instead of focusing on cutting employees, this case argues that there are other routes to success (even in difficult times). Why do you think this is true? Can you think of cases where it may not be true?

Source: N. Byrnes (2009). The Issue: Maintaining Employee Engagement. *Bloomsburg Businessweek, Interactive Case Study,* January 16. Retrieved from http://www.businessweek.com/managing/content/jan2009/ca20090116_444132.htm

SELECT MANAGE ~~WHAT?~~ DEBRIEFS

Taking Over as Manager: Building a More Motivational Workplace

This challenge is at the heart of what makes great management—establishing the type of culture and relationships where people are highly motivated to give their very best. While there are an infinite number of specific tactics you might employ, we think a good framework for addressing this challenge is the three-faucet analogy used in the text. That is, motivation essentially stems from three sources—the person, the job, and the manager—so a multidimensional approach that considers all three is likely to be your most fruitful approach to creating a motivational workplace.

Motivation from the Person. As popular theories of motivation demonstrate, different people have different needs, and even the same people can differ in their most driving motives at different times. The simple (but neglected) implication is to make a concerted effort to learn more about each individual you manage and to make such learning a continuous process. Frequently ask your associates about their goals and dreams and what they might find most stimulating in their work. As we note in the text, some people place a premium on achievement and recognition in their jobs, others put a priority on affiliation and belonging, while others want to have more power and control over what they do. So ask them directly what they expect of you and how they think you can help them in their work and career. Wherever possible, seek and select people on the basis of the energy and interest they show in the work you do.

The prior manager seemed to treat all people the same, and that is usually a grave motivational error. The goal is equity—not equality—and never underestimate the power of equity perceptions in influencing behavior. If people think they are treated fairly, you can get them to jump high hurdles for you. If they think your management behavior is not equitable, watch out!

Motivation from the Job. A second source of motivational options is the job itself. Not surprisingly, some job characteristics are far more motivating than others, and a terrific evidence-based framework exists for thinking about those aspects that might be influenced to enhance motivation. The five key characteristics are skill variety, task identity, task significance, autonomy, and feedback. The most motivating workplaces are where people feel like their jobs are stimulating, not boring, so look for ways to build those five elements into the jobs your people are doing.

Motivation from the Manager. Here again, there are many tactics you could deploy, but a focus on two general areas will serve you well. First, very soon after you take the job, begin the process of establishing SMART goals for your unit and all individuals in your unit. Goals are both informational (they clarify what you want done) and motivational (they stimulate action). The power of effective goal setting in inducing higher performance is as close to a management "law" as exists. Indeed, if you are truly serious about establishing a more motivational context here, it might constitute managerial "malpractice" not to utilize the power of goal setting.

Second, and relatedly, pay particular attention to how rewards (and punishments) are distributed in your group. First, aim to remove any de-motivators that may be keeping people from making more of an effort and achieving higher performance. Then aim to create a context where you tie rewards to desired performance. A good maxim is to "reward your doers." Who is doing the best work, and are they promptly, visibly, and significantly rewarded for doing so? It seems that was not the case under the prior manager, which had the resulting dampening effect on motivation.

Dealing with the Unmotivated Person

The best motivation model for diagnosing this type of situation is expectancy theory, which suggests that people are not motivated when they (1) don't know specifically what they are supposed to do; (2) don't think they are capable; (3) don't see any outcome (reward or punishment) tied to a behavior; or (4) don't value the reward/outcome that is attached to the behavior. So the equation $M = E \times I \times V$ helps us diagnose why this CPA may not be motivated to give his best, and, in turn, what might help motivate him to do so.

Expectancy. Does he know what high performance (organizationally and individually) looks like? Does he think he can do it? Few people will engage fully unless they have some ownership in the outcomes they are seeking and believe they can achieve them. In this case, there is little sense of collective goals or individual accountability

(continued)

(continued)

for such goals. If this guy is not sure what it is he can do to contribute, then it is unlikely he will be giving his best effort. So one key here is to clarify his expected performance outcomes, and get his input on it and personal statements that he understands and feels he can achieve those outcomes.

Instrumentality.   Does he believe that motivated effort will be linked to rewards or any sanctions attached to low performance? People will not be motivated in situations where there are ambiguous or nonexistent links between performance and specific outcomes. A recurring maxim of motivation is that "what gets measured and rewarded gets done." That linkage seems to be missing here, and is therefore certainly part of the low motivation.

Valence.   Does he value the rewards in place? People will not engage fully if the rewards (or punishments) are not sufficiently important to them. That is, do they feel that what they receive (which may be experience, money, opportunity, or a whole host of other outcomes) warrants the effort to come and participate?

Since any motivation is a function of all three factors, this associate will need to have high positives on all three. For example, even if he has high expectancy and high instrumentality, he still won't participate if they are completely neutral in valence.

The best way to address low motivation is to first diagnose (there should be no treatment without a diagnosis), in as realistic a way as possible, why it is that people do not give their best effort. Then match your recommendations to those diagnosed problems and come up with as many realistic, creative, and truly plausible ways in which to motivate people to give their very best.

Enriching the Boring Job

The most critical thing is to understand what it is that makes a job interesting or enriched in the first place (and why the lack of it makes one boring and maybe even demeaning). Fortunately, one of the most robust models in the organizational literature is the job characteristics model, which concisely outlines those very characteristics, and further outlines how the characteristics lead to meaningfulness, responsibility, and a knowledge of results, which in turn induce greater satisfaction, motivation, and effectiveness.

The five characteristics are skill variety, task identity, task significance, autonomy, and feedback, and the challenge is to be creative in how those characteristics could be increased in this context—with the result being a more interesting and ultimately productive secretarial job. Your text includes specific examples of how the characteristics can be practically increased.

- **Combine tasks (affects skill variety, task identity, and task significance):** Take on more different things to do—computer or otherwise—cross-training on different roles.
- **Group tasks into natural work units (affects task significance and task identity):** Team up with other clerical folks and rotate tasks—this mainly gives the employee a support group and less isolation.
- **Give contact with customers (affects skill variety, autonomy, and feedback):** Work with the people in your organization to interface with the end-users of what you do.
- **Vertically load jobs (affects autonomy):** Add in new roles and expand beyond current roles so she is not labeled and stuck just in traditional clerical work.
- **Open feedback channels (affects feedback):** Develop a scorecard to be completed by all those she works for so she can get a more thorough and timely perspective on what she is doing well and how she can improve.

A subtle nuance is that enrichment needs to be balanced with efficiency. That is, while there is substantial evidence that enriched jobs create positive outcomes, they also run the risk of lowering efficiency and overall organizational productivity. That is, the designers of jobs low in those characteristics are not all evil but usually just looking for high efficiency and low cost. It is not some insidious plot to abuse people or treat them like drones or bore them to death or something just as bad. Rather, in a competitive world they are simply adapting Henry Ford's discovery that specialization leads to higher efficiency in a number of dimensions.

The point is that such specialization also can lead to some dysfunctional outcomes associated with boredom and repetition and so on. So the persistent challenge for job designers is to try to balance specialization and its efficiency outcomes and job enrichment with its quality, turnover and absenteeism reduction, and citizenship benefits. If something along those lines is not done in this current case, the outcome will very likely be the loss of a productive employee and the high turnover costs associated with bringing in a replacement.

CHAPTER

7

Managing Employee Performance

OBJECTIVES

KNOWING

DOING

After reading this chapter, you should be able to:

KO 7-1 Define organizational citizenship and state its importance to organizational functioning.

KO 7-2 Describe the major steps in the performance-management cycle.

KO 7-3 Describe the advantages and disadvantages of different performance assessment methods.

KO 7-4 Understand the most prevalent errors in performance assessment.

KO 7-5 Articulate the key factors that contribute to effective performance feedback.

KO 7-6 Contrast consultative and expert coaching.

DO 7-1 Manage employee attitudes to reduce turnover.

DO 7-2 Set clear performance expectations.

DO 7-3 Evaluate job performance using multiple methods and multiple sources of data.

DO 7-4 Overcome common errors in observing performance.

DO 7-5 Deliver effective performance feedback to a peer or an employee.

DO 7-6 Diagnose employee problems and manage them with performance improvement discussions and training.

DO 7-7 Make a reassignment or termination decision.

Case: The Dallas Mavericks

A recent article in the field of human resource management is entitled *Everyone Hates Performance Evaluation* and it has become very popular among managers and employees alike. The reason for the popularity is that most of us have had (or know of) negative experiences with performance evaluation and thus the title resonates with us personally. Performance evaluations are often disliked because they tend to be subjective and often not related to important performance objectives. For example, all too many performance appraisals rely solely on subjective individual traits like initiative or professionalism or, even worse, attractiveness, height, or charisma.

Aware of the common weaknesses in evaluation, and how those weaknesses manifest themselves in the evaluation of professional basketball players, Mark Cuban, the owner of the Dallas Mavericks NBA basketball team, decided to do things a different way. Partnering with Wayne Winston, a professor of decision sciences at Indiana University, and author of the book *Mathletics*, Cuban sought to evaluate his players in a more objective way—one in which their evaluation was not tied solely to individual statistics.

< < EVERYONE HATES PERFORMANCE EVALUATION—BUT THEY REALLY SHOULDN'T

1. How are professional basketball players typically evaluated, and what are problems/limitations with those typical appraisals?

2. If you were a team owner, on what measures would you want your players evaluated?

3. Would it be worth a significant investment in performance evaluation? Why or why not? What benefits could be achieved?

1. Critiquing an Existing Performance Evaluation Form

Shown in the following is an authentic reproduction of the performance appraisal used for the servers at a typical chain restaurant (disguised here as "Chez Beaumaire"). Recognizing that you have recently completed a management course and are up to date on the latest evidence and best practice, your boss asks you to do three things:

1. Briefly make the case for him that effective performance appraisal is important enough that the managers at his restaurant should care enough to improve their form. Illustrate your arguments specifically in terms of the positive outcomes for that restaurant (critique the existing form with respect to its strengths and weaknesses: What does it help them accomplish? How does it limit them?).

2. Make recommendations for improvement—including some examples or illustrations of things you think would better help them meet their performance evaluation objectives. Be sure to include an explanation of why your improvements are better than what they currently do and also why these improvements will not create an overwhelming amount of extra work or hassle.

CHEZ Beaumaire
Server Performance Evaluation

\# of hrs worked/wk _____

Direct supervisor _____

Performance Evaluation (Please rate against all other servers previously assigned to you)

	Poor		Average		Outstanding	
Customer service	1	2	3	4	5	6
Willingness to perform assignments	1	2	3	4	5	6
Able to perform assignments	1	2	3	4	5	6
Punctuality	1	2	3	4	5	6
Cooperativeness	1	2	3	4	5	6
Initiative	1	2	3	4	5	6
Attitude	1	2	3	4	5	6
Overall evaluation	1	2	3	4	5	6

Recommendations/comments

_____

I HAVE DISCUSSED THIS PERFORMANCE EVALUATION WITH THE ABOVE SERVER

_____ Yes _____ No   Signature _____ Date _____

2. Evaluating Job Performance

Last summer, you were an intern at Techlo, a logistics company catering to the high-tech industry. The internships were extremely attractive with high pay and great perks. One reason the internships are so attractive is that of the three interns Techlo takes each summer, at least one is traditionally offered a job after graduation. In fact, you took a job offer and you've been working for Techlo for one year. Given your clear understanding of the intern role, your boss assigns you the responsibility of managing the new interns. Critical to this role will be to evaluate their performance over the four-month internship. Your boss will use your evaluation as the primary factor in determining which intern will be invited to join the firm full-time after graduation.

How should you determine the best-performing intern? How can you ensure the process for evaluating the interns' performance is fair? Are there typical mistakes managers often make in these situations? The interns are all very talented, so what might help you distinguish good from great?

3. Managing Both the Problem and the Star Employee

Your assistant operations manager, Ken, is truly a great guy. Everybody loves him. He's funny, very social, and good-looking. He also seems to be a great source of support for other employees. Indeed, several fellow employees would claim Ken among their best friends. Ken seems to have everything going for him. There is only one problem—Ken doesn't get results. In the two years Ken has worked in your store, he has never once met a single goal. You've met with him on numerous occasions about his performance, and each time he tells you the same thing, "I'll work on it, boss. You don't have to worry about me." After these conversations, Ken puts in a few good weeks and sometimes shows improvement. Shortly thereafter, however, his performance slides again.

What steps should you take to deal with Ken's subpar performance? What needs to be done first? How strict or harsh should you be? Should you be concerned about damaging the positive employee feelings toward Ken? One of Ken's peers, Venkat, is very quiet and reserved but has had exceptional performance over the last year. In what ways should you manage Venkat differently than you do Ken?

4. Conducting an Effective Performance Appraisal Feedback Session

You have been a supervisor of three people for the last year and next week is scheduled to be your first formal feedback session. You generally hated these sessions before you became a manager and you're really nervous and hoping they go well. What should you hope to accomplish? What are the key rules and important tactics to keep in mind? What are the most common and insidious traps that often characterize these sessions?

Introduction

The best managers know that their success stems largely from their people and they clearly understand three fundamental principles about effective management:[1]

Principle 1: Management is the intervention of getting things done through others.

Principle 2: Managers need their people more than those people need the manager.

Principle 3: Managers get rewarded for what their employees do, not for what the managers do.

Put simply, the job of managers is to make their people as successful as possible. Managers only succeed when their people succeed. Although that may seem straightforward, it is often one of the most difficult realizations for successful individual contributors making the transition to a management role: learning to get things done through other people—performance management.

Helping employees succeed through performance management involves setting expectations for employees, assessing their job performance, and providing effective feedback. This process forms the basis of the relationship between employee and manager, and nothing is more important to a manager's success than that relationship. Employees rely on this relationship to understand their performance, obtain rewards, seek advancement, and gain social support. Managers rely on this relationship to effectively structure and delegate work, generate ideas, and solve problems. Thus, it's not surprising that performance management is not an event or two but really a day-to-day practice that results in stronger manager–employee relationships and results.

The challenge of becoming effective in managing employee performance, however, lies in the inherent discomfort involved in judging others. Whether it's assessing an employee's performance or delivering negative feedback, most people are not naturally comfortable playing such a role. There is a certain appeal to simply holding people accountable for results (which, by the way, is not as easy as it sounds) and ignoring the behaviors and processes they use to attain such results. However, that approach ignores the value of performance management, which, when done effectively, can dramatically improve individual performance.[2] Unfortunately, though we know a great deal about what makes for effective performance management, such information is often ignored in favor of intuition and "commonsense" approaches. Indeed, common sense often leads to dysfunctional practice and is one of several myths (seen in Myths 7.1) that contribute to misunderstandings and lower-than-desirable performance.

?¿ MYTHS 7.1   Myths of Performance Management

- **People are naturally good observers of behavior.** Although most people *think* they can make accurate judgments about others' behavior or intentions, the fact is that without concerted discipline and utilization of some evidence-based methods, most human beings are miserable at accurately judging others' behavior.

- **Performance management is mostly common sense.** While most everyone wishes that were true, the reality is that a majority of people are less than satisfied with the way they are managed. Recent reports suggest an "under-management" phenomenon, noting that as few as 10 percent of managers practice the most basic elements of effective performance management on a consistent basis (see Management Live 7.1).

- **Feedback is always effective.** Conventional wisdom states that providing feedback to employees about their performance should generally lead to performance improvement. Yet substantial research reveals that poorly administered feedback can actually lead to *decreased* performance![3]

- **Performance management is only for low performers.** All players can benefit from a good coach—not just the struggling ones. Some people will need more time dedicated to them than others, but a great coach can decipher when and what type of coaching each employee requires.

- **Performance management is HR's responsibility.** Although a human resources department in an organization can support a manager's efforts, the primary responsibility for managing others' performance lies with managers. This myth is often believed because managers want to believe it—and who wouldn't want to delegate such an important but also complex task? Great HR departments and managers know that for employees to be most effective, they need a manager committed to performance management.

KO **7-1**

DO **7-1**

Job Performance

Before we discuss the details of the performance management process, it's important to understand the nature of performance itself. In fact, when asked, "What is it that managers *manage* anyway?" the short answer is simply "job performance."

Job performance consists of two major components: **task performance** and **contextual performance.** Task performance refers to the core substantive or technical tasks that are essential to any job. As we'll discuss in this chapter, all jobs have a set of critical job tasks.[4] Task performance, then, involves employees' behavior in accomplishing these tasks. Typically, managers are concerned with how effective and efficient employees are in accomplishing their critical job tasks—where **effectiveness** refers to the results an employee achieves and **efficiency** refers to the amount of resources dedicated to attain the results. Ideally, managers want employees to be both highly effective (that is, meet or exceed their goals) and highly efficient (meaning they expend as few resources as possible). Sometimes, however, these two aspects of task performance may be at odds. For example, consider the employee whose job it is to craft highly specialized products or services, such as an executive chef. The chef may waste considerable resources (for example, throwing away an expensive cut of meat that wasn't prepared to a certain standard) in making sure that the end product is highly effective. Conversely, consider the sales employee who spends very little money on entertaining clients but is not very effective in actually closing any new business. Most managers must deal with the inherent tensions in balancing these two key results of task performance. Regardless, task performance is generally considered to be "the bottom line" for most managers, and any good manager can expect to spend substantial time paying attention to his or her employee's task performance.

The second component of job performance is that of contextual performance, also known as **organizational citizenship behavior (OCB).** OCBs are employee behaviors that contribute to the overall effectiveness of the organization but are not formally required or considered part of an employee's core tasks. Examples include volunteering to work on a project that is not part of one's job, helping a co-worker learn a new task, and following organizational rules and procedures. Based on this description, it shouldn't surprise you that OCB has often been referred to as "good soldiering" (see Table 7.1 for examples of OCBs). Unlike task performance, where job tasks differ greatly depending upon the job or occupation, OCB tends to be common across many jobs and occupations.

Importantly, managers typically want "good citizens," not simply because they're nicer to be around but because OCB contributes to the effectiveness of an organization, even though such behavior is often less obvious and is certainly more indirect. For example, recent meta-analyses (including more than 50,000 people in total) examining the consequences of OCBs found that OCBs are strongly related to increased individual task performance, unit or department performance levels, as well as organizational productivity and profitability.[5] Further, when employees engage in OCBs, they were found to be less likely to quit or be absent from work, and to have customers who are more satisfied. Thus, the evidence is clear that managers ought to be concerned with not only the results employees produce but also how they contribute to the organization in ways that don't always show up in a job description.

Practice this!
Go to www.baldwin2e.com

TABLE 7.1 Organizational Citizenship Behavior (OCB)[6]

Altruism. Behaviors that have the effect of helping a specific other person with an organizationally relevant task or problem.

Civic Virtue. Behaviors regarding responsible participation in the political life of the organization. Civic virtue implies a sense of involvement in what policies are adopted and which candidates are supported. Behaviorally, civic virtue takes such mundane forms as attending meetings, reading mail, discussing issues on personal time, voting, and "speaking up."

Conscientiousness. Employee behavior that goes well beyond the organization's role requirements, in the areas of attendance, taking breaks, and obeying organizational policies.

Courtesy. Actions such as touching base with those parties whose work would be affected by one's decisions or commitments. Providing advance notice, reminders, and passing along information are all examples of courtesy.

Sportsmanship. Behavior indicating an individual's willingness to tolerate less-than-ideal situations by not filing petty grievances or complaining about minor issues. An employee who exhibits sportsmanship behavior can be described as being a good sport.

Job Attitudes

Although it's common for managers to talk about an employee's "attitude problem," such a phrase makes little sense. **Attitudes** are appraisals or evaluations of people, objects, or events. All of us possess attitudes on any number of topics from religion and politics to television and sex, and yes even managerial practices. When it comes to work-related attitudes, one of the more prevalent errors made by managers is to assume that peoples' attitudes and behaviors are always highly correlated. We falsely assume, for instance, that poor job satisfaction will always be associated with poor job performance. Unfortunately, attitudes can be quite complex and just because a person possesses a strong attitude doesn't mean that her behavior will be consistent with that attitude. For example, you may hold the attitude that it's imperative people start being more environmentally responsible. Despite this attitude, you may engage in behaviors that would be inconsistent with such a strong belief such as using that unrecyclable coated-paper coffee cup you may be drinking from right now!

Because behavior doesn't always follow attitudes doesn't mean, however, that managers should ignore employee attitudes. To the contrary, managers should care about employee attitudes because attitudes play a key role in employee behavior. More specifically, some job attitudes are associated with **withdrawal behaviors,** whereby individuals are more likely to avoid or leave the work situation altogether. Withdrawal behaviors, such as turnover and absenteeism, or even counterproductive work behaviors (for example, theft) are not only expensive but can be highly disruptive as well. Conversely, some positive job attitudes are associated with employees demonstrating extra effort or engaging in OCB. Thus, understanding, monitoring, and managing key employee attitudes alongside of performance management can greatly increase a manager's success.

One major obstacle to understanding attitudes, however, is determining how best to collect information about employee attitudes. Although it might be tempting to simply ask employees directly (for instance, "Are you satisfied at work?") or indirectly (for example, give them a survey asking such questions), employees are not likely to be forthcoming to questions that are not anonymous or where the manager could easily tie responses to a particular employee. Given these challenges, managers should seek outside groups to help elicit employee attitudes. This could include an organization's human resources or organization development department or a consulting firm specializing in organizational focus groups or surveys. These professionals are trained to understand the many potential social and ethical pitfalls associated with collecting employee attitudes and feeding back the information to managers in ways that will be productive and safe for all involved.

With this in mind, in the following we describe three critical job attitudes to pay close attention to: job satisfaction, organizational commitment, and organizational cynicism.

Job Satisfaction

We're fairly certain you've heard the many platitudes regarding job satisfaction such as "Happy workers are productive workers!" Such conventional wisdom captures the concept of **job satisfaction** or how an individual feels about his or her job. In its simplest form, job satisfaction is a global assessment of all aspects of one's work role. Job satisfaction can also be viewed as an appraisal of specific aspects of the job role including satisfaction with one's pay, co-workers, supervision, promotional opportunities, and the work itself. Despite conventional wisdom about happiness and performance, decades of research have shown that job satisfaction is only moderately related to job performance.[7] However, the relationship between satisfaction and performance is stronger for jobs that are more complex because they offer employees more autonomy to make decisions about their work.

For some time, there was debate about whether job performance might be the cause of increased job satisfaction (for instance, "I perform well so therefore I am happier about my job"); however, a recent large-scale study seems to suggest that, by and large (there are some exceptions), it is satisfaction that helps enable performance.[8] Practically speaking, however, managers should not expect that attempts to simply "make people happy" on the job are a prescription for improved performance. Indeed, many organizational interventions have failed because they were built on the all-too-simple premise that making employees happy is the key to success. You already know, for instance, that while an individual may not be satisfied with his overall level of pay, what matters most is how equitably he is paid compared to others in similar jobs.

As noted earlier, great managers pay close attention to satisfaction because of the potential consequences beyond job performance. For example, satisfaction has been associated with increased customer satisfaction and loyalty.[9] Further, research has shown that satisfaction with the work itself is strongly associated with increased motivation and involvement on the job, and decreased turnover intentions. Similarly, satisfaction with one's supervisor is highly correlated with increased engagement in OCBs, while satisfaction with co-workers is strongly associated with team cohesiveness.[10] This research clearly demonstrates the need for managers to understand not just whether or not employees are satisfied but the exact nature of their job satisfaction.

Organizational Commitment

Organizational commitment is an attitude representing the extent to which an employee identifies with his organization and desires to remain a member of the organization. Generally speaking, there are three different forms of organizational commitment attitudes, each one representing a particular aspect of commitment.[11] **Affective commitment** represents an emotional attachment to the organization. People who are affectively committed want to stay with the organization because they feel a personal connection with people (for instance, "I have good friends at work") or experience enjoyment from membership. **Normative commitment** is a wish to stay with the organization out of feelings of obligation (for example, "My boss gave me a chance when no one else would; I will never leave her"). **Continuance commitment** is a desire to stay with the organization because the costs of leaving outweigh the benefits (for instance, "I received $20,000 in tuition reimbursement, which I will owe back if I don't stay another two years").

Although all three represent various means of commitment to the organization, some have noted that continuance commitment is less about commitment and more about a feeling of being "handcuffed" to the organization. Not surprisingly then, research shows that individuals who possess higher continuance commitment are less likely to quit but more likely to be lower performers![12] That is, when people feel like they have no other choice than to remain with the organization, their performance suffers. The strongest findings for commitment, however, seem to emerge more from affective and normative commitment. Like job satisfaction, research has shown that employees who are more strongly committed to the organization show lower levels of absenteeism and turnover, and for some employees higher job performance. Further, research has shown that managers can have a strong influence on employees' level of commitment by engaging in important leadership behaviors such as setting high expectations, providing a compelling vision, and stimulating new ideas.[13] See Chapters 8 and 9 for a more complete discussion of how to increase employee commitment.

Organizational Cynicism

Everyone knows someone who seems to be overly critical of any new idea or proposed effort. Such an attitude may be indicative of **organizational cynicism** which is generally defined as an attitude of contempt, frustration, and distrust toward an object or multiple objects.[14] Importantly, cynicism in organizations is not the same thing as healthy "skepticism," where an individual is playing devil's advocate with the intent of improving a decision or being critical in order to explore assumptions underlying a particular effort. Rather, organizational cynics display a deep loss of faith or confidence in management's ability to do the right thing. So, regardless of how rational or thorough a particular decision might be, the organizational cynic isn't "buying it."

As you probably can guess, organizational cynicism is an attitude that can quickly become a toxic influence in work groups. Research has shown that organizational cynicism is associated with decreases in organizational citizenship, job satisfaction, organizational commitment, motivation, intentions to quit, and intent to create change. Further, scholars have also shown that cynicism among managers results in lowered performance evaluations of managers by senior leaders in the organization. Thus, whether manager or employee, cynicism seems to have mostly harmful effects in organizations.[15]

When asked about cynics in their organizations, we bet most managers would assume that cynicism is a personality trait and therefore "once a cynic, always a cynic." To the contrary, research has shown that in fact cynical attitudes are largely shaped by experiences in the work context.[16] Such experiences can include organizations achieving consistently poor results, layoffs, repeated failed change efforts, breaches of implicit employment contracts, and excessive executive compensation.[17] Thus, while it would be easy to dismiss a cynic as someone who was born to criticize or be negative, cynics tend to instead be well-intentioned individuals who have felt the organization (specifically managers) has broken too many promises. The good news here is that despite the poor influence cynics have in the organization, managers can work to reshape their experiences by establishing credibility and trust over a period of time. The major trap in turning around the cynic is to blame the cynic for her poor attitude. Again, cynicism usually results from a long history of unmet expectations. Thus, managers should start by accepting blame themselves for the organization's poor performance in keeping its promises. Tool Kit 7.1 discusses methods for effectively managing the organizational cynic.

KO 7-2

Performance Management: The Day-to-Day Work of Great Managers

The essential elements of performance management can be concisely framed in a simple diagram (see Figure 7.1) of the **performance management cycle (PMC).** Generally stated, the primary role of a manager is to establish expectations, assess performance, and provide feedback and development. Even though this sounds like a simple process, see Management Live 7.1 to see how infrequently these performance management basics are actually practiced.

⚒ MANAGER'S TOOL KIT

Tool Kit 7.1 Managing the Organizational Cynic[18]

A few key strategies can be employed when managing the organizational cynic within the context of organizational change.

1. **Deal with the past.** The past is always at the heart of cynicism. It is past mistakes, failed attempts, and so forth that reduce a manager's overall credibility. Thus, a manager must first attempt to regain that credibility—to be seen as honest and competent. Start by admitting your mistakes. You might be inclined to say, "But I wasn't even around when these past events happened!" It doesn't matter—the reality is you are management now and you represent all that transpired with management then. Take action to rectify any negative consequences from past failures and say "I'm sorry" when hardships or bad feelings are present.

2. **Involve cynics in change efforts.** The cynic has insight into where mistakes have been made and as some research indicates is likely to provide much more feedback on how to avoid mistakes in the future. The trap here is to ignore the cynic, to marginalize him. This will only serve to reinforce his cynical perceptions.

3. **As you plan a change initiative, don't make future promises you can't keep.** Another trap in managing the cynic is to over-promise the benefits of a particular change effort in the hope that she will be "won over." Even if the change effort is successful, there are likely to be aspects that were subpar.

4. **Over-communicate.** Cynics will interpret silence from their manager as an indication that once again, the organization is hiding things or not being fully transparent. Be honest and communicate what you do and don't know.

5. **Involve cynical "converts."** Sometimes the best people to turn around cynics are those who were known to be cynical in the past but have since become champions of the organization's efforts. Bring these folks into discussions to talk about how the organization has found ways to be successful.

Yet for many managers hiring their own people is a luxury; most managers inherit a group of employees. There are, of course, no guarantees that the previous manager took careful steps to assess candidate potential in the selection process. Thus, great managers must learn to manage performance regardless of the circumstances they inherit. This includes evaluating performance as well as learning how to manage and develop employee performance. Through the PMC, managers set clear performance expectations early and often. In addition, they frequently assess performance and provide the feedback necessary to keep employees on

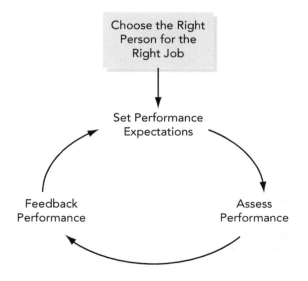

FIGURE 7.1
The Performance
Management Cycle
(PMC)

⇆ MANAGEMENT LIVE 7.1

The "Under Management" Epidemic

According to Bruce Tulgan of Rainmaker Thinking Inc., all good managers should master five *management basics:*

1. Make clear performance statements.
2. Set measurable goals and hold people accountable for those goals.
3. Accurately monitor and evaluate work performance.
4. Provide clear feedback about performance and improvement.
5. Distribute rewards and punishments fairly.

Following these management basics produces "engaged" employees who are motivated and productive. Yet Tulgan's research showed that few managers actually do these management basics regularly.

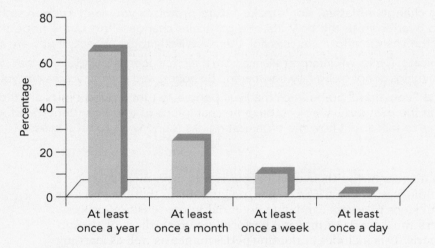

The problem Tulgan uncovered is that, while good management boils down to a handful of critical behaviors, few managers are willing to do what is necessary to engage in those behaviors. Whether it is due to a lack of time, lack of skill, or the fear associated with judging people, "under management" is widespread.

track. When performance is achieved, great managers recognize and reward achievement. When expectations are not met, great managers diagnose the performance deficiency and repeat the PMC. Doing so sometimes may involve reassigning an employee to a job that more appropriately utilizes the employee's skills. In some cases, it could involve terminating the employment relationship.

DO 7-2   Setting Expectations and Evaluating Performance

Performance standards should never be a surprise, because nothing frustrates employees more than not knowing what is expected of them. Expectations should never be set informally through hallway conversations or periodic e-mails; rather, they should be established through a formal meeting with each employee. Discussions should include expectations for the context of work (such as when the workday begins and ends), how work gets done (for example, telephone versus face-to-face sales calls), and actual work goals (complete 42 sales calls per month for existing customers). The goal should be to establish a *mutual performance contract*. This is not an employment contract, but a document that stipulates performance expectations. To create this contract, you will need to structure exactly what it is you want to communicate regarding performance. Topics to address in this contract discussion include:

- Critical job tasks
- Performance goals
- Professional conduct
- Resource requirements
- Developmental goals

Remember, this is a mutual process. Great managers make this conversation two-way by inviting employees to identify their expectations for the manager as well as their own personal performance.

Ensuring Goal Commitment

Recall from Chapter 1 the power of goal setting. This is one opportunity to put that technique into practice and tie it to performance standards and rewards. Setting SMART goals isn't enough; managers also need to gain employees' commitment to those goals. The mutual contract discussion is the perfect time to start enhancing employees' commitment to goals by engaging in the following behavior.[19]

- **Make it public.** Public goals increase goal commitment by creating an environment in which the employee is accountable to more than herself.
- **Be supportive.** When managers are supportive of employees' goals, they express confidence in the employee that he can attain the goal.
- **Tie to vision/mission.** Goals become more meaningful to employees when they are clearly relevant to the organization's mission.
- **Set goals, not actions.** Sometimes employee work needs to be structured. In many cases, setting the goal is all that is required, and letting employees determine how to get there, and what actions to take, can increase commitment.
- **Track progress and give feedback.** Employees will be more committed to goals accompanied with regular feedback whereby they can assess their progress. More on feedback is provided later in the chapter.
- **Ensure resources.** Few employees will be committed to goals that require unattainable resources. The role of a coach is to ensure the proper resources (time, money, education, technology) are available or readily attainable.
- **Remove obstacles.** Managers must pave the way for employees by removing organizational obstacles. It is the role of a coach to advocate for employees and to deal with the political roadblocks that could keep them from meeting their goals.

KO **7-3**

KO **7-4**

Observing and Assessing Performance

According to a survey of employees in Fortune 500 companies, both managers and employees alike have a particular disdain for performance evaluation.[20] People prefer not to be told about deficiencies, don't like vague performance standards, feel vulnerable without control, and fear evaluations will not be related

DO **7-3**

DO **7-4**

to their actual performance but based more on their personal relationship with their managers. For their part, managers dislike playing the role of judge, fear lawsuits, feel evaluation takes too much time, and that they have inadequate skills to differentiate performance. All of this is unfortunate as effective evaluation plays a central role in improving and sustaining employee performance.[21] To that end, overcoming these barriers and learning the basics of good performance evaluation are critically important.

Defining Job Performance Criteria: Behavior and Results

Practice this!
Go to www.baldwin2e.com

No matter what performance management assessment techniques you use, you must seek to capture employees' results and the processes used to obtain those results. Most jobs have some objective outcome or results and require certain behaviors to obtain those results. For example, litigation attorneys have some clear results, such as the number of cases won and settlements reached. Of course, some jobs might require a bit more ingenuity in finding the results to be measured. For example, customer service agents are primarily responsible for solving customer problems. Results might include the percentage of problems solved the first time versus those escalated to a specialist, or ratings from customer service surveys. To find the results for any job, ask the following questions:

- *If this employee performs poorly, what would suffer?* For example, would customer service or repeat business suffer? How about revenue? What about customer satisfaction?
- *What will this employee's performance make possible and for whom?* For instance, will good performance lead to increased unit performance? What about lower turnover or increased receivables?

A common mistake in performance management occurs when managers *exclusively* pay attention to employee results. Although results are critical, great managers know there are many ways to get those results—and that achieving them in the right way should be rewarded. For example, customer service representatives should engage in behaviors like answering the telephone promptly, using professional language, and asking questions that elicit the root of the problem. These are not actual results, but effective behaviors that lead to desirable outcomes. To identify the important *behaviors* associated with performance, ask these questions:

- *What are the most critical steps involved in achieving results?*
- *If this employee doesn't do the most critical steps, will he still be able to succeed?*

Using a results–behavior matrix is one way to visually classify and assess how an employee's performance behavior and results work together. Note that in Figure 7.2 the upper right-hand corner of the figure represents employee performance that achieved results through strong behavior. The lower left-hand corner represents the opposite: poor results and poor behavior. For most managers, these two boxes represent easy performance-related decisions. The upper right should clearly be rewarded with high performance assessments; the lower left certainly deserves lower performance marks.

More difficult, however, is what to do with employee performance that falls in the other two boxes of the figure. Take the lower right-hand corner, which represents good results attained, but through poor behavior. For example, Ted has the best sales numbers in his region. Unfortunately, Ted got those results by

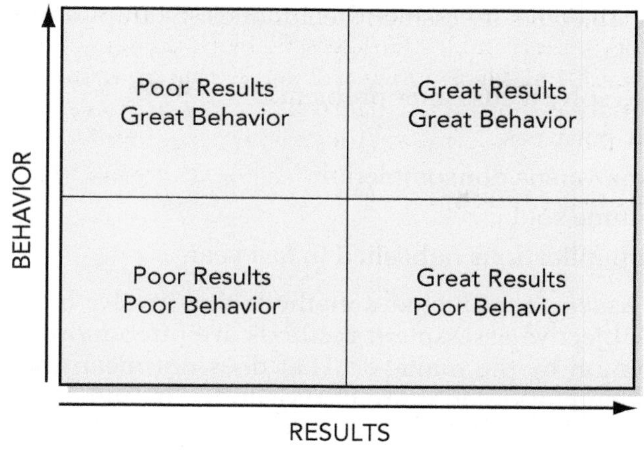

Poor Results
Great Behavior

Great Results
Great Behavior

Poor Results
Poor Behavior

Great Results
Poor Behavior

BEHAVIOR

RESULTS

FIGURE 7.2
The Results–Behavior
Matrix

stealing contacts from other sales reps and making promises to customers the company couldn't deliver. Is Ted a good performer? Probably not. Few managers would endorse his behavior as worthy of praise and would likely view his process as harmful to the organization. Looking at Ted's results alone, however, would have masked critical performance information.

Just as difficult is the upper left corner which represents the person who is exhibiting good behavior but not getting results. For instance, Maria has demonstrated she can build strong relationships with her clients, but can't seem to close the deal and make the sale. Is Maria a good performer? Here again, probably not. Results matter and achieving those results is part of performance. Unlike Ted, however, her behavior may lead her to results the right way, and she should certainly be recognized for her strong process.

Assessing Behavior, Not Traits

The appropriate performance management mantra remains the same: good assessment of future potential and current performance focuses on behavior and actual results, not traits or personal characteristics. Unfortunately, substantial research shows managers are highly influenced by traits or non-job-relevant information that reduces the accuracy of their assessment.[22] For example, many companies routinely ask managers to assess items such as dependability, initiative, and energy. But what does dependability mean? What would good dependability versus bad dependability look like? Instead of simply measuring the trait of dependability, the challenge is to determine what you mean when you say, "I want dependable employees." You might mean you want people who arrive on time, accomplish work without frequent reminders, and meet deadlines. These things are measurable! You can track timeliness, working without reminders, and meeting deadlines.

Using Multiple Methods to Assess Behavior and Results

There are multiple ways to assess employee behavior and results, and using multiple methods results in a more complete understanding of performance. In the broadest sense, evaluation methods can be categorized as either objective or subjective.

Objective assessment includes methods based on results or impartial performance outcomes. These are usually easily identifiable since they represent employee output that is visible and countable. Results performance is typically measured using objective assessment techniques. Examples of objective assessment include:

- Minutes to solve a customer problem.
- Sales calls per week.
- Completion versus noncompletion.
- Dollar volume sold.
- Research publications published in last year.

Subjective assessment includes methods that involve human judgments of performance. Subjective assessment methods are often more contentious since they involve opinion by the manager. That does not mean they are not useful. Many aspects of employees' jobs are not easily "seen" and can't be counted. For example, objectively quantifying a consultant's relationship with clients is difficult. Yet the behavior involved in building strong client relations is central to successful consulting performance so subjective assessments often play an important role. However, since we already know managers do not always make accurate judgments of employee behavior, understanding the implications of the different types of subjective assessments is critical. Typically, managers will employ two types of subjective assessments, separately or in conjunction with one another. These are known as absolute and relative standards. An **absolute subjective assessment** involves comparing an employee's performance to that of a "model" described in the performance statement, whereas a **relative subjective assessment** compares an employee's performance with another employee's performance to determine the level of performance. Let's look at some ways of accomplishing both.

Absolute Assessment Techniques

Practice this!
Go to www.baldwin2e.com

- **Graphic Rating Scale.** The most common form of absolute assessment (and evaluation in general) is known as a **graphic rating scale.** The graphic rating scale is used to assess how much of a particular behavior an employee displays on some graduated scale. For example, a manager might rate the level of customer service displayed by an employee on a scale from poor (1) to excellent (5).
- **Behaviorally Anchored Rating Scale (BARS).** Much like behavioral interviews, a **behaviorally anchored rating scale (BARS)** compares job behaviors with specific performance statements on a scale from poor to outstanding (or similar sets of descriptors). Although BARS assessments require a little time to develop, they are the best way to keep assessments focused on behavior and provide a little higher precision than graphic rating scales. Thus, like the graphic rating scale, a manager may rate an employee's performance in customer service on a scale from poor to excellent, but unlike the graphic rating scale, each point on the scale would be behaviorally defined (e.g., 1 = poor; employee ignores customer requests).

Relative Assessment Techniques

- **Ranking.** A **ranking** technique is a simple relative assessment. Managers use this technique by listing all employees from best to worst. The technique is quite good for distinguishing high- and low-performing employees, but difficult for assessing employee performance in the middle of the group.

- **Forced Distribution.** The **forced distribution** technique, also known as **topgrading,** requires managers to assess employees based on pre-determined evaluation categories and to force employees into these categories to form a desired distribution. Only a certain percentage of employees may achieve each evaluation category. For example, three performance levels may exist in a company—poor, good, and outstanding—and only 20 percent of all employees can be rated as outstanding, 70 percent as good, and 10 percent as poor. See Management Live 7.2 for more on topgrading.

Using Multiple Sources of Data or People

Few managers have the luxury of observing their employees' work throughout an entire day, much less an entire year. Thus, effective performance management involves collecting data from others about the employees' performance that can help confirm or disconfirm a manager's own observations. For example, it would be inadequate for a manager to observe her staff accountant for an hour and assume she has all the data required to evaluate performance. Other sources of data are necessary.

Peers, subordinates, project leaders, and customers can help a manager better assess her employees. Note, however, that all sources have their limitations. For instance, an employee's peers work daily with the employee and see his behavior

⇄ MANAGEMENT LIVE 7.2

The "Topgrading" Debate

Few areas of management development have generated more passionate recent discourse among academics and business professionals than that of forced distribution, or topgrading, performance management practices. Forced ranking refers to systems in which individuals are ranked in comparison to one another. Some managers, like high-profile former GE executives Jack Welch and Larry Bossidy, have extolled such practices as efficient and pragmatic means of "rewarding your doers" and "muscle-building" your organization. These and other authors often point to the success of General Electric, in both building shareholder value and developing executive talent, as evidence of the efficacy of forced ranking practices.

Many other organizations such as Heinz and SIRVA have instituted performance management initiatives based in whole or part on the process popularized by Welch and Bossidy. Even highly prestigious universities like Princeton are now topgrading. Princeton restricts the number of A's to 35 percent of the student body each semester. Many students who earn high marks (say, 93 percent) will receive a letter grade of B!

Others, like well-known authors Jeffrey Pfeffer and Malcolm Gladwell, condemn forced ranking as dysfunctional and suggest that such systems will be hazardous to an organization's culture. They choose *their* examples from among such organizations as Ford Motor Co. and Enron, which have had well-publicized *unsuccessful* experiences with forced ranking systems. Among those critical of forced ranking, some take issue with the philosophy of the practice, while others contend they agree with the objectives but "not the way it is often done."

So who is right? As is typically the case, the answer probably lies somewhere in the middle. The effectiveness of topgrading appears to depend on *who* is being topgraded and the culture of the organization. Cultures that are highly competitive and attract performance-oriented individuals are likely to see benefits from topgrading. In contrast, group- or team-oriented cultures would likely reject topgrading because it may be seen as pitting employees against each other. So as in many areas in management, the "right answer" depends, in this case, on the goals of the organization and what type of organizational culture it is trying to build.

firsthand. Common sense would dictate giving his peers a survey and using the results as a measure of performance. Yet evidence shows that, when peers know their ratings are used to evaluate another co-worker's performance, they provide inaccurate ratings. In some cases, they may "play" the system depending on how much they like or dislike their co-worker.[23]

Here are a few tips on how to use multiple sources of data.

- **Observe Behavior over Time.** A single observation of behavior is never enough. Make time to see performance. This may mean going along with an employee to meet a customer, working with an employee on a project, or asking for monthly progress reports.

- **Take Notes.** Research shows that managers who keep a diary or journal on each employee make more accurate performance ratings and reduce the burden associated with the evaluation process. Start a file on each employee. Schedule an hour each month to record each employee's successes and challenges over the last four weeks. Include any positive and negative data you received about the employee's performance.

- **Ask for Customer Feedback.** Customers, internal and external, should be included in assessing part of the employee's performance. This can be as simple as a few short survey questions, given periodically throughout a performance period.

- **Allow for a Self-Evaluation.** Employees themselves are a good source of data. They can highlight achievements they've made that managers may not often observe. Allow each employee to self-evaluate his or her performance.

- **Monitor Common Errors.** No matter what the source of data, if those data come from people, they are likely to have some error or inaccuracies associated with them. In Table 7.2, we discuss some of the common errors and what to do about them.

TABLE 7.2   Common Errors in Observing Performance and How to Correct Them

Manager's Error	What It Means	Technique to Correct
Halo Effect	• Judging all aspects of behavior or traits on the basis of a single trait or behavior. • Can be either positive or negative.	Use multiple raters of performance.
Leniency and Severity	• Consistently rating groups of employees as all high performers or as all low performers.	Use multiple raters of performance and a forced distribution or ranking technique.
Central Tendency	• Consistently rating all employees as average. • Only using the middle of the rating scale; no high or low ratings.	Use a forced distribution or ranking technique.
Recency or Primacy	• Evaluating employee on only the most *recent* or *initial* performance, rather than performance for the entire evaluation period. • Could lead to false high or low ratings.	Use frequent evaluations, and require raters to maintain logs over the entire rating period.
Similarity or Contrast	• Bias due to the perceived similarity or difference between the rater's job behavior and the employee's job behavior. • *Similarity* bias will lead to inflated ratings. • *Contrast* bias will lead to deflated ratings.	Raters can be trained to correct for bias.

Providing Effective Feedback

The purpose of feedback is to influence future behavioral change, and it can do so if done properly.[24] If done improperly, feedback can actually decrease performance or reinforce poor behavior.[25] Feedback works because it generates energy that serves to motivate the individual receiving it. Feedback also guides behavior in certain directions when motivation to behave is already present. For example, feedback can serve to generate motivation by disconfirming an individual's perception and creating reward expectations. Further, it directs behavior where motivation exists by calling attention to problems that need correcting and where learning needs to occur.[26] In addition, feedback contributes to building strong interpersonal relationships. Thus, feedback can serve as a valuable tool to keep employees on track or get them back on track toward achieving their performance goals.

"The deepest principle of human nature is the craving to be appreciated."

—William James

The Principles of Good Feedback

Let's elaborate on the critical elements of *effective* feedback:

- **Be specific.** Specific feedback is more effective than vague feedback. People respond most favorably to direct examples of their past behavior.

- **Focus on the problem rather than the person.** Feedback steeped in personal opinion and unconstructive criticism (for example, "You seem lazy") is unproductive.[27] Feedback should focus on the task not the person. Avoid people's perceived motives or attitudes.

- **Maximize absolute feedback; minimize relative feedback and comparisons to others.**[28] Feedback that says, "Tyler, you just need to be more like Marcus," won't be heard. Focus on whether Tyler is meeting *his* performance goals.

- **Avoid absolutes.** Unless you work side by side with an employee daily, you can't possibly observe everything. So don't imply you can by using absolute words like "always" or "never."

Practice this!
Go to www.baldwin2e.com

- **Be timely.** Feedback is most effective when it is presented close in time to the actual behavior.[29]
- **Focus on the future.** Feedback is inherently backward-looking, but what was done in the past is done. Your role is to influence future behavior by focusing on what can be done to correct undesirable behavior and continue desirable behavior.
- **Include information for improvement.** Telling an employee that her behavior is unproductive won't help unless the employee understands why it is unproductive. Effective feedback includes a statement regarding ways to improve the behavior toward performance.

Doing Feedback Well

Using the preceding guidelines, we have synthesized a few simple steps to keep in mind as a primer to most effectively deliver feedback:[30]

1. State the behavior you observed.
2. Describe the impact on self or others.
3. Provide information for improvement or explore improvement with the employee.

To further help you see how important phrasing feedback is, we've provided some examples of how to, and how not to, give feedback:

Ineffective Feedback: "You don't handle your people well; you're dictating, not managing."

Effective Feedback: "I've noticed you tend not to involve your employees in making decisions. This doesn't allow them the opportunity to express their own views. In the future, I'd like to see you provide more opportunities for employee input."

The difference between the two examples is clear. In the ineffective feedback example, the employee is given a vague and general statement that is overly evaluative. In all likelihood, the employee will walk away with little information to improve performance. The effective feedback example clearly articulates the behavior observed, describes the impact of the behavior on others, and gives direction for the future. Here's another example:

Ineffective Feedback: "Your presentation of the data was unorganized."

Effective Feedback: "When you create charts with formats different than the rest of the team's, it causes confusion in data interpretation. Stick with the standard format to alleviate such confusion."

> "You have to get ongoing feedback to push you out of your comfort zone."
>
> —Kevin Sharer, CEO, Amgen

Again, the effective feedback example is highly specific and behavioral and allows for immediate correction and future focus. Managers often find themselves delivering ineffective feedback when they are angry with an employee. Instead of communicating that anger, however, managers simply provide curt and unproductive statements, masking what they really want and need to say. According to managerial psychologist Edgar Schein, this withholding of negative information that needs to be said does more harm than good. Communicate your anger about the employee's behavior, and don't lose sight of good feedback principles. Here is an example of communicating your anger in a productive way:[31]

Ineffective Feedback: "You really blew that meeting John. You lack initiative and are just not aggressive enough for this kind of work."

Effective Feedback: "John, I'm pretty upset about what you've done. When we got stuck on the ABC project, you seemed willing to let matters drift instead of coming up with a proposal for how to confront the problems and move forward. When the other division challenged the direction you were going, you backed off instead of showing them why your solution was the right one. I have seen both of these patterns on other projects and am concerned about the lack of initiative and assertiveness that is implied by such behavior."

Unfortunately, although the principles are relatively simple, delivering effective feedback is hard to do and people often react negatively to receiving it.[32] Many become defensive, due to our human instinct to protect our self-image. Because defensiveness can lead to anger, managers are often reluctant to say what people need to hear. As such, quality feedback for improvement becomes obscured and hidden in platitudes and niceties. Even well-intentioned and confident managers fight their discomfort because they know how difficult it is to get candid feedback heard and acted upon. For an example of how to run a performance appraisal meeting well, see Tool Kit 7.2.

Managing Perceptions of Fairness in Performance Management

Managers find managing performance and giving feedback to be so difficult in part because of the enormous burden of responsibility it represents. Performance management activities involve some of the most important and sensitive decisions

MANAGER'S TOOL KIT

Tool Kit 7.2   Managing the Performance Appraisal Meeting

If you've done your job through the performance management cycle, running a good performance appraisal should be rather easy because your employee will know exactly where she stands prior to that meeting, based upon your continual feedback about performance against her goals. Here are the basic steps in conducting the meeting.

1. **Set the agenda and location.** Clarify expectations for the meeting and set the process, including where the meeting will take place. We like neutral territory such as a conference room. Employees often wonder how much they'll be able to talk or what managers expect from them in the meeting itself. We like managers who are very clear about what will happen, for instance, "We'll use this meeting to review your goals from the past year (10 minutes), discuss your performance against these goals (20 minutes), . . . ," and so forth.

2. **Review expectations.** Take a few minutes to simply state the goals and criteria upon which performance was evaluated. Again, this should not be surprising given your frequent feedback and early expectation setting.

3. **Allow the employee to review his performance.** Give your employee the opportunity to review his performance against the standards set in his own words. One easy way of doing this is to have the employee provide a self-evaluation ahead of the meeting and to review it with the manager during the meeting. Don't debate his evaluation, but rather actively listen, take notes, and encourage elaboration where necessary.

4. **Provide evaluation.** Acknowledge accomplishments and discuss positive and negative feedback based upon the data you've collected to measure performance. This is the time to comment on all aspects of performance, including professionalism and citizenship. Remember to focus on behavior and job tasks!

5. **Engage in discussion about the future.** Now it's time to set future goals which could include improvement in any of the previous areas (for example, particularly with respect to professional development). You're now starting the performance management cycle anew.

within organizations, such as promotions, performance assessments, and pay decisions. The visibility of these activities makes performance management a highly scrutinized aspect of management. Indeed, substantial research shows people respond favorably to fairness but are also highly sensitive to being treated in ways they perceive as unfair. More specifically, when employees view their job situation as "fair," they are less likely to withdraw from their work and more likely to be satisfied, perform better, and contribute to the organization beyond their stated job requirements.[33] Thus, maintaining a persistent focus on fairness is a hallmark of a good manager. As discussed in Chapter 4, perceptions of fairness are based on three primary factors: (1) the presence of a defined *process*, (2) a clear and communicated rule or decision model for distributing rewards, and (3) demonstrated respect for people.

- **Use a fair, defined process.** Employees view performance management as fair if they have input into the policies and procedures used to make decisions. In addition, employees want to see that the process is applied in a standard way. For example, evaluating two employees in the same job role using different performance standards is likely to lead employees to view the process as unfair.

- **Distribute rewards and resources fairly.** Employees will view performance management as fair when rewards and resources that follow from performance assessment are distributed fairly. This includes paying close attention to the three potential rules for allocating rewards discussed in Chapter 4: (1) the **equity rule,** where resources and rewards are distributed to employees based on their *contributions*, (2) the **equality rule,** where resources and rewards are distributed so that each employee gets the same outcome regardless of contributions, and (3) the **need rule,** where resources and rewards are distributed to those who need them most. For a practice to be just, it doesn't have to follow all three rules, but should follow at least one. For example, offering health benefits to some employees and not others violates the equality rule. Giving everyone a bonus, regardless of performance, violates the equity rule.

- **Demonstrate respect.** Respect comes in many forms. First, managers must treat people with dignity when evaluating performance. Not all employees are stellar performers, but they are all humans, so treat them as such. Second, provide solid explanations and rationale for all performance management decisions. Employees understand that not all performance-related decisions are positive. What they won't understand is why you won't share the basis of your evaluation and the rationale for your decisions.

DO **7-6**

DO **7-7**

Dealing with the Problem Employee

"Managing is like holding a dove in your hand. Squeeze too hard and you kill it; not hard enough and it flies away."

—Tommy Lasorda

The logical assumption behind feedback is that providing information about performance will lead to performance improvement. But what if, after multiple attempts to correct poor or inadequate performance through feedback, nothing improves?

We use the term *problem employee* to denote an employee who after repeated feedback interventions has not improved performance. Note, we caution managers to not confuse this term with "bad person" or other disparaging or demeaning labels. Like Ken in the Manage *What?* scenario at the beginning of this chapter, there are plenty of wonderful people who simply don't perform. The

MANAGEMENT LIVE 7.3

Revenge of the Plant Workers

A study by Professor Jerald Greenberg shows quite clearly the often hidden costs associated with perceptions of unfairness. In his research, two plants in the same company were anticipating a 15 percent pay cut for their workers. The pay cut was temporary and was to last 10 weeks. In plant A, management provided detailed explanations about why the cuts were necessary and how they would work. In addition, management expressed a great deal of regret in their announcement, acknowledging the sacrifice they were asking employees to make. In plant B, however, only a brief explanation was given, and management did not apologize or communicate regret for the decision.

Prior to these announcements, inventories (tools, supplies, and so on) in the plants were counted and were roughly equal. After the announcement, researchers measured the inventories and found that while both plants experienced theft, plant B had a significant increase in "missing" inventory (from 3 percent normally to 8 percent after the announcement) compared to plant A. Apparently, employees in plant B who felt a sense of unfairness in the pay cut sought retribution by stealing inventory.

The lesson is simple: Taking time to explain decisions and making decisions transparent go a long way in promoting fairness and keeping employees committed to the well-being of the organization.

Source: Greenberg, J. (1990). Employee theft as a reaction to underpayment inequity: The hidden cost of pay cuts. *Journal of Applied Psychology*, 75, 561–568.

problem with the problem employee is that he can't or won't change his behavior to meet acceptable levels of performance. The key to dealing with these problem situations is to determine the true source of the low performance and intervene to correct it. Great managers apply a disciplined framework for improving performance, which includes three fundamental steps: (1) diagnose the problem, (2) hold a performance improvement discussion, and (3) provide training when appropriate.

Diagnose the Problem

When multiple feedback attempts have failed, it is important to dig deeper and seek the reason for such failure. Recall that performance is a function of motivation, ability, and opportunity. No amount of feedback can replace talent, skills, and abilities, nor will it replace real opportunities to practice and improve. Managers must also turn the spotlight on themselves and ask what role they play in their own employee's performance failure. Sometimes, a simple reality check about this role is helpful. For example, perhaps the goals set for the employee are unattainable given the resources available. Although it is tempting to simply blame the employee for performance failure, it is not always a "person" issue. In Tool Kit 7.3, we provide a series of key questions and corresponding actions to understand the root cause of a performance failure.

Hold a Performance Improvement Discussion

When a manager can say that (1) the employee's performance is below expectations, (2) multiple opportunities for performance improvement have been provided, (3) the major cause of the performance deficiency is due to the employee,

Tool Kit 7.3   Analyzing a Performance Problem[34]

This guide highlights the key questions to ask regarding a performance problem and shows the general actions to take, depending on the response.

Question to Ask	If . . .	Action to Take
Does the employee know what is expected of him or her?	No	Reinforce expectations and seek mutual understanding of those expectations.
Does the employee know performance can be improved?	No	Tell the employee there is room for performance improvement.
Are there obstacles the employee faces beyond the employee's control?	Yes	Remove the obstacles. If it can't be done, revise the performance expectations to take this into account.
Does the employee know how to improve? Does the employee lack particular skills necessary to perform?	Yes	Provide training and practice opportunities to acquire skills.
Do negative consequences follow good performance?	Yes	Reinforce good performance with positive consequences.

and (4) the employee wants to improve her performance, a face-to-face discussion should take place. The steps and content of the discussion are outlined as follows.[35]

1. **Agree on the Problem.** Agreement suggests that the manager and employee have a shared understanding that a problem exists and the nature of that problem. This sounds simple, but many managers fail in this step because they tell the employee, "We've got a problem, your performance is low," and then try to fix it. Performance management experts note the employee must truly agree that his behavior is problematic and has important organizational and personal consequences. That is, the employee must "own" the problem and understand that it is hers to reconcile. Until there is agreement about the problem, no further discussion can occur.

2. **Mutually Discuss Problem Solutions.** The key question that needs to be answered is "What will you (the employee) do differently now that you understand the problem?" Non-behavioral responses and solutions are not effective. For example, "I'll work harder, boss," and "I'll move some things around in my schedule and take care of this" are not solutions but rather responses that generally don't lead to behavior change. An effective collaborative process requires the manager and employee to generate behavioral options and arrive at a solution.

3. **Create an Action Plan.** Recall from Chapter 6 on motivation that specific action plans must follow specific goals. Once an option has been selected, an action plan must be devised that the employee will commit to using to improve performance. Action plans must include (1) steps for improving (exactly what will be done and when), (2) a timeline (with dates tied

to each action step), (3) the resources required, including additional skill development if necessary, and (4) a plan for follow-up and evaluation. The fourth component is often overlooked. It is critical to document the plan and have the employee periodically demonstrate that she is moving in the right direction.

4. **Provide Ongoing Feedback: Reinforce Improvement.** As the person attempts to improve performance, the manager must provide feedback letting the employee know if improvement is truly occurring. In doing so, the manager is reinforcing such improvement. If improvement is occurring, then the manager's role is simply to state that she sees improvement and to recognize that improvement verbally. For example, "Looks like you have made significant strides in the percentage of clients retained since our discussion, great work!" If improvement is not occurring, the manager needs to communicate this observation immediately. Great managers do not reward zero improvement. That is, they do not tell an employee "good job" when it hasn't happened. Of course, providing encouragement is helpful ("I know this is going to be difficult to break your previous habits, but you have a good plan, and sticking to it will improve your chances") as long as it communicates that anything other than performance improvement is not acceptable.

Train Employees When Appropriate

Although managers are quick to embrace training programs, it is important to note that training is a solution to only one category of problem: namely, skill deficiency. Skills are behaviors that can be learned and practiced for consistent results. If there is an absent skill, provide training. Otherwise, do not waste time and money investing in training as a cure-all approach. This is an extremely important point and deserves to be restated. Since training will not cure all problems, it should not be "prescribed" when the ailment is not the lack of a specific skill—to do so is managerial malpractice.

↹ MANAGEMENT LIVE 7.4

Problem Employees: Invest or Divest?

In their popular book, *First, Break All the Rules*,[36] based on extensive research by the Gallup Corporation, authors Marcus Buckingham and Curt Coffman passionately argue that the reason organizations are so inefficient is they simply don't understand people. Most organizations, they claim, are built on two flawed assumptions about people. The first flawed assumption is that people can learn to be competent in any area they choose. The second is that people's greatest area for growth lies within their personal weaknesses. The message to managers is clear: Invest in your high performers and divest the low ones. Divesting would involve helping low performers find a job that more appropriately matches their talents rather than waste considerable company resources on attempting to develop employees outside their talent areas. The Gallup researchers note that sometimes a low performer *can* be put back on the right track. But this process is damage control and should not be confused with development. That is, the person has the talent to perform the job, but needs some slight remediation to align that talent productively with the organization's goals. In contrast to the flawed assumptions, Gallup notes that the world's best managers are guided by different assumptions that (1) each person's talents are enduring and unique, and (2) each person's greatest room for growth is in the areas of his or her greatest strength.

Making a Reassignment or Termination Decision

As one of our colleagues is fond of saying, "Sometimes Humpty Dumpty falls off the wall and *can't* be put back together." In other words, if successive attempts to manage the problem employee have not led to improvement, great managers recognize the current situation cannot continue. As a general rule, a manager can recognize this situation when she is more heavily invested in the employee's performance than the employee is. That is, when the manager is putting in more effort than the problem employee to correct the problem, reassignment or termination is likely appropriate.

Sometimes great employees are promoted or moved into roles where they become poor employees. Take, for example, a highly productive industrial engineer who is promoted to managing a group of industrial engineers and then fails miserably as a manager. He is still a great engineer, despite the fact that he has failed as a manager. Thus, termination is not always the answer; sometimes reassignment to old positions or different posts in the organization that better utilize the employee's talent may be more appropriate. Don't lose a great employee because someone made a poor staffing decision!

At the same time, retaining those who do not improve after ample time and resources are provided hurts everyone involved. The organization suffers from lower-than-expected performance that can drain the pool of available resources. Managers' own resources are spent disproportionately on the problem person, making it difficult to advance efforts toward accomplishing goals. Co-workers of the problem employee often harbor resentment toward managers and the organization for retaining someone who does not pull his own weight. And the problem employee himself may also lose out on authentic opportunities to succeed in other environments or types of work. In general, the longer a problem employee stays without improvement, the more likely it is that the work environment will suffer for all involved.

The Termination/Reassignment Discussion

Few managerial situations are feared more than that of telling an employee he or she is to be let go.[37] Managers often fear the employee will protest and the situation will become ugly. Yet if the manager has truly done her job through the performance management cycle (PMC), the decision to terminate should not shock or surprise the employee; rather, it will be seen as consistent with the manager's approach throughout. Nonetheless, few managers like to actually deliver the news. Even when termination or reassignment is the right and appropriate thing to do, it is still difficult and thus conducting the termination or reassignment meeting takes preparation and forethought (see Tool Kit 7.4 for a checklist).

Recognition and Reinforcement: Managing the Star

Although rarely acknowledged, managing a star employee can be just as difficult as managing the problem employee. We use the term *star employee* to denote the person who consistently performs beyond expectations. Misperceptions of managing stars include beliefs that "stars" are completely self-motivated, will continue to perform regardless of how they are managed, and require little

MANAGER'S TOOL KIT

Tool Kit 7.4 Terminating or Reassigning an Employee

Termination or reassignment should always be done with dignity and concern for others. Keep in mind that termination in particular has broad effects on people's families, peers, and co-workers, so taking it seriously is important. Here are the critical steps in terminating or reassigning an employee:

- **Be Prepared.** Have all your documentation regarding the employee's performance on hand and summarized in a form that can be quickly delivered. This includes the dates of each performance improvement discussion and the feedback given in each discussion.

- **Set the Right Tone: Get the Job Done.** This is not a time to schmooze or ask about the employee's family or personal life. Professionalism dictates the meeting should always be conducted face-to-face and in private and scheduled to last for 10 to 15 minutes at the most. In addition, do not attempt to relate your own termination stories or provide vague statements like "I know this is probably hard for you"—these are likely to make the situation worse.[38]

- **State the Reality.** Use effective feedback techniques. Without evaluating the person, state the reality of the situation. For example, "Jim, as you know, I have been concerned about your performance over the past eight months, and we have met on three separate occasions to address it. Despite repeated attempts to improve performance, I have not seen such improvement to date. As I indicated in our last meeting, the next step would be separation. Thus, I have made the decision to terminate our employment relationship. And this decision is final." Do not blame others involved or sidestep the issue; be direct.

- **Review Next Steps.** Organizations structure their severance and termination policies differently. The key here is to ensure you are prepared to tell the employee exactly what he is entitled to receive from the organization. Do this in writing and give a copy to the employee. In addition, it is important to tell the employee what to do next. For example, "OK, Jim, after we finish our meeting here, I'd like you to take 30 minutes to collect your things, return your keys, and leave the building."

attention and resources. The evidence regarding managing stars suggests a more complex picture.

First, star employees may come to possess an overdeveloped sense of entitlement. They may believe their high performance merits treatment beyond what may be feasible or reasonable.[39] Second, star performance may be a function of external rewards and not intrinsic motivation. Remove the rewards (say, in difficult economic periods) and performance may decline.[40] Third, many stars have difficulty seeing the contribution others make to their own success and may be inclined to alienate co-workers and clients. Fourth, managers often allocate more resources toward problem employees, reducing attention to stars and thus offering fewer opportunities for visibility and growth. Under such circumstances, stars may be more likely to leave the organization and seek opportunities elsewhere.

Put simply, star performance does not necessarily equate to "easy to manage." Of course, most managers prefer to have the difficulties associated with stars than those associated with problem employees, but are not well informed as to how best to manage their stars.

Understanding Star Performers

Research has provided a relatively clear picture of what stars value and how to induce the highest performance and commitment from them:

- **Learning Orientation.** Star performers seek environments where they can learn and develop their skills. This includes working for managers who provide regular performance feedback that helps them exploit their strengths and improve their weaknesses.[41]
- **Selective Hiring.** Star performers want to know the manager they work for is actively seeking to hire only the best, to create a group of motivated and talented people to share the workload.
- **Rewards and Recognition.** Star performers prefer to work in environments that reward individual performance and provide a high degree of recognition for their efforts. Rewards and recognition may be in the form of frequent fast-track promotions, performance-based pay, and praise and public recognition.[42]
- **Challenging Job Assignments.** Star performers tend to want increasingly challenging work assignments that expand their areas of performance achievement and expertise.[43]

Engaging the Star Performer

"What every individual needs—is to be recognized, by their leader and their peers, for outstanding individual performance."

—Vince Lombardi

Based on the preferences of star performers, we recommend important steps to ensure your star performers stay engaged and performing as stars. As we discuss in Chapter 9 on leadership, all people respond best to rewards that are contingent upon performance. That is, stars in particular want to know their exceptional outcomes will be met with rewards and recognition. Simply stated, great managers reward "doers." In fact, nothing is likely to burn out your star performer as much as equal rewards, whereby everyone receives the same reward, regardless of performance. Remember, fairness in distributing performance rewards is achieved by providing rewards commensurate with effort and results.

One common mistake managers make is to leave their star performers alone, assuming that the stars will continue to perform with a hands-off approach. While a star performer certainly will not appreciate micromanagement, it is not true that the star prefers *no* management. To the contrary, great managers are fully involved in providing challenging job assignments to star performers to feed their need for challenge and learning. Challenging job assignments generally have one or more of the following characteristics:[44]

- **Transitional.** Assignments that involve unfamiliar, new, or broader tasks. Such assignments also involve proving one can handle the added pressure. Examples include being the inexperienced member of a team and taking a temporary assignment in a different functional area.
- **Change-Oriented.** Assignments that challenge through added responsibility to create change in the organization, to grapple with recurring organizational problems, and to handle problems with people. Examples include launching a new product, hiring new staff, resolving employee performance problems, or facilitating the development of a new vision or mission statement.
- **High Level of Responsibility.** Assignments that involve high stakes and visible results, heavy time investment, diversity of responsibility,

and external pressure. Examples include taking a visible assignment with tight deadlines, representing the organization externally, or managing additional responsibilities following a personnel restructuring.

- **Non-Authority Relationships.** Assignments that require influencing others without positional power. Examples include presenting a proposal to top management, serving on a cross-functional team, or managing an internal project such as a company event.
- **Obstacles.** Assignments that provide challenge through exposure to adverse situations like financial concerns, lack of top management support, and great diversity of opinions regarding project directions. Examples include working with a talented but difficult boss, ambiguous projects, or starting a new project with few resources.

Coaching for Employee Growth

KO **7-6**

Many people turn to their managers to provide support and guidance to navigate more effectively in an organization. And if you were to ask 10 people what they think a great coach does, you'd probably get 10 fairly similar responses: give advice. Although coaching does often involve giving advice, great managers know that advice often falls short in efforts to help *develop* employees, to help them learn. When people give advice on solving problems (or avoiding them), they do so from their own personal experience base. That is, their advice is formed by their own assumptions about the way the world works.

In his groundbreaking book, *The Fifth Discipline*, Peter Senge argues that most people spend the majority of their work life dispensing advice or advocating their own position about the world. He notes, however, that problems are often highly distinctive, and just because a method solved a similar problem in the past does not in any way guarantee it will work in the future—especially for someone else. In the end, the advice may make the advice-seeker feel better and give her something to do, but it won't necessarily help her learn to solve the problem for herself in the future. That is, the goal of managing employees for growth and development is to *help people build their capacity to develop and solve their own problems more effectively.*

A simple example can show why giving advice doesn't always work the way we think. Say you have a son in third grade who is just learning to multiply and divide fractions. One day, your son says, "Gosh, I'm stuck. I really don't know how to solve this math problem. What should I do?" As a parent, you have a few options:

Option 1: *Retreat.* Tell your son, sorry, but you can't help him; it's his homework and he must struggle to do it himself.

Option 2: *Take Action.* Solve the problem for your son. Take his pencil and simply do it for him, saying, "See what I did there? Now go finish the rest."

Option 3: *Consult.* Ask your son several questions about the problem that might help him solve the problem on his own, such as, "What have you tried? Have you seen this type of problem before? How did you solve the earlier problem? Are there similar rules that may apply?"

Few parents could stomach Option 1; it's just too cold. Option 2, however, is much more palatable and seems quite reasonable. Yet, in reality, the person being helped in this option is not the son, but the parent. The parent dives into

"If it's free, it's advice; if you pay for it, it's counseling; if you can use either one, it's a miracle."

—Jack Adams

TABLE 7.3   Expert vs. Consultative Coaching

Expert Coaching		Consultative Coaching
Based on my experience, I would tell your co-worker to let you drive this one.	vs.	What criteria are you using to make your choice?
Budgeting always works better if you solidify your alliances early.	vs.	What are the possible political ramifications of not talking with folks about the budget ahead of time?

action, reducing the anxious feelings over seeing his or her son struggling and needing help. Although the child may get by with what the parent has done, it is unlikely he has learned how to solve similar problems in the future. Option 3 offers a chance to help the child learn through discovery and develop the capacity to solve similar problems in the future.

Coaching employees for growth is no different, albeit the problems that arise may be more complex. As a developmental coach, you have a few modes of operation that can make for successful manager–employee relationships. The first mode is known as expert coaching. An **expert coach** dispenses advice, instructs, and prescribes. The second mode is known as consultative coaching. A **consultative coach** helps the employee explore alternatives and challenges the employee's thinking through asking questions. Table 7.3 shows a few differences in these two approaches.

So which is better? That depends on the problem to be solved by the employee. We have developed a few guidelines to help guide you in your choice of which approach to take.

Use the *expert coaching* approach when:

- The problem and solution are simple and clear (for example, following federal regulations).
- There are "right" answers (for instance, accounting rules).
- The employee is a novice and needs to be given a lot of structure.

Use the *consultative coaching* approach when:

- The problem and solution are ambiguous (many factors are involved and one solution won't fix everything).
- The problem continues to reappear; past attempts to solve the problem have failed.
- There is relatively less urgency; work output can wait.

Coaching vs. Mentoring

Although great coaches help people develop, coaching should not be confused with mentoring. **Mentoring** is an intense, long-term relationship between a senior, more experienced person **(mentor)** and a more junior, less experienced person **(protégé)**.[45] Mentoring differs from coaching in at least two significant ways. First, the goal of mentoring is focused on an employee's overall development, not necessarily on day-to-day performance. Second, mentors are typically *not* the employee's direct supervisor. As such, mentors and protégés (those being mentored) generally have a relationship quite different from that of employee and supervisor. Coaching, on the other hand, is about day-to-day work and is focused directly on job performance.

> CASE CONCLUDED

Inspired by emerging evidence-oriented evaluation examples in other sports (see Moneyball), Cuban and Winston were most interested in measuring a player by how well the *team* did with that player on the court, after accounting for the other players on the court with him. The Mavericks' "plus/minus index" adjusts for how good the team is without the player on the court as well as for the opponent and for game situations. (Without such adjustments, players on a top team like the Los Angeles Lakers would all look good, because the Lakers so often dominate.)

While Professor Winston is quick to point out that no system is perfect, he believes the system he derived for the Mavericks beats other player evaluations because it can reflect *defensive* prowess. It's with defense, Winston says, that plus/minus "really shines," because defensive stats such as blocked shots, rebounds, and steals can't encapsulate a player's worth. Cuban also defends the system from skeptics, saying it is not for ranking players by talent or for trades, but for determining good lineups and tracking player development. "It's a system you use to see how [players] are being used and contributing in the short term, and how good they are over the long term."

Professor Winston adds, ". . . optimizing your spending under the salary cap in professional basketball is really critical." Winston explains: "The whole issue for me is getting beyond player performance as defined by box scores and other traditional measures. For me, it's about determining the contribution the player makes toward the team's success. Then I can parse out what he is worth. A given team only wins so many games, so the holy grail is figuring out how many wins each player can create. Once you know that, team owners can really make smart decisions. They could say that a certain player is worth five wins, but he can be signed for half as much money as a player who is worth seven wins. That's a better buy. The owner is getting more player for the dollar." Being efficient with the money you have is the key to being successful in professional sports. But he warns that "math is a tool, not an end-all solution. You want to think in terms of multiple inputs, and good mathematical analysis is just one tool to be used in the evaluation process."

The proof of the value of the Mavericks' evaluation system is clear to see. During the last 10 years the team has systematically improved their winning percentage from 49 to 69 percent and won the team's first NBA championship in 2011.

Questions

1. In what ways does the Mavericks' system of evaluation address the most common problems with performance evaluation?

2. Why are people so skeptical of objective data, often choosing to use far more subjective metrics in their own evaluations?

3. What concerns or questions would you have about using *only* this type of information in performance evaluation?

4. What lessons can be learned from this article in creating an evaluation for first-line managers?

5. What kinds of metrics in a business organization might capture the same spirit as a basketball plus/minus index?

Sources: Wayne Winston **www.kelley.iu.edu/ugrad/spotlights/ spotlight_wayneWinston.cfm; http://blogs.wsj.com/numbersguy/ mark-cubans-surprising-player-performance-numbers-580/tab/print/**.

Concluding Note

The key principles of performance management are relatively simple to understand but are a challenge to consistently execute. Execution of those principles, however, is among the most powerful levers a manager can have in driving higher performance. The most important recurring lessons of good performance management include the following:

- **Set Performance Expectations Immediately.** Remember that "settling in" sends the wrong message. Use the power of goal setting to get performance up and running.

- **Give Feedback Early and Often.** The more information employees have about how they are performing at any given time, the less you will have to manage their performance. When employees don't receive feedback, they will seek it out, sometimes from unreliable sources.[46] So don't wait until the end of the year to give feedback; it will lose its motivating potential.

- **Focus on Behaviors, Not Traits.** Don't evaluate people; evaluate their performance. Observe behavior frequently and take notes.

- **Assess Both Behavior and Results.** Remember, just because employees hit their target goals does not necessarily mean they are outstanding performers. Understand the full range of performance by taking into account *how* they achieved those goals.

- **Identify and Rectify Performance Gaps.** When a performance gap exists, revisit the goal contract with the employee and agree upon interventions for closing the gap. Remember, training is not always the answer!

- **Allow for Productive Failures.** Employees need to know it is acceptable to fail or to miss the mark. What is unacceptable is to not learn from this failure and to repeat mistakes frequently. Great coaches help employees learn from their mistakes and never repeat them.

- **Reward Desired Behavior and Ensure It Repeats.** If you really want people to perform, make their rewards contingent upon reaching performance goals. Be careful that you are rewarding the behavior you desire and not inadvertently another behavior.

- **Make It Just.** Whatever you do, no matter what type of assessment is involved, ensure that the process, outcomes, and interactions with employees are perceived as fair. Fairness, not equality or happiness, is the key to great performance management.

KEY TERMS

absolute subjective assessment 250
affective commitment 243
altruism 241
attitudes 242
behaviorally anchored rating scale (BARS) 250
civic virtue 241
conscientiousness 241
consultative coach 264
contextual performance 240
continuance commitment 243
courtesy 241
effectiveness 240
efficiency 240

equality rule 256
equity rule 256
expert coach 264
forced distribution 251
graphic rating scale 250
job performance 240
job satisfaction 242
mentor 264
mentoring 264
need rule 256
normative commitment 243
objective assessment 249
organizational citizenship behavior (OCB) 241

organizational commitment 243
organizational cynicism 244
performance management cycle (PMC) 244
protégé 264
ranking 250
relative subjective assessment 250
sportsmanship 241
subjective assessment 250
task performance 240
topgrading 251
withdrawal behaviors 242

Besides getting less vacation than workers in many other countries, Americans often don't use all the time that they do get, and what vacation they take is spent in small slices and often in contact with the office, according to most surveys on the subject.

An important distinction for workers in the United States is that there is no federal law mandating that companies pay employees for time off or that they grant them a minimum amount of vacation days unpaid. This is not the case in most of the rest of the world.

The typical practice in the United States—among large companies anyway—is 15 days paid vacation and 10 days of paid holidays for full-time employees with 10 years of tenure, according to a survey conducted by human resource consulting firm Mercer. Another study, however, by the Center for Economic and Policy Research (CEPR), found the norm to be much lower when considering companies of all sizes and workers of all tenures: 9 days of paid vacation with 6 days of paid holidays. It also estimates that almost one in four U.S. workers don't get any paid days off at all. To provide some context for this, all members of the European Union, by contrast, must provide workers with a minimum of 20 paid vacation days a year plus public holidays. Some specific examples from other countries include Finland with 30 required vacation days and 14 public holidays,

France with 30 vacation days and 10 public holidays, and Australia with 20 vacation days and 11 public holidays. In fact, of the countries surveyed, only countries like Vietnam, the Philippines, and Thailand have less vacation than the United States.

To compound the problem, most vacation time is accumulated in the United States based upon tenure. So, for example, an employee may get 10 days of vacation until she has more than 5 years of tenure, at which time she would get an extra 5 vacation days. Joe Robinson, who runs the Work to Live Campaign and advocates for a minimum paid-leave law in the United States, contends that a vacation system based on tenure, which is typical at U.S. companies, leaves U.S. workers with consistently low vacation benefits given how frequently people change jobs during a career.

While it is not legally required, Procter & Gamble has taken a slightly different approach to the vacation issue. In May of 2004, P&G's senior management orchestrated a company-wide important announcement: There would be time off for good behavior. P&G workers learned they had been

CASE
< < Extra Time Off at Procter & Gamble

granted a two-day vacation bonus, a reward for the company's sustained excellent performance over the previous four years, during which time P&G's stock rose from $60 a share in the mid-2000s to more than $106 a share in May 2004. "We've never before offered a company performance award such as this, but you've earned it," the chairman wrote to employees in an e-mail. Employees will have the option of taking two days' pay instead of the time off. A spokesman for P&G said that the cost of the bonus "will be in the millions, though it isn't material from an accounting standpoint." The cash involved would be equivalent to a less than 1 percent bonus. Nevertheless, P&G's gesture had people pondering the value of time off as a motivational tool.

Discussion Questions

1. Do you think P&G's "across the board" days off reward will motivate employees to perform?

2. What principle of distributing rewards is P&G using?

3. Do you think that making vacation contingent upon performance is a good or bad idea? Why?

4. How do you think top performers are likely to react?

SELECT MANAGE ~~WHAT?~~ **DEBRIEFS**

Critiquing a Performance Evaluation Form: Debrief

a. *Briefly argue why performance appraisal is important enough that the managers at this restaurant should care enough to improve the system.*

b. *Critique the form with respect to its strengths and weaknesses. What does it help them accomplish? How does it limit them?*

The overall reason is that very important administrative and developmental decisions are made on the basis of performance appraisal information and hence they would want evaluation to be as accurate and fair (reliable and valid) as possible. More specifically, those decisions could include pay, promotion, discipline, awards, training, establishing expectations, and feedback. With respect to this restaurant, they may want to have some profit sharing or merit-based pay and they are certainly interested in feedback and development (of mostly young, inexperienced servers). They might also be interested in awards or providing recommendations of different sorts, and probably would benefit from establishing clear customer service expectations.

The form is a classic example of a solely trait-based form with all the associated weaknesses. About all it helps them accomplish is to give a numeric score, it does give a rating of all servers, and it is the same for everyone, so it might be used to compare employees for administrative decisions. It is also certainly easy to understand and is not time-consuming to complete. With respect to limitations, it very much limits them in terms of establishing expectations, giving any type of meaningful feedback, or making reliable and valid administrative decisions—because it is so subjective and thus prone to different interpretations of the same labels (for example, initiative). It also would not stand up well in a discrimination court case.

c. *Make recommendations for improvement—including a sample form/process that you think would better help them meet their objectives. Be sure to include an explanation of why your improvements are better than what they currently do and also why they will not create an overwhelming amount of extra work for them.*

They clearly have to get away from traits (a common source of consistency problems) and move toward objective results and/or behavioral indicators. They may also want to think about more tailored (often behavioral) appraisals for different jobs or job classes. Ultimately, they want some type of combination of behavioral and objective results. Objective results might include the total revenue at his tables, total tips, broader restaurant revenues for the evening, cost cutting and waste reduction, attendance/on-time records, and other items. Behavioral items can be derived by taking the trait names and expanding them to specific behaviors. For example, customer service might include behaviors like smiles at customers when welcoming them; promptly checks with them just after they sit down; fails to bring their check after they have completed eating. Similarly, initiative might include behaviors like takes on additional tasks when assigned tables are not occupied; asks manager if he can contribute in other ways when not busy; fills water and drinks for fellow servers when sees the need; and so on.

Evaluating Job Performance: Debrief

This is another scenario where "common sense" and past experience are too often *not consistent* with the evidence regarding how to make the most accurate evaluations. And given what is at stake for these interns, you will want to make every effort to make your evaluations as fair and legally defensible as possible. The two main lessons to keep in mind are (1) define your performance criteria in terms of results and behavior—not solely personal traits, and (2) look for multiple sources of data for your evaluations.

Most jobs have some objective outcomes and require certain behaviors to obtain those outcomes. In an effort to determine some appropriate results measures, you might ask, Who do these interns serve? What will their performance make possible and for whom? What would suffer if they performed poorly? For short four-month roles like these, it may require some ingenuity in coming up with objective results to be measured, but it is worth the effort. One way to get outcome data is to identify "customers" of the interns' work (whether those customers are external or internal to the firm) and gather performance and satisfaction data from those customers.

Although results are a critical element in any good performance evaluation, it is also true that many factors in organizations can influence (some would say bias) results achieved (for example, projects assigned, department, luck), so it is important to also have some evaluation of behaviors or "how results were achieved." To reveal key behaviors, ask: What do the most successful people in this role do so well and frequently? Conversely, what are the behaviors that doom the less successful people in that role? For example, effective nurses review forthcoming treatments with patients, check for an understanding of the procedures to be followed, respond promptly to requests for pain treatment, follow up with patients to ensure compliance with their medication schedule, and so on. Those are not actual patient outcomes, but they are behaviors that lead to better outcomes.

The essential point is that *both* the outcomes and the behaviors are important to a comprehensive evaluation. Results/outcome evaluations are best for making administrative decisions, and behavioral evaluations are particularly good for providing feedback about why a certain rating was given and how someone can do better. In this case, those interns *not selected* will likely be frustrated and eager to get feedback as to why they were passed over; thus some behavioral evaluation information would be particularly useful here.

The second major thing to keep in mind, and which might not be intuitively apparent, is to seek input on these interns' performance beyond that from their immediate supervisor (in this case, you). For example, can you collect any feedback from their peers or other people they worked with, or interacted with, in their time at the firm? It may also be useful to have them complete a self-evaluation just to be sure you uncover major accomplishments that might not otherwise have been noted.

The most significant traps are just the inverse of the two major recommendations. First, resist the temptation to rely solely on subjective trait evaluations (for example, attitude, initiative, professionalism) because those terms are vague and do not have shared meaning. Such trait-oriented measures also have a poor record of support when challenged in the courts. Second, do not limit your evaluation data to just one immediate supervisor. Aim to collect data from multiple people and sources whenever possible.

Managing Both the Problem and the Star Employee: Debrief

In essence, what you have here is a "problem employee" and a "star employee," and the basic framework for dealing with a "problem" is:

- Agree on the problem
- Mutually discuss solutions
- Create an action plan
- Provide ongoing feedback—reinforce improvement

Here again, presenting that basic framework is a great start, but the best answers will specify actions and illustrate how management should approach Ken, doing so in a way that yields higher performance from him. The context is authentically complex: Ken is beloved by other workers so you do not want to destroy your culture—but you also need to send a message that performance is critical around here. So any vague soft-pedaling will not serve your purpose and will probably be dysfunctional. You need to tell Ken what he does not want to hear and yet do it in a way that he will respect you, not be defensive and disruptive, work harder with a focus on performance goals, and *deliver* performance. And he needs to know what will happen (and when it will happen) if he does not do those things.

Some potentially good ideas are to be sure to reference and build on Ken's strengths and find some way to use his good relations with others to help him reach those performance targets. They should also be consistent with the rules for giving good feedback in how they talk with Ken.

Venkat, on the other hand, is a "star" employee and the evidence suggests that he will respond best to several different things:

- **Learning orientation.** Opportunities to grow and get better and become even more valuable and deserving of more pay.
- **Selective hiring.** He wants to work with winners and he is quite interested in how you will deal with Ken. He is not amused by Ken's lovable low performance and it bugs him to think that Ken would get the same rewards that he (Venkat) gets despite a much greater focus and success in delivering performance outcomes.

(continued)

(continued)

- **Reward and recognition.** A critical trap is simply to let Venkat do his thing and get out of his way. Stars do not want close monitoring, but they do want to be recognized and rewarded. And the more specific the praise and rewards, the better. It shouldn't be "You're doing a great job" but "Thank you for the exceptional work on the Ben Dover account—that saved us in excess of $6,000 alone and qualifies you for an additional gain-sharing bonus."

- **Challenging job assignments.** Such as the following:
  - Transitional assignments
  - Change-oriented
  - High-level of responsibility
  - Non-authority relationships
  - Chance to overcome obstacles

Using Power and Influence

OBJECTIVES

KNOWING　　　　　　　　　　**DOING**

After reading this chapter, you should be able to:

"You cannot be successful in our group without building power and being able to influence customers and associates, whether or not you have any direct authority. Without power and influence, managers are not much use to anyone around here."

—Scott Pickering, Vice President of Sales, Urogyn Medical, Inc.

KO 8-1 Differentiate the concepts of power, influence, and authority.

KO 8-2 Explain how patterns of dependence in organizations act as sources of influence.

KO 8-3 Describe the role of norms and conformity on behavior.

KO 8-4 Recognize the effectiveness of various forms of influence tactics.

KO 8-5 Explain the key influence principle for each type of social influence weapon.

KO 8-6 Articulate methods for fostering a good relationship with one's manager.

KO 8-7 Describe at least five professionalism tactics for improving your impression.

DO 8-1 Use influence tactics and "weapons of social influence" to influence others informally.

DO 8-2 Influence your boss to adopt a given idea.

DO 8-3 Demonstrate competence and consistency in professional behavior.

DO 8-4 Build positive relationships with employees and co-workers.

DO 8-5 Create a memorable and positive first impression.

DO 8-6 Expand your personal network.

Case: KLOUT

The world is full of followers. But truly influential leaders remain an elusive commodity. Nowhere is this more evident than in the world of social media. Today's most progressive marketers believe that connecting with one influential leader, that one real beacon in a given niche, is worth at least a thousand followers. And that's where KLOUT comes in. KLOUT (a play on the concept of clout) was originally conceived as a way for frequent Internet users to gauge their personal influence and perhaps use it as a sort of "badge of honor" if their influence was deemed substantial. Founders Joe Fernandez and Binh Tran quickly discovered, however, that the system could be a gold mine for marketers looking to locate the true influential whales in a vast sea of little fish.

KLOUT has created an intricate (and secret) rating system that scores a person's "worth" in the social media world. It analyzes not only how many followers you have, but *who they are* and the type of content both you and your followers post, click on, or tweet. Originally, the system was devoted primarily to Twitter use, but KLOUT is now analyzing Facebook data—and YouTube, LinkedIn, MySpace, and Digg aren't far behind. When it comes to clout, the more the better.

1. What is influence, and what is the fundamental premise of a system like KLOUT?

2. How have technology and social media changed the nature of networking and influence? How does online influence differ from influence in an organizational context?

3. Do you buy the fundamental notion that influence matters on the Internet and different people are more or less influential?

4. Identify people you think have great online influence and would likely have correspondingly high KLOUT scores.

1. Influencing Without Formal Authority

You are the leader on a marketing project that requires a great deal of graphic design and production work to be successful. You have design people in the firm but they do not formally report to you and seem to have little urgency to get your work done. You are irritated by their lack of help and know they are not nearly as busy as they let on, but you have no authority to tell them what to do or threaten them with anything they care about. You are reluctant to go over their heads to their boss out of fear such a move would alienate them and compromise the level of effort and quality they would ultimately bring to the project.

To meet deadlines, you need some of the work done within a month. How might you get the graphics folks energized to complete your work? Are there any specific tactics you could use to get them moving? Are there any common but counterproductive tactics you should definitely avoid?

2. Selling an Idea to Your Boss

You have read a lot about the most successful companies and have picked up an idea you think would work well in your unit (operations) of the firm. Specifically, you think your department should go to an "open office" design whereby all the cubicles would be taken out and replaced with more modern collaborative workspaces. You have a host of good reasons why this would be a good idea for your unit, but your boss is a little old-fashioned and unlikely to buy into the idea. While she has always claimed she has an open-door policy and is "constantly on the lookout for good ideas," your past attempts have been met with comments like, "Interesting idea, we'll have to look into that," "Maybe sometime in the future we could do something like that," and "We don't have the budget for that right now, but it is a great thought."

If you really want to see this idea come to pass, how would you prepare to sell this to her? Where should you start? What would be some of the key factors to consider? Are there any tactics you should definitely avoid because they would be likely only to hurt your chances of her approval?

3. Making a Positive First Impression

Ever since you were a young child, your passion has been music. You love music in all its forms, play an instrument yourself, and want to make your passion your vocation—your dream is to work in the music industry. However, once in college you quickly learned that, because so many people share your dream, it is exceptionally difficult to get a job in the music industry. As luck would have it, however, your current management professor has two personal friends who are senior officers (one in human resources, the other in marketing) at Sony Music, and he has invited them to make a presentation to your class. Knowing of your lifelong interest, he has asked if they would be willing to spend half an hour with you after the presentation and they have agreed. How would you prepare? How would you try to make a good first impression? How might you appropriately try to leverage your professor's relationship? Would there be any absolute taboos (things never to do) or common mistakes to avoid here?

4. Building a Personal Network That Enhances Your Power

After your first six months at a public accounting firm, you are starting to see it will be very difficult to stand out until you really know the ropes and feel more connected, like all of your more senior associates. All but one of your colleagues at work have been at the firm for more than five years. Your fear is you will always be seen as a newbie around the firm. You also know you will have a far better chance of getting things done and moving up if you have a network of people within and outside the firm who mentor, coach, and support you. You are not really willing, however, to wait five years for that to happen.

Where would you start in your attempt to get more connected? What specific ways would make people want to be associated with you? How would you go about building a network?

Introduction

Although sometimes considered to be a "necessary evil" or the "unsavory" side of organizational life, skilled use of power and influence is critical to both personal and managerial success. For managerial purposes, **power** can be defined as the ability to exert influence to control others or events, and the capacity to defend against the influence of others.

Who has power in organizations? What are the sources of that power? What strategies will broaden our networks and increase our own power? What specific tactics have been shown to yield the most influence, especially in cases where we

"We have learned that power is a positive force if it is used for positive purposes."
—Elizabeth Dole

lack formal authority? How do we manage upward and navigate the political realities of organizational life? This chapter focuses on addressing these questions.

Authority and Influence

Although formal authority is often confused with power, it is just one *type* of power. More specifically, **authority** is the type of power a person possesses due to his position. In other words, a mother has the authority to make decisions for her five-year-old daughter solely because she is the child's mother. Similarly, a supervisor has the authority to discipline an employee who has been late to work. A company president has the authority to sign a legal contract as a representative of the company.

Influence, on the other hand, is the *use* of power. **Influence** is power *in action*, and influence tactics serve as the means by which managers gain and exercise power. While authority can be an important tool, great managers realize they need more than just authority to be effective. Therefore, understanding what power is, where it comes from, and the most effective tactics to get beyond authority to influence others is a key to great management. Since it is unlikely most of us will ever have enough formal authority to command wide-ranging action (particularly early in our careers), building personal skills associated with power and influence is important for both you personally and the organizations for which you work.

Dependence and Networks

KO 8-2

As a starting place, it is important to note that power is relational. That is, power only exists where there are at least two people, and is a property of the relationship between people. A useful and popular way to think of power is that it is based on **dependence.** Dependence leads people to do things they may not otherwise do ("I am dependent upon Jennifer for babysitting so I will buy my new car from Jennifer's husband," or "Anne controls my raises so I will pay close attention to what Anne says"). Understanding such relational dependencies is key to understanding your own power and the power of others. It is also a useful starting point for determining the influence tactics that can help you build broad networks and influence others to get things done. To be effective in your use of power and influence, it is important for you to understand the patterns of dependence in an organization; it can also help you understand and navigate the organization's political landscape. To diagnose interdependence, ask the following questions:

1. Whose cooperation will I need to accomplish what I am attempting?
2. Whose support will be necessary to get the appropriate decisions made and implemented?
3. Whose opposition could delay or derail what I am trying to do?
4. Who will be impacted by what I am trying to accomplish? More specifically, will anything change regarding (a) their power or status, (b) how they are evaluated or rewarded, or (c) how they do their job?
5. Who are the friends and allies of the people I have identified as influential?

Research has shown that people who have power and use it effectively attain desired jobs more quickly, make more money, and are promoted more quickly than people without power. While this might not be particularly surprising on the surface, the way it plays out is not always obvious or self-evident. For instance, conventional wisdom suggests that it is "who you know" that leads to getting a job. Although this is sometimes the case, of course, research suggests new jobs are more often the product of the **"weak ties"**[1] of the indirect relationships one possesses rather than the **"strong ties"** of direct relationships. In other words, people ultimately tend to get jobs through a friend of a friend (weak ties) and not through people they know directly (strong ties). The implication is that having positive relationships with many people, and people who are well-connected, is an important strategy for finding a job.

Not very long ago, the concept of strong and weak ties was pretty esoteric to most people. Recently, however, this has all changed because of social networking. It is largely this "weak tie" phenomenon that has led to the success of social networking sites like LinkedIn. A close examination of LinkedIn reveals that it is really a network management tool where people can recommend one another and build their professional networks in a very tangible manner. In terms of personal networks, Facebook serves a very similar role. In fact, the suggestions of people you may know come from the idea of weak ties. The suggestions provided by Facebook are based on friends of your friends. The more friends of yours who are friends with a certain person, the more likely that person will be recommended to you as a friend. Beyond LinkedIn and Facebook, however, this networking ability also allows Amazon.com to make book suggestions, Netflix to make movie recommendations, and a whole host of other applications—the importance of many of which is not yet fully understood due to its unfolding nature. For some specific examples of how social networking can pay off in the job market, see Management Live 8.1.

The reasons why weak ties are so important may not be immediately evident. First, it is important to understand that weak ties grow exponentially when your immediate network grows. This is because each person you know has ties to numerous other people who all become weak ties in your network (for example,

⇄ MANAGEMENT LIVE 8.1

Successful Uses of Personal Networks Through LinkedIn

The following cases are a few ways that social networking websites like LinkedIn can be effective when it comes to finding a job or otherwise enhancing one's career. These examples are taken from LinkedIn's website, but they are indicative of success stories using a number of other social media as well.

Liz Manning of Seattle, Washington

Liz saw an article in the paper about a new company and she said to herself, "I want to work there." She went to LinkedIn and found one of the founders of the company and sent him an InMail. He wrote back and appreciated her interest, but they had no openings at the time. Then she saw an ad on Craigslist for an opening at this company a couple of months later and this time the LinkedIn toolbar on the side of her screen showed that she was a 2nd-degree link to the cofounder. One of her old co-workers had just added him to her network. She sent him another InMail (and mentioned their common connection) and got a call for an interview within a day and landed the job. The company provides "senior transition coordination." This was exciting for Liz because she just worked on "transitioning" her mother into a retirement community, so helping other people transition their parents was a perfect personal fit for her as well."

Steve Weinstein of Milwaukee, Wisconsin

The recruiter for Cooper (Steve's current employer) did a search for marketing communications people in the metro Milwaukee area, and found Steve, among others, who fit the bill for the position that Cooper had open. Steve went in, interviewed for the job, and landed it. Now he's the Manager of Marketing Communications at Cooper Power Systems and he also is a member of the LinkedIn Milwaukee Group.

Chuck Hester of Raleigh, North Carolina

Chuck's connections on LinkedIn helped him land his current job. After relocating his family to North Carolina from California, Chuck began using LinkedIn to reach out to marketing professionals in the area. Among them was the chief executive of iContact, an e-mail software company where Chuck is now the corporate communications director.

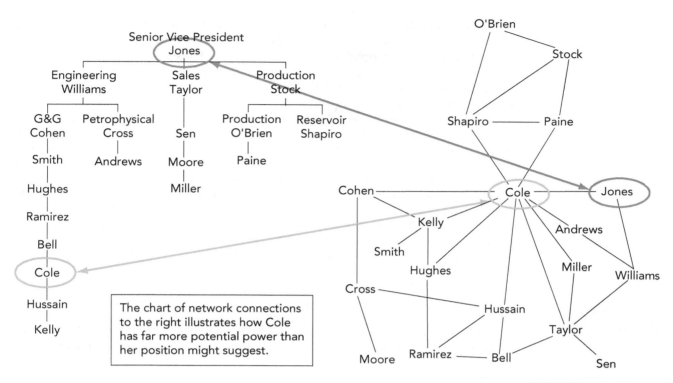

The chart of network connections to the right illustrates how Cole has far more potential power than her position might suggest.

FIGURE 8.1
Who Has the Power Is Not Always Obvious

see Figure 8.1). For instance, just getting to know one person could add 50 or 100 weak ties if that new friend is well connected. In addition, weak ties serve as an important information-gathering tool. Weak ties allow a person to collect information from a much broader network than those with fewer weak ties,

?¿ MYTHS 8.1 Myths of Power and Influence

- *Power and influence are inherently "corrupt."* An old but true axiom is that power can be used for good or evil. Great managers use their power to exert influence to accomplish *positive* change in organizations.

- *Rationality is the best form of influence.* We're taught to give people data, to influence others through the use of facts and figures. It turns out, however, that despite the popularity of the rational approach to influence, emotional approaches often win the day. People want to be inspired, challenged, and moved.

- *Power stems solely from one's position.* Title alone is only one form of power, and it does not in any way guarantee success toward influencing others. Some of the most powerful people in organizations have unimpressive titles—for example, secretary or help-desk specialist. However, such folks often have great influence in organizations.

- *Involving others and sharing power weakens your own position.* By and large, sharing power only *increases* your own ability to influence. Showing people you don't need to be protective because you are confident in your abilities and approaches increases your credibility and future influence potential.

- *First impressions and good manners are old-fashioned.* Hardly! Managing the impression you make always matters greatly in your ability to influence others. This includes all aspects of your work life, such as how you answer your telephone, what clothes you choose to wear, and how you introduce yourself to key clients or your boss's boss.

which provides a significant competitive advantage, an advantage that has been shown to result in both higher wages and a higher likelihood of being employed.[2]

Thus, people with broader networks have more power and an increased number of options, making them more valuable to their organization. In this light, it should not be surprising that power holders are often able to utilize their power to negotiate higher wages. Organizations are rightly willing to pay more for a person with the power and influence to get things done. For the organization, the powerful person is likely to be able to accomplish more and bring in additional resources. Thus, paying more for power would seem to be a wise investment that provides handsome returns for an organization.

Finally, research has also shown that people with well-developed power networks receive earlier promotions, have increased career mobility, and higher managerial effectiveness.[3] In short, power is advantageous to many important outcomes, and thus active efforts to gain and manage your power are a step toward a successful managerial career.

Practice this!
Go to www.baldwin2e.com

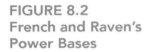

The Sources of Power and Influence

Even a casual observer would notice that some people in organizations are far more able to make things happen and get what they want done than others. Think for a moment about your personal situation, your family members, and your friends. Are some of them consistently more able to get things done and to bring together the resources they need? From your personal experience, you will probably notice that the people who are able to "get things done" are not always the ones with formal authority. Understanding differences in personal power bases, networks, personal professionalism, and the ability to use social influence effectively is central to using power effectively in organizations. We expand on these four areas next.

Bases of Power

The most widely known and accepted classification of power is French and Raven's model of the five **power bases,** first introduced more than 50 years ago.[4] Their classification has stood the test of time and become the way in which authors and practicing managers most often think about power. The five bases are reward, legitimate, referent, expert, and coercive power. (See Figure 8.2.)

Reward Power. A point emphasized throughout this text is that rewards are powerful motivators of behavior. Put simply, people are inclined to do things that will bring them rewards. Rewards can come in many different forms. In fact, anything we find desirable can be a reward, be it a new Lamborghini, a

**FIGURE 8.2
French and Raven's
Power Bases**

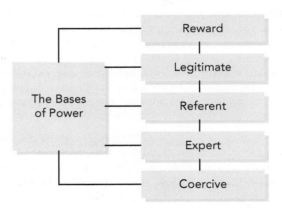

promotion, a good grade on a test, or a pat on the back. What is really important is that the reward being offered is desirable to the person you want to influence. **Reward power** is thus the ability to provide others with rewards they desire in exchange for work you need accomplished.

In order to increase your reward power base, you do need to control some rewards, and this may take a certain amount of creativity depending on your position. Remember, however, that social reinforcements (feedback, compliments, and so on) can be very effective rewards in some cases and that many rewards do not need to be expensive or linked to your position in the hierarchy. Simply stated, the best way to build reward power is to actually reward people, and the reality is that "if you don't use it, you will lose it." Few managers that have not paid anyone a compliment or provided some form of reward to people in the past five years would be seen by employees as having a strong reward power base (even if they have significant budget control).

Legitimate Power. **Legitimate power** is that which is invested in a role or job position (often called authority). Politicians, police officers, and managers all have legitimate power. The legitimacy generally stems from some higher hierarchical level or legal mandate. A police officer has legitimate power to arrest you by virtue of laws made by elected officials. The legitimate power of a manager ultimately comes from the company's owners or shareholders.

A common seduction of legitimate power is to neglect the reality that the influence associated with a role most often really stems from that position, not the *person* in the position. When people either fall from power or move onto other things, they can be surprised that those who used to fawn at their feet no longer do so. Legitimate power is often sufficient to gain compliance behavior but is less effective in inducing engaged and committed action.

Building legitimate power is often thought of as the most difficult power base to increase. This is because of its close tie to one's position in the organizational hierarchy. Remember, however, that taking a leadership role on high-profile projects and being associated with important divisions within a company do not always require receiving a formal promotion, but can be effective ways of increasing your legitimate power.

Referent Power. Unlike legitimate power, **referent power** is highly associated with the person and not the position. Referent power stems from another person either admiring you or wanting to be like you. It is the power of charisma and fame and is commonly (although often curiously) wielded by celebrities as well as others in highly visible roles. No one really believes Brett Favre is an expert on jeans, Danica Patrick is a web guru, or that William Shatner is really a knowledgeable travel consultant. However, they are highly successful at selling products because of their referent power.

In the workplace, referent power is normally associated with respect and a good working relationship. In other words, we are generally more willing to respond to a request from a person whom we admire and respect than from someone we do not know or dislike. You don't have to be friends with someone to have referent power—plenty of people are highly respected, but not necessarily liked. Referent power is one more reason why having a positive working relationship with your colleagues, bosses, and subordinates is extremely important.

Unlike legitimate power, referent power is directly under your immediate control. To increase your referent power, you need to be trusted and respected. By being seen as approachable, fair, friendly, and competent, you will build your referent power and be more effective in the process. In fact, much of this textbook is geared toward helping you do exactly these things.

"I have as much authority as the Pope, I just don't have as many people who believe it."

—George Carlin

Practice this!
Go to www.baldwin2e.com

Expert Power.   Much like referent power, **expert power** is normally associated with a person and not closely with the rank of a position. When a person possesses knowledge and skill someone else requires, then she has expert power. This common form of power is the basis for a large proportion of human collaboration, including in most companies where the principle of specialization allows large and complex challenges to be undertaken.

Expert power is relevant across a wide variety of situations. Trade unions often use expert power when they encourage their members to strike for better pay or working conditions. Many information technology (IT) departments within companies are powerful due to their specialized knowledge. Expert power is also at work when you go to a doctor and she prescribes medication; you tend to accept the prescription because the doctor is supposed to "be the expert."

The most common ways for people to build their expert power is through education. Be it a college degree, advanced degree, or specific certifications (for example, a CPA or a CFP), education is key. Beyond the role of education, however, obtaining specific, scarce knowledge is a great way to increase your expert power. For example, a low-level computer programmer can have the most power in the company when a system for which she is responsible fails. Become a technical expert in your field and you will likely find your expert power in the organization will increase.

Coercive Power.   **Coercive power** can be associated with either a person or the rank attached to a person's position. This is the power to force someone to do something against his or her will. Coercion often involves physical or verbal threats. It is the power of dictators, despots, and bullies. Coercion can result in physical harm, although its principal goal is to influence action. Demonstrations of personal harm are often used to illustrate what will happen if compliance is not gained.

In the workplace, coercive power can be thought of as coming in the form of disciplinary actions, demotions, or job loss. Generally, being threatened with firing is considered the most extreme form of coercive power, although threat of legal action may be used as a severe coercive inducement as well.

Actually building coercive power can be a tricky business and is not something we would recommend in most instances. As you might imagine, building coercive power tends to undermine some of your most powerful sources of positive power. More specifically, building coercive power by "flexing your muscles" and disciplining people or assigning unpleasant work duties will likely reduce your referent power significantly. To effectively manage coercive power, the best idea is to be fair and consistent when standards are not met. We recommend building and using coercive power sparingly, perhaps only when it is absolutely necessary that you receive 100 percent compliance (for instance, legal or safety compliance). In this way, people know that although you do not make it a practice to coerce behavior regularly, those who violate critical standards will receive a commensurate response. Remember that you don't have to use power to hold power. That people know you could coerce them is often enough to gain compliance.

KO 8-3   Norms and Conformity

Another subtle but very powerful form of influence is found in behavioral norms. Whether overt or just understood, every group and organization possesses a set of **norms,** a code of conduct about what constitutes acceptable behavior. Some norms will be strictly adhered to while others permit a wide range of behavior, but these norms have a significant influence on behavior in organizations. Usually, sanctions from the group (such as disapproval) are applied in the case of deviations from the norm.

To illustrate, think back to the days in which you dared a friend (or maybe even "double-dog dared" if you grew up in one of our neighborhoods) to do something outrageous. Such dares—like streaking naked though campus or eating bizarre amounts of restaurant condiments—are dares because they represent behavior that some reference group deems as *inappropriate* (would there be any other reason to drink an entire container of maple syrup?). Organizations of every kind are filled with such norms.

For example, if you show up late to a meeting when the norm is to be on time, most people in the group are likely to give you the "you're late" look. These looks are designed to let you know you are violating a rule and that you should not have done so. Norms are frequently associated with clothing, language (slang, cursing), Internet usage, the open expression of feelings, promptness, interrupting or challenging leaders, volunteering one's services, avoiding conflict, and so on. Many such norms are implicit, and new members may find it difficult to adjust—there rarely is a nice documented set of rules. Nonetheless, norms have great influence on workplace behavior.

From a managerial perspective, norms can be the source of both desirable and undesirable forms of influence. For example, you may want your employees to show up every Sunday for work. However, because this is not a general societal norm, you will certainly be met with resistance. Breaking norms makes people feel uncomfortable. The next time you get on a crowded elevator, start off by turning and facing the *back* of the elevator. Then, after a few seconds, start looking people in the eye. We guarantee you will not only make other people feel uncomfortable, but we suspect you will feel exceptionally awkward in bucking established norms. The important lesson is that most behavior is likely to happen "inside the norms," so it is always important to know what those norms are and how difficult it can be to influence people to break those norms.

Stemming directly from the influence of norms is the notion of conformity. **Conformity** is defined as a tendency to believe, behave, and perceive in ways that are consistent with group norms. Conformity enables us to feel as if we fit in, to feel comfortable with other people, and to have well-understood codes of conduct in society at large. Conformity is an important influence on the actions of people, especially when no formal authority or power is present. Two striking examples of the extraordinary influence of conformity are provided in famous experiments conducted by Muzafer Sherif and Solomon Asch.[5]

In Sherif's study, people were invited to estimate the amount that a point of light moved and to do so in a context where each participant could hear the estimates of other participants. Results showed that group members' estimates converged on a middle-of-the-road "group estimate" indicating the presence of a persuasive urge to conform. Asch conducted a set of similar experiments focused on social pressures to conform. In his experiments, several people were seated around a table and all but one were actually in on the experiment (that is, they were working for the experimenter as confederates). The group was shown a display of vertical lines of different lengths, and each participant was asked to say which line was the same length as another displayed line. One after another, the confederate participants chose the same (but wrong) line as that which was identical in length to the other displayed line. The only real participant sat in the next to last seat so that all but one of the confederates had given an answer prior to his choice. (See Figure 8.3.)

Incredibly, in repeated trials of the experiment, the real participants frequently picked the same incorrect line as the confederates, even though it was apparent to outside observers that the choice was clearly wrong. In fact, the unwitting participants (each of whom participated in a number of trials) conformed to the group response in 32 percent of the trials and 74 percent of the participants conformed at least once. It should be noted that recent research has

Practice this!
Go to www.baldwin2e.com

FIGURE 8.3
The Lines from
the Asch Study

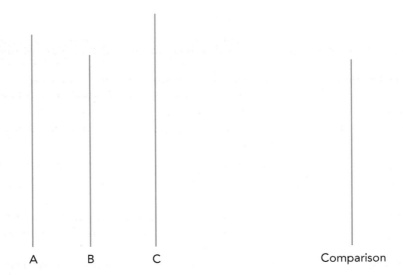

FIGURE 8.3
The Lines from
the Asch Study

shown some reduction in conformity since Asch's studies in the 1950s.[6] Nevertheless, his studies were instrumental in demonstrating the subtlety of conformity, a deceptively powerful source of influence.

One distinction between the tasks used by Sherif and Asch was the ambiguity involved. In Sherif's task, the light appeared to move but actually did not (this is known as the autokinetic effect). In this case, people looked to others because they were uncertain about what actually happened. In Asch's study, there was no ambiguity involved; people clearly answered due to social pressure. Thus, this points to two important times when people look to others, but for very different reasons. In many ways, the aftermath of 9/11 serves as an excellent illustration of both of these types of influence. People were unsure as to what happened, so they looked to others to make sense of the event. Then legislation and other rules passed quickly (some of which have since been revoked) due to the social pressure that followed.

DO **8-1**   Influencing Without Authority

Thus far, we have focused on understanding what power and influence are, where they come from, and how to develop them. The applied managerial skill, however, is how to use influence to get real and positive things accomplished through others, particularly in those cases where you have no legitimate power from your position. In short, you want to learn to influence without authority. In the following, we present the supporting evidence for several approaches and tactics that have been demonstrated to be successful in such cases.

KO **8-4**   Frequency and Effectiveness of Different Influence Tactics

A variety of different tactics are used to influence others, the most common of which are described in Table 8.1.

Research regarding these nine influence tactics has uncovered interesting and important findings. First, some tactics are used far more commonly than others, and certain tactics are also used much more frequently on particular targets (superiors, peers, or subordinates). Most importantly, some of the tactics are considerably more effective in achieving desired outcomes than others.[7]

TABLE 8.1   The Range of Influence Tactics[8]

Influence Tactic	Description
1. Rational Persuasion	Using logical arguments and facts to persuade someone your request will result in beneficial outcomes.
2. Pressure	Using demands or threats to get what you want.
3. Personal Appeal	Appealing to someone's loyalty or friendship with you to get him/her to do something.
4. Exchange	Offering an exchange of favors to get what you want.
5. Ingratiation	Using praise or flattery to put someone in a good mood prior to making a request.
6. Coalition	Seeking the help of other people to get someone to do what you want, or using the support of other people to get someone to agree with you.
7. Legitimizing	Establishing the legitimacy of a request by appealing to authority or pointing out its consistency with existing values or norms.
8. Consultation	Seeking someone's participation in planning or developing something that he/she will ultimately need to buy into.
9. Inspirational Appeal	Arousing an individual's enthusiasm by appealing to values, ideals, and aspirations.

Practice this!
Go to www.baldwin2e.com

More specifically, evidence shows that rational persuasion and pressure are the most frequently used influence tactics.[9] Interestingly, the other seven tactics are employed relatively rarely. With respect to the targets of influence attempts, downward influence (trying to influence a subordinate) is the most common, representing about 42 percent of the overall attempts. Upward influence (trying to influence your boss) was second, and lateral influence (trying to influence a peer) was the least common. Given the disproportionately large amount of time spent with peers, this finding is somewhat surprising.

The relative effectiveness of tactics can be defined as the reaction of the influence target in one of three ways: resistance, compliance, or commitment.

- *Resistance.* The influence target is opposed to carrying out requests and will resist accomplishing what is being requested.
- *Compliance.* The target is willing to do what the influencer asks, but is not enthusiastic about it. Compliance is characterized by doing only that which is required by a request—and nothing more.
- *Commitment.* The target agrees with a request or decision from the agent and strives to carry out the request or implement the decision with energy and engagement. The target complies with the request and will often go beyond and do more than is requested.

Of course, commitment is the most effective and desirable of the influence outcomes. However, compliance may often be acceptable and may sometimes be the best that can be achieved. For example, a supervisor may be responsible for overseeing that several relatively unpleasant tasks get completed. It is unlikely anyone will be "committed" to cleaning the bathroom or to filling out an expense report, so in such cases, compliance is likely the maximum outcome. Nonetheless, gaining commitment is the gold standard of influence attempts and should be sought at every available opportunity.

Table 8.2 presents data from research that has studied the effectiveness of the nine influence tactics presented in Table 8.1.[10] Note that personal appeal, consultation, and inspirational appeal all have "commitment" as their most likely outcome and thus are deemed the most effective of the tactics. On the other end, rational persuasion, pressure, ingratiation, and coalition are all linked most frequently with "resistance."

By bringing together the two questions of most interest—"Which tactics are most frequently used?" and "Which tactics are most effective?"—an important disconnect should be apparent. That is, the most frequently used tactics are among the least effective, and those used most infrequently are among the most effective! This would certainly seem to be a case where, in the words of Will Rogers, "Common sense ain't so common."

This disconnect between what is done most often and what works best leads to the obvious question of "Why would people do something that is not effective?" In our previous discussion of conformity, we referred to cases where the task was ambiguous (for example, the "moving light"). In the case of influence, whether a tactic works or not can be unclear to people observing (especially because of the time lag between the attempt and the result). As a consequence, we will look for meaning from others, and if others are using rational persuasion, we will use it as well. Now, however, you know better, so you do not need to "follow the crowd" in using ineffective influence techniques.

The lessons for students of influence should be clear. Do not necessarily do what you see others doing but rather do what works! Why the emotional appeals (for instance, inspirational appeals and personal appeals) work so well is because they are consistent with what we know about persuasion. That is, there is both a rational and an emotional component that leads to change.[11] But research suggests that managers generally invest most of their influence efforts on the rational aspect, even though emotional elements often lead most directly to change. Consider what persuades you most, a 100-page report full of charts and graphs or a passionate appeal to your heart? With all this said, we don't want to give the impression that rational persuasion should never be used. To the contrary. As it turns out, your boss is likely to give you a higher performance evaluation and more rewards when you use rational persuasion.[12] So the best idea is to make an emotional appeal and then briefly give people access to the rational persuasion evidence you have collected.

TABLE 8.2   Consequences of the Nine Influence Tactics

Tactic (listed in order of use frequency)	Outcomes (%)		
	Resistance	Compliance	Commitment
Rational Persuasion	**47**	30	23
Pressure	**56**	**41**	3
Personal Appeal	25	33	**42**
Exchange	24	**41**	35
Ingratiation	**41**	28	31
Coalition	**53**	44	3
Legitimizing	44	**56**	0
Consultation	18	27	**55**
Inspirational Appeal	0	10	**90**

Most people are heavily persuaded by emotional appeals for at least two reasons. First, emotional appeals establish a sense of urgency and help bring people together. Second, it is generally believed that thoughts and emotions are closely interrelated, and sometimes they may be in conflict. When there is a strong relationship between rational and emotional components, impacting the emotions will usually bring the rational elements into line (people convince themselves that something is a good idea and then justify it with data). If, however, thoughts and emotions are not in full agreement, appealing only to rational issues leaves the possibility open that people will reject the change based on an emotional objection (in other words, "I don't like the way this change feels")—something which cannot easily be overcome by data.

Closely related to influence tactics are a collection of behaviors broadly labeled *political skills*. **Political skills** combine the most effective influence tactics, resulting in a "disarmingly charming and engaging manner that inspires confidence, trust, and sincerity."[13] Like it or not, politics often play an important role in the work environment. It is often the case in organizations where the needs of two parties do not align. For example, with respect to resource allocation (pay raises, budget dollars, office space, new equipment), people and groups are often pitted against each other and respond by looking out for their own interests and ignoring those of others and the overall organization. In these cases, using the most effective influence tactics can be especially important to your ultimate success or failure in the organization. One of the most potent forms of political skill behavior involves methods for influencing without direct authority—a concept known as **social influence.** When used appropriately, social influence can help an individual achieve positive and ethical outcomes in organizations. In the next section, we describe the most important social influence behaviors.

Social Influence Weapons[14]　　　　　　　　　　　　　　　　　　KO 8-5

Many eager but inexperienced workers often find themselves in a bit of a quandary, anxious to get things done, but too junior in the organization to possess any real legitimate or formal authority. That is, it is often the case that we find ourselves asking the question "How am I supposed to get things done if I don't have the authority to influence people?" This is an important issue and one that thankfully has received a great deal of attention. The study of social influence provides a solid, research-backed series of tools to help people influence others in the absence of formal authority.

To better understand how people are able to influence without authority, the work of Robert Cialdini is considered to be "state of the art." Cialdini has summarized more than 50 years of research to better understand the basic principles of influence. And the best news is that these principles can be taught, learned, and applied. Cialdini's six principles include (1) friendship/liking, (2) commitment and consistency, (3) scarcity, (4) reciprocity, (5) social proof, and (6) appeals to authority.

Principle 1: Friendship/Liking

The central principle behind friendship and liking is that we tend to like others who like us. And once others like us, we're more likely to be effective in influencing them. Although mere attractiveness certainly plays a big role in liking (see Management Live 8.2), it by no means tells the whole story. We also like people because of their similarity to us, and the flattering treatment they direct toward us. The fact that we have a greater liking for those similar to us has been repeatedly demonstrated, and the wide range of comparison factors people consider in determining who is like them include age, race, gender, religion, politics, and even cigarette smoking habits.[15] People also *do* respond favorably to flattery. In a famous example, Joe Girard, who is billed as the World's Great Salesman by the Guinness Book of World Records, claimed the secret to his success was sending out a monthly card to 13,000 former customers that simply said, "I like you." The point here is that to really get others to like us, we need to uncover genuine similarities and offer praise when it's genuine.

The truly amazing thing is that even in cases where flattery is obvious and where the person clearly has a motive to manipulate another person, flattery can increase liking. In a controlled study where people received personal feedback from men who needed favors from them, the men who only provided positive feedback were better liked even though it was clear they had something to gain by using flattery.[16] In other words, we are influenced by people who like us, are similar to us, and who flatter us.

"My love for you really has less to do with how I feel about you, and more to do with how you make me feel about me."
—Unknown

Principle 2: Commitment and Consistency

The key principle behind commitment and consistency is that once we make a choice, we're more likely to remain consistent with that choice. Cialdini explains that:

> Once we make a choice or take a stand, we will encounter personal and interpersonal pressures to behave consistently with that commitment. Those pressures will cause us to respond in ways that justify our earlier decision. We simply convince ourselves that we have made the right choice and, no doubt, feel better about our decision.[17]

One classic example of how commitment and consistency can be used as influence weapons is what is known as the "foot-in-the-door" technique. Here a small request is made and granted, and is then followed by a larger request. This technique has been used by salespeople to get your commitment to buy first because they know once you've made the commitment to buy, you are far more likely to continue to buy. This is why nasty and unethical sales techniques like lowballing (i.e., you agree to an offer and the salesperson then adds unattractive details) and the "bait and switch" (i.e., you've shown up at the store ready to buy the advertised sale item only to learn it no longer exists, but the upgraded model is in stock) are so effective.

"Clothes make the man. Naked people have little or no influence on society."
—Mark Twain

What is really important about all of these techniques is gaining some small degree of commitment that can then be turned into something larger. A great

⮄ MANAGEMENT LIVE 8.2

Do Looks Really Matter?

However unfair, research evidence is clear that "looks matter!" In a recent summary of studies[18] that examined the effects of attractiveness, the researchers found that:

- Attractive individuals fared better than their less attractive counterparts in a variety of job-related outcomes.
- The attractiveness effect existed even when a lot of job-relevant information was available (so people viewed the attractiveness as being relevant even when performance levels were known).
- The biasing effect of attractiveness was present for professionals as well as for college students.
- The attractiveness effect was just as strong for attractive men as for attractive women.
- The attractiveness effect seems to be weakening over time (that is, it is not as strong as it was 20 years ago), but it is still quite significant.

Other studies have shown that attractive people are assumed to be more talented, kinder, more honest, and more intelligent than people who are less physically attractive.[19] Keep in mind these are major influences and not just relevant in some obscure cases. This effect holds for such far-reaching areas as politics (where physically attractive candidates get many more votes than unattractive ones[20]), salaries for jobs (where attractive individuals get paid 12 to 14 percent more than their unattractive co-workers[21]), and court cases (less attractive defendants are twice as likely to avoid jail as unattractive defendants). This effect also starts very young in life (elementary school teachers assume attractive children are better behaved[22] and more intelligent[23] than their less attractive classmates) and continues through adulthood.

The Relationship Between Attractiveness and Salary

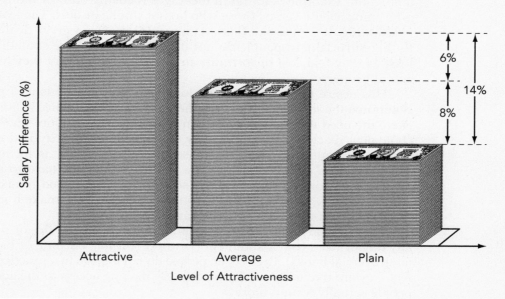

example of this type of influence can be seen in a classic study conducted by Steve Sherman, a psychology professor at Indiana University.[24] Dr. Sherman called a sample of local residents as part of a survey and asked them to predict what they would say if asked to spend three hours collecting money for the American Cancer Society. Notice that he did not actually ask them to collect money, but just to indicate what they would say if they were asked to volunteer. Because people did not want to appear uncharitable, a large number of people said they would volunteer. A few weeks later, the American Cancer Society called these people. As a result, there was a 700 percent increase in volunteers as compared to an earlier solicitation. You see, people really do strive for consistency!

Consistency is no less powerful in the workplace. Assume that you are a new sales manager and you have an employee who has had three straight quarters of low sales. Many new managers would be tempted to give a final warning before terminating. Contrast this approach with the use of commitment and consistency, where you meet with the sales employee, discuss the reasons for the underperformance, and have her articulate a plan for improvement. Next, ask the employee to put the plan in writing and then send it to you. Once you have the written plan and the employee has explained it, you share the plan with your boss and maybe a few other key managers in the area. You and the other managers let the struggling employee know that the plan looks great and that each of you are there to help her should she run into obstacles. Your employee has now made an active commitment and will generally act in a manner consistent with the plan because she wrote the plan and others are aware of it. That is a smart way to influence while building goodwill and strong relationships.

Principle 3: Scarcity

Despite what some economics classes may have you believe, individuals are not always rational in their decision-making processes (see Chapter 3). This makes scarcity all the more powerful when it is used to wield influence. Interestingly, people are particularly sensitive to a perceived loss—more so than they are to a perceived gain of the same magnitude. Studies in medicine have shown people are more likely to fully engage in their prescribed treatment when the message received is framed in terms of what they could lose by not doing so rather than in terms of what they gain from compliance. For example, a poignant example is found in messages focusing on how many years are cut off a smoker's life versus those who do not smoke or quit. The lesson is that the positioning of a message (loss versus gain) makes a great deal of difference. Rather surprisingly, people do not need to actually *have* something to fear its loss, as they fear lost *opportunity* in much the same way they fear the loss of actual property.

This desire to preserve our options is a main component of **psychological reactance** theory, which proposes that whenever free choice is limited or threatened, the need to retain our freedom makes us want it more than before.[25] Psychological reactance makes us very susceptible to scarcity and can cloud our judgment significantly. Take the case where a company is hiring new college graduates. The company makes the assertion that you have to make up your mind in a day or two because it has so many other qualified candidates and only a few openings. The scarcity of the job opening tends to make it more attractive (even though it may not be) to job candidates.[26]

Scarcity also helps explain why attempts to ban activities or products generally do not work (think about efforts to prevent flag burning or banning specific controversial books). Even when people do not engage in a practice, they want to feel they are free to do so if they wish. By making access to the activity "scarce," people actually want it more!

There can be great personal advantage in using the principle of scarcity. For instance, knowing a specific computer language your company uses, but that is known by relatively few people, may make you irreplaceable. The ability to speak well in front of an audience may be a very scarce commodity in some contexts. By developing skills that are scarce, you increase your value and potential influence.

Another area where scarcity can often be of value at work is the scarcity of information. For example, let's say you've got an early look at a report from your senior management. It's not confidential, but you want to use scarcity to influence others to support the report's conclusions. Get your people in a room and say, "I just received this and it won't be distributed to anyone until next week, but it's important and I wanted all of you to get an early look." The information will be seen as being of more value because of its exclusivity and more likely others will pay attention to it.[27]

Principle 4: Reciprocity

The basic principle behind reciprocity is that people generally repay actions in kind. This basic premise is so widespread that sociologists and cultural anthropologists worldwide have found it to be universal across all human societies. The interdependencies created by reciprocity allow for division of labor and the creation of an organized society. If people did not generally reciprocate others' actions, we would face a chaotic environment. It is the very widespread acceptance of reciprocity that makes it a particularly strong influence weapon.

The reality in most reciprocity-based influence attempts is that the person being influenced often did not request the service or action in the first place.

A clever and familiar example of this is a tactic used by a Boy Scout troop in their attempt to sell candy bars door-to-door. Using the door-in-the-face technique, the scouts first asked for a relatively large donation for an event the majority of targets would have zero interest in attending. When that offer was inevitably declined, the scouts were trained to then follow with, "If you don't want the tickets, will you at least buy some chocolate bars? They are only $1.00 apiece." Notice that this creates the appearance that both people are "giving in." In reality, the scout meets his objectives, while the buyer does not.

Managerial approaches such as "stretch goals" are examples of influence that capitalize on the reciprocity principle. Performance targets like "100 percent customer satisfaction" or "zero defects" are unlikely to ever be fully realized. However, by setting an extremely high goal at first, managers succeed in getting commitment to higher performance than would otherwise have occurred.

Resisting this form of influence can be very difficult, but a fundamental understanding at least makes you more aware of the possibility of being unwillingly trapped. Cialdini suggests we "accept the offers of others but to accept those offers for what they fundamentally are, not for what they are represented to be."[28] In other words, if the initial favor turns out to be some form of deception, we should respond as if someone is trying to take advantage of us. By looking at the influence attempt for what it is, rather than what it pretends to be, we are better able to respond in an appropriate manner that we will not regret later.

Reciprocity can also serve as a very legitimate and important tool in your "managerial tool kit." By supporting others when they need it, by making yourself available with your expertise, and by doing the "little extra things" that need to be done, you will build a greater reservoir of influence. If you have taken care to treat other people well, it is likely others will reciprocate this treatment when you need it most. A specific example of this is being helpful and sharing resources with your colleagues or other departments. When they thank you for your assistance, just be sure to follow it up with, "Always glad to help. I know how important it is, and if I were in the same situation, I know you'd help me, too." This action solidifies the reciprocity.[29]

Principle 5: Social Proof

Social proof is based on the reality that we tend to view actions as more acceptable to the degree that we see *others* performing them in the same or similar situations. In a classic study, researchers canvassed neighborhoods door to door asking for donations from residents. The researchers showed residents a list of their neighbors who had already donated to the cause. The results revealed that the longer the list of donors, the more likely residents were to donate.[30]

More recently, Cialdini conducted research at a hotel chain where the hotel was trying to increase reuse of towels by their guests. In one condition, they placed cards in the rooms saying, "Help save the environment. You can show your respect for nature and help save the environment by reusing your towels during your stay." This was associated with a 38 percent reusage rate among guests. Another condition used a card that read, "Join your fellow guests in helping to save the environment—Almost 75 percent of guests who are asked to participate in our new resource savings program do help by using their towels more than once. You can join your fellow guests to help save the environment by reusing your towels during your stay." This resulted in 48 percent of the guests choosing to reuse their towels. The difference here is simple: The second condition harnessed social proof—"If others think (and act) in a way to reuse towels, I should, too."[31]

Social proof is most influential under two conditions: (1) *uncertainty*, when people are unsure about what to do or the situation is unclear and can be interpreted in multiple ways, and (2) *similarity,* where people are more likely to follow the lead of people who are like themselves. As a result, this makes social proof an excellent description of what happened in the Sherif studies (that is, the "moving light"), which were discussed earlier in this chapter.

The methods for using social proof in a positive manner are relatively straightforward. You need to have vivid examples with rich details and be able to cite several instances where your recommendation has been effective. Also, staying on point (using a few themes over and over) tends to reinforce the idea and make it more likely to be accepted by others. It may be even more effective to let other people serve as examples of social proof. If you have had a difficult time getting buy-in for a new project from a few of the engineers, ask a senior engineer who is well respected by her peers to make the case and explain why the project is a winner; this may serve you better than trying to make the case yourself.

Principle 6: Appeals to Authority

The central principle of appeals to authority is that people generally defer judgment to others whom they believe are experts or authority figures. The tendency to obey legitimate authority comes from early socialization where we learned to obey our parents and teachers. Of course, the tendency to obey authority is actually very important to the safety of a child (for instance, listening to others may stop a child from running into the street) and to the smooth functioning of society (people generally accept court decisions because they view the process as legitimate). Like all social influence weapons, appeals to authority can be used for good or manipulation. Some variations of this weapon include things like "snob appeal" in which influence is based on appealing to people's sense that they are somehow better than others. An example of this is the marketing of the American Express Centurion Card (also called the Black Card), which is reserved for very high-income clients. Their website reads "Rarely seen, always recognized. Available by invitation only, The Centurion Card is the world's rarest American Express Card and confers a level of service that can be extended only to selected individuals worldwide." Other examples include appealing to tradition (e.g., "That's the way it's always been") or to things that are novel since "newer" is seen as "better." For instance, we are sure that no one reading this book would get a new smartphone due to its ability to do something you never use, such as a forward-facing camera for videoconferencing, but we are sure that you know of people who *would* do this (some sarcasm intended).

The trick to using authority effectively on the job is to let people know your strengths and expertise without coming off as a "bragger." Good ways to do this include recounting prior projects or telling short stories about accomplishment and the role you played. In general, disclosing personal information about yourself is a good way to let people know your strengths and what you are capable of accomplishing.

Appeals to authority are made most powerfully when they concern obeying the requests of genuine authorities who possess recognized knowledge and wisdom. Problems arise, however, when we obey authority as a mindless shortcut. Accepting false authority in an unquestioning manner is a formula for manipulation.

Research has shown three kinds of symbols are most dangerous in creating artificial authority: (1) titles, (2) clothing, and (3) automobiles. In separate studies investigating the influence of these symbols (titles, clothing, automobiles), people who possessed one or another of them (and no other noteworthy credentials) were granted more obedience by others.[32] Moreover, in each case, the obeying persons underestimated the effect of authority pressures on their behaviors.

That is, the people influenced generally believed that the symbols made no difference, but they actually did. It seems entirely irrational that the type of automobile a person drives would signal his or her authority, but the evidence supports it nonetheless.

We can defend ourselves against the unwanted effects of authority by asking two simple questions: Is this authority truly an expert? How truthful can we expect this expert to be in this case? The first question directs our attention away from the simple symbols and toward evidence for authority status. The second advises us to consider not just the expert's knowledge in the situation but also his or her trustworthiness in this instance. Legitimate appeals to authority can be a useful tool of influence. But be ever vigilant in ensuring your "authorities" and those of others are truly worthy of the label.

The social influence weapons offer proven strategies for influencing others when you do not have the formal authority to do so. Using the influence weapons, however, takes some thought and practice. Just as importantly, you need to be on the lookout for people trying to influence you in unwanted or undesirable ways. We have found it interesting how once you understand and recognize the basic social influence tactics how often you can see their use around you, and how effective you can be through their use.

Managing Your Boss

KO **8-6**

DO **8-2**

Many people report difficulty with the idea of "managing" their boss. This can result in a norm of politeness, where people are always courteous to their supervisors but are reluctant to pass along information that might distress them.[33] However, as one researcher put it:

> Effective organizational functioning demands that people have a healthy *disrespect* for their boss, feel free to express emotions and opinions openly, and are comfortable engaging in banter and give-and-take.[34]

"Accomplishing the impossible means only that the boss will add it to your regular duties."

—Doug Larson

When we explain the preceding point to students, we often get looks of disbelief. Upon further reflection, however, this finding is not so surprising. If you consider the relationship between you and your boss to be like any other relationship, communication is always an important factor of success. By engaging in the behaviors just described, the amount of communication is enhanced, and this gives both parties (meaning you and your boss) more to base feelings of trust upon. However, if an employee "clams up," this deprives the boss of the required information to have an effective relationship. In fact, research indicates that the frequency and depth of effective communication between supervisor and subordinate increase each person's trust for the other, enhance managers' willingness to act on their employees' suggestions, and actually make the manager more effective.[35] When managers don't get feedback from their subordinates regularly, it can have a negative effect on the whole organization. As mentioned in the decision-making section in Chapter 3, one study found that, of 356 decisions made in firms without significant upward communication, one-half of those decisions failed.[36]

The reality is that in almost all situations, you will have information your supervisor needs to effectively do her job. Further, your boss depends on you to make her look good, meaning your relationship with her is one of reciprocity. Your ideas have value because you are likely closer to the customer than your boss can be. You can actually help your supervisor become a better manager by giving feedback, provided you put it in a way that is constructive and that she will be willing to hear and act on.[37]

General Strategies for Managing Your Boss

Of all of the management "gurus" out there, perhaps Peter Drucker has had the largest impact on the day-to-day practice of management. Almost 60 years ago, Drucker wrote that "few managers seem to realize how important it is to manage the boss or, worse, believe that it can be done at all. They bellyache about the boss but do not even try to manage him (or her). Yet managing the boss is fairly simple—indeed, generally quite a bit simpler than managing subordinates."[38] Just as is the case in so many areas, Drucker's words here are very wise.

Keep in mind, however, that what Drucker is referring to is not about how to be a "brown noser," and you should not mistake the information in this section as being a "primer in sucking up to the boss." To the contrary, Drucker argued that "one does not make the strengths of the boss productive by toadying to him. . . . One does it by starting out with what is right and presenting it in a form which is accessible to the superior."[39]

Building on the work of Drucker, the following are a few guiding principles that have been proposed as fundamental to managing your boss.

- It is important to understand your boss's mindset and see the world through his lens. What is important to him? What are her goals and objectives, and how does your work contribute to those? What are his pressures? What are her strengths and weaknesses? If you understand these fundamental things, you can frame your communication in an appropriate way. You can appeal to shared values, or explain how your idea can create value relevant to your boss.[40]

- Aim to communicate in your boss's preferred style. Is your boss a listener or a reader? Each of us has a particular way in which we prefer to receive information, and that is usually the channel we choose to communicate with other people. If your boss consistently initiates face-to-face communication, this is likely the best way to proceed with a request. On the other hand, if your boss is a reader, it is a good idea to provide her with information in writing prior to a meeting, so she has a chance to fully absorb it.[41] But don't make this a guessing game. Ask your boss how he or she likes to communicate best and act accordingly.

- Understand yourself. The exercises and suggestions in Chapter 1 gave you a head start on this. Understanding your personal strengths, weaknesses, pressures, and goals helps you prioritize what requests you make of your boss, and gives you context when she approaches you with new challenges or opportunities.[42]

- It is very important to manage your boss's time effectively. Remember that you likely represent only 1 percent of his problems, so don't take up 25 percent of his time. The simpler the problem or issue at hand is, the less time you should have your boss spend on it. So the more you prepare, summarize, and synthesize information and options, the better off you will both be. A good practice is to book your boss for a series of short meetings over a period of time. This way, you are able to chart progress, and not have to wait weeks until decisions can be made to finalize a decision or a project that needs your boss's input.

"Listening, not imitation, may be the sincerest form of flattery. If you want to influence someone, listen to what he says. When he finishes talking, ask him about any points that you do not understand."

—Dr. Joyce Brothers

Managing Your Boss Through Effective Communication

So, when approaching your supervisor, what are the best communication strategies? We provide step-by-step advice on how to do this in Tool Kit 8.1.

⚒ MANAGER'S TOOL KIT

Tool Kit 8.1 **Steps for "Managing Your Boss"**

1. **Begin with the end in mind.** Have a clear vision of your recommendation, including its strategic importance, and say it up front. Some phrases that might help you begin the conversation are "I've noticed we have a problem with X and I have a solution I'd like to propose," and "You mentioned that one of our strategic goals for this year is X and I have an idea of how we can do that." That way your boss will listen because she knows where you are headed and you won't waste her time.

2. **Do not confuse raw data with useful information.** Your job is to integrate data and turn it into a meaningful story, not to dump everything you have learned into your boss's lap. So be selective, be visual, group the data, bring out what is essential. Data overload creates stress, which in turn can create denial, rejection, and numbness. Effective employees show up with useful information and are able to convey the results in an easily digestible form.

3. **Outline both costs and benefits, being as specific as you can about both.** Don't forget about intangible but important costs such as time and allocation of resources.

4. **Ask for input.** As a general rule, if you are going to approach your boss with a problem, come prepared with a recommendation as well. Your solution may not be the one that is ultimately implemented, but showing your boss that you are capable of understanding a problem and its consequences is important to your career.[43]

Professionalism: A Source of Trust and Respect

KO **8-7**

DO **8-3**

As noted earlier, power and influence are properties that come from relationships between people. Your power and influence will therefore be tightly linked to your ability to create strong and positive relationships. You must proactively and consistently work on building such relationships—they just don't happen on their own. That may seem obvious, but unfortunately studies show that nearly half of new management hires fail in their first jobs because of their inability to build good relationships with bosses, peers, and subordinates.[44]

"People do not care how much you know, until they know how much you care."

—Unknown

When most people talk about influential managers, they tend to focus on personal characteristics and most frequently cite traits that relate to trust and respect. For example, when describing effective managers, people commonly say things like:

- "He was highly organized and did what he said he would do."
- "She was tough, but fair and honest, and I respected that."
- "He always went out of his way to say thank you for the things I did."
- "She sent the most caring and comforting note when my dad died."

Conversely, when describing ineffective managers, people commonly say things like:

- "He was scattered and unfocused, and did not follow up on commitments."
- "She would tell you anything to keep you happy—she sucked up to upper management and was a phony with us."

- "He took the credit for our work."
- "He knew nothing about me and never seemed to appreciate anything I did."

So what do the trusted and respected managers consistently do that those less successful do not? The managers who get the highest marks from their people are often not the most brilliant, or the most versed in managerial knowledge. Rather, they are those who have devoted themselves to building relationships that bring out the best in people, and they know how to navigate social situations. We call that capability **professionalism.** When athletes are described as being "professional," it means they play the "right way," make others around them better, and represent themselves and their team well. Just as importantly, they do not do insensitive or immature things that damage their reputation or that of the team. Professional managers are the same.

Professionalism is the source of trust and respect; it brings out the best in others and strengthens your reputation and that of your organization. It is also an area where blunders can be fatal to a management career. While it can take months or years to fully gain the trust and respect of others, one breach of trust or one disrespectful outburst can damage a relationship for a lifetime. Though professionalism can include a wide variety of elements, a synthesis of the many popular management guidebooks and manuals reveals that the core of professionalism concerns how you manage your relationships, your etiquette, and your social network. Attention to building and refining competence in those areas will ultimately determine the level of trust and respect you will earn as a manager.

DO 8-4   Building Positive Relationships

Clearly, different managers have different styles and there is no "one best way" to build relationships. However, three general strategies consistently emerge as critical to creating positive relationships:

1. Get to know your people.
2. Show appreciation.
3. Under-promise and over-deliver.

"What's done to children, they will do to society."

—Karl A. Menninger, psychiatrist

Although many different labels have been used to describe those strategies, those three are the essential tools for managers most adept at relationships. Conversely, a neglect of such strategies often leads to relationship breakdowns and the derailing of otherwise promising management careers (see Management Live 8.3).

Getting to Know Your People: Showing Genuine Interest in Others

You cannot manage well without knowing those you manage. Therefore, the single most important professional behavior is to get to know those with whom you work. Unfortunately, demanding goals and busy schedules often make it difficult for managers to find the time to sit down with their people and get to know them well. A great sadness at funerals is that people often say they learned more about a deceased individual in an hour-long service than they did after working with him or her for 30 years or more. At the frantic pace of business today, learning about others is unlikely to occur naturally. Therefore, great managers proactively create opportunities to "stay in the loop" and keep abreast of the lives and concerns of their people. Specific behaviors useful to getting to know your people include:

"If there is any one secret of success, it lies in the ability to get the other person's point of view and see things from that person's angle as well as from your own."

—Henry Ford

Practice MBWA: Management by Walking Around. Make yourself visible by regularly talking and visiting with people. Every day, make a point to get out of your regular office or workstation and visit with people in your workplace. If your people are not in the same physical location, then call and still occasionally visit. Don't limit your visits to just those at your level or higher.

⇄ MANAGEMENT LIVE 8.3

Managers Relating Badly

The success rate for new managers is disturbingly low, largely because of a failure to build positive relationships with people. Here are a few of the most frequent and damaging relationship mistakes that managers make:

- **Taking Credit for the Work of Others.** A death sentence for relationships. Great managers obsess over showing appreciation and delight in the fact that their workers feel they are not taken for granted.

- **Failing to Follow Up on Commitments.** Quickly undermines trust and creates a culture lacking in accountability. Better not to commit than to offer a promise and not live up to it. Always live by the principle: Under-promise and over-deliver.

- **Trying to Show Everyone Who's in Charge.** One of the unfortunate misconceptions of young managers is that they need to convey complete control. They often feel any admission of weakness, or revealing a limitation, is dangerous and probably inappropriate. Contrary to such notions, the reality is you will almost certainly be more effective when you behave authentically. So apologize when you are wrong, and do not feel you have to disguise all weaknesses.

- **Refusing to Ask for Help.** You are not alone. Think of your group as a team and ask for their help. As a general rule, people want to help, and it is being left out of the loop that is far more damaging.

- **Overreliance on Title.** Perhaps the hardest lesson for young managers to learn is that a management title does not elicit automatic respect and obedience. Actions speak louder than words. If you show a level of competence, and demonstrate the skills that come with your title, the respect of your workers will follow.

For example, secretaries and service staff often have surprising influence in organizations and, more importantly, are interesting people in their own right.

MBWA sends positive messages to people. It reveals your interest in them and in their work, and it says you don't consider yourself "too good" to spend time with them. MBWA also enables you to stay in touch with what is going on in your department, section, or unit. So make time every week to spend time with people and aim for some contact even if you work at home or in a virtual environment. Some executives (Herb Kelleher of Southwest Airlines is a famous example) are beloved by people in their organizations because they take the time to visit with, and take a sincere interest in, people at all levels. That is a strategy worth emulating. See the series of steps that follow to better understand how to practice MBWA:

"You can observe a lot just by watching."

—Yogi Berra

Get Your Hands Dirty. One of the most common complaints of frontline workers is that their managers do not fully understand what they (the workers) really do. One good way to avoid that perception is to actually sample and *do* the employees' jobs on occasion. Plop down in front of the computer, pick up the telephone to deal with a customer complaint, or review a project chart. Sample their job enough to show your interest in it and to understand how it works. Think of it as a great way to connect with your frontline people and to gain a firsthand understanding of exactly what they are dealing with during a typical workday. Experience what they go through in their jobs, and you will have a much richer understanding of their circumstances, be able to relate to them much better, and almost certainly gain their appreciation as well.

"Seek first to understand, then to be understood."

—St. Francis of Assisi

Arrive Early to Work and Meetings. Make it a point to arrive at least 10 to 15 minutes early for work and meetings, and visit with people at that time. Similarly, *after* meetings or other more formal events, do not always rush back to your workspace. Linger occasionally and talk shop with people there. The casual time spent in informal contexts is often the easiest and most comfortable time to get to know people. If this feels like too great a loss of "productive" work time, remind yourself that time spent building relationships is perhaps *the* most productive management work.

Talk a Little About Yourself. People are more willing to share their own journeys with someone who has proven willing to share a bit of his or her own. So let people know about your hobbies, kids, or pets. Having some understanding and connection to your life will empower people to open up about their own lives as well. Of course, be careful not to talk so much about yourself that you are perceived as self-involved and narcissistic.

Be Authentic; Do Not Fake It. Seek to learn about others with enthusiasm and a desire to know and get the best from them as they are, not as you would want them to be. Whatever you do, *do not fake it*. If you do not have some authentic curiosity and interest in others, you will have a difficult time building relationships.

Show Appreciation. Probably the easiest yet most neglected tool for building good relationships is to more frequently use the words "thank you." A lack of appreciation is the cause of innumerable relationship breakdowns, and appearing to have taken credit for others' work is among the surest ways to sabotage relationships. It is easy to forget to show appreciation and just move on to the next challenge. But great managers know that appreciation is the lubricant of positive relationships and are obsessive about showing it to their people whenever they can.

So take the time to pass along credit and compliments to those who have made a contribution to your cause. Always speak well of your people and point out their accomplishments to any interested party.

Under-promise and Over-deliver. Especially for new managers, the innate desire to please and be liked, and to be viewed as top performing, often creates a pressure to over-promise. However, respect comes not from idealistic intentions—however noble—but from doing what you say you will do—when you say you will do it. Indeed, there are few relationship killers like unmet expectations. People can put up with a lot, provided they feel they are being told the truth and promises made are kept, even if they originally desired something more.

Great managers, therefore, are acutely aware of the importance of managing expectations. They also know the most raving fans and highest customer appreciation often stem from delivering *ahead* of promised commitments.[45] Since the same logically holds for personal relationships, you should aim to make only those commitments, promises, and deadlines you can meet or exceed—and aim to restrict a very natural inclination to promise what you cannot deliver. It bears repeating—great managers under-promise and over-deliver!

DO 8-5   ## Power Etiquette and First Impressions

For many of us, the terms *manners* and *etiquette* have a way of prompting thoughts of stuffy formal events and seemingly ridiculous, outdated conventions. Yet an understanding of modern business etiquette simply enables you to conduct yourself with ease, style, and confidence. Manners do not make you stuffy, obnoxious, or overly formal. They make you more comfortable in situations because you know exactly what to do. Indeed, as the family and social institutions that once taught manners decline in influence, a personal command of business etiquette is now one very good way to *set you apart* from others. In other words, exhibiting strong business etiquette allows you to "fit in" and feel comfortable with expected norms.

Of course, there are many written and unwritten rules and guidelines for etiquette and no possible way to know them all. Possibilities to commit a *faux pas* are limitless, and chances are, sooner or later, you'll make a mistake. But it is less important that you might use the wrong fork and more critical you have a polished introduction of yourself, can use and recall names with ease, and can convey the right impression with your dress and manners. In short, we labeled this section *Power Etiquette* because our focus is on just a few areas of etiquette we believe have a direct and powerful impact on your success as a manager.

First Impressions and Introductions.

It's often very difficult to overcome a poor first impression, regardless of your knowledge or expertise. So the first rule of management etiquette is to understand the power of that good first impression and to be sure to polish your approach. People make extraordinary assumptions about your professional credibility and potential performance based upon your appearance and behavior during your first meeting or meetings.

A variety of research studies support the power of first impressions, but we are particularly taken by one very simple investigation. In that study, participants were given a description of an individual with the following order of adjectives: *intelligent, industrious, impulsive, critical, stubborn, envious.* The researchers then gave the same description of this individual to other participants, but merely reversed the *order* of the adjectives to *envious, stubborn, critical, impulsive, industrious, intelligent.* Both sets of participants rated how likely it would be they would be friends with the person. Those with the first order of description were significantly more likely to be friends than those given the second ordering—even though both descriptions had the exact same descriptors! When positive information is given first, people are more likely to ignore later negative information. First impressions are truly important and carry considerable weight.

"Manners open doors that power, position, and money cannot."

—Dana Casperson

Much of your first business impression will be based on elements such as handshake, introductions, and clothing. A handshake is almost always appropriate, so develop a good firm handshake and make a practice of rising to shake hands with anyone who enters your office or room, whether male or female. You will also want to develop a ready and refined introduction.

The goal is to make a short but memorable impression. You should generally include some hint to help people remember you and to provide a tidbit of information to draw others into a conversation. Your self-introduction may vary according to the setting and the people you are meeting. A brief, finely tuned introduction is particularly useful when networking, beginning a conversation, or meeting someone new.

Beyond your own introduction, it is also wise to increase your skill and comfort level at introducing *others*. It is all too common for young managers to overtly avoid introductions because they are uncomfortable with how best to do it. An introduction is a courtesy to help people feel more comfortable when they meet for the first time, and it is an opportune time to demonstrate your professional acumen. Of course, some people have a knack for bringing others together, and there clearly is an art to good introductions. However, introductions really are not hard to make if you follow the three simple guidelines presented in Tool Kit 8.2.

✖ MANAGER'S TOOL KIT

Tool Kit 8.2   Making Introductions

1. Aim to help facilitate easy and comfortable conversation between the people by weaving in information regarding their backgrounds or accomplishments.
2. Try to state each name at least a couple of times to give each the best chance of picking up on the name.
3. In the business world, defer to office seniority and age (not gender or social standing). This means that you introduce the younger person to the older person, and not the other way around.

Learn and Use Names.   It has often been said a person's name is to that person the sweetest and most important sound in any language. However, like many others, you may likely struggle to remember names or have even noted you are "bad with names." How many times have you met someone and five minutes later not remembered that person's name? While remembering names in a general way is certainly a valuable social skill, it can be *vital* to a successful management career. Remembering names and faces is a priceless and rare quality—and thus a great competitive advantage in the workplace. (Remember how important scarcity can be in making it influential.)

"Of course I remember you. You're Parasaurolophus.
I always make a point to remember names."

© Ted Goff, *The New Yorker Collection*, www.cartoonbank.com

"No matter how much memory and power we put into computers, few things are as impressive as someone walking up to you and remembering your name."

—Ben Rosen, Chairman Emeritus, Compaq Computer Corp.

Fortunately, remembering names is a skill accessible to all of us. But, like all the skills we discuss here, it takes a willingness to invest one's time and discipline and consistently apply a few simple memory techniques. Perhaps the best memory framework is one used to dramatic effect by Benjamin Levy, a world-renowned magician and performer. As part of his act, Levy starts out his routine by asking every member of his audience (often well over 100 people) to state their name to him. He commits all those names to memory and then reveals those later in the performance. Levy's book describing his model was named as one of *Fortune* magazine's top 75 business books of the last 75 years. His model is appropriately abbreviated as FACE—focus, ask, comment, employ—and is described in Tool Kit 8.3.

MANAGER'S TOOL KIT

Tool Kit 8.3 The FACE Method for Remembering Names

- **Focus.** The first mistake most of us make is a failure to truly focus. When trying to remember a name, the first key is to intently lock in on the name at the first opportunity. So the first objective of remembering a name is to recognize the critical importance of locking it in at the first opportunity. The moment will pass instantaneously, so you have to target your attention intensely knowing that, like your locker number or your student identification number, you will need that name later.

- **Ask.** Ask to clarify that you have heard the name correctly. This gets you involved with the name and activates the memory process. A side benefit is it conveys to the other person you really care.

- **Comment.** Make some comment that will help cement the name in your memory. For example, "Paris, like the city?" Tie it to something familiar, a question, or something that will elicit a bit of further discussion. Doing that will help lock it into your memory.

- **Employ.** A terrific aid to memory is taking new material and teaching it to someone else. That is what happens when you introduce someone you've just met to someone else. It also gives you the opportunity to use the name again.

Far too many managers, young and old, resort to the excuse that they are "just not good with names." Discipline yourself to use the steps of FACE, and you will stand out as one of those magical people with a knack for names.

Building Your Social Network. Few great managers have ever achieved success on their own. Rather, they build and nurture a **social network** of people whom they can learn from, turn to for advice and support, and use as resources throughout their career. An important property of power is "the ability to mobilize resources to get things done," and social networks are immensely useful to that end.[46] See Management Live 8.4 as a networking example.

Fortunately, building a social network to enhance your power and influence is not a complex undertaking, but does take superior persistence, organization, and follow-up. A few simple steps can provide an excellent basis for building a good social network.

First, it is important to have a positive outlook on needing help and about soliciting support. Many people make the mistake of assuming that needing help is a sign of weakness. As a result, they do not reach out to others and thus fail to make important connections. The truth is most people you might seek for your network have been in similar places in their careers and will often gladly offer assistance whether it is arranging for personal introductions or providing advice and counsel. In general, all people like to feel needed, and involving them in your personal network is not likely to be an unwanted imposition. Just remember to "ask for a little," and it will often lead to much greater support.

Second, be sure to get beyond your organization and become active in industry or other professional events. Clubs and professional associations offer excellent ways both to add to your expertise and to meet others in your field of interest. Make it a point to meet and talk to at least a few new people each month, and don't forget to get business cards. Always follow up with the people you meet in a quick next-day e-mail. The goal is to make an impression so they will remember you the next time you contact them.

"Part of my concern about names is that I know how I feel when somebody I've met before does not know my name. It's like saying, 'I didn't bother—you must have had so little consequence in what you were saying or what you were doing, I don't even remember who you are.'"

—Steven Gluckstern, CEO, Zurich Global Asset Management

DO 8-6

"Old Girls Network" Helps Bring Young Women into Technology Jobs[47]

According to a report by the American Association for University Women Educational Foundation, the adventure games and programming challenges that attract young men to computers can serve to repel girls. In fact, most women enter information technology (IT) jobs via different paths than men, the report found.

Word of these differences has encouraged female "techies" to band together to help others break into the IT field. Networking groups are revolutionizing the way women learn new technical skills and ultimately find jobs. These groups are also reaching out to children who may have a knack for technology. A good example is Web Women, an online mailing list for women interested in Internet-related careers. They recently sponsored a Take Our Kids to the Web day.

According to Eve Simon, creative director at Interactive Applications Group, a Washington, DC, firm that creates websites for foundations and nonprofits, "An old girls network is a really powerful tool." That notion gains support from DC-area hiring managers who overwhelmingly say they prefer to bring on candidates who are referred by current employees. It is also supported by research conducted by professors at Stanford Business School on the hiring patterns and organizational structures of Silicon Valley technology companies.

Leslie Forte comments that, in her eight years in the IT field, she has endured countless slights, mostly from people who didn't think she fit the stereotype of an IT person. She balances the negatives with the acknowledgment that she has benefited from her network of support, which has helped her move from the help desk, traditionally a low-status position in IT, into a manager's role. Forte's boss tells her she's been rewarded because she can work comfortably in the world of computer hardware and still display soft skills, like communication. "What you're going to need is people to communicate the technology and teach people how to use it to change their lives," she says, "and for that, you're going to need people who are good with other people."

Third, to manage the contacts you have made, use a "black book," phone, tablet, or some other organizer that includes the names and contact information for those in your network. There will come a time in your career when knowing these people will pay off (with a job lead, a recommendation, advice), so it is important to keep your contacts "fresh." Proactively seek reasons to contact the people in your network (acknowledge an event or recognition they received, briefly report on a personal accomplishment, give them some grief on a favorite sports team defeat) and send an occasional e-mail or make an occasional phone call so your information is up to date and to make sure you are not forgotten.

We have seen many students confuse having a lot of Facebook friends with necessarily having a large social network. As a good test of your social network, think of how many of your Facebook friends would show up to help you move to a new apartment? While getting people to help you move may seem to be a pretty high hurdle, next think of how many people in your social network could you get to come to a party at your place this weekend? We have seen people with over 600 "friends" who sit home on Saturday night with nothing to do. Ask yourself, "Is this an effective social network"?

Finally, perhaps the most important lesson is that, just as the key to making friends is to first *be a friend*, your network will only grow to the extent you give as much as you gain. So look for opportunities to meet with and support *others* in their work.

As evidence of just how important personal networks are to career success, consider a study conducted at a major consulting firm.[48] The study was designed to determine any distinctive characteristics of high performers in terms of individual expertise, technology use, and personal networks. Results indicated that neither level of expertise nor skilled technology use differentiated average performers from high performers. It was solely the presence of larger and more diversified personal networks that differentiated the top performers from the average and low performers. Despite such findings, many of us spend an exorbitant amount of time and effort building our technical abilities and almost no time or effort building and maintaining our personal networks. Do not fall prey to that trap. Dedicate yourself to building a personal network from today forward.

Managing Facebook and Other Social Media Sites. A Harris Poll conducted in 2009 for CareerBuilder.com found that 45 percent of employers use social networking sites to research job candidates and another 11 percent who were not using them planned to start doing it. This was up from just 22 percent in 2008. Of those employers who used online sources to check on job applicants, 29 percent used Facebook, 26 percent used LinkedIn, and 21 percent used MySpace. Another 11 percent searched blogs and 7 percent followed job applicants on Twitter. Not too surprisingly, this was particularly common for employers in information technology and professional and business services.

Many students do not realize that many of the things they put online are there "forever." Of the employers who screen social media sites, 35 percent reported that they found content on a site that caused them to not hire a candidate. Some examples of why candidates were not hired included provocative or inappropriate pictures, drinking or drug use, bad-mouthing former employers, poor communication skills, discriminatory comments, lying about qualifications, and sharing confidential information from a previous employer. When it comes to communicating with an employer, similar patterns can be seen, and employers did not hire candidates because they used an emoticon (for example, a smiley face) or text language (GR8, BRB, or U) in an e-mail or job application.

While it may seem like you would be well advised to just stay away from social media altogether, that is not likely possible or necessarily desirable. There are positive consequences of employers screening your profiles, as 18 percent of employers found content that caused them to hire candidates. The most common reasons included that the profile provided a good sense of fit, it supported the professional qualifications, showed creativity, solid communication skills, and that the candidate was well-rounded. So, when it comes to managing your social media, Rosemary Haefner, Vice President of Human Resources at CareerBuilder, recommends the following DOs and DON'Ts to keep a positive image online:

- DO clean up digital dirt BEFORE you begin your job search. Remove any photos, content, and links that can work against you in an employer's eyes.

- DO consider creating your own professional group on sites like Facebook or BrightFuse.com to establish relationships with thought leaders, recruiters, and potential referrals.

- DO keep gripes offline. Keep the content focused on the positive, whether that relates to professional or personal information. Make sure to highlight specific accomplishments inside and outside of work.

- DON'T forget others can see your friends, so be selective about who you accept as friends. Monitor comments made by others. Consider using the "block comments" feature or setting your profile to "private" so only designated friends can view it.

- DON'T mention your job search if you're still employed.

> CASE CONCLUDED

So how are marketers and others thinking of using the KLOUT measurement of influence in the social media world? Marketers can use it to target influencers, of course, but there may also be other applications as well. For example, the Palms Hotel and Casino in Las Vegas is working on "The KLOUT Klub," which they claim will "allow high-ranking influencers to experience the Palms' impressive set of amenities in hopes that these influencers will want to communicate their positive experience to their followers." Presumably, only those with abnormally high KLOUT scores will be granted admission to the club. In the future, it may be the deciding factor in the battle over the Kingpin Suite or free tickets to Cirque de Soleil.

According to *AdAge* magazine, the primary downside of KLOUT is that it is a form of putting all your eggs in one basket. Says one expert, "KLOUT is like having just one credit monitoring company. You might do spectacularly well or have a terrible ranking but the validity of the ranking system itself has yet to be proven, at least until you have another service to compare it to. . . ." Along the same lines, KLOUT can certainly conjure up a rather scary, "Big Brother" scenario. Suppose your bank decides to use KLOUT scores to determine the interest on a mortgage loan? Or your real estate agent does

not find you "KLOUT worthy" to live in a certain neighborhood?

For some, the whole idea of ranking people by KLOUT scores, and then offering rewards to the top of the list, smacks of the immaturity of high school. "*Want to sit with me at lunch? Hang on while I check your KLOUT and then we'll talk . . .*" KLOUT is just one more example of innovations stemming from the Internet that create complicated scenarios for us all.

Questions

1. What type of applications could you see for KLOUT in your world? Would you be comfortable using KLOUT scores as one measure for selecting officers of a student club looking to expand its membership? Why or why not?

2. What are the potential downsides of KLOUT? Could you envision people trying to artificially manipulate and enhance their KLOUT scores?

3. How do people consciously increase their power in a firm? How does that relate to increasing your KLOUT score.

4. View the celebrity KLOUT indices from 2011 listed next. What can you conclude? What kinds of business decisions might those indices affect?

Name	KLOUT Score
Justin Bieber	99
Ashton Kutcher	97
Kim Kardashian	93
Rev Run	92
Jimmie Fallon	90
Lady Gaga	90
LeBron James	85
Snoop Dogg	84
Britney Spears	80
Ellen Degeneres	80
Reggie Bush	76
Lance Armstrong	75
Oprah Winfrey	65

*Most people have KLOUT scores under 20.

Source: From Kathlene Hestir, http://kathlenehestir.com/2010/07/13/how-klout-scores-work/. Reprinted with permission.

Source: Adapted with permission from Marketing Pilgrim Internet Marketing News Blog, October 5, 2010, http://www.marketingpilgrim.com/2010/10/want-a-vegas-upgrade-get-klout.html.

Concluding Note

Power is not a dirty word. In fact, it is rather essential for great management. To be effective, managers need to go beyond their formal authority and understand the influence tactics—social, political, and otherwise—that have been found to be most effective in gaining commitment. Professionalism is the source of trust and respect; it brings out the best in others and strengthens your reputation. However, like power and influence, it is also an area where blunders can be highly detrimental to a career. Skilled use of power, influence, and professionalism is the hallmark of all great managers.

KEY TERMS

authority 275
coercive power 280
conformity 281
dependence 275
expert power 280
influence 275
legitimate power 279

norms 280
political skills 285
power 274
power bases 278
professionalism 294
psychological reactance 288
referent power 279

reward power 279
social influence 285
social influence weapons 285
social network 299
strong ties 275
weak ties 275

CASE
Are 5,001 Facebook Friends One Too Many?

The British anthropologist and Oxford professor Robin Dunbar has posed a theory that the number of individuals with whom a stable interpersonal relationship can be maintained (read: friends) is limited by the size of the human brain, specifically the neocortex. "Dunbar's number," as this hypothesis has become known, is 150.

Facebook begs to differ.

What would be an impressive, even exhaustive, number of friends in real life is bush league for Facebook's high rollers, who have thousands. Other social networks use less-intimate terminology to portray contacts (LinkedIn has "connections," Twitter has "followers"), but

Facebook famously co-opted the word "friend" and created a new verb.

Friending "sustains an illusion of closeness in a complex world of continuous partial attention," said Roger Fransecky, a clinical psychologist and executive coach in New York (2,894 friends). "We get captured by Facebook's algorithms. Every day 25 new people can march into your living room. I come from a

failed Presbyterian youth, and there was a part of me that first thought it was impolite not to respond. Then I realized I couldn't put them all in a living room—I needed an amphitheater."

Facebook discourages adding strangers as friends, adding that only a tiny fraction of its 400 million users have reached the 5,000 threshold, at which point Facebook wags its digital finger and says: That's

(continued)

(continued)

enough. The company cites behind-the-scenes "back-end technology" as the reason for the cutoff, implying that the system will implode at the sight of a 5,001st friend.

What may seem surprising is that the subset of people with sizable lists is not limited to unemployed 20-somethings, commandeering tables at Starbucks and deluding themselves that they're "networking," social or otherwise. The high-users include plenty of grown-ups with real jobs and, seemingly, better things to do with their time than updating their "status" for strangers, former colleagues, and camp buddies from 300 years ago.

"At one point, I arbitrarily decided that for every new friend I confirmed, I had to delete one, like people with small closets do with their clothes," said Kurt Andersen (3,072), the host of *Studio 360* on public radio. "I devoted an entire weekend to going through them. But it made me feel like a 14-year-old girl: 'I'll be friends with you but not with you.'"

Facebook friends grow like kudzu for a variety of reasons, often personal or professional marketing—a proxy for the exchange of business cards (so old school). As in life, social networking lends itself to expanding social circles with like-minded people, so there are analogous Facebook cabals for foodies, literati, political junkies, perhaps gardeners, probably plumbers, and definitely Civil War reenactors (whose membership seems to be self-selected from former high-school audiovisual clubs).

If Facebook is a place of indiscriminate musings and minutiae, where people report their every thought, mood, hiccup, cappuccino, increased reps at the gym, or switch to a new brand of toothpaste, why not indiscriminate friendships? Why deny the little frisson of pleasure when your page proclaims you are "now friends with John Smith and 27 other people?"

Facebook's announcements and "suggestions" for new friends help to fetishize those numbers, although few will admit to an ego-gratifying interest in attaining the mythical quota of 5,000, like the Ryan Bingham character of Up in the Air, who's obsessed with reaching 10 million frequent flier miles.

As a metric for status or worth, Facebook has the ability to reduce its adult users to insecure teenagers, competing for high SAT scores or a seat at the cool kids' cafeteria table.

"I'm a Facebook friend of Bob Dylan, which probably means I have a deeply meaningful relationship with his publicist," said Daniel A. Farber (1,762), a law professor at the University of California, Berkeley. "I was hoping to impress my wife. And on the scale of things I've done to impress her, it's pretty good."

Jeffrey Wolf, a Bay Area real estate broker, claims, among (4,447) others, Alicia Keys, Alicia Silverstone and Alicia Witt as friends—and that's just the A-list. "I wanted to get Rachel Maddow," he said, "but she doesn't take friends."

Administering such a prodigious inventory—tending to requests from impending friends, let alone communicating with extant ones—is strenuous.

"Normally I start hitting it about 10 o'clock at night, and if I do it right, I can be done by 1 a.m.," Mr. Wolf said. "Anybody in his right mind would consider abandoning it."

What Mr. Andersen, the radio host, calls a graceful number of Facebook friends is a mutable concept. "I was grossed out when I first saw people with as many or fewer friends than what I have now," he said. "There's some optimal number, but I don't know what it is."

A large number (3,811) feels like the extension of a community for Hilary Rosen, managing partner of the Brunswick Group, a public strategy firm in Washington that has done consulting with Facebook. "When I went to work at Huffington Post, Arianna told me, 'Darling, you must confirm everybody,' and for the most part, I follow Arianna's rule," Ms. Rosen said. "But there's a core group that gets more attention, just like there used to be brown edges around some cards in my old Rolodex."

In his book *How Many Friends Does One Person Need?* Professor Dunbar stands by his number, acknowledging that digital resources help us keep in touch but fail to substitute for face-to-face relationships with loved ones who are sources of mutual support in a flesh-and-blood world.

Or, as Dr. Fransecky said, "I need friends that I can scratch and sniff."

Discussion Questions

1. After reading the chapter, do you think that 5,000 "friends" make you more "connected" than 4,000 "friends"? Than 2,500? Than 1,000?

2. Dunbar's number suggests that humans can only have 150 stable interpersonal relationships and that this number is limited by the size of the human brain. What is your experience with this number? Do you feel you have 150 "stable interpersonal relationships" or anywhere near that number?

3. From a power and influence perspective, are there many benefits to having friends that you cannot "scratch and sniff"? What types of power are derived from having a lot of interpersonal connections?

Source: Adapted and excerpted from "Are 5,001 Facebook Friends One Too Many?" by Aimee Lee Ball, *New York Times*, May 28, 2010.

SELECT MANAGE *WHAT?* DEBRIEFS

Influencing Without Formal Authority: Debrief

This type of scenario is faced daily by people in organizations and is therefore perhaps the most important of all power and influence skills. Obviously, because you do not have authority associated with your position, or any ability to reprimand the folks in graphics for not helping you, you must turn to other means to enlist their support.

Research on influence tactics is interesting in that it reveals that the most used tactics are often the least effective in gaining commitment. Specifically, people tend to rely on rational persuasion and pressure when the evidence suggests that those more often lead to resistance. The more effective strategies are those that rely on personal and social influence. In this case, your best bet for convincing the graphics group to help you out of this jam resides in one or more of three influence strategies:

- *Friendship/Liking.* Put simply, we are influenced by people who like us, are similar to us, and who flatter us. A traditional adage is that you get more flies with honey than with vinegar and, like it or not, it's true. So look for ways to establish personal relationships with the folks in graphics and search for common interests and connections. People are influenced by friends—so be a friend.

- *Commitment and Consistency.* Do not ask for their full commitment on the project immediately. Start by asking for something small, commend them for the work, and then gradually work up to the full request. Evidence suggests that once people have agreed to help, at even a small level, they will be more likely to offer further assistance. If you can just get the group started and modestly engaged on your work, then your chances of getting them to jump in and complete it are significantly enhanced. In this same vein, you might use the principle of reciprocity to get them on board. That is, you might describe the full set of work you have forthcoming and due, but would not want to burden them with it all on short notice—just this one reasonable project at this time. The effect is that you seem to be compromising. The hope is that they will reciprocate, in gratitude for you not dumping all the rest of your work on them at such a busy time, and take on the one project you put on their plate.

- *Social Proof.* Look for ways to send the signal to graphics that it is not just your group (with no authority or clout) but others more influential who want this project done well and on time. For example, can you get a senior leader or a key customer voice in the discussion? The goal is to have graphics feel that their completion of this project is important to other key stakeholders and thus should be prioritized more than they otherwise might.

(continued)

(continued)

Selling an Idea to Your Boss: Debrief

The importance of managing "up" is sometimes not fully understood by young managers and yet is critical to effectiveness. This is another case where you have no authority and thus cannot rely on organizational hierarchy or your control of rewards/sanctions to gain you any influence. In fact, any attempts to try to pressure or threaten would be ill-advised and likely career threatening.

The first key to influencing your boss is to first understand her mindset. Be sure you are fully aware of what is important to her. What are her goals and highest priorities, and how does your work contribute to those. What are her pressures and what is keeping her most occupied? If you understand these fundamental things, then you can frame your communication in an appropriate way. You can appeal to shared goals and values, or explain how your idea can create value that is relevant to her.

Second, have a clear vision of your recommendation, including its strategic importance, and say it up front. Some phrases that might help you begin the conversation are "I've noticed we have a problem with . . . and I have a solution I'd like to propose" or "You mentioned that one of our strategic goals for this year is . . . and I have an idea of how we can do that." That way your boss will listen, because she knows where you are headed and that you won't waste her time. Always outline both costs and benefits, being as specific as you can about both. Don't forget about costs such as time and allocation of resources. As a general rule, if you are going to approach your boss with a problem, come armed with a recommendation as well. Bosses are famous for saying "I have plenty of problems. What I need are solutions." Your solution may not be one that ultimately actually gets implemented, but showing your superior that you are capable of understanding a problem and its ramifications could prove to be an asset to your career.

Finally, communicate in your boss's preferred style. Is your boss a listener, or a reader? Each of us has a particular way in which we prefer to receive information, and that is usually the channel we choose to communicate with other people. If your boss consistently initiates face-to-face communication, this is likely the best way to proceed with a request. On the other hand, if your boss is a reader, it is a good idea to provide her with information in writing prior to a meeting, so she has a chance to fully absorb it. But don't make this a guessing game; ask your boss how he or she likes to communicate best since we all have very different preferences. And once you have presented your recommendation, ask for input. Organizations desperately need people capable of managing up; thus you want to learn what went well, and what did not, and use the opportunity to refine your approach for your next episode.

Building a Personal Network That Enhances Your Power: Debrief

While too often dismissed as frivolous and superficial, your efforts to build relationships will likely define your career—so it is never too early to start your network and to increase your competence in doing so. In fact, someone in this scenario would be well advised to expand the time they spend establishing and nurturing a personal network and avoid focusing solely on their own personal development.

Networking has enjoyed a surge in popularity and a number of bestselling books and seminars have emerged touting the many secrets to effective networking. In reality, however, a few simple and practical strategies have stood the test of time and are the building blocks of strong personal networks.

- *Be bold in asking for help.* Everyone has been in this same place at some point in their career and people are remarkably willing to help and "give back"—but they have to be asked. One good maxim is to start by asking for a little. That is, request a 10-minute phone conversation or a short informational interview (with no resumés or job leads requested). Such requests are more likely to be accepted and they often lead to follow-up opportunities of greater depth.

- *The best way to receive is to give.* It should never simply be about getting what you want. It's about getting what you want and making sure that the people who are important to you get what they want, too. Look for opportunities to help others make contacts and build their networks—they will likely reciprocate.

- *Never eat alone.* The death trap in trying to build a strong network is to disappear. So constantly be looking for chances to invite someone to lunch, join in on a group dinner, bring bagels in the morning prior to work so folks will gather. Look for the professional and civic organizations you can join and keep your calendar full. And think about how you can bring others together (for example, two of your contacts that have not met join you for lunch).

- *Get organized and keep track.* Be obsessive about creating and maintaining your personal "data base." Over time, nothing will be more valuable to your professional future. So get organized and create a recording system that enables you to rapidly store and receive (and keep fresh) the contact information for your growing network of friends and contacts.

- *Ping consistently.* Finally, constantly be on the lookout for opportunities to contact the people in your network (for example, acknowledge an event or recognition they received, briefly report on a personal accomplishment, reference something in the news you know they would find of interest). This has often been stated as looking for reasons to have a conversation, so send an occasional e-mail or make a brief phone call to stay in touch. In today's jargon, this is called "pinging" and is essential to make sure your network is up to date and you are not forgotten in the clutter of everyday life.

CHAPTER

9

Leading Others

OBJECTIVES

KNOWING   DOING

After reading this chapter, you should be able to:

KO 9-1   Explain the full range of leadership approach to leadership.

KO 9-2   Articulate how personal traits are related to leadership effectiveness.

KO 9-3   Describe the basis of transactional leadership.

KO 9-4   Describe the primary behaviors associated with transformational leadership.

KO 9-5   Describe the relationship between transactional and transformational leadership.

DO 9-1   Display transactional leadership behaviors in order to build trust.

DO 9-2   Exhibit transformational leadership behaviors.

DO 9-3   Create a development plan to improve your leadership skills.

Case: Google

n early 2009, statisticians from Google's corporate headquarters (known as the Googleplex) embarked on a plan code-named Project Oxygen. Their mission was to devise something far more important to the future of Google Inc. than its next search algorithm or application. They wanted to build better *bosses*.

So, as only those from a data-mining giant like Google can do, they began analyzing performance reviews, feedback surveys, and nominations for top-manager awards. They correlated phrases, words, praise, and complaints.

Later that year, the "people analytics" teams at the company produced what might be called the Eight Habits of Highly Effective Google Managers.

Now, brace yourself. Because the directives might seem so obvious—so, well, *duh*—it's hard to believe that it took the mighty Google so long to figure them out:

- "Have a clear vision and strategy for the team."
- "Help your employees with career development."
- "Don't be a sissy: Be productive and results-oriented."

The list goes on, reading like a whiteboard gag from an episode of "The Office."

"My first reaction was, that's it?" says Laszlo Bock, Google's vice president for "people operations," which is Googlespeak for human resources.

But then Mr. Bock and his team began ranking those eight directives by importance. And this is where Project Oxygen gets interesting.

For much of its 13-year history, particularly the early years, Google has taken a pretty simple approach to management: Leave people alone. Let the engineers do their stuff. If they become stuck, they'll ask their bosses, whose deep technical expertise propelled them into management in the first place.

But Mr. Bock's group found that technical expertise—the ability, say, to write computer code in your sleep—*ranked dead last* among Google's big eight. What employees valued most were even-keeled bosses who made time for one-on-one meetings, who helped people puzzle through problems by asking questions, not dictating answers, and who took an interest in employees' lives and careers.

"In the Google context, we'd always believed that to be a manager, particularly on the engineering side, you need to be as deep or deeper a technical expert than the people who work for you," Mr. Bock says. "It turns out that that's absolutely the *least important thing*. It's important, but pales in comparison. Much more important is just making that connection and being accessible."

1. Briefly summarize what Google found in their quest to uncover the best bosses.

2. Describe the best or worse boss you ever had. Is it consistent with Google's findings?

3. What do you think would be your strongest skill as a potential boss?

309

1. Making the Transition to a Leadership Position

You have been working for four years in a bank branch located in the front section of a large grocery store. For the last two years, the branch has been underperforming and a poor place to work—tellers show up late, cash drawers are often out of balance, and the customer service numbers for your branch are in the bottom quarter when compared to other branches of your bank. As a result of these problems, the branch manager was removed from your branch. Today, the regional manager offered you the job on an interim basis. The terms of your job include a three-month trial period, and if all goes well, you will be made the branch manager. You know that the problems in your branch stem in part from the lack of trust and respect for the prior branch manager. While you know the employees will be happy the old boss is gone, you are not sure how they will feel about your promotion to be their new manager.

So where would you begin? How would you go about building a solid foundation of trust in your leadership? How would you address the poor financial performance? Considering you were just recently a peer of your associates, and now their manager, would there be any critical things to do or not to do?

2. Leading People to Performance Beyond Expectations

After your first two years as manager of a local pizza franchise store, performance is in the upper third of all stores in the firm, turnover has been low, and you enjoy good relations with your employees. However, you want to be better than just good—you want your store to be seen as great! You currently have a capable workforce, even some who are seemingly interested in moving up in the company, but right now they appear relatively content to just keep doing what they are doing. For your own career progress, you know that to really move up you will need to get your store to have higher performance and a more notable profile in the company. Your boss has assured you that if you are able to "do great things" with your store, there will be a wide variety of options open to you within the company. You like the company and believe your boss, but are struggling to determine how to get higher performance out of your people and further your own leadership plans.

What would you do to energize your employees to take it up a notch and perform above expectations? What do leaders that transform situations like this really do? Are there any common traps to avoid making the situation worse instead of better?

3. Leading People Older than Yourself

You got a great education and really dedicated yourself in your first few years in your job. Your boss saw positive things in your future and so you were promoted, over several folks much older, to be the leader of your group. You are really excited but also quite anxious about leading people older than you are (some as much as 25 years or more) and who also have far more experience in your firm. Is it really that different than managing those younger? What will be the keys to your success in managing people older than yourself? What are the most common traps?

4. Developing Yourself as a Leader

Even though you have been moderately successful, you are not "coming along" in your career as quickly as either your boss or you had hoped. Two years ago, becoming the regional sales manager looked like it was about three years away. Now it seems like it could be five years away. You frequently overhear your boss and his boss saying, "We have plenty of good managers but few real leaders." The inference is that you and your colleagues either do not have, or have not shown, "the right stuff" of leadership.

What does it mean to be a leader? Can it be learned? How might you demonstrate it for your superiors? What specific actions could you take that have been shown to help build real leadership capability?

Introduction

Of all the topics in this book, leadership probably receives the most attention in the "popular press," and companies spend incredible sums of money trying to develop "leaders" and "leadership." Despite this considerable attention, most people still have a number of misconceptions about leadership and tend to have a very difficult time succeeding in leadership roles.

The concepts of "leader" and "leadership" have been around for literally thousands of years (there are even Egyptian hieroglyphs associated with them),[1] and yet perceptions vary widely regarding what leadership is and how it can best be developed. The focus of this chapter is on the wide range of competencies related to leadership effectiveness. Current leadership research recognizes that leadership is not genetic or a mysterious gift bestowed on just a few.[2] It is not just one thing but a comprehensive *set* of personal characteristics, skills, and behaviors that can be learned (although some are more amenable to learning than others) by anyone with the desire to do so. Consistent with our book title, the question is "What do those managers who are great leaders know and do?"

Of the many definitions of leadership, we tend to like Churchill's concise notion that "leadership is taking people in a direction they would not otherwise go." That is, **leadership** is the ability to influence people to set aside their personal concerns and support a larger agenda—at least for a while. The most effective leaders motivate people to perform above and beyond the call of duty, and enhance group success. Leadership effectiveness is not simply who exerts the most influence or emerges to control the group, but who can achieve high group performance over time.

A great deal of attention has been devoted to the distinction between leadership and management. Although it's popular to think of "leaders" and "managers" as different people or people who do different things, little research supports such a distinction. In fact, despite the popular notions, leadership can actually be considered a subset of effective management. Indeed, across five or more decades of research examining the major requirements of effective management, leadership is always seen as part of the managerial role.[3] That is to say that a manager is not being entirely effective if she ignores the importance of leadership as a central part of her role. To be certain, effective leadership is not a proscribed role and non-managers can display and enact leadership. Put simply, leaders may not be in a managerial role, but effective managers are almost always effective leaders. So how important is leadership to the managerial role? It is important enough that we dedicate an entire chapter to enacting leadership.

Leadership Matters

Leadership development is a multibillion-dollar industry in both the United States and Europe, and the amount of attention being paid to leaders and leadership has exploded in other parts of the world as well. In fact, due to rapid economic development, leadership development has become extremely important in India and China.

The reason for all of this focus on developing leadership skills is that effective leadership is paramount for the success of organizations and the well-being of employees and citizens. Recent meta-analyses conducted of the leadership literature make it easy to see why so much attention gets paid to organizational leadership and its development.[4] Leadership behavior has been linked to a wide variety of important outcomes across a wide variety of companies. In fact, leadership behaviors have been shown to be important for organizational success across industry types (such as for profit, not-for-profit, government, and others) and across national boundaries. Increasing evidence even suggests effective leadership is one of the best sources of sustainable competitive advantage an organization can have over its competitors.[5]

Effective leadership makes great things happen. Indeed, the most important achievements of humankind are associated with people who influenced others to achieve more than they thought was possible. On the other hand, the lack of inspired leadership has probably been responsible for more failed careers and unhappy employees than any other cause.

One interesting indication of the popularity of leadership today is that a quick search on Amazon.com reveals well over 68,000 books currently available on the topic.[6] Just for fun, we went ahead and playfully categorized some of those many books in Management Live 9.1.

"Projects, budgets, and facilities can be managed. People need to be led."

—Ross Perot

"Leadership is like beauty; it's hard to define, but you know it when you see it."

—Warren Bennis

"The question, 'Who ought to be boss?' is like asking, 'Who ought to be the tenor in the quartet?' Obviously, the man who can sing tenor."

—Henry Ford

Categorizing the Vast Array of Leadership Books

To help navigate the great number of books on leadership, we thought that providing a classification of these books would be illustrative. While this is presented largely in fun, it does show the extremely broad range of books available. It also demonstrates the intense demand for leadership knowledge.

Numbers
- *Executive Charisma: Six Steps to Mastering the Art of Leadership*
- *Leadership Wisdom from the Monk Who Sold His Ferrari: The 8 Rituals of Visionary Leaders*
- *Leading Every Day: 124 Actions for Effective Leadership*

CEOs
This category was way too large, so we just include a small sample of Jack Welch books here!
- **29 Leadership Secrets from Jack Welch*
- *Get Better or Get Beaten! 31 Leadership Secrets from GE's Jack Welch*
- *Jack Welch and the 4 E's of Leadership*

Laws
These can also be considered a subset of the numbers category.
- *The 21 Irrefutable Laws of Leadership*
- *The 9 Natural Laws of Leadership*
- *The Stuff of Heroes: The Eight Universal Laws of Leadership*

Presidents of the United States
- *Cigars, Whiskey and Winning: Leadership Lessons from Ulysses S. Grant*
- *John F. Kennedy on Leadership: The Lessons and Legacy of a President*
- *Lincoln on Leadership: Executive Strategies for Tough Times*

Religion and Spirituality
- *Dynamic Spiritual Leadership: Leading Like Paul*
- *The Maxwell Leadership Bible: Lessons in Leadership from the Word of God*
- *They Smell Like Sheep: Spiritual Leadership for the 21st Century*

Secrets
- *The Leadership Secrets of Billy Graham*
- *The Leadership Secrets of Colin Powell*
- *The Leadership Secrets of Santa Claus*

---

* Denotes the winning book. This falls into the numbers, secrets, and Jack Welch categories all in one brief title.

Note: In the first edition of this text, we had an idea for a book titled *The 12 Secret Laws of Millard Fillmore's Spiritual Army* (with a forward by Jack Welch). We have since reconsidered and are now thinking that *The 365 Spiritual Laws of Steve Jobs* (with a forward still being written by Jack Welch) may be more marketable.

In reviewing the extraordinary range of publications on leadership, two observations stand out. First, leadership clearly matters and people are eager for ways to learn about how to more effectively lead and improve their groups and organizations. Second, the multitude of lists, models, laws, and so on make it hard to know what is really associated with leadership effectiveness and supported by more than just opinion. In this chapter, we use the best evidence available to provide guidance regarding the essential conditions and leader behaviors associated with leadership effectiveness. Our goal, then, is not just to help you learn the most effective knowledge and behavior associated with great leadership, but also to help you consume leadership books and research more effectively. As noted, leadership is an area where there is a great deal of misinformation, and myths abound. Myths 9.1 identifies a few of the most common leadership myths. A first step toward understanding effective leadership is to first understand what is *not* true.

The Full Range of Leadership

KO **9-1**

As presented in Myths 9.1, one persistent misnomer in casual discussions of leadership is that effective leadership is comprised of just *one* general skill or competency. This gives rise to questions of whether leadership can really be taught. Of course,

---

?¿ MYTHS 9.1   Leadership Myths

- **Leaders are born, not made.** Leadership is multidimensional and consists of a range of skills, competencies, and behaviors. Genetics play some role, of course, but mostly in terms of personal traits and what makes someone *emerge* as a leader or gain the admiration and respect of followers. Ultimate leadership effectiveness is almost exclusively related to leader behaviors (what leaders do) and those behaviors are generally learnable.

- **Leaders must be charismatic.** While some great leaders are exceptionally charismatic, a large number of others are not. Charisma is often problematic because two people may observe the same person and disagree as to whether he or she is charismatic. Also, charisma may be helpful or harmful, depending on the situation, and charisma is certainly not a necessary condition for effective leadership.

- **Leaders don't delegate the important stuff.** Leaders delegate the right work to the right person. They share work and responsibilities to get the job done, and doing this doesn't reduce their credibility. Delegation is an important tool for effective leaders to develop the talents of the people around them.

- **Leadership exists only at the top.** Even though we are all familiar with the names of celebrity CEOs and businesspeople (such as Bill Gates, Jeff Bezos, or Jack Welch), effective leadership is demonstrated by scores of people whose names you have never heard. Effective leadership can be found at all organizational levels and is *everyone's* business.

- **Leadership incompetence results from too little of "the right stuff."** An emerging body of evidence suggests leadership failure is more related to having undesirable qualities and exhibiting toxic behaviors than it is to lacking desirable ones. Sometimes having *the wrong stuff* can be just as detrimental as any right stuff we may be lacking.[7]

- **Leaders need to keep others at a distance.** Forming close relationships is actually an important key to building relationships with high leader-member exchange (LMX). These effective relationships are associated with improved employee work attitudes and performance and should be encouraged, not banned.

some personal characteristics like integrity and decisiveness are not particularly responsive to change. However, leadership is multidimensional (not just personal characteristics) and many interpersonal and organizational leadership skills—such as diagnosing follower performance, tying rewards to performance, and creating collective goals—are certainly open to teaching and learning. With that in mind, we think it is most useful to address a wide variety of leadership competencies.

With respect to personal characteristics, the action focus is mostly on understanding the personal traits of importance and becoming more self-aware about your own personal profile so you can adapt when necessary and put yourself in positions where you are most likely to succeed. With respect to behavior, the key is to learn and practice those behaviors that promote positive transactions and transform people to go above expectations. (See Management Live 9.2 for a simple but powerful example.)

Consistent with the theme of this book, and the goals of this chapter, we are presenting what research and practice have found to be the most straightforward and up-to-date approach for understanding and practicing effective leadership. Although some of the ideas have been researched for over 50 years, the overall approach has been developed over the last 20 years and has enjoyed both research support and success in practical application. When asked how to guide a person in a management position toward "what to do" to be successful, the combination of building a solid foundation and then focusing upon more advanced leadership behaviors offers the most solid, research-backed, behavioral prescriptions. This combination is broadly referred to as the **full range of leadership approach.**[8] In order to describe this full range approach, we begin by addressing personal characteristics and transactional leader behaviors. The remainder of the chapter is dedicated to learning transformational leader behaviors.

⇄ MANAGEMENT LIVE 9.2

R. Seshasayee of Ashok Leyland

As managing director of Ashok Leyland, a leading transportation company in India whose buses carry 70 million people a day, R. Seshasayee was faced with reinvigorating the company to restore its performance after a few down years. An interview with Seshasayee suggests leadership in an Indian transportation company requires many of the same abilities as it does anywhere else in the world, or in most any workplace situation.

Seshasayee asserts, "Outstanding leaders are those who set audacious objectives and get people to own and achieve them." He continues by suggesting that leadership requires three essentials:

> [First is] setting a goal which seems impossible or needs a fundamental leap; second is to communicate to people and inspire them that the task is not so daunting; and the third is to be a living example of what can be done so that followers can refer to the leader's life and his actions and see the way to behave in given circumstances.

The leadership practices of Seshasayee go beyond the "big picture" issues described earlier. One of his favorite practices is to use small notes as motivational tools. He describes a habit of using pink notes as recognition tools.

> There was this employee who wrote a good report on something. I sent him a note saying that it was a "great delight to read this report. Good show." Later, this person left us and went to West Asia. Many years later, I ran into him in an airport and after chatting with him, he brought out his wallet and showed me the pink slip—he had preserved it all those years! The message is that little things can have a tremendous impact on people. The basic issue is to be able to relate to and touch people.

Source: Kamath, V. (2002). Leadership has to touch people. *Praxis,* 3 (4), 22–29.

Personal Characteristics of Leaders

KO **9-2**

Early leadership research looked at successful leaders in detail to see how they differed from people who were not leaders. This early approach (starting around 1850) became known as the Great Man theory of leadership[9] (there was little thought of women leading in those days) and was based on the premise that leaders both were more capable and possessed a different set of traits than followers.[10] In other words, leaders are born, not made. Interestingly, this approach was popularized by Sir Francis Galton, Charles Darwin's cousin. Today, this approach remains quite popular and implies that a particular set of traits offers some magic formula for success. This viewpoint can be seen in the titles of many popular books on leadership, which purport to have identified a set number of traits for successful leadership.

Many popular books on leadership make it sound like there is a small set of leadership traits (such as honesty, charisma, extraversion) that make a person into a successful leader. If only it were that easy. This is not to say, however, that a person's traits do not matter in the leadership process—they do. They just do not matter in the way most people think.

Important Personal Traits in Leadership

Like so many things in life in general, and managerial skills in particular, the evidence regarding traits is a bit more complex than all those popular press book titles suggest. While it is true that leadership is in part who you are, scientific reviews of the Great Man theory indicate traits alone won't guarantee effective leadership. In fact, the association between traits and leadership effectiveness is considered to be weak. Rather than the mere possession of these traits, it's what people *do* with those traits that matters most. Traits are, however, good predictors of **leadership emergence,** rather than leadership *effectiveness.* In other words, a set of traits has been found to be important in influencing others' *perceptions* of leadership. People who possess certain traits may be more likely to be perceived as a leader by others, but these people are no more likely to be effective in a managerial role. Possession of these traits, however, seems to be linked to who will ultimately attain a managerial role and who will not.

As an example of leadership emergence, think of the last time you were put into a group of people that you did not know well. After interacting for a little while, you formed an idea about most of the people in the group. Now think about what those perceptions were based upon and what type of person you would identify as a leader. A few people probably said very little and just observed while a few others did most of the talking. Of the people that did most of the talking, one or two of them probably seemed to be a bit smarter than the others and were more engaging speakers. When asked who was a leader in this group, very few people would identify the people who didn't speak or who didn't seem to be very engaging. As a result, a pretty consistent pattern emerges for the people who fill leadership roles, and that pattern is discussed next.

Although it is true that there is no definitive set of traits that guarantee leadership effectiveness, it is not true to say that personal characteristics do not matter in a well-rounded discussion of leadership. More specifically, the following traits have been found to matter in an important way:

- intelligence
- dominance
- sociability
- self-monitoring

"As a young marine I learned firsthand that leaders are not born, they are made. Anyone can become a stronger leader. It's your character and abilities that make you a leader, not your job title."

—Courtney Lynch, organizational consultant

"There are many qualities that make a great leader. But having strong beliefs, being able to stick with them through popular and unpopular times, is the most important characteristic of a great leader."

—Rudy Giuliani

- high energy or drive
- self-confidence
- tolerance for ambiguity

All of the preceding traits do a pretty good job of predicting *who will rise* to a formal leadership position. In looking at this list, these findings appear to be quite reasonable. For example, would you think a person who was bright, self-confident, had a high energy level, and so on, would be more likely to both want and be granted a management position than his or her counterparts (people who are not particularly intelligent, lack self-confidence, are socially passive, and so on)? This does not seem provocative in any way. What is more surprising to most people is that these characteristics do not make a person noticeably more likely to be an effective leader once the person reaches a managerial position. This makes the full range of leadership particularly important when it comes to understanding effective leadership. It goes well beyond the assumption that once a person reaches a formal position he or she will magically be effective.

Characteristics That People Admire

An additional way of looking at leadership traits is to examine the personal characteristics that people admire in their leaders. Although this approach may be somewhat problematic because it is not linked to whether the person is actually effective or not, it can still be useful, so we better understand what people are looking for in their leaders. (See Management Live 9.3 for a somewhat surprising characteristic associated with success.)

⇤⇥ MANAGEMENT LIVE 9.3

Death as a Characteristic of an Effective Leader?

On November 7, 2000, Melvin (Mel) Carnahan was elected to the U.S. Senate as a senator from Missouri. Mel Carnahan had been in a close race with John Ashcroft (who later was named the attorney general of the United States) and trailed by several percentage points in polls taken about two months before the election. During the last few months, however, Carnahan put on a surge and ultimately beat out Ashcroft for the Senate seat. What was Carnahan's political strategy? What did Carnahan do to overcome his opponent's lead? Well, Mel Carnahan died in a tragic plane crash just three weeks prior to the election.

Scott Allison and Dafna Eylon of the University of Richmond have been researching just how such an odd turn of events can happen.[11] In laboratory experiments, Allison and Eylon presented study participants with a written description of a man named Erik Sullivan. After providing a list of impressive accomplishments relating to Erik's role in building a successful company, the researchers manipulated one important piece of information and had half of the people respond to each story. In one situation, Erik died years after he retired, and in the other case, Erik was still alive. The results of this study showed that people formed significantly more favorable impressions of Erik Sullivan when they believed he was dead than when they believed he was alive.

Allison and Eylon use the term "death positivity bias" as the inflation in ratings associated with a person's death. The authors suggest a few different explanations of the effect may be relevant. First, the social norm of respecting the dead is very strong in most cultures. Another explanation for the death positivity bias comes from commodity theory, which posits that any commodity's value increases to the extent it is no longer available. Since the death of a person is clearly an example where the person's leadership is no longer available, others may value it more highly. Perhaps most importantly, these findings illustrate the often unreliable and biased nature of trait perceptions.

Leadership authors Jim Kouzes and Barry Posner[12] started with a simple idea: They surveyed business and government executives all over the world and asked them, "What values (personal traits or characteristics) do you look for and admire in your superiors?" They have had more than 78,000 people on four continents respond. From those responses, they developed a list of 20 characteristics. The top four characteristics (all supported by more than 50 percent of the respondents) were:

- honest
- forward-looking
- inspiring
- competent

For students, the evidence on leadership traits and leadership emergence offers some important lessons. First, this is a prime example of the inaccuracy (or at least incompleteness) of common sense, in that commonly understood leadership traits are not good predictors of leadership effectiveness. Second, it suggests a wonderful diversity in the types of people who have the capability to be effective leaders. Third, traits that people often associate with successful leaders (self-confidence) may just end up being biases or errors people make when they are evaluating others. For instance, how many times do you think someone doesn't get a leadership position because they didn't "look or act" like a leader in a job interview? How much real leadership talent goes unrecognized because it is hidden in "packages" that do not fit most people's stereotypes of what makes an effective leader? Great managers are able to show people they have what it takes even when they do not fit the preconceived mold. And the best way to accomplish this is to *behave* as an effective leader—the topic of the remainder of this chapter.

"Common sense is the collection of prejudices acquired by age eighteen."

—Albert Einstein

Transactional Leadership

KO **9-3**

DO **9-1**

Now that you have a better understanding of the role that personal characteristics play in the leadership process, the foundation-forming leadership behaviors need to be addressed. In the final analysis, the evidence is clear that great leadership is more about what one *does* than who one *is*. And research has shown that the basic "doing" of effective leadership involves two primary behaviors: (1) behaviors that focus on the task at hand, and (2) behaviors that focus on the relationship between leader and follower. In other words, leadership involves influencing people to attain goals not just by giving them directives (task behaviors), but also by supporting the employee (relationship behaviors). Though the behaviors we discuss will be a bit more complex, the foundation of great leadership is built on these two areas of leader behavior.[13]

Leading Through Transactions

Recall that a critically important role of people management positions is to motivate others (see Chapter 6). Since many approaches to motivation (especially expectancy theory) view motivation as a process by which people put forth effort due to their belief that something positive will come from their effort, the importance of trust between a manager and his or her employee cannot be overestimated. Would you expend energy for a person you did not trust? You would probably fear being exploited or taken advantage of by another person. As such, you might do everything possible to minimize your exposure to that person.

Since few people are willing to be influenced by someone whom they do not trust or believe does not have their best interest at heart, it is important for managers to build this level of trust in their employees. **Transactional leadership** serves to build these important influence components. Transactional leader behavior represents an exchange, or a transaction, between the leader and follower. This exchange pursues a cost-benefit, or economic exchange, strategy, whereby the leader exchanges rewards and treatment for desirable services (performance, effort, participation) from the subordinate.

Leader-Member Exchange

"Your job gives you authority. Your behavior gives you respect."

—Irwin Ferderman, CEO, Monolithic Memories

These transactional leadership behaviors are important because they provide a solid foundation for the relationship between the employee and manager, and great managers realize the employee-manager relationship is the most important relationship to get right. There are numerous benefits—to employee, manager, and organization—of having a positive, constructive relationship between employee and manager, commonly referred to as **leader-member exchange (LMX).**[14] More specifically, strong leader-employee relationships have been linked to increased employee citizenship behavior, higher employee performance ratings, increased employee satisfaction, reduced employee turnover, and a host of other positive consequences.[15] LMX is largely influenced by the types of exchanges or transactions that take place between employees and their managers. To establish a positive LMX, it is important that an employee can trust the manager (and transactional leader behaviors are important tools to make this happen). Employees who have positive relationships with their leader are referred to as members of an in-group. On the other hand, employees who do not enjoy a high-quality exchange are referred to as members of the out-group. When high-quality LMX occurs, the in-group employees receive increased formal treatment (money and public recognition, for example) and informal treatment (favorable projects, and so on).[16] These in-group members feel obligated, as a result of positive treatment by their leaders, to respond by working harder to benefit the leader and others in the work setting as a means of reciprocation.[17] Basically, building a strong LMX relationship is central to managerial effectiveness.

Transactional Leader Behaviors

Although numerous behaviors can be considered **transactional leader behaviors,** Bernard Bass, the major contributor to the transactional leadership approach, suggests that management-by-exception (putting out fires and taking corrective action when problems occur) and **contingent reward behavior** (rewarding an employee for doing a good job) are two of the most effective transactional leader behaviors. The important links between these behaviors and motivation are obvious. These behaviors help to clarify exactly what is wanted and what behavior is desired or not desired by the manager. Many people have made the parallel that management-by-exception is generally consistent with the idea of **contingent punishment**—providing an aversive consequence to reduce the frequency of a behavior.[18]

"A pat on the back is only a few vertebrae removed from a kick in the pants, but is miles ahead in results."

—W. Wilcox

Of these two main transactional leader behaviors, research has shown contingent reward behavior consistently results in positive consequences in both employee attitudes (job satisfaction, organizational commitment) and employee behaviors (job performance, organizational citizenship).[19] Further, contingent reward behavior is an important way to build LMX. Management Live 9.4 shows an interesting example of contingent reward behavior in action. Contingent reward is an essential part of effective leadership because it accomplishes the

MANAGEMENT LIVE 9.4

It Works for Shamu—Why Not You?

Have you ever wondered how they train killer whales to jump over a rope at SeaWorld and other amusement parks? Or for that matter, how they train dolphins to walk on the water and wave to the audience? Do you think they hang a rope 20 feet over the pool and then shout to the whale, "Up, up, up!"? Of course not, but that is exactly how many ineffective managers treat their employees.

The way Shamu (the world's most famous killer whale) and fellow killer whales are actually trained to jump over a rope is by starting the learning process with the rope *under* the water. When the whale swims over the rope, it gets rewarded. Then the rope is gradually raised. Each time the whale swims over it again, a reward is given. This continues until the whale is leaping out of the water! Now think how often managers give a reward only when the final goal is reached. Would it be more effective to provide rewards along the way as well? The killer whales seem to think so—and by the way, so do people!

important goal of linking performance and rewards for the employee (see the discussion of positive reinforcement in Chapter 6). This linkage is important because contingent rewards serve as a feedback loop that provides learning for both the employee and the organization as a whole. Thus, employees learn to see a positive relationship between what they're doing right and the rewards they receive (this is also consistent with the social learning approach of Bandura, discussed in Chapter 1). In most organizations, leaders control the available rewards to some extent. Since rewards are a powerful tool for showing employees what the leader desires, the use of contingent reward behavior may have important consequences for the company's overall culture, performance, and, ultimately, its long-term survival.

In terms of being an effective distributor of contingent rewards, we can provide detailed step-by-step guidance. To do this, see Tool Kit 9.1.

Much in the same manner that behavioral researchers know a great deal about how contingent reward should be distributed, the application of contingent punishment is also "tried and true" when it comes to its usefulness in managerial practices. To effectively provide contingent punishment, a manager should take the steps provided in Tool Kit 9.2.

MANAGER'S TOOL KIT

Tool Kit 9.1   How to Provide Contingent Rewards

1. Describe the desired behavior (push high-margin products, help others, share expertise with marketing task force).
2. Explain the benefits that the desired behavior will cause (increased profits, happier people, improved customer service).
3. Explain rewards associated with the desired behavior (increased performance ratings, raises, bonuses, promotions, more responsibility, interesting work assignments).
4. Provide examples and answer questions regarding desired behaviors.
5. Monitor behavior and reward desired behavior.
6. Follow through with the reward promised should the desired behavior occur.

MANAGER'S TOOL KIT

Tool Kit 9.2   **How to Provide Contingent Punishment**

1. Meet privately. Never punish in public.
2. Describe the undesirable behavior (poor customer contact, not meeting sales goals, bypassing safety policies).
3. Explain the problems the undesirable behavior is causing (low employee satisfaction, customer complaints, lost sales).
4. Allow questions and opportunities for clarification.
5. Explain consequences if the undesirable behavior does not change (probation, formal discipline procedures, termination).
6. Provide examples and time for questions regarding desired behaviors.
7. Monitor behavior and reward desirable behavior.
8. Follow through with the appropriate response to behavior (aversive consequences if the behavior has not changed, or positive outcomes if the behavior has changed).

The Role of Transactional Leader Behaviors

Transactional behaviors play an important role in effective leadership in at least three ways. First, as we have stated, they establish credibility, trust, and respect for one's manager.[20] When a manager makes promises and more importantly keeps those promises, an employee learns to trust what his manager says. Second, transactional behaviors form the foundation upon which other effective behaviors are built. As we will see, without a trusting relationship, few employees will take a manager seriously—a critical requirement for more advanced leader behaviors. Third, transactional behaviors establish fairness in the workplace. For example, when expectations are not being met (poor performance, unsafe practices, and so on), addressing the problem quickly and fairly is vital to establishing and maintaining a sense of fairness among employees. To ensure that sense of fairness, great managers need to sometimes use management-by-exception, or contingent punishment.

In a plant where one of this book's authors has conducted a great deal of training, a member of a generally well-performing group engaged in some potentially dangerous behavior while driving a forklift (chasing another person and encouraging other forklift drivers to race). In this case, many managers make a fundamental error; they ignore the behavior and say, "Overall, he is a good guy. I don't think he will do those things again." These types of behavior need to be addressed, and ignoring them is a recipe for failure down the road.

This type of wishful thinking on the part of the manager presents a twofold problem. It sends a message to the employee that this type of behavior is acceptable—maybe not desirable, but acceptable nonetheless. Second, and more problematic—and consistent with Bandura's social learning theory from Chapter 1—it can also send a message to others that the workplace is not fair ("He gets away with these things because the supervisor likes him. If I did that, I'd be fired"). In this case, however, the manager called the employee in, had

"Leadership without mutual trust is a contradiction in terms."

—Warren Bennis

a brief discussion where the rules for effective negative feedback were followed well, and the behavior did not recur. More importantly, the employee understood why the behavior was reckless and others knew the issue had been handled fairly. Thus, great managers get involved early and correct problems before they become too large to handle.

Some people may be surprised that more managers do not intervene early in cases like that described earlier. In our experience, regretfully, early intervention is rare for numerous reasons. One reason is that confrontation is uncomfortable for most managers, so they look for reasons to avoid potentially difficult situations. Further, the manager may believe that the behavior will stop on its own. This is possible and it has probably happened before, so the manager holds onto the hope that a problem will "take care of itself." Lastly, managers often fail to intervene because they fear that their own manager will not support them. So, while early intervention is certainly the best course of action and actually facilitates addressing problems while they are still relatively small, it is not that surprising that many managers are lulled into a very passive and ultimately self-defeating course of inaction.

When leaders perform these transactional leader behaviors well, they provide themselves with an excellent foundation. At this point, basic performance issues are addressed, relationships should be positive and productive, and employees have a sense they are being treated fairly. Great managers, however, know that what differentiates them from the rest of the pack is the ability to get people to go above and beyond expectations. In other words, it is not about getting people to do what is expected of them; it is about getting people to exceed expectations. To motivate their people to do this, great managers know people need to be able to change quickly, adapt to new demands, and seek out new challenges. Transactional leader behaviors are the way to build a solid foundation, but they will not deliver performance beyond typical expectations. Once a solid foundation has been established through transactional leadership behaviors, great managers use transformational leader behaviors to get their employees to go beyond the call.

"No one enjoys addressing others' deficiencies. But failure to do so sends the message that people are on track when they really aren't. And that may be the greatest disservice a leader can do to someone else."

—Eric Harvey

"You do not need leadership to eat a warm cookie."

—Scott Adams

Practice this!
Go to www.baldwin2e.com

Transformational Leadership: Getting Performance Beyond Expectations

Once a solid foundation has been established, **transformational leader behaviors** "seek to arouse and satisfy higher needs, to engage the full person of the follower."[21] Transformational leader behaviors engage the whole person by asking followers to transcend their self-interest for the sake of the team or organization and by raising employee awareness about the importance and values of goals. It should be noted that many different researchers have derived behaviors consistent with Bass's definition of transformational leader behavior. The contents of these different models, however, are actually quite similar. Professor Phil Podsakoff and his colleagues at Indiana University noted this similarity and presented a model of six transformational leader behaviors that do a great job of synthesizing the different transformational leadership models:[22]

- **Articulating a Vision.** Behavior that allows the leader to identify new opportunities for his or her group and talk positively about what that means for them.
- **Providing an Appropriate Model.** Behavior that sets an example for employees to follow that is consistent with the values the leader espouses.
- **Fostering the Acceptance of Group Goals.** Behavior aimed at promoting cooperation among employees and getting them to work together toward a common goal.
- **Communicating High-Performance Expectations.** Behavior that demonstrates the leader's expectations for excellence, quality, and high performance on the part of followers.
- **Providing Individualized Support.** Behavior that indicates the leader respects followers and is concerned about their personal feelings and needs.
- **Providing Intellectual Stimulation.** Behavior on the part of the leader that challenges followers to reexamine assumptions about their work and rethink how it can be performed.

Transformational leadership was once thought to be a heroic type of leadership performed only by gifted people at the top of organizations. More than 30 years of research, now suggests it is not restricted to any particular function, managerial level, or type of organization. Most importantly, the six transformational major behaviors just related appear to be quite responsive to learning. All of this is good news when you consider the great benefits that follow from engaging in these six transformational leadership behaviors.

For example, in a study of 1,539 people, Podsakoff and his colleagues found the transformational leader behaviors were associated with increased employee satisfaction, employee trust in their leader, and job performance (Figure 9.1).[23] Figure 9.1 shows that transformational leader behaviors are not just "nice to do" but have been shown to significantly improve work outcomes that matter! Other research has shown the effectiveness of transformational leadership in all sorts of industries and organizations. Here is just a sampling of that research:

- Methodist ministers rated high in transformational leadership had greater Sunday church attendance and membership growth.[24]
- In multiple banks, financial performance and commitment increased for 20 managers trained in transformational leadership versus the performance of a group of managers who did not receive the training.[25]

FIGURE 9.1
Average Correlations Between Transformational Leader Behaviors and Satisfaction, Trust, and Job Performance[26]

- A positive relationship was found between the transformational leadership behavior and organizational innovation for the CEOs of Taiwanese electronics and telecommunications companies.[27]
- Transformational leadership was positively related to acquisition acceptance, supervisor-rated performance, and job satisfaction during a major aquisition.[28]
- German bank unit performance was higher in banks led by transformational leaders.[29]
- Sales managers who used transformational leadership behavior had sales representatives that had increased sales performance.[30]
- Shift teams from a UK chemical processing plant engaged in more proactive performance when they received higher levels of transformational leadership from their supervisors.[31]

In other words, when leaders engage in transformational leadership behaviors, employees are more satisfied, more optimistic about the future, less likely to leave their jobs, are more likely to trust their leader, and perform at higher levels than employees who work for leaders who do not display these key behaviors.

As we noted, an important consequence of performing transformational leadership is that followers tend to give their transformational leader extra effort or performance beyond stated expectations. As noted in Chapter 7, this extra effort comes in the form of **organizational citizenship behavior (OCB).** Again, these are discretionary behaviors (not required to perform one's job) that are beneficial to the organization but not explicitly recognized by the formal reward system. Leading OCB researcher Dennis Organ conceptualized the ideas behind OCB and asserted that, overall, OCBs "promote the effective functioning of the organization"—and it is easy to see why.

Articulating a Vision

Articulating a vision has long been recognized as an important leadership behavior. Podsakoff and his colleagues defined the behavior as being aimed at "identifying new opportunities for his or her unit and developing, articulating, and inspiring others with his or her vision of the future." While the ability to develop a vision that will capture people's hearts and minds may be beyond our scope here, the ability to communicate such a vision is exactly what research

evidence suggests you can be taught.[32] More specifically, to increase your ability to articulate a vision you should:

- Repeat the vision often.
- Explain the significance of the vision.
- Appeal to your audience's values.
- Use metaphors.
- Use emotional appeals.
- Speak in positive terms.
- Use the term "we" instead of "I."

Additional research suggests effective visions should be appropriate for the level of the employee to which they are being communicated and that they should not contradict higher-level visions. In other words, when a first-line supervisor communicates a vision to her work team, it should be put into different terms than how the CEO originally presented the company's vision, but also should not work against it. For example, the vision that Jack Welch presented for General Electric—"to create the world's most competitive enterprise"—would need to be converted into action by the lower levels of the organization. In this case, a lower-level maintenance supervisor may have presented the vision to his employees as "We need to constantly maximize our machine uptime if we are going to make this place as competitive as it can be."

Great managers also realize visions need to be described in future terms and be short. The best visions tend to lend themselves to creating a mental image in the mind of those who hear them. The mental image helps create enthusiasm and assists in directing the day-to-day actions of the group.

Some additional specific techniques for effectively articulating a vision on the job include:

- Create a positive picture of the future for the work group.
- Stand up for what is important.
- Adjust plans and action as necessary in dynamic situations.
- Communicate the strategy of the organization as a whole and make sure your actions are in concert with that overall strategy.
- Involve the right people in developing the strategy for your area.

Providing an Appropriate Model

As mentioned earlier, **providing an appropriate model** is leader behavior that sets an example for employees to follow that is consistent with values the leader and the organization espouse. Why role modeling is such a powerful tool can be further explained by Bandura's social learning model (originally discussed in Chapter 1). Basically, role modeling sets an environmental cue in the mind of a person that this behavior is important and should be emulated. Thus, if a leader has done a good job expressing a vision, and then behaves in a way consistent with that vision, these messages come together in employees' minds and provide a clear message this vision is important and that others are treating it that way. See the following list for how to provide an appropriate model.

- Be clear about your expectations of other people.
- Hold yourself to the same standards and expectations to which you hold others.
- Be consistent in your display of the desired behavior.

- Remember that even small indiscretions can have major consequences. For instance, if you were trying to encourage cost savings, staying in an expensive hotel would undermine your credibility.

- Perform desirable behaviors where they can be observed. If no one sees you doing something positive or knows about the behavior, the positive behavior cannot serve as a model.

Consider for a moment what happens when people in leadership positions do not provide appropriate models to their employees. Assume that the vision of your company is to achieve "success through wasting nothing." The company posts "success through wasting nothing" banners around the offices, you get new business cards with the vision printed on them, and you see the company is recycling their paper now to underscore the importance of the vision. Now suppose you learn the CEO and her family are using the corporate jet to take a family vacation to Fiji and that this costs the company $100,000. What would the CEO's behavior do to your motivation? If you are like most people, this type of behavior would send a message that "success through wasting nothing" must only apply to the average worker. It is also likely you would now view the entire vision as a joke and behave in ways contrary to what the CEO espoused.

"Nothing is so potent as the silent influence of a good example."

—James Kent

Providing an appropriate model is important not only for senior executives, but for anyone in a leadership position. The old adage "Behavior speaks louder than words" is true, and even seemingly innocent behavior can speak volumes. For instance, if you stress being on time to other people, you had better be on time yourself. Kouzes and Posner provide a straightforward prescription for effective leader modeling: DWYSYWD—Do what you say you will do. They point out that DWYSYWD has two essential elements—*say* and *do:*

"If you're not excited, how can you get others excited? People will know. It's like how kids and dogs can sense when people don't like them."

—Carol Bartz, CEO Autodesk

> To set an example, leaders must be clear about their values; they must know what they stand for. That's the "say" part. Then they must put what they say into practice: They must act on their beliefs and "do."

Fostering the Acceptance of Group Goals

Fostering the acceptance of group goals is behavior on the part of a leader aimed at promoting cooperation among employees and getting them to work together toward a common goal. The most common example of this behavior is the setting of a **superordinate goal.** Superordinate goals are achievable only when *all* group members exert effort; individual effort alone will not result in goal achievement.

Importantly, these superordinate goals can be either top-down or bottom-up in nature. For example, a newspaper in Washington was in danger of closing because it was consistently losing money, as most readers in the area subscribed to the much larger *Seattle Times.*[33] The smaller newspaper's staff held brainstorming sessions to come up with ways of saving the paper, and a superordinate goal was set around establishing a new identity for the paper. The superordinate goal was that the paper should become "the source of news for the county." In other words, a decision was made to change the emphasis of the paper to county-specific news (the county had more than 900,000 residents). As a result, the paper became profitable and remains so at this time.

Fostering the acceptance of group goals works because the process brings people together to accomplish feats they previously thought were not possible. Group goals provide a sense of purpose, a rallying point, and common objectives to groups of people who are all too often caught up in internal competition and political infighting. Another specific reason getting people to accept group goals works is that the goals have a self-managing feature about them. They serve as useful benchmarks to let people know how they are doing by thinking about whether or not the goal has been accomplished (see both Chapter 1 and Chapter 5 for further discussion of the importance of goals). For specific guidelines on fostering the acceptance of group goals, see the following list.

- Set a goal that requires people to cooperate.
- Make sure that the goal is SMART (specific, measurable, attainable, relevant, and time-bound).
- Encourage people to work together by moving them closer together, and by encouraging informal contact (lunches, after-work gatherings).
- Continually remind people that everyone is "in it together" and that success for each person depends upon the group's success.

Communicating High-Performance Expectations

High-performance expectations are behaviors that demonstrate the leader's expectations for excellence, quality, and high performance on the part of followers. In other words, great managers know that if they expect a lot out of people, they are likely to get it. Yet setting high-performance expectations for many managers is counterintuitive. They often fall into the trap of thinking, "I'll set the bar low so my employees can feel success," or "I'll meet my quarterly goals by not challenging people and getting some quick wins." The evidence is clear, however; if you want high performance, setting the performance bar low will do one thing—produce low performance.

The reason why communicating high-performance expectations works is due in part to the Pygmalion effect. Basically, the **Pygmalion effect** (also called a self-fulfilling prophecy, and named after the character from Greek mythology who "willed" his stone beloved to come alive) is based on the premise that:

- We form certain expectations of people.
- We communicate those expectations to others through behavioral cues.
- People tend to respond to these behavioral cues by adjusting their behavior to match them.
- The result is that the original expectation comes true.

It should be pointed out that self-fulfilling prophecies have been shown to work across a wide variety of situations. And when we say a wide variety of situations, we don't just mean with different types of people, doing different jobs, in different types of organizations. While all of these are true, the effect goes much further. Even rats respond to self-fulfilling prophecies![34] Further, these self-fulfilling prophecies are incredibly powerful, as evidenced by the following research findings:

1. High-performance expectations lead to higher performance.
2. Low-performance expectations lead to lower performance.
3. Better performance resulting from high expectations leads people to like someone more.
4. Lower performance resulting from low expectations leads people to like someone less.

Put simply, if you truly think a person will succeed or fail, she generally will! There are several ways to actually communicate to others your expectations of them. When you set challenging goals or express confidence in another person's

"You have to expect things of yourself before you can do them."

—Michael Jordan

"High expectations are the key to everything."

—Sam Walton

"Treat a man as he is and he will remain as he is. Treat a man as he can be and should be, and he will become as he can and should be."

—Johann Goethe (1749–1832), German poet, novelist, playwright, courtier, and natural philosopher ability, you are communicating an expectation. When you assign tasks, you are providing a measure of your expectations. Regardless of which of the preceding behaviors you use to communicate high-performance expectations (the more behaviors, the better), you want to be aware of your expectations and engage in frequent checks regarding others' expectations of themselves. Great managers understand that a key to getting high performance is to set the bar high. When the people around you start to set their own bars high as a result of your actions, consider this the ultimate success of communicating high-performance expectations. For some specific suggestions as to how to communicate high-performance expectations, see the following list of behaviors:

- Set high standards for your people.
- Communicate the high standards and your confidence in their ability to achieve those standards.
- Let people know you are there to help them accomplish the high performance.
- Encourage workers to seek you out for help whenever they feel it would be helpful.

Providing Individualized Support

Providing individualized support is leader behavior that indicates he or she respects followers and is concerned about their personal feelings and needs. It shouldn't be surprising that this type of behavior is effective; individualized support makes people feel valued, capable, and liked. There is perhaps no more central explanation to an effective relationship than mutual liking.

Examples of individualized support can readily be seen. Some are heroic in scope, but most are relatively simple. By placing yourself in the position of the other person (using empathy), you are better able to consider what the person may need. If you realize that person has been under a great deal of stress at work, finding out what you can do to help is an important means of showing individualized support. It requires being attuned to employees' needs and paying attention to what people are saying and doing. Other everyday examples include:

"You can't be a good leader unless you generally like people. That is how you bring out the best in them."

—Richard Branson

- Genuinely caring and showing compassion in actions.
- Encouraging continuous development and growth of employees.
- Making interpersonal connections with employees (such as asking about a nonwork activity that is relevant to the person like a movie, sporting event, concert, and so on).
- Sending the message "I care about you and am looking out for your best interest."
- Being sympathetic to the problems faced by employees.

These behaviors are not complex, yet the payoff for understanding the unique needs of each employee is great. Research shows that providing individualized support can actually serve as a major buffer to employee stress and burnout. Further, individualized support has been shown to be associated with increased employee citizenship behavior, increased employee job satisfaction, enhanced organizational commitment, increased employee organizational citizenship behavior, and improved performance. Here are some further ways to provide individualized support:

- Work to build positive relationships with others so they feel comfortable approaching you.

- Determine how much support and what type of support each person needs. This can be done by observing employees' behavior as well as asking each person what he or she needs from you.
- Encourage the continuous development and professional growth of others.
- Show you care about others by genuinely caring and showing compassion in your actions.
- In all interactions with employees, you should be sending the message "I care about you and am looking out for your best interest."

Providing Intellectual Stimulation

The final transformational leader behavior identified by Podsakoff and his colleagues is intellectual stimulation. **Intellectual stimulation** is defined as leader behavior that challenges followers to reexamine assumptions about their work and rethink how it can be performed. Leaders who engage in intellectually stimulating their employees refuse to accept remarks like "That's the way we've always done it," or "I'm not sure. That's not my job." These are clear signs employees are not being asked to question old assumptions. Great managers know that without intellectual stimulation, employees become cogs in the wheel, resigned to performing their jobs with little passion or inspiration. In most cases, a little stimulation can go a long way.

Some of the most intellectually challenging people we have heard of happen to work in the restaurant industry. This may not be a coincidence. Think about how much competition most restaurants face—and when good restaurants stop reinventing themselves, they tend to stagnate and not be as successful as they once were. A great example of intellectual stimulation can be seen by the practices of Allen Susser of Chef Allen's in North Miami Beach. Susser gives servers and cooks $50 each to dine at any restaurant with cuisine similar to that of Chef Allen's. Employees return with a short written and oral report on what they have learned.

Another example can be seen in the actions of Matthew Mars and John D'Amico, proprietors of Chez Francois restaurant in northern Ohio. Every January and February they close their restaurant and travel around the world looking for new ideas to bring back and inspire their staff with. In recent years, they have traveled to Argentina, France, Italy, Mexico, Miami, New York, and Las Vegas to see what new ideas and trends they could identify. Keep in mind, this is to run a

"Innovation comes from people meeting up in the hallways or calling each other at 10:30 at night with a new idea, or because they realized something that shoots holes in how we've been thinking about a problem. It's ad hoc meetings of six people called by someone who thinks he has figured out the coolest new thing ever and who wants to know what other people think of his idea."

—Steve Jobs

MANAGER'S TOOL KIT

Tool Kit 9.3   Common Ways of Showing Intellectual Stimulation

Common ways of showing intellectual stimulation include:

- Encouraging the imagination of employees.
- Challenging the old ways of doing things.
- Looking for better ways to do things.
- Encouraging your followers not to think like you.
- Being willing to take risks for potential gains.
- Sending the message "If we change our assumptions, then . . ."
- Making it acceptable to fail if learning from the failure takes place.

restaurant located in a town of about 11,000 people! This translates into a creative menu with recipes that are not seen anywhere else in the region. Not surprisingly, Chez Francois has become a destination for people in the region and is one of the top restaurants in the state of Ohio.

Regardless of the industry, it is always important to keep an eye out for innovative or potentially useful ideas. The real power, however, comes from organizations of people who are all observing what is going on around them and who feel free to share these observations.

To intellectually stimulate others on the job, Kouzes and Posner in their book *The Leadership Challenge* offer some additional specific suggestions:

- Send people shopping for ideas.
- Put idea gathering on your agenda.
- Make it safe for others to experiment.
- Create an environment where new ideas are encouraged and implemented (solicit ideas from people, reward new ideas, implement new ideas even if they only make small changes to show ideas are taken seriously).
- Eliminate firehosing (the process of dousing good ideas with reasons why they will not work).
- Honor your risk takers.
- Debrief every failure as well as every success.
- Encourage possibility thinking ("What if . . .?").
- Send the message to others: "If we change our assumptions, then . . ."

Putting the Full Range of Leadership into Action

The combination of transactional and transformational leader behaviors offers leaders a powerful set of tools. The full range of leadership model is based on the idea that leaders need to use transactional leader behaviors to build trust and to ensure fairness in the work setting. Then the transformational leader behaviors can be used to build upon this basic fair exchange to get workers to excel by inspiring them with treatment that goes beyond the basic exchange of treatment for performance. Thus, it is the pairing of the transactional leader behaviors (needed to put a good foundation in place) and the transformational leader behaviors (needed to satisfy the higher-level needs of employees) that will allow leaders to be maximally effective. This is something that great managers know and put into action!

Practice this!
Go to www.baldwin2e.com

Obviously, leadership is a complex subject and there is a great deal of information to digest. However, it can be manageably boiled down to trying to increase your competence across the three dimensions of leadership: personal characteristics, transactional behaviors, and transformational behaviors. Within the domain of personal characteristics, your charge is to know yourself and act in ways proven to earn admiration. Recall that the recurring traits people admire in leaders are integrity, decisiveness, competence, and the ability to be forward-looking. For an example of someone who effectively uses the full range of leadership see Management Live 9.5 about Jeff Bezos, the CEO of Amazon.com.

Finally, strategize how you can bring the transformational behaviors to life in your situation. Can you identify and transfer a compelling vision people will want to sign on for? What are your collective goals? How are you supporting others? In what ways are you seeking to provide intellectual stimulation to your associates, and so on. The full range of leadership approach is not a simple cookbook recipe, but an evidence-based model of leadership effectiveness that can and should guide your thinking about how to go forward in a leadership position.

⇄ MANAGEMENT LIVE 9.5

Jeff Bezos and the Full Range of Leadership Model

Without doubt, most successful leaders rely upon a combination of transactional and transformational leader behaviors in their day-to-day actions. One case, however, that deserves special mention is Jeff Bezos, the CEO of Amazon.com.

There is no question that Bezos uses transactional leadership and analytical tools effectively. He likes to enumerate the criteria, in order of importance, for every decision he has made—even why he married his wife. The No. 1 reason for that particular choice? He wanted someone who would be resourceful enough to get him out of a third-world prison!

When it comes to being the CEO of Amazon.com, Bezos manages by the numbers. According to Steve Risher, Amazon.com's former vice president of marketing who now teaches business at the University of Washington, "There are fun moments in the four-hour meetings [at Amazon.com], but they aren't fun meetings. If someone comes in without the numbers, it can get ugly pretty quickly." Another indication of Bezos' numerical focus is one of his favorite phrases when someone has a good idea: It's "We can measure that," according to Patty Stonesifer (a former Microsoft executive who's now an Amazon.com director). But, she adds, "It's one thing to be a data junkie who just looks at history, but Jeff takes a prospective view. He takes risks and he changes and changes." It is the combination of these skills that has made Jeff Bezos a successful leader for Amazon.com.

As a prime example of Bezos' ability to convey vision and get people to think about things in new ways, in 2005 Amazon was faced with whether it should make its huge warehouse of data available to outside parties— that is, data that had taken more than 10 years and $1 billion to build, organize, and safeguard. At the end of a spirited debate, Bezos jumped up from his seat and, mimicking a flasher opening up a trench coat, declared that Amazon would "aggressively expose ourselves!" This move will undoubtedly open different possibilities for Amazon and change the way it does business. While this move will certainly be a risk, it also provides an opportunity for new growth and undoubtedly will get Amazon's employees to think about their business in new ways. This is what makes Bezos a good example of a leader who establishes a transactional base and then excels with transformational behaviors.

Source: Deutschman, A. (2004). Inside the mind of Jeff Bezos. *Fast Company*, 85, 52.

DO **9-3**   ## Becoming a Leader

> "Leaders develop themselves."
>
> —Warren Bennis

Leadership development is a lifelong journey and it is never too early to start. The primary responsibility for your leadership development rests with you. This is largely true of all professional development, as 70 to 80 percent of learning occurs on the job and informally.[35] At the same time, successful organizations are very aware that in order to have a strong pipeline of leaders, they must put in place a variety of tools and programs that can facilitate personal growth. For example, one recent study of corporate leadership development asked 350 organizations, "What programs or activities have most positively impacted the development of leaders in your company?" A summary of the results is presented in Figure 9.2.

Although that study was targeted to organizational leadership development efforts, the findings have direct implications for your own personal development. For example, consistent with the theme of this book, all successful development efforts start with assessment. So getting external feedback from multiple sources (360-degree feedback) can be a strong catalyst for personal growth. Further, an assertive effort to get cross-functional roles and stretch assignments seems to be a leadership development facilitator. Third, a very clear message from those findings is you do not develop as a leader by *yourself*.

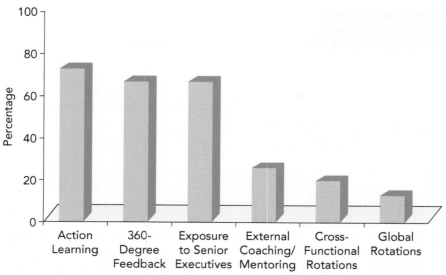

FIGURE 9.2
Key Actions That
Impact Leadership
Development Success

Notes: Adapted from Linkage Inc., Best Practices in Leadership Development (2000).

Rather, those with a mentor or mentors and a network of support are more likely to build leadership capacity early in their careers.

The most important thing for your leadership development, however, is to actively engage in leadership opportunities wherever they might present themselves. These opportunities may be within the context of an existing job (project assignments, job rotation, task force or other special teams) or a social organization. For students, the leadership chances may be in a club or other extracurricular role. Becoming an effective leader is about stepping up and being willing to lead people in a new direction. Put simply, leadership competence comes to those who choose to lead.

Key Actions That Impact Leadership Development Success

Because experience and hands-on learning are so important to developing leadership capabilities, experts in the area of leadership development have suggested that there are essentially five types of on-the-job experiences.[36] One such type of experience is that of *job transitions*. Here, leadership capabilities are developed by broadening one's knowledge base and expanding the functional skill set beyond one's immediate role or technical training. Job transitions provide a situation whereby the manager is a "fish out of water" and must learn to manage in an environment in which he or she may not be the resident expert. Example job transitions include:

* Being the inexperienced member of a project team.
* Taking a temporary assignment in another function.
* Moving to a general management job.
* Managing a group or discipline you know little about.
* Moving from a line job to a corporate staff role.
* A lateral move to another department.

Another experience is that of leading or *creating change*. This form of experience challenges people to start something new or fix long-standing problems. Such an experience allows individuals to practice leader behaviors like transformational leadership to influence others to engage in the work differently. These experiences often come with specific and challenging goals such as "reduce our waste by 20 percent" or "design a new shipping scheme without incurring additional costs." Examples of job assignments that involve creating change include:

- Launching a new product, project, or system.
- Serving on a reengineering team.
- Facilitating the development of a new vision or mission statement.
- Dealing with a business crisis.
- Handling a workforce reduction.
- Hiring new staff.
- Breaking ground on a new operation.
- Reorganizing a unit.
- Resolving subordinate performance problems.
- Supervising the liquidation of products or equipment.

Leadership experiences that also aid in development stem from assuming a *high-level of responsibility.* These job assignments often involve taking on a highly visible project or working outside one's regular role to assume part of someone else's role. For example, when an organization decides to restructure, in many cases people are asked to take on additional responsibilities, which may have the effect of increasing one's visibility in the organization. Such examples may include:

- A corporate assignment with tight deadlines.
- Representing the organization to the media or influential outsiders.
- Managing across geographic locations.
- Assuming additional responsibilities following a downsizing.
- Taking on a colleague's responsibilities during his or her absence.

Significant development can also come from *managing boundaries* and working in situations where one lacks formal authority. These types of assignments challenge managers to interface with key stakeholders outside the firm such as customers or unions. In doing so, the manager learns to manage "laterally," which for most managers requires developing a new skill set. Of particular importance is honing one's skills in influencing others who do not directly report to the manager, such as those sitting on a cross-functional project team. Examples of managing boundaries might include the following assignments:

- Presenting a proposal to top management.
- A corporate staff job.
- Serving on a cross-functional team.
- Managing an internal project such as a company event or office renovation.
- Working on a project with a community or social organization.

Finally, leaders develop through experiences designed to increase their exposure to diversity in people and contexts. This most certainly involves leading in context, where people are quite different than the leader herself, such as a global assignment. Working across cultures helps the leader understand her work from different perspectives, and it challenges assumptions she may have about people. Such assignments might include:

- Taking an assignment in another country.
- Managing a work group made up of people with racial, ethnic, or religious backgrounds different from your own.
- Managing a group that consists largely of expatriates from other countries.

- Working on a training and development project designed to help employees make transitions to global assignments

Beyond these types of job assignments, one type of experience may be significantly valuable to developing leadership capabilities but is the hardest to synthesize: namely, hardships. Hardships represent difficult situations in which a manager must overcome substantial obstacles in order to achieve results. Further, such hardships almost certainly involve situations in which most people simply quit trying, blame others, or play the victim and avoid the challenge altogether. Yet, for those who persist and find new ways to adapt to the reality of the situation, the learning can be incredibly powerful. For example, working for a difficult boss or in a situation where there is unclear direction from management can be frustrating and demoralizing. Similarly, being asked to start a new project with few resources or little foreseeable payoff can make the most industrious employee want to stop trying. All great leaders face such obstacles at one time or another. To the extent to which you can turn these obstacles into learning opportunities, the more likely you are to strengthen your hardiness and capability to lead across any situation.

There are three main things to realize if you are serious about building your leadership abilities. First, it is never too early to start. Second, it is your responsibility, not a company's, to develop your leadership behaviors. This will only continue to increase as job security within organizations becomes even rarer than it is today. Third, it is important to realize that a great deal is known about what to do and how to do it. For some guidance in how to develop your leadership abilities, we encourage you to undertake the process described next.

Unlike many other areas of personal skill development, developing yourself into an effective leader will likely take years to accomplish, rather than weeks or months. As a result, a long-term plan is needed to do this effectively. This plan should consist of the items explained in Tool Kit 9.4.

 **MANAGER'S TOOL KIT**

Tool Kit 9.4 The Leadership Development Plan

Your leadership development plan should consist of at least the following items:

1. Initial Diagnosis: What do you value? What do you want out of your career? Where do you see yourself in 5, 10, and 20 years?

2. Assessment: Seek feedback from others and utilize as many tools as possible (personality measures, career preferences) to enhance your understanding of yourself.

3. Design: While it is impossible to create a detailed plan for the next 20 years, you can seek out opportunities that will help you fill in the gaps in your background compared to the requirements of the positions you seek.

4. Implementation: Take advantage of opportunities when they present themselves. Even if the timing may not be great, sometimes people only get a few major chances in their lifetimes. When key mentoring opportunities, job rotation chances, or global assignments present themselves, these opportunities need to be seized when they help contribute to your personal development.

5. Support: Continually seek out feedback and development opportunities. Many successful leaders have had to take a wide variety of job assignments so they have a better understanding of the business and increased visibility in their corporate environments.

6. Evaluation: Every few years measure your progress. Are you ahead of schedule or behind? Why? What opportunities should you be seizing that you are not? Only through ongoing evaluation will you be able to continually develop your leadership abilities.

CASE CONCLUDED

Project Oxygen is noteworthy for a few reasons, according to academics and experts in this field.

Human Resources has long run on gut instincts more than hard data. But a growing number of companies are trying to apply a data-driven approach to the unpredictable world of human interactions.

Project Oxygen is also unusual because it is based on Google's own data, which means it will feel more valid to those Google employees who like to scoff at conventional wisdom.

Given the familiar feel of the list of eight qualities, the project might have seemed like an exercise in reinventing the wheel. But Google generally prefers, for better or worse, to build its own wheels.

"We want to understand what works at Google rather than what worked in any other organization," says Prasad Setty, Google's vice president for people analytics and compensation.

Once Google had its list, the company started teaching it in training programs, as well as in coaching and performance review sessions with individual employees. And it paid off quickly.

"We were able to have a statistically significant improvement in manager quality for 75 percent of our worst-performing managers," Mr. Bock says.

Google executives say they aren't crunching all this data to develop some algorithm of successful management. The point, they say, is to provide the data and to make people aware of it, so that managers can understand what works and, just as important, what doesn't.

Google tries to point out predictable traps in performance reviews, which are often done with input from a group. The company has compiled a list of "cognitive biases" for employees to keep handy during these discussions. For example, somebody may have just had a bad experience with the person being reviewed, and that one experience inevitably trumps recollections of all the good work that person has done in recent months. There's also the "halo/horns" effect, in which a single personality trait skews someone's perception of a colleague's performance.

D. Scott DeRue, a management professor at the Ross School of Business at the University of Michigan, applauds Google for its data-driven method for management. That said, he noted that while Google's approach might be unusual, its findings nevertheless echoed what other research had shown to be effective at other companies. And that, in itself, is a useful exercise.

Questions

1. What sets apart those that are most effective as managers?
2. Who in your circle would you consider a leader and why?
3. Why would you want to lead?
4. In what ways are Google's findings consistent or different from the evidence in your text chapter?

Concluding Note

Dare to Lead

Some would say leadership is the most important yet elusive skill set in all of management. There is no question that organizations of all kinds are desperate for good leadership—so the need is large, and the opportunity is great. Effective leadership consists of multiple dimensions and is a function of personal characteristics as well as transactional and transformational behaviors that influence positive action in others.

In this chapter, we have reviewed the evidence base for different leadership dimensions and have hopefully stimulated thought about what it takes to earn respect and take a group in a direction they would not otherwise go. Now summon your resolve and dare to lead at your next opportunity.

< < CASE
Volunteering Abroad to Climb at IBM

In July, a team of 8 to 10 IBM employees will travel to Ghana to help tiny businesses make their operations more professional. Another team will help entrepreneurs seek microloans in Turkey, while yet another will create training programs on information technology in Vietnam.

The projects, which were devised by IBM's citizenship group and are being coordinated through nonprofit organizations, have all the trappings of corporate philanthropy. But that is not why they were created, or how they are being used.

"This is a management development exercise for high-potential people at IBM," said Randy Mac-Donald, senior vice president for human resources.

Many multinational companies insist that promising executives do stints in their overseas offices. And many will free up employees to do pro bono work at community organizations. But IBM's program, which it calls the Corporate Service Corps, stands out on several counts. It uses the volunteer ethos to bring together employees who might

otherwise never meet, even as it gives IBM a high profile in countries where it does not yet have a significant presence.

"IBM doesn't have a big footprint in a lot of these places," said Kevin B. Thompson, the senior program manager in corporate citizenship who is running the Service Corps project. "And their experiences will be a lot more useful than research that says, say, that the Internet has a 12.7 percent penetration rate."

Management experts say IBM is onto something.

"As a development tool, this is a four-for-one," said Allan R. Cohen, dean of the Olin Graduate School at Babson College, near Boston. "It's stretching to work in another culture, to work in a nonprofit where the measurement of accomplishment isn't clear, to take a sabbatical from your everyday routine and

to learn to accomplish things when you can't just bark orders."

Indeed, Paul Ingram, a management professor at the Columbia Business School, is planning a similar program for this fall, in which executives attending the school's Senior Executive Program will work with nonprofit groups in New York. Because 80 percent of the students are not from the United States, the New York location is outside their comfort zone.

"The fact that you are an excellent programmer or salesman, or can lead a project in your own area and culture, doesn't mean you can be a great leader outside of your technical or cultural expertise," he said.

That is IBM's logic as well. The company views the Service Corps as a way to learn how well employees work with strangers, in strange lands, on unfamiliar projects. And

(continued)

(continued)

it plans to use that knowledge to customize further development programs for the participants.

Clearly, the Service Corps concept sits well with IBM employees. More than 5,500 of them, from more than 50 countries, applied for the program. IBM narrowed the pool to those who had been designated as fast-trackers, who had familiarity with volunteerism, and who submitted the best short essays on how participation would help them develop as leaders. The applications of those that passed that first cut were sent to the heads of IBM's eight geographic regions, who chose which of their employees to send.

The final list comprises 100 people from 33 countries, who will form 12 teams that will be deployed to projects in Romania, Turkey, Vietnam, the Philippines, Ghana, and Tanzania. IBM said it would select another 100 before the end of the year and have a total of 600 participants over the next three years.

The first projects will not begin until July, but the team members are expected to immediately begin studying the countries they will visit and their cultures.

They will also begin interacting with one another, possibly through a virtual venue, similar to Second Life, that IBM will set up. Each team will have electronic "facilitators," executives who are well versed in the countries they will visit and the types of businesses they will be advising.

After their four-week trips, the participants will go through two months of intensive debriefing to discuss what they learned about leadership—and about the countries they visited.

"It feels good to help in a developing country, even as you enhance your career," said Julie T. Lockwood, 31, a supply chain manager at IBM in Boulder, Colo., who will be on the Ghana team. "This will help my internal resumé more than an assignment in a developed country."

Discussion Questions

1. How does the IBM model help to build leaders? Are there similarities to leadership development discussed in the chapter?

2. The focus on helping in international situations offers an important piece of the IBM leadership development puzzle. From the company's perspective, what is important about international experiences, and can those experiences also be gained through certain types of domestic projects?

3. Do you agree with Julie Lockwood, who suggests that "this will help my internal resumé more than an assignment in a developed country"? Why do you think this is the case?

4. Do you think that assignments in less developed places provide more or less opportunities to engage in transformational leadership behaviors? Be sure to give specific examples to support your answer.

Source: Adapted and excerpted from "Volunteering Abroad to Climb at IBM," by Caludia Deutsch, *New York Times*, March 26, 2008.

SELECT MANAGE WHAT? DEBRIEFS

Making the Transition to a Leadership Position: Debrief

The transition from individual contributor to leader is among the toughest to make. Given the problems in this bank unit, and the lack of trust and respect for leadership that has emerged, your first priority should be to focus on the *transactional* elements of leadership—establishing expectations, rewarding your doers, and providing some meaningful consequences for those who are not performing.

So spend some time learning how your unit will be judged and also understanding what some of the obstacles to achieving that performance have been. Define success by clarifying a few key goals (for example, financial performance, customer satisfaction, employee engagement) with specific targets that you want to achieve.

Devote your time to communicating those goals and to finding ways to help your people reach them. Send very clear signals by rewarding those who contribute to the goals you are seeking but also by identifying and creating improvement plans for those who do not. Do not rush to fix everything; indeed, take some time to really listen to your people and be sure you understand what they are facing in their jobs.

Trust stems from several sources including the integrity of the leader and a sense that she has a sincere interest in leading the group to higher performance. So be visible, walk around and talk with people, even do their jobs on occasion (pick up a phone, wait on a customer, and so on). When people complain about their manager, it generally involves a sense that the manager is not visible, not communicating a vision for the group, not caring about the lives of her or his people, or is being unfair or dishonest. So establish clear goals, regularly monitor progress toward those goals, and consciously get out among the people in this bank branch to know them better, learn what enables and frustrates their job performance, and how you can enable them to reach unit goals.

Key things not to do here would be to assume you are still a peer and obsess over trying to be liked, pleasing everyone and being a good friend. People will be looking to see if you "play favorites"; therefore, it is critical that you apply the same level of standards and expectations to all of your people. The shift from individual contributor to manager is rife with challenges, and demands that you be vigilant in applying the fundamentals of good transactional leadership. It is sometimes noted that it is lonely at the top. While you need not abandon friendships or become distant, you do now have a different role and you will have to act as such if you hope to be successful.

Leading People Older than Yourself: Debrief

This frequently ranks as one of the most difficult and anxiety producing of all the challenges facing young managers. However, as the ranks of older workers increase, many young managers are likely to find at least some of their employees to be older. It can be an uncomfortable, even counterproductive, situation but fortunately there are some good time-tested strategies.

The first rule is to not obsess over age differences. What people of any age want from a leader is that the leader manages effectively, makes it easy for everyone to do their best, and shows respect for the people he or she is leading. If you are confident and open-minded and solicit feedback regularly, then whether your followers are older or younger is not all that important. That said, there are some unique challenges in working with people older than you are and a few good tips include:

- *Be cautious about assumptions.* It is easy to fall into assumptions like older workers are harder workers or that they are difficult to train or will resent your fast progress or whatever. Aim to be open-minded and not ruled by such assumptions and stereotypes. Your older workers are individuals just like everyone else in your group. Treat them as such.

- *Openly acknowledge, don't hide, the age differences, and seek to better understand.* Recognize that older workers' social and work experiences are not the same as yours, and respect those differences. Learning about their personal and professional values and goals will help you develop more meaningful leadership approaches. When people are 10, 20, or even 30 years older, they likely have different needs and expectations from their leader and the organization. They may need different benefits, different work schedules, and even different leadership styles, depending on their age and stage of life. Good leadership requires adapting your style to all different followers anyway, so age is just one of those differences.

- *Respect their wisdom; value their opinions.* Most older workers have a wealth of knowledge and experience that they would love to pass on. Give them the opportunity to do so and your leadership will benefit.

- *Shoot straight with them.* Age and maturity will make them less intimidated by any manager and aware that no situation is ever perfect. So be honest with them (but respectful) and you will receive honest reactions.

- *Do not play games because of intimidation.* It is natural to be somewhat intimidated by an older team member, but that should not lead to dancing around an issue or failing to address a conflict or low performance. People with life experience can usually see through that type of behavior and will lose respect for you if do not shoot straight.

- *Stand your ground, but do it respectfully.* If you are in the leadership position, then do your job. Older generations were raised in an era where they expect you to lead, but are perhaps even more sensitive to

(continued)

(continued)

respect. If someone is older, most likely she or he will be more sensitive to a younger leader being disrespectful, and react negatively when you are not respectful.

- *Be patient and flexible with them.* Sometimes older team members may not be as culturally, technologically, or trend savvy, but can generally make up for it by adding to the team in other ways. They may need different forms of communication or you may need to explain something in a different context.

The challenge of leading people beyond your age is not uncommon and it's not insurmountable. It takes just the right mix of thoughtfulness, tact, and strategy on your part and it can be highly rewarding when done well.

Developing Yourself as a Leader: Debrief

Being a leader means, as Winston Churchill so eloquently put it, "taking people in a direction they would not otherwise go." That is, leadership is more than just executing a defined course of action. It is charting a new direction and inspiring people to pursue that path. A nice three-part scorecard of leadership effectiveness includes (1) exceeds results expected, (2) generates high follower satisfaction, and (3) followers indicate a high level of willingness to continue with you as leader.

Many elements contribute to leadership development, including enhanced self-awareness and a supportive network that includes mentors and effective leaders you can model and learn from. So take seriously the charge to know yourself and your strengths and think about the kinds of situations where you would be most likely to lead effectively. This young person would be well advised to draft a leadership *story* that describes a situation where he was faced with a team challenge and perhaps ultimately stepped up to direct the group in a way that led to goal accomplishment. Writing such a story forces reflection on who we are and how we might lead and is among the best (yet strangely neglected) tools for developing as a leader. Further, he should seek out those with a record of leadership success and look for opportunities to meet with them and learn from their experiences.

But by far the most critical element in becoming a leader is to "dare to lead." That is, you have to find ways to get yourself in positions of leadership and practice the craft. Former GE CEO Jack Welch talked of the power of "popcorn stands"—relatively modest organizational units at GE—for the leadership development of young executives. Welch rightly believed that the best way to develop leadership skill is to be "at the front" leading something—but where the risk and cost of failure is relatively low to the firm and the person. In this same vein, progressive recruiting companies now often ask for a list of campus leaders and create a closed list to interview those on that list—believing that if these young people have some leadership experience while on campus they will have an easier path to leadership in the firm. The point is that no one magically transforms into a great leader. You learn to lead by leading—seeing what works for you and what does not. So the lesson is to find opportunities, no matter how small, to see if you can influence people in a way they would not otherwise go.

10

Team Effectiveness

"If you are not an effective team player in our organization, you are destined to fail. We build it into our reward systems and we promote those who have it. Most people who have worked in a number of teams think they are pretty good team players. They are not. At least not with respect to what we demand of our teams. I did not get nearly enough team training in college and I would recommend that any person who wants to work here, or places like this, take every opportunity to experience teams and get some practice in helping make them effective."

—David Pierce, CEO of Advection.Net

OBJECTIVES

KNOWING

After reading this chapter, you should be able to:

KO 10-1 Describe the potential of teams to exceed the performance of individuals.

KO 10-2 Recognize the disciplines of effective teams and dysfunctions of ineffective teams.

KO 10-3 Identify the key behaviors displayed by good team members.

KO 10-4 Describe team-building interventions that have been shown to stimulate team performance.

KO 10-5 Describe the key differences between virtual and face-to-face teams.

DOING

DO 10-1 Apply rules for determining the appropriateness of using a team.

DO 10-2 Solve common team problems.

DO 10-3 Lead an effective team meeting.

DO 10-4 Apply evidence-based tactics to improve a team's creativity.

DO 10-5 Lead an effective virtual team to overcome a given problem.

1. Helping the Highly Cohesive but Low-Performing Team

"I don't know what the problem is," says a member of a team formed two months ago. "We don't bicker or fight, and we all get along so well. We seem like a very cohesive team, we are really well organized, and we have great members. But the products of our work are disappointing." Another member puts it a bit more succinctly, "I love our team, but our performance stinks."

Assuming that the team does have capable members, what would be potential causes of the team's low performance? How would you go about trying to diagnose what is wrong? What suggestions would you give the team for ways they might go about producing higher-quality outcomes?

2. Getting a Team Started: Leading the First Meeting

One of the more difficult moments is when a team first meets and tries to figure out what they are supposed to do and how they will work together. You have just been assigned to a new team, but after all the members arrive at the first meeting you find no one really wants to say much and you fear this team has a good chance of failing. If your goal is to help make this group a high-performance team, what strategies would you recommend to get them kick-started and on their way to being effective?

3. Dealing with a Problem Team Member

You have been working as part of a five-person team for several months, and it is now painfully clear to you and three other members of your team that the fifth member is not motivated and is just not "pulling his weight." One of your teammates wants to "kick the slacker off the team" and you are prepared to do that if the person continues to contribute so little to the team's performance. The poor performer, however, was included on the team because of his excellent skills and expertise that, if applied, could help you greatly. So your first preference would be to keep the team together, motivate this member to contribute more fully, and generate higher performance as a unit.

So where would you start? How might you approach the problem member with the issue? Are there others you would involve? Are there particular traps to avoid here?

4. Forming and Leading a Virtual Team

You work for a multinational firm and have been asked to form and lead a virtual team composed of representatives from across the firm, to make recommendations for how to improve employee wellness, and ultimately reduce health care costs for the firm. You have been part of many face-to-face teams before but you suspect this virtual teaming may be an entirely different challenge. Is it? What are the particular challenges of virtual teams? What strategies would you use to avoid the known obstacles and maximize the chance your team will be successful.

Introduction

Teams are a hot topic these days, but they represent a paradox. When they are effective, teams can make better decisions than individuals and greatly outperform their best member. Teams can often generate higher productivity and more rapid innovation and creativity, especially for complex work. They can also create more satisfying work environments and places where people are attracted to work and stay. Jon Katzenbach and Douglas Smith, authors of *The Wisdom of Teams*, have even suggested that teams are the single best tool organizations have for meeting today's performance and change challenges.[1]

One terrific example of adaptive teamwork can be found at Southwest Airlines. Under the leadership of airlines industry maverick Herb Kelleher, Southwest became the most consistently profitable, productive, and cost-efficient carrier in the airline industry. It has also earned the Triple Crown award for best on-time performance, baggage handling, and customer satisfaction for several years running.[2] A financial analyst once asked CEO Kelleher if he was afraid of losing

"Great teams can outperform collections of individuals, even when the individuals are more talented."

—John Chambers, CEO, Cisco Systems

control of the organization. Kelleher told him he has never had control and never wanted it. "If you create a team environment where the people truly participate, you don't need control. They know what needs to be done, and they do it. And the more that people will devote themselves to your cause on a voluntary basis, a willing basis, the fewer hierarchies and control mechanisms you need." Southwest Airlines is a great example of creative team building on a very large scale.

But while teams hold great potential for positive outcomes, they also frequently fail.[3] For most people, the very word *team* produces both positive and negative reactions. Although it is said that "two heads are better than one" and that "many hands make light work," we are also warned that "too many cooks spoil the broth." For every case of team success, there is an equally compelling example of team failure. Although some people are energized by teamwork and excel in teams, others are not well suited to teamwork and dislike being part of a team.

Experience suggests there are several common misconceptions and unfounded assumptions regarding what makes teams effective. And since a key step to behaving effectively is to first recognize and avoid what *not* to do, a brief description of five of the most pervasive myths about teams is presented in Myths 10.1.

> *"A camel is a horse put together by a committee."*
>
> —Sir Alec Issigonis

When Do Teams Make Sense?

KO **10-1**

With some proclaiming the wonders of teams, and others pointing to their limitations and failures, how do we decide when and where teams are most appropriate? Teams make the most sense for particular objectives and under certain

---

?¿ MYTHS 10.1 Myths of Teamwork[4]

- **Teams are always the answer.** While stirring sports and military analogies can lead us to believe that teams are universally wonderful, they are often *not* the best way to accomplish a task. If the proper conditions for teamwork are not present, you are better off making individual assignments.

- **The key to team performance is cohesiveness.** It is common for people to talk about their best team experiences in terms like "We all got along so well" or "Everybody liked one another." But high cohesion is not a sufficient, or even the most critical, element for great performance. It sometimes even causes teams to make bad decisions and flounder.

- **The team leader is the primary determinant of team performance.** Team leaders have an important role, especially at the beginning. But teams with leaders who control all the details, manage all the key relationships, and present all the ideas are usually underproductive.

- **The more the merrier.** Though it would seem that adding people to a project is always helpful, teams lose some of their effectiveness when they get too large. The larger a team gets, the harder it becomes to keep people working on the same page, informed of what is happening, and personally invested in the team's performance.

- **The best individual performers will create the highest-performing team.** The highest-performing teams have *complementary* members, willing and capable of playing different roles, and are often *not* characterized by the highest level of individual talent.

circumstances.[5] In other words, teams do not represent a solution for all situations and should not be thought of as a "miracle cure."

First, teams are better when no individual "expert" exists. When there is no clear individual expert to handle a problem situation, teams tend to make better judgments than the average individual acting alone. With a team, labor and information can be shared, more knowledge and information can be applied to a problem, a greater number of alternatives can be examined, and tunnel vision can be avoided.

Second, teams are often superior in stimulating innovation and creativity. Teams are better when risk is desirable. Because of their tendencies to make more extreme decisions, teams are often more creative and innovative in performing tasks than individuals.

Third, teams can help create a context where people feel connected and valued. Human beings crave contact with other human beings and teams can serve to create a sense of community and support, reduce work stress, and perhaps induce people to join or stay in a particular role.

The first team skill, then, is the ability to assess whether or not a team is even appropriate. If you cannot clearly point to the existence of one or more of the three preceding conditions, do *not* create a team. At their worst, teams slow decision making, create confusion, take up too many organizational resources, and serve to detract from individual effort. The key is to use them when they make sense and to understand what makes them high performing. Even if a team is not appropriate, a meeting still may be needed. Later in the chapter, we provide a set of guidelines in Tool Kit 10.2 to increase the effectiveness of any meeting.

Different Teams—Different Challenges

In thinking about team effectiveness, it is also useful to be clear on the type of team under consideration. Most teams can be classified in one of three ways: teams that *recommend* things, teams that *make or do* things, and teams that *run* things.[6] While many other descriptive distinctions exist, our experience is that this simple classification is the most useful and action-oriented in that each type of team faces a unique set of challenges to be most effective.

Teams That Recommend Things.
These teams include task forces and project groups asked to study and solve particular problems. Teams that recommend things almost always have predetermined completion dates. Two critical issues unique to such teams are the necessity of getting off to a fast and constructive start and *execution*. That is, dealing with the handoff required to get the recommendations actually implemented. For recommending teams to be most effective, the team must have a clear charter and include members with the skills and influence necessary for crafting practical recommendations that will carry weight throughout an organization. There also must be attention paid to the handoff from the team to those actually responsible for the implementation. The more it is assumed that recommendations will "just happen," the less likely it is that they will. The more involvement task force members have in implementing their recommendations, the better.

Teams That Make or Do Things.
These teams include people on or near the frontlines who are responsible for doing the basic manufacturing, development,

operations, marketing, sales, service, and other value-adding activities of a business. Teams that make or do things tend to have no set completion dates because their activities are ongoing. Teams that make or do things are the most effective when they deal with "critical delivery points"—that is, places in the organization where the cost and value of the company's products and services are most directly determined. Such critical delivery points might include where accounts get managed, customer service is performed, or products are designed. If performance at critical delivery points depends on combining multiple skills, perspectives, and judgments in real time, then the team option is the smartest one. If it does not, then you are probably better off with individual rather than team assignments.

For teams that make or do things to be most effective, a relentless focus on performance is required. If leaders fail to pay persistent attention to the link between teams and performance, then it is far too easy for a team to struggle and the responsibility for outcomes to be diluted.

Teams That Run Things. This refers to teams that oversee some business, ongoing program, or significant functional activity. Despite the fact that many leaders refer to the group reporting to them as a team, few groups really are. Although they may seemingly be grouped together in some organizational chart or structure, they are often not a team in any real sense. Indeed, when such teams exist, the main issue such teams face is determining whether a real team approach is the right one. Many groups that run things would be far more effective as working groups or individuals than as teams. The key judgment is whether the sum of individual efforts will suffice for the performance challenge at hand or whether the group must deliver substantial incremental performance requiring real joint work products. Although the team option has the *potential* for greater performance, it also brings more risk, and managers must be brutally honest in assessing the trade-offs.

We believe that every organization faces specific performance challenges for which teams are the most practical and powerful vehicle for achieving desired goals. The challenge, however, is to recognize when and where a team might provide unique potential to deliver results. The first and most critical lesson of team effectiveness is to deploy teams strategically, and only when they are the best tool for the job at hand.

High-Performing Teams

KO **10-2**

KO **10-3**

DO **10-1**

While the word **team** is used in several different ways, we use it specifically to refer to a group of people who are collectively accountable for definable outcomes and have a high degree of interdependence and interaction. By our definition, a team is not just people who work for the same manager or whose workspaces are located near one another. Rather, a team is a group that shares responsibility for producing something together. People often confuse interdependence with personal contact. Simply working closely with others, however, does not make a team. Teams are unique because each member cannot complete the work without the work of other members.

As we noted earlier, just because a team is brought together hardly ensures it will be high performing. In the following, we highlight what defines a high-performance team and the key characteristics, or disciplines, contributing to such performance.

"Wearing the same shirts does not make you a team."

—Steve Buchholz and Thomas Roth, authors of *Creating the High Performance Team*

The High-Performance Team Scorecard

Before we are able to identify whether or not a team is high-performing, we need to identify the dimensions by which the performance of a team should be measured. A useful tool for doing this is a team scorecard. A scorecard for determining whether a team is high-performing consists of three dimensions:[7]

- **Production Output.** The products or outcomes of the team meet or exceed the standards set in that context. For example, a manufacturing team that exceeds its quota would get high ratings.
- **Member Satisfaction.** Being part of the team provides people with satisfaction. Members find belonging to the team to be a good experience both professionally and personally.
- **Capacity for Continued Cooperation.** The team accomplishes its tasks in a way that will maintain or enhance its ability to work together in the future. That is, effective teams do not exhaust all their resources and goodwill, but get better at working together for the next project and continually strive to learn from mistakes.

A high-performance team, then, is one that produces high-quality work but also has members who derive value from being part of the team and who are able to learn from each project in ways that make them able to cooperate even better in the future. Any team can stumble onto some success. Great teams, however, strive to understand the reasons behind their performance so they are able to consistently repeat that success.

The Five Disciplines of High-Performing Teams

One look at the hundreds of books devoted to teams would reveal a bewildering list of characteristics that are allegedly critical to creating high performance. Obviously, every team and context is different, and so it is impossible to specifically pinpoint any one ideal team success profile. However, recent research on teams has concluded that, across many different types of teams and contexts, five disciplines consistently emerge as essential to high performance: (1) small size, (2) capable and complementary members, (3) shared purpose and performance objectives, (4) productive norms and working approach, and (5) mutual accountability (Figure 10.1). Other commonly identified disciplines (for example,

FIGURE 10.1
Five Disciplines of High-Performing Teams

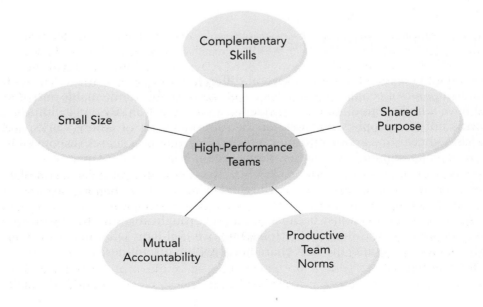

openness and communication) remain important, but none are as critical or as manageable as these five.[8]

What stands out about this short list is that none of the five disciplines are provocative, novel, or difficult to understand. But isolating and understanding the essential disciplines have proved to be much easier than actually *applying* those disciplines to achieve team performance. *Disciplines* is absolutely the right word because it conveys the importance of consistent application as opposed to just knowing or identifying the characteristics.

Team expert Jon Katzenbach likes to make this point using an analogy from weight-loss efforts. That is, there are only a very few simple, widely known, and accepted behaviors for losing weight based on some essential principles (for example, eat less, eat more wisely, exercise more). However, if you do each of those three things only once, and then check them off your list, you will not lose weight. Only through repeated and disciplined application of all three can you expect to meet significant weight-loss goals. Similarly, it is only through the repeated and disciplined application of the team dimensions that your team will achieve high performance. Simply stated, the research suggests you really have to get high scores on all of the disciplines, and do so consistently, if you want to deliver team performance.[9]

Small Size

It is seductive to believe that if two heads are better than one, maybe 15 heads would be better than 5. That is, however, not the case. Just as one glass of wine a day is good for your heart but five probably isn't, there is a point of diminishing returns with respect to team size and performance. Research has shown that, on average, people working in smaller groups work harder, engage in a wider variety of tasks, assume more responsibility for the team's performance, and feel more involved with the team.[10] The larger a team gets, the harder it is for people to meet either in person or virtually, gain shared understanding and commitment, share leadership roles, and so on.

We think Amazon CEO Jeff Bezos' "two-pizza group" is an appropriate guideline.[11] High-performing groups rarely consist of more than 10 people and ideally are between 5 and 8 members. If you have some influence over team size, aim for the smallest number of people who would bring enough complementary skills to accomplish the objectives. Do not be seduced into thinking more is better, and if a natural grouping exceeds 10, break it into smaller subgroups.

Capable and Complementary Members

People commonly believe they are good team players and have strong team skills because they get along well with others or have always been well liked. However, as noted by former Atari CEO and current CEO of Advection.Net, David Pierce, in the opening quote of this chapter, that perception is often inaccurate. The reality is that teamwork is *not* for everyone, and some people are far better suited to making team contributions than others but their identity is often not obvious. A typical team selection trap is to neglect consideration of specific skills and instead opt for people who either are readily available or seem to have the right functional background.

Of course, every team needs enough functional or technical skills to complete their required tasks. If the team's job is house construction, then a collection of chemists is unlikely to be optimal. However, it is not enough for team members to simply perform their functional area of expertise. The team also needs task management and interpersonal skills, and it is often much more elusive to determine whether potential members have those skills.

Fortunately, while "good team player" may seem like a rather fuzzy and ill-defined notion, recent research work has begun to very clearly identify the skills

"We have always found that people are most productive in small teams with tight budgets and time lines and the freedom to solve their own problems."

—John Rollwagen, CEO, Cray Research

"I believe in the 'two pizza' group. If you can't feed the group with two pizzas, it is too large."

—Jeff Bezos, CEO, Amazon

"There is no 'I' in team. But there is an 'I' in win."

—Michael Jordan

and competencies that characterize effective team members.[12] For example, team researchers have developed a 35-question paper-and-pencil test that assesses how an individual responds to a variety of common teamwork situations.[13] The test measures five dimensions of teamwork knowledge, skills, and abilities (KSAs) and 14 specific teamwork competencies (see Table 10.1). Research studies have shown that scores on the teamwork test are related to team effectiveness as measured by peers and supervisors.[14]

Other recent research has shown general cognitive ability and the personality characteristics of conscientiousness and agreeableness to be associated with higher team member ratings and performance outcomes.[15] The implication of these findings for team performance is to not take for granted that people have the requisite skills to excel on a team. Look for ways to gather information about potential team members in order to make informed and systematic judgments about selection rather than rely solely on gut feel or demonstrated functional expertise or superficial personality judgments. In other words, most of the subjects in Chapter 12 can help you select people who are likely to be strong team members, but this is not an area where intuition or "gut feelings" represent best practices.

"Teams do not really become successful until they have rejected a candidate for their team."

—John Mackey, CEO, Whole Foods Market

In thinking about team composition, it is also important to recognize every successful team needs a mix of skills and talents to deliver its performance objectives. That is, the key is not necessarily to search for people who bring high levels of *all* skills. Since people more often excel in limited areas, the focus should be on diversifying the team and considering multiple dimensions and potential interactions rather than solely evaluating members on their individual merits. As coach Rockne astutely noted in the nearby margin quotation, just having a set of individual stars is not the key to success. It is *complementary* members—capable of playing roles and who together bring technical, problem-solving, and interpersonal skills—who are the key to team success. A truly great example of this was seen when the Greek national basketball team beat a team of NBA all-stars 101-95 in 2006. It is important to note that the Greek team did not have a single NBA player on its roster. "We have to learn the international game better," U.S. coach Mike Krzyzewski said. "We learned a lot today because we played a team that plays amazing basketball and plays together."

"As a coach, I play not my eleven best, but my best eleven."

—Knute Rockne

TABLE 10.1   The Knowledge, Skills, and Abilities (KSAs) Requirements for Teamwork

KSA	Description
Conflict Resolution	The KSA to recognize and encourage desirable, but discourage undesirable, team conflict.
Collaborative Problem Solving	The KSA to recognize the obstacles to collaborative group problem solving and to implement appropriate corrective actions.
Communication	The KSA to listen non-evaluatingly and to appropriately use active listening techniques.
Goal Setting and Performance Management	The KSA to help establish specific, challenging, and accepted team goals.
Planning and Task Coordination	The KSA to coordinate and synchronize activities, information, and task interdependencies between team members.

Source: From M.J. Stevens, M.A. Campion, 1999, "Staffing Work Teams: Development and Validation of a Selection Test for Teamwork Settings," *Journal of Management*, 25 (2), 207–228. Reproduced with permission of Sage Publications, Inc. via Copyright Clearance Center.

MANAGEMENT LIVE 10.1

Warren Buffett on Working with Winners

My managerial model is Eddie Bennett, who was a batboy. In 1919, at age 19, Eddie began his work with the Chicago White Sox, who that year went to the World Series. The next year, Eddie switched to the Brooklyn Dodgers, and they too won their league title. Our hero, however, smelled trouble. Changing boroughs, he joined the Yankees in 1921, and they promptly won their first pennant in history. Now Eddie settled in, shrewdly seeing what was coming. In the next seven years, the Yankees won five American League titles. What does this have to do with management? It's simple—to be a winner, work with winners.

Source: Berkshire Hathaway. (2003). Letter to the Shareholders. *2002 Annual Report*. Omaha, NE.

Of course, many groups and managers do not have the opportunity to provide input on selecting their team members. But having the right skill sets in the team remains one of the disciplines of high performance—without that, no amount of process excellence will suffice. So it often makes sense to better understand the skill sets that exist in an assigned team and to consider strategies for filling gaps or reducing redundancies. There is also the possibility that existing members might learn and grow into the skills the team ultimately needs. For a quick related story, see Management Live 10.1.

Shared Purpose and Performance Objectives

High-performing teams have both a clear understanding of the purpose of the team and a belief that the goal is worth pursuing. The best teams are also able to translate their purpose into a clear understanding of the outcome-based goals to be achieved. Indeed, there is growing consensus among team experts that the single most powerful engine for teams is a clear and compelling performance challenge. Without a clear performance imperative, little else matters. High-performing teams know explicitly what they are expected to accomplish and how they will be measured and evaluated as a team.[16]

One of the more straightforward, but curiously neglected, prescriptions is to articulate *outcome*-based, rather than just *activity*-based, goals (see Table 10.2). This is a point similar to one discussed in our chapter on motivation. **Outcome-based goals** describe the specific outcomes by which success will be determined, while **activity-based goals** describe just the activities. Marriott Hotels, for example, uses their Guest Service Index to assess performance of their hotel service employees. FedEx has a similar measure whereby employees evaluate their managers. Outcome-based goals answer the questions: How would we know success? or When would we declare victory? Unless a group comes to terms with their specific goals, the group's members are destined to struggle and are unlikely to ultimately achieve high performance. To be blunt, if you cannot create shared performance objectives, disband the team.[17]

Just as goals strengthen the motivation of individuals, they can also enhance the motivation in groups. For example, in a study of U.S. Air Force personnel, a goal-setting and feedback program increased productivity by 75 percent.[18] In a study of the Notre Dame University hockey team, specific goals for aggressive behavior led to a 141 percent increase in legal body checking over two years.[19] Studies of United Way campaigns have found those communities that set challenging financial goals for their campaigns had better results than those with lower goals.[20] Obviously, group goals can have significant effects.

"The single most important factor for effective teams is that they have a clear goal. When they don't have a goal, they tend to flounder, because they have nothing to work toward."

—Jeff McHenry, Director of Executive Development, Microsoft

TABLE 10.2   Examples of Outcome vs. Activity Goals[21]

Outcome Goal: Win three new accounts in the next quarter.

Activity Goal: Develop a plan for winning new accounts.

Outcome Goal: Reduce the average duration of patient days by one day over the next five months.

Activity Goal: Save money through reducing patient days.

Outcome Goal: Cut in half the time it takes to process and approve new software licenses.

Activity Goal: Reengineer the new software license process.

Outcome Goal: Improve the retention rate among top-rated performers by 20 percent this year without incurring any additional salary or benefit costs.

Activity Goal: Make this company the best place to work.

Outcome Goal: Generate at least one-fifth of our revenue from products less than two years old.

Activity Goal: Build a culture of innovation and new product development.

Practice this!
Go to www.baldwin2e.com

Team Development

The development of teams typically occurs in four phases, and key to the journey to high performance is the establishment of shared and productive norms and a working approach whereby the team can effectively manage—not eliminate—conflict.

One way to improve the internal operations of teams and facilitate team effectiveness is to recognize different stages of team development. Team effectiveness may be influenced by how well members and leaders deal with the problems of each stage of development. The five stages of group development are forming, storming, norming, performing, and adjourning.[22] All high-performing teams ultimately go through the first four stages, while some unsuccessful groups never make it past the forming stage. A key teamwork skill is to help accelerate the process of development.

"The life expectancy of a team is about eight months. The next year, it's a whole new team."

—Mike Krzyzewski

- **Forming Stage.** In the forming stage of group development, a primary concern is the initial entry of members into a group. At this point, individuals ask several questions as they begin to identify with other group members and with the group itself. Among their concerns are: "What can the group offer me?" and "What will I be asked to contribute?" People are interested in discovering what acceptable behavior is, determining the real task of the group, and defining group roles.

- **Storming Stage.** The storming stage of group development is a period of high emotion and tension among the members. Hostility and infighting between members may occur, and the group typically experiences some changes. Membership expectations tend to be clarified and further elaborated. Attention tends to shift toward obstacles standing in the way of group goals. Outside demands, including performance pressures, may create conflict in the group during this stage. Conflict may also develop over leadership and authority, as individuals compete to impose their preferences on the group and to achieve their desired status position.

- **Norming Stage.** The norming stage is the point at which the group begins to come together as a coordinated unit. The interpersonal probes and jockeying behavior of the storming stage give way here to a precarious balancing of forces. The group as a whole will try to regulate behavior toward a harmonious balance. Minority viewpoints and tendencies to deviate from or question the group direction will be discouraged. Indeed, holding the group together may become more important to some than successfully working on the group's tasks. The sense of premature maturity needs to be carefully managed as a stepping-stone to a higher level of group development and not treated as an end in itself.

- **Performing Stage.** The performing stage of group development sees the emergence of a mature, organized, and well-functioning team. The team is now able to deal with complex tasks and to handle membership disagreements in creative ways. Structure is stable, and members are motivated by group goals and are generally satisfied. The primary challenges of this stage relate largely to continued work on task performance but with a strong commitment to continuing improvement and self-renewal.

- **Adjourning Stage.** The adjourning stage of group development involves completing the task and breaking up the team. A planned conclusion usually includes recognition for participation and achievement and an opportunity for members to say personal goodbyes. The most effective interventions in this stage are those that facilitate task termination and reduce apprehension in members in moving on to other assignments.

Productive Norms.   **Norms** are generally unwritten rules or standards of behavior that apply to team members and can be either prescriptive—dictating what should be done—or proscriptive—dictating behaviors that should be avoided. Norms allow members to predict what others will do, help members gain a common sense of direction, and reinforce a team culture.[23] Teams operate with many types of norms (communication, punctuality, level of formality), but among the most critical are those related to effort, meetings, and trust. Examples of productive and unproductive team norms are presented in Table 10.3.

Teams with norms that encourage preparedness and hard work on behalf of the team tend to be more successful in accomplishing their tasks. In a high-performing team, when someone violates a team norm, other members typically respond in ways that attempt to enforce the norm. These responses may include subtle suggestions, direct criticisms, reprimands, or even expulsion from the team. Strong norms create a team culture where members can rigorously challenge each other without taking it personally or getting upset and defensive. Make no mistake, the difference between teams that achieve high performance and teams that don't is very often the productive norms that are established and enforced.

Mutual Accountability

In high-performing teams, members pull their own weight, are rewarded for contributing, and challenged for slacking. Effective teams are characterized by high mutual trust among members and are concerned about the team's culture. High performance is rarely achieved if there is not a belief that members can be trusted and will act in the best interests of others on the team. Effective teams find a way to reward those who contribute, and accountability is determined in part by the team reward structure.

There are two fundamentally different types of team rewards: cooperative and competitive.[24] **Cooperative team rewards** are distributed equally among team members. That is, the group is rewarded as a group for its successful performance, and each member receives exactly the same reward. This type of reward structure does not recognize individual differences in effort or performance.

TABLE 10.3   Examples of Productive and Unproductive Team Norms

Common norms in work teams deal with relationships with supervisors, colleagues, and customers, as well as honesty, security, personal development, and change. The following list gives examples of how such team norms may be both positive and negative.

Organizational and Personal Pride Norms

- Productive Norm: Around here, it's a tradition for people to stand up for others who are unfairly criticized.

- Unproductive Norm: In our team, it is everyone for herself.

Performance Excellence Norms

- Productive Norm: In our team, people always try to improve, even when they are doing well.

- Unproductive Norm: Around here, there's no point in trying harder—nobody else does.

Teamwork Norms

- Productive Norm: Around here, people are good listeners and actively seek out the ideas and opinions of others.

- Unproductive Norm: In our team, it's dog-eat-dog and promote yourself.

Leadership Norms

- Productive Norm: Around here, people respect leaders and seek to take leadership roles.

- Unproductive Norm: In our team, everybody avoids the burden of leadership.

Punctuality Norms

- Productive Norm: To be on time is to be late; to be early is to be on time.

- Unproductive Norm: Don't worry about showing up on time. Nothing ever gets accomplished in the first 10 minutes anyway.

Straight Talk Norms

- Productive Norm: In this team, people say what they mean and mean what they say. We do not walk on eggshells.

- Unproductive Norm: Around here, if you use enough business jargon, you can "BS" your way through anything.

Productivity Norms

- Productive Norm: In our team, people are continually on the lookout for better ways of doing things.

- Unproductive Norm: Around here, people tend to hang on to old ways of doing things even after they have outlived their usefulness.

Cooperative reward systems ignore the possibility that some members make greater contributions to group task performance than others. This type of inequity can de-motivate team members who are high performers (see Management Live 10.2).

Under a **competitive team rewards** system, members are rewarded for successful performance as individuals on the team. They receive equitable rewards that vary according to their individual performance. It provides a strong incentive for individual effort. It can also pit members against each other.

Competitive team rewards differentially reward team members based on their effort or performance. While competitive team rewards may please high performers, they may also undermine the team's cohesiveness.

Which of these two reward systems is most appropriate depends on the degree of task interdependence. Pairing cooperative rewards with low interdependence will encourage unnecessary cooperation, may stifle individual performance, and may also promote social loafing. A similar mismatch can occur when competitive rewards are coupled with high interdependence. In this case, members desiring to secure a payoff from their own efforts will detract from the collective spirit of the team.

⇆ MANAGEMENT LIVE 10.2

Cooperative Team Rewards in Action[25]

R.R. Donnelley & Sons is one of the largest commercial printers in the United States, with products including books, catalogs, direct mail, and phone books. R.R. Donnelley has a very interesting strategy for implementing cooperative team rewards.

At Donnelley, the team reward system is based on a "game" concept. A Donnelley press operator created one game called NASCAR '98 with help from his frontline peers, all stock car racing fans. For the game, a "racing crew" consisted of a team working on an offset press. The game's purpose was to reduce materials waste, and the goal of the game was to reduce waste compared to the previous year.

Each press crew chooses a real NASCAR driver and a Matchbox car, which are then displayed on the wall. Velcro on the bottom of the cars allows the cars to stick onto the Velcro track. Cars are positioned on the track based on how the press they represent is doing that month against its own waste-reduction goals. Competition against the team's prior performance is the main idea because Donnelley wanted to make the goals purely collaborative; they did not want inter-team competition.

There is a winner each month—the press that performs best against its own goals. Each winner receives an actual NASCAR checkered flag, which many of the winning press operators hang in the work areas. In addition, the winning team is featured in the Gallery of Winners photo display next to the scoreboard for the entire year. These monthly winners also receive $40 individual gift certificates that each team member can use at a local shopping mall. If other press crews beat all of their goals in a given month, but aren't the overall department winner, each crew member receives a $20 gift certificate.

Playing the games has taught the workforce about Donnelley's business in ways classroom training never could. Not only do the games increase awareness of strategic business goals, but they're also much more fun and engaging than classroom training. Perhaps most importantly, the games provide a context where cooperative rewards have proven to be appropriate and motivational.

In many team-based organizations, reward structures are constructed so that at least some portion of team members' pay is contingent on the performance of the team as a whole.[26] This promotes cooperation and reduces the incentive for competition among members. How rewards are allocated should also be based on how demonstrable (easily observed) the individual contributions are. In the case of a baseball player, for example, it is relatively easy to demonstrate individual performance. However, for a football player, performance is often heavily dependent on how other players performed; thus, cooperative rewards are more appropriate.

Because team performance is more difficult to track and the actions that people take and the results of the team are often blurry, the use of several sources of appraisal (such as peers and customers) makes particular sense with teams. Peer evaluations can allow members to get direct feedback about their performance and help a team enforce performance norms. Tool Kit 10.1 is a behavior-based set of items useful for peer evaluations of team members.

In short, the high-performing team challenge can be boiled down to (1) keep the group small, (2) focus on complementary skill sets, (3) set clear outcome-based goals, (4) enforce productive norms and conflict management, and (5) match rewards to contributions, making at least some portion cooperatively based (see Table 10.4).[27]

It all sounds simple enough. However, ... simple rules. ...mind you that the battle is maintaining the discipline to ...

> *"I don't give Cs in this course, but you do."*
>
> —Professor explaining the importance of team peer evaluations to her students

Tool Kit 10.1 How to Evaluate Peer Team Members

This team member:	Always				Never
1. Consistently shows up to meetings on time.	5	4	3	2	1
2. Demonstrates flexibility in setting meeting times.	5	4	3	2	1
3. Prepares work assignments prior to meetings.	5	4	3	2	1
4. Contributes a shared amount of the workload.	5	4	3	2	1
5. Encourages innovation among team members.	5	4	3	2	1
6. Maintains focus on team goals.	5	4	3	2	1
7. Maintains an appropriate balance between talking and listening.	5	4	3	2	1
8. Changes his or her opinion when appropriate.	5	4	3	2	1
9. Communicates ideas effectively.	5	4	3	2	1
10. Shows respect for all team members.	5	4	3	2	1
11. Provides feedback effectively.	5	4	3	2	1
12. Is receptive to, or nondefensive about, feedback.	5	4	3	2	1

TABLE 10.4 Dysfunctions vs. Disciplines of a High-Performing Team

The keys to effective teams are not particularly elusive or hard to know—but they have proven to be exceptionally hard to do. The following list aligns the most common and insidious team traps or dysfunctions[28] with the team discipline and action strategy that can help teams be effective and enjoyable. If your team is working well, you're probably practicing all of these in some fashion. If your team is experiencing difficulty, check each step as a team, and you'll most likely figure out what needs to be worked on to bring about success.

1. **Teams get too big.** Keep to an optimal team size (3–10). "If we have too many members, we'll assign subgroups and choose representatives to be a small coordinating team."

2. **Casual or convenient team assignments.** Obsess over team membership and aim to ensure complementary skill sets. "We have the technical (functional), problem-solving, and interpersonal skills we need. Based on this work, no one is redundant; everyone has unique skills to contribute."

3. **Inattention to results.** Establish a shared purpose and clear outcome. "Here are *our* goals and here are *my* individual roles and outcome goals." "We will measure our success by . . ."

4. **Absence of commitment and trust.** Establish productive norms and a working approach. "We enforce norms regarding effort, meetings, and conflict management. We encourage spirited discussion and confrontation but with personal support. Our meetings are tight and disciplined."

5. **Unclear or diluted accountability.** Create mutual accountability. "Here's what we're accountable for, why we have to do it together, and how we are each rewarded if we succeed."

Managing Threats to Team Performance and Decision Making

DO **10-2**

Just as a company can become more profitable in two ways—increasing income or decreasing costs—a team can improve its performance through either building synergies (those activities that go better in a team compared with individuals working independently) or reducing threats. Threats refer to anything that can go wrong with a team. It may often be easier to control threats than stimulate synergies.[29] In the following, we identify the most common threats to team performance—information processing biases, social loafing, and social conformity—as well as strategies for controlling them.

Over the last 50 years, research on group dynamics has revealed that the effects on people of being in a team are exceptionally powerful and sometimes even scary. Four illustrations are:

- **Risky Shift.** When people are in groups, they make decisions about risk differently than when they are alone.[30] In the group, they are likely to make riskier decisions, as the shared risk reduces personal risk. On the other hand, group members may not want to let their colleagues down and hence can become risk-averse (sometimes called *cautious shift*). The bottom line is that when individuals come together in a team, they often make more extreme decisions than they might as individuals.

- **Innocent Bystander.** Membership in a team can sometimes create a **diffusion of responsibility,** whereby members feel their personal responsibility is limited because others will step up and act. An extreme state of diffusion of responsibility among people is known as the **innocent bystander effect.**

- **Choking.** As human beings, we are born with an innate tendency to be stimulated when others are watching. Indeed, one of the great promises of teams is they promote **social facilitation,** whereby individual motivation and performance are enhanced by the presence of others. The presence of others can create so much pressure and anxiety, however, that team members' performance can actually be hindered or below what they could do in isolation. This effect is commonly known as **choking** and research has found it is particularly likely when people are not experts at the tasks at hand.[31]

- **Escalation of Commitment.** A situation where team members will persist with a losing course of action, even in the face of clear evidence of their error, is known as **escalation of commitment,** which we discussed in Chapter 3 as an individual decision bias as well. Perhaps worst of all, the bigger the investment or the more severe the potential loss, the more prone team members are to escalation.[32]

- **Conformity and Obedience.** A team member who has neither the ability nor expertise to make decisions, especially in a crisis, will leave decision making to the group and its hierarchy. As discovered in the famous studies of Stanley Milgram,[33] and replicated often since then, it is surprisingly easy to induce people to view themselves as instruments for carrying out another person's wishes—and therefore no longer see themselves as responsible for their actions. Once this critical shift of viewpoint has occurred in people, the potential for truly objective team decision making is severely diluted.

Practice this!
Go to www.baldwin2e.com

Information Processing Biases

Most people take communication for granted in their interaction with team members, but of course nothing magical happens just because you get together. Indeed, one of the most difficult challenges is to overcome naturally occurring information processing biases, including narrow perspectives and uneven communication.

First, people are remarkably poor at seeing others' perspectives. For example, people who are privy to information and knowledge they know others are not aware of still tend to act as if others *are* aware of it, even in cases where it would be impossible for the others to have such knowledge.[34] Studies show we often grossly overestimate the overlap between our knowledge base and that of others.[35] Further, people wrongly assume others share the same underlying assumptions about the world.

Second, left unmanaged, in any team a handful of people will do the majority of talking, and this inevitably leads to uneven communication. For example, in a typical four-person group, two people do over 70 percent of the talking. Of course, this is not always dysfunctional, but some evidence suggests the people doing the talking may *not* be the most informed about the problem.[36] Moreover, the power of team decision making is lost if one or two people dominate the discussion or overly influence decisions.

A persistent threat to be addressed is that unique information does not always emerge in team interactions because team members are more likely to discuss information that everyone already knows rather than the unique information each may have. Thus, decisions will be biased in the direction of whatever information happens to be commonly shared. This often means that technical information is not given the weight it should have because it may be held by only one member, and teams often fail to make the choices that would have been supported if all members had full information about those choices.[37]

Effective teams are able to muster the discipline to efficiently process the information that resides within the team and involve all members in generating ideas and making decisions. High-performing teams direct discussion toward unique information, minimize status differences, and frame tasks as problems to be solved (via accumulated evidence) rather than opinion-based judgments to be made. To ensure you get the relevant information into team discussions, make frequent use of "go-arounds" (formally allowing each member air time) and direct solicitations of those with known interests and expertise.

Another category of threats is social in nature and include social loafing (people will opt to be free-riders) and conformity (people make poor decisions in an effort to be liked or accepted by the team).

Social Loafing and Self-Limiting Behaviors

Perhaps the most well-known and despised threat to effective team process is known as **social loafing** or, more simply, free-riding. Most of us are well acquainted with this phenomenon based on prior experiences in teams. Max Ringelmann first formally identified this tendency in a simple experiment. He asked people to pull as hard as they could on a rope, first alone and then in a group. He found the average individual effort dropped as more people joined the rope pulling task (see Figure 10.2).[38]

Today, the term **Ringelmann effect** is used to describe the situation in which some people do not work as hard in groups as they do individually. The cause of the effect is a lack of actual or perceived individual accountability. On the one hand, a social loafer may recognize that his or her contributions are less noticeable in a group setting; on the other, a social loafer may simply prefer to let others carry all or most of the workload given the task at hand.

As a general rule, most of us want equitable work sharing and detest free-riders. Team members are commonly concerned they will be left doing all the work and getting little or no credit. This can lead to what is known as "sucker aversion." Because everyone wants to avoid being taken advantage of, team members hedge their efforts and wait to see what actions other members will take. Obviously, when everyone does this, no one contributes. When people see others not contributing, it confirms their suspicions and they try to avoid being a sucker ("I'm no sucker. If these guys aren't going to contribute, why should I?"). Almost anyone that has ever been on a team-based class project is familiar with social loafing. Our experience is that in school-based group projects the most talented students are often the *least* satisfied with teamwork because of having to carry "slackers" and having to do a disproportionate share of their team's work.

Perhaps the best strategy for addressing social loafing is **identifiability.** That simply means to find ways to get each member's contribution to a task somehow communicated or displayed where others can see it. In such cases, people are less likely to loaf or slack off than when only overall group performance is made available. A team contract that stipulates consequences for free-riders and

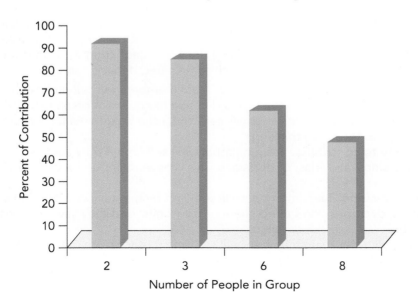

FIGURE 10.2
Social Loafing
Increases as a Function
of Group Size[39]

peer evaluations are good identifiability strategies and can help avert free-riding. Social loafing may also be reduced if the task is sufficiently involving, attractive, or intrinsically interesting.[40]

A related team dysfunction is known as **self-limiting behavior** which occurs whenever team members choose to limit their involvement in the team's work.[41] While similar to social loafing, self-limiting behaviors are a bit different. Social loafers try to make sure that no one detects that they are withholding their efforts and the payoff is that they get away with it. Self-limiters, however, overtly reduce their involvement in team activities because they just do not see any payoff to participating. For example, a team member might say, "The last time we did this it was just a waste of time—no one listened to our suggestions—so why bother?"

Social Conformity

Another recurring pitfall of teams, though sometimes subtle, frequently constrains the effectiveness of good decision making. **Social conformity** involves social pressures to conform to the perceived wishes of the group. That is, members of a team strive so hard to maintain harmony and cohesion they end up avoiding the discomforts of disagreement.[42] But in so doing, they make poor decisions. Social psychologist Irving Janis called this **groupthink**—the tendency of members in highly cohesive teams to lose their critical evaluative capabilities.[43] Janis noted that pressure to conform in highly cohesive teams causes members to self-censor personal views and become unwilling to criticize views offered by others. Desires to hold the team together become more important than the quality of the decision under consideration. To avoid unpleasant disagreements, there is an overemphasis on concurrence and an underemphasis on realistic appraisals of alternatives. Such situations can result in poor decisions.

⇄ MANAGEMENT LIVE 10.3

When Team Members Raise the White Flag[44]

As noted earlier, high-performing teams thrive because of the presence of a shared performance goal and sense of accountability and commitment. The presence of several factors can dilute that commitment, cause self-limiting behaviors, and amount to what some team observers call "raising the white flag" (that is, analogous to surrendering in a battle). Among the conditions most likely to cause such self-limiting behavior are:

- *The presence of someone with obviously superior expertise.* Team members will self-limit when another team member is highly specialized enough to make a decision or comment on an issue.
- *Presentation of a compelling argument.* Team members will self-limit if the arguments for a course of action are very persuasive or similar to their own thinking.
- *Lacking confidence in one's ability to contribute.* Team members will self-limit if they are unsure about their ability to contribute to discussions, activities, or decisions. This is especially true for high-profile decisions.
- *An unimportant or meaningless decision.* Team members will self-limit by mentally withdrawing or adapting a "who-cares" attitude if decisions don't affect them or their units, or if they see a connection between their efforts and their team's successes or failures.
- *A dysfunctional decision-making climate.* Team members will self-limit if other team members are frustrated or indifferent, or if a team is floundering or disorganized.

Source: Adapted from Mulvey, P. W., Veiga, J. F., and Elsass, P. M. (1996). When teammates raise a white flag. *Academy of Management Executive,* 10 (1) 40–49.

One of the most famous examples of groupthink is the presidential advisory group that almost led President John F. Kennedy into invading Cuba and potential nuclear war in the 1961 Bay of Pigs affair. The first Challenger space shuttle disaster was another groupthink situation in which NASA officials disregarded engineers' concerns and placed great pressure on them, ultimately leading them to change their initial no-launch decision despite evidence-based concerns.

A form of social conformity related to groupthink is known as the **Abilene paradox.**[45] The paradox drew its name from an exceptionally clever parable describing four adults sitting on a porch in 104-degree heat in the small town of Coleman, Texas, some 53 miles from Abilene. They are engaging in as little motion as possible, drinking lemonade, watching the fan spin lazily, and occasionally playing a game of dominoes. The characters are a married couple and the wife's mother and father. At some point, the wife's father suggests they drive to Abilene to eat at a cafeteria there. The son-in-law thinks this is a crazy idea but doesn't see any need to be obstinate, so he goes along with it, as do the two women. They get in their car with no air conditioning and drive through a dust storm to Abilene. They eat a rotten lunch at the cafeteria and return to Coleman exhausted, hot, and generally unhappy with the experience.

It is not until they return home that it is revealed that *none* of them really wanted to go to Abilene—they were just going along because they thought the others were eager to go. That hidden pressure toward agreement is an insidious pitfall for many groups. Contrary to our basic human fears that conflict will lead to our team's ultimate demise, it is sometimes precisely the opposite! Often the real performance threat to a team is the inability to manage *agreement*. If you would like to experience the paradox firsthand, just suggest that your team order a couple of pizzas for their next meeting and then ask them, "What would you like on them?" We suspect that the ultimate pizzas delivered are unlikely to be what any member would have ordered individually. Of course, this may represent effective compromise. It also may reflect members' desire to go along and do what others want—a formula for poor group decisions.

So how do you avoid the various forms of social pressure to conform? Of course, you can never fully inoculate a team from a bias toward agreement, but Table 10.5 outlines several actionable steps that can help a team steer clear of Abilene and the consequences of groupthink.

TABLE 10.5 Strategies to Help Teams Avoid Social Conformity[46]

- Ask each team member to be a critical evaluator.
- Encourage a sharing of objections.
- Don't let the leader become partial to one course of action.
- Create subgroups with different leaders to work on the same problem.
- Have members discuss issues with outsiders and report back.
- Invite outside experts to observe and react to group discussions.
- Have a different member act as "devil's advocate" at each meeting.
- Write alternative scenarios for the intentions of competing groups.
- Hold "second-chance" meetings once an initial decision is made.
- Make use of pre-votes and anonymous decision votes.
- Use electronic meeting formats.

⇆ MANAGEMENT LIVE 10.4

How Teams Can Have a "Good" Fight

Effective team leaders know that conflict in a team is inevitable. Reasonable people, making important decisions under conditions of uncertainty, will almost always have honest disagreements over the best course of action. And we know that without some conflict, groups can lose their effectiveness. Teams whose members challenge one another and create a broader range of options to consider ultimately make better decisions. The alternative to conflict is not usually agreement but rather apathy and disengagement.

Unfortunately, however, conflict can also be unproductive and ultimately disastrous for a team. A comment meant as an informative remark can be interpreted as a personal attack. Frustration over difficult choices can evolve into anger directed at colleagues. So the challenge is to keep constructive conflict over *issues* from degenerating into dysfunctional conflict between people. Put another way, the goal is to encourage team members to argue without destroying their ability to work as a team.

In a comparative study of 12 teams, a group of researchers found that the highest-performing teams were able to treat conflict in consistent and recurring ways. More specifically, the authors distilled a set of six tactics characteristic of teams that found a way to "fight" productively.

- They work with more, rather than less, information.
- They develop multiple alternatives to enrich debate.
- They establish and keep coming back to common goals.
- They make an effort to inject humor into the team discussions.
- They maintain a balanced corporate power structure.
- They resolve issues without *forcing* a consensus.

These tactics work because they keep conflict focused on issues; foster collaborative, rather than competitive, relations among team members; and create a sense of fairness in the decision-making process.

Source: Condensed from Eisenhardt, K. M., Bourgeois, L. J., and Kahwajy, J. L. (2009). How management teams can have a good fight. Boston: Harvard Business Publishing.

KO **10-4**

DO **10-3**

Effective Team Interventions

Given an understanding of the basic disciplines of high-performing teams and the most common and insidious threats that derail them, we felt it was important to explore what can be done to effectively intervene to stimulate performance and avoid dysfunctions. We highlight five types of interventions that have proven useful in building various aspects of high-performance teams: (1) holding effective meetings, (2) understanding member profiles, (3) building team cohesion, (4) conducting after-action reviews and process checks, and (5) dealing with a free-rider.

Holding Effective Meetings

If there is a universal complaint among people in organizations, it is that they attend too many meetings and most of those meetings stink! So one straightforward way to improve any team is to focus on limiting the number of meetings—and making those you do have maximally effective.

First and foremost, get in the habit of starting every meeting by asking: (1) What are the two or three most important things we need to get done at this meeting? and (2) How much time does everyone have? Just that opening can help create the sense of direction and urgency that helps avoid the wasted time and lack of direction characterizing all too many meetings. If you feel a need to socialize (which is often entirely appropriate to help build team spirit and morale), focus on the goals of the meeting first; then socialize. But try to keep it short—shorter is always better. Try to do a few things at a brisker pace. Tool Kit 10.2 is a synthesis of the best ideas for running a meeting. Many of the most effective managers keep similar tools as tent cards on their desk or laminated cards in their purse or wallet to keep them on track whenever they gather their team together.

Understanding Member Profiles

Most of us intuitively sense a team will perform better if the members get to know one another. While certainly true at some level, the unfortunate reality is what we ultimately come to know about others is often superficial (family, hobbies) and has little to do with how we might function effectively together in a team. For some guidance on how to behave appropriately on a team, see Tool Kit 10.3.

One tool widely used in helping teams build better understanding of each other on such dimensions is the Myers-Briggs Type Indicator (MBTI) assessment of style preferences. As discussed in Chapter 1, the MBTI is widely used as a stand-alone individual assessment of one's personality preferences. Yet it can also be useful for team building. That's because the MBTI reveals individual preferences with respect to important team-related interactions such as how people prefer to gather information, order discussion, and make decisions.

Collectively reviewing the different MBTI profiles in a team can have a variety of potential benefits, including identifying sources of conflict, providing a basis for improving communication patterns, distributing work according to preferences (assuming people agree with their preference profile), supplying a framework to better understand and resolve conflict, and increasing understanding of how to best utilize all members for useful and effective problem solving.

> *"Our team is well balanced. We have problems everywhere."*
>
> —Tommy Prothro, Former Professional Football Coach

MANAGER'S TOOL KIT

Tool Kit 10.2   How to Run an Effective Meeting

- *Always* work from an agenda, ideally distributed in advance, but at least established at the very start of the meeting.
- Appoint a scribe to record the discussion and outcomes of the meeting.
- Use "go-arounds" and direct solicitations of those with known interests and expertise to ensure you get all relevant information into the discussion.
- Explicitly attach action assignments to specific members and get public ownership (in front of the group) of their willingness to complete the task by a deadline date.
- Even in a short meeting, avoid leading all the discussion yourself. Maximize participation by inviting members to lead different aspects of the discussion.
- Push the team to stay focused on the key meeting objectives identified at the start. Use "parking lots" for good off-task ideas and defer discussion until future meetings.
- Close every meeting with a brief review of what was accomplished, clearly reiterate any action items and which members "own" those items, and push to schedule a time for the next meeting.

Tool Kit 10.3   How to Be a Great Team Member[47]

In today's team-oriented workplaces, it is now commonplace for job candidates to be asked in an interview *"Tell me about a recent time where you were part of a team and describe your role and contribution."* Some progressive organizations even construct assessment exercises known as leaderless group discussions (LGDs) and observe candidate behavior in those exercises. In any case, if you want to be a part of great teams, you need to be a great team player yourself. Teams need members who perform both task and maintenance (interpersonal) roles, and the best contributors are individuals who know what they do well and can match that to the needs of their team. The following is a set of team member behaviors that are commonly used in assessing teamwork performance. It also makes a nice team audit or checklist for assessing contributions of members and the gaps that, if filled, might help a team function more effectively.

Task Roles	Interpersonal Roles
• **Initiating:** Suggesting new goals or ideas.	• **Encouraging:** Fostering team solidarity by reinforcing others.
• **Information seeking:** Clarifying key issues.	• **Harmonizing:** Mediating conflicts.
• **Opinion seeking:** Clarifying attitudes, values, and feelings.	• **Compromising:** Shifting one's own position on an issue to reduce conflict in the team.
• **Elaborating:** Giving additional information about points made by others.	• **Gatekeeping:** Encouraging all team members to participate.
• **Coordinating:** Pulling together ideas and suggestions.	• **Reflecting:** Pointing out the positive and negative aspects of the team's dynamics and calling for change if necessary.
• **Orienting:** Keeping the team headed toward its stated goals.	• **Standard setting:** Expressing, or calling for discussion of, standards for evaluating the quality of the team.
• **Recording:** Performing a "team memory" function by documenting discussions and outcomes.	
• **Challenging:** Questioning the quality of the team's method, logic, and results.	

Building Team Cohesion

The extent to which members of a group actually conform to its norms is strongly influenced by the group's level of cohesiveness—the degree to which members are attracted to, and motivated to remain part of, a group. Persons in a highly cohesive group value their membership and strive to maintain positive relationships with other group members.

The more difficult it is to get into a group, the more cohesive the group typically becomes. The hazing through which fraternities put their pledges is meant to screen out those who don't want to "pay the price" and to intensify the desire of those who do to become fraternity actives. But group initiation needn't be as blatant as hazing. The competition to be accepted to a good medical school results in highly cohesive first-year medical classes. The common initiation rites—applications, test taking, interviews, and the long wait for a final decision—all contribute to creating this cohesiveness.[48] For specific ways to build team cohesiveness, see Tool Kit 10.4.

MANAGER'S TOOL KIT

Tool Kit 10.4 How to Build Team Cohesiveness

- Schedule social time together.
- Get agreement on group goals.
- Focus attention on competition with outside groups.
- Reward members for group results (cooperative rather than competitive rewards).
- Reduce contact with other groups.
- Create a sense of performance "crisis."

The opposite steps may be taken to reduce the cohesiveness of a group. Such actions may become necessary when members of a highly cohesive group are operating with negative performance norms and the efforts to change these norms have failed.

Members of highly cohesive groups tend to be concerned about their group's activities and achievements. In contrast to people working in less cohesive groups, they tend to be more energetic, less likely to be absent, are happier about group successes, and more upset about failures.[49] However, as noted in the section on myths, cohesive groups do not always result in high performance. The critical question is whether the cohesiveness supports high-performance task outcomes. Figure 10.3 helps to answer the question: "How do different norms and levels of cohesiveness combine to influence performance?"

When the performance norms encourage performance and the group is cohesive, the figure shows this to be the best-case or high-performance situation. But in highly cohesive groups, where norms exist that discourage performance, the group is less likely to perform well. This creates the worst-case or low-performance situation in the figure. Members will behave in ways that conform to shared low-performance expectations.[50] The bottom line is that cohesion

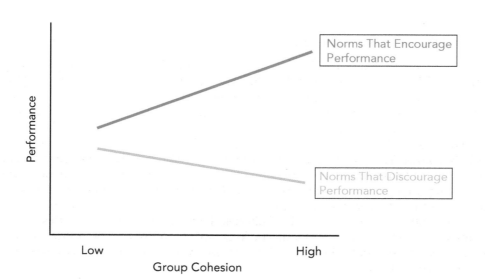

**FIGURE 10.3
Cohesiveness and
Performance Norms**

MANAGEMENT LIVE 10.5

Safe Return Doubtful

One of the most powerful historical examples of extraordinary cohesion emerging in a team is the story of Sir Ernest Shackleton and his voyage to Antarctica. The story has been chronicled in an IMAX film and is the focal point of an innovative management training program created by Philip Morris Co. In the course of the training, managers are asked to place themselves in the roles of members of Shackleton's expedition, and it becomes a rich and authentic illustration of the power of a common purpose.

One of the more interesting aspects of the adventure was that Shackleton advertised for his crew with an ad that read: "Join an Antarctic Expedition! We promise you: low pay, poor climate, and *safe return doubtful*." Yet he still got well over 5,000 applicants! If people perceive an opportunity for an adventure and share in the values and common purpose, it is remarkable what they will tolerate and sacrifice on behalf of the team.

Source: Block, P. (2000). Safe return doubtful. *AQP News for a Change*, June, 1–3.

is important for team performance, but the norms present in the group will dictate whether or not that cohesion is channeled toward high or low performance. Remember, although norms are unwritten, they have a powerful influence on people who simply want to do most anything to avoid the discomfort of breaking those norms. So, while it's important to increase cohesion in the group, it is equally important to pay attention to the types of norms (that is, productive versus unproductive) being set.

Conducting After-Action Reviews and Process Checks

The ability to learn from experience and work smarter as a group is an essential element of high performance. Great teams have "productive failures," whereby mistakes are not seen as a cause for punishment but opportunities for growth and development. High-performing teams do not repeat their prior mistakes; they learn from them!

Military commanders have long recognized that, in life-or-death situations, making the same mistake twice, or not learning from prior failures, can be catastrophic. Tool Kit 10.5 is adapted from a U.S. Army best practice and represents a targeted process for ensuring that teams are conscious about what they are doing well—and not so well (see Chapter 3 for further description of After Action Reviews).

Dealing with a Free-Rider

With respect to dealing with social loafing, you should consider three preliminary steps before approaching a slacking teammate. The first step is to correctly state the issue in terms of the demonstrated behaviors, not labels like "unmotivated" or "lazy." Second, ask yourself whether it is legitimate for you to give feedback about the perceived problem. That is, does the behavior affect the team's or other members' ability to get results, or is the behavior damaging a working relationship within the team? Third, consider whether you have collected a *balanced* set of facts about the situation? Often when we draw conclusions (as reflected when

⚒ MANAGER'S TOOL KIT

Tool Kit 10.5 Conducting a Team Process Check

To help assess whether your team is operating effectively, have each team member complete a process check form, rating the team's functioning on a 10-point scale on a set of dimensions that ensure good team functioning. Questions might include:

- How satisfied are you that your ideas are heard by the team?
- Are our team outcome goals clear and understood by all team members?
- Rate the quality of decision making in the team.
- How well does the team follow its agenda and meet agreed-upon deadlines?
- How well does the team follow its own ground rules?
- How well does the team fully utilize people's skill sets?
- Rate your level of comfort in asking other team members for help.
- How well does the team resolve differences of opinion?
- Overall, how would you rate the quality of the team's functioning ability?

general labels are used to describe a situation), we really don't have adequate facts upon which to make an informed judgment.

One strategy for trying to actively reduce loafing is to address the issue before it happens, by creating spoken norms within the team. That is, before a goal gets set, a task is assigned, or work divided, the team might discuss and agree upon the consequences for members who do not pull their own weight. This type of **social contracting** can help create a higher level of accountability and will allow for a common reference point all members can refer to should freeloading occur.

Thomas Watson, founder of IBM, was once asked, "Mr. Watson, how many people do you have working for you?" His response: "About half."

Creativity in Teams

DO **10-4**

As global competition rises and organizational challenges become ever more complex, there is an increasing premium on *creativity* in teams. Creativity is bringing into existence a new or novel idea, and this ability can often be hard to cultivate in teams. It might be tempting to think creativity stems from a lack of structure and procedure, but managing for more creativity in teams is not all about "letting go." Teams that produce creative results generally have an environment that encourages and rewards creativity—they don't just *hope* it happens. As management expert Peter Drucker has said, "Most of what happens in successful innovations is not the happy occurrence of a blind flash of insight but, rather, the careful implementation of an unspectacular but systematic management discipline."

The two critical success factors that promote more creativity in teams are (1) a climate of trust and risk taking, and (2) the disciplined use of creative problem-solving tools and processes.

Practice this!
Go to www.baldwin2e.com

A Climate of Trust and Risk Taking

Creative teams have safe environments marked by openness, mutual trust, and a willingness to challenge each other's ideas. On such teams, members are willing to share information and to fully express differences in assumptions and

TABLE 10.6   Idea Growers vs. Idea Killers

One of the keys to creativity is to use language that embraces and encourages creative ideas rather than prematurely suppresses them. The following are two sets of common phrases in organizations:

Idea Killers
• We tried it before.
• That will never work.
• It would cost too much.
• That's not our job.
• You can't do that here.
• Our customers would never go for that.
• That's not how we have always done it.
• What we have is good enough.
• You may be right, but . . .
• If it ain't broke, don't fix it.

Idea Growers
• How could we improve . . .?
• Who else can build on that?
• How many ways could we . . .?
• May I ask a question?
• What have we missed?
• Who else would be affected?
• What would happen if . . .?

Source: Gorman, C. K. (2000). *Creativity in business: A practical guide for creative thinking.* Menlo Park, CA: Crisp Publications.

interpretations. Team members see mistakes as learning experiences and part of the creative process. The team avoids "idea killer" phrases and places a premium on "idea growers" (Table 10.6).

Creative Problem-Solving Techniques

Having a set of techniques to help take advantage of the different talents of your team is a second key to creative team problem solving. Among the most successful methods for generating creative thought are an encouragement of divergent thinking, subdivision, analogies, and problem reversal.

Divergent Thinking

Most intuitive attempts to solve problems rely on **convergent thinking**—starting with a defined problem and then generating alternatives to solve it. Convergent thinking is oriented toward deriving the single best (or correct) answer to a clearly defined question. It emphasizes speed, accuracy, and logic and focuses on accumulating information, recognizing the familiar, reapplying set techniques, and preserving the already known. It is based on familiarity with existing knowledge and is most effective in situations where a ready-made answer exists and needs simply to be recalled from stored information.

Divergent thinking, by contrast, involves producing multiple or alternative answers from available information. It requires making unexpected combinations, recognizing links among remotely associated issues, and transforming information into unexpected forms. Answers to the same question arrived at via divergent thinking may vary substantially from person to person but be of equal value. They may never have existed before and thus are often novel, unusual, or surprising.

"Creativity is more than just being different. Anybody can be plain weird, that's easy. Making the simple awesomely simple, that's 'creativity.'"

—Charles Mingus, jazz legend

Subdivision

One technique to stimulate divergent thinking is **subdivision,** or the process of breaking things, such as problems, products, or services, into their smallest component parts or attributes. Once a problem or item is subdivided, think about changes to each individual part, including those that seem on the surface like they could never work. The number of alternatives generated is likely to be far greater, and often the best creativity stems from the wild and "out there" ideas included in a longer list.

In a similar fashion, it can be useful to have a question checklist to push creative buttons in a team. Useful questions for prompting creativity include:

- What else could this be used for?
- What else could be used instead?
- How could it be adopted or modified for a new use?
- What if it were larger, thicker, heavier, or stronger?
- What if it were smaller, thinner, or lighter?
- How might it be rearranged or reversed?
- In my wildest dreams, how would this problem be resolved?

Analogies

Developing creative ideas when you are starting with a blank slate is tough. Today it is popular jargon to "think outside the box," but some recent authors have argued that at times it is more helpful to think inside the box or at least conceptualize a different box.[51] Consistent with that notion, one well-tested technique for improving creative problem solving involves using **analogies.** The goal of analogies is to help make the strange familiar or the familiar strange. That is, team members put something they don't know in terms of something they do, or they expand thinking by taking a familiar issue and relating it in a new or distinctive context. Some good questions to ask when forming analogies are:

- What does this remind me of?
- What does this make me feel like?
- What is this similar to?
- What *isn't* this similar to?

Many creative solutions have been generated via the use of analogies. FedEx was modeled after the hub and spokes of a wheel. Taco Bell, in turn, used the FedEx model as an analogy to help conceive how to get small stores in diverse locations the inventory they needed. When using analogies, it is important to find analogs that can be readily visualized or pictured by your audience (for example, soccer games, crowded malls, making breakfast).

For example, imagine that you work at a bank and your top marketing person comes to your team with an idea to redesign the customer service areas of

"Analogies, it is true, decide nothing, but they can make one feel more at home."

—Sigmund Freud

the bank. She says, "We want the bank to be less formal—hipper and cooler and more inviting to our young professional customers." How do you envision the new space?" We suspect that your mind is probably a blank. On the one hand, you have a blank slate to work from and no constraints—but the lack of constraints can be paralyzing, not liberating. Moreover, your team might sit at the conference-room table and nod together at the idea of "being more inviting to young professionals," but secretly the team members are envisioning success very differently. One member imagines piping in music, while another conceives of a playroom for children, while a third is dreaming of a more friendly and outgoing bank teller staff.

But what if your marketing person had started with an analogy like, say, "We want our customer service spaces to be more like Starbucks and less like the Post Office." Suddenly it is just so much easier to picture the goal. However, also notice that the Starbucks vision is constraining and takes options off the table—yet it is those very constraints that in some cases will dramatically improve the chances your team will hit the goal.[52]

Problem Reversal

A final technique for generating creative ideas is **reversing the problem.** As we discuss in Chapter 3, reframing a problem is sometimes all it takes to redirect energy toward creative solutions. So take a problem and think of the opposite approach, and force seemingly unrelated attributes together. For example, suppose you work at a restaurant and are faced with the problem that guests are unhappy with the service. Maybe one angle would be to treat the guests as *servers* and allow them to help prepare and serve their own meal (open grills are now very popular). ATMs were conceived in that same way (that is, have less employee service and more convenient opportunity for customers to serve themselves). The idea is to reverse or contradict the existing understanding of a problem to expand the alternatives considered. So maybe the way to higher student satisfaction is to make a course *harder*, not easier, or perhaps the service in a retail store is *too* fast, or a map *too* detailed. Such differing perspectives often challenge and provoke and can serve to enhance team creativity.

KO **10-5**

DO **10-5**

Virtual Teams and Meetings

Not long ago, the mention of a team evoked images of a group of people in a nice meeting room, huddled around a conference table, with someone writing notes on a flip chart. Today, teams are often **virtual teams,** with people working in remote locations. Virtual arrangements can save time and travel expenses and can allow people to belong to a team whether or not they live or work in close proximity to each other. Virtual membership also allows people to more easily accommodate their personal and professional lives.[53]

"Technology . . . the knack of so arranging the world that we don't have to deal with it."

—Max Frisch, Swiss author, 1957

While much has been made of the virtual revolution and the need to develop a new set of virtual skills (virtual communication skills, virtual collaborative skills, and so on), the truth is that the five fundamental disciplines of high team performance remain the same. Indeed, the most significant difference is that, because people are dispersed and there is no naturally occurring monitoring and social pressure, virtual teams demand even *higher attention* to those disciplines. That is, for virtual teams to achieve high performance it is even more critical to ensure that the group is kept to a manageable number, the right members are selected, goals and norms are established and shared, a productive working approach is facilitated, and members feel a mutual accountability for team outcomes.[54] Table 10.7 is a summary of lessons learned from a research study conducted on multiple virtual teams at Sabre Corporation.

TABLE 10.7 Conventional Wisdom, Team Challenges, and Lessons Learned from Sabre

Conventional Wisdom	Virtual Team Challenge	Lessons Learned from Sabre
Building trust in virtual teams is extremely difficult, given the limited face-to-face interaction.	Establishing trust based on performance consistency rather than social bonds.	• Rapid responses to virtual teammates foster trust. • Establishing norms around communication patterns is key. • Team leaders play important roles in reinforcing timeliness and consistency of team interaction. • Levels of trust based on performance compensate for lack of social interaction.
Virtual teams will struggle with creating synergy.	Overcoming group-process losses associated with virtual teams.	• Extensive training in virtual teamwork helps overcome process loss. Training in virtual team leadership, conflict management, and meetings management is particularly valuable for overcoming process loss. • Adaptation of decision-making software facilitates problem solving and decision making.
Virtual team members experience isolation and detachment.	Creating a virtual environment of inclusiveness and involvement.	• Consider individual differences in preferences for working virtually when selecting virtual team members. • Give virtual team members a realistic preview of the potential for feeling detached. • Team leaders play a critical role in maintaining continuous contact with remotely situated virtual team members. • Redesign job assignments to provide virtual team members with occasional face-to-face customer contact to reduce isolation. • Convene face-to-face meetings for virtual team members of company-sponsored conferences.
Because of the need to communicate via information technology, selection of virtual team members overemphasizes technical skills and underemphasizes interpersonal and teamwork skills.	Identifying virtual team members who have a healthy balance of technical and interpersonal skills.	• Use behavioral interviewing techniques and simulations as part of the selection process. • Use panels of current virtual team members to help recruit and select new team members and ensure the appropriate balance of technical and interpersonal skills. The panel approach has the additional benefit of building support and facilitating socialization of the newly selected virtual team member.
Assessment and development of virtual team members are very limited in the virtual team environment.	Establishing the appropriate quantitative and qualitative data for accurate assessment of virtual team members.	• Use of a comprehensive "balanced scorecard" approach provides valuable quantitative data on team performance. • Monitor group communication archives to assess subjective factors, including idea generation, leadership, and problem-solving skills.
	Developing creative approaches for providing feedback, coaching, and support for virtual team members.	• Use team member peer reviews to assess contributions to team effectiveness. • Use "richer" communication media, including video-conferencing, for performance evaluation feedback. • Identify online training and development resources to address virtual team members' knowledge, skills, and abilities in need of further improvement.

Source: Adapted From Table 1 of Kirkman, B. L., Rosen, B., Tesluk, P. E., Gibson, C. B., and McPherson, S. O. (2002). Five challenges to virtual team success: Lessons from Sabre, Inc. *Academy of Management Executive,* Vol. 16, No. 3, August, 67–79.

For example, one study of 29 virtual teams that communicated strictly by e-mail over a six-week period found that the most successful teams shared three specific characteristics. First, they began their interactions with a series of social messages—introducing themselves and providing some personal background—before focusing on the work at hand. Second, they set clear goals and roles for each team member, thus enabling all team members to identify with one another. Third, all team members consistently displayed eagerness, enthusiasm, and an intense action orientation in their messages (mutual accountability).[55]

Electronic Meetings

Whether a team is geographically dispersed and primarily virtual or not, some evidence suggests that electronic meetings (systems that allow for simultaneous discussions) can be superior to face-to-face gatherings, at least for certain types of group tasks. The major advantages of electronic meetings are anonymity, honesty, and speed. Participants can anonymously type any message they want and it flashes on the screen for all to see. It also allows people to be honest without penalty or the pressures of social conformity. And it's fast because chitchat is eliminated, discussions don't digress, and many participants can "talk" at once without stepping on one another's toes.

More specifically, some studies have found that electronic meetings can be as much as 55 percent faster than traditional face-to-face meetings.[56] On the other hand, electronic meetings are not always advisable. For example, they are not good for establishing relationships, dealing with sensitive issues, or persuading a team to fully commit to a course of action. The bottom-line implication is that it makes sense to use electronic meeting technologies for one part of the team process. If you really want to get creative, innovative, high-quality ideas, then electronic discussion is clearly better than verbal discussion. On the other hand, if you want to build a good team, strengthen the relationships, and allow for opportunities for mentoring and individual growth, verbal discussion is better. Table 10.8 provides a nice template for determining whether an electronic or face-to-face meeting would be most productive.

TABLE 10.8   When to Meet Face-to-Face vs. Electronically

Face-to-Face

- For first meetings when team members are trying to create a common identity, establish goals, and hammer out a productive working approach.
- When the goal of the meeting is to persuade members to commit to a particular course of action.
- When the team must deal with highly sensitive issues.
- When conflicts must be resolved.
- When the team is acknowledging important milestones or celebrating successes.
- When privacy and confidentiality of team discussions must be maintained.

Electronically

- When generating new ideas.
- When the goal is fact-finding or solving problems that have one right answer.
- When gathering preliminary information and opinions prior to a face-to-face meeting.
- When keeping team members informed between meetings.
- When the goal is to reduce status effects or groupthink.

MANAGEMENT LIVE 10.6

The Golf Scramble: The Underlying Magic of Teams at Work[57]

In its usual format, the game of golf is among the most individual of all sports. Every shot is under the control of the player and, unlike say tennis or baseball, even the behavior of opponents has no bearing on one's individual play. Team scores are really just the collection of scores of all members. But the popular "scramble" format changes all that. In a scramble format, players in a foursome hit their own ball but then play the next ball from the best position of all four shots. That is, even if you shanked your own drive, you get to grab your miserable ball and place it right where the best shot of your team landed. If you have ever played in such a format, we suspect that, like us, you would notice some of the magic of teams at work. For example, in one recent scramble event, the first author made the following observations. Each of our four team members had some terrible shots, some decent shots, and occasionally some really good shots—which provided the opportunity to both laugh at and praise each other. We offered advice to each other as well as made joint decisions about which ball was in the best position for our next shot. At the end of the round, we tallied our score and found that we were three shots under par—far better than any one of us could ever have done individually, and far more fun. When they work like this, teams can be magic.

CASE CONCLUDED

Formed in 1995, Team Concepts specializes in bringing the Olympic notions of high performance and inspirational and transformational leadership into corporate culture. Rowing, movie-making, festival games, stock car racing, and more provide the catalyst for creating teams with synergy. Dan Lyons' Team Concepts combines the Outward Bound experience, business school concepts, and motivational speaking into one. He further incorporates his own experience as a world-class rower—and the sport of rowing itself—as one of the purest examples of teamwork.

So what is the secret sauce of finding synergy? Lyons' core philosophy is embodied in *The Eight Secrets of High Performance Teams,* his brief description of the essentials for realizing the latent potential of individuals and teams. "Competition is in everybody," Lyons says. "But it gets a bad name because some compete outside the rules. Competition is not philosophical; it's very practical—just like capitalism, because in 100 percent of the cases, capitalism has won."

The beauty of rowing as a context for learning team performance is that it absolutely demands coordination and "flow" with teammates to achieve high performance. Indeed, those acting alone, no matter how intense, strong, or technically proficient, generally *detract* from the speed of a boat.

When conducting his team-building sessions using crew boats, Lyons randomly assigns teams and the random assignment inevitably creates some imbalances in size and athleticism—but it doesn't matter. Among novice rowers, says Lyons, any team that truly trusts each other and achieves flow can easily defeat a team of highly athletic members.

Team Concepts' Eight Secrets of High-Performance Teams:

Secret 1: Everyone wants to be part of something bigger.

Secret 2: Everyone wants to feel valued.

Secret 3: Define performance objectives. Clearly articulate specific team objectives, including the expected time frame for achieving those objectives; create challenging and achievable objectives.

Secret 4: Ennoble the effort. Paint a verbal picture of what the future could look like, helping individuals see themselves within that picture; highlight the team's intrinsic value in its historical and organizational framework.

Secret 5: Empower individuals within team synergy. Provide the framework for individual accomplishments that support team objectives.

(continued)

> CASE CONCLUDED *(continued)*

Secret 6: Emphasize personal responsibility, challenging individuals to make a commitment to excellence. Develop the value of the team's objectives within individual members.

Secret 7: Celebrate the journey. Win every day, and create awareness of the rewards that occur along the journey.

Secret 8: Positive, engaged energy. Draw the best from others by showing the best from yourself.

Questions

1. What do the examples of lower-talented crew teams defeating more talented ones teach us about measuring and assembling teams? Are there strategies for selecting the best teams rather than just the best individuals?

2. Based on what you learned in this chapter, what would you recommend to Coach Preczewski for improving the performance of his Varsity boat?

3. Given that top individuals have the greatest *potential* for performance, what are possible strategies or interventions to help them reach that potential?

4. Critique Team Concepts' list of high-performance teams. What is most important in that list? What might be missing? Which of those is most difficult to achieve?

Source: Snook, S., and Polzer, J. T. (2004). The Army Crew Team. *Harvard Business Review Case # 9-403-131*, March 30.

Concluding Note

"Nothing great was ever achieved without enthusiasm."

—George Bernard Shaw

As we have repeatedly emphasized throughout this book, many principles and tools of great managers are very straightforward and make so much intuitive sense that they start to sound easy—and that is a grave trap. Team building is exceedingly hard work and it takes time and discipline. Remember that not all great team members or team processes started that way. The predictable reality is you will be part of teams that flounder and your results will sometimes be disappointing. One goal you should have with any team you join is to learn something you can take with you as you navigate a world filled with organizational teams that could use your help. When things do not go well, ask yourself (and your team), "What can we learn from this?" and go on bravely with a tolerance and enthusiasm for the struggle. In the end, few things are more satisfying and outright fun than being on a team that really works.

KEY TERMS

Abilene paradox 359
activity-based goals 349
adjourning stage 351
analogies 367
choking 355
competitive team rewards 352
convergent thinking 366
cooperative team rewards 351
diffusion of responsibility 355
divergent thinking 367
escalation of commitment 355

forming stage 350
groupthink 358
identifiability 357
innocent bystander effect 355
norming stage 350
norms 351
outcome-based goals 349
performing stage 351
reversing the problem 368
Ringelmann effect 357
risky shift 355

self-limiting behavior 358
social conformity 358
social contracting 365
social facilitation 355
social loafing 357
storming stage 350
subdivision 367
team 345
virtual teams 368

> < < **CASE**
> ## Small Teams, No Titles: Life at W. L. Gore[58]

The classic Gore culture began in the basement of the home of Bill Gore, who left DuPont in 1958 to create his own enlightened version of the workplace. Gore built the company upon four core principles—fairness; the freedom to encourage others to grow in knowledge, skill, and responsibility; the ability to honor one's own commitments; and consultation with others before taking action that could affect the company "below the waterline." Instead of the typical corporate hierarchy, he created a "flat lattice" organization that had not only no titles, but also no chains of command or predetermined channels of communication.

In Gore's model, associates communicate directly with one another and are accountable to their peers rather than bosses. Ideally, leaders in the company emerge naturally by demonstrating special knowledge, skill, or experience—"followship."

The $1.84 billion company's flat organizational structure makes it exceptionally nimble. "If someone has an idea for a new product, they don't have to go up a hierarchy to find some boss to approve it," says John Sawyer, chairman of the department of business administration at the University of Delaware. "Instead, they have to find peers in the organization who support the idea and will work with them. That open style of communication allows ideas to come up from the bottom."

The company developed shred-resistant Glide dental floss, for example, after an associate wondered whether Gore's industrial fibers could be used for cleaning teeth as well. Engineers at Gore's Flagstaff, Arizona, plant worked for three years on their own to develop plastic-coated guitar string before they offered the product of their inspiration to the company, which successfully marketed it.

In his bestselling book *The Tipping Point*, author Malcolm Gladwell describes Gore's traditional practice of limiting the size of its plants to roughly 150 workers, because that was the largest group of people who could know one another well enough to converse in the hallway. Today, however, human resources associate Brinton works in a plant with more than 300 fellow associates. More important, associates in multiple countries may have to work together to service a single multinational client. In addition to encouraging the old hallway chats, Gore now has regular plant communications meetings where leaders share with the associates news about company performance, discuss safety, and introduce new workers.

"It's a challenge to get bigger while staying small," Brinton says. Associates still work in small teams and frequently meet face to face—though in some cases the teammates may be on several continents and do much of their communicating by phone or e-mail. "It's tough to build relationships by e-mail," Brinton says. "For us, that's a work in progress right now. We do bring global teams together physically on a fairly regular basis." Brinton can't calculate the expense of such travel, but says it is substantial.

In recent years, Gore has also begun subjecting its product development process to more discipline, the University of Delaware's Sawyer says. While associates still initiate their own projects and build support for them, an evaluation team measures their progress against metrics or goals that must be reached in order for a project to progress.

Gore's recruiters still spend months and sometimes years filling job vacancies because it isn't easy to find people who not only have the right skills, but also are temperamentally and intellectually suited for the unorthodox environment. "It isn't a company for everyone," Brinton says. "It takes a special kind of person to be effective here—someone who is really passionate about sharing information, as opposed to controlling it. Someone

(continued)

(continued)

who can handle a degree of ambiguity, as opposed to 'Here's my job and I only do these tasks.' Someone who's willing to lift his or her head up from the desk and see what the business's real needs are."

These days, Gore associates use the company intranet to seek out opportunities elsewhere in the organization, but personal relationships still remain at the core of the company's development process— the relationship between an associate and his or her sponsor, and the relationships among sponsors. "The sponsor's role is to be broadly knowledgeable about the business, to be able to help the associate find opportunities," Brinton says.

While other companies have instituted small, self-managed teams and some other aspects of Bill Gore's philosophy, no imitator has taken those concepts as far as the company he founded, says Henry Sims, Jr., a professor of management at the University of Maryland's graduate business school and an expert on self-managing teams. "One of the things that's different about Gore is that they started with this philosophy," Sims says.

"There's a lot of evidence that these small, empowered teams can be very effective, but they take a great deal of time and attention to develop. And changing to that system requires a period of difficult and frustrating transition," he says. "Once teams reach a mature stage, as they have at Gore, they can do things a lot better. They can produce products at a lower cost, bring in new processes more rapidly and smoothly, innovate more quickly."

Discussion Questions

1. Gore's philosophy is focused on interpersonal relationships so much so that accountability is said to be to peers rather than one's supervisor. Are there any possible disadvantages to this approach?

2. What effective team principles or practices is Gore using?

3. What do you think it takes to be successful at Gore? How much do you think you could personally achieve in their environment?

SELECT MANAGE *WHAT?* DEBRIEFS

Helping the Highly Cohesive but Low-Performing Team: Debrief

This is a situation for which clarifying and emphasizing the disciplines of high-performance teams can be very useful. The first step would be to articulate the team's lack of performance in a few sentences. Describe in some detail what is happening, the nature of the low performance, and when and how frequently the difficulty occurs. Then take the disciplines in Figure 10.1 in turn. Is the team too large? Does it really have the member skill sets needed? Are the outcome goals clear and shared? Does the team have effective information processing and meeting disciplines (given the expressed love, it seems likely there may be an aversion to productive task conflict here), and is there a sense of mutual accountability for outcomes?

Raise those questions in a team process check (Tool Kit 10.5). Begin talking with team members about their perceptions of the team's functioning. You might say, "I don't think the team is functioning as well as we could be. How do other team members feel?" If a number agree with you, ask the team to take 10 minutes to identify ways to solve the problem and get some agreement as to what the team should do differently.

Experience has shown that the biggest "bang for the buck" is likely to come from clarifying outcome goals and ensuring they are shared by all. Ask team members to independently describe what they see as the team's goals. Listen carefully for assumptions and interpretations. You may be surprised at the differences in perceptions that team members have regarding the goals of the team. After you have discussed the goals, write them down and give a copy to each team member. Building on that information, ask team members to describe their roles and responsibilities as they relate to the tasks at hand. Some will likely not understand the full scope of their responsibilities (for example, that they must communicate to other team members outside of team meetings when their work impacts others). Reexamine the process steps/milestones the team has set out to complete the required output. Are the necessary steps in place to deliver the quality of output required? Have breakdowns occurred that have not been addressed? Remind them that the team is going to be held accountable for its work and institute a peer evaluation tool as you go forward so there is a known sense of identifiability for individual contributions.

Getting a Team Started: Leading the First Meeting: Debrief

Most teams take far too long to come together, determine their mission and objectives, and produce productive outcomes. Therefore, a good start is critical to get some immediate traction. So begin with good meeting proto-col: Ask the team members about their time constraints and then throw it open for a discussion of what you hope to get accomplished in your time together. Clearly, the single most important priority has to be to get a shared understanding of the purpose of the team and the performance outcomes that the team will be asked to meet.

Given it is a first meeting, after the initial agenda clarification it would be a good idea to spend some time try-ing to accelerate the *forming* stage of group development. So propose an ice-breaker and facilitate the process of helping the group get a sense of who is in their team, and what the different members bring to the challenges ahead. It is likely too early to begin to specify roles, but do assign any tasks to specific members and ask them to report at the next meeting. Close the meeting with a review of what was accomplished, clearly reiterate any action items and which members "own" those items, and push to schedule the time for the next meeting.

Dealing with a Problem Team Member: Debrief

It is important to make two initial points. First, your assumption that this person is unmotivated may not be true, and it is unclear what "pulling their weight" actually means. What form is "unwilling to work" taking? These are labels and are not helpful in diagnosing a problem, if there is one. So the first step in any problem-solving model is to accurately state the problem.

To start thinking about this issue, collect some facts. How has the person contributed to the team? (Be fair and give credit where credit is due.) Specifically, what work has he completed and what work has he not com-pleted? How has his work met or not met expectations? Are you asking him to work outside his area of expertise? If he was "pulling his weight," what would he specifically be saying or doing? How has his not "pulling his weight" impacted the performance of the team? How has the unwillingness to work demonstrated itself in his behavior? Does he refuse to take an assignment? Does he not show up for meetings? Is he joking or socializing during meetings? What specifically are you going to ask him to do or not do in the future? Do others feel the way you do about the person?

Recall from the chapter on motivation that motivating isn't something you do to another person, but rather something you *discover* about that person. To discover what motivates this person, you need to observe, listen, and ask. What topics, ideas, and things does the employee get excited (in a positive way) about? What does he frequently talk about? What does he spend time doing? In what subject areas is he an expert? How does he describe himself? Spend some time talking with him outside of project work and maybe over a soda or cup of coffee.

This is also a good place to introduce some greater level of identifiability—where his work (or lack thereof) can be made more visible to group members.

CHAPTER

11

Resolving Conflict Through Negotiation and Mediation

OBJECTIVES

KNOWING   DOING

After reading this chapter, you should be able to:

KO 11-1 Differentiate between task and relationship conflict in organizations.

KO 11-2 Identify your preferred conflict resolution style.

KO 11-3 Describe the conditions under which negotiation is appropriate.

KO 11-4 Describe the stages of win–win negotiation.

KO 11-5 Identify the steps of the mediation process.

DO 11-1 Diagnose the cause of conflict in a dispute situation.

DO 11-2 Adjust your conflict resolution style to appropriately meet the needs of the situation.

DO 11-3 Detect the negotiating tactic being used by another party in a given negotiation.

DO 11-4 Facilitate a resolution of a conflict situation using a superordinate goal, negotiation, and/or mediation approach.

DO 11-5 Mediate a workplace dispute.

"Win–win negotiating is not just academic talk to us. We need more people who are good at protecting the firm's interest without alienating our clients and associates. When we can bring in people who really 'get it,' everybody is much better off. Those who 'don't get it' don't last very long in this business."

—Sherri Bachmann, Managing Partner, Bachmann Global Associates

Case: The National Football League Players Association

Any casual bystander observing the 2011 NFL lockout would intuitively conclude that the leverage in that situation was heavily skewed toward the owners of the NFL teams. With very deep pockets earned from other sources, the owners were well positioned to withstand a locked out 2011 season. But, with income only from their playing contracts, could the players?

From the moment he was elected executive director of the NFL Players Association in March 2009, DeMaurice Smith took the long view when it came to negotiations with the owners on a new collective bargaining agreement. And his mantra—Hope for the best, plan for the worst—is a very useful one for effective negotiating. It's one of the reasons that slightly more than a year ago he received approval from his executive committee to secure insurance that would pay each player roughly $200,000 if there was no football in 2011.

Smith had disclosed the fund to only a handful of people outside of the executive committee. However, with negotiations seemingly at a standstill late Wednesday night July 13, 2011, the decision was made to play one of their aces in the hole. So, in the relative quiet of the sides' New York City bargaining room the next morning, Baltimore Ravens cornerback Domonique Foxworth informed the owners of the previously secret lockout fund.

Was that the shove in the back that moved the sides closer to a potential agreement? Only the owners know for sure, but a source close to one of them said the disclosure definitely got that side's attention.

> ## < < CAN YOU GET A GOOD DEAL WHEN THE OTHER SIDE HAS MORE POWER?

1. Why was Mr. Smith's move to confidentially secure an insurance policy so valuable as a negotiating tool in this case?
2. What strategies can you use to help determine others' positions?
3. How do you determine your own starting position?

1. Resolving a Team Dispute

You are a team leader and just returned to your office after a miserable meeting. At the end of the meeting, one of the members, Pat, stood up and said some very offensive and controversial things. Jordan briefly responded and stormed out. You asked for other feedback and rebuttal, but no one else said anything and the meeting was adjourned. But you have already gotten an e-mail from two other members claiming they were offended and felt "silenced" and that you better do something about this or they will take their concerns to a higher level.

Given that this has been a very productive team, how do you go about holding it together? What steps should you take? Would you bring Pat and Jordan together, and if so, how would you mediate the meeting? Would you involve others? What traps would you want to avoid that would likely only escalate the dispute?

2. Negotiating an Agreement Between Conflicting Parties

You are the chair of the student facilities committee at the Ballton learning-living center (dormitory) on your campus and find yourself in the middle of a sticky debate. When it was built in the 1940s, the hallmark of the center was a clock tower that has now fallen into disrepair, to the point of leaking and causing water damage. The clock tower was originally paid for by a special gift from the Ballton family, a large and continuous donor to the university to this day. Rumor has it that the key donors in the family are quite disappointed the tower has been neglected.

Part of your committee is adamant about the importance of repair, not only to appease the Balltons, but also for the historical significance of the structure and the aesthetic attractiveness of the center. The other part of your committee is equally adamant and wants to spend only the absolute minimum necessary to repair the leak and use the remainder of your budget dollars on the improvement of other facilities, including revamping the workout and recreational rooms in the lower level of the center. One member of that group is particularly vocal and you overheard him comment that "it would be stupid to spend the money on something nobody in the dorm uses or cares about."

You know both sides have compelling arguments and it would not be wrong to take either side. So how would you go about negotiating a plan that would potentially satisfy both factions of your committee? Where would you start? How would you go about structuring a negotiating process here? What traps would you want to avoid to not further polarize the groups? What if you were to make a decision yourself and tell both sides to deal with it?

3. Starting from a Position of Strength

Although you are very young, your boss has a lot of faith in you. She has scheduled a long-planned African vacation and has asked you to lead the contract negotiation with a potential new vendor which will take place while she is gone. You have never managed a negotiation like this and you know you tend to seek compromise too quickly. Recognizing that you have to get the best deal possible for the firm, and your reputation and your boss's are on the line, what steps should you take to be sure you go into the negotiation with the best chance of success?

4. Getting Beyond Failed Negotiations

You are assistant manager at a large retail store where two of your sales associates, Chris and Terry, have been at each other's throats to the point where the conflict is now affecting work at the store and bothering others. When it first started, you brought the two together for a meeting, but you did not really know what to do and did not take an active role, and the meeting was essentially a disaster. Because they are part of your unit, the store manager has told you to "please deal with this ASAP and let me know what I can do to help."

So what would you do? What would be your first actions? How would you structure a mediation meeting that would be more likely to yield better results than last time? Any traps to avoid? Would you ask your boss to help in some way?

Introduction

An inescapable reality for anyone who works with people in organizations is **conflict.** Conflict can take many forms: It may be a disagreement about how to complete a task or allocate money or a personality clash between two associates, but it is an inevitable part of organizational life.[1] As we will see, conflict is not always bad for a group or organization, but improperly diagnosed or left unchecked, it can be a highly destructive force. Too much conflict potentially creates a toxic workplace environment where satisfaction and performance are low and absenteeism and turnover are high. Great managers know this and take great care to prevent conflict from becoming a destructive force.

Conflict, of course, is a big topic, and entire college courses are devoted to coverage of conflict negotiation, mediation, and resolution. However, from a skills perspective, there are a few points that are key for managers.

First, all conflict is not the same. Thus, knowing the different types and sources of conflict is useful as a diagnostic aid when faced with disputes and disagreements.

Second, there is a significant body of evidence regarding different *styles* of conflict resolution and their relative pros and cons. An understanding of your own style preferences and an awareness of the different styles available (and the importance of adapting one's style to the situation) are important conflict management tools.

Third, a significant portion of a manager's job involves negotiations. Negotiating with senior management about budget allocations, negotiating with employees regarding deadlines and reasonable expectations, negotiating with clients regarding their expectations and what you can effectively deliver. Since such a large part of managers' jobs involves negotiations of one type or another, having a basic grasp of how to effectively negotiate is critical.

Fourth, there are few more unnerving events for new managers than being thrust into conflict situations and being asked to mediate between conflicting parties. Conflict situations are often highly charged and emotional and can cause a great deal of stress. Hence, an understanding of the fundamental principles of mediation is critical for success in such contexts. In short, managers do not have to have the solution to every conflict. They should, however, be capable of diagnosing conflict and facilitating resolutions and agreements.

This chapter is focused on the competencies just discussed, but first note the common myths associated with these areas, which are shown in Myths 11.1. Remember that an important step toward doing the "right thing" is knowing what not to do.

"Where all think alike, no one thinks very much."

—Walter Lippmann

- *Conflict is always dysfunctional.* Conflict can be destructive; however, in the right form and managed well, it can also stimulate innovation and improve group decision making.

- *Conflict is generally a "personality" problem.* Most conflict has less to do with personality and more to do with different ideas of how to accomplish work and competition for scarce resources. A recurring lesson of conflict management is how best to separate the people from the problem.

- *Negotiation creates a winner and loser.* Sometimes there will be a winner and a loser, and sometimes people have to agree to disagree or find an equal place to call it a draw. But the ultimate and often possible resolution is to break out of a win–lose mindset and seek outcomes where both parties feel like winners.

- *You should always negotiate.* Oftentimes, negotiation is in your interest. There are a whole host of other times, however, when you should not engage in negotiation because you have nothing to gain, and possibly something to lose.

- *Good conflict mediators are born, not made.* Some people do have personal traits that make them well suited to bringing people together (grandmas often have this knack). But like almost everything else we have addressed in this text, effective mediation is a learned skill. The evidence is clear that those who wing it are generally far less successful than those who learn and execute a known set of effective principles.

KO **11-1**

DO **11-1**

Types of Conflict and Their Effects

At the most general level, two kinds of conflict occur in organizations.[2] **Task conflict** occurs over tasks, ideas, and issues and is divorced from evaluations of people's character. **Relationship conflict** is personalized and, therefore, highly threatening and damaging for personal relationships, team functioning, and problem solving.

To use a medical analogy, conflict can be compared to cholesterol: Both have good and bad forms (and in case you were wondering, HDL is the good cholesterol and LDL is the bad cholesterol). Relationship conflict is the "bad conflict." It threatens productivity and interferes with the effort people put into a task because they are preoccupied with retaliation, increasing their personal power, or attempting to restore cohesion, rather than working on the task. For the most part, relationship conflict is probably what comes to mind when you think about conflict. It causes managers significant stress and is generally associated with negative consequences.

In contrast, task conflict can be seen as the "good conflict." It can be beneficial to more effective decision making and problem solving and can lead to greater accuracy, insight, and innovation.[3] Task conflict may induce a healthy level of constructive criticism and the stimulation of more spirited and evidence-based discussion. In other words, task conflict is what managers may want to stimulate to "shake things up." Stimulating relationship conflict, on the other hand, is a recipe for disaster.

In one study of 48 top management teams' decision-making quality and team member commitment, team members were asked to assess how much relationship conflict (anger, personal friction, personality clashes) and task conflict (disagreements over ideas, differences about the content of the decision) was present in their respective groups. Results showed the presence of task conflict was associated with higher decision-making quality, higher commitment, and more decision acceptance. In contrast, the presence of relationship conflict significantly reduced those same outcomes.[4]

To suggest that task conflict is always desirable, however, is a bit of a simplification. De Dreu presents convincing evidence that there exists a curvilinear relationship when it comes to task conflict.[5] Too little task conflict is bad because people are not being challenged and problems are not being addressed, but too much task conflict can also be problematic. When very high levels of task conflict occur, it is difficult to get agreement on how to proceed and the process can degenerate. Recent research paints an even more complex picture of the role that task conflict plays in teams. From a meta-analysis of 116 studies, researchers found that task conflict and group performance were more positively related when the association between task and relationship conflict was relatively weak. In other words, when conflict about the task is not connected or tied to specific people (i.e., "It's a bad idea, and its typical coming from you"), then conflict around the task can be useful in promoting group performance. This research also found that task conflict is likely to be more beneficial for top management than for non–top management teams, and when group performance is measured in terms of financial outcomes or decision quality.[6]

Table 11.1 outlines several of the more evidence-based positive and negative consequences of conflict in the workplace. Consistent with the preceding findings, other studies have found a low to medium level of task-related conflict can stimulate more careful thinking and conscientious work.[7] Other evidence has found a leading cause of business failure is too much *agreement* among top management; thus, task conflict that fosters alternate viewpoints and less complacency can be very useful.[8]

While task conflict can and does have beneficial effects, and the good conflict/bad conflict distinction has been conventional wisdom for many years, task conflict certainly does not *always* have such effects. Indeed, the potential damaging effects of conflict were highlighted in a recent meta-analysis that examined 28 separate studies of conflict in teams and found the presence of conflict in work teams has a generally detrimental effect on team member satisfaction and often even on team performance.[9]

These most recent findings confirm that relationship conflict is certainly dysfunctional in organizations and that too much task conflict is generally bad as well. Findings on the beneficial effects of a small to moderate amount of conflict are mixed. Factors that help to explain when and where task conflict may be

Practice this!
Go to www.baldwin2e.com

"Don't be afraid of opposition. Remember, a kite rises against, not with, the wind."

—Hamilton Mabie

TABLE 11.1 Positive and Negative Effects of Conflict

Positive Effects of Conflict	Negative Effects of Conflict
Brings problems into the open that might otherwise be ignored.	Can lead to negative emotions and stress.
Can motivate people to try to understand others' positions and ideas.	Often reduces communication between participants, which can hurt work coordination.
Encourages people to voice new ideas, facilitating innovation and change.	May cause leaders to avoid participative leadership and instead rely on "top-down" authoritarian decisions.
Forces people to challenge their thinking and assumptions, often improving the quality of decisions.	Can result in negative stereotyping and workgroup divisions, since members of opposing groups tend to emphasize the differences between themselves and the opposition.

TABLE 11.2   Effects of Conflict on Teams

Conflict Type	Project Stage (High-Performing Teams)		
	Early	Middle	Late
Relationship	Low	Moderate	Moderate
Task	Low	Moderate	Low
Conflict Type	Project Stage (Low-Performing Teams)		
	Early	Middle	Late
Relationship	Low	Low	High
Task	Moderate	Moderate	Very High

beneficial are the timing and handling of the conflict in the course of a decision process. That is, *when* the conflict occurs (early or late in the process) and *how it is addressed* by the manager or team seem to be important to whether task conflict ultimately has good or bad effects.

For example, one recent study explored the conflict profiles of a set of both high- and low-performing teams over a 13-week period.[10] As shown in Table 11.2, the intriguing results suggest high-performing teams had very little conflict *early* in the project, whereas conflict in the low-performing teams was present from the beginning. During the middle period of the project, the high-performing teams experienced moderate levels of conflict, whereas the low-performing teams maintained a relatively consistent level of conflict. Finally, late in the project the low-performing teams had a high degree of conflict, whereas the high-performing teams experienced much less. These findings and others are important in managing conflict because they prescribe when and how it can be either beneficial or detrimental.

Managing Conflict

So what do great managers do when conflict arises? Clearly, the goal isn't to eliminate conflict (that's impossible anyway) but to manage it in a way that minimizes its harm to engagement and performance. An important first step in this direction is to be able to diagnose a conflict situation to determine its source. That is, consistent with the evidence-based approach to management, there should be no treatment without diagnosis. To do so is managerial malpractice!

DO 11-1

Diagnosing Conflict Sources

As noted, the first diagnosis to make about a conflict is whether it is focused on the relationships or on the tasks. Relationship-centered disputes can be nasty—they stem from what has transpired between two or more people and often deteriorate into name-calling sessions or even worse. These are disputes about things like accusations of harm, demands for justice, or feelings of resentment, and are often played out in confrontations where emotions run high. Relationship conflict is sometimes outside the manager's scope to mediate and the best solution may well be to separate (reassign, relocate) the conflicting parties if no reasonable working solution can be found.

"There is an immutable conflict at work in life and in business, a constant battle between peace and chaos. Neither can be mastered, but both can be influenced. How you go about that is the key to success."

—Philip Knight, former CEO, Nike

Task-centered disputes, on the other hand, are debates over competing ideas, proposals, interests, or resources. They can be, though not always are, conducted in a healthy manner. Usually during such conflicts, emotions run "cooler" than they do in relationship-centered disputes, and participants are generally more receptive to solutions.

Several questions are useful starting points for diagnosing conflict and represent the major sources of conflict. These questions can be seen in Tool Kit 11.1.

Informational Factors

Informational factors come into play when people have developed their point of view on the basis of a different set of facts. The parable of the blind men and the elephant vividly illustrates this point.[11] The parable describes a group of blind men who happen upon an elephant. When they encountered the animal, each approached a different part of it: One felt the elephant's trunk, another its leg, another its side, another its tail, and so on. Consequently, each man believed the elephant was something different: The one that felt the trunk argued that the elephant was like a snake, while the one who felt the leg maintained it was more similar to a tree trunk. Because each of the men had a different piece of information about the elephant's body, they had vastly different interpretations of its nature.

Such differences in information are often the source of conflict. In an organization, if two people have different information about, say, the budget allocations for a project or the deadline for filling a customer request, they are likely to find themselves in conflict as a result of their different understandings.

"Get your facts first, and then you can distort them as much as you please."

—Mark Twain

Perceptual Factors

Perceptual factors exert their influence when people have different images or interpretations of the same thing. In this instance, each person selects the data that support his or her point of view and tend to devalue information that does not support it. Say, for example, you have an instructor who assigns a team paper with no set page limits. When you ask for clarification on the length, the instructor tells you that she doesn't think you can cover all the information in less than seven pages. It is very likely that members of your work team could disagree on what this means: Some will contend the paper is to be seven pages long; others will argue it probably needs to be longer to fulfill the instructor's expectations. You all have the same objective (if somewhat vague) information, but you interpret it differently. This difference in perception is a common source of frustration and conflict.

MANAGER'S TOOL KIT

Tool Kit 11.1 Diagnosing the Conflict Source

- Do the disputants have access to the same information (informational)?
- Do the disputants perceive common information differently (perceptual)?
- Are the disputants significantly influenced by their role in the organization (role)?
- What stressful factors in the environment might disputants be reacting to (environment)?
- In what way do disputants' personal differences play a role in the dispute (personal)?

Practice this!
Go to www.baldwin2e.com

Role Factors

Role factors have the potential to contribute to conflict when people believe their roles within an organization are somehow in conflict or that the "turf" associated with their position is being challenged. This may occur when division managers believe they have to fight for their work unit in budget allocation meetings, but it can also occur at the interpersonal level. Assume your best friend becomes your boss. It is not hard to see how the roles of friend and boss might be difficult to navigate in this circumstance. A similar problem can occur between the role of parent and friend, of boss and employee, and a host of other combinations. While many people can work through such conflicts, the possibility of conflict certainly exists when incompatible roles are imposed on an interpersonal relationship.

Environmental Factors

Several environmental factors can cause, or at least intensify, conflict. When an organization is forced to operate on a shoestring budget, its members are more likely to become involved in conflict over scarce resources. Scarcity of any kind tends to lower the levels of trust people have in one another, which in turn increases the potential for conflict. For example, in recent years a number of state governments have had furlough programs to help them close budget deficits. These furlough programs have had the effect of reducing employee pay and putting significant stress on everyone from the Department of Motor Vehicles, to police officers, to college professors (and even students).

Another environmental factor is uncertainty. When people feel uneasy about their status in an organization, they tend to become anxious and more prone to conflict. This kind of "frustration conflict" often occurs when employees experience rapid repeated change in their environment. If task assignments, management philosophies, work procedures, or lines of authority are changed frequently or with little notice, the resultant stress can cause sharp, bitter conflicts over seemingly trivial problems.

Finally, an important aspect of conflict stemming from the environment is the degree to which competition is present. In many instances, a little healthy competition can be an inducement for higher effort and engagement. For example, creative sales managers routinely develop contests to stoke the competitive juices of their people who respond because they want to win any game. Unfortunately, it is also possible that competition can interfere with overall group success. Often called a **mixed-motive situation,** employees are placed in a position where they are rewarded if they compete aggressively but told they should work toward the department's overall outcome as a whole.[12] As you can imagine, competing can often be a **zero-sum game,** whereby the success of one employee means the failure of another. Such situations can lead to intense conflict when one employee leads another to believe they are both working toward the common good, and the latter employee finds out later that the other employee was in it for himself.

Personal Factors

Personal factors are perhaps the most intractable of conflict sources. Conflicts stemming from incompatible personal values are very difficult to resolve. They can become highly emotional and take on moral overtones. In this kind of conflict, disagreements about *what is factually correct* can easily turn into bitter arguments over *who is morally right.*

Other types of personal factors that can contribute to conflict include different personalities as well as differing long- and short-term goals for the parties

"Science cannot resolve moral conflicts, but it can help to more accurately frame the debates about those conflicts."

—Heinz Pagels

involved. Interestingly, even cases where people are very much alike and want to play the same role (for example, two people want to set the agenda or "take charge") can lead to conflict. When facing a particular conflict, understanding the five potential sources is a good first step in diagnosing the situation and deciding on a course of action. Armed with an idea of what the nature of the conflict is, you can then move into conflict management mode.

To help you keep track of the type of conflict and its source, you can use a simple checklist like the one presented in Tool Kit 11.2. This can serve as an important start in ultimately resolving the problem at hand.

Matching Conflict Styles with Situations

KO **11-2**

DO **11-2**

As with most situations where people are involved, there is no one best way to manage conflict, either as an involved adversary or as a neutral third party. Rather, there are several styles and strategies you can use, and their effectiveness for you will depend on a variety of factors. One of the most well-known assessments for measuring your conflict style is the Thomas-Kilmann Conflict Mode Instrument. That assessment is based on a model of five conflict-resolution strategies: competition, accommodation, avoidance, compromise, and collaboration. Although most people find they have one dominant conflict management style, you might find your preferred style is balanced between two or more. This may indicate flexibility in your conflict management style and may help you adapt your style as the situation dictates—an important capacity for most effective conflict management. Figure 11.1 provides an overview of the five conflict management types and how the styles relate to one another.

"You can't shake hands with a clenched fist."

—Indira Gandhi

Two often misunderstood points regarding conflict management styles are important to keep in mind. First, there are no necessarily good or bad styles. That is, *all* five styles can lead to successful outcomes; it just depends on the situation. So the key is to develop the ability to recognize when a style would be appropriate and be able to adapt your style to that circumstance. There are, however, ineffective techniques of applying any of these conflict management styles, which you would be better off avoiding. These are illustrated in Table 11.3.

"The direct use of force is such a poor solution to any problem, it is generally employed only by small children and large nations."

—David Friedman

Second, conflict styles are preferences, your natural reactions, or behavioral responses. For example, if your natural style is to avoid conflict, it does not mean

MANAGER'S TOOL KIT

Tool Kit 11.2   A Conflict Grid

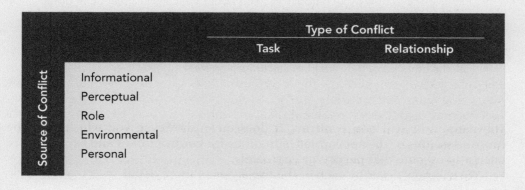

Source of Conflict	Type of Conflict	
	Task	Relationship
Informational		
Perceptual		
Role		
Environmental		
Personal		

FIGURE 11.1
The Thomas-Kilmann Conflict Resolution Grid

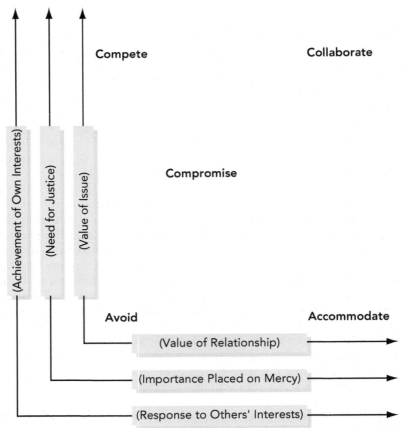

Adaptations of Kilmann Grid by Pepperdine University Straus for Dispute Resolution.

TABLE 11.3   *Ineffective* Conflict Management Techniques

- After listening to the other person for a short time, begin to nonverbally communicate your discomfort with their position, for example, sit back, fidget, shake your head, and so on.
- Have serious conflict management conversations in public places, or with frequent interruptions.
- Discourage the expression of emotion. While you don't want people to get overheated, it is often inappropriate to require them to be dispassionate.
- Minimize the seriousness of the problem, particularly if someone else brought it to your attention.
- Publicly or privately make derogatory jokes about the conflict situation or other parties to the conflict.
- Express displeasure that conflict is being experienced. Remember, conflict can be a *good* thing too.
- Tell the other party they are irrational or incompetent.

you cannot, or will not, confront. It does mean, however, you will have to be more conscious of the appropriate situations for confrontation and expend more energy to execute that particular approach.

We will now describe each of the five styles in more detail.

Competition

Competition is characterized as being dominant and nonsupportive. In this mode, individuals pursue their own concerns relatively aggressively, often at the expense of other people's concerns. This is a power-oriented mode, where people use whatever power seems appropriate to win their position—their organizational status, their ability to be persuasive, or even coercive. Competing could mean standing up for your rights, defending a position you believe is correct, or simply trying to win.

Although you might think a competitive strategy would be outdated in today's collaborative, team-based business environment, that is not the case. Many situations make it absolutely necessary to use this kind of style.

Consider situations where someone has to be in charge to effectively coordinate complex systems—for example, situations where safety is on the line. Would we really want an air traffic controller trying to negotiate with every pilot who is landing a plane? Similarly, the competition approach may be helpful when you notice a dispute has perception issues that need to be resolved. If two of your associates disagree about your desired work standards, it would be appropriate for you to assertively make your wishes known so that they can be on the same page. Likewise, it is appropriate to use the competitive style on important issues when unpopular actions need implementing, such as cost cutting, enforcement of unpopular rules, or discipline. Competition also can be valuable against people who take advantage of noncompetitive behavior.

However, appropriate competition can be effective in some circumstances; it can also be highly unpopular. With that in mind, here are a few tips for using this approach most effectively:

- **Be direct.** Use declarative and precise statements, and keep them simple. Make sure people know *exactly* what you want them to do. This is not the time for ambiguity or showing others you are unsure. For example, say you see a child about to run into the street in the path of an oncoming car. Your best response would be a loud, clear, "Timmy! Stop right there!"

- **Explain later.** To avoid having to use this technique often, take a minute to explain your rationale to the other person once the emotions or stress of the conflict situation have diminished. For example, once you have caught your breath and slowed your heart after Timmy's near miss, it would be a good idea to explain basic traffic safety principles.

- **Use this strategy selectively.** We all know people who yell direct commands about every little thing. Over time, we tune them out; their competing conflict management style loses its effectiveness when they use it too often. This is a good weapon to have in your arsenal when you really need to use it, but using it too often can damage your work team's morale and lessen your personal credibility in future conflicts. Think about it. If you bark commands at Timmy all the time, he is less likely to respond when he absolutely must.

Accommodation

Accommodation is behaving in a supportive, submissive, unassertive, and cooperative manner. It is generally the opposite of competition. When accommodating, individuals neglect their own concerns to satisfy the concerns of others. There is an element of self-sacrifice in this mode. Accommodating might take the form of selfless generosity or charity, obeying another person's order when you would prefer not to, or yielding to another person's point of view. Basically, when someone goes along with you when you are in competition mode, they are in accommodating mode.

Put simply, if this is your most frequent conflict management style, others will ultimately not respect you at work. They may like you a lot, but chances are good you (and ultimately the people you represent) will eventually be exploited. Fortunately, most people who practice accommodating in their interpersonal conflicts can easily make the transition to a more assertive style by recognizing that, when they accommodate everyone else's interests at work, they are essentially cheating the people they represent. One of your primary duties as a manager is to protect the interests of your organization and your workers, and it is difficult to do this through constant accommodation.

So when *is* accommodation a viable option, and how do you do it effectively should you choose to use it? Accommodation is a good idea if an issue is just not that important to you. Say, for example, one of your people wants to come in at 8 a.m. rather than 8:30 a.m., leaving a half hour earlier in the afternoon. Ask yourself, is this a big deal? If it isn't critical the person be in the office at the close of business, why not take the opportunity to accommodate him?

Similarly, occasional accommodation is good when you engage in a series of negotiations with another person. Giving in on issues that aren't that critical can earn you "goodwill points" that could prove useful in future encounters. Finally, accommodation is also a good strategy if you think your safety could be jeopardized and someone else knows more about the situation than you do. For example, accommodation is the perfect strategy for those rare occasions when a firefighter gives you instructions to leave a burning building. More pragmatically, accommodation may be an appropriate strategy if there are status or power differences in a dispute, and you are simply outranked by the other person. Accommodation is also a good idea when you find out you are wrong, since it allows a better position to be heard and allows you to simultaneously learn and show your reasonableness.

In these or similar circumstances, here are some strategies for using accommodation effectively in your managerial role:

- **Acknowledge the accommodation.** We don't mean you should try to make yourself out to be a martyr, but it is important to let the other person know you are consciously giving her what she wants.

- **Have a rationale.** Remember that one of the most important things you need to do as a manager is to treat all people fairly. If you accommodate the wishes of one employee, you need to have a reason that is palatable to other employees if you hope to avoid their resentment or looking like you are playing favorites. Similarly, having a rationale will help you decide what to do if other people ask for the same accommodation.

Avoidance

Avoidance is behaving in a submissive, nonsupportive, unassertive, and uncooperative manner. People in this mode do not immediately pursue their own concerns or those of the other person. They simply do not address conflicts. Avoiding might take the form of diplomatically sidestepping an issue, postponing an issue until a better time, or simply withdrawing from a threatening situation.

As we have previously noted, managers who ignore or fail to manage conflict are likely to incur the disadvantages of conflict without enjoying any of the advantages. If this is your dominant reaction to conflict, you might want to consider role-playing or practicing other conflict styles so you become more comfortable actually engaging in conflict.

"All problems become smaller if you don't dodge them, but confront them."

—William F. Halsey

Still, in some isolated situations, avoiding is a good strategy. Basically, you can use avoiding as a way of delaying issues until they are more appropriate to address. If an overworked, overstressed co-worker on a tight deadline starts to argue with you, it might not be a bad idea to simply walk away, pledging to address the issue at a specific but later time. Similarly, if a conflict has information issues, your best strategy might be to provide everyone with the same information and then insist on some reflection time before the discussion continues. Sometimes, having time to reflect on a dispute can help the parties absorb new information without feeling defensive about it. Avoiding is also appropriate when an issue is trivial, or more important concerns are pressing. Similarly, this strategy is useful when others can resolve the conflict more effectively. For example, it might not be appropriate for you to try to manage a conflict occurring between people with whom you are not directly involved.

If you are going to employ the avoidance strategy, here are some guidelines to do it effectively:

- **Set time limits.** Rather than merely saying you will deal with a conflict *later*, specify (in your own mind, if not with the other parties) when you will get back to it—and then do it. Allowing conflicts to fester for too long only makes them more difficult to handle in the long run.

- **Set goals for the time out period.** It is important that people know what they are supposed to be working toward while they are avoiding a conflict. If they should be absorbing new information, getting additional information, or even just calming down, be sure everyone knows what they should try to accomplish.

Compromise

Compromise is an intermediate style. The objective of people who use this style is to find some expedient, mutually acceptable solution that partially satisfies everyone involved. It falls into the middle ground between behaving in a supportive and nonsupportive manner and between behaving in a dominant and submissive way. Compromising might mean splitting the difference, exchanging concessions, or seeking a quick middle-ground position.

When is it appropriate to use the compromising style? If the conflict involves scarce resources that cannot be expanded, then some form of compromise is usually required to reach a fair outcome. For example, if the organization's budget only allows two new employees to be hired, and three managers each need a new employee, they are going to have to negotiate to determine the best distribution of the limited number of people that can be hired. Compromise is also most appropriate when the conflict has significant role factors. If you are a party to the conflict simply because of your position in the organization, then you will likely find yourself in a position where you will need to also defend your own department's interests against the competing demands of other departments. Compromise also works to obtain temporary solutions when some interim action must be taken but future study is required. It is also a good way to arrive at solutions when you are under time pressure. As a last resort, compromise also can be utilized when previous attempts at collaboration or competition are unsuccessful.

Collaboration

Finally, **collaboration** represents behaving in both a dominant and supportive, and assertive and cooperative, manner. It is the opposite of avoiding. Collaborating means digging into an issue to identify the underlying concerns of the two conflicting individuals and then finding an alternative that meets both sets of concerns. Collaborating might take the form of trying to learn from each other in the course of a disagreement or jointly seeking solutions to problems involving scarce resources. Collaborators value the insight they gain from learning about others' interests and perspectives. They enjoy taking a creative approach to problem solving and won't leave the table until everyone is fully satisfied with the outcome.

A collaborative negotiation is one in which both parties consider their relationship and the outcome so important that they must work together to maximize both. The collaborative negotiation is also referred to as *win–win* because it strives to ensure both sides achieve winning positions. Collaborators focus their attention on creative problem solving, rather than the competitive tactics of compromising.

Collaboration is often touted as the most important conflict management strategy in organizations, with good reason. Collaborative approaches to conflict management take relationships into account, and allow for healthy debate and the expression of diverse ideas within the confines of mutual respect and a commitment to ultimately reaching a solution under which everyone benefits. Collaboration is appropriate when part of your objective is to learn more about the other party, when you wish to merge insights or perspectives from other people or groups, or when you need to work through feelings that have interfered with a relationship. Collaboration also has the benefit of making people feel committed to the solutions decided on, since they feel they have been part of the decision-making process. Consequently, collaboration is particularly useful when you need to gain commitment by incorporating everyone's concerns into a consensus decision. We should note, however, that collaboration—though one of the most positive options in this arsenal of approaches—is also the most time-consuming.

"Truth springs from argument amongst friends."
—David Hume

Table 11.4 provides a concise summary of the five conflict approaches and the appropriateness of their use in different situations.

While adapting your conflict style to the situation is the ideal, the reality is that it is often difficult to do. Unfortunately, evidence suggests that the conflict style we actually use is often based less on the situational considerations outlined in Table 11.4 and more on either our dominant style or the positions of the parties involved. For example, one study found that, despite widely varying types of conflict, people tended to use their one dominant style.[13] Other evidence, summarized in Figure 11.2, reveals that the choice of conflict management strategy is heavily influenced by whether the conflict is with a boss, co-worker, or employee. Note that when a conflict is with a boss, people try to "convince" less frequently than if the conflict were with employees.

TABLE 11.4   When to Use Each of the Conflict Management Styles

Situational Consideration	Competition	Accommodation	Avoidance	Compromise	Collaboration
Issue Importance	High	Low	Low	Medium	High
Relationship Importance	Low	High	Low	Medium	High
Relative Power	High	Low	Equal	Equal	Low-High
Time Constraints	Medium-High	Medium-High	Medium-High	Medium-High	Low

Situational considerations are defined as:

- Issue Importance: How important is the disputed issue? (High — Extremely important; Low — Not very important)

- Relationship Importance: How important is the relationship? (High — Critical, ongoing, one-of-a-kind partnership; Low — One-time transaction, for which there are many other alternatives available)

- Relative Power: What is the relative level of power, or authority, between the disputants? (High — Boss to subordinate; Equal — Peers; Low — Subordinate to boss)

- Time Constraints: To what extent is time a significant constraint in resolving the dispute? (High — Must resolve the dispute quickly; Low — Time is not a salient factor)

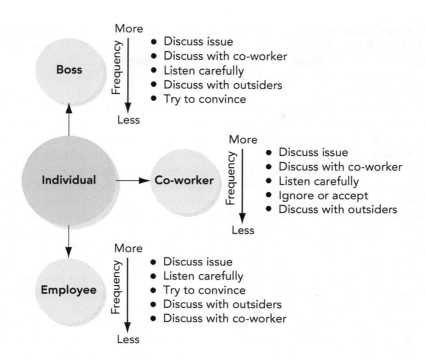

FIGURE 11.2
How People Actually
Respond to Conflict

Seeking Superordinate Goals

One universal strategy that is valuable across all styles and situations is seeking a **superordinate goal.**[14] A superordinate goal is an objective so valuable to both parties that it transcends the dispute. As one example, social scientists have learned that one way to reduce conflict between some groups (and individuals) is to have them work together on a project of mutual interest. The project must be of high importance and value to each party and cannot be completed without the successful input from both parties. Management Live 11.1 is a classic illustration of a superordinate goal being used in a youth group context.

Effective Negotiations

KO **11-3**

KO **11-4**

People commonly think of negotiation as something that takes place in a limited set of arenas such as international diplomacy, organized labor, or car dealerships. However, in reality, most of us negotiate many times each day. For example:

- We negotiate with associates to get them to take on a new assignment or to take a trip to another city.
- We negotiate with our manager to get assigned to high-profile projects.
- We negotiate purchases from vendors as well as discounts and deals.
- We negotiate deadlines with customers, colleagues, or vendors.
- We negotiate in group meetings to get other people to support our proposed initiatives.

To Negotiate or Not? Recognizing Negotiation Situations

Two points regarding the recognition of negotiation situations are important. First, it is important to question whether an issue that appears to be nonnegotiable or that someone states as being so truly is. For instance, if you have a job

"In business, you don't get what you deserve, you get what you negotiate."

—Chester Karrass

↦ MANAGEMENT LIVE 11.1

The Robbers Cave Study and the Superordinate Goal[15]

In 1954, researchers Muzafer and Carolyn Sherif set out to study prejudice in children's social groups. With a group of 22 boys at a Boy Scout camp at Robbers Cave State Park in Oklahoma, the Sherifs split the boys up into two groups (the Eagles and the Rattlers) and set up four days of competitions between the groups, promising rewards such as medals and camping knives to the winners. As the competition proceeded, conflict between the two groups developed. The conflict was first evidenced by the boys' incessant taunting of those outside their own group. As the competition continued, the conflict intensified and the Eagles burned the Rattlers' flag. Seeking retribution, the Rattlers trashed the Eagles' cabin. The groups became so aggressive with each other that the researchers had to physically separate them.

In order to reduce the conflict, the Sherifs first attempted to allow the boys from each group to talk with each other or have contact. This only served to intensify the situation. Next, the Sherifs forced the boys to work together to accomplish superordinate goals such as repairing a broken-down vehicle. These superordinate goals drastically reduced the conflict between the two groups. The lessons from the Robbers Cave study play out in organizations today. It's not enough to put people in a room and tell them to get along. A manager must discover a common purpose that employees can rally behind and thus transcend their disputes.

offer and the company has indicated the salary is nonnegotiable, you should fully consider and investigate whether that is really the case. If salary truly is nonnegotiable, maybe the amount of vacation, expense accounts, or a company vehicle *are* negotiable items, which may lead to significant increased value for you.

"Only free men can negotiate."
—Nelson Mandela

Second, if there is no way to create added value for yourself in a negotiation, you should not be negotiating in the first place. For instance, a supervisor should never negotiate over a safety rule or unexcused absences from work. Similarly, parents are often duped into negotiating things with children that should have been clearly stated as nonnegotiable (for example, wearing seat belts, eating junk food before dinner). In such cases, negotiating only undermines legitimate authority and can add no value. Even worse, negotiating in these cases can actually lead to having to negotiate for everything. This is not a path you want to travel down.

Practice this!
Go to www.baldwin2e.com

We negotiate in order to get a better outcome than we could get if we did not negotiate. Therefore, it is critical to know what alternative we will be left with if we *cannot* reach a negotiated agreement, or what is known as the **best alternative to a negotiated agreement (BATNA)**.[16] Like many cases, to negotiate or not can be thought of as a cost-benefit analysis. If the benefit of a negotiated solution compared to your BATNA is larger than your costs of negotiating, then negotiating should be done. To calculate the benefits of negotiating, consider:

- The current BATNA
- The likelihood of favorable negotiated outcomes
- The direct costs of negotiating (travel, personnel, meeting facilities, and other items)
- The indirect and opportunity costs (the lost work time of personnel, secretarial support, and so on)

Then, if the incremental benefits (negotiated outcome minus BATNA) are greater than the incremental costs (direct plus indirect costs), then negotiating makes sense. If not, the effort of negotiating may not be worthwhile. This provides you with a straightforward and amazingly powerful decision rule to help you negotiate when you should, and maybe even more importantly, to prevent you from negotiating when you should *not*.

The Negotiation Scorecard: Outcomes of an Ideal Negotiation

Before we can start the negotiating process, we need to know what an effective negotiation should produce. In this case, the scorecard for an effective negotiation consists of three outcomes:[17]

1. **All parties believe they made a good deal.** Ideally, you want the other parties to believe they have helped themselves—rather than hurt themselves—by working with you.

2. **The relationship is maintained or even improved.** Usually you negotiate with people you have ongoing relationships with so you hope to sustain a positive relationship after the negotiation is complete.

3. **Each negotiator's constituents are satisfied with the agreement.** When you negotiate, other people have to accept the agreement you reach. Examples include your boss, partners, employees, or customers.

The most successful negotiations are characterized by all three of these outcomes.

Win–Win Negotiation

Largely because we are all intimately familiar with courtroom debate and high-profile negotiations in the news, we commonly assume a competitive or "win–lose" approach to the negotiations we regularly face. Buying a car is a common example of this. If you choose a competitive strategy to negotiate, you have to accept the possibility of losing. **Win–lose negotiation** means someone has to lose in the negotiation process, and odds are it will sometimes be you.

However, in many situations, the possibility of losing is not acceptable. Examples of such situations include negotiating with:

- Your boss
- Your peers, both individually and as a group
- Major clients your company has had for multiple years
- Potential partners for long-term ventures

"If you are planning on doing business with someone again, don't be too tough in the negotiations. If you're going to skin a cat, don't keep it as a house cat."

—Marvin S. Levin

With some of these—for example, a major client—you don't even want to accept the possibility that the *other party* will lose. Parties who lose in negotiation often seek other relationships, and you clearly don't want that with a major client. So, while you might use a win–lose approach to negotiate for a car deal or to decide a lawsuit, in ongoing relationships you ultimately want "win–win" outcomes, where both parties walk away from the agreement feeling good about it and believing the relationship has been maintained or even improved. Remember, when people feel they have lost, they are not likely to want to do business with you again or may even be looking for ways to get even. Neither of these outcomes is good for building long-term relationships.

Win–win negotiation is focused on cooperative problem solving. This does not mean you give in or compromise easily just to maintain a good relationship with the other party. It means you treat the conflict as being separate from the relationship and work to seek a mutually acceptable solution to the conflict. The way to maintain the relationship is not to win the fight, but to solve a problem, in a way that meets the needs of both parties and creates value for both. You don't need to defeat the other party; in fact, the best way to get them to agree to a settlement that benefits you is for the settlement to also benefit them. In win–win negotiation, a critical challenge is to propose a solution that helps the other party meet their needs, along with your own. Table 11.5 presents the characteristics of win–win negotiations. A collaborating conflict management style best represents the win–win approach to negotiations.

Although every negotiation has unique features, effective interactions share the common elements of preparation, execution, and evaluation. In this section, we touch on key points and skills associated with each of these elements. The goal is for you to become a more effective negotiator in a variety of settings.

DO **11-3**

DO **11-4**

Stages of Effective Negotiations

As a way of attempting to resolve conflicts, negotiations are generally thought of as the most common and easily implemented remedy. Like any good tool, negotiations involve a series of steps that, when done properly, will help increase the likelihood of success. The major steps involved with the negotiation process can be broken down into preparation, understand needs, list and discuss options, process tactics, ending, and evaluation (Figure 11.3).

Negotiation Preparation

People who frequently negotiate (such as purchasing agents or insurance adjusters) say in surveys that the most important part of negotiation is the planning and preparation.[18] Even though it is extremely important, negotiators from many other countries have the impression that Americans don't take the task of negotiation planning seriously enough. It is very easy to be careless or superficial in this step, so don't fall into that trap. The following tips apply to good negotiation preparation.

Organize the Issues

Begin by identifying and defining the issues. For example, if you are being asked to take a promotion and transfer to São Paulo, Brazil, you need to list the issues you want to bring into the negotiation. You will likely want to discuss pay, moving expenses, how much time you will have to move, and the expenses of travel if your family moves at a different time than you do, among other issues. Try to consider the issue from multiple levels. Are you negotiating just your move to Brazil or also your future with your current firm? This may not always be obvious at first, but some serious thoughts about these types of issues can prove useful.

You will want to list the issues in writing. Organize the issues into priorities. For a few issues, simply order 1, 2, 3, and so on. For more issues, divide them into high- and low-priority groups. This is also a good place to utilize the decision-making skills that were presented in Chapter 3.

TABLE 11.5   **Characteristics of Win–Win Negotiation**

- A focus on common interests rather than differences.
- An attempt to address needs and interests rather than bargaining positions.
- A commitment to helping the other party meet their needs also.
- An exchange of information and ideas.
- The creation of options for mutual gain—creating value for both parties.

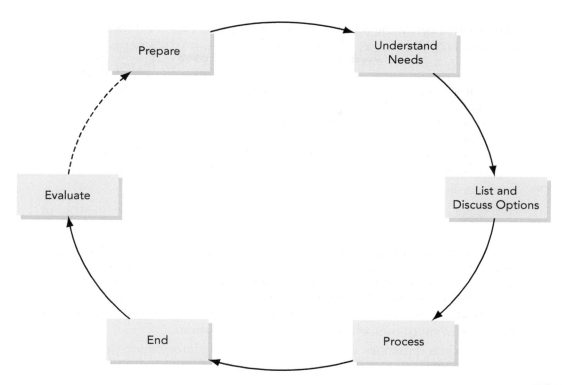

FIGURE 11.3
The Stages of the
Negotiation Process

Talk to Other People Who Have Information You Need

1. **Seek out other people you know who have conducted similar negotiations.** For example, if you are being asked to take that transfer to Brazil, look for people you know who have been asked to take international transfers. You want to ask these people what issues were negotiable for them and what issues were not. Ask them about the agreement they reached. This is analogous to buying a house. If you've done this a few times, you know some issues are negotiable and some aren't. Don't reinvent the wheel; learn from other people's experiences. This is especially important because it is unlikely you will have a good knowledge base of firsthand information if you've never been in this type of situation before. By finding out as much as possible from people who have experience, you will put yourself in a much stronger position.

2. **Talk to your constituents.** When you negotiate, you usually represent constituents who must accept the agreement you reach. For the move to Brazil, it may be your spouse and children. If you are negotiating a new hire, it may be the HR department or your boss. If you don't address your constituents' concerns in the negotiation, you'll have difficulty reconciling them later.

3. **Talk in advance to the other parties.** In some formal situations such as international diplomacy, it makes sense to agree on the topics to be negotiated (and not negotiated), timetables, schedules and locations of meetings, deadlines, and who may attend the meetings. Many of the negotiations you will be involved in are not this complex, but some are. If they do become complex, consider whether these sorts of agreements before the negotiation would be useful.

Practice this!
Go to www.baldwin2e.com

Research the Parties You'll Be Negotiating With

Like you, the other parties involved are only going to negotiate if they believe they can serve their interests better by negotiating than by not negotiating. In other words, if they don't believe that their BATNA can be improved through negotiating, they shouldn't be sitting there in the first place. Therefore, gaining an understanding of their interests will be helpful to you. If they have chosen to negotiate with you, they have a reason they are willing to negotiate. You have more to work with if you understand that reason.

"To measure the person, measure their heart."

—Malcolm Forbes

It also is helpful to know whether each of the other parties plans to use a competitive or cooperative approach to the negotiation. To help determine that, consider five indicators (see also Table 11.6):

1. Learn their reputation. Do they have a pattern of being competitive or cooperative in past negotiations?
2. Do the issues seem to be scarce resources like money or time? If so, they may move toward a competitive style.
3. Do you believe they have an interest in maintaining a good relationship? Such an interest suggests a cooperative approach.
4. Is this an ongoing relationship or a one-time negotiation? Parties are often more competitive in one-time negotiations.
5. Do you think they will trust you with all the information they have on the topics to be negotiated? Lack of trust and information hoarding are characteristic of competitive negotiations.

Consider Your BATNA (Best Alternative to a Negotiated Agreement)

The BATNA is the yardstick against which you measure any possible agreement.

- An agreement better than your BATNA should be accepted.
- An agreement worse than your BATNA should not be accepted.

By putting a little different twist on our example of a transfer to Brazil, we can see how the BATNA works in practice. Let's say you are trying to get an

TABLE 11.6   Types of Difficult Negotiators[19]

- **Aggressive Opener.** Negotiator unnerves others by making nasty comments about their previous performance or other remarks to belittle the opponent.
- **Long Pauser.** Will not answer immediately; appears to give comments substantial thought with long silences; hopes silence will get the other side to reveal additional information.
- **Mocker.** Mocks and sneers at the other party's proposals to anger the other side so that they will say something they may later regret.
- **Interrogator.** Challenges all comments with searching questions meant to suggest the other party has not done their homework; contests any answers and asks the opposition to explain further what they mean.
- **Sheep's Clothing.** Appears to be reasonable while making impossible demands.
- **Divide-and-Conqueror.** Produces dissension within other party to create internal conflict; allies with one member of the team and tries to play him or her off against the other members of the team.
- **Dummy.** Pretends to be dense and by doing so exasperates the opposition in hopes of drawing out more information or lulling the opponent into a false sense of superiority.

employee, Bob, to accept a promotion and transfer to go to São Paulo, Brazil. You want Bob for the promotion because he seems to have the right skill set to be successful. Unfortunately, Bob may not want to go to Brazil, and his skill set is already highly marketable in his current city. Let's say that if you can't get Bob to go to Brazil, your best alternative is Pat from a local office. Pat has relatives in Brazil and is interested in going there. Pat would do an acceptable job, but in your estimation, Pat is not as good a match for this assignment as Bob.

In this case, Pat is your BATNA. This is the yardstick against which you measure the possible negotiated agreement with Bob. If you have to agree to buy Bob's house, give him a $40,000 pay raise, and wait two months to get Bob to go to Brazil, you compare that against having Pat in the job in São Paulo.

If your BATNA is very good, you are in a strong negotiating position when you meet with Bob. However, if your BATNA is not acceptable to you, you must be more willing to make concessions to Bob. A good BATNA reduces your dependence on the other party, and remember that dependence is an important determinant of power. Whenever possible, you want to avoid negotiating when you have a very weak BATNA. Having a weak BATNA is the hallmark of a desperate person. A very weak BATNA can lead you to accept very undesirable situations. A person driving across the desert does not have a very good BATNA when he pulls up to the only gas station for 100 miles and the gas gauge reads "empty." In much the same manner, a person with only one job opportunity does not have much ability to negotiate for more desirable terms than those that are initially offered.

"The best way to make a good deal is to have the ability to walk away from it."

—Brian Koslow

Understanding the Needs of Other Parties

Many people begin negotiating by stating their positions. Positions are what people claim they want. For example, "I want you to accept a promotion to lead our office in São Paulo, Brazil. I want you there two weeks from today." Unfortunately, positions don't really give much information. They tell what we want, but not the true underlying *reasons* why we want it.

If we are going to view negotiation as a mutual problem-solving situation, we have to share information so the other party understands the problem to be solved. In the Brazil example, it may be that our current manager, who was doing a very poor job, just resigned unexpectedly. It's a good opportunity to replace a poor performer, but we need a seasoned person who can move quickly. If we share these underlying needs with the other party, they are more capable of helping solve the problem.

If they know our true needs, they have the ability to offer possible options we may have never considered. For example, "I don't want to go to São Paulo to manage the operations there. However, I would consider going for a temporary assignment for six months to train a new manager." That option might be better than your BATNA. If you consider Bob's offer of going for six months better than sending Pat, then Bob should be sent because this is better than your BATNA.

So try to never begin a negotiation by stating positions. Begin by discussing the needs and interests of the parties. Listening to their needs and interests is critical. Many skilled negotiators rank listening as being one of the most important negotiation skills.[20] Being able to "put yourself in their shoes" is critical to creating a win–win solution.

List and Discuss Possible Options

Once the parties have an understanding of the needs and interests of each other, you are ready to move to discussing options. Options are possible solutions or parts of possible solutions. Given that we negotiate multiple issues,

"Problems cannot be solved from the same level of awareness that created them."

—Albert Einstein

a partial solution that addresses one issue is often a helpful building block for a complete solution. Generating multiple creative options to discuss is a source of power for a negotiator. If you can offer four or five possibilities that meet the needs of both parties, then you have great potential to control what the solution looks like. However, this only works if you are committed to finding a solution that lets all parties meet their needs. We can't forget that the other party only wants to reach an agreement with us if the agreement creates value for *them.* This is because others are rarely motivated to do things that only benefit you!

Complex negotiations often happen in stages across time. Once you understand the other parties' interests, this might be a good time to pause the negotiation and let each party discuss possible options with their constituents. You also might find this to be a good time to do additional research on the issues and alternatives to negotiating a settlement with this party (for example, discussing the proposed project with another potential partner).

Choosing Among the Options

As you continue discussing options with the other party, it is often helpful to talk in **hypotheticals.** An example might be to ask, "If we were able to move the roll-out date forward by six months, would you be able to commit more engineers to the project?" Using hypotheticals lets you explore creative possibilities with less pressure and helps both parties think through issues they may not have previously considered. This process can be helpful in the generation of new solutions and new opportunities. Mutual gain can often be created when the priorities of the two parties are different. For example, the other party may want an immediate startup date for the project, to balance off personnel demands on other projects. Maybe the startup date is not important to you because your segment of the project begins during the second month of the project. Trade-offs may work here because the priorities are different.

To be successful at this stage, look for ways to improve options that are already on the table. You can create considerable goodwill if you point out to the other party how their idea could be altered to serve their needs better without causing you any harm. Conversely, you may see ways to serve your needs better without negatively affecting their outcome.

Use of Objective Standards and Norms

The vast majority of people we negotiate with want to appear reasonable. Therefore, when confronted by what appears to be reasonable standards, most negotiators will have difficulty ignoring those standards. The key then is knowing where to look for these standards and norms.

Try to look for objective standards or precedents that are supportive of what you want in a negotiation. For example, "I thought you gave a 10 percent discount to all customers who place orders this large." If that standard is true, the other party feels unreasonable if they don't give you the same discount. Having a good grasp of your industry and what your competitors are offering is extremely helpful in this situation.

However, be aware that multiple objective criteria might apply to a negotiation. For example, "Yes, but we don't give the 10 percent for the initial order because of the overhead costs in setting up the account. We do give the 10 percent in subsequent orders." Obviously, you want to look for the objective criteria most consistent with your needs. Be aware that the other party you are negotiating with has constituents that they must satisfy. Sometimes they are looking for you to give them the objective standards they can use to go back and convince those constituents.

Employing Process Tactics During Negotiations

Once you have your list of options on the negotiating table and are discussing them, consider employing the following process tactics to achieve your objectives.

Look for Key Information from the Other Party

Information is the lifeblood of negotiation. As the negotiation opens, you want to start looking for information. Ask probing questions: why, how, what if, what would be wrong with, and so on.

Since a strong BATNA provides an advantage, you would like to determine your negotiating party's BATNA. For example, let's say you are trying to decide between three job offers. Do these companies have other job candidates in mind? If so, what are the qualifications of the others? If one of the companies has no other good candidates, that helps your negotiating position. If the company has other qualified and attractive candidates, you should know that early in your negotiation. More specifically:

1. You want to understand the other party's underlying needs and interests. Like you, they have decided to negotiate for some reason. You have more information to work with if you understand that reason.

2. If they have a deadline, you want to know it. For example, do they need to reach an agreement before their flight to London tomorrow? Evidence shows people will make more concessions as their deadline approaches. Not all negotiators have a deadline, but if they do, you want to know it.

"Information is a negotiator's greatest weapon."

—Victor Kiam

Making Concessions

People enter negotiations expecting concessions to be made on both sides. With that in mind, experienced negotiators will always leave themselves room to make at least some concessions.

There is clear evidence that parties feel better about a settlement when the negotiation had a progressive set of concessions than when it did not. This is because negotiators want to believe that they are capable of shaping the other's behavior. When one person makes a concession and the other does not, reciprocity is not fulfilled (see Chapter 8) and the party who made the initial concession can experience a deep-rooted sense of betrayal. It is very frustrating to negotiators to see they have not shaped the outcome and influenced the other negotiator's behavior.

In the 1950s, GE used an extremely aggressive tactic in negotiating with its labor unions. The company claimed it had done all the appropriate research, its offer was fair, and the offer represented a nonnegotiable final offer. This was referred to as GE's "take it or leave it" strategy and was later called "Boulwareism" after GE's labor negotiator Lemuel R. Boulware.[21] Regardless of the offer's actual fairness, the unions hated this tactic because they felt they had no influence on the other party or outcome. It should be pointed out that a "take it or leave it" or Boulwareism approach is generally seen as a case of negotiating in bad faith and is not recommended. Remember that in an ideal negotiation all parties believe they have made a good deal. *How* you go about negotiating can influence that perception. Management Live 11.2 gives an interesting example of how everyone can be better off by obtaining an outcome that is **Pareto efficient.**

One common question concerns what to do if the opposing side is more powerful. There is no easy answer, but your best strategy is to be very clear on your BATNA. The better your BATNA, the better your position. So search for ways to improve your BATNA and be prepared to predict *their* BATNA. A related question

⇄ MANAGEMENT LIVE 11.2

Pareto Efficiency

The ultimate goal of negotiations is to be Pareto efficient. A Pareto-efficient outcome (the term is named after Italian economist Vilfredo Pareto who brought us the Pareto (80–20) rule as well!) is one in which two parties reach an agreement resulting in both parties being better off and no other change to the agreement could bolster both equally (in other words, one party would ultimately benefit more). If there is an outcome that would have made both better off, the decision reached is not Pareto efficient.

Consider Barry and Nancy, who are going out to dinner. Barry likes Indian food best but cannot eat Chinese food. Nancy greatly prefers Chinese food but finds Indian dishes too hot. There is a range of possible solutions. They could go to a Chinese or Indian restaurant or choose among numerous other types of cuisine. They find Italian food acceptable but both prefer Thai to Italian.

It is possible to plot out all of these choices on a graph. On one axis are Barry's preference values. On the other axis are the values Nancy attaches to each preference. For Barry, Indian food has the highest value, Thai is next, then Italian, and Chinese last. For Nancy, Chinese is highest followed by Thai, Italian, and Indian last.

In this case, we conclude that Thai Pareto exceeds Italian. That is, a decision to go to a Thai restaurant results in both Barry and Nancy being better off than if they had gone to an Italian restaurant. The Thai choice is also Pareto efficient because the only choice that is better for Barry (Indian) leaves Nancy worse off. Similarly, the only decision better for Nancy (Chinese) leaves Barry worse off.

Collectively, negotiators "leave money on the table" when they settle for a Pareto-inefficient agreement. Pareto notions are a good mindset for seeking win–win agreements.

is what if the other party won't participate in a win–win process? In such cases, your best option is to try to place the focus on the integrity of the process instead of the opposing positions. If you really feel unable to keep the negotiations going in the right direction, you may want to consider using a third party to facilitate the negotiation.

Some Common Forms of Leverage

Discussions of who has more power among negotiating parties and who will not negotiate are related to leverage. Leverage refers to the principle of using a small advantage, or merely a perceived advantage, to gain a much larger benefit. Leverage in negotiations can take several forms, a few of which we highlight here.

Leverage of Legitimacy. The goal of this form of leverage is to give the impression an issue is not negotiable. To the extent that the other party believes it is nonnegotiable and does not attempt to negotiate, you have been successful. If a customer goes into an appliance store planning to buy a refrigerator, the store may have a very official-looking price tag on each refrigerator that says "Holiday Sale $759.99." Most people will not attempt to negotiate the price of the refrigerator in such cases because it appears nonnegotiable. Often, however, more things truly are negotiable than generally believed.

In any case, there are two lessons to learn about the leverage of legitimacy.

1. ***Make it look nonnegotiable.*** If you don't want something to be negotiated, think of ways to make it appear nonnegotiable. Vendors do this by having an "official price sheet." They are attempting to give the

impression that the terms of the sale are not negotiable. If the customer agrees to the sale without challenging any of the items in it, they have been successful in establishing legitimacy.

2. **Ask.** There is generally no or minimal risk in asking whether an issue that appears to be nonnegotiable truly is. If the vendor absolutely will not sell for any other price, you'll pay the same price whether you ask or not. If a vendor absolutely will not waive the restocking fee for returns, you haven't lost anything by asking.

Leverage of Timing.   A common tactic in negotiation is to get up to leave, saying, "Let me think about it. I'll be back." This has traditionally been a very effective tactic when buying a new car because salespeople do not want to see a customer who is willing to buy walk out the door. A variation of this tactic can be used by telephone as well.

You may gain several benefits by using this tactic:

1. You control the timing of when the negotiation will continue.

2. You get the opportunity to collect your thoughts and plan the next step in negotiating. This is particularly useful in complex negotiations.

3. You gain an opportunity to consult with other people, possibly including your own constituents, and collect further information.

4. You can use the time to talk to other parties to see if a better deal is possible elsewhere.

5. You can put pressure on the other party, if the other party is facing a deadline. For example, if a delegation has traveled from Argentina to discuss a joint venture with you, they incur a cost by extending the negotiation and letting you control the timing. This same principle may hold for sales quotas and the ending of a month or a quarter.

The Leverage of Limited Authority.   All things being equal, most people would say they prefer more authority to less. However, in negotiation, we gain an ironic benefit by having our authority limited by our boss or by some other entity.

For example, if you have been interviewing candidates for a job and have decided which one to make an offer to, your boss telling you a maximum salary to offer gives you an advantage. You are less pressured to accept an agreement you, your boss, and possibly others don't want. Your bottom line is carved in stone by someone else. You can even say, if pushed, "I wish I could help you, but my hands are tied. If it were up to me, I'd accept your offer." Another common example of this tactic occurs when a purchasing agent suggests that she has the authority to make the deal for $50,000, but will need additional clearances if the price is $55,000. In this case, the purchasing agent is unable to make any further concessions, so the logical route of progress is for the other party to make concessions.

As you might suspect, overuse of this tactic can frustrate the other party so much that they break off negotiations if they have a reasonable BATNA. If this tactic is used on you, one response is to attempt to circumvent the person with no authority and negotiate with the person who *has* authority.

Some Specific Process Tactics and How to Respond

Silence.   While it may sound a little odd, in the negotiation process, silence can be your strongest tool. All too often, negotiators do poorly because they "talk too much." If you've made an offer and you're waiting for a response, just sit back and wait. This is also a common tactic to use when you don't like what your counterpart has said. Most people feel uncomfortable when conversation ceases, and they start talking automatically to fill the void. Almost without fail, your counterpart will start whittling away his or her position when you use this tactic. In a wide variety of situations, consider the application of this tactic.

An example of using this tactic is the lack of response when a salesperson presents an initial offer. Often, your silence will make the salesperson uncomfortable and she will begin to provide more favorable terms because she is concerned that your silence is a signal of your unhappiness, and a salesperson will not want the potential client to leave. During the negotiation, you may make a proposal and find the other party remains silent. This can be very difficult to handle and often signals disapproval to the inexperienced negotiator. Just as nature abhors a vacuum, so silence induces the need in people to talk.

So what if you find yourself negotiating with a person who understands the importance of silence as well as you? Rather than wasting time in silence, restate your offer. Don't make suggestions; just repeat your terms. This maneuver forces the other person to respond, and more often than not, the person responds with a concession. If you have a proposal to make, make it and ask the other side how he or she feels about it. Having asked the question, sit back and wait for the answer. Whatever you do, don't change your offer because this could seriously weaken your position.

The Good Guy/Bad Guy Routine.   This tactic is often used in movies and sometimes in actual interrogations. The idea is that one detective person seems unreasonable and inflexible, while the other tries to make it look like he or she is on the suspect's side. The basic idea here is to gain the confidence of the suspect by conveying that you care about his or her well-being. This tactic is designed to get the suspect to make concessions without the other side making any in return. While this tactic is most famous in movies, it can also happen in interpersonal and business negotiations. The idea of "My boss doesn't want to do this" or "You will have much better luck dealing with me than the other guy" is to get another person to make a concession because that person feels that he is at an advantage as long as he is negotiating with the "good guy."

If you find yourself on the receiving end of the good guy/bad guy routine, your best option is to simply ignore it. Recognize the routine for what it is, but do not get pulled into it by allowing the "good guy" to influence your decision. The most effective response is to let your counterparts put on their show, while you stay focused on your own interests.

The Wince.   The wince is any visible negative reaction to another person's offer. For example, you might act stunned or surprised when your counterpart presents his initial offer. This tactic lets your counterpart know that you believe the offer is "out of range," and this is not a dishonest or contrived act in itself. Wincing at the right time can save you a great deal of money and gain you much better terms in some cases. It is just important to remember that when deals are negotiable, your counterpart will normally start high. Where wincing becomes a real challenge, however, is when it is theatrically performed.

Of course, you won't always be the wincer. Many times, especially in the sales profession, you'll be on the receiving end of the wince. You are normally best served by going into a mode of silence. Force the other person to articulate her displeasure and do not begin making concessions due to the negative facial expressions or body language of the other person. This is a place where it is best to close your mouth and force your counterpart to act.

The Trial Balloon.   This tactic presents a question designed to assess your negotiating counterpart's position without giving away your plans. You may ask your counterpart, "Would you sign a contract today if the terms are good?" or "Would you be interested in some financing options?" These types of questions are effective ways of gaining additional information by keeping your counterpart talking, and they do not commit you in any way because they are not actual offers on your part. It is important to note that this may be very consistent with win–win negotiating by bringing more options to the table.

When you're on the receiving end of a trial balloon question in a competitive setting, do not feel like you have to answer the question thoroughly. If, however, you are in a collaborative setting, feel free to answer the question and pose your own trial balloons in response. For example, if someone asks, "Would you consider financing the house yourself?" respond, "Well, if I did, what would your offer be?" This both builds the information available and puts the ball back in the court of your counterpart.

Bait-and-Switch.   The bait-and-switch tactic should be avoided because it is inherently dishonest, but this does not mean that others will not try it when you are negotiating with them. Your counterpart may try to attract your interests with one great offer, but then hook you with another mediocre one. This is a common tactic in print advertising, particularly among mattress stores. A common practice is to have a bed advertised for some outrageously low price, but when you go to the store, you find that the bed is actually a piece of foam two inches thick.

If someone does use this tactic against you, you will inevitably fare poorly unless you can recognize it is happening. When you do recognize it, run (don't walk) away from your counterpart. It is a sure sign that your counterpart does not have a genuinely good deal, because if he did, he would not resort to the bait-and-switch.

Outrageous Behavior.   Many students may be surprised by this, but outrageous behavior is a common tactic and one that is employed in college faculty meetings frequently. Outrageous behavior can be categorized as any form of socially unacceptable conduct intended to force the other side to make a move, such as throwing a fit of anger or bursting into tears. As most people feel uncomfortable in these situations, they may reduce their negotiating terms just to avoid them. The authors of this book have seen people pound the table, jump up and down, swear, turn red, and perform just about every tantrum-like behavior imaginable.

While it is extremely tempting to get locked into an emotional battle with people who employ this tactic, the most effective response to outrageous behavior is none at all. Just wait for the fit to die down before reacting, because emotional negotiations can result in disaster. It is not your job to comfort the other person and if the person is really "outrageous," you probably should not be negotiating with this person anyway.

Red Herring.   During the negotiation process, a red herring refers to one side bringing up a relatively minor point to distract the other side from the more important issues at hand. Most ethical negotiators agree that this tactic is exceptionally sleazy and cannot be considered an action of someone acting in good faith. If your negotiation is bogged down with a minor problem (or a series of minor problems), and your counterpart insists on settling it before talking about substantive matters, then you are probably seeing the use of a red herring tactic.

Because the use of red herrings generally signals a breach of good faith, this should be a signal to you to proceed with great caution. The best course of action is to suggest setting the issue aside temporarily to work out other details. If this consistently fails, then you should remove yourself from the negotiation because it will prove very difficult to improve upon your BATNA if the other party is negotiating in bad faith.

The Written Word.   This is a tactic to make it appear that the terms are not negotiable, when they may truly be negotiable. When the terms of a deal are written out, they appear to be nonnegotiable (especially if they are put into legal terms). For example, when was the last time you negotiated a lease, or a loan, or even a service contract that was typed up in advance in an official-looking document? You probably assumed these deals were nonnegotiable, and for some reason most people make the same mistake of accepting terms that appear in writing. It is important to remember that many more things are negotiable than you generally assume. Let your counterpart know that you find some part of the terms unacceptable and that if she is not willing to negotiate these terms, that you will find another person who will be open to negotiating. While this may not work, it will let you know whether there is room for negotiation, or whether you should look elsewhere.

"During a negotiation, it would be wise not to take anything personally. If you leave personalities out of it, you will be able to see opportunities more objectively."
—Brian Koslow

Bluffing.   With all of the recent attention to Texas Hold'em poker, you may be wondering about the stone-cold bluff. Bluffing is a common tactic in negotiation, but be aware that bluffing incurs two risks. First, heavy-handed bluffing can strain relationships. Remember that one outcome of the ideal negotiation is that the relationship is maintained or even improved. Bluffing is an especially high-stakes risk in ongoing relationships. Second, if the bluff fails, the negotiation can be over. In this case, you may have sacrificed an outcome superior to your BATNA because of the failed bluff.

As an example of overplaying a bluff, assume you tell a vendor you absolutely must have shipment within 48 hours or there is no deal. However, you are bluffing. You know this is the only vendor that can fill your order with the specifications you want and that you would wait as long as necessary to get the order from this vendor. You just bluffed to get a faster shipment. Suppose the vendor replies, "We absolutely can't ship it that fast; I guess we'll have to lose out on your order. Maybe we could do business in the future." At that point, you begin to backpedal and the vendor realizes you were bluffing—and that they can make the delivery any time they want. If you were heavy-handed in the way you posed your bluff, you may have even strained the relationship. In that case, the vendor may choose not to expedite the order at all. The failed bluff showed the vendor that it didn't need to negotiate to get your business.

The End of the Negotiation

As a negotiation draws to a close, always keep multiple issues on the table until the very end. That gives you the opportunity to make trade-offs so each party believes they made a good deal. If you let the end of the negotiation come down to one issue, with all other issues taken off the table, you'll have much more difficulty reaching an agreement whereby both parties believe they made a good deal.

Basically, by leaving as many issues on the table as possible, it gives you more potential options in putting together a final agreement.

Once you have made an agreement, you'll want some level of documentation of the terms of the agreement. This might range from a verbal agreement and handshake to a formal contract prepared by attorneys. You'll need to decide what level of documentation you want. Either end of the continuum carries a risk.

If you ask for the agreement in writing:

- You can offend the other party. This is a particularly common problem in cross-cultural negotiation. In many cultures, a personal relationship of trust is paramount, and asking for a contract prepared by attorneys is offensive because it implies a lack of trust in the relationship. This is especially true in Japan and many South American countries.

- You strain the relationship. Think of what it would do to the relationship if you negotiated with your spouse over the specifics of an upcoming vacation and then insisted on putting the terms of the negotiation in writing.

If you don't ask for the agreement in writing:

- The other parties can later disagree about the terms of the agreement.
- One or more parties may back out of the agreement.
- The resources you are investing are at more risk.
- Your constituents, particularly your boss, may not be satisfied with a verbal agreement.

Evaluate How Well It Went

Most negotiators naturally neglect thinking about the process of negotiation itself. Instead, they focus exclusively on the content of the specific negotiation—the problem, their needs, the issues, the proposals, and the counterproposals. As the stakes get higher, the process gets pushed even further into the background.

When the negotiation is over, however, it is always a good idea to take time to analyze how the process went. Think about your strategy and tactics. In retrospect, were they appropriate? What information was critical to the process, and how did you seek it? Did you recognize the strategy and tactics used by the other party? Did you respond effectively to that strategy and those tactics? If this was a negotiation in an ongoing relationship, what did you learn that might help in the next negotiation? Did the other party use any tactics you would like to adopt into your negotiating style?

In evaluating a negotiation, it is useful to debrief any negotiation experience using a scorecard like the one in Table 11.7. You may need to modify the scorecard for specific instances, but the framework provided here is pretty flexible and generally will do a good job of letting you know whether or not the negotiation was truly a win–win outcome.

In Table 11.7, a truly win–win deal should not have any entries in the "no" category. One or two "maybes" may exist, but ideally, a "yes" should appear in every row.

This is yet another situation where it's important to learn from our experiences. We all know people who repeat the same mistakes. In negotiation, learning from your mistakes means analyzing the process afterward when you have time to focus on process. Evidence shows that superior negotiators are more likely than average negotiators to analyze the negotiation process after the negotiations are over (see Table 11.8).

"I am a woman in process. I'm just trying like everybody else. I try to take every conflict, every experience, and learn from it. Life is never dull."

—Oprah Winfrey

TABLE 11.7   The Negotiation Scorecard

In evalauting a negotiation, it is useful to debrief any negotiation experience using a scorecard like the one below. You may need to modify the scorecard for specific instances, but the framework provided here is pretty flexible and generally will do a good job of letting you know whether or not the negotiation was truly a win–win outcome.

	Yes	Maybe	No	Not Relevant
All parties believe they made a good deal				
You believe you made a good deal				
Your boss believes you made a good deal				
The other party believes they made a good deal				
The relationship is maintained or improved				
You wish to do more business with the other party				
The other party wants to do more business with you				
Constituents are satisfied with the deal				
Your constituents (boss, peers, partners, and other stakeholders) are satisfied with the deal				
The other party's constituents are satisfied with the deal				

TABLE 11.8   Actions of Superior Negotiators[22]

Evidence shows that superior negotiators demonstrate behaviors average negotiators are less likely to exhibit. Compared to average negotiators, they:

In negotiation planning:

- Consider more possible solutions and options.
- Spend more time looking for common interests.
- Think more about long-term consequences.

In the actual negotiation:

- Are more likely to begin by taking a cooperative rather than competitive stance.
- Make fewer immediate counterproposals.
- Make a greater effort to understand the other party's interests.
- Ask more questions, especially to test understanding.
- Are less likely to describe their offers in glowing, positive terms.
- Have a greater frequency of topic changes.
- Summarize the progress made during the negotiation.

KO 11-5

Mediation

DO 11-5

While we certainly hope for a win–win result from the negotiation process, to imply that all negotiation creates a happy ending is utter nonsense. Negotiation between parties often breaks down or creates unsatisfactory outcomes. Fortunately, if negotiation does break down, you are not entirely out of options. Perhaps the most straightforward of those options is some form of mediation using a third party (maybe you, if you have two conflicting associates). Mediation has a long history of facilitating conflicts and can sometimes create the discipline and focus to resolve a dispute when negotiation has failed.

When Is Mediation Used?

Mediation can be used in a great number of areas. To keep the situations as easy to understand as possible, we will group the situations where mediation is often used into two specific categories: non-business and business settings.

Non-Business Settings

The most common situations where mediation is used (at least in the United States) are for divorce and child custody. Mediation offers a couple the chance to define what is most workable for their particular situation and to tailor an agreement that reflects their own circumstances. Compared to the courts, the privacy of mediation can make it easier for people to discuss emotional matters and give the parties more control over the process and outcome. In general, parties wish to avoid going to court because a court-imposed solution may leave everybody unhappy.

Beyond divorce and child custody cases, mediation is also frequently used to settle interpersonal arguments (for example, between roommates, friends, or family members), in a school or university setting (say, peer mediation in both high schools and universities), criminal cases (for instance, minor nonviolent crimes are often referred to mediation to ease the burden on the court system), and community situations (such items as land use, zoning, and nuisance complaints). The primary goal in all of these cases is to settle a dispute in a structured manner that gives the party some measure of control in the process. Also, a significant goal of mediation is to reduce the burden on the courts and to provide a more cost-effective means of settling disputes than is normally possible once attorneys and the court system become involved.

Business Settings

The goals in business settings remain the same as in non-business settings: to keep some control of the process and to settle disputes in a cost-effective manner. In business settings, the mediation cases that get the most attention are collective bargaining between labor unions and management. Other common examples of mediation in a business setting occur for contract disagreements; insurance claims; construction issues involving architects, builders, and owners; real estate disputes; and cases between landlord and tenant, consumer and merchant, and farmer and lender.

For our purposes, however, the most relevant form of mediation in a business setting is that of workplace mediation. Problems between business partners, co-workers, or supervisor and employee are often mediated to correct particular problems and continue productive relationships. It is important to know that while mediation can be a very formal procedure, less formal mediations happen all the time. Every time there is a dispute between co-workers and another person steps in, this can be considered mediation of some sort. Our real challenge is to understand the mediation process as completely as possible and then be able to employ its guidelines so we can help others settle their disputes, or play a constructive role in the process when we are engaged in a dispute that requires some form of mediation.

In some cases, a mediator is an outside party who specializes in helping people in conflict reach an amicable agreement. In other cases, it can simply be a manager with two conflicting associates or a friend trying to help resolve a dispute between two other friends. A mediator is typically necessary where a lack of trust between two parties makes negotiation ineffective. In such cases, only when the disputing parties feel there will be some sense of fairness and justice will disputes be resolved.

Trust Building: The Foundation of the Mediation

An effective mediator must convince the parties to trust him or her, then to trust the negotiation process itself, and finally to begin to trust each other.[23] To help the parties involved trust the mediator, a few important guidelines for the mediator include:

- Choose a comfortable neutral space away from any party's "turf."
- Schedule short meetings and be involved as little as possible.
- Listen with an open mind and do not say much.
- Be respectful and express only positive opinions of the parties involved.
- Emphasize a desire to help. Do not pick sides.
- Assure parties that all conversations are held in strict confidence.
- Be a role model and build a strong reputation for staying on task and doing what you say.

Trust in the process is facilitated by focusing only on procedural matters in the beginning. For example, getting parties to agree on where to hold the meetings and using some ground rules for discussion may help convince them the process will work. It is best to avoid all substantive issues until both parties have made some small agreements. These small successes build momentum that a solution is possible.[24]

An effective mediator also (1) is dogged in learning and applying facts, (2) frames the disputed claims into the real issues, (3) maintains neutrality, and (4) seeks to understand the underlying interests of each party, validating both sides. These skills are nicely illustrated in Management Live 11.3 which appears later in this chapter.

The Mediation Process

Mediation is a well-studied and constantly practiced process. As a result, it has well-defined steps and procedures. To best understand the mediation process, it helps to break it down into four major steps. These four steps are (1) stabilize the setting, (2) help the parties communicate, (3) help the parties negotiate, and (4) clarify the agreements. We will address each of these areas in turn next.

Stabilize the Setting

First, it is important to consider where the parties have been before they reached mediation. In general, mediation occurs because there has been a problem that the parties have been unable to solve themselves. So it is best to think of mediation as "Plan B" and "Plan A" was a failure. In personal lives, divorcing couples go to mediation to avoid costly legal battles, child support amounts are sometimes determined through mediation, and other issues relating to the custody and care of children are often determined through this process.

In order to stabilize the setting, there is a series of step-by-step procedures in which to engage. While all of these may not be necessary every time, the following steps provide a "cookbook" approach to stabilizing the situation so that meaningful progress can be made.

- Greet the parties.
- Indicate where each of them is to sit.
- Identify yourself and each party by name.

- Offer water, paper and pencil, and patience.
- State the purpose of the mediation.
- Confirm your neutrality.
- Get their commitment to proceed.
- Get their commitment that only one party at a time will speak.
- Get their commitment to speak directly to you.

The preceding steps serve to make the parties feel comfortable and also get them to make initial agreements. Even if it is only getting people committed to the process and to some basic ground rules, these are important steps to making real progress toward resolving more substantive disputes between the parties.

Help the Parties Communicate

It is important to remember that the parties in negotiation are generally there because they have not been able to work the problems out themselves. So the situation is often contentious. In such a case, your fairness is of utmost concern and may require you to go to great lengths to show that you are impartial. Follow the steps in Tool Kit 11.3 to help the parties communicate.

Help the Parties Negotiate

Once you have identified the issues and had the parties set the priorities on the issues and demands at hand, it is time for you to assist the parties in their negotiation. Remember, you want to help the parties toward a win–win solution, so the

MANAGER'S TOOL KIT

Tool Kit 11.3 Mediation Guidelines

- Explain the rationale for who speaks first.
- Reassure them that both will speak without interruption, for as long as necessary.
- Ask the first speaker to tell what has happened.
- Take notes and respond actively (for example, "Yes," "I see," "Continue," "How did that make you feel?").
- Calm the parties as needed.
- Clarify with restatements.
- Focus the narration on the issues in the dispute.
- Make sure you understand the story by summarizing (eliminate all disparaging references here).
- Thank this party for speaking, the other for listening quietly.
- Ask the second speaker to tell what has happened, and follow the same list of instructions as you did for the first speaker, from taking notes to thanking both parties.
- After both speakers have had their say, ask each party in turn to clarify the major issues to be resolved.
- Inquire into basic issues, probing to see if something else, instead, may be at the root of the complaints.
- Define the problem by restating and summarizing.
- Conduct private meetings if needed.
- Summarize areas of agreement and disagreement.
- Help the parties set priorities on the issues and demands.

advice from earlier in the chapter is extremely relevant to this step in the process. To help the parties negotiate you should:

- Ask each party to list alternative possibilities for a settlement.
- Restate and summarize each alternative.
- Check with each party on the workability of each alternative.
- Restate whether the alternative is workable.
- In an impasse, suggest other alternatives.
- Note the amount of progress already made, to show that success is likely.
- If the impasse continues, suggest a break or a second mediation session.
- Encourage them to select the alternative that appears to be workable.
- Increase their understanding by rephrasing the alternative.
- Help them plan a course of action to implement the alternative.

Clarify the Agreement

The final and maybe most important part of the process is to clarify the agreement. After the hard work that has gone before (see Management Live 11.3 for an example of the mediation process), too many mediated solutions fail because the parties depart unclear as to exactly what was agreed to. By removing uncertainty and ambiguity from the agreement, a good mediator can help the parties forge a solution that will be more adhered to and will reduce the likelihood of future disputes. To clarify the agreement effectively, the mediator needs to:

- Summarize the agreement terms.
- Recheck that each party understands the agreement.
- Ask whether other issues need to be discussed.
- Help them specify the terms of their agreement.
- State each person's role in the agreement.
- Recheck with each party that each knows when to do certain things.
- Explain the process of follow-up.
- Establish a time for follow-up with each party.
- Emphasize that the agreement is for the parties, not for the mediator.
- Congratulate the parties on their reasonableness and on the workability of their resolution.

⇄ MANAGEMENT LIVE 11.3

Mediation in Action

Several years ago, a large trucking company received a call from a customer that a truck had recently caused damage to the customer's loading dock, but that the trucker would not compensate the manufacturer for the repairs. After some discussion, mediation was recommended.

The opening statements were predictably accusatory, with the manufacturer expecting compensation and the trucking outfit denying any involvement. The mediator sought and introduced the undisputed facts that emerged in the discussion to help both sides understand what really happened and when.

The mediator listened as each side presented its position and then followed up with a line of questions designed to reframe the discussion in terms of issues. The manufacturer stated that the container door swung open as the truck pulled out, damaging the frame and bending the rails that allow the steel shutters to seal the opening, resulting in several thousand dollars of damage. On the other hand, the trucking outfit noted that several days had gone by before it was notified of a claim, and it was not sent any evidence of the damage.

Through each party's responses, the mediator began to clarify each party's underlying interests. While it was obvious the manufacturer wanted monetary compensation, the trucking outfit wanted to be sure that the manufacturer was not taking advantage of them. In essence, the trucking outfit was not inclined to accept any liability for the events in question before being shown it was responsible.

The mediator then validated the motivations and acknowledged the feelings of each party explicitly, giving all sides a reason to buy into the mediation and continue. When both sides agreed that it is industry standard for the truck driver to be responsible for properly securing the container door before departure, and the mediator pointed out that the driver would be unlikely to volunteer information to his own employer about any sort of incident, the trucking outfit agreed to settle the matter upon two conditions. One was a follow-up discussion with the driver who had handled that day's shipment, and the second was receipt of the manufacturer's internal documentation (including pictures) noting what had happened.

This mediation was successfully concluded in under an hour and did not require further mediator intervention to uphold the bargain. Without the mediation, the conflict would likely have deteriorated to the detriment of both parties—not only would the trucking outfit have lost a valued customer, but the manufacturer would also have limited its own scheduling options and pricing power by severing all ties to an established local trucking outfit. In this case, the relationship between the trucking outfit and the manufacturer was preserved and the parties were able to continue working together going forward, to their mutual benefit.

Of course, things don't always work out so smoothly. However, they are far more likely to work out if you avoid the tendency to wing it in the pressure of conflict situations and instead practice the known principles of mediation success.

> CASE CONCLUDED

The common perception was that the players' solidarity would crumble once they started missing paychecks. However, the foundation beneath that line of thinking would be as solid as Jell-O if the players could couple the insurance with a large financial award from U.S. District Judge David Doty, who previously ruled the owners had illegally created a $4.3 billion lockout fund for themselves by renegotiating their TV deals at the expense of the players.

"Players Association leadership looked into this as a last possible resort to keep players together in case games would be missed," one players-side source said of the insurance war chest. "It was never intended to be used as a bargaining chip or negotiating point until things became critical."

If the sides could not advance negotiations, then the possibility of hundreds of millions of dollars being lost to canceled preseason games was real. And if the owners allowed the impasse to get that far, what was to stop them from testing the players' pain threshold by extending the lockout into the regular season?

The Players Association began informing its membership about the insurance fund once it looked like some paychecks could be missed. There's no way to know whether it was the final oomph that pushed negotiations onto positive ground, but it's hard to believe it didn't have some impact, considering the talks were "not in a good place" for much of the prior negotiations period.

Questions

1. Describe the concept of BATNA and how it applies to the NFL Players position in this case? Why is it such a powerful idea?

2. What are the first steps in "getting your way"?

3. Are there any special steps to be taken if you know you are lower in power than your other negotiating party?

Concluding Note

Conflict situations are inevitable and frequent in organizational life, and generally they are among managers' most unnerving experiences. Two fundamental guidelines are to always diagnose before acting and to know the different alternatives for conflict resolution so you can adapt your own natural inclinations as appropriate. Becoming familiar with a few simple but powerful principles for negotiating agreements and mediating disputes is also critical to competence in managing conflict. Perhaps the most important lesson is that conflict can be a powerful source of growth. That is, properly managed, it can be an opportunity to implement change in the way people interact and improve their problem-solving skills. It can also result in increased innovation and strengthened relationships. To quote William Ellery Channing, "Difficulties are meant to rouse, not discourage. The human spirit is to grow strong by conflict."

KEY TERMS

accommodation 387

avoidance 388

best alternative to a negotiated
  agreement (BATNA) 392

collaboration 389

competition 387

compromise 389

conflict 378

hypotheticals 398

mixed-motive situation 384

Pareto efficient 399

relationship conflict 380

superordinate goal 391

task conflict 380

win–lose negotiation 393

win–win negotiation 393

zero-sum game 384

< < CASE
How the Marriage Proposal Became a Negotiation
The question, like the ring, used to be a surprise

In 1972, on a park bench in Birmingham, Alabama, Garner Lee Green's father proposed to her mother. The proposal came out of the blue. She said yes.

"That doesn't happen to people anymore," says Ms. Green, who is 30. And it certainly wasn't the way her husband asked her to marry him several years ago. The two of them talked for a long time about how and when the proposal would happen. "I was ready before he was, so we had to come to a meeting of the minds about a time frame.

The negotiations lasted about six months," Ms. Green says.

She is not the only one who missed what used to be a classic big moment. Those romantic tales that get passed among friends and relatives—"One day he just showed up with a ring! I was completely surprised!"—are relics of the past. We've gone from popping the question to a long conversation, hammering out the details of when and how the engagement will happen.

Amanda Miller, a sociology professor at the University of Central Oklahoma, conducted a study about how proposals are made among cohabiting couples. The result, titled "Waiting to Be Asked," found that couples not only work together as a team to set the date, but some women actually script the proposal first, telling their boyfriend something like: "I'd always wanted to be proposed to on Christmas morning in front of family."

The engagement negotiation is not some repackaged version of the female proposal or part of an ultimatum. This new ritual simply points to a less unilateral and more pragmatic approach. In a world where two young people are juggling goals, the proposal language sounds something like: "I'll be finishing up medical school, and then I'll be doing my residency, so maybe we can do the wedding between the residency and my fellowship. So what if you propose in June?"

Consider the case of 29-year-old Ethan, a GMAT tutor in New York City (he asked that his last name not be used because details of his proposal process are not known to his future in-laws). He says he and his fiancée talked about all but one thing ahead of time: "Essentially, the diamond was the only element of the proposal and the wedding that we did not negotiate."

And then there's Casie Zimmerman, a 27-year-old lawyer in New Orleans who is engaged to her boyfriend after dating him for five years. Their discussion was a now-typical one about how to shoehorn a wedding into career plans. "He wanted to finish law school and pass the bar before he proposed, and I wanted it to happen before I took a job in a new city, so we had a lot of back-and-forth on how it would happen." As part of the contemporary transparent process, Ms. Zimmerman's now-fiancé instructed her to go pick out rings in advance.

So how is all this bargaining affecting gender dynamics? "The norm that the man has to take control of the proposal has been greatly undermined and eroded," says Kathleen Gerson, a professor of sociology at New York University. "Women want to feel they have more control of where a relationship is going instead of waiting to react."

Yet the gender dance is still being worked out. Josh Brentan, who blogs at thegroomwithaview.com, proposed to his girlfriend in July after an open discussion about getting engaged. "But I was happy that I could surprise her with the actual proposal. It's nice to still have some proprietary feeling over it," he says. Ms. Green's husband has said he feels slightly cheated that he didn't get to surprise her with his proposal.

Even so, do not mistake this for a level playing field. While there is more negotiation and compromise about the marriage time-table, Ms. Miller says her research showed that the man still holds the power to shut down the marriage conversation. Men in their 20s and 30s don't seem to view the backroom negotiation as emasculating or ceding their turf to a generation of empowered women either. On the contrary—all this talking may have simply eliminated the only scary aspect of a proposal for a man: that the woman will say no.

"You do not propose to a woman without absolute assurance that she'll say yes," says Ethan, and Mr. Brentan agrees. "I liked that Erica, my fiancée, brought up the topic of marriage with me first. It was nice knowing, before I proposed, that she wanted to spend the rest of her life with me."

Ms. Seligson is the author of *A Little Bit Married: How to Know When It's Time to Walk Down the Aisle or Out the Door* (Da Capo Press).

Discussion Questions

1. Do you think that viewing a marriage proposal as a negotiation is a good idea or not? Support your answer by providing likely outcomes.

2. Using the material from the chapter, can you build on the case to provide other "nontraditional" examples of where win–win negotiations may be possible?

3. If negotiation does not work in this example, would you recommend going forward to the mediation process? Why or why not?

SELECT MANAGE *WHAT?* DEBRIEFS

Resolving a Team Dispute: Debrief

Based on the information you have, this is not an issue that you should hope will just "work itself out." Instead, you will need to actively intervene if your goal is to keep this team together and functioning productively. And prior to embarking on a strategy to resolve this dispute, it would be good to know your own dominant conflict management style. This type of situation can be very tense and it may require direct conversations that can be challenging to those with a preference for compromise or conciliation—so know your style and what you are most likely to resort to if pressed. That way, at least you will be cognizant of when you may be asked to go "against style" and the extra preparation and energy that it may consume.

In any case, the first thing to do is to promptly arrange individual meetings with Pat, Jordan, and the other members of the team who contacted you and noted their dissatisfaction. Start with other team members and describe your reaction to Pat's actions and indicate your commitment to enforce team norms and a willingness to move quickly and forcibly with those who violate those norms. Also, be sure to invite input. Ask about the specific nature of their concerns and how those concerns could be resolved to their satisfaction. Is this task conflict or relational conflict (much harder to resolve)? Be clear that you communicate that you want their input but will make no decisions until you collect sufficient data and hear all perspectives.

Once you have met with all other concerned team members, meet with Pat and tell him directly that his actions were a violation of team norms and cannot be tolerated. Ask for his input on what he thinks can be done to help restore the group to productive functioning. Ideally, he will be remorseful and perhaps willing to apologize to the team and indicate a willingness to move forward—indeed you might want to require this of him as a condition of continued team membership.

At the next scheduled meeting of the team, you need to be clear that the working norms of the group were violated and that, as team leader, you will not stand for future outbursts or team disruptions of this kind. However, you also know that the team has been productive in the past and that pressure and deadlines can create friction that otherwise would not exist. Moreover, people make mistakes. So, given some remorse, an apology, and team member willingness to give Pat a second chance, your hope is that the team can get back on course. By addressing the issue right away and showing a willingness to fully understand and deal with it (that is, discussing the undiscussables), you have a much better chance of getting members to put this incident behind and go forward.

Negotiating an Agreement Between Conflicting Parties: Debrief

This type of situation, where both sides have good arguments and there is no obvious right solution, is particularly common in organizational situations. Unfortunately, the search for agreement too often takes the form of *positional* bargaining whereby each side opens with their position on an issue and tries to convince the other. This is generally an *ineffective* way of reaching agreements—it tends to encourage stubbornness and often harms the parties' relationship.

As chair of this committee, both the issue and the relationships are very important to you and so you are therefore eager to avoid positional bargaining and find a collaborative solution. Your goal is to get your committee members to think of each other as partners in problem solving rather than as adversaries in a negotiation. With that in mind, the four fundamental principles of effective negotiation (sometimes called principled negotiation or collaborative conflict resolution) are particularly applicable. Specifically, (1) separate the people from the problem; (2) focus on interests rather than positions; (3) generate a variety of options before settling on an agreement; and (4) insist that the agreement be based on objective criteria.

First, you want to attempt to separate the people from the problem. In this case, the problem is that you have a number of worthy uses for limited resources, including a leaky tower that some important folks would like to see fixed. You have people who already feel strongly about what to do (and not do) and so they will tend to take any challenges to their position as a personal attack. Ideally, you want to foster a discussion that focuses on solving this problem and not solely on advocating preconceived arguments. Thus, it might make sense to hold a meeting without the strongest advocates present or at least ask opposing parties to articulate the other's case. Whatever you do, it is critical that you talk about different ideas and arguments without associating them with any names or members.

Second, good agreements stem from a focus on the parties' interests, rather than their stated positions. A good way to get at interests is to ask, "Why do you take that position?" Responses to that question often yield a glimpse into other positions that might satisfy that interest. In this case, the positions are (a) use all the money to restore the clock tower, and (b) use just enough to fix the leak. Other interests are likely things such as focus on current students in the dorm, honor our commitments, respect tradition, represent the desires of the majority, keep donors happy, and so on. Once you get such interests expressed and in the open, it is far easier to apply the third principle, generate creative options.

When the parties' interests differ, they should seek options in which those differences can be made compatible or even complementary. The key to reconciling different interests is to "look for items that are of low cost to you and high benefit to them, and vice versa." Each side should try to make proposals that are appealing to the other side, and that the other side would find easy to agree to. There are no easy answers, of course, but your only chance of getting a win–win agreement is to get beyond the two opposing positions that are in play right now.

Finally, it might be helpful here to spend some time in a shared search for some objective criteria to help decide the reasonableness of any decision reached. The parties must agree which criteria is best for their situation. Criteria should be both legitimate and practical. Benchmarking data from like situations, research findings, and legal precedent are possible sources of objective criteria. Rather than agreeing on substantive criteria, the parties may create a fair procedure for resolving their dispute. For example, children may fairly divide a piece of cake by having one child cut it, and the other choose her piece. In this case, an objective criterion might be something like "For every dollar spent on historical preservation, one is also spent on current student needs." The idea is that if we can agree to some objective standard decisions based on reasonable standards, this will make it easier for the parties to agree and preserve their good relationship.

Getting Beyond Failed Negotiations: Debrief

This is the type of miserable situation dreaded by most young managers, and, to be frank, there may be no way to resolve this beyond terminating the employment of one or both of the associates in question. However, particularly if they are productive in their respective jobs, you should hope that this will not be necessary and so your best bet is to apply the guidelines associated with effective mediation. If you are going to be effective in this situation, you must convince both Terry and Chris to trust you and the mediation process, and finally to begin to trust each other. Among the key rules to follow are:

- Choose a comfortable, neutral space away from any party's "turf."
- Shorter is better. Schedule short meetings and be involved as little as possible.
- Listen with an open mind and do not say much.
- Be respectful and express only positive opinions of the parties involved.
- Emphasize a desire to help—do not pick sides.
- Assure parties that all conversations are held in strict confidence.
- Be a role model and build a strong reputation for staying on task and doing what you say.

Trust in the process is facilitated by focusing only on procedural matters in the beginning. For example, getting parties to agree on where to hold the meetings and using some ground rules for the discussion may help convince them that the process will work. It is best to avoid all substantive issues until both parties have had some small agreements. It is these small successes that build momentum that a solution is possible. An effective mediator also (1) is dogged in learning and applying facts, (2) frames the disputed claims into the real issues, (3) maintains neutrality, and (4) seeks to understand the underlying interests of each party—validating both sides.

It probably would be a good idea to involve your boss in a meeting—following the same guidelines. That way, both Terry and Chris understand the seriousness of the issue and the willingness of management to devote time to creating a more harmonious working environment.

CHAPTER 12

Recruiting, Selecting, and Retaining Talent

OBJECTIVES

KNOWING   DOING

After reading this chapter, you should be able to:

"You can dream, create, design and build the most wonderful place in the world, but it requires people to make the dream a reality."

—Walt Disney

KO 12-1 Articulate the essential steps in recruiting and selecting employees.

KO 12-2 Describe effective recruitment and selection methods.

KO 12-3 Articulate the most important aspects of employment law.

KO 12-4 Explain the key elements in retaining talent.

DO 12-1 Create an evidence-based recruitment strategy.

DO 12-2 Create a strategy to increase diversity in an applicant pool.

DO 12-3 Create a realistic job preview for a new position.

DO 12-4 Write a behavioral interview question.

DO 12-5 Use evidence-based methods to retain talented employees.

Case: Google, Microsoft, Southwest Airlines, and Doubletree Hotels

Making selection decisions remains one of the most misunderstood and poorly executed of all management endeavors. And it takes on particular importance where jobs are highly desirable and people will go to great lengths to obtain those jobs (and perhaps even stretch the truth and inflate their credentials on resumés and in unstructured interviews). So how do progressive firms go about making selection decisions that will most likely result in productive workers? Consider the cases of four such firms.

Google. While once obsessively focused on raw technical skills, Google now looks for more multidimensional candidates and does so by relying less on traditional screening tools like resumés, unstructured interviews, and reference checks—and more on bio-data, structured interviewing, and work samples. Desperate to hire more engineers and sales representatives to staff its rapidly growing search and advertising business, the firm has created an automated way to search for talent among the more than 100,000 job applications it receives each month.

It begins by asking job applicants to fill out an elaborate online survey that explores their attitudes, behavior, personality, and biographical details going back to high school. Among the types of questions asked are: Have you ever made a profit from a catering

HOW DO YOU PICK PEOPLE FOR JOBS AT PLACES WHERE EVERYONE WANTS TO WORK?

business or dog walking? Do you prefer to work alone or in groups? Have you ever set a world record in anything? The answers are fed into a series of formulas created by Google's mathematicians that calculate a score—from 0 to 100—meant to predict how well a person will fit into Google's chaotic and competitive culture.

"As we get bigger, we find it harder and harder to find enough really talented and qualified people," said Laszlo Bock, Google's vice president for people operations. "With traditional hiring methods, we were worried we will overlook some of the best candidates. For example, we have found unstructured interviews to be terrible predictors of performance," Mr. Bock said.

Microsoft. Microsoft has long held that brains alone are not enough. You aced math. You can write code in your sleep. You'd kill to work at Microsoft. So tell me this: Why are manhole covers round? Or, how many gas stations are there in the United States? Or . . .

Microsoft's interview process is notoriously rigorous. Part oral exam, part brainteaser, and part personality

test, the software developer's inquisition of computer talent is like an Olympic decathlon designed to discover those people whose "skullware" is fast, flexible, and above all creative. While other companies look just for technical expertise and experience, the Redmond software giant is keenly screening for a broader skill set as well.

A Microsoft structured interview can range from the typical computer science question about bit counting and link lists to brainteasers involving ski lifts, look-alike coins of varying weight, or balloons that move in mysterious ways. Another form of question is more like a sampling of candidate creativity—often a multipart exercise that requires quick access to your mental architecture. One interviewer, for instance, asks candidates to plan the ideal shower, and then to modify the plan to accommodate a handicapped user. Other interviewees have been asked to come up with designs for houses and TV remote controls.

The purpose of these mental gymnastics is to discover applicants who can thrive at Microsoft's supercharged Redmond corporate
(continued)

campus, where caffeine-fueled programmers can find themselves working 16-hour days on programs that will eventually earn hundreds of millions of dollars in revenue. To come out on top in the interview, you must display an ability to think creatively rather than simply provide the right answer.

The interviews, and the process behind them, speak volumes about Microsoft's curious corporate culture. In most companies, the human resources manager interviews candidates and then sends them off to a senior executive. At Microsoft, geeks rule. Human resources personnel do the preliminary vetting, but junior software engineers and program managers, as young as 24, also do the interviewing.

In testimony to the peculiar folklore of the company, there is even a kind of pantheon of defunct "Microquestions." The best known of these is probably the conundrum about manhole covers and why they are round. The answer, you wonder? Because a square cover on a square manhole would be dangerous. Rotate the cover 45 degrees, tilt it on its side, and it could fall in.

1. Even otherwise very good managers often have a hard time fully understanding findings from selection research. What lessons from that research have served Google and Microsoft so well?

2. What are the most common selection traps and misconceptions that Google and Microsoft are avoiding with their innovative tactics?

3. Why have firms like Google and Microsoft moved away from relying on resumés and unstructured interviews when making their hiring decisions?

4. If you really wanted a job at Microsoft, how would you most effectively answer questions like "How many gas stations are there in the USA?" or "How many ping pong balls will fit in a school bus?" or "How much would you charge to wash all the windows in Seattle?" or "How would you move Mount Fuji?"

MANAGE WHAT?

1. Expanding Your Pool of Candidates: Using Effective Recruiting Tactics

You fully recognize that the best way to get good employees is to be able to choose from many. However, your company is not a well-known firm and you frequently get very few candidates for your open positions. What are the best practices in recruiting and what do the best firms do? Does it make sense to seek employee referrals? What are common traps and mistakes in recruiting for new talent?

2. Choosing the Best Person for a Role

You have just been promoted to the position of sales manager with a large salary increase, the potential for a nice bonus, and responsibility for four sales representatives who will now report to you. As part of your new job, your boss asks you to hire a fifth sales representative in response to the rapid growth of the company. "In fact," he adds, "I've got a stack of resumés in my office for you. All you have to do is interview a few candidates and pick the best one."

How would you go about filling the new sales position? Are there typical mistakes managers make in this type of situation that you should aim to avoid? What type of information would you hope to gather on these job applicants? How might you best determine who would be the highest performer?

3. Conducting a More Effective Selection Interview

The unfortunate reality is that a monkey, throwing darts at a list of candidates on the wall, would have a chance of finding the best performer on that list roughly equal to many of the selection methods commonly in use today. Chief among the culprits is the unstructured interview (for example: Tell me about yourself? What are your greatest weaknesses? Why did you pick your major? etc.) which is among the most widely used forms of interviewing. While you have been interviewed in that way for all your jobs to date, you personally want to do better and conduct more useful interviews. So how should you go about increasing the effectiveness of your interviews? What are the major differences between unstructured and structured interviews? How should you frame your questions?

4. Retaining a Talented Employee

It's Monday morning and you're swamped. It's three days before "Black Friday" and your 45 store employees are frantically preparing for the 4 a.m. opening. As you finish getting through the morning's e-mails, someone knocks on your door; it's Jessica, your star marketing associate. Despite being busy, you always make time for her as Jessica has personally been responsible for some of the store's most successful marketing campaigns. "Hi Jessica. Getting excited for the end of the week?" you say with energy. "Well, to tell you the truth, I've been feeling a bit unappreciated of late, particularly around the busy season," she remarks.

As you lean back in your chair, she describes in detail her dissatisfaction with her pay relative to others, the amount of time she works, and the lack of respect of her own direct reports. She ends by remarking, "I've always been honest with you and so I feel compelled to let you know I'm on the market and had an interview last week." You think to yourself, "How could this be? I've never heard any complaints from her and she's such a great employee." What can you do to keep Jessica? How might you ensure that you retain your other talented employees? What traps should you avoid in putting together a retention strategy?

Introduction

There is perhaps no more important task for a manager than selecting employees. As we have noted throughout this book, organizations succeed through people.[1] Clearly, having good people (or preferably great people) is an important key to success for any business, but in far too many cases, managers ignore the human part of the equation and are convinced that it's through their financial controls, or their information systems, or their manufacturing processes that success is obtained. What these managers (and oftentimes their entire organizations) forget is that underlying each of these important systems are the people that design, maintain, and utilize these systems. In other words, without the people, none of these other issues really matter. In this chapter, we step through how to recruit, select, and retain the talent you want. Because these processes determine who you have in your organization, their importance cannot be overemphasized. Before we can focus on how to accomplish these objectives, we want you to take a look at Myths 12.1 to get an idea of what *not* to do.

Selecting People for Roles

Choosing the Right People for the Right Jobs

Making selection decisions remains one of the most misunderstood and poorly executed of all managerial endeavors. Managers are often bombarded by consultants who claim to hold the secrets of successfully choosing the right people for various roles. So how can you know who is telling the truth?

First, keep in mind that, no matter what people may say, there are no mind-reading exams, no five-minute magic tests, no one best personality, and no million-dollar interview questions that will help you successfully choose the right person for a role. Rather, a disciplined and systematic approach will increase your chances for success. Second, if you read the chapter on solving problems, you already know that judgments about who will be successful in organizations are subject to a great deal of personal bias and error. To be sure, even the best selection tactics are subject to some error—that is, no method is foolproof. However, substantial research indicates that the more managers rely on mechanical (that is, statistics, objective indicators, and so forth) rather than subjective methods (in other words, judgments based upon one's experience), the more likely

By and large, executives make poor promotion and staffing decisions. By all accounts, their batting average is no better than .333; at most, one-third of such decisions turn out right, a third are minimally effective, and one-third are outright failures.

—Peter Drucker

KO **12-1**

KO **12-2**

KO **12-3**

DO **12-1**

?¿ MYTHS 12.1   Myths of Recruitment, Selection, and Retention

- **Recruiting is a short-term activity.** Unfortunately, most managers approach recruitment as a short-term task. That is, when a job becomes vacant, recruitment begins. Yet research shows that one of the most effective practices affecting firm performance is succession planning—a deliberate attempt to assess the "bench strength" of the organization and plan for filling roles before they become available.[2] Effective recruitment is proactive, not reactive.

- **Personality is the best predictor of job performance.** Most managers, even human resource managers, agree with this basic premise.[3] Research, on the other hand, makes clear that applicants' cognitive ability, job knowledge, and skills are much better predictors of who will be a good performer on the job than individual personality. It's seductive to want to place a primary emphasis on personality in hiring employees; unfortunately, to do so is likely to net poorer results.

- **Good recruiters "sell" their organizations to good candidates.** While we all want to put our best foot forward in an interview situation, giving an unrealistic view of the workplace is not a recipe for success when making a hiring decision. Although we may be tempted to answer candidate questions with responses like "Sure, there is a great support for families here" and "Everyone goes out after work and it is a really collegial place," candidates who accept job offers on such faulty information will quickly realize that they were lied to. Providing a realistic job preview is considered a best practice when it comes to hiring.

- **People are naturally good at judging talent.** Although most people *think* they can make accurate judgments about others' behavior or intentions, the fact is that, without concerted discipline and utilization of some evidence-based methods, most human beings are miserable at accurately predicting others' future behavior. For example, interviewers often spend the majority of their interview time confirming what they assume to already know about the job candidate rather than trying to *disconfirm* their assumptions.[4] One study even showed that, the more the *interviewer* spent time talking during the interview, the more highly that interviewer rated the job candidate's potential![5]

- **Money is the only way to retain talent.** Although it is true that paying talented employees competitively aids in retention, it's only one piece of the retention puzzle. For example, more important than the level of pay is how pay is delivered; star employees want their pay to be based on merit and delivered contingent upon performance. In addition, talented employees want frequent performance feedback and access to increased developmental opportunities. Thus, simply focusing on the level of pay may be a misguided approach to retention.

they are to make the right choice.[6] Our goal here is to help you improve your odds in selecting the right people by demystifying the process and demonstrating what works and, possibly more importantly, what does not.

Selection Is Prediction

Before discussing selection methods, it's important to step back and look at what managers want to accomplish with respect to the selection process. Most broadly, when making a selection decision, managers are actually attempting to predict future employee success in the organization. As a result, selection efforts target two important aspects of employee success:

- **Future Job Performance.** Selection methods allow managers to assess potential employees' fit with the overall job requirements. That

is, managers must decide whether or not job candidates possess the right mix of knowledge, skill, and ability to successfully perform the job.

- **Future Person–Organization Fit.** Selection methods help both the candidate and the manager determine whether the candidate will fit the organization's culture. Even the most highly capable job candidates can fail within an organization when the culture of the organization (such as long-hour expectations) is not aligned with the candidates' work preferences.[7]

Thus, an effective selection process involves a systematic approach to identifying a strong pool of qualified candidates, and collecting data about the candidates' knowledge, skills, and abilities in order to assess these two aspects of fit. Achieving a good fit sounds pretty simple, but managers typically have relatively little information at their disposal to help accurately predict the future. One of our colleagues is fond of saying that most employment decisions are made with less information than people have when buying a car. Actively collecting data will help form a more complete picture of the candidate and help predict success with more accuracy. Following a four-step selection process can greatly increase a manager's ability to collect the right data and use that information in a productive manner (Figure 12.1). We will now explain these four critical steps in more detail.

Practice this!
Go to www.baldwin2e.com

Clarify the Job Context

Before reviewing resumés, interviewing candidates, or giving any job-related test, you need to understand the context in which the job takes place. Remember, the goal of recruitment and selection is to determine which job candidate is likely to succeed in the organization, in terms of both job performance and overall fit with the organization. Therefore, managers must be able to communicate key elements of the work environment and their own working style as outlined in step 1 of Figure 12.1: knowing yourself, the job, and the law.

If you get the right people on the bus, the right people in the right seats, and the wrong people off the bus, then you can figure out how to take it someplace great.

—Jim Collins

Know Yourself and What Kind of Boss You'll Be

Hall of fame basketball coach Bob Knight is well known for his firm and sometimes controversial tactics. Over the years, people have certainly protested

STEP 4: Decide on Methods and Assess
- Get the Most from Interviews
- Include Methods Beyond the Interview

STEP 3: Recruit Talented Applicants
- Use Effective Recruitment Practices
- Manage the Organization's Image
- Determine the Best Recruiters
- Create a Realistic Job Preview (RJP)

STEP 2: Establish a Process
- Standardize It
- Involve Others

STEP 1: Clarify the Job Context
- Know Yourself
- Know the Job
- Know the Law

FIGURE 12.1
The Steps to a Great Hire

different aspects of his approach, but one thing he did indisputably well is let players know what to expect prior to joining the team. Knight knew exactly what experience players would have playing for him and those players got exactly (for better or worse) what they were told in advance—no surprises. As a result, he had one of the highest retention (graduation) rates of all coaches.[8]

Potential employees need to know what it will be like to work for a manager. A simple exercise to start down the path of understanding what type of boss you'll be is to answer the following question: *Why should anyone want to work for you?* If you can successfully—honestly and with some objectivity—answer that question and understand the possible ramifications of the answer, the next step is to communicate it effectively to candidates. We'll come back to this point a bit later.

Know the Job Well

Although it seems self-evident selection decisions would be based on job descriptions, they often are not. Rather, managers commonly plunge right in looking for the "right person" without having defined what the "right person" actually means. Great managers spend time describing and defining the job to be filled. Most often referred to as a **job analysis,** this process involves collecting information about what tasks (actual work) and knowledge, skills, and abilities (KSAs) are required for the job. The result of a job analysis is a job description that will help the hiring manager focus the recruitment and selection efforts and provide a basis for communicating essential responsibilities to candidates.

To complete a job analysis and write a job description, managers should gather information about the job from many different sources, including job incumbents (people doing the job currently), customers, previous job descriptions, training materials, and performance appraisals. Unfortunately, those in positions of responsibility often do not have a good understanding of what employees actually do "in the trenches." The key then to completing a strong job analysis is to be thoughtful in the process, which almost always requires interviewing a few incumbents about what they do. A great aid in job analysis is the U.S. Department of Labor's online resource known as O*NET, described in Management Live 12.1. Note that while O*NET descriptions are useful for those analyzing jobs, they also can be helpful to job candidates who are trying to best position their credentials as fitting with the requirements of specific jobs.

⇄ MANAGEMENT LIVE 12.1

O*NET

Writing a job description does not have to be an overly time-consuming process. The U.S. Department of Labor has created an extensive resource that can provide the basis of a manager's job analysis process. This online resource is known as O*NET, or the Occupational Information Network. It is described as "a comprehensive database of worker attributes and job characteristics. O*NET will be the nation's primary source of occupational information."

According to the O*NET website: The network offers a common language for communication across the economy and among workforce development efforts. It provides definitions and concepts for describing worker attributes and workplace requirements that can be broadly understood and easily accepted. Using comprehensive terms to describe the KSAs, interests, content, and context of work, O*NET provides a common frame of reference for understanding what is involved in effective job performance. The goal of O*NET's common language is straightforward: improve the quality of dialogue among people who communicate about jobs in the economy, generate employment statistics, and develop education and training programs. It provides the shared foundation of language upon which to build private- and public-sector workforce development efforts. Employer hiring requirements will have the same meaning for human resource practitioners, workers, education and training developers, program planners, and students.

A searchable keyword database at http://online.onetcenter.org helps individuals browse through the database of occupations.

Source: U.S. Department of Labor, National O*NET Consortium. O*NET OnLine [Interactive web application]. Available at http://online.onetcenter.org.

After completing a job analysis, the job description almost writes itself. Job descriptions do not need to be exhaustive and probably shouldn't be. They should simply describe the most critical job tasks, KSAs, and other contextual information about the job. At a minimum, a good job description should contain the following information:

- Critical or essential job duties and tasks
- Knowledge, skills, and abilities (KSAs) required
- Working conditions
- Educational requirements
- Physical demands
- Legal or company policies or requirements

The last bit of information—legal issues—leads us to the third aspect of clarifying the job context.

Know the Law

The great myth about employment law is that it is overly restrictive and serves as a barrier to making the right selection decisions. Managers fret over what questions can be legally asked of job candidates and worry about potential discrimination suits tied to evaluating performance. Clearly, abiding by employment law has important implications for an organization's risk exposure, both financially and by reputation. However, less understood is that the law also helps, not hinders, good recruitment and selection practice. The reason is that employment law requires managers to focus solely on information that is *job-related*,

TABLE 12.1   Employment Law Basics

Under employment law guidelines, discrimination is considered to be present regardless of intent. Intentional discrimination, or **disparate treatment,** is said to occur when a manager or organization intentionally discriminates by using race, ethnicity, gender, national origin, or religion as a factor in deciding who is selected for a position. When a male manager decides to hire a male over a more qualified female because he "prefers to work with men," he is engaging in disparate treatment. **Adverse impact** is the discrimination that occurs when the use of a standard procedure has a discriminatory effect on one or more individuals or groups. An example would be firefighters using a simulation to test job candidates' physical abilities (for example, swinging a sledge hammer 40 times in a row), which causes adverse impact for women. The test does not intentionally discriminate, but, because it's based on physical abilities such as strength, it often does discriminate. Key guidelines to avoid disparate treatment and adverse impact follow:

- **Keep It Job-Related.** As mentioned, the best way to avoid legal problems is to ensure that all practices are truly job-related. Avoid asking candidates about their personal lives and issues that have no relationship to the job (marital status, children, home location, and so on).

- **Treat All Candidates the Same.** Discrimination occurs when one candidate gets a leg up on another because a manager gave preferential treatment.

- **Use Valid Predictors.** Valid employment tests predict job performance (statistically speaking) consistently and with accuracy. Don't use predictors that do not have some supporting evidence of their reliability and validity in predicting job performance.

- **Don't Discriminate.** Do not make decisions on the basis of race, age, nationality, sex, religion, or disability. To do so puts you and your organization at risk and takes your eye off what is really important.

which helps actively reduce natural biases by deterring the use of information not directly related to the job requirements. Table 12.1 discusses the basics of employment law.

Once you have clarified the context of the job, you're ready to move on to the next step in the selection process.

Establish a Process

The second step in selecting employees is establishing a process for making your decisions. Establishing a process *before* you decide to hire an employee is beneficial for several reasons. First, when a position becomes open or is newly created, there is usually a heightened sense of urgency to fill it *now*. This sense of urgency usually leads people to skip critical steps that would help avoid a poor selection decision. Second, in employment law cases, the courts typically want to see that an organization has a plan—that is, that the company has a process it uses uniformly and does not stray from.

Third, the best job candidates prefer a transparent (no hidden features) selection process. A manager who can articulate exactly what the process is and how it will transpire makes a good impression on candidates.[9]

Standardize It

Let's say you need to buy a new car. Based on price and features, you narrow your choices down to two cars: a Honda Civic and a Toyota Corolla. You decide to test-drive the two cars. When you test-drive the Honda, you drive down a long stretch of highway. A few hours later, you test-drive a Corolla down a back road full of potholes. That night, you determine the Honda has a better ride and can't wait to buy it. Have you drawn the appropriate conclusion?

Of course not—and yet this is exactly the mistake many managers make when it comes to selection. They use an unstandardized selection process. If you want to be able to say one candidate is better than another, you must ensure your process is standardized. Of course, the process may vary based on job type but should be consistent for all candidates for any one job. For instance, a selection process for a regional sales manager may differ greatly when compared with that of a staff accountant in the same organization. Tailoring the process to the job naturally makes the process that much more job-related—a factor we have already emphasized as being important.

Taking time to hire selectively and getting it right the first time pays off.[10] Regardless of how long the process takes, however, applicants should always be kept informed about the process and where they stand at any given time. Research shows that highly qualified and marketable applicants often assume something is wrong with a company that does not provide this type of information in a timely manner.[11] Conversely, applicants often disproportionately favor a firm that promptly and professionally manages the critical contacts that the firm has with them in the selection process.

We have learned the hard way that "no hire" is ultimately better than a bad hire.

—HR Vice President

Involve Others

While an applicant may be targeted to work directly for the hiring manager, that applicant will also ultimately work with others in the firm. So involve those "others" in the process. They may be co-workers, subordinates, internal customers, or experienced employees who know the culture well. Involving others allows the candidate exposure to a variety of people and jobs in the organization and allows many people to help assess the candidate's future potential. But remember what was just discussed about standardization: Others should be involved in the same way for each candidate.

Recruit Talented Applicants

Recruiting talented employees is a long-term activity and one in which great managers are continuously engaged. That is, strong recruitment is built upon the effort undertaken when there are no vacancies: through building social networks, determining the capabilities of current employees, and planning for the future. In fact, succession planning or long-term recruiting has been shown to have a strong impact on a firm's bottom line.[12] With that said, people do leave jobs, and when they do it can create great difficulty for managers. Being prepared ahead of time by having up-to-date job descriptions based upon job analyses discussed previously is a great start. From there, real recruitment begins.

The overall purpose of recruitment is to increase the pool of qualified applicants and decrease the pool of unqualified applicants. In doing so, managers hope to accomplish a few important goals. First, there is a real concern about costs. While it would be nice to take out a full-page ad in *The Wall Street Journal* or have a big splash on Monster.com for every job opening, such expenditure would not likely be prudent (or necessarily effective, as we discuss next). Second, since turnover is one of the highest costs an organization can incur beyond payroll and benefits, attracting employees who not only will perform but will fit with the organization's culture is an important consideration. As such, the tactics used to effectively recruit employees are varied depending on the situation; however, some practices have been shown to be more effective than others.

DO **12-2**

DO **12-3**

Effective Recruitment Practices

Recruitment activities may be divided into two broad categories of formal or informal tactics. Formal tactics involve posting job ads on internal systems or on recruitment websites, whereas informal tactics include networking and referral-based approaches. Although there are no hard and fast rules to recruitment approaches, research indicates that, in general, informal tactics tend to be more effective.[13] Regardless of the tactic, two main themes of effective recruitment are the treatment of applicants and the quality of the information about the job.[14] This is perhaps why one of the most effective recruitment practices is that of employee referrals, which ask current employees to seek out others who would both be qualified for the job and be a good fit with the organization. With referrals, an applicant is likely to receive excellent treatment by organization representatives since the applicant is a friend or acquaintance of a current employee. In addition, the referring employee is likely to have spent considerable time describing the workplace in great detail, providing important information about fit with the organization. Tool Kit 12.1 describes the important characteristics of a solid employee referral program.

Beyond employee referrals, the most important advances in recruitment are in social media tools, with organizations' websites providing only a starting point for such technology. To be sure, research is clear that having an easy to navigate and informative website is critical to the recruitment

MANAGER'S TOOL KIT

Tool Kit 12.1   Creating an Employee Referral Program

Employee referral programs are relatively easy to establish. The trick is to make sure your employees are sufficiently motivated to act as recruiters. Most importantly, your employees must be well informed about the jobs in which you are recruiting. In addition, they need to be armed with job descriptions and other job information (for instance, locations, hours, and so forth) that would allow them to answer potential applicant questions. Effective programs also include the following:[15]

(1) **Make rewards real.** The best programs give the referring employee a cash incentive for referral. Depending on the job, successful referrals (for example, ones that stay with the organization past a certain probationary time frame like six months) could pay upward of $5,000. Typically, referral programs pay around $1,000 for referrals that result in an actual hire.

(2) **Tailor the program to each job.** Do not have the same program for all jobs. Use the referral program to target hard-to-fill jobs, particularly those in tight labor markets where highly skilled individuals are difficult to find.

(3) **Make it highly visible in the organization.** Publicize your program as much as possible so that even employees from other areas of the organization have an opportunity to provide you with quality referrals.

(4) **Track from where/whom best referrals come.** You will find that some employees are natural recruiters. Track over time who these folks are and make it worth their while to continue their efforts. In addition, you may find a theme regarding from where your best applicants are referred. For example, there may be a particular organization, training program, association, or even social club where quality applicants continually originate.

(5) **Consider "referral goals."** Make it everyone's job to constantly be on the lookout for exemplary employees, even when no job is available. In this way, you can build a solid database of high-quality applicants for when a job is available. Consider setting some targets for employees regarding a total number of referrals they are required to make annually.

process.[16] But great managers are turning to social media to keep their recruiting engine turning. Social media such as LinkedIn, Facebook, and so forth, though new and innovative, work on very simple principles of network quality (discussed in Chapter 8). That is, you will find great applicants not necessarily from your close friends, but from your friends' friends (what are called "weak ties"). Social media tools simply facilitate this age-old networking process. Some interesting research is now uncovering some of the ways to utilize social media most effectively. One study, for example, found that testimonials provided by employees are most effective when they are posted on websites or blogs outside the organization. Apparently, applicants believe that these "word of mouse" testimonials are more trustworthy when they aren't sanctioned by the organization.[17]

Recruiting Recent Graduates

In some cases, recruiting the "old-fashioned way" is still required. For example, if you want to be first to see the best graduating candidates from the local university, be prepared to meet quarterly with the head of the business placement office and develop a strong relationship. This might include some volunteer work on your part, such as speaking in a class and inviting students to your organization. Another critical way to build relationships with universities is through projects, "service-learning" experiences, or internships. Whatever the arrangements, great managers know that when students have the opportunity to demonstrate their capabilities in the organization, both student and manager learn whether the fit will be a good one. When recruiting recent graduates, you might be inclined to ignore factors such as grade point average in favor of other factors like leadership in extracurricular activities and work experience. This would be a mistake. In fact, research shows that GPA is a strong predictor of job performance for recent graduates within five years of undergraduate graduation and even more important for recent graduates of master's degree programs.[18] Despite this fact, recruiters rarely pay any attention to GPA, preferring to use less valid indicators of future success.[19] Thus, don't resort to stereotypes that would characterize "A" students as "book smart, not street smart." On the contrary, all things being equal, high-achieving students are more likely to perform well on the job.

Managing the Organization's Image

Information provided by organizations during a recruitment effort has a strong impact on applicants' evaluations of fit. Research has found that the image projected by the firm influences applicants' initial reactions. This is particularly true for applicants with increased job opportunities, since they are more attentive to, and influenced by, early recruitment activities. Not surprisingly, applicants get "turned off" by organizations early on and never come back to give the firm a second chance. What drives away talented recruits the most? First, poor treatment on a site visit is an immediate red flag for many applicants. If applicants encounter rude "screeners" such as receptionists or human resource personnel, they are likely to assess the job negatively. Second, timelines are a critical source of negative reactions. For instance, applicants infer negative outcomes from long delays, even if the delay is real (for example, the final approval from a job hasn't been determined). Such delays reduce the willingness to accept future job offers and the most marketable job seekers assume that something is wrong with the organization. Third, confusing, complicated, or out-of-date information sends a signal to applicants that the organization isn't on top of its game. Fourth, the appearance and behavior of recruiters greatly impacts applicants' impressions.[20] All this means that while others may be involved in the process, the

TABLE 12.2   Recruiting Diverse Applicants

Although there is little empirical research directly addressing the question of how best to attract diverse applicants to an organization, some recent research by Derek Arvey and Patrick McKay summarizes the literature to date in order to draw conclusions about tactics that are likely to increase attraction. Here are some of the key conclusions taken from their research of activities, which will convey to minorities that the organization values diversity:[21]

- **Use Target Media.** Placing recruitment ads in targeted media.
- **Use Inclusive Statements.** Presenting inclusiveness policy statements in ads.
- **Target Recruiting.** Recruiting at predominantly minority or female institutions of higher education.
- **Use Diverse Recruiters.** Employing female or minority recruiters.

manager must keep a close watch on how job incumbents, co-workers, human resource professionals, and even administrative staff interact with and respond to applicants. To not do so puts the best candidates at risk for exiting the process early. In Table 12.2, we offer some practical guidance specifically for improving recruitment of diverse applicants.

Of course, these tactics manage the impression given by an organization. If upon meeting with organizational representatives different messages (even subtle ones) are provided, candidates will recognize that the organization is mostly putting on a show with respect to its commitment to diversity. Thus, there is no substitute for an *authentic* commitment to diversity.

The Manager as Recruiter

Recruiters are a mixed blessing in organizations. To be certain, they fulfill an important role by sourcing candidates, and saving managers time and effort in sorting through resumés. In many cases, however, the recruiter is not highly familiar with the job and does not work in the future job incumbent's immediate environment; yet he is often the first contact applicants have with the organization. Thus, recruiters serve an important role in communicating the nature of the job and the information that applicants use to determine fit. Indeed, research shows that applicants view recruiters as a "signal" of unknown aspects of the firm.[22] Not surprisingly then, some recruiters are seen as more credible than others. For example, human resource and corporate recruiters are seen as less trustworthy and credible about the job than are job incumbents or future peers.

Another potential problem with recruiters is that they have been shown to make inferences about candidates' abilities solely from resumés, which may or may not be correct.[23] One recent study found, for instance, that while recruiters may indicate to applicants that they are seeking individuals with strong interpersonal or leadership skills, they actually endorse and recommend applicants on the basis of technical skills.[24] All of this is to say that although it is attractive to want someone else to do recruiting for you, great managers do not abdicate this responsibility, with the understanding that nobody else can describe the job like a boss and future co-workers. In doing so, managers are able to provide applicants more accurate information in determining fit and hopefully reduce future turnover. This accurate description of the job is one of the critical steps of the recruiting process, known as a realistic job preview.

Create a Realistic Job Preview (RJP)

DO 12-3

Recall the last product you bought from an actual salesperson. Did the individual tell you the product was the best on the market and that it had everything you'd want? If you're like us, more than once, we've purchased a product like that only to find it wasn't everything we wanted. Strictly "selling" a job to applicants rarely works out. At the same time, providing little to no information about the job doesn't work either. Great managers describe the job in detail to candidates. This process is more akin to arranging a good marriage than selling a product. In doing so, it is in the manager's best interest to present an accurate and realistic description of the job to the candidate, who, like the manager, is trying to determine fit and future potential. Evidence generally supports the use of **realistic job previews (RJPs)**.[25]

- Applicants receiving RJPs are significantly less likely to drop out of the selection process.

- RJPs presented to applicants prior to hiring are associated with lower turnover *after* they have been hired.

- Though pre-hire RJPs are not associated with increased job performance post-hire, an RJP provided after an applicant is hired is associated with higher job performance.

- RJPs increase the job acceptance rate among applicants with no prior exposure to the job, and decrease the job acceptance rate among those with prior exposure.[26] Thus, RJPs can help to improve applicants' decisions about job fit, especially when they are already familiar with the job.

- Providing an RJP verbally is generally more effective than handing an applicant a brochure with a job description or having the candidate view a videotaped presentation.

To help you with actually preparing a realistic job preview, a worksheet is provided in Tool Kit 12.2.

Decide on Methods and Assess

Once you've done your homework on establishing the basic process, you can move to tailoring your methods for specific searches, and then on to the actual assessment. How much time you spend and what type of assessment method you choose depend greatly on the details of the job situation. Clearly, hiring extra staff for the holidays requires different assessment methods than selecting a district manager. That is not to say you should not assess your part-time holiday help; rather, the amount of time and number of methods you choose may be less. One thing is certain, however: It is imperative you collect data beyond the information readily available from resumés, prescreening processes, or basic job applications.

Great managers utilize multiple methods for collecting data about the applicant's suitability for the job. The process of selection should both be standardized and include methods such as interviews, work samples, and ability tests. Great managers attempt to select methods that reduce their own biases, are legally sound, are based on solid evidence, and make business sense (that is, are cost-effective and worth the time and effort). Here are a few guiding principles to follow for the most effective selection process:

- **First, define performance.** If you can't define what success looks like on the job, then you'll never be able to predict it.

- **Use different methods for different jobs.** Rarely is one method appropriate for all jobs.

MANAGER'S TOOL KIT

Tool Kit 12.2   Providing a Realistic Job Preview

Most job candidates should be given a realistic job preview (RJP). Here are the minimum topics that should be presented to each job candidate. Finish the following sentences and then use them to discuss the job with each candidate.

- The essential responsibilities of the job are _____
  _____
  _____.

- The expectations for hours worked, travel, and working conditions are _____
  _____
  _____.

- The top five positive and five negative aspects associated with performing the job are _____
  _____
  _____.

- The top five positive and five negative aspects of working for the organization are _____
  _____
  _____.

- The top five positive and top five negative aspects of working for me are _____
  _____
  _____
  _____.

- The benefit package includes the following: _____
  _____
  _____.

- **Use reliable and valid methods** to predict future job success. Just remember, no method is perfect—some, however, are supported by a body of evidence, while others are not.

- **Collect multiple pieces of data** before drawing conclusions. If an applicant seems like she will make a poor accountant in an interview, suspend judgment until she has completed other tests that might serve to disconfirm your judgment.

- **Defy conventional wisdom,** as it can often lead to wrong conclusions when assessing employees, though it often *feels* right. A number of studies have found a large gap between what methods people *think* are effective and those that evidence shows are *actually* effective.[27] To put the preceding points into practice requires some important knowledge about the relative usefulness of performance predictors. A great deal of research has been done on the relative value of the various types of methods or predictors. That is, some predictors are more useful than others along several dimensions, including:

  - **Validity.** How well, statistically speaking, the method predicts future job performance. This is usually the most important factor and the one related most to legal defensibility.

- **Fairness.** The degree to which the method avoids adverse impact (unintentional discrimination).
- **Feasibility.** The degree to which the method can reasonably be employed in different situations, and its overall cost.
- **Face validity.** The degree to which applicants *believe* (whether it actually does or not) the selection method fairly measures requirements for the job.

In Table 12.3, we show the major employment testing methods and a rank order based on their validity,[28] as well as information regarding fairness, feasibility, and face validity. As can be seen in Table 12.3, validity evidence is strongest for work samples, cognitive ability tests, and structured interviews, and is much less so for references and years of experience. The unfortunate irony, of course, is that the volume of usage in organizations today is *inversely* correlated with the evidence. That is, the least valid measures are often the most used. One reason for this can be seen in the chart. Tests such as reference checks, assignment of points to training and experience, and years of education are all easily collectable and face valid. The more valid predictors shown in Table 12.3 can be difficult to administer and more costly and time-intensive. A full examination of each predictor is beyond the scope of this chapter; however, we provide some details on some of the best predictors: (1) structured interviews, (2) performance tests (work samples and assessment center), (3) cognitive ability tests, and (4) personality assessments. For an efficient way of determining which selection method should be used in what type of job, see Tool Kit 12.3.

Getting the Most from Interviews

Few managers would be willing to hire an applicant sight unseen, and thus almost all organizations use some form of employment interview.[29] Interviews can be effective tools for predicting future job success, but should not be used to measure all types of job requirements. In general, the interview is a highly effective method for measuring job knowledge and interpersonal skills.

Practice this!
Go to www.baldwin2e.com

TABLE 12.3 Selection Method Effectiveness

Selection Method (Ranked from Best to Worst for Validity)	Fairness	Feasibility	Face Validity
1. Work Sample	High	Moderate	High
2. Cognitive Ability Test	Low	High	Moderate
3. Structured Interview	Moderate	High	High
4. Job Knowledge Test	High	High	High
5. Assessment Center Evaluation	Moderate	Low	High
6. Biographical Data	Moderate	Moderate	Low
7. Personality Assessments	Moderate	High	Low
8. Reference Check	High	High	High
9. Training and Experience Points	High	High	High
10. Years of Education	High	High	High
11. Graphology (Handwriting Analysis)	Low	Moderate	Low
12. Flip of a Coin	Low	High	Low

MANAGER'S TOOL KIT

Tool Kit 12.3   Choosing the Right Assessment Method for the Job

Choosing the right person for the right job requires applying appropriate assessment methods. That is, some methods are better than others for particular jobs. Unfortunately, many factors make this decision complex, including the time frame to hire, the resources available, the size of the applicant pool, and type of job (for example, seasonal help versus a full-time salaried position). At a minimum, structured interviews and a background check should be completed on all final candidates. Using other methods in addition will also improve prediction. Based on existing research regarding the validity of different assessment methods:

- The assessment for *any* job should generally include:
  - Structured interview
  - Cognitive ability test or other indicator of cognitive ability
  - Measure of conscientiousness
  - Background check
- Jobs with a great degree of *interpersonal interaction* (customer service, sales, and so on) should add:
  - Work sample or simulation
  - Measures of agreeableness and extraversion
- Jobs with a high degree of *technical knowledge* required (such as engineer) should add:
  - Work sample
  - Job knowledge test
- *Managerial* jobs should add:
  - Work sample
  - Assessment center or simulation exercises

Never wear a backward baseball cap to an interview unless applying for the job of umpire.

—Dan Zevin

When going about the interview process, it is important to distinguish between two general types of interviews:

- The **unstructured interview,** whereby the interviewer and applicant have a conversation that is unscripted. That is, the interviewer may have some general topics she wants covered, but it is unscripted.
- The **structured interview,** whereby the interviewer follows an interview script designed specifically to target certain KSAs required for the job, asking the same questions of all job applicants.

Recalling our car buying example, you probably won't be surprised to hear that structured interviews are much more valid predictors of performance than unstructured ones because they are standardized and maintain an interviewer's focus on job-related questions.[30] Though some research has shown that under very limited circumstances unstructured interviews can be effective, the evidence strongly supports structured interviews.[31] Despite the fact that structured interviews are much more valid than unstructured ones, too few managers employ such structure in their interview practice,[32] in effect trading off validity for the freedom of asking anything of anyone. This trade-off comes at a high price, namely, the ability to predict future success—your primary goal as a hiring manager!

Behavior, Behavior, Behavior

DO **12-4**

Though it may seem counterintuitive, when trying to predict future job performance the challenge is to pay less attention to how applicants describe themselves and rather focus on their behavior. For example, consider the following typical exchange in a selection interview:

Interviewer: Please describe your primary strengths as a sales representative.

Applicant: I'm a people person! Put me with people and I am at my best; I'm golden. People love me and I love them.

Interviewer: OK, great. So you love people. Why is that a particular strength in this case?

Applicant: Well, you see, sales reps must interact well with people: customers, managers, other reps, suppliers—so people skills are incredibly important. I can't stress that enough—no two ways about it.

Interviewer: Right, makes sense.

Aside from a pleasant conversation, what have we learned about this candidate's suitability for the job of sales representative? First, we learned how *he* describes himself. Second, we learned what *he* thinks is important for the job. Third, *he* is in control of the interview. In other words, we haven't really learned anything that will help us distinguish whether he is more or less capable of doing this job than are other candidates. Effective interviewing is all about *behavior*. Focus on what an applicant *can* or *did* do, rather than what she *says* she can do.

Great managers commonly use two types of structured interviews as valid predictors of job performance.[33] **Situational interviews** include hypothetical scenario questions that ask candidates to describe in detail how they would likely behave in such a situation. **Behavioral interviews** include questions that ask candidates to recount actual instances from their past work or relevant experiences relative to the job at hand. Both forms of structured interviews work well because they focus on behaviors or **behavioral intentions** (the motivation and thoughts that are immediate precursors of a person's actual behavior) and acknowledge the reality that past behavior is a strong predictor of future behavior.[34] Some recent research has found that for high-level positions behavioral interviews are more effective than situational, while the reverse is true for lower-level positions.[35]

One of the particular challenges of behavioral interviews is how best to evaluate the range of responses. One proven way is to use a number system from worst answer to best answer and jot down some potential responses that correspond to each of those categories of response. In general, the more detail an applicant provides, the better the response. If an applicant can't provide a detailed response after follow-up questions, it's less likely he has actually done the behavior in question. Use the information from the job analysis to help match possible responses with level of quality. Tool Kit 12.4 demonstrates how to construct and evaluate behavioral interview questions, including using the STAR (situation, task, action, result) method. See Management Live 12.2 for some good examples of what *not* to do when it comes to interviewing.

As I grow older, I pay less attention to what people say, I just watch what they do.

—Andrew Carnegie

Important Interview Reminders.   Beyond using structured approaches, there are a few important reminders to highlight in regard to conducting interviews.

- **Avoid non-job-related questions.** Here again, keep it job-related and focused. Your results will be better and you'll avoid possible legal recourse by applicants.

- **Use panel (group) interviews wisely.** The more people that crowd a room and "interrogate" applicants, the less likely the interview will be a

MANAGER'S TOOL KIT

Tool Kit 12.4   Creating and Evaluating a Behavioral Interview Question

An easy way to remember how to conduct a behavioral interview is using the STAR method. STAR is an acronym for situation, task, action, and result. Using the STAR framework can help you formulate a strong behavioral interview question based on the knowledge, skills, and abilities (KSAs) you are attempting to measure. For example, if you wanted to measure teamwork skills, you might ask:

(S) Describe a time when you were asked to be part of a team.

(T) What task were you and the group charged with doing?

(A) What did you ultimately do to accomplish the task?

(R) What results did you achieve?

To evaluate a response on a behavioral interview question,[36] a scoring guide must be developed. A basic scoring guide should differentiate between poor, good, and outstanding responses. On a piece of paper, draw three columns and label them Ineffective, Effective, and Highly Effective. Next, brainstorm behaviors representative of each category and record them. Assign scale points to each category, recognizing that some behaviors under Effective are more or less effective than others, but are still not Highly Effective or Ineffective. Finally, leave room at the bottom to take notes. Listen to candidates' responses and record them. Go back later and evaluate the quality of the responses.

Example of STAR Rating Form for Teamwork Question

Ineffective			Effective			Highly Effective		
1	2	3	4	5	6	7	8	9

Ineffective	Effective	Highly Effective
• Unable to describe the purpose of the team and his or her own role in it.	• Described the purpose of the team and own role.	• Described how role on team contributed to task accomplishment.
• Did not display awareness of others' viewpoints.	• Related effectively to people of differing backgrounds and interests.	• Worked very effectively with people of differing backgrounds and interests.
• Emphasized differences and criticized others.	• Sometimes used others as problem-solving resources.	• Viewed others as valuable problem-solving resources and leveraged their abilities to achieve key objectives.
• Took all the credit for successes of the group.	• Shared credit for group tasks.	• Rewarded others when their efforts made substantial contributions to the group task.
• Changed mind in face of opposition.	• Mentioned an awareness of others' viewpoints.	• Consistently demonstrated an awareness of others' viewpoints and feelings and modified own position when appropriate.
• Ignored disagreements in the group.	• Highlighted and summarized areas of agreement with others.	• Raised and discussed difficult issues/disagreements to find common ground.

⇄| MANAGEMENT LIVE 12.2

Animals, Superheroes, and Other Themes

"What kind of animal would you be and why?"

For whatever reasons, many managers have a favorite interview question like the one above, which they believe helps them identify the strongest job candidates. Although it is tempting to employ such novel or "out of the box" questions, they often do not serve to differentiate candidates in desired ways. For example, one manager we have worked with likes to ask candidates for a marketing position, "Who is your favorite cartoon superhero and why?" He fully believes this question tests the creativity necessary for his marketing job. Before accepting his premise, however, we would encourage consideration of a few fundamental questions.

First, what is a "good" response? When asked, the manager said there was no right answer; he wanted to see the applicant's creative thinking process. But notice that the question doesn't ask for applicants to detail how they arrive at their conclusion or what criteria they use. Second, this question is likely to be measuring something entirely different than creativity—that is, one's familiarity with cartoons and the time spent contemplating those cartoons. Is that what this manager intended?

It is easy to fall into this trap. One way to avoid it is to ask yourself for every question, "What am I really measuring when I ask . . .?" Stick to structured, job-related questions, and you will improve your ability to predict high performance. We like to say that interview questions are expensive; if you want to get the most return on your investment, spend questions wisely and precisely! And for the record, we like superhero Professor X for his ability to read minds (and extremely bad handwriting).

Some Popular but Questionable Interview Questions

- If you were a car, what kind of car would you be?
- What's your favorite color and why?
- If you could go back in time and meet anyone, who would you meet and why?
- If aliens landed and offered you any position on their planet, what position would you ask for?
- A plane crashes on the border between the United States and Canada. Where should they bury the survivors?
- Give me two reasons why I should *not* hire you.

valid predictor.[37] Involve other people with multiple small-group interviews, but avoid interview sessions with three or more. Applicants tend to prefer one-on-one, face-to-face interviews.[38] However, telephone interviews can often be just as effective as face-to-face meetings.[39]

- **Do not over-weight negative information.** Interviewers tend to give much more weight to negative information revealed by an applicant than positive—so much so that it often requires twice as much positive information to overcome a single piece of negative data.[40]

- **Be aware of subtle biases.** As we mentioned, interviewer ratings are too often influenced by things like applicant attractiveness, similarities in race and gender, and nonverbal behavior such as eye contact.[41] The more aware an interviewer is of these subtle influences, the less likely he is to fall prey to them.

Beyond the Interview: Other Effective Assessment Options

Interviewing generally reveals an applicant's job knowledge and interpersonal skills, but other tests are helpful in evaluating other skills the applicant needs to perform the job well, such as technical and managerial skills. These skills are specific job behaviors a person has learned to perform with consistent results. For example, an architect clearly needs to be able to read architectural drawings accurately. A flight attendant needs to know how to open the emergency exit door on an airplane. A teacher needs to be able to speak clearly in front of a group. Tests designed specifically to measure these "hands-on" skills are known generally as **performance tests** and are highly predictive of future job performance.

Performance Tests.   A performance test is one in which applicants must demonstrate their capabilities for the job by *doing* something. One type of performance test is known as a **work sample.** Work sample tests are literally samples of the work involved in the performance of a specific job. Underlying them is the assumption that performance obtained under realistic work conditions should be a strong predictor of work on the job. Athletic tryouts or musical auditions are good examples of work samples. Constructing a work sample does not need to be complicated—just follow these steps:

1. *Select the Sample.* Using the information from the job description, pick one or two essential job tasks.
2. *Define Performance.* Determine what results a candidate needs to obtain on these job tasks to be considered "excellent" through "poor."
3. *Create a Realistic Environment.* Provide the job candidate with the most realistic possible setting in which to perform the selected work sample.

To illustrate the construction of a performance test, let's take the example of an applicant for a sales representative job:

Step 1. We select one of the key tasks of this job, which is to make a sales presentation to a prospective client.

Step 2. We decide that to be considered excellent, the applicant must do all of the following: (a) establish a rapport with the customer, (b) determine the customer's product needs and requirements, (c) communicate the products available to meet the customer's needs, and (d) ask for questions or concerns from the client.

Step 3. We design a short scenario to provide the applicant with information regarding the customer and the products, and a time limit of 30 minutes to prepare. The applicant would then "in character" make a sales presentation to our "customer." This takes a bit of preparation, but as can be seen, it doesn't require weeks and can be highly effective in predicting future success.

Other performance tests such as assessment centers measure more managerial-related skills, such as delegating, planning/organizing, making decisions, and taking the initiative. An **assessment center** (a method for evaluating managerial applicants, not a location) is a collection of work samples that mimic "a day in the life" of a manager (for example, group discussions, employee feedback meetings, oral presentations, and in-basket exercises). Performance in the exercises is usually evaluated by trained raters who in some cases are more senior managers from the same firm as those being assessed. Although assessment centers are highly valid predictors, especially for managerial jobs, they are often quite expensive to develop and conduct. See Management Live 12.3 for more on assessment centers.

Talent wins games, but teamwork and intelligence wins championships.

—Michael Jordan

Cognitive Ability, Integrity Tests, and Personality

Perhaps the most widely discussed and misunderstood selection methods are tests of cognitive ability and personality. Misperceptions abound about the usefulness of these types of tests; however, cognitive ability measures are often the most valid predictors of performance when used appropriately. **Cognitive ability** or General

MANAGEMENT LIVE 12.3

Assessment Centers: Uncovering Managerial Talent

Assessment centers are not for everyone. But when it comes to predicting managerial talent early in employees' careers, assessment centers are hard to beat. The earliest uses of assessment centers can be traced to Germany during World War I, followed by the adoption of the technology for use in World War II by the United States and Great Britain. Specifically, the OSS (the precursor to the modern CIA) used assessment centers to select appropriate candidates for spying activities during World War II.

Basing their work on the earlier military applications, in 1956 AT&T conducted the best-known study of assessment centers (called the Management Progress Study) to investigate changes in managerial skills as managers moved through their careers. This led to the use of assessment centers as an aid in selecting first-line supervisors, higher-level managers, and other specialists. Subsequently, more than 1,100 U.S. organizations have utilized assessment centers for selecting and developing managerial talent.

More recently, assessment centers have been used in educational settings to provide critical feedback to business students regarding managerial skill strengths and weaknesses. Students receive objective, behavioral feedback about their managerial skills, which serves as a starting point for their development in college and beyond. Recent research has shown that students who perform well in collegiate assessment centers are offered higher starting salaries than those performing poorly. In addition, research shows students who demonstrate high skills in an assessment center receive promotions more quickly over a five-year post-graduation period and are more satisfied at work than their low-skill peers.[42] Thus, assessment center exercises can be powerful tools to help students identify their managerial strengths and weaknesses early in their career, providing focus to their business studies and preparing them for future success.

Mental Ability represents a person's ability to learn and acquire cognitive skills, including verbal, mathematical, spatial, and logical reasoning. Tests of cognitive ability tend to be strong predictors of future success because they measure how effectively individuals can acquire job knowledge used to perform on the job.[43]

Let's say you want to cause an uproar at your next family gathering. Simply tell your family members that cognitive ability is one of the best single predictors of job performance across most jobs, and then look out for flying food. Despite the hot debate in the United States about intelligence and intelligence testing, the evidence is clear: Cognitive ability is a valid predictor of job performance even when the applicant pool is already restricted to high intelligence,[44] such as in the case of graduates from elite law schools or medical students applying for medical residency positions. Researcher Sara Rynes and her colleagues summarized the vast body of research stating, "Deliberate attempts to assess and use GMA [general mental ability] as a basis for hiring should be made for *all* jobs. Failure to do so leaves money on the table." Cognitive ability can be quite efficiently assessed using short timed tests such as the Wonderlic Personnel Test (WPT). The WPT takes 12 minutes to complete and is relatively unobtrusive from an applicant's perspective.[45] For an interesting summary of the Wonderlic scores of a number of NFL quarterbacks, see Management Live 12.4.

So why doesn't everyone use cognitive ability tests? The answer is twofold. First, a great deal of misunderstanding regarding their usefulness permeates all levels of organizations. For example, in one survey, even high-level human resource executives demonstrated misperceptions about the validity of testing cognitive ability.[46] Second, cognitive ability tests may cause an adverse impact on hiring certain minority groups. Thus, organizations hoping to increase the diversity of their applicant pool will need to search for other ways to measure

MANAGEMENT LIVE 12.4

How Smart Is Your First-Round Draft Pick?[47]

Quarterback Eli Manning scored a 39 on the Wonderlic Personnel Test (WPT) before the 2004 draft. That's about 10 points higher than most other draft picks who take the 50-question, 12-minute test. The question is, Why do NFL players need to take an intelligence test? Team owners, it seems, place a great deal of stock in the test and believe in its validity in predicting the future performance of players. "Selecting a new quarterback is like hiring a president for a company," says Michael Callans, president of Wonderlic Consulting. "They need to lead, think on their feet, evaluate all of their options, and understand the impact their actions will have on the outcome of the game." Cognitive ability tests like the WPT help owners evaluate a player's cognitive and reasoning ability, which can help determine whether they have the skills to follow directions and react to their situation—all critical field skills. Despite the lure of using intelligence, research has shown that intelligence is less important for football player performance. Although intelligence seems to be important for successful performance of most jobs, playing football isn't one of those![48]

Famous NFL Quarterbacks and Their Wonderlic Scores

Name	Wonderlic Score
Eli Manning	39
Drew Bledsoe	37
Aaron Rodgers	35
Tom Brady	33
Steve Young	33
John Elway	30
Drew Brees	28
Mark Sanchez	28
Ben Roethlisberger	25
Brett Farve	22
Michael Vick	20
Dan Marino	16
Vince Young	16

Note: The average college graduate score is 25, with a standard deviation of 6.

cognitive ability so as to not discriminate. Here are a few recommendations to follow regarding the use of cognitive ability tests:

- **Job Complexity.** The more complex a job, the more important cognitive ability becomes. For most managerial positions, cognitive ability is an excellent predictor and should be used.
- **Diversity Goals.** If increasing minority representation in organizations is a top priority, use other predictors that are highly correlated with cognitive ability but cause less adverse impact, such as job knowledge tests, work samples, and simulations.

- **Experience.** Some research indicates significant experience can compensate for lower levels of cognitive ability. Thus, an experienced applicant with lower cognitive ability may perform as well as one with higher cognitive ability.

Integrity tests are designed to detect and predict deviant behaviors on the job. Such behaviors could include outright violations of the law such as theft, but also include more subtle counterproductive actions such as abuse of resources (for example, consistently rounding up expense reports or making personal copies at work), physical aggression, and inappropriate language. Two types of integrity tests exist, overt and personality-based tests. Overt integrity tests directly ask applicants about their attitude toward theft and the occurrence of previous theft behaviors. For example, an overt test might include a question such as, "Have you ever overcharged someone for your personal gain?" Personality-based integrity tests do not ask about deviant behaviors directly but seek to identify certain traits that have been linked to several related employee behaviors that are detrimental to an organization. The assumption is that employee misbehavior is just one element in a larger syndrome of antisocial behavior or organizational delinquency and that common personality patterns can be identified through the use of certain personality inventories.

Do integrity tests actually make accurate predictions of "bad behavior" at work? The answer, which is surprising to most people, is a resounding "Yes." The evidence generally suggests that overt integrity tests are excellent predictors of counterproductive behavior and theft. Even more, these tests are better at predicting such behavior for jobs that are higher in complexity.[49] Interestingly, although integrity tests are designed to predict bad behavior at work, they are a moderately strong predictor of job performance. In many cases, if a manager were to use a measure of cognitive ability and an integrity test for a highly complex job, the manager might be able to account for close to 50 percent of the variance in the future performance of the applicant. This is an incredibly high prediction from two simple and cost-effective tests. Here again, however, we should note that the appropriateness of any test (interview or otherwise) should always be determined in reference to the job analysis that was performed for the job.

The use of **personality assessments** for selection is highly misunderstood and often inappropriately used. In Chapter 1, we discussed the major classifications of personality, including what has become known as the Big Five personality factors. Recall that we never recommend using a single predictor to select an employee. Regardless of how strong or valid a predictor may be, multiple data points are always preferable. With that in mind, personality tests can often add some predictive value to a selection process. Of course, not all personality factors are relevant for all jobs. In particular, the evidence shows that certain factors of the Big Five personality traits may be more or less important depending on the type of job. Based on that research, a measure of conscientiousness makes sense as part of a selection process for almost any job.[50] In addition to conscientiousness, other personality dimensions can be valuable for select job classes, such as:

- **Sales-oriented jobs** might also include a measure of extraversion and emotional stability or "potency" (persisting in the face of obstacle).
- **Customer service jobs** might add a measure of agreeableness.
- **Management trainee jobs** might usefully assess agreeableness, extraversion, and openness to experience.

Despite the research just mentioned, it is important to note that although most managers believe personality is the most important factor in predicting future success, the most recent evidence suggests that in fact personality is rarely related even moderately to future performance.[51] Further, many personality tests such as the Myers-Briggs Type Indicator (MBTI) or the DiSC were not developed with the intention of predicting job performance and in fact are not recommended for use in selection.[52] Because of their popularity, however, many managers are inclined to use them to select employees. The bottom line here is that while it may be intuitive to want to capture personality in predicting future performance, we caution you against the usefulness of most personality measures in predicting future job performance. With that said, personality can be effective in understanding fit with a particular job or organizational environment.

Retaining Your Best Talent

KO **12-4**

DO **12-5**

Give a man a "why" and he will find a "how."

—Anonymous

Before determining how to retain talent, it's important to understand why people tend to separate from organizations. Two forms of turnover occur in organizations: voluntary and involuntary. **Voluntary turnover** occurs when the separation is based upon an employee's choice to leave for any number of reasons spanning personal and professional issues. **Involuntary turnover** occurs when the separation is initiated by the organization due to poor performance, downsizing, and so forth. Most of the time, voluntary turnover is not desired and the organization stands to lose a great deal. For example, when an employee chooses to leave the organization, it is likely to incur significant financial costs estimated at one- to two-thirds the departing employee's salary. In addition, there are social costs to employees who enjoyed good working relationships with the departing person; costs to employees who must pick up the workload caused by a job vacancy; and missed opportunity costs, especially for revenue-producing roles. Thus, determining how best to retain your talent is a key managerial capability. Yet, it's essential to understand that not all employees are equally likely to leave. That is, when all else is equal, low and high performers are much more likely to voluntarily quit than are average performers. Low performers often receive poor evaluations and smaller-than-average pay increases, prompting them to look elsewhere before the company makes that decision for them. High performers are looking for a way up, not necessarily out. Given that they often possess superior job skills, high performers are more likely to have increased external opportunities and actively seek those out. Average performers (and we need people who do their jobs competently, if not exceptionally) tend to be comfortable in their positions and their earned outcomes.[53] Although these are of course generalizations, the lesson is this: Ignore your talent and it will leave.

Research has examined the many reasons why high-performing talent quits, and the results are rather interesting. As seen in Figure 12.2, some research shows that high performers that quit tend to be *less* satisfied compared to lower-performing quitters with respect to learning new skills and promotions received. High performers also tend to quit when their superior performance is not recognized by timely salary increases or when equal pay raises are given regardless of each employee's performance.[54] Of course, pay seems to be an important factor in why people stay or go. However, you might be surprised to learn that pay satisfaction is not necessarily derived from the overall level of pay, but rather whether or not people feel like they are compensated equitably compared to others in similar job roles. In fact, people stay in low-paying jobs with the comfort of knowing that everyone else is paid rather poorly as well! In addition, people tend to be more satisfied with their pay when it is contingent upon performance.[55] Contingent pay creates a sense of fairness and individual control over pay outcomes. High performers in particular are highly sensitive to equity and want to be sure they are paid accordingly for their performance. For additional specifics on understanding the needs of star performers and the types of job assignments to engage them, please see Chapter 7.

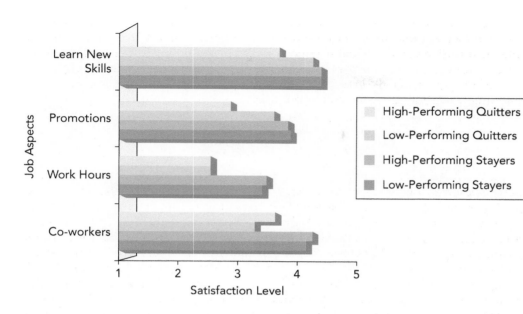

FIGURE 12.2
Relationship Between
Satisfaction and Job
Aspects for Different
Performance Levels

 CASE CONCLUDED

Southwest Airlines. Unlike Google and Facebook, Southwest Airlines is not pursuing technical experts that have broader skills as well. Instead, they screen for *attitudes* such as unselfishness, flexibility, fun, initiative, and a propensity to take risks. To do that, they start by designing targeted questions to get at the specific attitudes they want. For example, Southwest has a culture that values "doing whatever it takes" to satisfy customer needs. So their structured interview questions often include queries like "Tell me about a time when you broke the rules, flexed a policy, or went above and beyond the call of duty to meet a customer's need." They try to avoid a common interviewing flaw of projecting, telling the applicant that a willingness to do whatever it takes is important in our company, and *then* asking the hypothetical question, "So what would you do to go above and beyond the call of duty to satisfy a customer?"

Other questions designed to find ideal employees for Southwest include:

- Tell me about the last time you broke the rules to serve a customer in need. (flexibility; judgment)
- Tell me how you recently used humor to diffuse a tense situation. (fun)
- Tell me about a time when you went beyond the call of duty to assist a co-worker when you

received no recognition or no credit. (unselfishness; teamwork)

- Give me an example of how you've worked with an extremely difficult co-worker. How did you handle it? (adaptability)
- Tell me about a time when you made a serious mistake with a customer or a co-worker. How did you reconcile it? (ability to admit mistakes)
- Tell me about the last time you tried something new or took on additional responsibility when there was no guarantee for success. (willingness to take risks)

Note how the focus of those questions is more on what candidates have done in the past and less on predicting what they would do if they come to work for Southwest Airlines. Southwest knows well that people are always on good behavior during interviews and are often very good at rehearsing and preparing for interviews. But past behavior is the best predictor of future behavior, and interview effectiveness increases when the interviewer continues to draw applicants back to specific examples of how they have previously demonstrated the attitudes Southwest seeks most.

Doubletree Hotels. Doubletree Hotels, a popular hospitality firm, has implemented a peer

(continued)

> CASE CONCLUDED *(continued)*

interviewing process that allows their best employees to help select more employees like themselves. They began peer hiring first among their housekeeping staff. Up until then, turnover had been astonishingly high. Then they began having housekeepers interview prospective housekeepers. And because they spoke multiple foreign languages, they allowed them to interview in their own languages. They watched the results in amazement. Not only did turnover decrease to single digits, but the housekeepers were coming in on weekends, not clocking in (no pay), and shadowing the people they had hired. They knew that their peers would hold them accountable for hiring strong players, but they also wanted to make sure that the countrymen and -women they hired were successful in their jobs.

At Doubletree, they helped their frontline people do a good job with peer interviewing by setting up a structured interview for them to follow. This included several steps that are fairly easy to implement and that offer managers a great deal of insight into the nature of the work, the reasons for high turnover, and the people less prone to it.

Questions

1. Although the questions and assessments are in a modern context and may seem quite innovative, Google, Microsoft, Southwest Airlines, and Doubletree are really just applying very well-researched evidence on effective selection. What selection research lessons do you see in the practices of these firms?

2. Identify a very different type of firm and job (for example, sales, attorney, civil engineering) and use the selection lessons from these firms to design a valid structured interview.

3. Explain the statement "You hire for skills and then the whole person shows up."

4. Consider the following monologue from *The Social Network*, a film that tells the story of how Facebook started and ultimately thrived.

The candidates have 10 minutes to get root access to a Python web server, expose its SSL encryption and then intercept all traffic over its secure ports . . . but here's the beauty—every tenth line of code written, they have to drink a shot; and, hacking is supposed to be stealth, so every time the server detects an intrusion, the candidate responsible has to drink a shot. I also have a program running that has a pop-up window appear simultaneously on all five computers. The last candidate to hit the window has to drink a shot. Plus, every three minutes they all have to drink a shot.

The dialogue excerpt in this scene from David Fincher's *The Social Network* depicting early candidate selection methods at Facebook is both brilliant and telling. Assuming Facebook actually resorted to such eccentric selection practices, what type of selection predictor is this and how would you characterize its validity relative to other selection options? Explain.

Sources: From *The New York Times*, "Googles Answer to Filling Jobs Is An Algorithm," by Saul Hansell, January 3, 2007. © 2007 The New York Times. All rights reserved. Used by permission and protected by the Copyright Laws of the United States. And: Geek logic. *Canadian Business*, Vol. 68, Issue 8 (August 1995).

Concluding Note

One of our favorite bosses once remarked that when a manager does his or her job in recruitment, selection, and retention, he or she engages in very little "performance management." By this he meant that when we get the right people in the right roles, a lot of the problems associated with poor-performing employees go away. In this sense, one of the best approaches to managing people is to ensure from the beginning that you've got the best possible talent matched to the roles you manage. The evidence presented in this chapter is difficult to apply, however, and not because the evidence is not available. Rather, many organizations do not allow managers to engage in hiring, preferring human resource professionals to do the job for the manager. This is unfortunate as selection is truly a responsibility of management; great managers do not fully abdicate such responsibility to others. Yet, even if a human resource department or senior executive drives the overall process, any manager involved in the hiring process can apply aspects of the skills in this chapter. So, next time you're asked to sort through resumés, meet new college graduates, or interview a candidate for a position, remember the evidence presented here and apply it. You'll be thankful you did!

KEY TERMS

adverse impact 424
assessment center 436
behavioral intentions 433
behavioral interviews 433
cognitive ability 436
disparate treatment 424
face validity 431

fairness 431
feasibility 431
integrity tests 439
involuntary turnover 440
job analysis 422
performance tests 436
personality assessments 439

realistic job preview (RJP) 429
situational interviews 433
structured interview 432
unstructured interview 432
validity 430
voluntary turnover 440
work sample 436

 CASE
Staffing UnitedHealth Group[56]

Tom Valerius, the vice president of recruitment services at UnitedHealth Group, was rightly overwhelmed in early 2001. He was facing a massive staffing effort. By his estimates, more than 40,000 employees would have to be hired in the coming years to meet strategic business goals. With six corporate divisions and a presence in all 50 states, this would be no small task. For many companies faced with such decisions, the logical conclusion is to outsource the staffing function, thereby easily disengaging services when staffing needs are met.

Not so at UnitedHealth Group. Their concern was that by outsourcing recruitment and selection they might lose control of this critical function. As a solution, they decided to segment hires into two categories: those who would be staffed by an internal recruitment team, and those who would be recruited

through outsourcing partners. Under the new strategy, in-house recruiters replaced search firms to fill decision-making positions, such as managers and executives with salaries of $100,000 or more. All other openings—in information technology, administration, consumer services, and the call centers—would be staffed by outsourcing specialists. The logic behind this two-pronged approach was that UnitedHealth could maximize control over the quality of candidates in influential posts, while at the same time reduce expenses by filling mass staffing orders with outsourcing partners—a more cost-effective method.

In addition, the company decided to centralize its staffing operations.

Since UnitedHealth first brought the recruitment of high-impact positions in-house, its expenses have dropped to $2 million—a savings of $10 million.

Discussion Questions

1. What do you think about the decision to centralize the selection function? What role do you think managers play in this approach to recruitment and selection?

2. Do you agree with the logic to outsource lower-level positions?

3. How might outsourcing the recruitment/selection function affect the methods used to select people?

SELECT MANAGE ~~WHAT?~~ **DEBRIEFS**

Expanding Your Pool of Candidates: Using Effective Recruiting Tactics: Debrief

The first rule of good selection is to seek out where good candidates can be found and *obsess* over recruiting a larger pool from which to choose. Obsess is exactly the right word but rarely is it found in recruiting. The sad irony is that many organizations spend more time recruiting information to make a decision on a new coffee machine than they do in actively recruiting job candidates. That is particularly unfortunate because evidence shows that relatively low selection ratios (number of candidates selected divided by the number of candidates in the pool) are critical to improving selection over time. And the cost of a bad hire is astronomical, so most companies hardly want to just reactively take what is readily available to them.

So where might good candidates be found and how can companies get them interested in the opportunities they have to offer and pull them into their pool? Recruitment activities can be divided into two broad categories of formal or informal tactics. Formal tactics involve posting job ads on internal systems or on recruitment websites. Informal tactics include networking and referral-based approaches. Although there are no hard-and-fast rules to recruitment approaches, it is surprising to many young managers that informal tactics are generally more effective.

Regardless of the tactic, two main themes of effective recruitment are the treatment of applicants and the quality of the information about the job. This is perhaps why one of the most effective recruitment practices is that of employee referrals, which ask current employees to seek out others who would both be qualified for the job and be a good fit with the organization. With referrals, an applicant is likely to receive excellent treatment by organization representatives since the applicant is a friend or acquaintance of a current employee. In addition, the referring employee is likely to have spent considerable time describing the workplace in great detail and providing important information about fit with the organization.

It may also be useful to assemble a team of people who represent the best qualities of the people who currently hold the same or a similar position. Including the hiring manager and having them develop a job description that delineates the key responsibilities and outputs of the position are good ideas. Then define the behavioral characteristics of the person that is felt to be the ideal candidate. Finally, charge them with the job of finding a solid pool of candidates. There is an old adage in advertising that says, "*Half of every ad dollar is wasted; you just can't tell which half.*" The same thing could be said of recruiting. It is a lot of work and much of it will lead to nothing. But the payoffs in terms of effective selection and productivity in the organization are enormous.

Conducting a More Effective Selection Interview: Debrief

Traditional interviews can be significantly improved by (1) using a structured approach and (2) using the STAR method of interviewing. Structured interviews are much more valid predictors of performance than unstructured because they are standardized and maintain an interviewer's focus on job-related questions. Though some research has shown that under very limited circumstances, unstructured interviews can be effective, the evidence strongly supports structured interviews.

Unfortunately, despite the fact that structured interviews are much more valid than unstructured ones, few practicing managers choose to utilize them, trading in validity for the freedom of asking anything of anyone. This trade-off comes at a high price, namely, the ability to predict future success—your primary goal as a hiring manager. So, given you want to go your own way and do it right, the key is that when trying to predict future job performance, pay little attention to how applicants describe themselves and focus on their *behavior*. That is, focus on what an applicant *can* or *did* do, rather than what he *says* he can do. Great managers commonly use two types of structured interviews found to be valid predictors of job performance. *Situational interviews* include hypothetical scenario questions that ask candidates to describe in detail how they would likely behave in such a situation. *Behavioral interviews* include questions that ask candidates to recount actual instances from their past work or relevant experiences relative to the job at hand.

Both forms of structured interviews work well because they capitalize on behavioral intentions (that is, the motivation and thoughts that are immediate precursors of a person's actual behavior) and the notion that past behavior is often a strong predictor of future behavior. Some research now shows that, for high-level positions, behavioral interviews are more effective than situational ones, while the reverse might be true for lower-level positions.

When framing questions, a simple and straightforward approach is known as STAR, an acronym for **S**ituation, **T**ask, **A**ction, and **R**esult. The notion is that traditional interview questions often get at traits or personality characteristics, and what a candidate might be able to do—rather than behaviors and what the candidate has already done. With a STAR approach, the questions would not be, say, Are you a good team player? or Do you work well in teams? Rather, they would be (1) Describe a time when you were asked to be part of a team? (situation), (2) What task were you and the group charged with doing? (task), (3) What did you ultimately do to accomplish the tasks? (action), and (4) What results did you achieve? (results).

The STAR model is consistent with the notion that past behavior is the best predictor of future behavior and helps interviewers stay focused on observable behaviors rather than ethereal personal characteristics. Many of the most progressive firms train their recruiters in the STAR model and, therefore, a prudent strategy on the part of job candidates is to be prepared to present their records in a STAR-like format.

The first point is that though turnover has a generally negative connotation, it is actually a neutral term and needs to be qualified as whether it is a functional or dysfunctional turnover. That is, from an organizational perspective, turnover is dysfunctional when the firm loses someone it wants to retain. Functional turnover is having people leave that the firm either preferred to have go or was indifferent about. Retention efforts should obviously be focused on reducing dysfunctional turnover, and this scenario is a case of trying to retain a star, so it is clearly in that category.

Second, turnover and its more positive analog, retention, need to be actively managed. Often, people quit solely out of neglect and could have been retained had someone in the firm just modestly reached out. A good lesson is to think of top performers as assets of the firm, and thus everyone in the organization has a vested interest in retaining top performers and ideally will make efforts to do so.

As for the specifics of how to retain talent, some recent research has synthesized the elements that top performers most want in a job and organization. Those elements include:

- The opportunity to solve problems for customers
- Personal development and growth
- Recognition of work
- Working with winners
- An appropriate compensation contingent on performance
- Job continuity

That list is a great evidence-based start, but perhaps the most critical point is to treat individuals as individuals and not just as part of a group identity (in this case, high performers). Seeking to gain a greater understanding of this person and what she finds most attractive and satisfying about possible roles in your group would be your best strategy for success here.

CHAPTER
13

Culture and Diversity

KNOWING   **DOING**

After reading this chapter, you should be able to:

"If you do not manage culture, it manages you, and you may not even be aware of the extent to which this is happening."

—Edgar Shein, MIT professor

KO 13-1 Articulate how organizational cultures differ.

KO 13-2 Recognize the key factors involved in structuring an organization.

KO 13-3 Describe the importance of inclusive cultures to managers and organizations.

KO 13-4 Understand the select dimensions of people-first cultures that have been linked to high performance.

DO 13-1 Assess an organization's culture in relation to your own personal fit.

DO 13-2 Act in ways that facilitate rapid acclimation and socialization in a new context.

DO 13-3 Improve the productivity of a diverse team.

DO 13-4 Influence the cultural practices that are linked to healthy and high-performance outcomes.

Case: Zappos and Their "Quit Offer"

Tony Hsieh, CEO of billion-dollar e-tailer Zappos, is relentless in pursuing the ultimate experience for his customers. Included among Zappos' customer experience strategies are fast free shipping and a standing offer to cover any return shipping if a customer is dissatisfied for any reason at any time. Service representatives are given great leeway to make sure every customer is an *enthusiastic* customer. Thank-you notes to customers are common and the company folklore even includes an anecdote about a service representative who sent flowers to a customer whose mother had recently died.

But even in light of Zappos' customer service obsession, one practice is particularly bold and provocative—it's known as the "quit offer." When Zappos hires new employees, it puts them through an intensive four-week training program, immersing them in the company's culture, strategy, and processes. Then, about one week after completion of the program, Zappos makes the "offer," telling newbies, "If you quit today, we will pay you for the amount of time you have worked, plus a $3,000 bonus." In a *BusinessWeek* interview, Tony Hsieh reported that only 2 to 3 percent of people ultimately take the offer. The other 97 percent say no deal—and choose the job over the instant cash.

1. What is the underlying logic of the Zappos quit offer? Won't it be abused by people who apply for a job there just to get some gas money? Doesn't it seem silly and wasteful to induce people to quit who have already completed your training program?

2. What does the quit offer say about Zappos' confidence in their jobs and organization? Why do so few people ultimately take the offer?

3. Critique the following statement from Tony Hsieh: "If you really want to amaze your customers, a great way to start is to amaze your employees."

4. How might the quit offer give Zappos a business advantage over competitors?

< < A HIGHLY PRODUCTIVE CULTURE DISGUISED AS FUN AND WEIRDNESS

1. Will I Fit In Here? Decoding an Organization's Culture

Two of the most central lessons of organizational culture are that (1) different companies have very different cultures and subcultures, and (2) the fit between a person and the culture is a critical factor in determining job success and satisfaction. With that in mind, assume you have just received two job offers and both firms have offered the same pay, same job description, and same geographic location. So your hope is to begin to sort out which of those firms would be the best fit for you. What types of culture differences are most important in organizations? What questions would you ask? What would be the sources of information (systems, signs, traditions) you would seek to help determine the nature of each culture, and your potential fit?

2. Avoiding Culture Shock

You are very aware that fitting in and acclimating to a culture are critical to job success and satisfaction. In contrast, slow assimilation and "culture shock" are associated with slow advancement and derailed careers. You are the manager of an exciting new international branch of your firm in Seoul, South Korea. Given that you want your new people to assimilate quickly, get a fast start in their jobs, and jump-start their careers in the firm, what general strategies and specific actions will you take? Failures in this type of situation are very common, so where do you suspect most managers go wrong? Be specific in isolating a couple of the most important "must dos" and a couple of the taboos or "don't dos."

3. Making a Culturally Diverse Team Productive

You have just been honored by being appointed to one of three project action teams, chartered by your company's senior leadership officers, to work on a current strategic issue in the firm. You have been asked to complete your work in three months and make a presentation at the top management retreat in front of the CEO, the vice president of marketing, and other decision-makers. Your team's charge is to explore how your firm might better recruit the best young talent worldwide. The team is composed of eight people from across the company and is the most diverse team you have ever been on.

More specifically, the team consists of six men and two women; an age range of 24 to 62; three American Caucasians, one African American, one Hispanic American, and one national representative from each company unit in India, China, and Brazil, all of whom are currently on assignment in the United States. Everyone speaks English, although the Chinese woman seems exceedingly shy and not particularly comfortable with her language skills.

Recognizing it is demanding enough to achieve quality team outcomes with people you know well and understand, you are concerned it's going to be very difficult to pull this group together quickly, communicate effectively, and achieve the kind of work product you will want to present in three months. So what would you recommend that could help bring this team together? How would you attempt to minimize some of the communication and coordination challenges known to face diverse teams? Conversely, how might you best bring out the potential creativity and idea generation that is the promise of diversity? In short, what could you do to help create a productive and diversity-friendly team?

4. Building Your Own High-Performance Subculture

One of the most misunderstood and yet exciting research findings regarding culture concerns *subcultures*. Specifically, research has found that the cultural variance *within* companies (for example, between different McDonald's stores) is often as great as or greater than that *between* companies (McDonald's vs. Burger King). The same holds for different chapters of non-profit organizations, for individual churches in a national denomination, and for the same government function (for example, property assessment) in different city or county locations. What is exciting about this is that it suggests an overall company or top-down culture is not destiny and, in fact, individual subcultures exist and are greatly subject to the influence of the managers and workforce within a unit.

With that in mind, assume you work for one branch of a landscaping firm that has six branches in your state. Each branch has roughly the same annual revenue, organizational/cost structure, and retail presence, and all brand and marketing expenditures are handled at the corporate level. As a young and energetic go-getter, you would really like to make your branch the top performer in the state. So where do you start? Given that your branch seems almost identical to the other five branches, is there really anything you can do that would have much impact? What are the things that impact high-performance cultures and what levers to change them are available to you? In what ways would you seek to differentiate yourself from the other branches and why? What elements, if any, of high-performance cultures from well-known firms (for example, Starbucks, Google, SAS) would you try to emulate and how could those elements be adapted to fit this landscape business?

?¿ MYTHS 13.1 Myths of Culture and Diversity

- **All companies in certain industries or product categories are culturally similar.** Most people would be quick to recognize this as a myth but would still grossly underestimate just *how great* the cultural divide is between firms. Firms vary dramatically in their cultures and learning, so to recognize and assess such differences is an important skill.

- **Some people are just better at fitting in.** Like many myths, there is some truth in this statement. Personality differences in people are real and can certainly influence the ability and motivation to acclimate. Nonetheless, successful socialization and effective on-boarding are far more related to what you do (behavioral actions) than who you are (your personality profile).

- **New employees are lost initially and then within a few months are well socialized.** Many managers assume that when people are hired, they will have a brief period of getting socialized and then that process will be over. Evidence, however, suggests that this is not the case and that it takes from nine months to a year just to get back to where the person was in his or her first week.

- **The best inclusiveness strategy is to be "blind" to all differences.** This is often characterized as a noble and nondiscriminating strategy and yet is actually nonsense. The objective reality is that people do differ in many meaningful ways and our goal should be to recognize and effectively utilize those differences, rather than engage in a futile attempt to dismiss or ignore them.

- **Organizations have one culture.** While there can certainly be dominant values and patterns of behavior in firms, the exciting reality is that it is organizational *subcultures* that are often most influential in firms. That means that effective leaders and individual contributors can and do have significant impact on the subculture of their particular organization unit.

- **Organization culture is a strictly positive phenomenon.** Oh, do we wish this were true (and not a myth). Unfortunately, there is an all-too-common "dark" side of culture, whereby toxic, non-inclusive, and low-performance norms prevail in many organizations. Worse yet, there are companies where the cultures reward unethical, discriminatory, and immoral behavior. Culture is exceptionally powerful and can influence dysfunctional and evil action just as it can foster high performance and ethical practice.

- **Our group identities define us.** This is one of the most pervasive and destructive myths and is also known by a fancy name: *"the ecological fallacy."* Put simply, it is nonsense to say that all women, or all Asians, or all senior citizens share all the same characteristics—yet such stereotypical assumptions are common and insidious. Although some general shared patterns and characteristics are known, and can be very useful as starting points in working with diverse groups, a good maxim is to always judge people as *individuals* and not solely on the basis of their group identities.

Introduction

One of the textbook authors once worked in a large, Fortune 500 organization where people had a unique way of talking to each other. In fact, if an employee didn't speak this way, he or she might be seen by others as not fitting in. What was this way of speaking? Well, put simply, it was the use of extensive expletives. That's right, in this organization using expletives was a way of showing that you were tough, that you've been around the block, that you could handle things on your own, that you wouldn't crumble under pressure. Most importantly, it was a symbol that you were "one of the gang." When explaining such a phenomenon, you'd probably describe this way of behaving as part of the organization's culture. **Organization culture** represents a shared way of being, acting, and interpreting life in the company. You can't touch or feel this culture per se, but you certainly know it exists. Further, you will have probably heard stories about how this culture came to be like this. For example, this organization was originally founded by a blue-collar, "rough and tumble" fellow who prided himself on his aggressive tactics. He valued peoples' "straight talk" and didn't have much tolerance for formalized or overly complicated ways of speaking. His values regarding how people should speak to one another have remained in place even as the organization grew from a family business to a publically traded corporation.

Interestingly, although this aspect of their culture is pervasive, it doesn't necessarily mean that it is related to the organization's success. Herein is the difficult paradox of managing organizational culture: The very things that make a place unique may not necessarily be the things that make the organization successful. In this chapter, we try to help you understand the nature of organizational culture, how it develops and is reinforced. At the same time, we hope to offer you a perspective that culture is not something that is simply historical in nature, but rather an area that must be managed with care. Although few individual managers can change a company's culture alone, managers can build positive cultures within their own group and hope that their success is contagious beyond their department or unit.

KO 13-1   Understanding Culture and Its Importance in Organizations

When managers talk about culture, they are referring to the values, norms, and assumptions that influence their ability to make sense of events and guide people's behavior. Some of these elements of culture can be seen, while others exist in people's mental models or assumptions (see Chapter 4) about the organization. Edgar Schein in his extensive work on organizational culture describes culture as a pattern of basic assumptions which have (1) been invented, discovered, or developed by a given group as it learns to cope with problems of external adaptation and internal integration; (2) worked well enough to be considered valid; and (3) have been taught to new members as the correct way to perceive, think, and feel in relation to those problems. In other words, culture is a way of being that everyone agrees is important (not by voting, but by acting!) and should be taught to all members of the organization. In Schein's model of organizational culture, he describes the three levels of culture as they would appear to an outside observer from the most superficial and visible level to the deepest unobservable level.[1] Schein's model includes (1) **artifacts** or organizational attributes that can be observed, felt, and heard as an individual enters a new culture; (2) **values** or espoused goals, ideals, norms, standards, and moral principles—this is usually the level that is measured through survey questionnaires; and (3) **underlying assumptions** or the phenomena that remain unexplained when insiders are asked about the values of the organizational culture. According to Schein, the real essence of organizational culture lies in this third level.

The contents of each level can be seen in Figure 13.1. At the third and deepest level, the organization's tacit assumptions are found. These are the elements of culture that are unseen and not identified or even realized in everyday

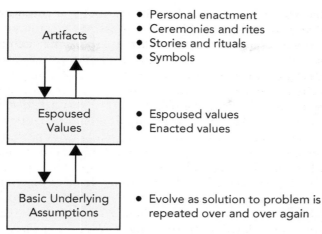

- Personal enactment
- Ceremonies and rites
- Stories and rituals
- Symbols

Artifacts

Espoused Values

- Espoused values
- Enacted values

Basic Underlying Assumptions

- Evolve as solution to problem is repeated over and over again

Source: From E.H. Schein, *Organizational Culture and Leadership,* Jossey-Bass, 1992, Figure 9. Copyright © 1992. Reprinted with permission of John Wiley & Sons, Inc.

FIGURE 13.1
Schein's Three Levels of Culture

Practice this!
Go to www.baldwin2e.com

interactions between organizational members. Additionally, these are the elements of culture that are often taboo to discuss inside the organization. This deepest level of culture becomes even more difficult to discern because the very people who have the experience to understand it best are often so immersed in the culture over time that it makes the deep level virtually invisible. As one wise observer once quipped, "People can't see their organizational culture in the same way that fish don't see water." Culture at this level is the underlying and driving element of organizational culture that is often missed by most managers and by most people studying organizational behavior.

Using Schein's model, understanding organizational behavior that appears to be counterintuitive or even full of contradictions becomes more possible. For instance, an organization can use team-oriented standards at the second level of Schein's model while simultaneously displaying curiously contradictory behavior at the third and deepest level of culture. At the surface, organizational rewards can imply that individual contributions are more valued than teamwork, but at the deepest level imply a close-knit family sense of team. This insight offers an understanding of the difficulty that organizational newcomers have when joining a company. The stated values of the organization may say one thing, but the deep assumptions that are enacted may be quite different. It also explains why organizational changes are often unsuccessful because the underlying assumptions are generally not understood before would-be change agents and many new managers begin their attempts to make changes.

Based upon Schein's work, we can begin to understand how cultures survive and thrive as specific and sometimes elaborate activities are enacted to maintain the culture that exists. For example, most organizations have ceremonies, rites, or rituals that serve to preserve culture. Figure 13.2 provides examples of various organizational rites and their purpose. One particularly important activity is that of storytelling. Telling stories helps to quickly and poignantly communicate values the organization seeks to embody. There are common types of stories told in organizations to communicate broad-level values on a range of issues, including stories about (1) managers, (2) getting fired, (3) dealing with relocation, (4) career paths for low-level employees, (5) dealing with crises scenarios, and (6) consequences for breaking rules.[2] At McDonald's, for instance, stories are told about how senior executives routinely started their careers as line-cooks and they proudly display buttons exclaiming "Up from Line." The obvious implication of such a story is to communicate that anyone can "make it" in the organization and that the company promotes its own. Please see Tool Kit 13.1 for techniques to improve your storytelling skills.

FIGURE 13.2
Example Organization-
al Rites

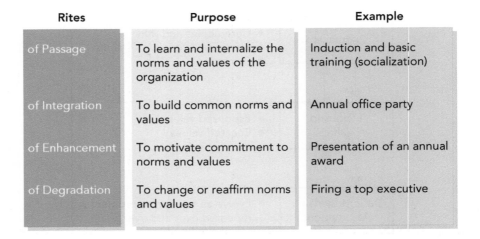

Rites	Purpose	Example
of Passage	To learn and internalize the norms and values of the organization	Induction and basic training (socialization)
of Integration	To build common norms and values	Annual office party
of Enhancement	To motivate commitment to norms and values	Presentation of an annual award
of Degradation	To change or reaffirm norms and values	Firing a top executive

Making a Cultural Choice: The Competing Values Model

Although many theoretical models of culture exist, one known as the Competing Values Model by Quinn,[3] has received considerably more attention than others. Like many models that are both useful and simple, the Competing Values Model categorizes cultures along two axes (see Figure 13.3). More specifically, one dimension depicts the degree to which a company values stability and control versus the degree to which it values flexibility and discretion. The other dimension represents the value placed on internal focus and integration versus the valuing of an external focus and differentiation. As you can see, the name "Competing Values" is a good one for this approach because like many other ideas in this book, there is a competition between two worthwhile objectives on each dimension. It is the decisions that the company makes on these major issues that ultimately determine "what kind of organization" it will be.

MANAGER'S TOOL KIT

Tool Kit 13.1   Improve Your Storytelling[4]

As we've noted throughout this book, much of effective management requires practice. Learning to engage in good storytelling is no different. This tool kit gives you some ideas about situations where storytelling can be practiced and used.

1. *Listen to stories and try storytelling yourself.* As you hear stories, try to apply the five-step framework. Ask people to help you improve your own stories by using the framework.

2. *Tell stories to others.* Find stories in the press, books, novels, and in personal experience. First read a story to build your comfort level; then retell a story that you've read using the five-step storytelling framework.

3. *Pair work.* Practice telling stories with just one other person.

4. *Field work.* Start telling stories more frequently to other organizational members, friends, and others.

5. *Keep a journal.* To have good material, it is important to write down stories that illustrate important points you would like to make on the job.

6. *Consider alternative perspectives.* Try thinking through the same story from different perspectives. Consider the boss, the co-worker, the employee, and the customer as important perspectives to take.

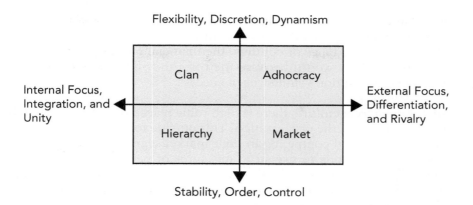

FIGURE 13.3
The Competing Values
Model of Culture

Keep in mind that like so many other areas, the Competing Values Model is not suggesting that there is a "correct" decision on either of these axes. To the contrary, the goals of stability and flexibility are both laudable ones—as are the goals of internal and external foci. The problem is you cannot have it both ways; the reality is that by choosing one we tend to lose the advantages of the other. In other words, to create stability, a company will generally have centralized decision making and a deliberate way of doing things. These companies tend to have more policies, and be more formalized. Once a company has opted for stability, this creates significant hurdles when it tries to be flexible and nimble in responding during times of change. Even more insidious in many ways is that the very issues that help define the company, and that may be responsible for its significant success, may ultimately make it unable to compete in a different environment.

An example of this can be seen in General Motors. By almost any measure, General Motors was the most successful for-profit organization on the planet. It reigned supreme for the better part of 50 years, and former U.S. Secretary of Defense Charles Erwin Wilson once remarked, "What is good for General Motors is good for the United States." General Motors, for many reasons, had a culture that valued stability. This was completely appropriate when the auto industry was basically controlled by a few large global companies and General Motors was the biggest of them. The rise of global competition, however, significantly changed the environment, and General Motors was forced into bankruptcy reorganization in 2009 (now General Motors has been reorganized as a smaller, more flexible company to try to compete in the very competitive global auto industry of the 21st century).

From the two competing values in the Competing Values Model, four different organizational cultures can be derived. These four cultures are referred to as clans, hierarchies, adhocracies, and market cultures. We will explain each of these cultures in more detail in the following.

Clan. In a clan culture, there is a strong value placed upon flexibility and an internal focus of the organization. These organizations tend to be friendly places to work with a high degree of individual development. As a result, leaders play developmental roles and are more likely to fill the role of mentor or coach rather than task master. Most promotion occurs from within the organization because the company has spent a great deal of time and effort developing their next generation of leaders. In these cultures, long tenures are relatively typical and organizational commitment and loyalty are high.

Hierarchy. In a hierarchical culture, there is a high value placed on stability and control with an internal focus. Compared to the other cultures, increased formalization tends to be the rule. The leadership role in a hierarchy consists primarily of organizing, monitoring, measuring, and evaluating the activities of subordinates. In these types of cultures, the financial and production functions tend to be relatively powerful because the roles they fill are highly valued and central to the organization's standards of success.

Market.   In a market culture, there is high value placed on control and stability, with a focus outside of the organization. This outside focus means that the company is directed toward competing in their market segments and the leadership of these companies tends to use strict measures of performance (for example, performance quotas) to control subordinate behavior. In a market culture, an employee's current contribution or performance is the most important factor for employee payment or promotion. As a result, market cultures can be difficult places to work for some, but they tend to be places where driven, competitive people thrive (see the discussion of topgrading in Chapter 7 for a further description of practices that are common in a market culture).

Adhocracy.   In an adhocracy culture, flexibility is valued and the focus is outside of the company. As a result, we have the opposite of a hierarchy-based culture. The role of the leadership team is more of an entrepreneurial role than one of controlling. The company's entrepreneurial focus is externally directed and the company is in constant competition to be the first one to market, with the most innovative ideas. In an adhocracy, risk taking is encouraged and innovation is valued. While certain people thrive in adhocracies, others may have a great deal of difficulty adapting to the uncertainty and fast pace. These tend to be relatively intense places to work, with top leaders who are often considered "visionary."

An Alternative View of Culture

Another simpler way of looking at organizational culture is to view it as a group's general reaction to stimulus consistent with the basic tenants of learning theory (see Chapter 6) and the behaviorist approach. Although this is a significant simplification, the work of behaviorists is rooted in the tradition of B. F. Skinner and looks to the consequences of behavior to understand why certain behaviors occur. In understanding culture, behaviorists view an organization's culture as the manifestation of the company's reward system.[5] From this view, an organizational culture is a group of people who have been trained, or who have simply learned from those around them, how to act in any given situation. In this way, corporate culture functions just as any social learning does. In many ways, this simple interpretation is very powerful and can help us understand the Quinn Competing Values Model even more deeply.

Linking values and reward systems is not a difficult task. In fact, if we value something, we tend to reward it. From the behavior of dogs (for instance, I give my dog a treat when he rolls over because I value obedience to my command), to children (for example, when my child says something funny, I laugh because I value humor in my child), to employees (for instance, our employees get sales bonuses for making their sales quotas because I value sales and the revenues they generate), the linking of values and rewards is both common and powerful.

In taking a more or less behaviorist view of culture, Kerr and Slocum presented an interpretation of culture where they saw the clan and market cultures above as being at opposite ends of the continuum about what is valued and rewarded.[6] Basically, they described the market culture as a culture that values performance, whereas the clan culture values loyalty. In looking at the characteristics of the two cultures, this is a compelling logic and one that makes the management of the cultures and any attempt to change cultures much more straightforward. Using a behaviorist view of culture, we need to change the reward system if we are going to change the culture. It is that simple (though doing this is not easy). From a behaviorist's view, trying to change culture without changing the reward system is an absolutely futile exercise that will end in failure.

Is One Type of Culture the Best?

At this point, most students have a rather obvious question in mind: "This is all very nice, but which culture is best? Which will lead to being most successful?" Like so many other issues discussed in this book, that question is actually akin to asking "What language is best?" or from a doctor's perspective "What's the best way to heal a patient?" Luckily, there is some pretty good evidence to help us structure a usable answer to this question. In a very interesting and impactful study, researchers examined a large number of companies, and then classified their cultures, and measured their performance. What they found was that there is not a best culture, but that the best culture depends on the structural characteristics of the industry in which the company competes.[7] In other words, what is needed is a match between the culture of the company and the type of industry in which the company competes. In their study, clans enjoyed superior performance when the industry was relatively stable and the barriers to entry were high (for example, cars, steel, and airlines). In these situations, the more clan-based cultures outperformed the more market-like cultures. In situations where the industry was engaged in more dynamic competition and where barriers to entry were low (such as web development, distributors, and professional service firms), companies with market cultures outperformed the more clan-like cultures.

Another issue to consider when trying to determine an appropriate culture is the complicating factor that almost no company is a "pure form" of any of the cultures described earlier. In other words, even companies that value external focus certainly still place some value on internal issues. Similarly, companies that value flexibility always have some practices that promote stability. The reason for this can be thought of as an effort to "hedge your bets." In other words, if you rewarded nothing but individual performance, you could easily run the risk of losing effective people who had been with the company for years but had a short-term setback.

From the preceding discussions, it is evident that culture impacts the behaviors of everyone in the organization—from the CEO to the new building maintenance guy. In some cases, however, the effects of culture on behavior are relatively weak, while in other cases they are extremely strong.[8] This leads us to the idea of strong and weak cultures. In a **weak culture,** there is a great deal of variance in the way people think and behave within the organization. In very **strong cultures,** this variance is much less. The idea of a subculture is a telling signal regarding a culture's overall strength.

Organizational Structure: A Key Cultural Ingredient

KO **13-2**

Inseparable from an organization's culture is its structure. Although there are many elaborate organizational structures being used today, the main concepts behind an organization's structure are relatively simple. **Organizational structure** can best be defined as the work roles and authority relationships in an organization.

These roles and relationships are particularly relevant in the field of organizational behavior because they have important effects on the behavior of individuals, teams, and the actions of the entire organization. When many people think of organizational structure, however, the first thing that comes to mind is the organization's hierarchy, which is graphically represented in an organizational chart. Three primary characteristics of organizational structure are the concepts of span of control, height, and departmentation.

When thinking about an organizational structure, the manager's **span of control** is the number of people that report directly to a single manager. So, in the case of a small retail store with 10 employees and one store manager, the store manager's span of control would be 10. While this may not seem like a very important consideration when thinking of a small retail store, the span of control becomes a major structural issue when larger organizations are the focus. In fact, the **height of an organization,** which is the number of hierarchical levels in an organization, is often determined by the span of control of the management members. At first glance, many students might think that the difference between five people reporting to a manager and seven people reporting to a manager is not that significant (it's only two people after all). In practice, however, increasing the span of control usually allows an organization to reduce the number of managers required and maintain a relatively flat or shorter organizational height. Thus, the span of control and the height of an organization are often inversely related, meaning that a small span is likely related to a taller organization height and a large span to a shorter organization height.

In addition to span of control and height, the form of departmentation a company chooses is another primary characteristic of an organization's structure. **Departmentation** refers to the grouping of resources (including people and technology) into work units. The most common forms of departmentation include organizing by function, by geography, by customer, by product, and hybrids of these four. Tool Kit 13.2 provides a quick guide to the most common forms of departmentation and the circumstances that best dictate their use.

Structure Influences Behavior

Many eager managers fall prey to a simple managerial trap when thinking about how best to structure their department. The trap is that they fail to realize that structure influences behavior. In 1971, Phillip Zimbardo, a Stanford University psychologist, conducted a now classic study known as the Stanford Prison Experiment.[9] Zimbardo and his team of researchers recruited 24 undergraduate students for the study who were randomly assigned to role play the part of either a prison guard or prisoner. The researchers created a simulated prison in the basement of the Stanford psychology building and even staged mock arrests at the participants' homes! Within one day of the experiment starting, the new "prisoners" endured humiliating treatment from the guards, and these newly appointed guards (who just 24 hours before were typical college undergraduates) developed an almost sadistic approach to dealing with the prisoners. On the second day of the experiment, a riot erupted. The guards voluntarily worked overtime and attacked the prisoners with fire extinguishers without the researchers' approval. Guards began to use physical punishment such as forcing endless pushups, removing prisoner mattresses, or prohibiting prisoners to urinate in a bathroom. Prisoners were only allowed to be addressed by their prison identification number (which they had to memorize and repeat constantly). The experiment became so out of hand that by day six, the researchers called it off.

MANAGER'S TOOL KIT

Tool Kit 13.2 Selecting Appropriate Organizational Forms

Organizational Form	Description	Use When . . .	Key Advantages
Functional	• Departments staffed by a specialist in an organizational function (for example, accountants work in accounting)	• The environment is stable or certain, the organization is small to medium-sized, routine technology is used, and goal is efficiency	• Promotes skill specialization • Reduces the duplication of resources • Promotes clear career ladders in large departments
Self-Contained Unit	• Also known as *Divisional* or *Product*, groups activities on the basis of products, services, customers, or geography	• The environment is rather unstable, the organization is large in size, technological independence is high, goals are product specialization and innovation	• Fosters an overall outcome and client focus • Allows for skill expansion and training • Promotes delegation of authority and responsibility • Heightens work involvement
Matrix	• Groups people by function for a specific project, product, or line of business	• The environment requires dual focus on product demands or technical specialization, pressure for fast information processing, and pressure for shared resources	• Specialized functional knowledge is readily available • Highly flexible—rapid response • Maximizes coordination and communication • Provides legitimate mechanisms for multiple sources of power

What is so fascinating about this study is that neither the prisoners nor the guards were given instructions on how to act. Yet, within hours of being assigned their roles, they acted according to their role—keep in mind these were normal, well-adjusted undergraduates. Although there are many things to learn from this experiment, one critical takeaway is the simple yet important idea: Structure influences behavior—put people in prisons and they will act like prisoners. In other words, situations (not people) often dictate behavior, and it's a fallacy to believe that people can accomplish goals regardless of their situational constraints. We are constantly amazed at the number of organizations that want nothing more than to have their frontline employees serve customers with delight. Yet their behavior is restricted by a structure consisting of endless series of red-tape approvals and "sign-offs" anytime they want to appease a customer. The reason that Ritz-Carlton is a model of customer service is that every employee has the ability and the obligation to satisfy the customer. Ritz employees are given funds to make this happen and can, at their *own* discretion, allocate those funds to a particular customer situation. Thus, for the Ritz to meet its goals of customer loyalty and satisfaction, they realized they had to structure employees' work by pushing much of the day-to-day decision making to lower-level employees. Conversely, if an organization has a strong need for safe operations (for example, a nuclear power plant), then acting like the Ritz is not likely to accomplish their goals. Instead, they ought to opt for intense monitoring and smaller spans of control.

The point is, in creating a desired organizational culture, you must align the structure of people's work with the mission, goals, and strategy you are trying to achieve. This point is too easy to overlook as companies often simply copy their competitors' structure or structure work in accordance with what is most expedient. An easy rule applies here: First decide what it is you're trying to achieve and then create the structure that allows people to achieve it. Don't create the structure and hope people will be able to work within that structure. Put differently, all great managers periodically review structure by asking, "What things stand in the way of my employees achieving their goals?" The answer almost always contains structural constraints. The good news here is that redesigning jobs and structuring a department's work (see Chapter 6) is well within the control of managers and relatively easy to do.

KO **13-3**

DO **13-1**

DO **13-2**

People Make The Place: Person–Organization Fit

It's clear that organizations do differ significantly in their types and strength of organizational culture. But to talk about differences in organizational culture is really to talk about differences in the collection of people that make up an organization. It is the people within the organization, how they act, react, and feel, that comprise the essence of organizational culture. Thus, one critical factor in designing and maintaining a productive organizational culture is to examine the fit between a given person and the organization (that is, everyone else), otherwise known as person–organization fit or **P-O fit** for short. P-O fit represents the extent to which a person's values, personality, and work needs are aligned with an organization's culture. Fit would be considered strong when individuals' most important values, for instance, are perceived as being important in the organization.

The ASA Framework

The concept of P-O fit was born out of the **attraction-selection-attrition (ASA) framework,** which suggests that individuals and organizations are attracted to each other based on similar values and goals.[10]

The idea of the ASA model is a simple yet very powerful one, and it gives us a useful lens for understanding everything from why a person interviews with a certain company, to who gets selected in the interviewing process, to who gets promoted, to ultimately who leaves the firm on either voluntary or involuntary bases. The basic ASA model argues that people are attracted to organizations that appear to have the same personal values as they have, people who are most like the current culture are selected, and those who do not ultimately share the same values and standards as the organization eventually attrition out of the organization. A brief example of these different stages helps bring the power of the ASA model to light.

Let's assume we have three different organizations. These three different organizations for the illustration are Harvard Medical School, the United States Army, and Google. Would you assume that applicants (that is, people trying to get in or be hired) to those three organizations are random individuals? In other words, pick any person you know, or even think about yourself. Is the chance of applying to those organizations equally likely for your friend (or you)? Of course not. The applicants for these three organizations are very likely entirely different groups of people with almost no overlap. This is because the people have self-selected toward organizations that they identify and want to be associated with. This is the power of attraction. Attraction begins the socialization process before people are even part of the organization. In the U.S. Army, for instance, most recruits know what they are getting into. They understand the time commitment and the dedication that being in the Army will require. People don't often join the Army to "see if they like it." If you find the values and the requirements of the Army to be similar to your values and skill set, you will consider joining the Army. If your values and skill set are the exact opposite of the Army's, it is very unlikely you would enlist.

In the same way, people are attracted to all different types of organizations. In college, people join fraternities or sororities if these organizations are appealing to them. This process continues through the rest of your organizational life as well. If you are a pre-med student with a strong academic record, then Harvard Medical School is likely an organization that holds great interest for you. But for most people, Harvard Medical School is not an organization to which they are attracted because they have different interests, values, and skill sets that are not good matches with Harvard's medical school.

The next step of the ASA model, selection, acts to further refine the initial group of applicants. So Google starts with a large group of smart, motivated, technically minded people, and then has to select a small portion of those people to become Nooglers (the term for new Google employees). From Chapter 12, the two goals of the selection process are to pick people who will be high performers but who will also fit with the culture. So, from the initial pool of very smart people, Google is able to pick the people who they think will fit in best. Now ask yourself a simple question: "Is someone who fits in likely to be similar to other people in the organization?" Of course they are. So, from the initial group, Google will then pick people who tend to be like the other people at Google. Mind you, this is not specific to any one organization, but it happens in all organizations whether or not people are aware of it while it is happening.

The last step of the ASA process is referred to as attrition. Over time, certain people will perform well, fit in, be rewarded, and likely be promoted. Other people will have a harder time fitting in with others, not building positive relationships with bosses (recall the **LMX** relationships discussed in Chapter 9) and subordinates, and not being valued and rewarded by the organization. Be it through voluntary (for example, a person looks for another job because she is unhappy where she is) or involuntary (for instance, she is fired) means, these people will tend to leave the organization over time.

So the ASA model helps us understand the process of how organizations create cultures through employees' evaluations of P-O fit. The punch line here is that when employees perceive a strong P-O fit, they are much more likely to be satisfied on the job, display increased commitment to the organization, and are far more likely to stay with the organization for the long term. Further, meta-analytic research shows that a strong P-O fit is related to increased displays of organizational citizenship behaviors.[11] Yet P-O fit is not associated with increased employee performance and it's important not to confuse the two. People may be a terrible fit for the organization but may still, in fact, perform quite well. Over time, however, the research on P-O fit would suggest that despite performing well, employees who feel like they are a mismatch for the organization are likely to eventually look elsewhere for employment. In Tool Kit 13.3, we

Tool Kit 13.3 Determining P-O Fit by Decoding Cultural Characteristics

Let's say you are in the final stages of considering multiple job offers and you're trying to determine how well you might fit in. The following are broad categories or characteristics of organizations that will help you determine the organization's culture. For example, you should ask people you meet with about the degree to which the organization encourages risk taking or is inclusive. These characteristics also provide a good platform to describe the company to others, particularly newcomers.

- **Innovation and risk taking.** The degree to which employees are encouraged to be innovative and take risks.
- **Attention to detail.** The degree to which employees are expected to exhibit precision, analysis, and attention to detail.
- **Outcome orientation.** The degree to which management focuses on results or outcomes rather than on the techniques and processes used to achieve those outcomes.
- **People orientation.** The degree to which management decisions take the employees into consideration.
- **Team orientation.** The degree to which activities are organized around teams rather than individuals.
- **Aggressiveness.** The degree to which people are aggressive and competitive rather than easygoing.
- **Stability.** The degree to which organizational activities emphasize maintaining the status quo in contrast to growth.
- **Inclusiveness.** The degree to which a diverse set of individuals can gain entry, acclimate, and thrive in the organization.

Each of these characteristics exists on a continuum from low to high. Assessing the organization on these eight characteristics then gives a composite picture of culture. That picture becomes the basis for determining your own or others' person–organization fit.

provide some dimensions that you can use to assess your own P-O fit within any organization.

Cultural Adaptation: Socialization and Onboarding Employees

The strong evidence supporting P-O fit means that contrary to popular belief, managers can have an influence on shaping their immediate organizational culture to create an environment whereby employees feel like they belong. This active process is known as **employee socialization** or the process of helping employees quickly adjust to and reinforce the central values the organization espouses. When employees join an organization, they are often overwhelmed by the ambiguity of their job, worried about whether they will be able to succeed, and concerned about being socially accepted by fellow employees. New employees must learn to deal with the fact that some of their initial expectations won't be met (but if they are given a good realistic job preview [or RJP, discussed in Chapter 12], fewer unmet expectations will exist in the first place). Further, they must adjust to routines in the organization for how people communicate with others. Perhaps most difficult is coping with anxiety about what their manager expects from them in terms of job contributions. In fact, research has shown that in the first month of employment, employees experience moderate levels of self-confidence, **role clarity** (understanding their job requirements), and perceptions of social acceptance. Yet, in months three to six, these three critical perceptions have diverged drastically. Role clarity plummets and feelings of social acceptance decrease as well. Self-confidence initially increases, but then also decreases drastically by month six. It takes anywhere from 9 to 12 months for employee feelings of role clarity and social acceptance to return to where they were during their first few weeks.[12] The point is that many managers are apt to believe that socialization is a static process whereby employees are lost initially, and then within a few months are perfectly socialized. The reality of this process, however, is far more complex and dynamic.

Given this protracted period for most employees, research on socialization has shown that when organizations engage in a systematic method to socialize employees, they are more likely to reduce the ambiguity of being new and increase perceptions of P-O fit. The key here is that a systematic method is used which implies that all new employees experience a standard process to learn about the organization immediately upon starting with the organization. This means that regardless of the type of job or firm, socialization must address some critical content, including (1) organizational mission and values; (2) job requirements; (3) networks and politics; (4) language or jargon; and (5) organizational history.

Most organizations will engage in socialization via a formalized program such as a new employee orientation. Unfortunately, for too many new employees these programs are a dry regurgitation of facts and distributions of large three-ring binders with things to "read." It doesn't have to be this way, of course, and progressive managers understand that they must personally contribute to getting their employees off to the right start. The single most harmful trap would be to stand aside and let your employees "get used to things" and ease them into the culture. To the contrary, on day one you should set expectations with your employees about performance and behavior (see Chapter 7 on performance management), provide them with challenging goals from the start (see Chapter 9 on leadership), and help them build their networks through mentoring and other opportunities to network inside the organization (see Chapter 8 on power and influence). As you can see, applying your knowledge about management to socialization just requires you to think about your new employees not as fragile individuals but as people who want to be challenged immediately and be steeped in the culture quickly to move past their anxiety of the unknown and start to feel like they fit in.

National Cultural Differences

Managing People from Different Cultures

The most well-known research on cultural differences was conducted by Geert Hofstede in his role as a psychologist for IBM. Hofstede collected data on employee values and perception of the work situation from more than 116,000 IBM employees in 64 countries. Based on his surveys, he identified five dimensions along which people from national cultures tend to differ (see Table 13.1).

1. Power Distance. Hofstede used **power distance** to refer to the degree to which people accept economic and social differences in wealth, status, and well-being as natural and normal. See Management Live 13.1 for an interesting example of how power distance can matter in an important way that is anything but obvious. Countries that allow inequalities to exist or believe they are natural are

Practice this!
Go to www.baldwin2e.com

TABLE 13.1   Hofstede's Cultural Attitudes Profile for 10 Countries

Country	Power Distance	Individualism	Masculinity	Uncertainty Avoidance	Long-Term Orientation
China	H	L	H	M	H
France	H	H	M	H	L
Germany	L	H	H	M	M
Indonesia	H	L	M	L	L
Japan	M	M	H	H	H
Netherlands	L	H	L	M	M
Russia	H	M	L	H	L
United States	L	H	M	L	L
West Africa	H	L	M	M	L

H = top third, M = middle third, L = bottom third among 53 countries and regions for the first four dimensions and among 23 countries for the fifth.

Source: Based on Geert Hofstede, Gert Jan Hofstede, Michael Minkov, *Cultures and Organizations, Software of the Mind,* Third Revised Edition, McGraw-Hill, 2010. Reprinted with permission of the authors.

high in power distance; those that dislike and prevent the development of strong inequities between citizens are low in power distance. Highly industrialized Western countries tend to score lower in power distance, while developing countries, particularly those in Latin America, tend to score higher on this measure. Application: According to Hofstede's model, in a high-PD country like Malaysia,

⇄ MANAGEMENT LIVE 13.1

Power Distance and Plane Crashes?

In his national bestselling book, *Outliers: the Story of Success,* Malcolm Gladwell proposed what he calls "The Ethnic Theory of Plane Crashes." Gladwell explored two plane crashes—one Colombian (Avianca Flight 52) and another, South Korean (Korean Air Flight 801)—and how the culture of the pilots perhaps contributed to each disaster. He focused on how well the pilots communicated with each other and with air traffic control. Poor communication in these examples, he argues, has to do with Geert Hofstede's concept of power distance (PD)—see the discussion regarding Table 13.1 earlier. Countries with a high PD generally value being more deferential toward authority, and thus not contradicting a superior (the U.S. and New Zealand both have a low PD).

Planes are flown safely when the pilot and co-pilot are in open and honest communication. And in cultures where it is difficult for a junior person to speak openly to a superior, plane crashes are more likely. Gladwell argues that since both Colombia and South Korea rank toward the top of the power distance spectrum, the subordinate members of their cockpit crews were unable or unwilling to speak up as assertively as they should have about safety concerns. Gladwell further delved into the history of Korean Air, which in the 1990s was plagued by a series of plane crashes. Investigators discovered that when Koreans spoke to each other in Korean they "were trapped in roles dictated by the heavy weight of their country's cultural legacy," which meant they were hesitant to challenge a superior directly. According to Gladwell, a number of plane crashes were likely related to the existence of power distance. Fortunately, once Korean Air figured out that their problem was cultural, they fixed it (via pilot training) and their safety rates are now equivalent to those around the world.

you would probably send reports only to top management and have closed-door meetings where only a select few powerful leaders were in attendance.

2. Individualism versus Collectivism.

This dimension focuses on the values that govern relationships between individuals and groups. Countries high in individualism value individual achievement, freedom, and competition. In countries high in collectivism, values of group harmony, cohesiveness, and consensus are very strong, and the importance of cooperation and agreement is paramount. In collectivist cultures, the group is viewed as more important than the individual. Japan epitomizes a country dominated by collectivist values, while the United States is the most-often-mentioned example of an individualistic country. Application: Hofstede's analysis suggests that in the Central American countries of Panama and Guatemala where the individualism scores are very low, a marketing campaign that emphasized benefits to the community or that tied into a popular political movement would likely be understood and well received.

Practice this!
Go to www.baldwin2e.com

3. Masculinity versus Femininity

Countries that are masculine-oriented value assertiveness, performance, and success, and are results-oriented. Countries that are feminine-oriented value warm personal relationships, and service and care for the weak. People from Japan, for example, tend to be masculine-oriented, while those from the Netherlands, Sweden, and Denmark tend to be feminine-oriented. Application: Japan is highly masculine, whereas Sweden has the lowest measured value. According to Hofstede's analysis, if you were to open an office in Japan, you might have greater success if you appointed a male employee to lead the team and had a strong male contingent on the team. In Sweden, on the other hand, you would aim for a team that was balanced in terms of skill rather than gender.

4. Uncertainty Avoidance.

People from different countries have been found to differ in their tolerance for uncertainty and their willingness to take risks. Countries low on uncertainty avoidance are relatively easygoing and comfortable with ambiguity (such as the United States and Indonesia); they also tend to be tolerant of differences in what people believe and do. On the other hand, those high in uncertainty avoidance (such as Japan and France) tend to be more rigid and intolerant of differences. In high uncertainty avoidance cultures, conformity to the values of social and work groups to which a person belongs is the norm, and structured situations are preferred because they provide a sense of security. Application: Hofstede's cultural dimensions imply that when discussing a project with people in Belgium, whose country scored very high on uncertainty avoidance, you should investigate the various options and then present a limited number of choices, but have very detailed information available on your contingency and risk plans. Note that there will also be cultural differences between French and Dutch speakers inside Belgium!

5. Long-Term versus Short-Term Orientation.

The last dimension that Hofstede identified concerns whether citizens of a country have a long- or short-term orientation toward life and work. A long-term orientation (LTO) derives from values that include saving and persistence in achieving goals. A short-term orientation (STO) reflects values such as a concern for happiness or stability and living for the present. Japan and Hong Kong are known for their high rates of per capita savings; they have long-term orientations. Citizens in the United States and France, on the other hand, tend to spend more and save less, reflective of their short-term orientation. Application: According to Hofstede's analysis, people in the United States and the United Kingdom have low LTO scores. This suggests that you can pretty much expect anything in this culture in terms of creative expression and novel ideas. The model implies that people in the U.S. and UK don't value tradition as much as many others, and are therefore likely to be willing to help you execute the most innovative plans as long as they get to participate fully. This may be surprising to people in the UK, with its associations of tradition!

One of the most important contributions of Hofstede's studies regarding working with diversity in teams is the notion of **diversity distance.** For example, a group that consists of Norwegians and Swedes is not as diverse as a group that consists of Norwegians and Saudis, which in turn is not as diverse as a group of Norwegians, Saudis, and Americans. Understanding such distance and some typical patterns of perceptions and motives can be useful as a starting point in working with team members from diverse cultures.[13]

Cultural norms play a large part in the mechanics and interpersonal relationships at work. When you grow up in a culture, you take your norms of behavior for granted. You don't have to think about your reactions, preferences, and feelings. When you step into a foreign culture, suddenly things seem different. You don't know what to do or say. Using Hofstede's cultural dimensions as a starting point, you can evaluate your approach, your decisions, and actions based on a general sense of how the society might think and react to you.

Of course, no society is homogenous, and there will be deviations from the norms Hofstede found. However, with this as your guide, you won't be going in blind. The unknown will be a little less intimidating and you'll get a much-needed boost of confidence and security from studying this cultural model.

The beauty of Hofstede's work is that beyond its descriptive power, it also offers a starting point for functioning effectively in diverse contexts. Table 13.2 is a synthesis of the applications of Hofstede's findings organized by the five dimensions of national culture differences he identified; also see Management Live 13.2 to think about how Hofstede's work is important in your own situation.

TABLE 13.2   Applications of Hofstede's Findings for Working with National Cultures[14]

	Characteristics	Tips
High Power Distance	• Centralized companies. • Strong hierarchies. • Large gaps in compensation, authority, and respect.	• Acknowledge a leader's power. • May need to go to the top for answers
Low Power Distance	• Flatter organizations. • Supervisors and employees treated as equals.	• Use teamwork. • Involve as many people as possible in decision making.
	Characteristics	Tips
High Individualism	• High valuation of others' time and need for freedom. • An enjoyment of challenges, and an expectation of rewards for hard work. • Respect for privacy.	• Acknowledge accomplishments. • Don't ask for too much personal information. • Encourage debate and expression of own ideas.

Low Individualism	• Emphasis on mastery and competence. • Work for intrinsic rewards. • Harmony is more important than honesty.	• Show respect for age and wisdom. • Suppress feelings and emotions to work in harmony. • Respect traditions and introduce change slowly.
	Characteristics	**Tips**
High Masculinity	• Men are masculine and women are feminine. • There is a well-defined distinction between men's work and women's work.	• Be aware that people may expect male and female roles to be distinct. • Advise men to avoid discussing emotions or make emotionally based decisions or arguments.
Low Masculinity	• Equality between the sexes. • Powerful and successful women are esteemed and respected.	• Avoid an "old boys' club" mentality. • Ensure job design and practices are not discriminatory to either gender. • Treat men and women equally.
	Characteristics	**Tips**
High Uncertainty Avoidance	• Very formal business conduct with lots of rules and policies. • Need and expect structure. • Feelings of nervousness spurn high levels of emotion and expression. • Differences are avoided.	• Be clear and concise about your expectations and parameters. • Plan and prepare, communicate often and early, provide detailed plans, and focus on the tactical aspects of a job or project. • Express your emotions through hand gestures and raised voice.
Low Uncertainty Avoidance	• Informal business attitude. • Concerned with long-term strategy rather than what is happening on a daily basis. • Accepting of change and risk.	• Do not impose rules or structure unnecessarily. • Minimize your emotional response by being calm and contemplating situations before speaking. • Express curiosity when you discover differences.
	Characteristics	**Tips**
High Long-Term Orientation	• Family is the basis of society. • Parents and men have more authority than young people and women. • Strong work ethic. • High value placed on education and training.	• Show respect for traditions. • Do not display extravagance or act frivolously. • Reward perseverance, loyalty, and commitment. • Avoid doing anything that would cause another to "lose face."
Low Long-Term Orientation	• Promotion of equality. • High creativity, individualism. • Treat others as you would like to be treated. • Self-actualization is sought.	• Expect to live by the same standards and rules you create. • Be respectful of others. • Do not hesitate to introduce necessary changes.

MANAGEMENT LIVE 13.2

Testing Hofstede's Findings in Your Own World

Take some time to review Table 13.1 for the various cultural dimensions Hofstede identified. Pay particular attention to the native countries of those you work with on a day-to-day basis.

In light of these scores, think about some interactions you've had with people in other countries. Does your conversation or association make more sense given this newly found insight? Challenge yourself to learn more about one culture in particular. If your work brings you in contact with people from another country, use that country as your point of reference. Apply Hofstede's scores to what you discover and determine the accuracy and relevance for you.

The next time you are required to work with a person from a different culture, use Hofstede's scores and make notes about your approach, what you should be prepared to discuss, and why you feel the way you do. Afterward, evaluate your performance and do further research and preparation for your next endeavor with that person.

KO 13-4

Inclusive Cultures

Characteristics of Inclusive Cultures

Inclusiveness is not just an idea or a burden. It's a competitive weapon.

—CEO, Fortune 500 Firm

connect

Practice this!
Go to www.baldwin2e.com

As noted earlier, inclusion (or lack thereof) is an important dimension of a company's culture. While it was once in vogue to speak of managing diversity, that terminology has rightly given way to the more apt managing *for* diversity or simply *creating inclusive workplaces.* Note that an organization may have diversity *without* inclusiveness. The mere presence of a workforce from many national, ethnic, and generational backgrounds doesn't necessarily mean that a business is genuinely inclusive. If the diversity of backgrounds doesn't impact organizational assumptions, values, and behaviors, it remains at best a neutral statistic, and at worst an obstacle to the organization's cohesiveness and success.

The full creative possibilities and payoff of inclusiveness can only be captured if it is deliberately practiced in all aspects of organizational life. The cost of anything less is an organization in which many people are not operating at their full potential, corporate cohesion is only at a surface level, and a narrow band of approaches and perspectives is used to address problems and respond to opportunities.

So what is it that makes a culture inclusive? Decoding an organization by looking at power relations, policies, practices, processes, and daily interactions can be quite complex, but a few central characteristics stand out.[15]

A Formal Corporate Statement

While it hardly guarantees action, in today's world the lack of a formal organizational commitment supporting inclusiveness can be seen as conspicuous by its absence. So make it official. If nothing else, it may prompt some action that occurs solely out of the desire to not seem hypocritical in having a statement of inclusion that is ignored or flaunted. Post inclusion statements in company policies and ensure there is an opportunity for them to be seen and heard by every organizational member.

An example of a diversity and inclusion statement developed at Coca-Cola Enterprises is:

Attracting, developing and retaining a highly talented and diverse workforce is one of our three strategic business priorities. To achieve this, we are committed to creating an inclusive culture—one that welcomes, values, and celebrates a workforce comprising employees of different ages, ethnicities, races, cultures, genders and sexual orientations.

Symbols, Rituals, and Stories

Do the symbols, stories, and rituals of the company speak to everyone—or do they reinforce in-group identities at the expense of others? Do recruitment, screening, evaluation, career-tracking, and promotion processes genuinely seek to develop diversity at all levels—or are there blinders that perpetuate stereotypical roles for different groups of people? Does the company promote after-hours social interactions and professional networking across cultural, occupational, and other subgroups—or does inclusiveness exist only in the immediate job and project context?

Are differing viewpoints and approaches to solving problems encouraged—or just the narrow band that fits the prevailing culture of the leadership or dominant social group? Are the differing strengths of diverse management styles acknowledged and emulated—or is there a single standard? Are different employee support needs, expectations, work patterns, and communication styles accommodated—or is there a one-size-fits-all approach to managing and developing people? Organizations that are serious about inclusiveness effectively integrate inclusive principles into all aspects of the organization, including designing structures and practices that support diversity, coordinating marketing efforts that consistently focus on creating, understanding, and serving diverse market segments, and thoughtfully managing international operations to ensure they are in compliance with cultural norms and expectations.

Provide Opportunities for Networks and Support

Employee networks are excellent tools to foster inclusion in the workplace. While some exceptions make sense, it is usually best to have it so that *any* employee (not just those of a targeted identity) can become a member of each group—and those outside the target group are particularly encouraged to join, allowing them to develop a stronger understanding of the challenges other employees encounter. Networks add more to an employee's work experience, fostering communication and relationship building. The information shared in these groups assists management in addressing issues and removing barriers to an inclusive workplace. Campbell's Soup Company in Chicago makes particularly good use of networks, including unique networks dedicated to African Americans, Asians, Latinos, GLBT, women, and American Indians/Aboriginals.

Carefully Considered and Customized Training Opportunities

Inclusiveness training can be successful or it can be a disaster—and there are many examples of both. To be effective, training needs to be customized to a particular organizational audience and avoid simple lecturing and "preaching" and rather include a variety of training methods—role play, classroom style, Q & A, and web-based learning. Indeed, some of the most effective inclusiveness learning opportunities do not happen in formal classrooms or traditional educational formats. Isolating and addressing diversity flashpoints and subtle signs of exclusiveness (see Management Live 13.3) are examples of such naturally occurring development opportunities.

As one illustration of how an organization can attack diversity flashpoints and exclusiveness, IBM launched eight executive-led task forces on women, men, African Americans, Hispanics, Asians, Native Americans, gays and lesbians, and people with disabilities. Ted Childs, vice president for global workforce

⇄ MANAGEMENT LIVE 13.3

Diversity Flashpoints and Signals of *Exclusiveness*

One of the most telling signals of an inclusive culture is, perhaps ironically, how *exclusiveness* is identified and addressed. Diversity flashpoints are those situations, often subtle but sometimes arresting, where exclusiveness occurs in organizational contexts, and the "moments of truth" where a truly inclusive culture is created. Typical examples of diversity flashpoints include statements like:

"That was so gay."

"No offense, but in this firm that is not really a job for a woman."

"We need fewer waspy white guys running everything."

"I am not prejudiced, I have lots of black friends, but I just do not think that black women make good attorneys for us."

"You know that some minority is going to get a token role so it will look good."

"He strikes me as a bit old to be pushing for that job."

diversity, explains: *"We asked [the task forces] to look at IBM through their constituency and answer, 'What was required for your group to feel welcome and valued throughout IBM?' and 'What could we do in partnership to maximize your productivity? How could the company better approach your constituency to influence your buying decisions?' The intent was for us to identify anything where change would make things better. We looked at recruiting, mentoring, stereotyping, and external agencies we should work with."* The results were rich: The company is still working to implement all of the recommendations from its task forces.[16]

Truly inclusive cultures are quick to identify, expose, and discuss such signals of exclusivity. Developing an inclusive culture requires effort from every member within an organization. *Would* you respond, and if so, *how* would you respond if you heard one of the preceding statements over lunch in your school or organization? Your response (or lack thereof) will be a critical signal of inclusiveness in your context.

Manager Accountability

Companies that are serious about inclusiveness put their money where their mouths are, making managers personally accountable and rewarding them for fostering inclusive cultures. For example, at Carrier Corp., a Syracuse, New York–based heating, air conditioning, and refrigeration firm, business unit presidents meet quarterly to track their progress in recruiting, retaining, training, and developing minority and female workers. Their performance in each of these areas is directly reflected in the presidents' annual performance bonuses.[17]

Top Management Models and Tone Setting

Culture is established and reinforced at the top of an organization, so it is critical that the most senior managers live and breathe inclusiveness—otherwise, all other efforts may be weakened or wasted. When top-level executives emulate the corporate culture, it's easier for employees to follow and commit to adopting the inclusive culture themselves. One great example of top-management embracing and exhibiting inclusiveness comes from Paul Hogendoorn, president of OES Inc. located in the United Kingdom, whose following quote illustrates one way that he sets the tone from the top to encourage an inclusive culture:

> When I make the rounds in the morning, I often say good morning in ten different languages. Of course "good morning" is just about the extent of what I am able to say in many of those languages, but it does put a few smiles on faces. Sometimes it takes intentionally role-modeling examples to illustrate the point that no one person is above any specific task, including myself. Although specific roles may have different values in an organization, as individuals, we are still equal.

The Payoffs from Inclusive Cultures

Tony Burns, former CEO of Ryder Systems, launched inclusiveness initiatives in his company long before he had any evidence that the initiatives would pay off. So why did he launch them? "Because it was the right thing to do," he replies. Moreover, there are laws that prohibit discrimination made on the basis of "protected characteristics" that have no relationship to job performance. There are six broad categories of protected characteristics, including race and color, gender, religion, national origin, age (over 40), and disabilities, and the laws do demand that all persons receive the same opportunities for employment—though no laws require that an employer give preferential treatment to any person or group of persons because of their protected characteristic.

The time is always right to do what is right.

—Martin Luther King, Jr.

So there are clearly moral and legal reasons to favor inclusive workplaces. But the really wonderful news about inclusiveness is that doing the right and legal thing also happens to be good business. That is, although moral and legal motives are important in their own right, inclusiveness has also been tied to revenue growth, profitability, and maximizing resource utilization.[18] For example, companies rated by "Best Companies for Asians, Blacks, and Hispanics" by *Fortune* magazine routinely perform well, beating or matching the S&P 500 each year.[19] Simply put, those organizations with inclusive cultures tend to be superior performers. Making the business case for inclusiveness often references metrics that include the following.

Reduction in Absenteeism and Turnover.   Research has demonstrated that, when people perceive themselves as being treated unfairly, they both tend to be absent more and are more likely to leave the company altogether.[20]

Marketing Advantages.   Multicultural decision-makers are a competitive advantage for any organization that wants to provide goods and services to a multicultural market. McDonald's restaurants in Israel initially fared poorly because the company did not understand the importance of serving kosher food.

On the other hand, there are numerous examples of marketing successes that can be directly traced to smart and inclusive cultures. Kentucky Fried Chicken was successful in Israel with kosher chicken, and United Airlines saw a significant increase in Hispanic customers when they installed a Spanish-speaking telephone reservation line.[21] Another example of a company that took full advantage of its diverse workforce is JCPenney. Here, African American members of the marketing staff knew that many African American women have a tradition of wearing white dresses to church on the fifth Sunday of the month. Consequently, the marketing staff created a fashion layout of very attractive churchgoers wearing white dresses from JCPenney, resulting in brisk sales of white dresses in Penney's top markets.[22]

Company Reputation. Many people from culturally diverse groups prefer to patronize organizations that have a good track record for inclusiveness. On the other hand, a reputation for exclusiveness can hurt a company's sales—for instance, thousands of Americans boycotted Cracker Barrel restaurants when company officials admitted to firing a number of employees because they were gay or lesbian, and hundreds of African Americans switched loyalties from Coca-Cola to PepsiCo because of repeated racial discrimination claims against Coke.[23]

Recruiting Advantages. A company that values inclusiveness expands its pool of potential applicants; companies that do not have fewer talented workers to choose from. A company's commitment to diversity sends a message to members of traditionally disadvantaged groups that they will be welcomed into the organization and allowed to work to their full potential.[24] Maria Elena Lagomasino, head of global private banking at Chase, sums it up this way: *"If you become known as a great place for women or Blacks or Asians, you'll attract the talent. They get a sense that they'll just be much happier in the company—and that's as important as title or money."*[25] Research suggests that a company's commitment to diversity communicates to recruits that its policies and procedures are designed to treat all employees fairly, thus making the organization more attractive as a potential employer.[26]

DO 13-3   Working Productively with Diverse People and Teams

It is never too late to give up your prejudices.

—Henry David Thoreau

Working with people very similar to us is tough enough; working with those who are *dissimilar* is often even more challenging. For most people, diversity issues are most pronounced with respect to working in teams. Current research suggests teams composed of individuals with diverse backgrounds face special challenges in functioning effectively, but also have potential advantages that can enhance their performance.[27] Group functioning is made more difficult because diverse people are less likely to see or understand situations in similar ways. People from like backgrounds trust each other more readily, while diversity increases the chance for misperception and confusion in the group process. Time spent by the group clarifying confusion thus increases the time needed to achieve outcomes and diminish productivity. Put simply, diversity makes communicating and reaching agreement within a group more difficult and time-consuming.

At the same time, diverse teams do also have the *potential* to achieve better outcomes than homogeneous teams because their wider range of human resources enables them to invent more options and create more solutions. Diversity makes it easier for teams to consider more ideas, avoid groupthink, and actively attend to fellow team members' ideas and contributions. Diversity is most advantageous for teams facing ambiguous and creative tasks. On the other hand, diversity is most challenging for teams facing implementation-type tasks that require reliable, fluid, and frequent interaction.

The managerial skill challenge, then, is to find ways to minimize potential process deficits and harness the potential of diversity to positively influence team outcomes. The successful diverse team is generally one in which members are *aware* of, and open about, important differences, not just surface ones, *understand* how those differences might influence team process and member engagement, and *take explicit action* to bring the team together and communicate most effectively (Figure 13.4).

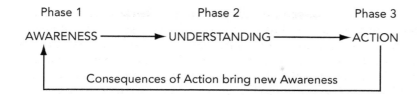

FIGURE 13.4
Phases of Success for a Diverse Team

Building Awareness

Any managerial focus on diversity should stem from the reality that not everyone is motivated by the same things, nor do they prefer to interact in the same way. At one level, this reality makes teamwork more difficult. But given both the productive potential of diverse teams and their inevitability in today's workforce, it does little good to worry about that. Rather, a first step in being diversity savvy is to be aware of the situation, embrace it, and make the most of it.

With respect to diversity awareness, three common traps often befall teams. One is a tendency to romanticize diversity, whereby *any* differences are deemed important and the presumption is that diversity somehow magically leads to positive team outcomes. That is nonsense. As noted earlier, the research is clear that diversity generally makes team challenges *more* demanding and, for some types of teams and team purposes, will be a detriment rather than an enabler.[28]

A second trap is to deny or ignore important differences and the potential for those differences to affect team process and outcomes. Being strictly "diversity blind" may sound like a fair and high-minded approach but, in reality, is often a recipe for team failure. People differ in important ways that impact their perceptions, motivations, and actions on behalf of a team. To neglect that reality is to destine teams to fail.

A third trap is that, when most people use the term "diversity," they are talking only about observable or **surface-level diversity.** Surface-level diversity refers to differences that are easily seen and generally verifiable via a quick assessment of physical characteristics, including gender, age, race, and national origin/ethnicity. However, diversity exists on many levels. Indeed, while surface-level diversity factors heavily into people's unique cultural background and experience, important diversity also exists below the surface and is not so easily observed. This type of diversity has been called **deep-level diversity** and reflects differences among people in such areas as attitudes, beliefs, knowledge, skills, and values.[29] This level of diversity can only be understood by seeking to learn about different perspectives and observing behavior over time. The most prevalent and insidious danger is to assume the surface-level diversity you *can* observe is indicative of a deeper-level diversity you *cannot* observe (Figure 13.5).

As you might suspect, people who make such assumptions and are only concerned with surface-level diversity miss the real underlying power associated with deep-level diversity. For example, research has shown that managers who want to form an effective diverse work team should do so on the basis of factors relating to differences in skills, personality traits, values, and attitudes, rather than surface-level characteristics.[30]

This is not to say that attention to surface diversity is never warranted. It clearly is a good place to start to ensure equity in the workplace. In too many cases, a history of exclusion and even discrimination has created a lack of representativeness of certain groups of minorities (for example, a glass ceiling exists where few women are in executive positions), and proactive attempts to create a more representative balance are appropriate. However, surface diversity is often treated as a more important indicator of deep-level diversity than it really deserves. A key to creating a diversity-friendly team is to recognize that diversity is more than surface or skin deep and that deep-level diversity is the key to more

It is not best that we should all think alike; it is difference of opinion that makes horse races.

—Mark Twain

FIGURE 13.5
Surface-Level and
Deep-Level Diversity

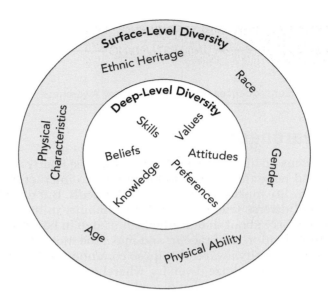

productive work environments. For some specific ways to get past surface-level diversity, see Tool Kit 13.4 and also look at Management Live 13.4 for a good example of a company's diversity philosophy.

True diversity awareness comes from a willingness to challenge assumptions and avoid stereotyping. However, it is critical to remember the perceptions and

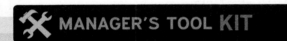

MANAGER'S TOOL KIT

Tool Kit 13.4   Getting Underneath Surface Diversity

To know that a person is of a certain race, gender, or ethnic background does not by itself tell us much about that person's perceptions, values, or behaviors. However, it clearly does alert us to possible *sources* of miscommunication. We can then take the opportunity to learn more.

The following list includes several practical strategies for learning more about those who differ from us. Not surprisingly, the key ingredient to establishing a relationship with people of difference is mutual respect and a desire for understanding.

- Create informal time together. Invite fellow members to meals—ideally in your home. Show respect for their culture and language and signal to them that you honestly want to learn about them and their culture. Ask, "How would I feel if I were in their shoes?"

- Learn how to pronounce names correctly. Their names are as important to them as yours is to you. Practice saying names until you get close to how they should be pronounced.

- When speaking English to people with limited English skills, do so slowly and clearly. Remember, raising your voice and speaking louder does not make English more understandable.

- Listen, observe, and ask a lot of questions. A key question might be, "Would you help me understand?"

- Be careful about promises. In English, we express the subjunctive (possibility, probability, or contingency) in a way that is sometimes misunderstood by internationals.

- Don't allow cultural differences or preferences to become the basis for criticism and judgments. Differences are neither good nor bad. What we do with them is the key. Seek and promote any organizational diversity initiatives (training seminars, mentoring, language seminars) that might help your cause.

MANAGEMENT LIVE 13.4

The Diversity Philosophy at Booz Allen Hamilton

A great example of the importance of broadly conceived diversity (that is, both surface- and deep-level) can be found in the following comments from Tony Mitchell, a managing principal for Booz Allen Hamilton Inc. "As a consulting firm, one of the most important aspects of our ability to support our clients is intellectual capital—or what we call *thought leadership*. Diversity comes into play here as diversity of thought. If we have people who all have the same backgrounds, who all went through the same type of formal training and education, and who all had the same experiences in terms of corporate America, we limit our ability to refine our thinking on how we can improve our clients' probability of success—no matter what the specific problem is. That includes diversity in the traditional sense of race and ethnic background, but we try to ensure that we capture diversity in the broadest sense."

Source: www.nytimes.com/marketing/jobmarket/diversity/booz.html.

behaviors of any particular individual of a given group may not conform to the averages or tendencies. As Table 13.3 illustrates, diversity awareness is fundamentally different than stereotyping.

Understanding Differences

The most prevalent myth about diversity is that people are more different than alike. It is tempting to assume that people's visible differences will somehow lead them to behave in a stereotypical way. The opposite, however, is frequently true. With respect to most of the surface-level dimensions of diversity, surprisingly few evidence-based differences are relevant to team performance.

Three surface dimensions where research *has found* interesting differences among people are ethnic heritage (culture), age, and gender. These research findings are intuitive to most managers who often note their most difficult challenges are (1) managing people from different cultures (which was addressed earlier in this chapter), (2) managing those with considerable age differences, and (3) communicating with the opposite gender.

TABLE 13.3   Diversity Awareness vs. Stereotyping

Diversity Aware	Stereotyping
Based on differences verified by empirical research on actual intergroup differences.	Frequently based on false assumptions and anecdotal evidence or even impressions, without any direct experience with a group.
Views cultural differences as neutral.	Judges traits of a group as positive or negative, or ascribes motives for group members' behavior.
Assumes a higher probability that members of a group share the traits of the group, but allows for individual differences.	Assumes characteristics thought to be common to a group apply uniformly to every member of that group.

Generational Differences

Another area where recent research has highlighted patterns of differences is on the core dimension of age (generation). Rather than relying solely on demographic birth patterns, author Claire Raines has identified four generations of workers.[31] Each has a unique history and set of common life experiences not shared by other generations. The evidence suggests these generational experiences shape work attitudes and perceptions in important ways. The four categories of generations are (1) Traditionalists, (2) Baby Boomers, or Boomers, (3) Generation X, or Xers, and (4) Millennials.

Every generation needs a new revolution.

—Thomas Jefferson

- **Traditionalists.** The Traditionalists were born between 1922 and 1943 and entered the workforce in the mid-1940s and 1950s. Often referred to as "the greatest generation" because of their survival and ingenuity during the years of the Depression and World War II, these workers tend to embrace strong work ethic values. These values include hard work, a conservative approach to business, and intense organizational loyalty. Not surprisingly, this generation tends to not be comfortable publicly questioning the hierarchical chain of command.

- **Boomers.** Born between the mid-1940s and early 1960s, Baby Boomers were named as a result of a large increase in the birth rate during this time period—some 4.3 million births per year at the trend's peak. Boomers' work values tend to focus on quality of life and nonconformance (think hippies and Vietnam War protests). At the same time, they seek recognition and also place value on respect.

- **Generation X.** The Xers were born during the mid-1960s through about 1980 and grew up in an era that saw a large increase in nontraditional families (single parenting). They watched as their parents underwent the downsizing of the 1980s and developed a new sense of values about the world of work, which included some cynicism toward organizations, a focus on work–life balance, flexibility, and loyalty not to the company but to relationships with others.

- **Millennials.** Born in the early 1980s through the turn of the century, Millennials are the first generation to be truly surrounded by technology and a media-driven world. They, like Xers, also tend to believe the work-place is not just a place to make money, but a place to express oneself and often socialize. In addition, Millennials place more value on global awareness, heroism, and goal achievement (see Tool Kit 13.5).

Gender Communication Differences

A third area of diversity understanding related to team functioning concerns gender—particularly communication style differences between men and women. For example, research observing men and women interacting in group settings has found that, for males, conversation is for solving problems, maintaining status, and preserving independence, not necessarily building closeness or community. For men, activities and doing things together are central, and just sitting and talking is not an essential part of closeness. Men are typically friends with other men they *do things* with. Females, on the other hand, use conversation to negotiate closeness and intimacy. For them, talk is the essence of intimacy, so building closeness and community means sitting and talking. Author Deborah Tannen succinctly describes these differences as "women talk to establish rapport . . . while men talk to report."[32]

From a team-building perspective, it is not hard to see how these differences can potentially influence the effectiveness of a gender-diverse team. In general, men will tend to be most focused on team *outcomes* and *solutions,* while women will be as concerned with the problem-solving *process.* Consistent with this, one study of team member perceptions (among men and women on the same set of teams) found male participants were most comfortable and satisfied with their team when the team's objectives were clarified to the greatest extent possible and the individual roles of team members were well defined.[33]

The quickest way to a man's heart is through his chest.

—Roseanne Barr

MANAGER'S TOOL KIT

Tool Kit 13.5 Six Principles for Managing Millennials

So how do you translate what you've read so far into your day-to-day life on the job? What do today's young employees want? If we're designing recruiting programs and management systems based on their values and needs, how do we proceed? What kind of work environments attract, retain, and motivate Millennial co-workers? Here are their six most frequent requests:

- **You be the leader.** This generation has grown up with structure and supervision, with parents who were role models. Millennials are looking for leaders with honesty and integrity. It's not that they don't want to be leaders themselves; they'd just like some great role models first.

- **Challenge me.** Millennials want learning opportunities. They want to be assigned to projects they can learn from. A recent Randstad employee survey found that "trying new things" was the most popular item. They're looking for growth, development, a career path.

- **Let me work with friends.** Millennials say they want to work with people they *click* with. They like being friends with co-workers. Employers who provide for the social aspects of work will find those efforts well rewarded by this newest cohort. Some companies are even interviewing and hiring groups of friends.

- **Let's have fun.** A little humor, a bit of silliness, and even a little irreverence will make your work environment more attractive.

- **Respect me.** "Treat our ideas respectfully," they ask, "even though we haven't been around a long time."

- **Be flexible.** The busiest generation ever isn't going to give up its activities because of work. A rigid schedule is a surefire way to lose your Millennial employees.

Women, on the other hand, were most comfortable when communication and other group maintenance activities were clearly valued in addition to task activities. Women were also more comfortable than men with collective, team-based evaluations and rewards. More specifically, "poor sharing of information" was the top reported problem for females, while for males the top problem was "unclear or inappropriate expectations." These findings seem consistent with the claim by gender theorists that women value relationships based on communication and understanding and that men's roles tend to be defined by role and status.

As with cultural and age generalities, it is worth noting once again that perceptions and behaviors of any particular individual of a given group may not conform to averages or tendencies. However, understanding the patterns that have been documented is useful to help move beyond surface levels of core differences (old/young; American/Chinese; male/female) to a richer understanding of how such differences may manifest themselves in team member perceptions and behavior.

Taking Action

Armed with an awareness of the diversity in your team and an understanding of both misconceptions and real differences in general populations, you can ultimately be more effective in trying to make a diverse team productive. Several prescriptions useful in that regard are highlighted below.

Heighten Attention to Good Management Fundamentals

At the most basic level, effective diversity management is simply good people management—only harder and more important without the lubricant of natural trust that comes from similarity. That means you need to focus on job-related behaviors and earn the trust and respect of others by treating them with respect and dignity. People of diverse backgrounds rarely need preferential treatment, just fairness. For example, if you need a good scribe or secretary, focus on the characteristics of the role, not on finding a young woman. If you need a team member to act in a leadership role, look closely at members' organizational and interpersonal skills, not at finding someone of a particular gender, race, or age. Do not succumb to allowing your stereotypical understanding of others, or your impressions based on superficial diversity, to bias your decisions. Put simply, the rules of good management do not change with diversity—they just take on added importance.

Actively Challenge Your Assumptions

Although relevant differences in diverse team members do exist (language, culture, generation), we often perceive differences that are really *not* there. For example, with respect to gender, researcher Janet Hyde has recently shown that, while men and women certainly do differ in some straightforward ways, they are more *alike* than they are different. In her research, Hyde reviewed some 45 meta-analyses (large studies of other studies—in this case, 124 results overall) examining research that investigated almost every potential gender difference, including cognitive abilities, communication, personality, psychological well-being, work behavior, motor skills, and moral reasoning. What she found is that 78 percent of all these studies found *no meaningful differences* between men and women. In other words, the data point more to similarities than differences.

Further, some disturbing research suggests perceptions of difference can influence important decisions. For example, an analysis of studies over a 20-year period showed that employees who were similar to their managers' ethnicity received higher performance ratings than employees who were dissimilar in terms of ethnicity.[34]

The key point here is that the reasons for differences in performance were not *because* of age, race, or gender, but because of *perceptions* that age, race, or gender matter in performance. Do not confuse the two. A belief that race matters is very different than whether it *actually* matters. Unfortunately, people often pay a high price for these mythical managerial perceptions about surface-level diversity.

Recall that the best managerial outcomes come from treating people as individuals and seeking to understand their unique styles, values, and motives. So discuss with each team member their expectations—what they need and don't need and how you can be most helpful to them. In turn, you should articulate your expectations as well.

Increase Interaction and Inclusion

Increasing interaction between individuals reduces the influence of stereotypes and improves team functioning. As people get to know others, stereotypes are replaced by more accurate knowledge of each other, which can result in reduced prejudice and greater cohesion. Be diligent about including diverse others in all key meetings and interactions. Unfortunately, diversity often makes us far less comfortable in interacting with others, and thus the level of communication is likely to be typically *less* in such teams, particularly initially. Moreover, based on past experience, diverse members may have a fear of exclusion, so it is doubly important to be sure all team members are included and important interactions are conducted in contexts accessible and comfortable to all.

With that in mind, be bold in trying to better know your team members and seek to recognize and uncover important differences. If you are in doubt, go ahead and ask! Most people will give you the benefit of the doubt if they sense you are respectful and making a good-faith effort to understand and be sensitive to their interests. Seek two-way understanding by sharing your perceptions and style preferences and actively inquiring and listening to other team members share their own. By initiating dialogue, you will aid your own understanding and establish stronger relationships with team members.

Building "People-First" High-Performance Cultures

DO **13-4**

Great strategy, breakthrough products, innovative technology, clever marketing, and even luck significantly influence organizational success. However, it is also true (but for some reason a much bigger secret) that people management practices are among the most important and sustainable source of competitive advantage in organizations today.[35] Recall from the first chapter that—more than product, industry, technology, or strategy—how people are managed in a firm has the most profound effects on numerous organizational outcomes, ranging from quality and productivity to the survival rate of new firms.[36] Despite such evidence of these successful practices, the number of "toxic" workplaces remains depressingly high. Reports of organizations where bosses scream at and threaten workers, allow little involvement in decision making, neglect the hiring process, horde information from associates, and otherwise fail to employ the skills covered in this text are all too frequent. In such cases, the results are predictable. Good people leave, and those that stay do not fully commit to the business and are far less inclined to recommend ways to improve the organization's products and services or work harder to satisfy customers.

In short, the kind of workplace that great management creates matters as much as or more than virtually any other organizational element. An environment

Don't make assumptions. Find the courage to ask questions.

—Don Miguel Ruiz

Practice this!
Go to www.baldwin2e.com

where people work with high levels of trust and support is likely to generate greater commitment and foster greater innovation and creativity. Investing time and resources into making a company a *great place to work* is likely to pay off with direct impact on the bottom line.

How Cultures and Subcultures Are Created: *You* Can Make a Difference

Creating a committed workforce and a high-performance culture is sometimes thought to be outside the control of individual managers, especially young managers with little experience in an organization. However, one of the most compelling findings of the Gallup research referenced in the accompanying Management Live 13.5 is that there is more variation in Q12 scores *within* companies than *between* companies. That is, within each of the more than 200 organizations analyzed, Gallup found some of the most-engaged groups and some of the least-engaged groups. Thus, high-performance cultures are not so much characteristic of an entire organization as they are within *particular units* or subcultures of an organization.[37] So it is quite possible to make the journey to great management, provided you have the awareness, the willingness, and a little courage to make it happen.

Examples of individual managers making a difference are all over. Author Marcus Buckingham tells the story of Ralph Gonzalez, a manager at Best Buy who was charged with resurrecting a troubled store in Hialeah, Florida.[38] He immediately named the store the Revolution, even drafted a Declaration of Revolution, and launched project teams, complete with army clothes. He posted detailed performance numbers in the break room and deliberately over-celebrated every small achievement. He gave every employee a whistle and told them to blow it loudly whenever they caught anybody (co-worker or supervisor) doing something "revolutionary." As a result of Ralph's efforts, the Hialeah store became one of Best Buy's best in terms of store performance and employee satisfaction.

Put simply there is no knowledge advantage without an *action* advantage. Knowing what to do but not doing it does not get you far. Our hope is that our demonstration of the connection between people management and organizational performance, and an awareness of management practices that really do make a difference, will help close the gap between knowing and doing in how we manage people.

The Characteristics of High-Performance Cultures

Demonstrated relationships between organizational success and people management practices rightly prompt questions regarding just what the most influential and important practices are. Of course, many management practices can be supported on a humanistic level, but ultimately carry no supporting evidence that they actually contribute to high-performance cultures. Those people management practices that *have* been shown to relate strongly to organizational performance should now be familiar since they really are just the organizational extensions of many of the individual managerial skills and practices discussed in this text.

Interestingly, there is an emerging body of research evidence that points directly to the impact of specific managerial practices known to be tied to organizational performance called **high-performance work practices.** These practices include, but are not limited to, the use of incentives, selectivity in hiring, succession planning, extensive training, and decentralized decision making. Scholars believe that high-performance work practices improve organizational performance in at least three ways. First, engaging in these practices is thought to provide employees with the critical knowledge, skills, and behaviors required to perform their jobs. Second, such practices heightened employees' motivation and opportunities to get the job done. Third, these practices are believed to improve the social dynamics in organizations, thereby promoting increased cooperation and communication.[39] Recently, empirical research has confirmed the value of these practices by examining high-performance practices against organizational financial metrics. Combs and colleagues conducted a large meta-analysis of the research examining the financial effects of high-performance work practices. Using data from over 19,000 organizations, representing 20 years of research (or 92 studies) of 13 high-performance practices, the researchers found that high-performance work practices have significant effects on organizational performance overall.[40] Figure 13.6 displays the results of their study. From the figure it becomes clear that when the 13 high-performance work practices are simultaneously deployed in a highly effective manner, organizations can exceed 15 percent increases in growth, productivity, and retention.

In particular, this study showed that all 13 practices were associated with increases in performance, but some practices were particularly strong. For example, engaging in a single practice such as human resource planning (also known as succession planning) can yield over 20 percent increases in financial performance. Therefore, given this impressive body of evidence that has explored these practices, we think any great manager should be aware of, and engaged in, trying to create such practices in his or her own organizational role. Recently, Professor Jeffrey Pfeffer of Stanford University synthesized the decades of research on these critical practices.[41] We draw upon his descriptive work in explaining eight of these key high-performance work practices.

Selective Hiring of New Personnel

Too many firms spend more time and energy picking a copy machine than they do hiring new associates. This is unfortunate because the linchpin for all people-first management strategies is a base of capable and willing (not necessarily extraordinary) people. The performance management skills shared in Chapter 12 are essential to creating a truly great place to work. It may often make sense to let high-performing peers participate in the hiring process because good people *hire other good people,* creating something of a rolling snowball effect whereby the organization keeps collecting more and more stars. Southwest Airlines even allows some customers to get involved in some phases of their flight attendant selection.

Firms commonly can get so desperate to fill a position that they go against their own guidelines. But a bad hire is far worse than no hire. Involve senior management and others to emphasize the importance of hiring.

Think of an extreme case of selective hiring. Have you ever seen the television show *The Apprentice* (not *"Celebrity Apprentice"*)? Donald Trump picks one

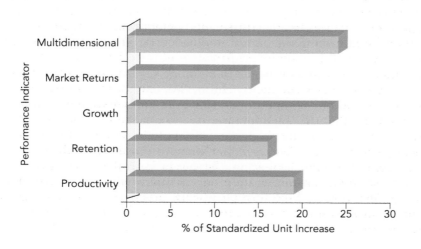

FIGURE 13.6
Effects of High-Involvement Work Practices

employee from an applicant pool of hundreds of thousands of people after seeing the finalists perform a series of difficult tasks. In this case, do you think Trump should be able to find a well-qualified person? We would certainly hope so! While it is very unlikely your company will be as popular as *The Apprentice,* selective hiring can be practiced in most organizations. Companies that really get this right, however, do not stop with the hiring; they continually adjust their hiring practices to make sure the people they get are successful in the jobs for which they apply.

Decentralized Decision Making and Employee Involvement

Assuming good people have been hired, great organizations then let those people go to work. These organizations may provide relevant training and give a lot of direction, but letting people do the job for which they were hired is just as important. This provides a sense of ownership and challenge and often supports a customer service orientation. By encouraging employees to go beyond the literal boundaries of their jobs, you gain not just a part, but the full potential, of their contributions to the organization.

An emphasis on decentralized decision making can take several forms. In some cases, it may involve the creation of self-managed teams, which may reduce the necessity of administrative oversight and closer customer contact. In other cases, it may simply mean giving associates greater discretion to use their heads in making good decisions—often to satisfy customers. For years, Nordstrom, a high-end department store, was famous for an employee manual that consisted solely of:

Rule 1: Use your good judgment in all situations.

Rule 2: Refer to Rule 1—there will be no additional rules.

Trusting people to use their brains and abilities has even broader effects than you may think. Because people tend to manage others the way they were managed, managing with a focus on trust helps build a positive organizational culture. A culture that allows for input and involvement in decision making has a cascading effect in an organization over time.

As is done to children, they will do to society.

—Karl Menninger

You can divide any working population into three categories: people who are engaged (loyal *and* productive), those who are not engaged (just putting in time), and those who are actively disengaged (unhappy and spreading their discontent). Some recent estimates suggest the U.S. working population is no more than 26 percent engaged and up to 20 percent actively disengaged. One of your most important tasks as a manager is to increase the percentage of *your employees* who are engaged.

Comparatively High Compensation Contingent upon Performance

Although labor markets are far from perfectly efficient, a relationship does exist between what a firm pays and the quality of the workforce it attracts. Put simply, higher wages attract more qualified people. A firm does not need to be at the *very* top; many other factors matter. But to the extent you can pay well, the better your chance of attracting the highly qualified, capable people your organization needs to be successful.

No matter how much we invest in our employees, they give us more in return.

—Robert Wegman, CEO, Wegmans Food Markets

An important distinction needs to be made regarding high wages. Decision-makers in organizations frequently claim, "We cannot be competitive if we pay higher wages than our competitors." However, such a statement may reflect a failure to understand that high labor *costs* are not the same as high labor *rates.* For example, at some of its properties, hotel chain Marriott hired fewer maids to clean rooms, but then paid a higher wage to those they did hire to do more rooms at a higher quality—creating a higher labor rate but sustaining a similar overall labor cost. The result was a group of maids who were more committed, produced higher-quality work, and ultimately satisfied more customers. In many cases, it is possible that high wages can be a win–win situation for the employee and the employer alike.

Of course, whatever the pay level, your main aim is to reward people for those activities and behaviors that are central to organizational performance. So, measuring what really matters, not just what your current software system can easily produce a report of, is absolutely critical. When it comes to managing people, many of the most progressive firms have developed unique standards of performance that often involve people, not just sales or technical accomplishments. For example, Pfeffer refers to the following measurements when discussing what separates "the best from the rest":[42]

- Hewlett-Packard evaluates managers on their *subordinates' assessment* of managerial behavior and adherence to HP values. FedEx has a similar leadership assessment process.
- Motorola has traditionally had a goal of giving each employee at least 40 hours of training per year, and measures managers by the proportion of their people who get that amount of training.
- Singapore Airlines spends 15 percent of its payroll costs on training. Most important, however, is that the firm takes its commitment to training seriously enough to track it.
- SAS Institute measures key employee turnover and holds all managers accountable for that metric. As a result, managers are acutely aware of the turnover rate and talk and strategize with others to keep the number down.
- Southwest Airlines tracks the number of its job applicants (currently more than 120,000 a year). Some would see processing so many applicants as a waste of resources, but Southwest views this activity as critical to ensuring access to the best possible workforce.

Extensive Training

Today's workforce is aware of the uncertainty of jobs and organizational success, and thus, more than ever, is acutely interested in growth and employment viability. The cost of training and educational opportunities for people can be high, but evidence suggests the investment is returned. A recent study by the American Society for Training and Development found that top-performing organizations consistently devoted a higher percentage of their budget to training and had a higher percentage of their total workforce involved in training compared to lower-performing companies.

Extensive training is an important piece to the overall puzzle. Training will allow employees to possess the skills they need to be fully engaged decision-makers. Training's effect should be enhanced performance that allows for higher wage rates to be paid.

An excellent example of an organization known for its training is Motorola. Motorola begins by taking a broad look at the goals of the organization and the current business environment. Then, to get a measure of where its current skill levels rank, the company reviews performance excellence scorecards and conducts interviews with senior management. The gaps identified from the scorecards and the interviews are then compared with current critical business goals to determine and prioritize individual, team, and the organization's learning needs. Training priorities and opportunities that align to critical business needs are communicated directly from senior leadership through manager briefings, e-mail messages, and quarterly town hall meetings. As a result of these communications, learning skill guides are created that list the company's priorities according to functions, groups, and regions. Employees can refer to these guides and identify training opportunities available for their own individual development needs.

At the individual level, Motorola identifies training needs through its Personal Commitment process. During this process, individuals discuss training and career development with their managers. Within these dialogues, career aspirations, feedback from managers, linkage with overall business and group objectives, and recommended training from the learning skill guides are covered. These plans are jointly reviewed and agreed upon by both the employee and the supervisor. Training opportunities for employees include instructor-led, classroom-based training, e-learning via the Web or CD-ROM, and self-study opportunities such as reading industry publications and participating in communities of practice.

Smart companies recognize that a significant commitment to employee training is critical to continued success.

Employment Security

From a simple psychological perspective, people will work more effectively when they can focus on doing their job rather than worrying about *keeping* it. Similarly, if employees are your company's greatest assets, then it makes sense to ensure they're not working for your competition. Keep in mind that if you have been selective about who you have hired—well-paid, involved decision-makers in whom you have invested a lot in training—why would we want them to worry about losing their job?

Although this may seem like common sense, many organizations practice uncommon sense and get sucked into the performance death spiral. For example, a first action of many new CEOs is to initiate layoffs. If competitive success is truly achieved through people, then it is important to build a workforce that can achieve competitive success and that others cannot readily duplicate. Ironically, the recent trend toward using temporary help, part-time employees, and contract workers, particularly when such people are used in core activities, flies in the face of the changing basis of competitive success. This trend raises questions about why these practices seem to be growing, what effects they have on the ability to achieve advantage through people, and what the implications are for organizations that might follow a different strategy.

Providing your people a sense of employment security is not always fully possible, but is a valuable practice worth striving toward. The practice of maintaining employment security does not mean poor performers have a job for life, quite the contrary. As we discussed in Chapter 7, effective performance management dictates communicating extensively to a company's star performers so they feel valued and are assured their jobs are secure. Valuing performance and rewarding the doers has positive effects on organizational culture. In contrast, tolerating slackers and deadwood can ultimately poison the culture; great managers actively manage poor performers to maintain a high-performing environment.

Reduced Status Distinctions and Barriers

The trappings of executive life are seductive at some level, but in reality most people *hate* status distinctions, and such distinctions generally depress morale, innovation, and people's satisfaction with their jobs. In short, people do not like to be reminded they are somehow lower in the pecking order than others.

Typical ways status is communicated include:

- *Dress.* Managers wear white hard hats in plants, while workers wear yellow, or managers wear ties, and employees are in company uniforms.
- *Parking spaces.* Executives have reserved spaces while others use an open lot.
- *Expense budgets.* While on company business, companies often have two different sets of standards for travel. Executives stay in expensive hotels and the company pays for expensive meals, whereas lower-ranking employees have strict limits and often have to go through a laborious process to get their reimbursements.

- *Benefit or compensation packages.* Managers are eligible for bonuses or stock options, while others are not. Also, large differences exist in executive pay when compared to average workers.
- *Office size and furniture.* Executives have corner offices, managers have offices, and the rest have cubicles.
- *Equipment.* Executives and managers often have huge computer monitors and up-to-date new computers, while employees, who use their computers for more of the day, have smaller screens and slower computers.
- *Access.* In many banks and other large headquarters buildings, executives have their own elevators with special key cards. These key cards guarantee that no other employees can access the floors on which the executives work or gain entrance to the executive dining area.

Clearly, the symbols of workplace status differences surround most people on a daily basis. A good example of an early company to remove most status differences is Wainwright Industries, headquartered in St. Louis, Missouri. Wainwright manufactures stamped and machined parts for customers in the automotive, aerospace, home security, and information processing industries. In 1994, the company won the U.S. National Institute of Standards and Technology's prestigious Baldrige Award. In 1996, Industry Week tapped Wainwright's company as one of the best-run plants in America. As part of creating Team Wainwright, all employees (including the CEO) wear the same uniform on the job. In addition, Wainwright has no assigned parking spaces, and all of the office walls were removed and replaced with glass so that anyone walking by a manager's office (including the CEO's) could see what that person was doing. Don Wainwright, the CEO, asserts: "If I can walk out on the shop floor and see what a person is doing, then anyone should be able to see what I am doing." This level of equality is rarely seen in U.S. companies, but does wonders for showing people that "everyone here counts regardless of status."

Extensive Sharing of Information Throughout the Organization

At the most basic level, you build trust by treating all members of an organization as though they can be trusted. This means, among other things, sharing information with everyone. When John Mackey, CEO of Whole Foods Market, was asked why his firm shared all of its performance information with everyone, and even made it possible for each team member to know the salary of everyone else in the company by name, he replied that to keep secrets implied the organization didn't trust those from whom information was withheld. Knowledge is power, and sharing information entails sharing power. Not sharing information suggests some in the organization can be trusted with its secrets, and others can't. This is the wrong message to send if you want to harness the efforts and energy of everyone in the organization.

You cannot build trust without treating people with respect and dignity. Layoffs in which those let go are immediately escorted off the premises by uniformed security guards send a clear signal of distrust. This process deprives those people who have been laid off of the opportunity to say goodbye and, more fundamentally, signals distrust and disrespect. Consider instead New Zealand Post, which in 1987 became a state-owned enterprise expected to operate on a profitable basis. It has since accomplished amazing things—for instance, actually *reducing* the cost of a stamp! People laid off were offered generous severance packages, given parties on their leaving, and were recognized for their contributions to the company. Indeed, the organization even let the staff help decide who would go and who would stay—for it turned out that some people the organization intended to keep wanted to leave or retire, while others wanted to stay.

Building trust also means taking the organization's values seriously. The 2005 annual report for AES Corp., one of the world's largest independent producers of electricity, discusses how well the organization is doing in living up to its four core values of safety, integrity, honoring commitments, striving for excellence, and having fun through work. Whole Foods Market's annual report prominently displays the results of its employee satisfaction survey. These organizations signal they take seriously their commitments to both their values and their people by publicly discussing where they are succeeding and where they are falling short—and what they are going to do about it.

Today, many firms spend a great deal of time benchmarking best practices in other companies. They want to know how they're doing relative to their peers. In reality, however, most managers can often learn much from examining what is done well in their own company. In other words, learn from your own people first.

As an excellent example of sharing information inside of the business, let's return to the example of Best Buy used earlier in this chapter. Interestingly, across 400 stores (which for all practical purposes are identical to each other), employees are engaged to vastly different degrees. In the Best Buy store that had the highest scores on the Gallup surveys, 91 percent of employees strongly agreed with the statement, "I know what's expected of me at work." In the store with the lowest score, just 27 percent agreed. What would account for those kinds of differences? How should a company like Best Buy or any other store for that matter capitalize on those types of discrepancies across locations? By the *sharing of information*. What do store managers in the store with a high level of engagement do differently from the store with low employee engagement? Are they using the same process to select their workers? Are they treating them the same? Probably not. But only through sharing this type of information will managers at the poor store be able to learn from managers at the successful store.

Corporate Examples of High-Performance Cultures

Managers in workplaces all across the world implement some of the practices described in this book. The rare company, however, has built a culture where these skills are implemented on an ongoing, consistent basis. That is, pockets of excellence exist all over, but truly excellent performance at the corporate level is still pretty rare. The companies discussed next provide illustrations of great people management practice and demonstrate how ordinary people can achieve extraordinary results.

- **Whole Foods.** Whole Foods, which grew in the 1990s from $100 million to $1 billion in sales—in the grocery business, no less—is rightfully well known for its use of self-managed teams. The company shares detailed performance and financial information with all its people—so much information that, because many people own stock in the company, all employees are considered insiders for purposes of Securities and Exchange Commission regulations. The company even makes data about individual salaries available to *all* its employees. It also shares productivity gains with its people through team-based incentive compensation, as part of fostering decentralized decision making.

- **The Men's Wearhouse.** The Men's Wearhouse has succeeded in the retailing industry, which is notorious for its use of part-time, low-paid, undertrained, and poorly treated help. The company has achieved this success by doing exactly the opposite of what the industry is known for:

It has invested heavily in training, uses relatively few part-time staff, pays above-industry-average wages, and encourages employee stock ownership. The company recognizes that what's important is not what people *cost*, but what they *do*.

- **AES Corp.** AES Corp., a global developer and operator of electric power plants, has succeeded by fostering radical decentralization, sharing financial and performance information (all of its people, as with Whole Foods, are also insiders), recruiting on the basis of cultural fit, and eschewing bureaucracy. How many companies with several thousand employees do you know that have no human resources staff and that make business development and strategic planning part of everyone's job, not just the responsibility of centralized staff?

Cultural Audits

When we think of audits, we generally think about financial audits. Basically, a financial audit is the review of a company's finances, resulting in a report on whether or not the financial statements of the company are relevant, accurate, complete, and fairly presented. From a managerial perspective, financial audits are important because they provide important measures, they give credibility, and they provide relevant information about areas that may need to be improved.

Cultural audits can be thought of much like a financial audit. The primary difference, however, is that a **cultural audit** evaluates a company's values and practices to ensure they are aligned with their corporate strategy. In other words, if we are a company that espouses low prices and sees the ability to provide low prices to our customers as our primary competitive tool, we need to know if our company's values and practices are really aligned with the idea of low prices or if we are just paying "lip service" to that ideal. So a cultural audit can be used to measure how far an organization's behavior matches its expressed values. The results of a cultural audit are used to make decisions for future investments, organizational changes, hiring, and to determine whether the organization is "on course" or whether significant cultural changes are needed.

An effective workplace cultural audit determines the overall working environment, identifies the unwritten norms and rules governing employee interactions and workplace practices, highlights possible barriers to effective work practices and communication, and makes recommendations for addressing identified problems. Not only will this help retain top performers; it provides a blueprint of what attributes to look for in applicants.[43] An important thing to understand about cultural audits is that the audit is not an end in itself. It serves as a starting point to address cultural strengths and weaknesses within your organization and to start the discussion on what needs to be done to facilitate organizational change. Management Live 13.5 shows some excellent areas to consider for an organizational audit, which the authors cluster under the concept of "engagement."

What is most impressive is how individuals' *subjective* answers to the Q12 index relate to *objective* business results. Indeed, the relationships between those questions and a variety of performance measures were substantial. For example, the most "engaged" workplaces (those in the top 25 percent of Q12 scores) were more likely to have lower turnover, higher-than-average customer loyalty, above-average productivity, and were more likely to report higher profitability.

⇄ MANAGEMENT LIVE 13.5

Twelve Questions That Matter to Culture

If you want to build the most engaged workforce, your first job is to help every employee generate compelling answers to 12 simple questions about the day-to-day realities of his or her job. These factors, maintain Marcus Buckingham and his colleagues at The Gallup Organization, determine whether people are engaged, not engaged, or are actively disengaged at work. Employees are fully engaged when they can answer each question with an emphatic "Yes!"

1. Do I know what is expected of me at work?
2. Do I have the materials and equipment I need to do my work right?
3. At work, do I have the opportunity to do what I do best every day?
4. In the past seven days, have I received recognition or praise for doing good work?
5. Does my supervisor, or someone at work, seem to care about me as a person?
6. Is there someone at work who encourages my development?
7. At work, do my opinions seem to count?
8. Does the mission or purpose of my company make me feel my job is important?
9. Are my co-workers committed to doing quality work?
10. Do I have a best friend at work?
11. In the past six months, has someone at work talked to me about my progress?
12. This past year, have I had opportunities at work to learn and grow?

Source: From *First, Break All The Rules*, by Gallup Press. Copyright © 1999 Gallup. Reprinted with permission. All rights reserved.

Common Areas to Assess in Cultural Audits

Since a cultural audit is the evaluation of a specific culture, the content of each of these audits should be different. In other words, what we measure needs to correspond to what is important at our company. There are, however, general areas that are evaluated during cultural audits because they are relevant for most all companies. These areas include, but are not limited to:

- Competitiveness
- Pay and benefits
- Working conditions
- Decision-making practices
- Co-worker relations
- Leadership behavior
- Client/stakeholder orientation
- Communication effectiveness
- Change orientation
- Teamwork
- Employee trust in the management
- Learning environment
- Respect for the individual

You may notice that the preceding list includes many of the exact topics we have covered in this book, either directly or indirectly. This is not an accident. In many ways, cultural audits represent a summary of a company's practices when it comes to managing their people. And remember that great cultures are not only important for big companies—Management Live 13.6 provides some great examples of smaller companies that also value culture.

Following Up a Cultural Audit

Chapter 14 deals directly with organizational change, and the entire chapter can be considered tightly linked to the results of a cultural audit. Here, however, it is important to provide some specific ways that companies frequently follow up on the

⇄ MANAGEMENT LIVE 13.6

The Unique High-Performance Cultures of "Small Giants"

One risk in books like ours, and business education in general, is that all the evidence and examples can be drawn from just a few hundred publicly held corporations. Unfortunately, there is precious little research on small businesses. One terrific exception is a book that reports on companies that chose not to grow big, but to grow better. The author has carefully researched about a dozen businesses of the wide variety of industries scattered across the United States that have all chosen to become better rather than bigger. In fact, their "betterness" has led to a fairly significant amount of growth in revenue and profit. More importantly, they have grown strong competitive barriers.

The author labels these firms *Small Giants* and they include Anchor Steam Brewing, Zingerman's Deli, and Clif Bar. The seven recurring elements that capture the cultures of these Small Giants are:

1. They consciously **questioned the usual definitions of success** and imagined different possibilities than the usual ones. This concept had surfaced in the world of professional businesses, such as CPAs, physicians, and architects, where people talk about having a profession rather than a job. One of the key distinguishing factors that turned up in different architectural firms is whether a firm considered itself a practice or a business. When it was a business, financial criteria were prime. When it was a practice, a whole variety of other criteria took precedence. Yes, of course, they needed to make a living, but making money was not the overriding goal.

2. The leaders had to overcome enormous pressures to take traditional paths to success. Often this meant **rejecting outside capital and growth opportunities** outside their usual geography.

3. Each company has an extraordinarily **intimate relationship with its local community** in which it does business.

4. Each company cultivated exceptionally **intimate relationships with customers and suppliers** based on personal contact, one-to-one interaction, and mutual commitment on delivering on promises.

5. They had **unusually intimate workplaces,** which were in effect functional little communities that strove to address a broad range of their employees' needs as human beings, including emotional, spiritual, social, as well as the economic ones. For those of you who know of the culture of Southwest Airlines, this is called relational coordination, which is built on the principle of caring for people in the totality of their lives.

6. This sample represents a **broad variety of corporate structures and modes of governance** that they have come up with to help them achieve their driving force.

7. The **passion that the leaders brought to what the company did**—they loved the subject matter, whether it was music, safety, food, lighting, special effects, or constant torque hinges. They had deep emotional attachments to their business, and this deep emotional attachment extended, as mentioned earlier, to employees, vendors, customers, and their community.

Source: Burlingham, B. (2005). *Small Giants: Companies That Choose to Be Great Instead of Big.* Portfolio; New York.

results of a cultural audit to show their usefulness and their role in building effective, high-performing cultures. The areas that follow are presented in order of the tenure of employees which is generally targeted. Thus, the following examples should give you a flavor of how systemwide the results of a cultural audience can be utilized.

- *Staffing.* When selecting new people, it is important to find people who will fit with the organization (P-O fit). The ability to find people who fit the values of the organization is very difficult, however, when the organization itself does not really understand its values. The results of a cultural audit can be useful in attracting and ultimately hiring people who have a vested interest and willingness to support and work toward the vision of the organization.

- *Onboarding.* Using the cultural audit findings, it is much easier to provide realistic job previews (RJPs), and set clear expectations of what is expected on the job. Also, because the audit provides information about group norms and shared values, these results should make a company's onboarding practices much more helpful to new employees and provide them with more precise information.

- *Team Interventions.* The results of cultural audits are commonly used to determine vwhether team training or developmental activities are needed. For instance, if the cultural audit shows that employees do not feel the teams are cohesive enough or that the expectations placed on teams are clear enough, these results provide direct input to improving the functioning of teams in the company. Chapter 10 addresses a wide variety of specific interventions that can be used for teams.

- *Leadership Development.* The roles of management members and the leadership behaviors they exhibit are often key components of cultural audits. Most companies consider the behavior of people in leadership positions to be critical to the culture of the organization, because these people are the "face" of the organization to most employees. In other words, if your company values inclusiveness and creativity, but a manager is not encouraging or supportive of those behaviors in his workgroup, this suggests a disconnect that needs to be remedied. Chapter 9 provides a host of specific actions to develop a company's leaders.

Concluding Note

When managers and their people take culture seriously, remarkable things can happen. People get fired up about their firms and their jobs, firms are drawn to support and reward those people in exceptional ways, and the job of manager is infinitely more fulfilling and rewarding. Managers who most contribute to high-performance cultures and great places to work share three things: (1) a belief in the power of people management to influence organizational success, (2) an understanding of the people management practices that most influence commitment and performance, and (3) motivation, even courage, to manage in a way that puts people first, even in organizations with little traditional support for such behavior.

KEY TERMS

adhocracy 454
artifacts 450
attraction-selection-attrition (ASA) framework 458
Boomers 474
clan 453
collectivism 463
cultural audit 485
deep-level diversity 471
departmentation 456
diversity distance 464
employee socialization 460
feminine orientation 463

Generation X 474
height of an organization 456
hierarchy 453
high-performance work practices 478
individualism 463
long-term orientation (LTO) 463
market 454
masculine orientation 463
Millennials 474
organization culture 450
organizational structure 455
P-O fit 458

power distance 461
role clarity 461
short-term orientation (STO) 463
span of control 456
strong culture 455
surface-level diversity 471
Traditionalists 474
uncertainty avoidance 463
underlying assumptions 450
values 450
weak culture 455

< < CASE
Socializing Expatriates Worldwide at PepsiCo

Pepsi offers employees many of the standard benefits. These include an attractive set of retirement, savings, and stock plans. They also offer their employees a collection of work/life benefits that include things like family leave, adoption assistance, auto and home insurance programs, tuition reimbursement, and access to employee assistance programs. On top of these, they even have discounts to movie tickets, cell phones, hotels, computers, and Broadway shows.

In addition to the common benefits mentioned, PepsiCo offers some specific programs designed to help their expatriate employees.

Two of the most popular types of programs are language training and expatriate family benefits. When it comes to the language training, this is considered very important to help the employees integrate better into their new environment. A final big piece of the expatriate socialization package, however, is that the company provides family benefits. When

sending expatriates abroad, it is important to remember that the relocation affects the whole family, especially the spouse. Family problems are one of the most common reasons for expatriates to leave their assignments earlier than was initially planned. To assist with the family relocation and ease tensions that go along with moving abroad, PepsiCo offers support and financial help in finding schooling for kids. Nonworking expatriate spouses sometimes receive help in finding unpaid activities (such as volunteer work or studies).

Some other aspects of Pepsi's program include benefits that many people may not readily think about. As part of their program to help expatriates adjust, employees are offered a health risk assessment that is available to spouses and partners as well. As an incentive, all participants get a reward of $100 in their health care spending accounts. For PepsiCo, however, their socialization attempts reach beyond their employees by facilitating spouse networking opportunities in local communities and developing a children's cultural integration program.

Some of Pepsi's other benefits, however, are less well known but are possibly even more important for the employees they target. More specifically, for expatriate executives at PepsiCo Inc. working in Mexico City, Pepsi offers more than language lessons to immerse them in national culture. Indeed, executives can join fellow PepsiCo employees for onsite Zumba lessons in their Latin dance fitness program. In Dubai, international employees participate in a World Cup soccer challenge and corporate Olympics. And in China, ping-pong tournaments help PepsiCo expats engage with local hires.

According to Pepsi, such athletic and social activities allow expatriates in a new country to adjust to culture shock as well as curb the impulse to work nonstop in a demanding new job.

Discussion Questions

1. What factors might you consider important in taking on an expatriate assignment for PepsiCo? Does PepsiCo's socialization program appear to address these factors?

2. What critical components might PepsiCo add to their program to "round out" the socialization process?

3. If you were to take an expatriate assignment in Latin America, how might national culture differences impact your transition?

SELECT MANAGE *WHAT?* DEBRIEFS

Will I Fit In Here? Decoding an Organization's Culture: Debrief

First, this type of cultural "audit" is a very good idea. The reality is that similar firms can be quite different in culture, and evidence suggests that both job satisfaction and organizational commitment are often heavily dependent on things that might not be readily apparent on the surface. Second, it is a good idea to get multiple inputs when seeking organizational information. That is, certain biases can cloud judgments, so it makes sense to get the cultural equivalent of second opinions in medicine.

The following are broad categories or characteristics of organizations that will help you determine the nature of the organization's culture. These characteristics also provide a good platform to describe the company to others, particularly newcomers.

- *Innovation and risk taking.* The degree to which employees are encouraged to be innovative and take risks.
- *Attention to detail.* The degree to which employees are expected to exhibit precision, analysis, and attention to detail.
- *Outcome orientation.* The degree to which management focuses on results or outcomes rather than on the techniques and processes used to achieve those outcomes.
- *People orientation.* The degree to which management decisions take into consideration the input of employees.

(continued)

(continued)

- *Team orientation.* The degree to which activities are organized around teams rather than individuals.
- *Aggressiveness.* The degree to which people are aggressive and competitive rather than easygoing.
- *Stability.* The degree to which organizational activities emphasize maintaining the status quo in contrast to growth.
- *Inclusiveness.* The degree to which a diverse set of individuals can gain entry, acclimate, and thrive in the organization.

Each of these characteristics exists on a continuum from low to high. Assessing the organization using these characteristics gives a composite picture of its culture. That picture becomes the basis for determining your own or others' person–organization fit. Armed with that information, you can be much more comfortable in determining which of your two job offers would be the best choice.

Avoiding Culture Shock: Debrief

Just like the shock that so often accompanies traveling to new countries or regions, organizational culture shock is very common among new employees. However, unlike the realization that you cannot get ice in your Coca-Cola or that you will eat your biggest meal at noon, the consequences of organizational culture shock can be devastating to people and careers. When employees join an organization, they are often overwhelmed by the ambiguity of their job, worried about whether they will be able to succeed, and are concerned about being socially accepted by fellow employees. Further, they must adjust to routines in the organization for how people talk with others. Perhaps most difficult is coping with anxiety about what their manager expects form them in terms of job contributions.

The good news is that managers can have an influence on shaping their immediate organizational culture to create an environment whereby employees feel like they belong. Indeed, research on socialization has shown that when organizations engage in a systematic method to socialize employees, they are more likely to reduce the ambiguity of being new and increase perceptions of fit. The key here is that a systematic method is used which implies that all new employees experience a standard process to learn about the organization immediately upon starting with the organization. This means that regardless of the type of job or firm, socialization must address some critical content, including (1) organizational mission and values, (2) job requirements, (3) networks and politics, (4) language or jargon, and (5) organizational history.

Most organizations will engage in socialization via some formalized program such as a new-employee orientation. Unfortunately, for too many new employees these programs are a dry regurgitation of facts and distributions of large three-ring binders with things to "read." But it doesn't have to be that way. Progressive managers understand that they must personally contribute to getting their employees off to the right start.

The single most harmful trap would be to stand aside and let your employees "get used to things" and ease them into the culture. To the contrary, on day one you should set expectations with your employees about performance and behavior, provide them with challenging goals from the start, and help them build their networks through mentoring and other opportunities to network inside the organization. Applying your knowledge about management to socialization requires you to think about your new employees not as fragile individuals but as people who want to be challenged immediately and steeped in the culture quickly to move past their anxiety of the unknown and to start to feel like they fit in.

Making a Culturally Diverse Team Productive: Debrief

Diverse teams have the potential for performance as high as or higher than that of homogenous teams, but diversity is harder to manage because of greater communication and interaction hurdles. Perhaps the most important lesson is that, at the most basic level, good diversity management is simply good people management. That means keep your focus on job-related behaviors and earn trust by treating others with respect and dignity.

The presence of diversity also accentuates the need for even greater focus on the fundamental team disciplines discussed in your text. More specifically, it is especially important to keep diverse teams small and pick members on the basis of some expertise other than just their diversity—though in this case the team has already been selected. Similarly, be obsessive about clarifying shared outcome goals and group norms of behavior.

With diverse group membership there is additional importance in being absolutely clear that everyone knows and agrees what the group is ultimately charged to accomplish, and how decisions will be made and work completed. Finally, seek mechanisms of mutual accountability. It is very easy in diverse teams for members to feel that their representation and input is enough. But without a shared stake in the outcome there is little chance that the promise of diversity will truly be achieved.

Although relevant differences in diverse team members do exist (for example, language, culture, generation), it is also true that we often perceive differences that are really *not* there. So one of the most important things to do in this case is to increase the interaction between individuals to reduce the influence of stereotypes and improve team functioning. As people get to know the others, stereotypes are typically replaced by more accurate knowledge that can result in reduced prejudice and conflict and greater cohesion. Be diligent about including diverse others in all key meetings and interactions. Unfortunately, diversity often makes us far less comfortable in interacting with others and thus the level of communication is likely to be typically *less* in such teams—particularly initially. Moreover, based on past experience, diverse members may have a fear of exclusion, so it is doubly important to be sure all team members are included and that important interactions are conducted in contexts accessible and comfortable to all.

With that in mind, be bold in trying to better know your team members and seek to recognize and identify important differences (see Tool Kit 13.4). If you are in doubt, go ahead and ask! Most people will give you the benefit of the doubt if they sense you are respectful and making a good-faith effort to understand and be sensitive to their interests. Moreover, increase the use of process checks to be sure the group is on target. Seek two-way understanding by sharing your perceptions and style preferences and actively inquiring and listening to other team members share their own. By initiating dialogue, you will both aid your own understanding and establish stronger relationships with team members.

Recall that the best managerial outcomes come from treating people as individuals and seeking to understand their unique styles, values, and motives. So discuss with each team member their expectations—what they need, don't need, and how you can be most helpful to them. In turn, you should articulate your expectations as well. People of diverse backgrounds rarely need preferential treatment, just *fairness*. For example, if you need a good scribe or secretary, focus on the characteristics of the role—not on finding a young woman. Do not succumb to allowing your stereotypical understanding of others, or your impressions based on superficial diversity, to bias your decisions. Once again, the rules of good management and good teams do not change with diverse people—they just take on added importance.

14

Making Change

OBJECTIVES

KNOWING   DOING

After reading this chapter, you should be able to:

KO 14-1 Compare different models of change.

KO 14-2 Explain the steps involved in the contracting process.

KO 14-3 Describe methods for collecting data in a change initiative.

KO 14-4 Describe the purpose of the most common change interventions.

KO 14-5 Recognize the signs of resistance to change.

DO 14-1 Apply a model of change to conduct a planned organizational change.

DO 14-2 Structure an organizational problem into an achievable change initiative.

DO 14-3 Collect and feed back data needed to increase change readiness.

DO 14-4 Provide feedback to a group about a change initiative.

DO 14-5 Build trust in an employee who is cynical of a given change initiative.

DO 14-6 Evaluate the results of a change initiative.

"It used to be that change leadership was restricted to people at the very top of the organization. Today, however, especially in a rapidly changing industry like telecommunications, we need people who can make change at every level. If you want to move up the ranks here, show that you can lead people to make a change."

—Matt Collins, Director of Marketing, Forum Nokia

Case: The Indiana Bureau of Motor Vehicles

I n 2010, for the second time in three years, the Indiana Bureau of Motor Vehicles (BMV) was awarded the International Customer Service Award, recognizing the agency for the best customer service in its industry throughout all of North America. Speaking at the award ceremony, Governor Mitch Daniels pronounced that "Indiana now has the best BMV anywhere on the planet." This comment evoked a roar from the crowd of BMV staff in attendance. Daniels continued: "You are the first repeat winner of this award in its history. And your transformation of the Indiana BMV from the worst to best motor vehicle agency in North America is one of the greatest public sector success stories we've ever seen."

What made that occasion and accomplishment so remarkable was that, just a mere five years earlier, the Indiana BMV was indeed considered to be, as Daniels alluded to, the very *worst* agency of its kind in the nation. It was despised by Hoosier residents statewide, and a newspaper article at the

time even quoted one customer who lamented that ". . . going to the BMV is worse than a trip to the dentist for a root canal. . . ." Moreover, fraud reports were rampant and costs were rising. So, upon taking the office of governor, Daniels found a BMV that was disdained by the public it was intended to serve, compounded by fraudulent practices and widespread mismanagement. Customer service quality was not measured and there were no reports of branch efficiency or effectiveness because such things were not recorded. Employee morale was low and there was a sense of resignment to the status quo. Moreover, the agency was hampered (as are many government agencies) with low resources and an intensely political climate. That is, any attempts to make significant changes (cost cuts) in branches would certainly be met by

resistance from state legislators of those districts.

1. How and why could service be so poor at such a visible government agency?

2. Many prior governors had publically recognized the problem and promised a focus on improvement in the BMV, but almost nothing had changed in 30 years. Why is it so hard to make changes in organizations—even in situations like the Indiana BMV where the problems are so visible and public? What are typical sources of resistance to change?

3. If you were appointed as commissioner of the Indiana BMV in 2005, where would you start? That is, what would be your primary change strategy and what would you try to address first? What would you communicate to the public about what you were trying to do?

1. Converting an Organizational Problem into an Achievable Change Initiative

It's your senior year of college and, in an attempt to build your resumé, you agreed to run for president of the campus professional business fraternity. No one else ran, so you won in a landslide. But now you are faced with a big challenge as your returning vice president tells you the organization is a mess. She further notes that nobody is motivated and the members just want something to put on their resumés. She observes it is really hard to get people to take initiative on fraternity events and that new membership and attendance at events dropped to an all-time low last term.

Clearly, this seems like a situation ripe for change management, but how would you proceed in ways that might really yield improvement? Where do you begin? What common traps should you avoid? Who, if anyone, would you want to involve in the process? What resistance might you predict? At the end of the year, how would you judge whether you were successful as a change agent?

2. Creating Urgency for a Change

You are in sales with a pharmaceutical firm and the major drug in your portfolio is one of three patented products that are widely prescribed by physicians (the other two are manufactured by two competitor firms). You are starting to see that the other firms are gaining an advantage with their aggressive and innovative promotion campaigns and marketing efforts. Sales of your product have not fallen off much yet, but you can see that the doctors you call on are starting to be more and more impressed with the competitor products, while interest in your drug is waning. Unfortunately, your superiors are complacent and do not recognize what is happening. Other salespeople have tried to make similar cases in the past but have often been dismissed as whiners (because their own sales were dropping) or as "Chicken Littles" who acted as if the sky was falling when it was only a passing phase that happens with all product cycles.

From your relatively low level in the firm, how might you build urgency for a change here? What might you do knowing you have little authority to get anyone to comply? What common traps should you avoid? Are there tactics that might seem intuitive or obvious but that might only raise resistance and create obstacles rather than urgency?

3. Dealing with Change Resisters

You are working as assistant manager in a restaurant where a new manager has just been hired away from a very popular and successful competing restaurant chain. The new guy is bright and energetic and eager to bring some of what he learned in his prior job to his new role. More specifically, he wants to overhaul the way your hosts and servers interact with diners. He is particularly interested in a team approach (whoever is available brings ready food to a table regardless of who took the order) and is encouraging more proactive exchanges with diners.

For example, he wants servers to make recommendations and encourage diners to try various specialty items on the menu. The recommended approach is not forceful or aggressive, but is a reasonable way of ensuring that guests are given every opportunity to sample some of the best food and drink and to help create a more memorable dining experience. You really like the new approach and think it can lead to higher store performance and ultimately translate into better bonuses and merit increases for the staff. But you know there will be resistance.

What different forms might the resistance take? What recommendations would you make for how to present the change in a way that might unfreeze that resistance? What common traps should you avoid?

4. Evaluating a Change Initiative

Your company has just spent a significant amount of money on a new enterprise software solution. Since you were an important part of the team that worked with the external consultants, your regional manager calls you in and gives you the following "opportunity." He asks you to complete an evaluation of how the implementation went. Basically, the company just spent a lot of time and money going through this process and they wanted to find out what worked and what didn't.

He explains to you that this could be particularly important because a number of other districts are considering implementing similar software solutions and they will be looking for guidance in this process. He tells you to "be honest" and to be "comprehensive." Other than that, he doesn't give you much guidance, but just sends you out with a note of encouragement saying, "This could be a good opportunity for you to gain some visibility, so let's see what you've got."

Where would you start? How would you structure such a task and what are some things to be sure that you include? How would you collect the information and be aware of various stakeholders' perspectives during the process?

Introduction

Making change is the appropriate title for this chapter, and it is rightly placed at the end of the book. It is the right title because, unlike many discussions of change in organizations, our focus is *not* primarily on large-scale organizational transformations or cultural shifts. Rather, our goal is to help you develop the skills of an effective change agent, whatever the scope of your desired change and regardless of your level in an organization.

Consistent with the chapter's opening quote, our belief is that change leadership can and does happen at every level in an organization. It *needs* to happen throughout an organization if the company is to thrive in today's business environment. Though few of us will soon be responsible for a new product launch, an international relocation, or a large-scale quality improvement effort, we will all have the opportunity to observe gaps in our organizations between *what is* and *what should be*. Even the lowest-level employees have the opportunity to facilitate, support, and execute change.

Making change is appropriately at the end of the book because it goes well beyond a one-dimensional skill or capability. It involves a reliance on practically every skill covered up to this point. For example, the successful change agent will often need to define and frame problems, communicate persuasively, motivate and lead others, manage conflict, build teams, and so on. Thus, you might think of making change as a capstone management skill and one that brings together many pieces of your journey in managerial skill development.

Managers in every type of organization (government, business, religious, family) have always struggled with change. The key element in change is people, and getting people to buy into a new way of doing anything is often difficult and inevitably involves resistance. As you saw in Chapter 1, significantly changing the behavior of a single person (yourself) can be exceptionally difficult work. Remember, changing yourself is easier than changing others because at least you want to change (assuming you are trying). Others, however, may not share this desire to change, which only amplifies the complexity of altering behaviors. This is one big reason why helping others change their behavior, in an effort to get something new accomplished in an organization, offers particularly thorny challenges.

Although getting people to change is undeniably challenging, much is known about change, why it fails, and when it succeeds. In this chapter, we review what is known about making successful change and present practical frameworks and tools that can help you develop a greater capacity to identify and create positive change.

The Challenge of Change

Any unit you join will surely have to change and adapt if it hopes to survive and thrive. Even for a company founded in the 1980s or 1990s, the need to change has probably made it almost unrecognizable to someone who had not seen it since it was started. Many types of changes can occur in organizations (new products, new work processes, new employees) and many of those changes are unplanned. That is, unplanned change is the result of external forces that require some reaction and organizational adaptation. Our focus in this chapter

?¿ MYTHS 14.1   Myths of Making Change[1]

- **Crisis is a guarantee of change.** Urgency is important, but crisis hardly ensures change will occur. Consider that 90 percent of patients who have had coronary bypass surgery *do not* sustain changes in the unhealthy lifestyles that worsen their severe heart disease and greatly threaten their lives.

- **Change has to start at the top.** Many very successful changes are "bottom-up" initiatives. In fact, while support from top management is often vital, change that has "bubbled up" from lower levels in the organization is frequently some of the most effective and rapid organizational change.

- **Fear is the best motivator of change.** It's too easy for people to go into denial over the bad things that might happen to them. Compelling, positive visions of the future are a much stronger inspiration for change.

- **Compelling facts are the key to change.** For better or worse, motivation for change is guided by emotions and stories, as much as, if not more than, by facts. When a fact does not fit how we make sense of the world, we ignore or reject it. Facts alone, without some personal emotional connection, rarely inspire significant change.

- **Old dogs can't learn new tricks.** Our brains have extraordinary plasticity, meaning we can continue changing and learning new things throughout our lives. The key is to have significant motivation and an understanding of the need for change; age has little to do with it.

"The evidence is overwhelming that the central challenge of change is not strategy or systems or culture. The fundamental problem is changing the behavior of people."

—John Kotter

is on *planned* change resulting from managers' and others' deliberate attempts to improve organizational operations.

In some cases, managers at higher levels have the power and influence to force change in an organization. That is, by virtue of their authority and control over key organizational reward systems, they can dictate a change from the top, and people in the organization will be forced to comply (at least temporarily). However, in most cases, particularly for lower-level managers and associates, the use of such methods is unlikely to lead to long-term success. Moreover, at lower levels, managers even lack the ability to get people to comply in the short term. And without some type of short-term success, long-term change is certainly doomed.

Before we focus on how to make change, it is a good idea to dispel a few of the more persistent myths that exist in this area (see Myths 14.1).

On a more positive note, while it is popular today to talk about the high failure rate of change, the evidence is that planned change efforts, relying on sound frameworks of the change process, have been quite successful. For example, several comprehensive reviews summarizing research evidence regarding the effectiveness of change interventions have found positive results. For example, one study identified 35 reported change interventions that were evaluated by rigorous methods. Using outcome measures such as performance, turnover, and productivity, researchers found there was significant positive change in 51 percent of the cases.[2] Other reviews have found gains in productivity associated with change interventions in over 80 percent of studies investigated.[3,4] So, while success in making change is far from a foregone conclusion, planned change does frequently work when it is executed well.

General Models of the Change Process

KO **14-1**

DO **14-1**

Practice this!
Go to www.baldwin2e.com

The reality is that many change efforts fail—even when it seems profoundly logical or imperative that change should succeed. This frequently occurs because change initiatives are often haphazard and not managed in line with best practices. Investment managers would not think of investing funds without considering models of risk, portfolio performance, and so on. Doctors would not prescribe medicine without evidence of the effects of the prescribed drugs. Yet change efforts are often curiously free of any adherence to the change process models shown to predict and explain when and how change occurs. Consistent with the evidence-based approach we take in this book, however, we aim to make sure that you do not repeat these errors.

In the following sections, we briefly explain several models of change that can help you think about how change happens. We then present a more specific framework for planned action and a set of practical strategies for converting an organizational problem into an achievable change initiative. The intention here is to help you both know (that is, know how change occurs) and do (bring about and successfully manage change).

Lewin's Unfreeze-Change-Refreeze Model

The renowned sociologist Kurt Lewin developed one of the most enduring conceptions of organizational change,[5] which was a direct extension of his *field theory*. In general, he conceived of fields of force that struggle to maintain the status quo as depicted in Figure 14.1.

Lewin's model described change as a three-stage process of unfreezing, changing, and refreezing. In Lewin's **unfreeze-change-refreeze model,** the first stage, *unfreezing,* involves overcoming inertia and breaking down existing ways of thinking. Resistance has to be overcome, and a readiness or willingness to get involved with a change has to be sparked. Lewin felt this stage is often neglected because eager and excited **change agents**—people responsible for making or communicating a change—often dive right in and try to sell their change without first diagnosing and dealing with the resisting factors.

The second stage is what Lewin called *changing* and refers to when the change intervention is started and ongoing. Changing is often a period of anxiety and tension as old ways are challenged and the reality of a new way is first truly experienced. New information and rewards are introduced and comfort zones are pushed. The third and final stage is what Lewin called *refreezing*. Ideally, a new mindset and behavioral pattern is created for those involved, and the change yields positive benefits for the unit or organization.

"There is nothing so practical as a good theory."

—Kurt Lewin

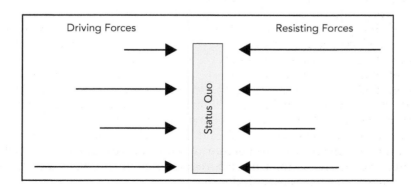

FIGURE 14.1
Lewin's Force Field Analysis

Lewin's model is always a good starting point in a situation where change is desired because it draws attention to the most important questions:

- What is preventing change and why hasn't it happened yet?
- What actions might influence change?
- How can change be sustained?

Based on his theory, Lewin developed the process for a **force field analysis** (see Tool Kit 14.1 for steps to conduct a force field analysis). Force field analysis is a powerful tool that can be used in a number of different situations. The basic premise is that, for every problem or current state of affairs (the status quo), a desired condition or future state also exists that has not been achieved. The status quo is held constant in an organizational system by two opposing forces: (1) driving forces (positive aspects of the problem), and (2) resisting forces (negative aspects of the problem). A force field analysis will help you understand all sides of the problem and where to begin looking.

Lewin argued that the effective path to change is to focus first and primarily on removing the restraining forces rather than trying to significantly increase the driving forces. While that may seem counterintuitive, the logic is that increasing the driving forces can often result in an increase in the resisting forces against the change—people dig in and push back. Removing the obstacles and restraining forces can, therefore, be the least disruptive and quickest path to change.

Although simple in concept, Lewin's model provides a general overview of change that has had profound influence on change research and practice. Indeed, most models of change developed since then acknowledge his influence and simply elaborate on his elegant three-stage model of the organizational change process.[6,7]

MANAGER'S TOOL KIT

Tool Kit 14.1   Conducting a Force Field Analysis

1. On a piece of paper or flip chart, write "Current State" at the top center and write your problem statement underneath. To the right of your current state, write your Desired Condition and write the ideal state if the problem were solved.

2. Draw a line down from the center of Current State. Label the left side Driving Forces and the right Resisting Forces.

3. Now answer the following questions and record the answers on the appropriate side. What are the *drivers*, those things that are driving you toward success and goal achievement? What are the *resisters* for the project or change effort, those things that are restraining you from reaching success and goal achievement?

4. Draw a horizontal arrow underneath each driver and restrainer that demonstrates the relative strength of each. Point the arrow toward the center. Your longest arrow indicates the strongest field of force that is currently operating. Similarly, the shortest arrow indicates the least powerful force. Thus, there should be a range of arrow lengths.

Now that you have a map of the various driving and restraining forces affecting your problem, as well as their varying levels of strength, you are ready to act. Now your team can make a game plan for how to diminish or remove the forces that are a barrier to your implementing your change.

Punctuated Equilibrium

Even though Lewin's work provides some great basics for understanding change, it likely lulls us into thinking that change is an orderly process where the steps are as easy as 1, 2, 3. This is a case where there is a legitimate tension between trying to be simple (because it is easy to use) and trying to be accurate (because it is correct). A specific limitation of Lewin's simple approach is that the status quo appears to hold for long periods of time, and then a gradual process of change alters that condition and creates a new status quo (which appears to then be stable for a relatively long period).

When it comes to technology and other significant organizational changes, however, Lewin's model does not seem to do a very good job of describing reality. A number of researchers have put forth an approach called punctuated equilibrium (see Figure 14.2).[8] In its simplest form, punctuated equilibrium suggests that there are significant periods of relative stability in an environment (for example, cell phone design and the ability of these phones were only marginally different between the early 1990s and the year 2000), but then revolutionary change jolts the environment significantly (in this case, the introduction of "smartphones"). So, rather than organizational change occurring in relatively smooth, planned steps, punctuated equilibrium argues that change happens in revolutionary "jumps," and jumps then introduce a "new normal." The idea of punctuated equilibrium is an important one for managers because it is helpful to recognize when a significant change is happening and when your organization is in a period of relative stability.

Bridges' Model of Transitions

An approach that adds further understanding to either the unfreeze-change-refreeze model or punctuated equilibrium is the **model of transitions** created by William Bridges.[9] The real contribution of Bridges' model is that it "humanizes" the change process. Bridges' model is important because it allows us to better understand what is actually going on during the change process by considering the transitions that people actually need to make during the process.

In studying a variety of failed change efforts, Bridges became convinced it is impossible to achieve any desired objectives without getting to the "personal stuff." Bridges asserts that *transition* is not the same as change. A change occurs when something in our external environment is altered, such as changes in leadership, organizational structure, job design, systems, or processes. Transition, however, is the *internal* process that people must go through to come to terms with a new situation.

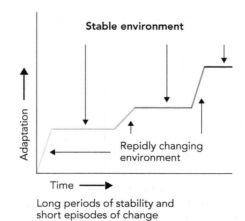

FIGURE 14.2
Punctuated Equilibrium

FIGURE 14.3
The Three Overlapping
Transitions in Bridges'
Model

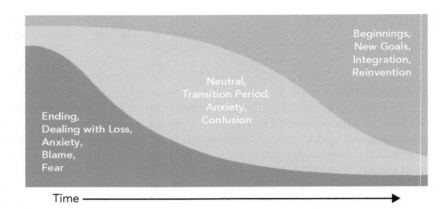

According to Bridges, individuals experience three stages of transition while undergoing change (Figure 14.3). Further, Bridges believes the failure to identify and prepare for the inevitable human psychological transitions that change produces is the single largest problem with most change initiatives—and why they too often fail. Although many changes can be physically put in place quickly, the psychological process of transitions takes time. Indeed, transitions can take a very long time if they are not well managed, so the *acceleration* of transitions becomes critical. Think about it: Companies just do not have the time to allow everyone "all the time in the world" to process and to dwell upon what is going on. If they did this, the competition would quickly leave them behind.

If any change is going to be sustained, people must own it. And unless they go through the inner process of transition, they will not develop the new behavior and attitudes the change requires. As a result, change efforts that disregard the process of transition are doomed. The critical lesson is both to recognize the nature of personal transition and to learn basic transition management strategies that can help accelerate the process. The specific strategies are presented in Tool Kit 14.2.

TOOL KIT 14.2   Using the Bridges' Model

According to Bridges' model, it is important for managers to:[10]

1. Identify who's losing what.

2. Accept the reality and importance of subjective losses. Don't argue with what your employees believe they are losing because loss is a largely *subjective* (rather than objective) experience.

3. Do not be surprised by "overreaction." What you may see as an overreaction is actually very normal. It is part of the process and should not be denied or belittled; it just needs to happen.

4. Acknowledge the losses openly and sympathetically. Do not worry about "stirring things up." In the long term, the real problem is to deny that things have changed.

5. Expect and accept the signs of grieving. People will go through anger, unrealistic bargaining attempts, anxiety, sadness, disorientation, and depression. Your job is to let people express these feelings and to accept these feelings as legitimate.

6. Compensate for the losses. Try to provide something to reduce the shift in balance. For instance, if a person's pay has been significantly reduced as part of a new work arrangement, try to provide a title that salvages some personal prestige for the person.

7. Give people information, and do it again and again. Keep people informed and share all of the information you possess. You cannot fall back on ideas like "They don't need to know" or "We don't know all the details ourselves yet."

8. Define what's over and what isn't. Be specific by letting people know exactly what they need to do, and what they should stop doing.

9. Mark the endings. Symbols and rituals are helpful in marking the end of something. An example here is to shred an old policy book or to take down one sign and replace it with another.

10. Treat the past with respect. Do not mock or disparage the past. It remains important to many people, and treating the past disrespectfully puts up a barrier between you and the people who lived through those times.

11. Let people take a piece of the old way with them. This may be a literal move (for example, the person's old chair) or a symbolic one (for instance, clothing with an old corporate logo after a merger).

12. Show how endings ensure the continuity of what really matters. The idea that the transitions are "allowing us to do what really matters" is an important one. Show how the new way is actually consistent with what has been happening all along.

Source: From William Bridges, 2004, *Managing Transitions: Making the Most of Change*, 2E, p. 100. Copyright © 2004 William Bridges. Reprinted by permission of Da Capo Press, a member of the Perseus Books Group.

Kotter's Eight Stages of Change

For many years, a leading authority on change has been John Kotter, a Harvard Business School professor. **Kotter's change model** is another useful way to think about the critical elements necessary to create successful change interventions.[11,12] Kotter's change model is based on analyzing where change initiatives go wrong, and then explains how to make effective change by steering clear of the pitfalls that unsuccessful changes suffer from. These stages can be seen in Figure 14.4.

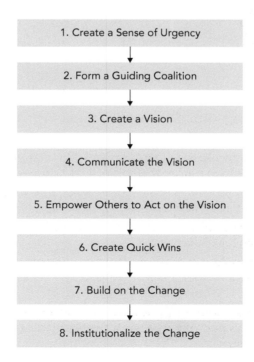

FIGURE 14.4
Kotter's Change Model

1. Create a Sense of Urgency
2. Form a Guiding Coalition
3. Create a Vision
4. Communicate the Vision
5. Empower Others to Act on the Vision
6. Create Quick Wins
7. Build on the Change
8. Institutionalize the Change

Create a Sense of Urgency

Kotter contends that raising a feeling of urgency is the first and most critical step in successful changes. Reports and spreadsheets are not enough; you need to demonstrate actions that make people aware—that even shock or jolt them—into understanding the need for the change you've determined.

The goal is to get people out of their established routines and comfort zones and ready to move. Kotter notes one way to do that is to create dramatic presentations with compelling objects that people can actually see, touch, and feel. He suggests showing customer service people a videotape of an angry customer rather than handing out a two-page memo filled with negative customer data. You want people telling each other, "Let's go, we need to change things!"

A favorite example of Kotter's is taken from an organization that had a very fragmented and disorganized purchasing system. One result of that poor system was that the company was paying significantly different amounts for the same products, but because people across units were not aware of what others were doing, few felt any pressing need for change. To heighten the sense of urgency, one middle manager in the company collected and made a display of all *424 different types* of rubber gloves the company regularly purchased and the wide range of prices paid for those gloves. The display was then prominently exhibited throughout the company to alert people to the reality that the firm was purchasing the same product from multiple vendors and at very different prices. Although many people in the company already knew there were significant problems with the purchasing system, the exhibit created a buzz and had people saying, "*Now* we have to do something!"

Form a Guiding Coalition (Identify Your Champions)

Every good change initiative needs a group of influential, effective champions. It is important to find the right people who are fully committed to the change initiative and who can help you influence others and manage resistance. Senior

"Change is not made without inconvenience, even from worse to better."

—Richard Hooker

managers with some clout in the organization are often good champions. However, in some cases the best champions are those thought to be skeptical of change or who would be seen as cynics or tough sells. For example, those responsible for addictive behavior counseling for teenagers often rely on recovering addicts—those who have experienced the lows of addiction firsthand—as champions of their message and sources of moving testimonials.

Create a Vision

While creating a shared need and urgency for change may push people into action, it is the vision that will steer them in the new direction. Kotter emphasizes that you want to construct a relevant vision that will help people visualize possible futures. The ideal is a clear picture of a post-change future, no matter how small, that can be articulated in one minute or written up on one page or less. To commit to change, people need a clear sense of where they are going and why that future state will be better, or the existing state more undesirable.

Communicate the Vision for Buy-In

Once a vision and set of goals have been developed, they must be communicated in order to promote understanding. Sending clear and credible messages about the direction and progress of change establishes buy-in, which in turn gets people ready to act.

You are generally best off keeping communication simple and heartfelt. Find out what people are really feeling and then speak directly to their anxieties, confusion, anger, and distrust. Aim to help people get information relevant to their specific needs. Do not rely on memos and reports that will simply get lost in the clutter. According to John Kotter, the total amount of communication going to the average employee in three months is 2.3 million words or numbers. The typical communication of a change project uses 13,400 words. That means that the change-associated communication the average employee sees is 0.58 percent of what that same employee sees overall. With that in mind, several elements of effective communication are key and can be seen in Tool Kit 14.3.

"The view only ever changes for the lead dog."

—Yukon Dog Sledder

Empower Others to Act

To empower means to bolster confidence that the job can be done and to recognize and reward in ways that inspire, promote optimism, and build self-confidence. Actively encourage input and participation of those who will be involved with the

TOOL KIT 14.3 COMMUNICATING TO AVOID CLUTTER

- **Simplicity.** Try to keep all jargon and technical terminology out of messages.
- **Analogy and Example.** A picture, chart, or illustration is worth a thousand words.
- **Multiple Forums.** Big meetings, small forums, memos, and newsletters are all effective for spreading the word.
- **Repetition.** Ideas sink in only after they've been heard many times.
- **Modeling the Way.** Visible people behaving inconsistently with the vision overwhelms other forms of communication.
- **Explanation of Seeming Inconsistencies.** Unaddressed inconsistencies undermine the credibility of all communication.
- **Give and Take.** Two-way communication is always more powerful than one-way communication.

change, be as open with information and feedback as you can, and keep making the case to resisters so they feel the need for change.

Rather than viewing empowerment as simply handing out power, Kotter describes it as removing barriers, or unfreezing those who you want to take part in the change effort. This is akin to Lewin's suggestion to aim to remove or diminish the resisting forces. This removing of obstacles helps inspire people to take action and avoid a "wait and see" approach.

Create Quick Wins

Creating short-term wins is a recurring method for success, and one emphasized by every popular model of change.[13] Short-term wins nourish faith in the change effort, emotionally reward the hard workers, keep the critics at bay, and build momentum. By creating short-term wins, and being honest with feedback, the change is seen as working and thus energizes people further.

If you can produce enough short-term wins fast enough, you can energize your change champions. So be on the lookout for small wins that are visible, timely, clear, and meaningful to others. Focus publicly on just 2 to 4 goals instead of 15, and make sure no new initiatives are added until one of those first goals is achieved and celebrated.

Build on Change and Don't Let Up

You're not done until the change has been entrenched in the organization. This is a good time to revisit Kurt Lewin's force field analysis. Frequently, successful change can slide back into past habits when the new behavior does not become commonplace. Successful change agents follow up regularly to ensure the new change remains supported, and continue to highlight small wins and progress in relation to goals.

Institutionalize the Change

The final and ultimate goal is to build a hardiness and capacity for future changes in your workplace. Successful efforts build on the momentum from one change to stimulate *other* needed changes and initiatives. Highlight the connections between making change and career success by finding ways to reward risk taking and change makers. Aim to help make your workplace a "change-ready" culture. Management Live 14.1 gives an interesting take on how Jack Welch viewed the issue of making changes work—and last.

McKinsey 7S Framework

Much in the same manner as Kotter's approach, the McKinsey 7S framework is based upon the idea of "alignment." Developed by Tom Peters and Bob Waterman in the early 1980s, the McKinsey 7S framework identifies seven key factors (which not surprisingly all start with the letter "S") that need to be aligned if an organization is going to be successful. As a result, companies need to manage change in a manner that creates and maintains the alignment between these seven S's. Importantly, these factors can also be used as the basis for alignment with individual or team projects, or most any other organizationally relevant activity. The seven factors are shown in Figure 14.5.

Taken individually, the 7S's refer to:

1. Shared values are the core values of the company that are evidenced in the corporate culture and the general work ethic. These are shown in the center of the framework because they are normally thought of as the glue that holds the 7S's together.

↹ MANAGEMENT LIVE 14.1

Schools, Media, and Police: Powerful Levels of Change

Former GE CEO Jack Welch once noted that the most rapid political and societal change has come about when a change maker sought and gained control over the schools, the media, and the police. Although not identical in form, corporations have their equivalents of all three, and therein lies a basic lesson for making change in organizations. Put simply, if you can exert influence over the schools, media, and police in your context, you have a very good chance of making change.

In organizations, schools include training and development seminars but also less formal discussion forums, e-learning, and on-the-job mentoring and coaching. The media include internal publications, employee magazines, newsletters, e-mail, and the grapevine. The police can be the accountants or managers who review decisions and control how money is spent and people are rewarded or sanctioned.

As a change agent you are looking for the most influential levers to get your change accomplished. And there are few more powerful levers in organizational life than the schools, media, and police. If you want to make change, find ways to influence what people are learning, and hearing, and how they are rewarded and punished.

Source: Tichy, N., and Sherman, S. (1994). *Control your own destiny or someone else will: Lessons in mastering change—The principles Jack Welch is using to revolutionize General Electric.* New York: Harper Business.

2. Skills represent the competencies of the company's employees.

3. Strategy is the plan being followed to gain an advantage over the company's competitors.

4. Structure signifies how the company is organized overall and who reports to whom.

5. Systems are the procedures that employees perform to get work accomplished.

6. Style is used to describe the leadership approach employed in the company.

7. Staff is the deployment of specific employees.

While the McKinsey 7S model is most often used at the corporate level of analysis, it works equally well within a specific workgroup. The real lesson here is that change cannot be done in an isolated manner. If we are changing one

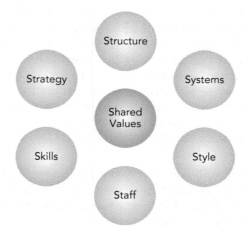

**FIGURE 14.5
The McKinsey 7S
Model**

issue (for example, shifting from salaried to commissioned salespeople), we also need to consider what else will need to be changed so that the system remains (or becomes) aligned.

A Practical Model of Planned Change

The models of change presented earlier hopefully stimulate ideas about why change often fails and how one might *generally* strategize to make a successful change in an organization. However, many inexperienced change agents need an even more concrete and practical blueprint. With that in mind, we present and illustrate a model of change here that draws heavily on the work of Lewin, Bridges, and Kotter, as well as Robert Schaffer, Peter Block, and others who have been influential in researching successful change.[14]

Reduced to the essential elements, all planned change efforts can be thought of in terms of:

1. Structuring the problem.
2. Contracting with key parties.
3. Collecting data and feedback.
4. Implementing interventions.
5. Evaluating and sustaining the change.

However, it is important to note that such discrete phases are isolated and separated only for purposes of explanation and illustration. Real change in organizations is rarely a straightforward linear process. It usually involves considerable overlap and skipping among the phases.[15] For example, data collection can easily lead to a restatement of the problem, more data can come to life in the process of an intervention, and so on.

DO 14-2   Structuring the Problem

Although sometimes unfortunately bypassed in an urgency to *do something* quickly, the first step in any effective planned change process is to structure the problem to be addressed.

Structuring a change problem involves addressing two fundamental questions:

- Who is (are) the customer(s) of the change?
- What is the scope of change (how broad, how much)?

Unless you explicitly address those questions, and structure the change initiative accordingly at the outset, you run the great risk of proceeding without a clear understanding of what you are trying to do or for whom you are doing it. Most change projects in organizations are likely to have a broader effect than originally thought and may produce unforeseen results. Further, change has a ripple effect, and even a small change in one part of an organization can have effects on individuals and groups in other areas. For these reasons, it is critical to clarify the nature of the problem and the relevant parties (often called stakeholders).

Using Appreciative Inquiry to Structure a Problem

While the PADIL model of problem solving (discussed extensively in Chapter 3) is undoubtedly an incredibly useful approach for structuring the problem, **appreciative inquiry** offers some unique perspectives when it comes to organizational change. Appreciative inquiry is an approach that attempts to focus on "what works" when it comes to people and their companies. At its heart, appreciative inquiry involves asking a series of probing questions that strengthen a system's positive potential.

Appreciative inquiry sets out in a very deliberate fashion to discover "what works" and to then tap into this "positive change core." While much of this may sound abstract, the process is not really very mysterious or very complicated. Basically, the stakeholders of the organization (usually focusing on all of the management and the employees) are brought together in a series of meetings and maybe even one large meeting. An agenda is then constructed that revolves around the following guidelines.

> **Wholeness.** All parts of the organization need to be involved. This means workers from all functions who barely know one another and people who work together every day. The purpose of "wholeness" is that it leads to trust and connectedness, and it forces people to see a purpose greater than their own. Obviously, if the goal is trust and connectedness, we cannot have certain groups (for example, engineering) left out while other groups (such as sales and marketing) dominate a discussion.

> **Discovery.** At the beginning of the session, participants explore their organization's "positive change core." They ask, Who are we? What do we do well? What are our hopes for the future? It is from the answers to these questions that everything else will be derived. It is important to notice that this meeting is not about "What is wrong here?" or "What needs to change?" Quite to the contrary, the entire tone is one of "What works?"

> **Dream.** After the discovery portion, participants break into groups and discuss the company's potential for positive influence and impact: What will the company look like in 2020? What will be happening in our industry environment? What are the best outcomes we can dream of? These breakout groups then report back to the other groups. The "dream" step allows for a goal to be created toward which the "what works" findings can be directed.

> **Design.** Participants focus on creating a company that incorporates the positive change core into every strategy, process, and system. The result: action-oriented statements of how the organization will function. This starts the movement toward making change.

> **Destiny.** At the end of the session, participants distill designs (from the previous step) into a list of "inspired actions." Task groups emerge around each action. If successful, these groups will sustain themselves long after the session ends.

As can be seen in Management Live 14.2, the issues of structuring a problem and getting people involved can often go hand in hand. While appreciative inquiry is certainly an important way of getting people involved and starting the contracting process, it is clearly not the only technique available. The next section addresses the second important step in the general mode of change presented in this chapter—contracting with those involved in the change.

Contracting with Those Involved in the Change   KO 14-2

Never try to make change alone. Any change done *to* people is less likely to be as effective as change in which people felt involved from the beginning. Far too often, a *joint* diagnosis of problems is neglected in favor of expediency or rapid

↤↦ MANAGEMENT LIVE 14.2

Leaders for the Long Haul[16]

When workers and executives from Roadway Express came together to strategize about the company's future, they made a startling discovery: Everyone wanted the same things. Here is Roadway's head-slapping realization: To compete in an industry in which net profit margins are less than 5 percent in a good year—let alone in a year when business is contracting—every one of its 28,000 employees must be a leader.

"Almost two-thirds of our every revenue dollar is consumed by wages and benefits," says Roadway president and COO, James Staley, 51. "There's not a lot of new technology that's going to make us more efficient. So future opportunities are going to come from our people being more involved in the business."

Now, together with David Cooperrider, an associate professor at Case Western Reserve University's Weatherhead School of Management, Roadway is bringing that premise to life on the loading dock. Using appreciative inquiry, the trucking giant has begun to engage its heavily unionized workforce in ways that hardly seemed possible just five years ago.

At the Akron terminal, that engagement began in January. A steering committee of workers from across the facility was put together to plan an offsite meeting aimed at setting a course for the future. Their first task was to decide who among the terminal's 687 employees would be invited to attend. The goal was to create a microcosm of the company, with workers from all departments and all functions and with varying degrees of empathy for Roadway's corporate objectives.

A few weeks later, 88 employees gathered at a local Holiday Inn for the three-day offsite conference. Then Cooperrider posed his first challenge: "Talk about a time when you felt the most alive, the most engaged, in your job at Roadway." The wording was purely intentional—a signal that this wasn't going to be the usual management–labor gripe session. Cooperrider's second challenge fed off the first: "Imagine that you've woken up after being asleep for five years. What would you want Roadway to look like?"

When participants paired off to discuss their responses, they made a surprising discovery. "It didn't matter what your job was," says John Duncan, 57, who has been a Roadway driver for 24 years. "Everyone wanted the same things." Things such as sustained growth, happy customers, and job security. In short, all of these employees wanted to win.

Over the next three days, the summit participants moved from mission to plan. They drew an "opportunity map" of needs and priorities, and voted on which ones were most pressing. Then they organized into seven action teams. One group would address the trust gap between management and the union. Another would devise strategies to turn drivers—the Roadway employees who have the most contact with the company's customers—into de facto sales reps. Other teams would address employee communications, performance measurement and monitoring, and education.

movement. However, by encouraging people to develop a shared view of what is wrong or what is needed, an initial commitment to change is more likely to be established and mobilized.

Peter Vaill has presented a convincing application of complexity theory and argues that no high-level manager can see what is happening with lower-level changes while they are occurring, and that these can only be seen in hindsight.[17] So what managers need to do is step back and allow frontline employees to handle the changes as quickly and as effectively as possible while giving them the support they need. This is difficult for many managers who feel that their job is to control all facets of work. The great manager realizes that he or she needs to contract closely with the employers and supervisors who are dealing with the problems on a day-to-day basis.

While the term **contracting** is often used to refer to an external vendor or consultant, it actually carries a much broader meaning. The idea is to get those connected to the change involved in doing a **gap analysis** together. That is, where are we now and where do we want to be? The more transparent (not hidden or kept secret) you make all information pertaining to the change and involve those who will be connected with the change, the better the chance for success.

Smart change agents also work to clarify their *own* role in the change process. That is, situations differ in their need for direct or supportive change consultation. Author Ed Schein has suggested the change agent role can vary from being a **"pair of hands"** (using your expertise to fix the problem yourself) to enacting a **doctor–patient relationship** (providing the diagnosis and recommended treatment) to acting as a **process consultant** (serving more as an advisor/facilitator of the process). The appropriate role will differ depending on the circumstances, of course, but assume people will be curious about your agenda and your role as change agent. So the more you are able to communicate this information to them, the more people will feel comfortable with the process and, again, will be more likely to embrace and commit to making the change.

As you may recall from the chapter on problem solving (Chapter 3), a recurring trap is to solve the *wrong* problem precisely. So, before you embark on setting goals and intervening, first connect with the key players to (1) understand their perspective on the problem(s), and (2) lay the groundwork for getting their commitment in finding a solution. Further, clarify your role and interest in the change and how you are personally involved and committed to seeing it through. See Management Live 14.3 for important issues related to the early stages of any consulting project.

> *"A big problem with both parents and managers is that they want to judge before they understand."*
>
> —Unknown

⇄ MANAGEMENT LIVE 14.3

Robert Schaffer's Five Fatal Flaws of Consulting

In many ways, the role of change agent can be likened to being an "internal consultant." A good consultant works with a client to frame a problem and gathers data to diagnose situations and propose potential solutions. Author Robert Schaffer, whose writings on change are among the most widely reprinted articles in *Harvard Business Review*, suggests the reason many change/consulting relationships fail can be traced to five fatal flaws. Of course, not every project is marked by all five flaws, but even a few can block the path to success.

- Projects are defined by the work to be done, not the *change results* to be achieved.
- The scope of the project ignores readiness to implement.
- Projects aim for one big solution rather than incremental small wins.
- Projects entail a sharp division of responsibility between client and consultant and little room for partnership.
- Projects make labor-intensive use of consultants rather than leveraged use, whereby the targets of change can become self-dependent.

By actively reversing each of the five flaws of conventional practice, Schaffer suggests that change initiatives can be set up to succeed, rather than fail, and are far more likely to truly reach the objectives for which they were designed.

Source: Schaffer, R. H. (2002). *High-impact consulting: How clients and consultants can work together to achieve extraordinary results.* San Francisco: Jossey-Bass.

Externalizing the Threat/Enemy

Any significant change effort will inevitably involve resistance. But one way to almost surely create *more* resistance is to frame the problem as caused from *within*. That is, if the motivation for the change is perceived as being the result of internal incompetence or negligence (for instance, by current staff or managers), then the change will almost certainly encounter defensive backlash from those very groups who will feel attacked and therefore look to undermine any change. So smart change agents attempt to *externalize* the enemy or threat—that is, provide an externally caused need for change. Good candidates for external enemies are competitors, market forces, rapid environmental shifts, government and regulation, higher customer demands, and simply "changing times."

If you really want to mobilize commitment, you need to be focused on an external enemy such as unforeseen competition. If together you are fighting an external threat, you have a much better chance of uniting and getting behind a change. Note that the root cause of the problem may very well be an internal issue or multiple issues. But getting people to rally early on in the process can help galvanize their attention toward ultimately solving the real issue at hand.

Defining Goals in Terms of Results Instead of Activities

Presuming you structure the problem and get the right people involved with energy to make change, the next key is to establish a set of measurable objectives. While that may seem obvious, it is often (if not usually) violated in the initiation of change projects. Change projects are too often defined in terms of activity or actions to be taken, and not in terms of specific outcomes or results to be achieved. Of course, the assumption always is that the activities will translate into the desired results. But that is only an assumption; it is rarely part of the formal framing of a change or contract. Indeed, making measurable results the primary immediate goal of a change project is one of the most important elements of successful change.[18]

The value of results-oriented goals is threefold:

1. They lead to more direct and urgent strategy development (How do we most directly and quickly achieve those goals?).
2. They lend themselves to more objective and meaningful evaluation and measurement (What has worked and not worked?).
3. They promote accountability and produce a healthy culture of ownership among those involved.

Not incidentally, achieving and celebrating real value-added outcomes is rewarding and often fun. When the goals are in terms of outcomes, you can take aim from the very first moment at achieving tangible results—not just programs, reports, or a set of recommendations.

Even with a focus toward the measurable, a second trap is to think solely of a *singular* goal. However, recent research has begun to demonstrate the value of a **balanced scorecard,** which argues for developing goals around *multiple* factors.[19] A balanced scorecard approach is based on the notion that a single goal may often be insufficient to truly assess the impact of an initiative. So, if you have a change project designed to get at a sales problem, then the goals might be in terms of sales performance, customer satisfaction, new accounts generated, and salesperson product knowledge (a balanced scorecard used by Southwest Airlines is show in Figure 14.6). If your change involves cost-cutting and budget savings, then goals might be in terms of dollars saved, budget efficiency, process

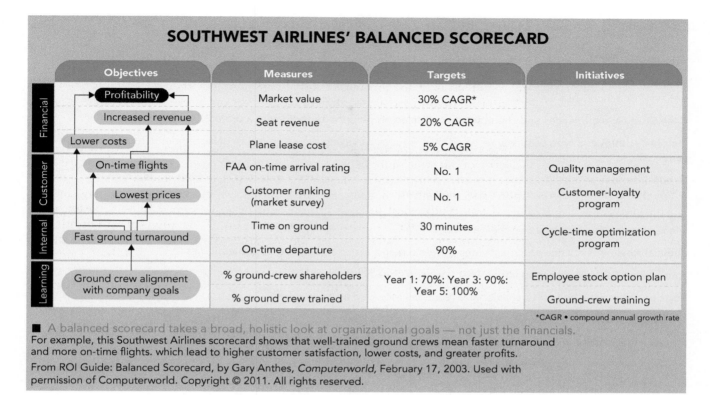

SOUTHWEST AIRLINES' BALANCED SCORECARD

	Objectives	Measures	Targets	Initiatives
Financial	Profitability	Market value	30% CAGR*	
	Increased revenue	Seat revenue	20% CAGR	
	Lower costs	Plane lease cost	5% CAGR	
Customer	On-time flights	FAA on-time arrival rating	No. 1	Quality management
	Lowest prices	Customer ranking (market survey)	No. 1	Customer-loyalty program
Internal	Fast ground turnaround	Time on ground	30 minutes	Cycle-time optimization program
		On-time departure	90%	
Learning	Ground crew alignment with company goals	% ground-crew shareholders	Year 1: 70%: Year 3: 90%: Year 5: 100%	Employee stock option plan
		% ground crew trained		Ground-crew training

*CAGR • compound annual growth rate

■ A balanced scorecard takes a broad, holistic look at organizational goals — not just the financials. For example, this Southwest Airlines scorecard shows that well-trained ground crews mean faster turnaround and more on-time flights. which lead to higher customer satisfaction, lower costs, and greater profits.

From ROI Guide: Balanced Scorecard, by Gary Anthes, *Computerworld,* February 17, 2003. Used with permission of Computerworld. Copyright © 2011. All rights reserved.

FIGURE 14.6
Southwest Airlines'
Balanced Scorecard

steps reduced, and so on. If your problem is declining membership in some unit, then the goals should be built around membership totals, new contacts made, and so on.

The common trap here would be to establish objectives that point to a new ordering or inventory system, a new commission structure for staff, or a new supplier selection process. Those may well be *paths* to results goals but, by themselves, these are activities, not results.

"First seek to understand, then to be understood."

—Stephen Covey

Collecting Data and Providing Feedback

KO **14-3**

DO **14-3**

DO **14-4**

Once we have structured the problem and contracted to determine our own role and that of others, it is important to collect information that will help determine what intervention or activities will be most likely to achieve the goals set and make effective change occur. One way to focus the diagnosis is to ask, "Where is the real pain we want to address?" The challenge is to look beyond the symptoms and identify the root issues that need to be targeted.

Different Methods of Collection

Numerous methods can be employed to collect information (as evidenced by the sampling of methods contained in Table 14.1). Even though there are a large variety of options available, it is usually preferable to use more than one method to obtain multiple data points or perspectives. This provides a sense of consensus that is impossible to have with only one method and makes gaining buy-in easier because the results are less subject to disagreement.

TABLE 14.1   Examples of Different Data Collection Methods

Advisory or Advocate Teams: ideas and viewpoints of selected persons.

Behavior Observation Checklist: a list of behaviors or actions among participants being observed. A tally is kept for each behavior or action observed.

Case Studies: experiences and characteristics of selected persons involved with a project.

Delphi Technique: a type of survey research that requires surveying the same group of respondents repeatedly on the same issue in order to reach a consensus.

Group Interviews: small groups' responses, opinions, and views generally collected in an open-ended format allowing the respondents to elaborate on their answers.

Individual Interviews: individual's responses, opinions, and views generally collected in an open-ended format allowing the respondents to elaborate on their answers.

Judicial Review: evidence about activities is weighed and assessed by a jury of professionals.

Knowledge Tests: information about what a person already knows or has learned.

Logs or Journals: a person's behavior and reactions recorded as a narrative.

Opinion Surveys: an assessment of how a person or group feels about a particular issue.

Panels, Hearings: opinions and ideas presented and elaborated upon in a structured discussion.

Performance Tests: testing the ability to perform or master a particular skill.

Physical Evidence: residues or other physical by-products are observed.

Q-sorts: a rank order procedure for sorting groups of objects. Participants sort cards that represent a particular topic into different piles that represent a series of categories to logically organize the results.

Questionnaire: a collection of questions that people generally respond to in writing.

Records: information from records, files, or receipts.

Self-Ratings: a method used by participants to rate their own performance, knowledge, or attitudes.

Simulations: observations of a person's behavior in simulated settings.

Time Series: measuring a single variable consistently over time (for instance, daily, weekly, monthly, annually).

Wear and Tear: measuring the apparent wear or accumulation on physical objects, such as a display or exhibit.

In most change settings, a multimethod approach will usually include interviews (conducted in either an individual or group setting) and some type of survey or questionnaire. Interviews offer many advantages such as gaining a wide range of information while simultaneously building a relationship with the interviewees. The people interviewed generally are those likely to be involved in the change process, and thus the change agent can spend time during the interview explaining his or her approach, which begins the necessary unfreezing process.

However, interviews also have their challenges and drawbacks. For example, arranging and conducting interviews can take a great deal of time, and the process itself can lead to bias and selective information. Therefore, although the interview is generally the starting point of data collection for most change, change agents should keep an eye toward using some of the other methods described in Table 14.1 to make sure their observations are collaborated by more than one method.

Understanding Before You Judge

A common postmortem observation of failed change initiatives is that the change agents were *quick to judge* but slow to really *understand* the context of their change. To keep you aware of that common oversight, we next describe some of the best approaches for getting a more thorough and actionable diagnosis.

- **Find out who benefits from the current situation.**[20] Rare is the change that does not create some "loser" (or at least a *perceived* loser) in the process. Such people can be the turning point for your change, so try to first understand who is going to *lose* the most from your proposal.

- **Write down everything you do *not* know.**[21] Ed Schein has proposed that one good way to stimulate good diagnosis and learning is to formally write down everything you really do *not* know about how a system or process works. Authentic inquiry and experience can significantly enhance the chance of a collaborative relationship with others and slow down a premature diagnosis when making transitions.

- **Use appreciative inquiry.** As discussed earlier in the chapter, appreciative inquiry involves looking for what is *right* and effective in any system.[22,23] As its name suggests, it is based on discovering the *best* of what works in an organizational context. Too often, attempts to introduce change send a signal that those involved have failed or that prior incompetence led to the need for change (that is, internalizing rather than externalizing the enemy). Appreciative inquiry seeks to highlight what is right and working and thereby avoid a strictly negative tone and emphasis on weaknesses. Appreciative inquiry recognizes that people are most motivated by their own stories of success and tries to use that to spur commitment to make something new, better, or more productive in the organization.

- **Discuss the undiscussables.** Author Roger Schwartz[24] has observed that change agents often choose not to discuss the most critical problems and issues because they seem delicate, political, or otherwise problematic. They reason that to raise such issues would only make some people feel embarrassed or defensive and to discuss them would not be sensitive or compassionate. The unfortunate result, however, is to overlook the *uncompassionate* consequences created by *not* raising undiscussables and a resulting failure to address the biggest obstacles to change. To raise an undiscussable issue with compassion for others and yourself, try using the following approach suggested by Schwartz: "I want to share some observations and raise what may be an undiscussable issue. I am not raising it to put people on the spot, but to see if there is an unaddressed issue that is preventing us from being as effective as we want to be. Here's what I've observed . . ."

Providing Feedback

A key change tool in the data collection process is to provide feedback of any information gathered. Feedback is an attempt to heighten awareness and build urgency for change. Energy created by feedback comes from two sources: the process and content. As noted earlier, people can be energized when they are involved, and when they see a gap between a current and a desired state. Probably the most important aspect of data feedback is to "get the system into the room."[25] That is, if there are people directly associated with the data, then these individuals should be present. In addition, if the group is to build their own capacity for solving problems, individuals who have the power to make decisions and affect change need to be present.

You always need to be aware, however, that people will bring various feelings into a feedback meeting. For example, there may be anxiety and defensiveness as well as hope that true change will occur. The key point is that if you are going to collect information in your organization, then you need to plan how you will feed that information back and to whom.

How to Present Data

While there are many thoughts about how to best present data, Peter Block's *Flawless Consulting*[26] approach is considered to be a best practice. Because of this, we will briefly explain his approach and then provide a detailed agenda explaining how to do it.

According to Block, it is vital to remember the purpose of presenting data in the first place. All too often, presenters become fascinated with the data and like to hear themselves speak. When data are being presented, too many people have the idea that "more is better" and that by drowning people in data they will show everyone how knowledgeable they are about a subject. The real point, however, is to focus attention on a manageable number of dimensions. So keep the feedback to 10 or fewer issues.

Once the number of areas has been defined, remember that the presentation does not have to be complete. By leaving areas for the audience to question, it allows the members to participate in the analysis. Remember that participation is key because you need their action to make the changes that will ultimately be needed. As a consequence of this, the final report should emphasize the role of the members, and not the role of the presenter. In cases of data feedback, the story is about the audience and the actions they are going to take in the future, not about the speaker.

With the understanding of presenting a focused message and that the purpose is to build commitment and buy-in on the part of the audience, the form of the feedback meeting can be set in a very specific manner. While it may sound kind of strange, to run an effective feedback session, there is a rather precise formula and it should be done in 60 minutes. A 60-minute time frame makes sure that the meeting "moves along" and that the group has time to ask questions, and so on. When meetings go too long, attention will wander and a great deal of momentum may be lost. To see the exact format of how to manage a feedback meeting, see Table 14.2.

TABLE 14.2   Feedback Meeting Agenda

Steps	Beginning	End
1. Restate the contract	The beginning	
2. State the structure of the meeting		3rd minute
3. Present diagnosis	4th minute	
4. Present recommendations		12th minute
5. Ask for client reactions	13th minute	30th minute
6. Halfway through the meeting, ask the client "Are you getting what you want?"	31st minute	
7. Decision to proceed		36th minute
8. Test for concerns of control and commitment	37th minute	54th minute
9. Ask yourself if you got what you wanted	55th minute	
10. Give support to the group		60th minute

Diagnosing Change Readiness

The best change in the world is only valuable if the targets of change are ready to accept, implement, and sustain it. Robert Schaffer uses the example of a home furnishing consultant who redesigned a family closet with new fixtures and organization schemes.[27] The family loved it and the project was deemed a smashing success, but a few weeks later the closet was just as messy as before the change. The problem was the family had not contributed to the solution and was not ready to sustain it. This example illustrates the importance of Lewin's notion of first *unfreezing* prior to any intervention.

Independent of the appropriateness of any change, the chance of success will be heavily influenced by what the targets of change are actually ready and able to do. Several researchers have pointed to the importance of a "felt need" or overt desire to make a change.[28] In the treatment of obesity and addictive behaviors, for example, it is well known that those patients who accept personal ownership of the problem ("I am Tim and I have a serious eating problem") and an overt desire to improve their condition are far more likely to actually succeed in a change than those without such a felt need. In organizational contexts, one element of readiness testing is an identification of the level of felt need among the people whose approval or cooperation will be essential for success. Other elements include the level of perceived support from management for the change and the existing cynicism regarding prior change initiatives (discussed in some detail in the section on managing resistance that follows). Often the readiness is higher if a change can be framed in terms of a small scope and a quick start.

Put simply, you want to be sure you do not embark on a well-intentioned change effort that is destined to fail. As discussed earlier, a force field analysis is a form of readiness assessment that focuses on finding and reducing forces leading to complacency and discovering whether people involved in a change will be sufficiently ready to carry it out. Common sources of complacency include an absence of urgency, measurement of the wrong performance indices, lack of feedback from external sources, a denial of problems, and too much conformity and acceptance of low-performance norms (also known as "happy talk").

Looking for Small Wins to Generate Momentum

A natural tendency in any change context is to think big and aim for a comprehensive solution to an identified problem. Once a need or problem is defined, most of us like to think in terms of a complete remedy. Why not fully solve the problem once we have identified it? However, it is short-term gains and highly visible rapid changes that will help embed the change and gather momentum. In other words, the big solution will often take so long that people will lose track of the solution. By proceeding with changes in smaller, more definable units, people have the chance to see progress, know why something happened, and then turn their attention to making more changes. So do not think solely of big gains and wide scope. Aim for small gains and short-term wins.

Implementing Interventions   KO **14-4**

Once we have a feel for our scope, goals, and rationale, the next step is to actually execute the alternatives that have the most potential to create the change we desire. When attempting to address some organizational problem, a change agent might reasonably ask, "What are my options?" or "What are the different things I might do to address any particular problem?"

"Anything not worth doing is not worth doing well."
—Unknown

"We do not have to change, because staying in business is not compulsory."
—W. Edwards Deming

Practice this!
Go to www.baldwin2e.com

Types of Interventions

Of course, an infinite number of specific change activities might be selected. However, work in the **organizational development** field has synthesized the types of change interventions into four distinct categories that can provide a good menu or starting point for the type of intervention you might undertake.[29]

Strategic

Strategic interventions might involve organization structure, reporting relationships, target markets and customers, and new product or service introductions.

- **Cultural Change.** Cultural change attempts to radically and fundamentally change the culture of an organization by changing the basic values, norms, and beliefs of its members. The goal is to improve organizational performance, but it should be evident that this is not a short-term effort. Cultural change needs to be measured in years, not weeks or months.
- **Open Systems Planning.** Open systems are largely influenced by the work of Peter Senge and his book *The Fifth Discipline.* A high-functioning system uses ongoing feedback among its pieces to keep everything in alignment and focused on achieving the overall goal of the larger system (this is usually the company). If any parts in the system become misaligned, the system adjusts to more effectively achieve its goals. The McKinsey 7S model is an example of an open systems approach to change.
- **Organizational Alliances.** Organizational alliances normally involve the coming together of two or more firms to create a new organizational entity (such as a joint venture), in which each company keeps its own identity. An example of an organizational alliance was NUMMI, where General Motors and Toyota developed automobiles together in California. The most common purpose of this type of alliance is to achieve joint strategic goals, to reduce risk, and to leverage resources for increased payoffs. These are particularly common when attempting to do business in a new market for a company (for example, many American companies have formed organizational alliances with companies in China and India).
- **Strategic Planning.** While there are many different versions of it, strategic planning is a process to help determine (1) where an organization is going over the next year or more; (2) how it's going to get there; and (3) how it'll know if it got there or not. The focus of a strategic plan is usually on the entire organization.

Social and Human Resources

Social and human resource interventions deal with culture, teamwork, selection, performance evaluation, training, and rewards. The focus is on how people communicate, solve problems, and are selected, trained, and rewarded.

- **Employee Assistance Programs.** These are support services that identify and resolve the concerns of employees that may affect performance. The specific services included in these programs vary widely, but commonly involve support for staff during periods of intensive change, counseling to tackle the problem of stress, returns to work, and eldercare initiatives. These programs normally also contain some type of provision to help employees with drug or alcohol problems.
- **Personal Coaching.** Coaching is a relationship between a client and a coach. It is based on the client's expressed interests, goals, and objectives. Personal coaching is a learning process where the coach uses inquiry, reflection, requests, and discussion to help clients identify personal and/or

business and/or relationship goals and develop strategies, relationships, and action plans intended to achieve those goals. A coach provides a place for clients to be held accountable to themselves by monitoring the clients' progress toward implementation of their action plans.

- **Mentoring.** Mentoring refers to a developmental relationship between a more experienced person (for instance, the mentor) and a less experienced partner (the mentee). Through ongoing personal exchanges, the mentee relies on the mentor's guidance to develop skills, perspective, and experience. Mentoring exists in many forms: formal or informal, group or one-to-one, structured or unstructured.

- **Self-Directed Work Teams.** Self-directed work teams represent an approach to organizational design that goes well beyond problem-solving teams. These teams are in-place work groups that work together to perform a function or produce a product or service. Self-directed work teams not only do the work but also take on the management of that work—functions formerly performed by supervisors and managers.

- **Team Building.** Team building refers to a wide range of activities for improving the performance of a team. These activities can range from relatively simple activities to complex simulations and multi-day team building retreats. Team building's focus is in bringing out the best in a team to ensure self-development, positive communication, leadership skills, and the ability to work closely together as a team to problem solve.

Structural

Structural interventions deal with changes in work area configurations, work-flow design, the division of labor, and so on. Some specific examples of these interventions include:

- **Balanced Scorecards.** The balanced scorecard is a tool that focuses on various overall performance indicators, often including customer perspective, internal-business processes, and learning and growth and financials, to monitor progress toward an organization's strategic goals. Each business unit throughout the company establishes its own scorecard which, in turn, is integrated with the scorecards of other units to achieve the scorecard of the overall organization.

- **Business Process Reengineering.** This approach intends to improve corporate performance by redesigning the organization's structures and processes, including, when necessary, by starting over and designing the organization from the ground up.

- **Downsizing.** When done correctly, downsizing focuses on making strategic cuts in certain areas that are not critical to the core operations of the organization. These reductions need to be consistent with an overall strategic plan and are intended to spur future growth, rather than acting as an attempt to "cut your way" to improved effectiveness.

- **Outsourcing.** Outsourcing involves a third party to carry out some tasks previously done by employees of the company. When done correctly, outsourcing allows companies to focus on key business issues while having the details taken care of by outside experts. This means that a large amount of resources and attention, which might fall on the shoulders of management professionals, can be used for more important activities that add increased value for the company.

- **Management by Objectives (MBO).** MBO attempts to improve corporate organizational performance by aligning individual and corporate goals throughout the organization. Ideally, employees negotiate their objectives with their supervisors so that maximum participation exists throughout the system. MBO includes ongoing tracking and feedback throughout the process to reach the agreed-upon objectives.

- **Organizing Tasks, Jobs, and Roles.** The most common form of structural organizing is done through job design. By conducting job analyses, the tasks performed by specific people can be reorganized to better support the overall objectives of the company while simultaneously creating more motivating work, as described in Chapter 6.

Technological

Technological interventions deal with tools, equipment and machinery, and computing systems.

- **ISO.** ISO is an internationally recognized standard of quality, and includes guidelines to accomplish the ISO quality standard. Organizations can be optionally audited to earn ISO9000, ISO9001, and related certifications.

- **Ergonomics.** Ergonomics is an entire field by itself. The goal of ergonomics in the workplace is to create safe facilities and designs that are comfortable to use by people at work and that contribute to comfort, efficiency, safety, and ease of use. A great deal of attention has been paid to the ergonomic design of desks, chairs, and computer equipment in recent years.

- **Six Sigma.** Six Sigma is a rigorous and systematic methodology that utilizes information (management by facts) and statistical analysis to measure and improve a company's operational performance, practices, and systems by identifying and preventing "defects" in manufacturing and service-related processes in order to anticipate and exceed expectations of all stakeholders to accomplish effectiveness. True Six Sigma refers to under 3.4 defects per million opportunities. So, if McDonald's was operating at Six Sigma quality with its French fries, this would mean that no more than three French fries out of a million would be burned!

- **Total Quality Management.** Pioneered by W. Edwards Deming, the basis of TQM is to reduce the errors produced during the manufacturing or service process. Total quality management is often associated with the development, deployment, and maintenance of organizational systems that are required for various business processes. The main difference between TQM and Six Sigma (which is a newer concept) is the approach. TQM tries to improve quality by ensuring conformance to internal requirements, while Six Sigma focuses on improving quality by reducing the number of defects throughout the process.

Obviously, there are an almost infinite number of things you might do in pursuit of change. The importance of the preceding categorization is that it helps structure decisions about what type of intervention to undertake in a concise and meaningful way. Depending on the nature of the organizational challenge, the resources you have at your disposal, and the scope of the effort, different interventions will be appropriate. Perhaps most importantly, many organizational challenges are likely to be solved using a combination of intervention types. The key then is to select a set of interventions and aim to ensure they are consistent and fit together. Interventions must be selected and coordinated carefully, since either an inappropriate intervention or the lack of consistent interventions (where they end up working against each other) will doom the effort.

Remember that the interventions presented here are only a small sample of the interventions available. We encourage you to do further research in this area to learn more about the intervention(s) that may be of most use to you. Trying to cover all of the interventions is well beyond the scope of the present text, but in providing you with a simple explanation, we hope to give you some initial guidance in the use of an appropriate intervention.

Framing, Reframing, and Selecting Interventions

Another useful model for thinking about change interventions is the **four frames model** developed by authors Lee Bolman and Terrence Deal.[30] They suggest that four frames exist in every kind of organization: structural, human resource, political, and symbolic. The four frames can be respectively likened to factories, families, jungles, and theaters or temples.

- The *structural frame* (factory) relates to how to organize and structure groups and teams to get results.
- The *human resource frame* (family) concerns how to tailor organizations to satisfy human needs, improve human resource management, and build positive interpersonal and group dynamics.
- The *political frame* (jungle) deals with how to cope with power and conflict, build coalitions, hone political skills, and deal with internal and external politics.
- The *symbolic frame* (theater or temple) focuses on how to shape a culture that gives purpose and meaning to work, to stage organizational drama for internal and external audiences, and to build team spirit through ritual, ceremony, and story.

Bolman and Deal suggest frames are tools that can help change agents identify the various options inherent in any situation. Their most powerful prescription is that of **reframing,** which means simply to explore organizational issues through multiple lenses or frames and to use those frames to uncover new opportunities and options in confusing or ambiguous situations.

Looking at situations through more than one frame can help you choose among different alternative approaches and not get mired or narrowly focused on a single frame that may seem intuitive or reflect solely your own personal style or orientation. Using multiple frames has been shown to lead to better decision making and fewer dysfunctional change efforts.[31] Conversely, the failure to see the world through more than one frame has been associated with many well-documented and notorious organizational blunders.[32]

To illustrate, suppose our focal organizational problem was the high student dropout rate at our university. The structural frame would lead us to investigate our current systems for helping struggling students and the efficiency of the existing bureaucracy. Questions asked might include: What is currently in place for students to get help? How easily can we identify and reach struggling students before it is too late?

A human resource frame would focus on the *students* themselves and the ways in which they are admitted into the university and graded and developed while they are on campus. Within that frame we might be interested in how students create support groups, find their identity on campus, and connect with others in the campus community.

A political frame would direct the focus toward the university culture and who really "owns" the problem of student dropouts. We might explore the reward system for faculty and others and even the *disincentives* to keep students in school (for example, a more elite student population, less remedial instruction, more time for research and consulting). How might different groups work together to help address the problem and what would be the rewards and incentives for doing so?

A symbolic frame would explore perceptions of how we label and discuss "at risk" students and the sense of embarrassment associated with needing help. How might we reduce some of the stigma attached to those needing remedial instruction and create a more inviting environment for those who need help so they will proactively seek it?

Focusing on the different frames makes it possible to reframe—that is, view—the same problem or challenge from multiple perspectives and avoid the quick intuitive calls that are often superficial and uninformed. When the world seems confusing and it is difficult to decide what to do, reframing is a powerful tool for gaining clarity, generating new options, and finding strategies that work.

The central enduring point is no one type of intervention or change approach is clearly best. The best intervention depends on the situation because interventions are not one-size-fits-all. The challenge, therefore, is to have one or more frameworks that help you generate and explore the range of options open to you. Both the typology of organizational development interventions and Bolman and Deal's four frames model are time-tested tools that are useful in that regard.

Communicating What You Are Doing

"There is no one best way. But all ways are not equally effective."
—Jay Galbraith

The mantra of successful real estate people is location, location, location. The analogous axiom for change agents should be communicate, communicate, communicate! Whatever you decide to do, a critical factor in your success will be how well you are able to communicate the whys and whats of your change intervention as clearly and as often, and in as many different ways, as you can. The best change agents think in terms of multimedia and use targeted communication. That is, an overall e-mail or memo is unlikely to successfully communicate your message. Rather, think of how you can really reach the targets of your change, authentically address their most frequently asked questions, and identify and leverage key people who might most effectively communicate your message (see Management Live 14.4).

MANAGEMENT LIVE 14.4

The Law of the Few: Finding Your Communication Champions

It is well known that one critical element in the communication of any message is the nature of the *messenger*. In his bestselling book, *The Tipping Point*, author Malcolm Gladwell makes a compelling case for the "law of the few," which refers to the reality that it is just a select few individuals who create epidemics and rapid societal changes. The key is to find those exceptional people or *senders* who are capable of starting epidemics. Gladwell specifically identifies three distinct types of senders, which he labels *connectors*, *mavens*, and *salespeople*. Connectors are people who know lots of people and have a particular knack of making friends and social connections. They have a link to many different worlds and an ability to bring them together. Mavens are information specialists who like to figure things out and, once they do, want to tell others about it too. Salespeople are those with the skills to persuade us when we are unconvinced of what we are hearing. From the perspective of a change agent, the lesson is that your biggest impact will come from concentrating your time and resources on connectors, mavens, and salespeople. Who are those people in your context and how do you find and energize them on behalf of the change you seek?

Source: Gladwell, M. (2000). *The tipping point: How little things can make a big difference.* New York: Little Brown.

Overcoming Resistance to Change

No matter how well planned your change efforts, you can't avoid resisters. Resistance is an inevitable reality of change management, and for any significant change there will be naysayers, cynics, victims, and people who will dig in their heels and push back. It is tempting to view opposition as being strictly negative and those resisting change as troublemakers or bad apples who need to be removed. However, we have been careful here not to talk about *eliminating* resistance but overcoming or managing it. There can, of course, be legitimate reasons to resist change efforts. For example, proposed changes may not be well directed and thus not worthy of support. Moreover, even when change is warranted, resisters can provide some of the best information for how to frame, communicate, and modify change initiatives for the better.

Resistance to change can come about for many reasons (see Table 14.3). However, resistance is usually related to uncertainty about the effects of the proposed changes or experience with previous changes that have failed. We all enjoy the comfort of established routines; therefore, any change in approach or scope can be disruptive and make us less productive and insecure in our activities. In general, resistance can be traced to people (1) not fully understanding the change or need for it ("I don't know what I will have to do"), (2) fearing they will not be able to thrive in the new changed reality ("I don't think I can do it"), or (3) not seeing any sufficiently rewarding or punishing consequences linked to the change ("What's in it for me?"). As one of our colleagues reminds us, people don't resist the change itself as much as they resist the threat of *being* changed.

"People do not resist change, they resist being changed."

—Unknown

"It's not like we don't know it's bad for us. It's written all over the can."

—B. J. Schumacher, a 23-year-old bull rider who was very upset over a decision that prohibited tobacco companies from handing out free samples of snuff to contestants

Accelerating Change, Reducing Opposition

Urgency—But Not Fear. It has become popular in discussions of change resistance to talk about "burning platforms" that force people to jump away from their comfortable positions. Burning platforms can work, but they can also create a panic that prevents action. Unless fear is converted to a positive urgency and with some speed, it can create a source of resistance rather

TABLE 14.3 Why People Resist Change

- **Loss of Control.** Individuals feel change is being done to them rather than done with or by them.

- **Loss of Face.** Changes being suggested can result in people losing face or status.

- **Loss of Identity.** People who build an identity around their role do not like any loss of symbols, tradition, or status.

- **Loss of Competence.** People do not like having their competence challenged by being put into situations where they lack the necessary competencies.

- **Excessive Personal Uncertainty.** The individual is not aware or is uncertain of how the changes will affect him or her.

- **More Work.** Change often brings fear of additional work for those involved.

- **Unintended Consequences.** Change in one area often has unintended effects in another.

than an impetus for action. With too much fear, some people will focus on the immediate source of anxiety and nothing else. Some will freeze, hide, or become self-protective. Fear can produce movement, but it is not the best sustaining force. It is urgency that sustains change; you do not want self-preservation as the No. 1 goal.[33]

In today's competitive organizational cultures, the reality is that organizations not only want and need to make change but want to accelerate the change process. A common situation facing managers is the need to bring about "big change fast." As Lewin noted, it may often be more productive to explore and seek to counter the resisting forces than it is to create a wave of momentum in favor of the change. Indeed, your best hope of accelerating the change process probably lies in the success of strategies to overcome resistance and several factors will affect the choice of how best to overcome resistance. Part of the skill of a change agent is recognizing the appropriate strategies to employ. Some common factors should influence the choice of these including:

> *The urgency of the need for change.* The stronger the threat or importance of change, the stronger the case for quick-change strategies.

> *The degree of opposition or resentment.* The more opposition you expect to the changes, the more appropriate are those strategies that involve the largest amount of key people. The rate of change also needs to be considered, as this strategy often takes longer.

> *The power of the individual/group initiating the change.* It may be possible to implement fast change strategies, even if there is opposition, if the individual or group initiating the change is powerful enough.

> *The necessity for information and commitment.* If the change can only be achieved and sustained by commitment and education of those affected (which is very often the case), full involvement in the change is essential.

In the end, the diagnosis of resistance and the effectiveness of strategies to manage it will be among the best predictors of your change success. Do not fear resistance. Resisters often hold a value many change agents never bother to harness. The key is to learn to isolate areas of resistance and then seek to understand them, make use of them, and strategize to most effectively manage and ultimately overcome them.

Strategies for Overcoming Resistance

There are six general strategies for overcoming resistance.[34]

Education and Communication

Coupled with education efforts, in the context of change, some experts have noted it is virtually impossible to *overcommunicate.* Let people know what and why at every opportunity. Some successful change agents post a regular frequently asked question (FAQ) in an attempt to keep people posted. The trap, however, is to focus solely on the frequency of the communication. As such, do not send out the same memo or communication every day assuming you will just pound the message into people's heads. It's the quality of communication that matters more than the frequency. So plan ways to communicate that are varied and tailored to different stakeholder groups.

Participation and Involvement

As emphasized previously, it is far more unlikely, even difficult, for people to resist changes they help bring about themselves. Participation enhances understanding and feelings of control. It also reduces uncertainty and promotes a feeling of ownership.

Facilitation and Support

By accepting people's anxiety as legitimate and appropriate, you have a better chance of gaining the respect and commitment needed to make the change work. When you acknowledge and respond to FAQs, a concern of the month, and other such needs for information, your approach provides people with the sense that their concerns are being heard and attended to. Testimonials from those at the front of the change can also be a powerful influence if used appropriately.

Negotiation and Agreement

Often necessary when dealing with powerful resisters, negotiation and agreement normally involve specific exchanges and incentives in return for a person's or group's agreement to support a change. Examples of this may include providing assurances certain employees will not be laid off as part of a restructuring effort or that a particularly powerful department head will be able to maintain her budget.

Manipulation and Co-optation

Manipulation and co-optation involve selectively using information and implied incentives. The aim—a risky one—is to get the compliance of resistant parties by promising them certain rewards and benefits linked to their "going along with" the change.

Explicit and Implicit Coercion

In some cases, the use of authority and threat of punishment may be necessary. As with manipulation, using coercion is a risky process because people will likely resent forced change. But in some situations speed may be essential and the changes will not be popular regardless of how they are introduced, so coercion is among the only options.

Although these six strategies have been described independently, they are not mutually exclusive, and a range of strategies can be employed to manage resistance. The key is to fully understand the pros and cons of each method and to be aware of your own change situation. Table 14.4 summarizes the six different methods and their advantages and disadvantages.

Managing Organizational Cynicism

In recent years, how people view their relationships with organizations has changed dramatically. Rampant mergers and acquisitions have often resulted in mass layoffs. And though labeled as "right-sizings" or restructurings, such changes have not been well received in the ranks of the workforce. Unethical corporate leadership, greed, and outsourcing have further contributed to employee negativity. Indeed, many employees have become increasingly cynical and the popularity of cartoon strips such as "Dilbert" and television shows such as *The*

TABLE 14.4   Different Approaches to Overcoming Resistance

	Approach	Commonly used when...	Advantages	Disadvantages
1	Education and Communication	There is a lack of information and analysis.	Once persuaded, people will often help implement the change.	Can be very time-consuming if many people are involved.
2	Participation and Involvement	The initiators do not have all the information they need to design the change, and others have considerable power to resist.	People who participate will be committed to implementing change, and any relevant information they have will be integrated into the change plan.	Can be very time-consuming if participants design inappropriate change.
3	Facilitation and Support	People are resisting because of adjustment problems.	No other approach works as well with adjustment problems.	Can be time-consuming and expensive and still fail.
4	Negotiation and Agreement	Some person or group with considerable power to resist will clearly lose out in a change.	It can sometimes be a relatively easy way to avoid major resistance.	Can be too expensive if it alerts others to negotiate for compliance.
5	Manipulation and Co-optation	Other tactics will not work or are too expensive.	It can be a relatively quick and inexpensive solution to resistance problems.	Can lead to future problems if people feel manipulated.
6	Explicit and Implicit Coercion	Speed is essential, and the change initiators possess considerable power.	It is speedy and can overcome any kind of resistance.	Can be risky if it leaves people angry with the initiators.

Source: Reprinted by permission of Harvard Business Review. Excerpt from "Choosing Strategies for Change," by J.P. Kotter and L.A. Schlesinger, March–April 1979. Copyright © 1979 by the Harvard Business School Publishing Corporation; All rights reserved.

Office are further evidence that people may hold rather negative impressions of managers and management.

From the perspective of a change agent, research on **organizational cynicism** has revealed at least three important considerations. First, such cynicism may be entirely rational. That is, a firm may well have a history of dishonesty and unmet promises, and thus resistance to a change effort may be based on past organizational behavior. Second, rational or not, cynicism's existence will heighten resistance. Salaried employees have often been found to be cynical about organizational change, perhaps because they are frequently the population that stands to be most directly affected. Third, cynicism is particularly difficult to overcome if prevalent in the organization's leadership. Cynicism among middle managers, for example, greatly magnifies the challenge of change in an organization.[35]

A cynical environment will make resistance even more pronounced and makes the importance of diagnosing and managing that resistance even greater. That said, some research has shown that cynics are often more deeply concerned about the organization and could, if turned around, make the best change agents.[36]

Evaluating and Sustaining Change Efforts

DO **14-6**

Successful change must have made meaningful progress on the results established at the outset. It is important to do some evaluation to verify success, identify needs for new or continuing activities, and improve your change process itself to help make future interventions more successful.

Any initiated change may produce unforeseen and potentially undesirable side effects in addition to the expected result. Further, change has a ripple effect, in that even a small change in one part of an organization can have effects on individuals and groups in other areas. For this reason, it is critical to get evaluation data from all stakeholders.

Frequently, a successful change can slide back into the past when the new behavior does not become tradition or "the typical way things get done around here." So it is important to remain diligent and attempt to create a new, sufficiently strong support for the change to remain. Do not declare victory too soon, because the resisting forces are always waiting to make a comeback.

Sustaining change is never easy. Peter Block notes that what makes sustaining change so difficult is our natural tendency to believe change can be installed, managed, engineered, and forgotten. That engineering model works well for solving mechanical problems, but is incomplete in trying to change human systems. Change cannot be installed and engineered, and so it always takes longer and is more difficult than people imagine.[37]

The best tool to actually evaluate a change depends upon the goals of the change and the goals of the organization. As a result, this makes the balanced scorecard an excellent technique for assessing what has worked, and what hasn't. Well-constructed balanced scorecards use two different sets of measures to get overall indications of performance. These measures are referred to as "lead measures" and "lag measures."

The problem with most measures of corporate performance is that they let us know how things *went*, not how things are *going to go*. So often, our standard measures of performance (personal sales, corporate earnings, and so on) do a great job of telling us how the last three months were, but are mute when it comes to how the next three months will be. **Lead measures** attempt to solve this problem. Based on a specific balanced scorecard, you may know that the number of hours spent with clients, the advertising dollars spent, and the calls received are all good indicators of future performance. They do not guarantee future profitability, but experience has shown your organization that they are pretty good predictors of performance three months into the future. So, if you can combine good lead measures (proven predictors of future performance) and important **lag measures** (often things like income, sales volume, market share, and so on), this gives you an excellent idea of how the company is really performing—this is the concept of the balanced scorecard.

Well, the same logic can be used for assessing a change. When any change initiative is begun, a series of goals should be identified (for example, reduced turnover, an increased number of new products, and so on). To effectively evaluate any change effort, managers need to refer back to the original goals and then look at the defined lead and lag measures. By paying special attention to the appropriate lead measures, great managers can "correct course" and manage more effectively to increase the chances of reaching the ultimate goal of the initiative. Without assessment, however, we never know whether or not the initiative was effective and we are unable to improve for the future changes, which will undoubtedly be needed.

"When it comes to improvement in processes, the low hanging fruit often keeps growing back."

— Roger Schmenner

Practice this!
Go to www.baldwin2e.com

> CASE CONCLUDED

The ultimate change process at the Indiana BMV stands as something of a blueprint as to how to transform a troubled organizational unit—whether it be a government agency or not. However, it is particularly instructive as a confirmation that substantive and lasting change can be made in nonprofit organizations with a long history of low performance.

What did the leaders of the BMV actually do to engineer such a remarkable turnaround? First, the governor coaxed a highly successful business leader, known for building high-customer-service cultures in the private sector, into taking the job as commissioner of the BMV. That commissioner first sought to fully understand and clarify the challenge and establish a sense of urgency for change. He quickly learned that customers of the agency were clear and consistent in revealing that quick visit times were far and away their top priority.

With that in mind, and following the change maxim that you cannot manage what you do not measure, he established and consistently communicated a set of critical outcomes and metrics that would allow him to measure and monitor progress on those outcomes—particularly related to transaction efficiency and customer satisfaction. A key part of that process was the introduction of a new software program, which ironically had been owned by the BMV for some time, that enabled far more efficient and integrated transaction processing.

The new commissioner recognized that he could not enact such a substantial cultural change alone, so he created mechanisms for associates at all levels to participate in the process. He established an employee council that met monthly with the commissioner and offered many suggestions that ultimately came to light in the agency. Some of those changes included revamping the physical layout of some branches to better process customers quickly, and the installation of cameras in every branch. The cameras had a direct feed to the commissioner's office in Indianapolis so that bottlenecks could be quickly recognized and addressed and outstanding and efficient service could be recognized. The commissioner further created and executed a bonus system to reward the fastest and most effective service associates. And, in the face of brutal political pressure, he even consolidated some branches and replaced those service representatives with the poorest service levels and little desire to improve.

By 2010, the results of the change efforts were impressive by any standard. The BMV now had metrics on over 100 key performance indicators and most had dramatically improved since 2005. For example, the average customer time per transaction had gone from over 40 minutes to under 5! Fraud and error rates were down dramatically and customer satisfaction and employee engagement were way up (remember those two tend to go together). The agency now posts a dashboard of all their key performance outcomes, and it was the sterling performance on those metrics that had earned it national recognition as the best in the country.

Perhaps most importantly, what they ultimately discovered was that the vast majority of people in any organization—even one as seemingly intractable as the BMV— want to work in a place where people care about customers and each other. They want to be fully engaged, take pride in their work, and feel the obligation to continually improve. In other words, just like we found in Chapter 13 with Zappos and others, it turns out that the best BMV associates are eager to work in a high-spirit and high-performance culture. And if you let them, they will even help you create it.

Questions

1. What are some transferable lessons of change that can be drawn from the remarkable transformation of the Indiana BMV?

2. Your text includes an illustration of how using the levers of "schools, media, and police" can be a powerful metaphor for making change. Explain in the context of the Indiana BMV.

3. How did the BMV commissioner try to create "urgency without fear" in this case?

4. Now that the BMV is running so well, what issues do you see in sustaining the change?

5. What common traps often befall organizations that are trying to maintain significant changes in process and culture?

Sources: www.nwitimes.com/news/state-and-regional/illinois/article_ab65d9c9-f809-53ca-931e-73bad2a8cefe.html; www.sagamoreinstitute.org/american-outlook/fall-2010/governing-matters/; www.wthr.com/story/13225281/indiana-bmv-gets-top-honors.

Concluding Note

Stay Focused on the Basics

Throughout this chapter we have presented several different frameworks, models, and charts, which can all become rather bewildering. Change in organizations is a complex process, making it easy to get overwhelmed and frustrated about how to actually proceed. Fortunately, although different writers and professionals certainly have multiple perspectives, the good news is that relatively few core ideas are repeatedly referenced. The following is a Top 10 list of the most fundamental lessons of change:

1. Change only when it is important. Do not change for change's sake.
2. Know your customer. If you don't have one, find one.
3. Seek participation and involvement in both planning and execution.
4. Define your change goals in terms of *results*.
5. Listen to learn about rationales for resistance, rather than getting defensive over them.
6. Make sure people know the *whys* of change.
7. Plan for, seek, and celebrate small wins in the process of change.
8. Communicate often with whatever you know, and in different forms.
9. Find the key champions for your cause.
10. Frequently highlight and discuss the post-change future.

In earlier times, a CEO or a few leaders at the top with a change agenda were enough. But now it takes a company *full* of change agents to really adapt and thrive in a competitive world.[38] There is no reason a young supervisor cannot be an agent of change in the way that hourly employees are treated, a young engineer cannot orchestrate the redesign of a quality control system, or a young restaurant manager can't champion a new way to serve diners. You do not need to be at the top to bring new ideas and enhance your organization. What you do need is an understanding of the process and a little passion to add value to your workplace. *No matter where you are in an organization, just do it.* In the end, the most important elements in your success as a change agent will be your heartfelt belief that change is possible and your motivation to make something happen. The world around you may seem like an entirely immovable place, but it almost never is. Intelligent action can make a difference with the right pushes in the right places. There is an extraordinary need for people who are willing and able to seek positive change in our world. So now go make change!

KEY TERMS

appreciative inquiry 508
balanced scorecard 512
change agent 499
contracting 511
doctor–patient relationship 511
force field analysis 500

four frames model 521
gap analysis 511
Kotter's change model 503
lag measures 527
lead measures 527
model of transitions 501

organizational cynicism 526
organizational development 518
pair of hands 511
process consultant 511
reframing 521
unfreeze-change-refreeze model 499

< < # CASE
Boldly Going Where No Stadium Has Gone Before

The Yankees, still looking for pitching help, detoured on Tuesday into discussions of wireless technology; the convergence of video, Internet, and voice; and killer apps.

None of that will be supplied by the free agent C. C. Sabathia, but by Cisco Systems, the high-tech behemoth, which has wired the new $1.3 billion Yankee Stadium with what it said was the most advanced technology ever embedded in a North American stadium.

"Yankee Stadium will be in a constant state of the artness," Lonn Trost, the team's chief operating officer, told a news conference at Cisco's office across West 33rd Street from Madison Square Garden. "Don't look up that word. It doesn't exist."

John T. Chambers, the passionate salesman who is the chairman of Cisco, offered a cinematic analysis of the company's installation at the new stadium, which he estimated cost $15 million to $16 million and is not part of a sponsorship. "Take the dream of *Star Trek* or other movies," he said in a voice suffused with the influence of his upbringing in West Virginia. "That concept is where we're going to go." He added: "It's going to change all of sports. I don't think I'm too bold in saying that."

The technological prowess acquired by the Yankees includes the ability to program 1,100 flat-panel, high-definition TV monitors with live game coverage, archival and highlight video, statistics, promotional messages, and weather and traffic updates.

The monitors will be located at concession stands, inside the 59 luxury and party suites, around the restaurants and bars, and in restrooms. They are designed to surround fans visually from the moment they walk into the stadium, especially when they stray from a direct view of the field. The team will be its own video puppeteer, controlling all the monitors centrally with the capabilities of offering different content on each one.

Each player will have a computer at his locker and all video instruction has been integrated into the Cisco system.

The luxury suites will be outfitted with special touchscreen phones that will let better-heeled fans order food and merchandise. And Cisco's videoconferencing technology will be installed in the stadium's business conference center, which will let it connect to a library in the Bronx (for students and community groups) and eventually to other locations in the city like hospitals, to let players and executives talk to fans.

"The ultimate fan experience is when Derek Jeter can help some kid in the Bronx learn long division" via videoconferencing, said Ron Ricci, the co-chairman of Cisco's sports and entertainment division, who said he learned arithmetic through baseball.

Ricci and Chambers said that the technology already wired into the stadium would eventually allow fans at the stadium, and at home and beyond, to connect the system's data and video to their home televisions and mobile devices.

"This technology is future proof," Ricci said. "It will be possible, at the next level, that fans at each seat will have an individualized interactive experience, perhaps ordering food and picking it up at the concession stands, most assuredly through your mobile phone."

He added: "I can't emphasize enough how important video is. It's the killer application. It's what fans want to see, to see more angles and do it on their terms." Some elements of the system, which Cisco began installing about two years ago as the stadium was being built, will take a while to be fully functional. Trost said his greatest concern was making sure the stadium opened on time, but insisted that elevating the fan experience— a phrase used repeatedly—was behind the Cisco strategy.

"We can't deliver the same thing every year," Trost said. "We try to deliver winning ballclubs and part of that is bringing in winning partners."

Chambers said that past experience told him he could not be certain how the technology would evolve or how envisioned uses would change over time. "Once you build the architecture," he said, "it's like highways. You can really go wherever you want."

The Yankees have created a technology subsidiary, which seems appropriate.

Trost said his high-tech learning curve ended in the 1960s with his mastery of the mimeograph machine. And Hal Steinbrenner, the Yankees' co-chairman, said of some of Cisco's technology: "I didn't know it existed."

Discussion Questions

1. The New York Yankees are one of the most valuable sports franchises on the planet. Why do they need to worry about change?

2. When dealing with a tradition-based game like baseball, do you think there are changes that the fans would not accept? What would be some examples? What would be some examples of changes that you think could be made, but would be pretty risky to make?

3. Overcoming resistance to change plays a big role in the success of most change initiatives. Identify reasons why resistance could be an issue among fans and then make recommendations as to how these different forms of resistance may be overcome.

Source: Excerpted from Boldly Going Where No Stadium Has Gone Before, *New York Times*, November 12, 2008.

MANAGE WHAT? DEBRIEFS

Converting an Organizational Problem into an Achievable Change Initiative: Debrief

This challenge strikes at the heart of making change—a declining situation with no clear owners of the problem. If you really hope to make a difference, and to be able to proudly cite your accomplishments at the end of the year, your best chance is to take a page from successful change agents who are masterful at (1) structuring problems, (2) contracting with the key parties, and (3) defining goals in terms of results, not activities.

As noted in your text, structuring a change problem involves addressing two fundamental questions:

- Who is (are) the customer(s) of the change?
- What is the scope of change (how broad, how much?)

Unless you explicitly address those questions, and structure the change initiative at the outset, you run the great risk of proceeding without a clear understanding of what you are trying to do or for whom you are doing it.

A second important recognition is that by encouraging people to develop a shared view of what is wrong or what is needed, an initial commitment to change is more likely to be established and mobilized. So try to always start a change by first involving and contracting with others. The more people involved early in the process, the more potential commitment there will be to support the ultimate changes. In this scenario, it would seem essential to meet any returning club officers, probably some of the members, and perhaps some of the other club presidents to get their perspective on running a successful student organization. So, before you embark on setting goals and intervening, it is important to first connect with the key players to (1) understand their perspective on the problem(s), and (2) lay the groundwork for getting their commitment in finding a solution. Further, clarify your role and interest in the change and how you are personally involved and committed to seeing it through.

With respect to problem structuring, about all we know is that our membership is not motivated and attendance at our events has been declining. That is often about as much information as exists in the first stages of change. So what might be our potential courses of change action? A reasonable preliminary list might include:

- Changing the nature, timing, and focus of our events. The business fraternity may not be offering an attractive variety of what the membership base wants.

(continued)

(continued)

- Changing our membership. It may be that we are not seeking or admitting the right member profile or perhaps admitting too few (or too many) new members in a given year.
- Changing our governance structure and/or accountability for results. The group may not be organized in a way that promotes the most directed effort from members or holds people accountable for not meeting commitments.

As you work through the analysis, other ideas will likely surface and the idea is to condense them into the shortest list possible. If you find that there are several additional options that you cannot readily categorize into one of those items, then simply create a new item called "other issues" and move on.

Presuming you structure the problem and get the right people involved with some energy to make change, the next key is to establish a set of measurable objectives. When the goals are in terms of results, you can take aim from the very first moment at achieving some tangible results—not just programs or reports or a set of recommendations. Even with a focus toward the measurable, a second trap is to think solely in terms of a *singular* goal. However, recent research has begun to demonstrate the value of a more "balanced scorecard," which argues for developing goals around *multiple* factors.

Based on the earlier discussion, at this business fraternity it would seem that a set of results goals might include a defined increase in member satisfaction, percentage increases in membership or attendance at key events, and so on. The common trap here would be to establish objectives that point to a new ordering or inventory system or a new commission structure for staff or a new supplier selection process. Those may well be *paths* to results goals but, by themselves, they are *activities* and not results.

Creating Urgency for a Change: Debrief

Raising a feeling of urgency is the first and most critical step in a successful change intervention. In this case, you are trying to "manage up" to get your superiors to see the urgency, so the challenge is particularly daunting. While there are many specific tactics you might try, as a general framework for action a few fundamental strategies should guide your efforts.

First, recognize that reports and spreadsheets are rarely enough to generate real urgency. So, while highlighting declining sales reports and market trends may be part of your approach here, you will need to find illustrations that touch emotion to make managers aware, and perhaps even shock or jolt them. The key is to "find the pain" and the means of getting people to feel that pain more directly. One way to do that is to create dramatic presentations with compelling features that people can actually see and feel. For example, can you get taped or transcribed testimony from a doctor (customer) who is dissatisfied with your product or is switching to the competitor?

Second, you probably do not see yourself as a storyteller, but you will want to become one if you are serious about this change. Considerable evidence suggests that a good story (or stories) can be a critical element in creating urgency for change. In this case, a carefully crafted and chosen story may help you translate the rather general and abstract (our products are slipping) into a meaningful message for others. For example, can you find a story of a similar product decline cycle (from your own firm history or elsewhere) and make it into a short cautionary tale that could happen here? Can you find a champion in the senior management of the firm and partner with him in communicating a story of decline and response to that decline? Seek to find out what your managers are really feeling and target your story directly to their most acute hopes and fears.

Third, if you are serious about getting some real urgency for change you have to find ways to *externalize* the enemy. That is, if the motivation for the change is perceived as being the result of internal incompetence or negligence (on the part of, say, current staff or managers), then the change will almost certainly encounter defensive backlash and defensiveness (from those very groups who will feel attacked and therefore look to undermine any change). So smart change agents attempt to provide an externally caused need for change. Good possibilities for external enemies are competitors, market forces, rapid environmental shifts, government and regulation, higher customer demands, and simply "changing times." Urgency will be killed if any of those that you hope will see the need instead feel that they are being singled out as the cause or reason that the change is required.

Perhaps the biggest trap here would be to create fear rather than urgency. That is, it is now popular in discussions of change resistance to talk about "burning platforms" that force people to jump away from their comfortable positions. Burning platforms can work, but they can also create a panic that *stops* action. Unless fear is converted to a positive urgency, and with some speed, it can create a *source* of resistance rather than an impetus for action. With too much fear, some people will focus on the immediate source of anxiety and nothing else.

Some will freeze or hide or become self-protective. Fear can produce movement but it is not the best sustaining force. Urgency sustains change—you do not want self-preservation as the number one goal.

Finally, remember that urgency will not be felt in the same way by all of your constituents. Put simply, what is urgent to one may not be urgent to another. So think of ways to segment those constituents and vary your messages of urgency accordingly.

Dealing with Change Resisters: Debrief

In this case, and many like it, the reality is that the status quo ("the way that it has always been done") will be very powerful, and thus resistance will almost certainly be substantial, even from among those who may think the change sounds positive. Resistance can come about for many reasons (see Table 14.3); however, it is usually related to uncertainty about the effects of the proposed changes. We all enjoy the comfort of established routines; therefore, any change in approach or scope can be disruptive and make us less productive and secure in our activities. In general, resistance can be traced to these causes: (1) people do not fully understand the change and/or the need for it (illustrated by comments like, "I don't know what I will have to do"); (2) they fear they will not be able to thrive in the new changed reality ("I don't think I can do it"); (3) they do not see any sufficiently rewarding or punishing consequences linked to the change ("What's in it for me"?).

Based on evidence derived from studies of successful and unsuccessful change initiatives, four strategies stand out as a means of getting this new serving process in place and accepted in your restaurant.

Education and Commitment

Even if the consequences of this change are generally perceived as positive, extensive education regarding what will be different will help reduce anxiety and ensure that people understand why it is being done, what will be expected, and how they will be supported and rewarded. Come up with a catchy new name for this new process (for example, "customer-first serving" or some such) and communicate regular briefings and a "Frequently Asked Questions" posting in an attempt to keep people abreast of what is happening and why.

Participation and Involvement

It is far more unlikely, even difficult, for people to resist changes they help bring about themselves. Participation enhances understanding and feelings of control. It also reduces uncertainty and promotes a feeling of ownership. So identify several key champions and actively solicit their support and help in the planning for the change roll-out. Give everyone in the restaurant some opportunity to express their views and offer input. Be clear that such input is a "voice not a vote," but be certain to offer feedback on how such voices were heard and how they informed the decision process.

Facilitation and Support

By accepting people's anxiety as legitimate and appropriate, you have a better chance of gaining the respect and commitment needed to make the change work. When you acknowledge and respond to FAQs, the concern of the month, and so on, it provides people with the sense that their concerns are being heard and attended to. Testimonials from those at the front of the change can be a powerful influence if used appropriately.

Negotiation and Agreement

The cold reality is that when dealing with powerful resisters, it may require specific exchanges and incentives in return for a person's or group's agreement to support a change. Examples of this may include providing assurances that certain employees will not be laid off as part of this effort, or that a certain manager can still utilize a favorite approach with certain customers, or whatever. Change has been likened to guerilla warfare, and successful change agents are on the lookout for compromises and agreements that can remove opposition and accelerate desired changes.

In the end, the diagnosis of resistance and the effectiveness of strategies to manage it will be among the greatest predictors of your change success. Do not fear resistance and do not feel as if it is a necessity to get "everyone" on board. In most cases, it is not necessary and may even be counterproductive to seek complete consensus. In any case, resisters often hold a value that many change agents never bother to exploit. The key is to learn to isolate areas of resistance and then seek to understand it, make use of it, and strategize to most effectively manage and ultimately overcome it.

ENDNOTES

Chapter 1

1. Rousseau, D. M. (2006). Is there such a thing as "evidence-based management"? *Academy of Management Review, 31,* 256–269.

2. Khurana, R. (2007). *From higher aims to hired hands: The social transformation of American business schools and unfulfilled promise of management as a profession.* Princeton, NJ: Princeton University Press.

3. Combs, J. G., Liu, Y., Hall, A. T., and Ketchen, D. J. (2006). How much do high performance work practices matter? A meta-analysis of their effects on organizational performance. *Personnel Psychology, 59,* 501–528; Huselid, M. A. (1995). The impact of human resource management practices on turnover, productivity, and corporate financial performance. *Academy of Management Journal, 38,* 635–672.

4. Greenberg, J. (1990). Employee theft as a reaction to underpayment inequity: The hidden cost of pay cuts. *Journal of Applied Psychology, 75,* 561–568; Griffith, R. W., Hom, P. W., and Gaertner, S. (2000). A meta-analysis of antecedents and correlates of employee turnover: Update, moderator tests, and research implications for the next millennium. *Journal of Management, 26,* 463–488; Judge, T. A., and Piccolo, R. F. (2004). Transformational and transactional leadership: A meta-analytic test of their relative validity. *Journal of Applied Psychology, 89,* 755–768; Podsakoff, P. M., Bommer, W. H., Podsakoff, N., and MacKenzie, S. B. (2006). Relationships between leader reward and punishment behavior and subordinate attitudes, perceptions, and behaviors: A meta-analytic review of existing and new research. *Organizational Behavior and Human Decision Processes, 99,* 113–142; Podsakoff, P. M., MacKenzie, S. B., Paine, J. B., and Bachrach, D. G. (2000). Organizational citizenship behaviors: A critical review of the theoretical and empirical literature and suggestions for future research. *Journal of Management, 26,* 513–563; Stajkovic, A. D., and Luthans, F. (2003). Behavioral management and task performance in organizations: Conceptual background, meta-analysis, and test of alternative models. *Personnel Psychology, 56,* 155–194.

5. Lombardo, M. M., Ruderman, M. N., and McCauley, C. D. (1987). Explanations of success and derailment in upper-level management positions. *Journal of Business & Psychology, 2,* 99–216; Lowe, K. B., Kroeck, K. G., and Sivasubramaniam, N. (1996). Effectiveness correlates of transformational and transactional leadership: A meta-analytic review of the MLQ literature. *The Leadership Quarterly, 7,* 385–425; Ng, T.W.H., Eby, L. T., Sorensen, K. L., and Feldman, D. C. (2005). Predictors of objective and subjective career success: A meta-analysis. *Personnel Psychology, 58,* 367–408.

6. Hershcovis, M. S., and Barling, J. (2010). Towards a multi-foci approach to workplace aggression: A meta-analytic review of outcomes from different perpetrators. *Journal of Organizational Behavior, 31,* 24–44; Hogan, J., Hogan, R., and Kaiser, R. B. (2010). Management derailment: Personality assessment and mitigation. In S. Zedeck (Ed.), *Handbook of industrial and organizational psychology,* Vol. 3, 823–895. Washington, DC: American Psychological Association; Judge, T. A., and Piccolo, R. F. (2004). Transformational and transactional leadership: A meta-analytic test of their relative validity. *Journal of Applied Psychology, 89,* 755–768; Podsakoff, P. M., Bommer, W. H., Podsakoff, N., and MacKenzie, S. B. (2006). Relationships between leader reward and punishment behavior and subordinate attitudes, perceptions, and behaviors: A meta-analytic review of existing and new research. *Organizational Behavior and Human Decision Processes, 99,* 113–142.

7. www.greatplacetowork.com; Levering, R., and Moskowitz, M. (2005). *The 100 best companies to work for in America.* New York: Penguin.

8. Rivikin, S. G., Hanushek, E. A. and Kain, J. F. (2005). Teachers, schools and academic achievement. *Econometrica, 73,* 417–458.

9. Ibid.

10. Carens, K., Cottrell, D., and Layton, M.C. (2004). *Management insights: Discovering the truths to management success.* Cornerstone Publishing: Dallas, TX.

11. Buckingham, M., and Coffman, C. (1999). *First, break all the rules: What the world's greatest managers do differently.* New York: Simon & Schuster; Devries, D. L., and Kaiser, R. B. (2003). Going sour in the suite. In Steckler, S., Sethi, D., and Prescot, R. K. (coordinators). *Maximizing executive effectiveness.* Workshop presented by the Human Resources Planning Society, Miami, FL.

12. Dierdorff, E. C., Rubin, R. S., and Morgeson, F. P. (2009). The milieu of management: Exploring the context of managerial work role requirements. *Journal of Applied Psychology, 94,* 972–988.

13. Ibid.

14. Lombardo, M. M., Ruderman, M. N., and McCauley, C. D. (1987). Explanations of success and derailment in upper-level management positions. *Journal of Business & Psychology, 2,* 99–216.

15. Briner, R. B., and Rousseau, D. M. (2011). Evidence-based I-O psychology: Not there yet. *Industrial and Organizational Psychology: Perspectives on Science and Practice, 4,* 3–22; Rousseau, D. M. (2006). Is there such a thing as "evidence-based management"?

16. Tetlock, P. E. (2000). Cognitive biases and organizational correctives: Do both disease and cure depend

on the politics of the beholder? *Administrative Science Quarterly, 45,* 293–326.

17. Meyer, et al. (2001). Psychological testing and psychological assessment: A review of evidence and issues. *American Psychologist, 56,* 128–165.

18. Roth, P. L., BeVier, C. A., Switzer III, F. S., and Schippmann, J. S. (1996). Meta-analyzing the relationship between grades and job performance. *Journal of Applied Psychology, 81,* 548–556.

19. Rynes, S. L., Giluk, T. L., and Brown, K. G. (2007). The very separate worlds of academic and practitioner periodicals in human resource management. Implications for evidence-based management. *Academy of Management Journal, 55,* 987–1008.

20. Whetton, D. A., and Cameron, K. S. (2005). *Developing management skills.* (6th ed.). Upper Saddle River, NJ: Pearson Prentice Hall.

21. Ibid.

22. Baldwin, T., Pierce, J., Farouk, S., and Joines, R. (2009–August). The curious elusiveness of applied management knowledge: A critical challenge for management educators. Paper presented at the annual meetings of the Academy of Management, Chicago, IL.

23. Baldwin, T. T. (1992). Effects of alternative modeling strategies on outcomes of interpersonal skill training. *Journal of Applied Psychology, 77,* 147–154.

24. Mabe, P. A., and West, S. G. (1982). Validity of self-evaluation of ability. A review and meta-analysis. *Journal of Applied Psychology, 67* (3), 280–296. See also, Bass, B. M., and Yammarino, F. J. (1991). Congruence of self and others' leadership ratings of naval officers for understanding successful performance. *Applied Psychology International Review, 40,* 437–454. Church, A. (1997). Managerial self-awareness in high performance individuals in organizations. *Journal of Applied Psychology, 82* (2) 281–292.

25. Bandura, A. (1977). *Social learning theory.* New York: General Learning. Bandura, A. (1986). *Social foundations of thought and action.* Englewood Cliffs, NJ: Prentice Hall.

26. Ibid.

27. Ibid.

28. Collins, D. B., and Holton, E. F. (2004). The effectiveness of managerial leadership development programs: A meta-analysis of studies from 1982 to 2001. *Human Resource Development Quarterly, 15* (2), 217–248. Baldwin, T. T., and Rubin, R. (2004). Making better managers: A meta-analytic review of management development interventions (1951–2003) and an agenda for future research. *Academy of Management Best Paper Proceedings.*

29. Manz, C. C., and Neck, C. P. (2003). *Mastering self-leadership: Empowering yourself for personal excellence.* (3rd ed.). New York: Pearson Prentice Hall. Manz, C. C., and Sims, H. P. (1989). *SuperLeadership: Leading others to lead themselves.* New York: Prentice Hall.

30. Ibid.

31. Edmondson, A. C. (1996). Learning from mistakes is easier said than done: Group and organizational influences on the detection and correction of human error. *Journal of Applied Behavioral Science, 32* (1), 5–28. Edmondson A. C. (1999, December). Psychological safety and learning behavior in work teams, *Administrative Science Quarterly, 44* (4), 350–383.

32. Latham, G. P. (2004). The motivational benefits of goal setting. *Academy of Management Executive, 18,* 126–130.

33. Locke, E. A., and Latham, G. P. (1990). *A theory of goal setting and task performance.* Englewood Cliffs, NJ: Prentice Hall.

34. Skinner, B. F. (1971). *Beyond freedom and dignity.* New York: Knopf.

35. Marx, R. D. (1982). Relapse prevention for managerial training: A model for maintenance of behavior change. *Academy of Management Review, 7* (3), 433–441. Marx, R. D. (1986). Self-managed skill retention. *Training and Development Journal, 40* (1), 54–57.

36. George, J. M., and Jones, G. R. (2002). *Individual difference: Personality and ability. Understanding and managing organizational behavior.* Upper Saddle River, NJ: Pearson Education, Inc. Digman, J. M. (1990). Validation of the five-factor model of personality across instruments and observers. *Journal of Personality and Social Psychology, 52,* 81–90. Barrick, M. R., and Mount, M. K. (1991). The big 5 personality dimensions and job performance: A meta analysis. *Personnel Psychology, 44,* 1–26. Barrick, M. R., Mount, M. K., and Strauss, J. P. (1993). Conscientiousness and performance of sales representatives: Test of the mediating effects of goal setting. *Journal of Applied Psychology, 78,* 715–722. Witt, L. A., Burke, L., Barrick, M. R., and Mount, M. K. (2002). The interactive effects of conscientiousness and agreeableness on job performance. *Journal of Applied Psychology, 87,* 164–169.

37. Lubinsky, D., and Dawis, R. V. (1991). Aptitudes, skills and proficiencies. In M. D. Dunnette, and L. M. Hough (Eds.), *Handbook of industrial psychology.* (2nd ed., Vol. 3, pp. 1–59), Palo Alto, CA: Consulting Psychologists Press.

38. George, J. M., and Jones, G. R. (2002). *Individual difference: Personality and ability. Understanding and managing organizational behavior.* Upper Saddle River, NJ: Pearson Education, Inc.

39. Fletcher, C., and Baldry, C. (2000). A study of individual differences and self-awareness in the context of multi-source feedback. *Journal of Occupational and Organizational Behavior, 73* (3), 303–319.

40. Ibid.

41. Hazucha, J. F., Hezlett, S. A., and Schneider, R. J. (1993). The impact of 360-degree feedback on management skills development. *Human Resource Management, 32* (2–3), 325–351. London, M., and Beatty, R. W. (1993). 360-degree feedback as a competitive advantage. *Human Resource Management, 32* (2–3), 353–372.

42. Van Velsor, E., Taylor, S., and Leslie, J. B. (1993). An examination of the relationships among self-perception accuracy, self-awareness, gender, and leader effectiveness. *Human Resource Management*, 32 (2–3), 249–263.

43. Roberts, H. V., and Sergesteketter, B. F. (1993). *Quality is personal: A foundation for total quality management*. New York: Free Press.

44. Buckingham, M., and Coffman, C. (1999). *First, break all the rules: What the world's greatest managers do differently*. New York: Simon & Schuster. Buckingham, M., and Clifton, D. O. (2001). *Now discover your strengths*. New York: Free Press. Clifton, D. O., and Nelson, P. (1996). *Soar with your strengths*. (2nd ed.). New York: Dell Books.

Chapter 2

1. DeFrank, R. S., and Ivancevich, J. M. (1998). Stress on the job: An executive update. *Academy of Management Executive*, 12 (3), 55–66.

2. Auerbach, S. M. (1998). *Stress management: Psychological foundations*. Upper Saddle River, NJ: Prentice Hall.

3. Chapman, K. (2005). Are you working too hard? *Harvard Business Review*, 83, 53–58.

4. Barling, J., Kelloway, E. K., and Frone, M. R. (2004). *Handbook of Work Stress*. Sage Publications.

5. Selye, H. (1974). *Stress without distress*. New York, NY: Lippencott and Crowell Publishers.

6. Weaver, J. (2006). Can stress actually be good for you? Retrieved 10/1/2010 from www.msnbc.msn.com/id/15818153/ns/health-mental_health/.

7. Lazarus, R., and Folkman, S. (1987). Transactional theory and research on emotions and coping. *European Journal of Personality*, 1 (3, Spec. Issue), 141–169.

8. Friedman, M., and Rosenman, R. (1974). *Type A behavior and your heart*. New York: Knopf.

9. Ibid.

10. Clark, L. K., and Miller, S. M. (1990). Self-reliance and desire for control in the Type A behavior pattern. *Journal of Social Behavior & Personality*, 5, 405–418.

11. Dwyer, D., and Fox, M. (2000). The moderating role of hostility in the relationship between enriched jobs and health. *Academy of Management Journal*, 43 (6), 1086–1096.

12. Christian, M. S., Bradley, J. C., Wallace, J. C., and Burke, M. J. (2009). Workplace safety: A meta-analysis of the roles of person and situation factors. *Journal of Applied Psychology*, 94, 1103–1127.

13. Burger, J. M. (1989). Negative reactions to increases in personal control. *Journal of Personality and Social Psychology*, 56, 246–256.

14. Baum, A., Cohen, L., and Hail, M. (1993). Control and intrusive memories as possible determinants of chronic stress. *Psychosomatic Medicine*, 55, 274–286.

15. Bandura, A. (1982). Self-efficacy mechanism in human agency. *American Psychologist*, 37, 122–147.

16. Stajkovic, A. D., and Luthans, F. (1998). Self-efficacy and work-related performance. A meta-analyses. *Psychological Bulletin*, 124, 240–261.

17. Lewin, J. E., and Sager, J. K. (2007). A process model of burnout among salespeople: Some new thoughts. *Journal of Business Research*, 60, 1216–1224.

18. Kanner, A. D., Coyne, J. C., Schaefer, C., and Lazarus, R. S. (1981). Comparisons of two modes of stress measurement: Daily hassles and uplifts versus major life events. *Journal of Behavioral Medicine*, 4, 1–39.

19. Zohar, D. (1999). When things go wrong: The effect of daily work hassles on effort, exertion, and negative mood. *Journal of Occupational and Organizational Psychology*, 72, 265–283.

20. Greenhaus, J. H., and Beutell, N. J. (1985). Sources of conflict between work and family roles. *Academy of Management Review*, 10, 76–88.

21. Jackson, S., and Schuler, R. (1985). A meta-analysis and conceptual critique of research on role ambiguity and role conflict in work settings. *Organizational Behavior and Human Decision Processes*, 36 (1), 16–78.

22. Ford, M., Heinen, B., and Langkamer, K. (2007). Work and family satisfaction and conflict: A meta-analysis of cross-domain relations. *Journal of Applied Psychology*, 92 (1), 57–80.

23. Hobfoll, S. (1989). Conservation of resources: A new attempt at conceptualizing stress. *American Psychologist*, 44 (3), 513–524.

24. Maslach, C., Schaufeli, W., and Leiter, M. (2001). Job burnout. *Annual Review of Psychology*, 52, 397–422.

25. Ibid.

26. Ibid.

27. Ibid.

28. Grandey, A. A. (2000). Emotional regulation in the workplace: A new way to conceptualize emotional labor. *Journal of Occupational Health Psychology*, 5 (1), 95–110.

29. Hochschild, A. R. (1983). *The managed heart: Commercialization of human feeling*. Berkeley: University of California Press.

30. Grandey, A. A. (2000). Emotional regulation in the workplace: A new way to conceptualize emotional labor.

31. Brotherridge, C., and Grandey, A. (2002). Emotional labor and burnout: Comparing two perspectives of "people work." *Journal of Vocational Behavior*, 60 (1), 17–39; Grandey, A. A. (2000). Emotional regulation in the workplace: A new way to conceptualize emotional labor; Pugliesi, K. (1999). The consequences of emotional labor: Effects on work stress, job satisfaction, and well-being. *Motivation and Emotion*, 23 (2), 125–154.

32. Ashforth, B. E., and Humphrey, R. H. (1993). Emotional labor in service roles: The influence of identity. *Academy of Management Review*, 18 (1), 88–115.

33. Morris, J. A., and Feldman, D. C. (1997). Managing emotions in the workplace. *Journal of Managerial Issues*, 9 (3), 257–274.

34. Karasek, R. A. (1979). Job demands, job decision latitude and mental strain: implications for job design. *Administrative Science Quarterly*, 24, 285–308.

35. Karasek, R. A., and Theorell, T. (1990). *Healthy work: Stress, productivity, and reconstruction of working life.* New York: Basic Books.

36. Fox, M., Dwyer, D., and Ganster, D. (1993). Effects of stressful job demands and control on physiological and attitudinal outcomes in a hospital setting. *Academy of Management Journal,* 36 (2), 289–318.

37. Ganster, D. C., Fox, M. L., and Dwyer, D. J. (2001). Explaining employees' health care costs: A prospective examination of stressful job demands, personal control, and physiological reactivity. *Journal of Applied Psychology,* 86, 954–964.

38. Karasek, R. A., and Theorell, T. (1990). *Healthy work: Stress, productivity, and reconstruction of working life.*

39. van der Doef, M., and Maes, S. (1999). The job demand-control (-support) model and psychological well-being: A review of 20 years of empirical research. *Work & Stress,* 13 (2), 87–114.

40. Cooper, C. L., and Cartwright, S. (1997). An intervention strategy for workplace stress. *Journal of Psychosomatic Research,* 43, 7–16.

41. Bollini, A. M., et al. (2004). The influence of perceived control and locus of control on the cortisol and subjective responses to stress. *Biological Psychology,* 67 (3), 245–260.

42. This discussion is condensed largely from the excellent 1994 book by Robert Sapolsky, *Why zebras don't get ulcers.* New York: W.H. Freeman and Company.

43. Stewart, D., and Winser, D. (1942). Incidence of perforated peptic ulcer: Effect of heavy air-raids. *Lancet,* 28 February: 259.

44. See for example, Sachser, N., Durschlag, M., and Hirzel, D. (1998). Social relationships and the management of stress. *Psychoneuroendocrinology,* 23 (8), 891–904. And DeVries, A. C., et al. (2003). Social modulation of stress response. *Physiology and Behavior,* 79 (3), 399–407.

45. Sapolsky, R. (1998). *Why zebras don't get ulcers.* 263–264.

46. See for example, Sachser, N., Durschlag, M., and Hirzel, D. (1998). Social relationships and the management of stress. *Psychoneuroendocrinology,* 23 (8), 891–904. DeVries, A. C., et al. (2003). Social modulation of stress response. *Physiology and Behavior,* 79 (3), 399–407. Auerbach, S. M., et al. (2005). Optimism, satisfaction with needs met, interpersonal perceptions of the health-care team, and emotional distress in patients' family members during critical care hospitalization. *American Journal of Critical Care,* 14 (3), 202–210. Boden-Albala, B., et al. (2005). Social isolation and outcomes post stroke. *Neurology,* 64 (11), 1888–1892.

47. Described in Sapolsky, R. (1998). *Why zebras don't get ulcers.*

48. Oudejans, R.R.D. (2008). Reality-based practice under pressure improves handgun shooting performance of police officers. *Ergonomics,* 51, 261–273.

49. Gucciardi, D. F., and Dimmock, J. A. (2008). Choking under pressure in sensorimotor skills: Conscious processing or depleted attentional resources? *Psychology of Sport and Exercise,* 9, 45–59.

50. Beilock, S. L., and Carr, T. H. (2001). On the fragility of skilled performance: What governs choking under pressure? *Journal of Experimental Psychology: General,* 130, 701–725. Beilock, S. L., and Gray, R. (2007). Why do athletes choke under pressure? In Tenenbaum, G., and Eklund, R. C. (Eds.), *Handbook of sport psychology* (3rd ed., pp. 425–444). Hoboken, NJ: Wiley.

51. Jordet, G. (2009). When superstars flop: Public status and choking under pressure in international soccer penalty shootouts. *Journal of Applied Sport Psychology,* 21 (2), 125–130.

52. Ibid.

53. Maddi, S., Kahn, S., and Maddi, K. (1992). The effectiveness of hardiness training. *Consulting Psychology Journal: Practice and Research,* 50 (2), 78–86.

54. Brandon, J. E., and Loftin, J. M. (1991). Relationship of fitness to depression, state and trait anxiety, internal health locus of control, and self-control. *Perceptual and Motor Skills,* 73 (2), 563–566.

55. Craft, L. L., and Landers, D. M. (1998). The effect of exercise on clinical depression and depression resulting from mental illness: A meta–analysis. *Journal of Sport & Exercise Psychology,* 20 (4), 339–357.

56. Lupinacci, N. S., Rikli, R. E., Jones, C. J., and Ross, D. (1993). Age and physical activity on reaction time and digit symbol substitution performance in cognitively active adults. *Research Quarterly for Exercise and Sport,* 64, 144–150.

57. Shepard, R. J. (1999). Do work site exercise and health programs work? *The Physician and Sportsmedicine,* 27, 48–72. Frew, D. R., and Bruning, N. S. (1988). Improved productivity and job satisfaction through employee exercise programs. *Hospital Material Management Quarterly,* 9, 62–69. Edwards, S. E., and Gettman, L. R. (1980, November). The effect of employee physical fitness on job performance. *Personnel Administrator,* 25, 41–61.

58. Neck, C. P., Mitchell, T. L., Manz, C. C., and Thompson, E. C. (2004). *Fit to lead: The proven 8-week solution for shaping up your body, your mind, and your career.* New York: St. Martin's Press. Neck, C. P., and Cooper, K. H. (2000). The fit executive: Exercise and diet guidelines for enhancing performance. *Academy of Management Executive,* 14 (2), 72–83.

59. Maddi, S., and Kobasa, S. C. (1984). *The hardy executive: Health under stress.* Homewood, IL: Dow Jones–Irwin.

60. Ibid.

61. Fredrickson, B. L. (2001). The role of positive emotions in positive psychology: The broaden-and-build theory of positive emotions. *American Psychologist,* 56, 218–226.

62. Tugade, M. M., and Fredrickson, B. L. (2004). Resilient individuals use positive emotions to bounce back from negative emotional experiences. *Journal of Personality and Social Psychology,* 86 (2), 320–333.

63. Covey, S. (1989). *The 7 habits of highly effective people: Powerful lessons in personal change.* New York: Simon & Schuster. Lakein, A. (1973). *How to get control of your time and your life.* New York: Signet.

64. Morgenstern, J. (2005). *Never check e-mail in the morning: And other unexpected strategies for making your work life work.* New York: Fireside Books.

65. Borst, J., Taatgen, N. A., and van Rijn, H. (2010). Problem representations in multi-tasking: An additional cognitive bottleneck. *Journal of Experimental Psychology: Learning, Memory, and Cognition,* 36 (2), 363–382. Ophir, E., Nass, C., and Wagner, A. (2009). Cognitive control in media multitaskers. *Proceedings of the National Academy of Sciences.*

66. Adapted from http://www.ehow.com/how_134144_write-effective-list.html, accessed 10/2/2011.

67. Allen, D. (2003). *Getting things done: The art of stress-free productivity.* New York: Penguin Books.

68. Lakein, A. (1973). *How to get control of your time and your life.* New York: Signet Publishing.

69. Cited in Kay, M. (1995). *You can have it all: Lifetime wisdom from America's foremost woman entrepreneur.* New York: Prima Lifestyles Books. pp. 68–69.

70. If you drop it, should you eat it? Scientists weigh in on the 5-second rule. (2003, September 2). *ACES News Services.*

71. Lakein, A. (1973). *How to get control of your time and your life.* New York: Signet Publishing.

72. Winston, S. (1991). *Getting organized: The easy way to put your life in order.* New York: Warner Books.

Chapter 3

1. Nutt, P. C. (1999). Surprising but true: Half the decisions in organizations fail. *Academy of Management Executive,* 13 (4), 75–90.

2. Bonabeau, Eric (2003). Don't trust your gut. *Harvard Business Review,* 81 (5), 116–123.

3. Kruger, J., Wirtz, D., and Miller, D. T. (2005). Counterfactual thinking and the first instinct fallacy. *Journal of Personality and Social Psychology,* 88 (5), 725–735.

4. Winerman, L. (2005). What we know without knowing how. *Monitor on Psychology,* 36 (3), 50–52.

5. Gladwell, M. (2005). *Blink: The power of thinking without thinking.* New York: Little, Brown & Company.

6. Argyris, C. (1985). *Strategy, change, and defensive routines.* Boston: Pitman.

7. In this section, we relied heavily on Max Bazerman's outstanding synthesis of the most important research on judgment biases and errors. Bazerman, M. (1998). *Judgment in managerial decision making.* (4th ed.). New York: Wiley & Sons. We also draw heavily on the work of Michael Metzger, Business Law professor at the IU Kelley School of Business where he teaches a highly acclaimed course on critical thinking.

8. Dawes, R. M. (2001). *Everyday irrationality: How pseudoscientists, lunatics, and the rest of us fail to think rationally.* Boulder, CO: Westview Press.

9. Kahneman, D., and Tversky, A. (1972). Subjective probability: A judgment of representativeness. *Cognitive Psychology,* 3, 430–454.

10. Gilovich, T., Vallone, R., and Tversky, A. (1985). The hot hand in basketball: On the misperception of random sequences. *Cognitive Psychology,* 17, 295–314.

11. Tversky, A., and Kahneman, D. (1974). Judgment under uncertainty: Heuristics and biases. *Science,* 185, 1124–1131.

12. Myers, D. G. (1980). *The inflated self.* New York: Seabury Press; Svenson, O. (1981). Are we all less risky and more skillful than our fellow drivers? *Acta Psychologica,* 47, 143–148.

13. Torngren, G., and Montgomery, H. (2004). Worse than chance? Performance and confidence among professionals and laypeople in the stock market. *Journal of Behavioral Finance,* 5, 148–153.

14. Breslin, J. W. (1995). Negotiation Journal editor dies in accident. *Negotiation Journal,* 11 (3), 195–200.

15. Plous, S. (1993). *The psychology of judgment and decision making.* New York: McGraw-Hill.

16. Christensen-Szalanski, J., and Bushyhead, J. (1981). Physicians' use of probabilistic information in a real clinical setting. *Journal of Experimental Psychology: Human Perception and Performance,* 7, 928–935.

17. For example, see Koriat, A., Lichtenstein, S., and Fischhoff, B. (1980). Reasons for confidence. *Journal of Experimental Psychology: Learning, Memory, and Cognition,* 6 (2), 107–118. Lichtenstein, S., and Fischhoff, B. (1980). Training for calibration. *Organizational Behavior and Human Performance,* 26, 149–171.

18. March, J. G., and Simon, H. A. (1958). *Organizations.* New York: Wiley.

19. Mitroff, I. (1998). *Smart thinking for crazy times.* San Francisco: Berrett-Koehler Publishers, Inc.

20. Adapted from http://www.nytimes.com/1996/05/12/us/boy-s-last-wish-sets-off-animal-rights-furor.html.

21. Vroom, V. H. (2000). Leadership and the decision making process. *Organizational Dynamics,* 28 (4), 82–94.; Field, R.H.G. (1982). A test of the Vroom-Yetton normative model of leadership. *Journal of Applied Psychology,* 67, 523–532.

22. Ibid.

23. Ibid.

24. Cited in Field, R. H., and House, R. J. (1990). A test of the Vroom-Yetton model using manager and subordinate reports. *Journal of Applied Psychology,* 75 (3), 362–366.

25. Judson, A. I., and Cofer, C. N. (1956). Reasoning as an associative process. *Psychological Reports,* 2, 469–476. Maier, N.R.F., and Burke, R. J. (1967). Response availability as a factor in the problem-solving performance of males and females. *Journal of Personality and Social Psychology,* 5, 304–310. Tversky, A., and Kahneman, D. (1981). The framing of decisions and psychology of choice. *Science,* 211, 453–458.

26. Taken from Jones, M. D. (1998). *The thinker's toolkit.* New York: Three Rivers Press.

27. Volkema, R. J. (1986). Problem formulation as a purposive activity. *Strategic Management Journal,* 7, 267–279.

28. Tversky, A., and Kahneman, D. (1981). The framing of decisions and the psychology of choice. *Science,* 211, 453–458.

29. Senge, P. M., Kleiner, A. M., Roberts, C., Ross, R. B., and Smith, B. J. (1994). *The fifth discipline fieldbook* (p. 90). New York: Doubleday.

30. Adapted from *What is systems thinking* (2006). Pegasus Communications. Pegasuscom.com.

31. Adapted from Senge, et al. (1994). *The fifth discipline fieldbook.*

32. Adapted from Hammond, J. S., Keeney, R. L., and Raiffa, H. (1999). *Smart choices: A practical guide to making better decisions.* Boston: Harvard Business Press.

33. Ibid.

34. Mullen, B., Johnson, C., and Salas, E. (1991). Productivity loss in brainstorming groups: A meta-analytic integration. *Basic and Applied Social Psychology,* 12 (1), 3–23.

35. Paulus, P. B., and Yang, H. (2000). Idea generation in groups: A basis for creativity in organizations. *Organizational Behavior and Human Decision Processes,* 82 (1), 76–87.

36. Thompson, L. (2003). Improving the creativity of organizational work groups. *Academy of Management Executive,* 17 (1), 96–111.

37. Jackson, S. E. (1992). Team composition in organizational settings: Issues in managing an increasingly diverse workforce. In S. Worchel, W. Wood, and J. A. Simpson (Eds.), *Group process and productivity* (pp. 138–173). Newbury Park, CA: Sage.

38. Sweetman, K. J. (1997). Cultivating creativity. *Harvard Business Review,* March–April, 10–12.

39. Ibid.

40. Nutt, P. C. (2004). Expanding the search for alternatives during strategic decision-making. *Academy of Management Executive,* 18 (4), 13–28.

41. Whetten, D. A., and Cameron, K. S. (2005). *Developing management skills.* Upper Saddle River, NJ: Pearson Education.

42. Russo, J. E., and Schoemaker, P.J.H. (1989). *Decision traps: Ten barriers to brilliant decision making and how to overcome them.* New York: Simon & Schuster.

43. Nutt, P. C. (2004). Expanding the search for alternatives during strategic decision-making. *Academy of Management Executive,* 18 (4), 13–28.

44. Cosier, R. A., and Schwenk, C. R. (1990). Agreement and thinking alike: Ingredients for poor decisions. *Academy of Management Executive,* 4 (1), 69–74.

45. Slovic, P. (1987). Perception of risk. *Science,* 236, 280–285.

46. Argyris, C., and Schon, D. A. (1978). *Organizational learning: A theory of action perspective.* Reading, MA: Addison-Wesley.

47. Senge, P. M. (1999). *The dance of change: The challenges of sustaining momentum in learning organizations.* New York: Currency/Doubleday.

48. Adapted from *The News Hour with Jim Lehrer,* "Medical Errors," February 7, 2005; transcript accessed from www.pbs.org/newshour/bb/health/jan-june05/errors_2-7.html.

Chapter 4

1. Veiga, J. F., Golden, T. D., and Dechant, K. (2004). Why managers bend company rules. *Academy of Management Executive,* 18 (2), 84–90.

2. McCabe, D. L., and Trevino, L. K. (1996). What we know about cheating in college. *Change,* 28, 28–34.

3. Taken from Trevino, L. K., and Brown, M. E. (2004). Managing to be ethical: Debunking five business ethics myths. *Academy of Management Executive,* 18, 69–81.

4. McCabe, D. L., Trevino, L. K., and Butterfield, K. D. (1996). The influence of collegiate and corporate codes of conduct on ethics-related behavior in the workplace. *Business Ethics Quarterly,* 6, 461–476.

5. Kidder, R. M. (1995). *How good people make tough choices* (p. 51). New York: Simon & Schuster.

6. Trevino, L. K., and Nelson, K. A. (1999). *Managing business ethics: Straight talk about how to do it right.* New York: Wiley.

7. Trevino, L. K., and Brown, M. E. (2004). Managing to be ethical.

8. Ibid. Here we rely heavily on the outstanding work of Kidder (1995). Kidder has framed ethical dilemmas as "right versus right" and provides excellent examples.

9. Carney, D. R., and Mason, M. F. (2010). Decision-making and testosterone: When the ends justify the means. *Journal of Experimental Social Psychology,* 46, 668–671.

10. Jones, T. M. (1991). Ethical decision making by individuals in organizations: An issue-contingent model. *Academy of Management Review,* 16, 366–395.

11. This framework for systematic ethical decision making is adapted from Trevino, L. K., and Nelson, K. A. (1999). *Managing business ethics.* Hoboken, NJ: John Wiley & Sons, Inc.

12. Hartman, L. P., and DesJardins, J. (2008). *Business ethics: Decision-making for personal integrity and social responsibility.* Burr Ridge, IL: McGraw-Hill.

13. Ibid. In addition, this section is adapted from our colleague and renowned business ethicist Dr. Laura Hartman's course notes. We are grateful for her willingness to share this material with the textbook authors.

14. Carney, D. R., and Mason, M. F. (2010). Decision-making and testosterone: When the ends justify the means. *Journal of Experimental Psychology,* 46, 668–671.

15. Kohlberg, L., Levine, C., and Hewer, A. (1983). Moral stages: A current formulation and a response to critics. Basel, NY: Karger.

16. Johnson, C. E. (2007). *Ethics in the workplace. Tools and tactics for organizational transformation.* Thousand Oaks, CA: Sage.

17. Robinson, S. L., and O'Leary-Kelly, A. M. (1998). Monkey see, monkey do. The influence of work groups on the antisocial behavior of employees. *Academy of Management Journal,* 41, 658–672.

18. Treviño, L. K., and Youngblood, S. A. (1990). Bad apples in bad barrels: A causal analysis of ethical decision-making behavior. *Journal of Applied Psychology,* 75, 378–385.

19. These studies conducted by John Darley and Bibb Latane began with the publication of Darley, J. M., and Latane, B. (1968). Bystander intervention in emergencies: Diffusion of responsibility. *Journal of Personality and Social Psychology,* 8, 377–383.

20. Latane, B., and Darley, J. (1970). *The unresponsive bystander: Why doesn't he help?* New York: Appleton-Century-Crofts.

21. Adapted by M. Donkin from Miceli, M. P., Van Scotter, J. R., Near, J. P., and Rehg, M. (2001). Responses to perceived organisational wrongdoing: Do perceiver

characteristics matter? In J. M. Darley, D. M. Messick, and T. R. Tyler (Eds.), *Social influences on ethical behaviour*, Mahwah, NJ: Lawrence Erlbaum Associates, 119–135.

22. Miceli, M. P., Van Scotter, J. R., Near, J. P., and Rehg, M. T. (2001). Individual differences and whistle-blowing. *Academy of Management Proceedings.*

23. Kidder, R. M. (1995). *How good people make tough choices* (p. 167). New York: Simon & Schuster.

24. "American seeks to weather the airline dip." (2004, September 13). National Public Radio.

25. Kahneman, D., Knetsch, J., and Thaler, R. (1986). Fairness as a constraint on profit: Seeking entitlements in the market. *American Economic Review, 76,* 728–741.

26. Colquitt, J. A., et al. (2001). Justice at the millennium: A meta-analytic review of 25 years of organizational justice research. *Journal of Applied Psychology, 86,* 425–445.

27. Bies, R. J., Martin, C. L., and Brockner, J. (1993). Just laid off, but still a "good citizen"? Only if the process is fair. *Employee Responsibilities and Rights Journal, 6,* 227–238.

28. Brockner, J., Konovsky, M., Cooper-Schneider, R., Folger, R., Martin, C., and Bies, R. J. (1994). Interactive effects of procedural justice and outcome negativity on victims and survivors of job loss. *Academy of Management Journal, 17,* 397–409.

29. Adapted from Greenberg, J. (2005). Managing behavior in organizations. Upper Saddle River, NJ: Pearson Prentice Hall.

30. Casio, W. (2005). Strategies for responsible restructuring. *Academy of Management Executive, 19* (4), 39–50.

31. Ibid.

32. Trevor, C. O., and Nyborg, A. J. (2008). Keeping your headcount when all about you are losing theirs: Downsizing, voluntary turnover rates, and the moderating role of HR practices. *Academy of Management Journal, 51,* 259–276.

33. Simmons, T., and Roberson, Q. (2003). Why managers should care about fairness: The effects of aggregate justice perceptions on organizational outcomes. *Journal of Applied Psychology, 79,* 455–460.

34. Bloom, M. (1999). The performance effects of pay dispersion on individuals and organizations. *The Academy of Management Journal, 42,* 25–40.

35. Anderson et al. (2010). CEO pay and the great recession. Institute for Policy Studies: Washington, DC.

36. Common concerns highlighted by Trevino, L. K., and Nelson, K. A. (1999). *Managing business ethics.*

37. Cawley, B. D., Keeping, L. M., and Levy, P. E. (1998). Participation in the performance appraisal process and employee reactions: A meta-analytic review of field investigations. *Journal of Applied Psychology, 83,* 615–633.

38. Rubin, R. S., Bommer, W. H., and Bachrach, D. G. (2010). Operant leadership and employee citizenship: A question of trust? *The Leadership Quarterly, 21,* 400–408.

39. Bowling, N. A., and Beehr, T. A. (2006). Workplace harassment from the victim's perspective: A theoretical model and meta-analysis. *Journal of Applied Psychology, 91,* 998–1012.

40. Willness, C. R., Steel, P., and Lee, K. (2006). A meta-analysis of the antecedents and consequences of workplace sexual harassment. *Personnel Psychology, 60,* 127–162.

41. Gajendran, R. S., and Harrison, D. A. (2007). The good, the bad, and the unknown about telecommuting: Meta-analysis of psychological mediators and individual consequences. *Journal of Applied Psychology, 92,* 1524–1541.

42. Dierdorff, E. C., and Ellington, J. K. (2008). It's the nature of the work: Examining behavior-based sources of work–family conflict across occupations. *Journal of Applied Psychology, 93,* 883–892.

43. Gajendran, R. S., and Harrison, D. A. (2007). The good, the bad, and the unknown about telecommuting: Meta-analysis of psychological mediators and individual consequences. *Journal of Applied Psychology, 92,* 1524–1541.

44. Adapted from Bollier, D. (1991). *Merck & Company.* Stanford, CA: The Business Enterprise Trust, as summarized in Trevino, L. K., and Nelson, K. A. (1999). *Managing business ethics.*

Chapter 5

1. Conger, J. A. (1998). The necessary art of persuasion. *Harvard Business Review,* May–June. Reprint 98304. Mayfield, M., and Mayfield, J. (2004). The effects of leader communication on worker innovation. *American Business Review, 22,* 46–51.

2. Graduate Management Admission Council (GMAC). (2006). *Corporate Recruiters Survey;* Van Velsor, E., and Leslie, J. B. (1995). Why executives derail: Perspectives across time and cultures. *Academy of Management Executive,* November, 62–72.

3. Mayfield, M., and Mayfield, J. (2004). The effects of leader communication on worker innovation. *American Business Review, 22,* 46–51.

4. Keysar, B., and Henly, A. S. (2002). Speakers overestimation of their effectiveness. *Psychological Science, 13,* 207–212.

5. Newton, L. (1990). Overconfidence in the communication of intent: Heard and unheard melodies. Unpublished doctoral dissertation, Stanford University, Stanford, CA.

6. Hanft, A. (2005). It's the sound bite, stupid. *Inc.,* June, 128.

7. Conger, J. A. (1998). The necessary art of persuasion. *Harvard Business Review,* May–June. Reprint 98304.

8. Hovland, C. I., and Weiss, W. (1951). The influence of source credibility on communication effectiveness. *Public Opinion Quarterly, 15,* 635–650; Hovland, C. I., Janis, I. L., and Kelley, H. H. (1953). *Communication and persuasion.* New Haven, CT: Yale University Press.

9. Wiethoff, W. E. (1994). *Writing the speech.* Greenwood, IN: Alistair Press.

10. Gladwell, M. (2000). *The tipping point.* New York: Little Brown & Co.

11. Heath, C., and Heath, D. (2007). *Made to stick.* New York: Random House.

12. Smith, L., and Fershleiser, R. (2009). *Six-word memoirs on love and heartbreak: By writers famous and obscure.* New York: Harper Perennial.

13. Bell, B. E., and Loftus, E. F. (1988). Degree of detail of eyewitness testimony and mock juror judgments. *Journal of Applied Social Psychology,* 18, 1171–1192.

14. Kaufman, B. (2003). Stories that sell, stories that tell. *The Journal of Business Strategy,* 24 (2) (March–April), 11–15.

15. Hedin, R. (2005). *Telling a good story.* Unpublished manuscript. Indiana University: Bloomington, Indiana.

16. Minto, B. (1996). *The Minto pyramid principle: Logic in writing, thinking, and problem solving.* London: Minto International.

17. Quoted in Matson, E. (1997). Now that we have your complete attention. . . . *Fast Company,* 7 (February/March), 124–125.

18. Chaiken, S. (1979). Communicator, physical attractiveness, and persuasion. *Journal of Personality and Social Psychology,* 37, 1387–1397. Eagly, A. H., Wood, W., and Chaiken, S. (1978). Causal inferences about communicators and their effect on opinion change. *Journal of Personality and Social Psychology,* 36, 424–435.

19. Bozek, P. E. (1998). *50 one-minute tips to better communication.* Menlo Park, CA: Crisp Learning.

20. Lovett, P. (1988). *Meetings that work: Plans bosses can approve.* Boston: Harvard Business Publishing.

21. DuFrene, D. D., and Lehman, C. M. (2004). Concept, content, construction, and contingencies: Getting the horse before the PowerPoint cart. *Business Communication Quarterly,* 67, 84–88.

22. Daft, R. L., Lengel, R. H., and Trevino, L. K. (1987). Message equivocality, media selection, and manager performance: Implications for information systems. *MIS Quarterly,* 11, 355–366.

23. Ibid.

24. Carlson, J. R., and Zmud, R. W. (1999). Channel expansion theory and the experiential nature of media richness perceptions. *Academy of Management Journal,* 42, 153–171.

25. Alge, B. J., Wiethoff, C., and Klein, H. J. (2003). When does the medium matter? Knowledge-building experiences and opportunities in decision-making teams. *Organizational Behavior and Human Decision Processes,* 91, 26–40.

26. Bolton, R. (1986). *People skills: How to assert yourself, listen to the others, and resolve conflicts.* Englewood Cliffs, NJ: Prentice-Hall, Inc.

27. Rice, E. J. (1998, May). Are you listening? *Quality Progress,* 31 (5), 25–29.

28. Robinett, B. (1982). The value of a good ear. *Personnel Administrator,* 27, 10.

29. Kanter, R. M. (1983). *The change masters.* New York: Simon & Schuster, 70.

30. Bormann, E. G., Howell, W. S., Nichols, R. G., and Shapiro, G. L. (1969). *Interpersonal communication in the modern organization.* Englewood Cliffs, NJ: Prentice Hall.

31. Eckman, P., and Friesen, W. (1971). Constants across cultures in the face and emotion. *Journal of Personality and Social Psychology,* 17, 124–129.

32. Morsbach, H. (1973). Aspects of nonverbal communication in Japan. *Journal of Nervous and Mental Disease,* 157, 265–272. Barna, L. M. (1988). Intercultural communication stumbling blocks. In L. A. Samovar and R. E. Porter (Eds.), *Intercultural communication: A reader* (pp. 102–125). Belmont, CA: Wadsworth.

33. McCaskey, M. B. (1979). The hidden messages managers send. *Harvard Business Review,* 57 (November–December), 146–147.

34. Kratz, D. M., and Kratz, A. R. (1995). *Effective listening skills.* Boston: McGraw-Hill.

35. Simons, D. J., and Chabris, C. F. (1999). Gorillas in our midst. *Perception,* 28, 1059–1074.

36. Pearce, C. G., Johnson, I. W., and Barker, R. T. (2003). Assessment of the listening styles inventory. *Journal of Business and Technical Communication,* 17, 84–103.

37. Kratz, D. M., and Kratz, A. R. (1995). *Effective listening skills.* Boston: McGraw-Hill.

38. Hamilton, M. A., and Stewart, B. L. (1993). Extending an information process model of language intensity effects. *Communication Quarterly,* 41, 231–246.

Chapter 6

1. Vroom, V. (1964). *Work and Motivation.* New York: Wiley. Locke, E., and Latham, G. (1968). Toward a theory of task motivation and incentives. *Organizational Behavior and Human Performance,* 3, 157–189. Adams, J. (1963). Toward an understanding of inequity. *Journal of Abnormal and Social Psychology,* 67, 422–436.

2. Blumberg, M., and Pringle, C. D. (1982). The missing opportunity in organizational research: Some implications for a theory of work performance. *Academy of Management Review,* 7 (4), 560–569.

3. Vroom, V. H. (1964). *Work and motivation.* New York: Wiley.

4. Adams, J. S. (1965). Inequity in social exchange. In L. Berkowitz (Ed.), *Advances in experimental social psychology,* 2. New York: Academic Press, 267–299.

5. Adams, J. (1963). Toward an understanding of inequity. 422– 436.

6. Markey, S. (2003). Monkeys show sense of fairness, study says. *National Geographic News,* September 17. Brosnan, S. F., and de Waal, F.B.M. (2003). Monkeys reject unequal pay. *Nature,* 425, 297–299.

7. Huseman, R., Hatfield, J., and Miles, E. (1987). A new perspective on equity theory: The equity sensitivity construct. *Academy of Management Review,* 12, 222–234.

8. Miles, E., Hatfield, J., and Huseman, R. (1994). Equity sensitivity and outcome importance. *Journal of Organizational Behavior,* 15, 585–596.

9. Ibid. Huseman, J., Hatfield, J., and Miles, E. (1985). Test for individual perceptions of job equity: Some preliminary findings. *Perceptual and Motor Skills,* 61, 1055–1064.

10. McClelland, D. (1975). *Power: The inner experience.* New York: Irvington.

11. McClelland, D. C. (1966). That urge to achieve. *Think*, IBM, 82–89.

12. Stuart-Kotze, R. (2006). Motivation theory. http: www.managementlearning.com.

13. Hulin, C. L., and Smith, P. C. (1965). A linear model of job satisfaction. *Journal of Applied Psychology*, 49 (3), 209–216.

14. Hackman, J., and Oldham, G. (1980). *Work redesign*. Reading, MA: Addison-Wesley.

15. Workman, M., and Bommer, W. H. (2004). Redesigning computer call center work: A longitudinal field experiment. *Journal of Organizational Behavior*, 25, 317–337.

16. From www.newport.com.

17. Ranky, P. G. (2004). *Total quality control and JIT management in CIM*. Ridgewood, NJ: CIMware.

18. From www.wainwrightindustries.com.

19. From www.phelpscountybank.com.

20. Milliman, J., Zawacki, R., Norman, C., Powell, L., and Kirksey, J. (1994). Companies evaluate employees from all perspectives. *Personnel Journal*, 73, 99–103.

21. Locke, E., and Latham, G. (1984). *Goal setting: A motivational technique that works*. Englewood Cliffs, NJ: Prentice Hall. Locke, E., and Latham, G. (1990). *A theory of goal setting and task performance*. Englewood Cliffs, NJ: Prentice Hall.

22. Latham, G. (2004). The motivational benefits of goal setting. *Academy of Management Executive*, 18 (4), 126–129.

23. Ibid.

24. Rubin, R. S. (2002). Will the real SMART goals please stand up? *The Industrial-Organizational Psychologist*, April, 26–27.

25. See, for example, Locke, E., and Latham, G. (1990). *A theory of goal setting and task performance*. Englewood Cliffs, NJ: Prentice Hall. Latham, G. (2002). The reciprocal effects of science on practice: Insights from the practice and science of goal setting. *Canadian Psychology*, 42, 1–11.

26. Earley, P., and Kanfer, R. (1985). The influence of component participation and role models on goal acceptance, goal satisfaction, and performance. *Organizational Behavior and Human Decision Processes*, 36, 378–390.

27. Ordóñez, L. D., Schweitzer, M. E., Galinsky, A. D., and Bazerman, M. H. (2009). Goals gone wild: The systematic side effects of overprescribing goal setting. *Academy of Management Perspectives*, 23 (1), 6–16.

28. Thorndike, E. L. (1911). *The elements of psychology*. New York: Seiler. Skinner, B. F. (1974). *About behaviorism*. New York: Random House.

29. Kerr, S. (1975). On the folly of rewarding A, while hoping for B. *Academy of Management Journal*, 18, 769–783.

30. *BusinessWeek* (1971, December 18).

31. Bateman, M., and Ludwig, T. (2004). Managing distribution quality through an adapted incentive program with tiered goals and feedback. *Journal of Organization Behavior Management*, 75 (23), 33–55.

32. Hantula, D., Rajala, A., Kellerman, E., and Bragger, J. (2004). The value of workplace safety: A time-based utility analysis model. *Journal of Organization Behavior Management*, 75 (21), 79–98.

33. Rohn, D., Austin, J., and Lutrey, S. (2004). Using feedback and performance accountability to decrease cash register shortages. *Journal of Organization Behavior Management*, 75 (22), 33–46.

34. Ludwig, T. D., Biggs, J., Wagner, S. and Geller, E. S. (2002). Using public feedback and competitive rewards to increase the safe driving behaviors of pizza deliverers. *Journal of Organizational Behavior Management*, 21, 75–104.

35. Nelson, R. (1994). *1001 ways to reward employees*. New York: Workman Publishing.

36. Nelson, B. (1999). Recognition plans can be simple, yet effective. *Charlotte Business Journal*, June 25.

37. Easterlin, R. (2000). Income and happiness: Towards a unified theory. *The Economic Journal*, 111, 465–484. Easterlin, R. (2001). Life cycle welfare: Trends and differences. *Journal of Happiness Studies*, 2, 1–12.

38. Whetten, D., and Cameron, K. (1998). *Developing management skills*. (4th ed.). Reading, MA: Addison-Wesley.

39. Podsakoff, P. M., Bommer, W. H., Podsakoff, N. P., and MacKenzie, S. B. (2006). Relationships between leader reward and punishment behavior and subordinate attitudes, perceptions, and behaviors: A meta-analytic review of existing and new research. *Organizational Behavior and Human Decision Process*, 99, 113–142.

Chapter 7

1. Fournies, F. F. (2000). *Coaching for improved work performance*. New York: McGraw-Hill.

2. Huselid, M. A. (1995). The impact of human resources management practices on turnover, productivity, and corporate financial performance. *Academy of Management Journal*, 38 (1), 635–672.

3. Kluger, A. N., and Denisi, A. S. (1996). The effects of feedback intervention on performance: Historical review, a meta-analysis and a preliminary feedback intervention theory. *Psychological Bulletin*, 119, 254–284.

4. Campbell, J. P., McCloy, R. A., Oppler, S. H., and Sager, C. E. (1993). A theory of performance. In N. Schmitt, Borman, W. and W. C. Borman (Eds.), *Personnel Selection in Organizations*. San Francisco: Jossey-Bass.

5. Posdakoff, N. P., Whiting, S. W., Podsakoff, P. M., and Blume, B. D. (2009). Individual- and organizational-level consequences of organizational citizenship behaviors: A meta-analysis. *Journal of Applied Psychology*, 94, 122–141; Nielsen, T. M., Hrivnak, G. A., and Shaw, M. (2009). Organizational citizenship behavior and performance: A meta-analysis of group-level research. *Small Group Research*, 40, 555–577.

6. Organ, D. W. (1988). *Organizational citizenship behavior: The good soldier syndrome*. Lexington, MA: D. C. Heath.

7. Judge, T. A., Thoresen, C. J., Bono, J. E., and Patton, G. K. (2001). The job satisfaction–job performance relationship: A qualitative and quantitative review. *Psychological Bulletin*, 127, 376–407.

8. Riketta, M. (2008). The causal relation between job attitudes and performance: A meta-analysis of panel studies. *Journal of Applied Psychology, 93,* 472–481.

9. Koys, D. J. (2001). The effects of employee satisfaction, organizational citizenship behavior, and turnover on organizational effectiveness: A unit-level longitudinal study. *Personnel Psychology,* 101–114; Griffith, J. (2001). Do satisfied employees satisfy customers? Support-services staff morale and satisfaction among public school administrators, students and parents. *Journal of Applied Social Psychology, 31,* 1627–1658.

10. Kinicki, A. J., McKee-Ryan, F. M., Schriesheim, C. A., and Carson, K. P. (2002). Assessing the construct validity of the Job Descriptive Index: A review and meta-analysis. *Journal of Applied Psychology, 87,* 14–32.

11. Meyer, J. P., Allen, N. J., and Smith, C. A. (1993). Commitment to organizations and occupations: Extension and test of a three-component conceptualization. *Journal of Applied Psychology, 78,* 538–551.

12. Luchak, A. A., and Gellatly, I. R. (2007). A comparison of linear and nonlinear relations between organizational commitment and work outcomes. *Journal of Applied Psychology, 92,* 786–793.

13. Avolio, B. J., Zhu, W., Koh, W., and Bhatia, P. (2004). Transformational leadership and organizational commitment: Mediating role of psychological empowerment and moderating role of structural distance. *Journal of Organizational Behavior, 25,* 951–968.

14. Andersson, L. M. (1996). Employee cynicism: An examination using a contract violation framework. *Human Relations, 49,* 1395–1418.

15. Rubin, R. S., Bommer, W. H., Dierdorff, E. C., and Baldwin, T. T. (2009). Do leaders reap what they sow? Leader and employee outcomes of leader cynicism about organizational change. *The Leadership Quarterly, 20,* 680–688.

16. Johnson, J. L., and O'Leary-Kelly, A. M. (2003). The effects of psychological contract breach and organizational cynicism: Not all social exchange violations are created equal. *Journal of Organizational Behavior, 24,* 627–647.

17. Andersson, L. M., and Bateman, T. S. (1997). Cynicism in the workplace: Some causes and effects. *Journal of Organizational Behavior, 18,* 449–460; Davis, W. D., and Gardner, W. L. (2004). Perceptions of politics and organizational cynicism: An attributional and leader–member exchange perspective. *The Leadership Quarterly, 15,* 439–465; Wilhelm, P. G. (1993). Application of distributive justice theory to the CEO pay problem: Recommendations for reform. *Journal of Business Ethics, 12,* 469–482.

18. Reichers, A. E., Wanous, J. P., and Austin, J. T. (1997). Understanding and managing cynicism about organizational change. *Academy of Management Executive, 11,* 48–59; Bommer, W. H., Rubin, R. S., and Baldwin, T. T. (2004). Setting the stage for effective leadership: Antecedents of transformational leadership behavior. *The Leadership Quarterly, 15,* 195–210.

19. Latham, G. P. (2004). The motivational benefits of goal setting. *Academy of Management Executive, 18* (4), 126–129.

20. Latham, G. P., and Wexley, K. N. (1994). *Increasing productivity through performance appraisal.* (2nd ed.). Reading, MA: Addison-Wesley.

21. Rynes, S. L., Gerhart, B., and Parks, L. (2005). Personnel psychology: Performance evaluation and pay for performance. *Annual Review of Psychology, 56,* 571–600.

22. Latham, G. P., and Wexley, K. N. (1994). *Increasing productivity through performance appraisal.* (2nd ed.). Reading, MA: Addison-Wesley.

23. Kluger, A. N., and DeNisi, A. S. (2000). Feedback effectiveness: Can 360-degree appraisals be improved? *Academy of Management Executive, 14* (1), 129–139.

24. Kluger, A. N., and DeNisi, A. S. (1996). The effects of feedback interventions on performance: Historical review, a meta-analysis, and a preliminary feedback intervention theory. *Psychological Bulletin, 119,* 225–284.

25. Ibid.

26. Nadler, D. A. (1977). *Feedback and organization development: Using data-based methods.* Reading, MA: Addison-Wesley.

27. Schein, E. H. (1999). *Process consultation revisited. Building the helpful relationship.* Reading, MA: Addison-Wesley.

28. Kluger, A. N., and DeNisi, A. S. (2000). Feedback effectiveness: Can 360-degree appraisals be improved? *Academy of Management Executive, 14* (1), 129–139.

29. Ilgen, D. R., Fisher, C. D., and Taylor, M. S. (1979). Consequences of individual feedback on behavior in organizations. *Journal of Applied Psychology, 64* (4), 349–371.

30. Hunt, J. M., and Weintraub, J. R. (2002). *The coaching manager: Developing top talent in business.* Thousand Oaks, CA: Sage.

31. Example taken from Schein, E. H. (1999). *Process consultation revisited. Building the helpful relationship* (p. 138). Reading, MA: Addison-Wesley.

32. London, M. (2003). *Job feedback: Giving, seeking and using feedback for performance improvement.* Mahwah, NJ: Lawrence Earlbaum Associates.

33. Colquitt, J. A., Conlon, D. E., Wesson, M. J., Porter, C., and Ng, K. Y. (2001). Justice at the millennium: A meta-analytic review of 25 years of organizational justice research. *Journal of Applied Psychology, 86* (3), 425–445.

34. Adapted from Orth, C. D., Wilkinson, H. E., and Benfari, R. C. (2001). The manager's role as coach and mentor. *Organizational Dynamics, 16,* 66–73.

35. Adapted from Fournies, F. F. (2000). *Coaching for improved work performance.* New York: McGraw-Hill.

36. Buckingham, M., and Coffman, C. (1999). *First, break all the rules. What the worlds' greatest managers do differently.* New York: Simon & Shuster.

37. Bayer, R. (2000). Termination with dignity. *Business Horizons, 43* (September–October), 4–10.

38. Flynn, G. (1995). Thirteen steps to a smoother termination. *Personnel Journal, 74* (10), 27–30.

39. Sussman, L., and Finnegan, R. (1998). Coaching the star: Rationale and strategies. *Business Horizons, 41* (March–April), 47–54.

40. Groysberg, B., Nanda, A., and Nohria, N. (2004). The risky business of hiring stars. *Harvard Business Review, 82* (5) (May), 92–99.

41. Lombardo, M. M., and Eichinger, R. W. (2000). High potentials as high learners. *Human Resource Management Journal, 39* (4), 321–329.

42. Trank, C. Q., Rynes, S. L., and Bretz, R. D., Jr. (2002). Attracting applicants in the war for talent: Differences in the work preferences among high achievers. *Journal of Business & Psychology, 16* (3), 331–345.

43. Ibid.

44. McCauley, C. D., Moxley, R. S., and Velsor, E. V. (1998). *The center for creative leadership: Handbook of leadership development.* San Francisco: Jossey-Bass.

45. Kram, K. E. (1985). *Mentoring at work. Developing relationships in organizational life.* Glenview, IL: Scott, Foresman.

46. Ashford, S. J., and Cummings, L. L. (1983). Feedback as an individual resource: Personal strategies of creating information. *Organizational Behavior and Human Performance, 32,* 370–398.

Chapter 8

1. Granovetter, M. S. (1973). The strength of weak ties. *American Journal of Sociology, 78,* 1360–1380. Granovetter, M. S. (1994). *Getting a job: A study in contacts and careers.* (2nd ed.). Chicago: University of Chicago Press.

2. Montgomery, J. D. (1992). Job search and network composition: Implications of the strength-of-weak-ties hypothesis. *American Sociological Review, 57,* 586–596; Montgomery, J. D. (1994). Weak ties, employment, and inequality: An equilibrium analysis. *American Journal of Sociology, 99,* 1212–1236.

3. Granovetter, M. S. (1994). *Getting a job: A study in contacts and careers.* (2nd ed.). Chicago: University of Chicago Press.

4. French, J.P.R., Jr., and Raven, B. (1960). The bases of social power. In D. Cartwright and A. Zander (Eds.), *Group dynamics* (pp. 607–623). New York: Harper & Row.

5. Sherif, M. (1935). A study of some social factors in perception. *Archives of Psychology, 27* (187), 17–22. Asch, S. E. (1955). Opinions and social pressure. *Scientific American, 193* (5), 31–35.

6. Bond, R., and Smith, P. B. (1996). Culture and conformity: A meta-analysis of studies using Asch's (1952b, 1956) line judgment task. *Psychological Bulletin, 119* (1), 111–137.

7. Yukl, G., Kim, H., and Falbe, C. M. (1996). Antecedents of influence outcomes. *Journal of Applied Psychology, 81,* 309–317. Yukl, G., and Tracey, J. B. (1992). Consequences of influence tactics used with subordinates, peers, and the boss. *Journal of Applied Psychology, 77,* 525–535.

8. Ibid.

9. Ibid.

10. Falbe, C. M., and Yukl, G. (1992). Consequences for managers of using single influence tactics and combinations of tactics. *Academy of Management Journal, 35,* 638–652.

11. Fox, S., and Amichai-Hamburger, Y. (2001). The power of emotional appeals in promoting organizational change programs. *Academy of Management Executive, 15* (4), 84–94.

12. Higgins, C. A., Judge, T. A., and Ferris, G. R. (2003). Influence tactics and work outcomes: A meta-analysis. *Journal of Organizational Behavior, 24* (1), 89–106.

13. Ferris, G. R., Perrewe, P. L., Anthony, W. P., and Gilmore, D. C. (2000). Political skill at work. *Organizational Dynamics, 28* (4), 25–37.

14. Throughout this section, we relied heavily on Cialdini, R. B. (2001). *Influence: Science and practice.* (4th ed.). Boston: Allyn & Bacon.

15. Hosoda, M., Stone-Romero, E. F., and Coats, G. (2003). The effects of physical attractiveness on job-related outcomes: A meta-analysis of experimental studies. *Personnel Psychology, 56,* 431–462.

16. For a detailed review of this literature, see Eagly, A. H., Ashmore, R. D., Makhijani, M. G., and Longo, L. C. (1991). What is beautiful is good, but . . .: A meta-analytic review of research on the physical attractiveness stereotype. *Psychological Bulletin, 110,* 109–128.

17. Efran, M. G., and Patterson, E.W.J. (1974). Voters vote beautiful: The effects of physical appearance on a national election. *Canadian Journal of Behavioral Science, 6,* 352–356.

18. Hamermesh, D. S., and Biddle, J. E. (1994). Beauty and the labor market. *The American Economic Review, 84* (5), 1174–1194.

19. Dion, K., Berscheid, E., and Walster, E. (1972). What is beautiful is good. *Journal of Personality and Social Psychology, 24,* 285–290.

20. Ritts, V., Patterson, M. L., and Tubbs, M. E. (1992). Expectations, impressions, and judgments of physically attractive students: A review. *Review of Educational Research, 64,* 413–426.

21. Furnham, A. (1996). Factors relating to the allocation of medical resources. *Journal of Social Behavior and Personality, 11,* 615–624.

22. Drachman, D., deCarufel, A., and Insko, C. (1978). The extra credit effect in interpersonal attraction. *Journal of Experimental Social Psychology, 14,* 458–465.

23. Cialdini, R. B. (2001). *Influence: Science and practice,* 53.

24. Sherman, S. J. (1980). On the self-erasing nature of errors of prediction. *Journal of Personality and Social Psychology, 39,* 211–221.

25. Cialdini, R. B. (2001). *Influence: Science and practice.*

26. Brehm, J. W. (1966). *A theory of psychological reactance.* New York: Academic Press.

27. Cialdini, R. B. (2001). Harnessing the science of persuasion. *Harvard Business Review, 79* (9), 72–79.

28. Cialdini, R. B. (2001). *Influence: Science and practice,* 53.

29. Cialdini, R. B. (2001). Harnessing the science of persuasion. *Harvard Business Review, 79* (9), 72–79.

30. Ibid.

31. Cialdini, R. B. (2005). Don't throw in the towel. Using social influence research. *Association for Psychological Science.* Accessed 8/31/11 from http://www.psychologicalscience.org/observer/getArticle.cfm?id=1762.

32. Bushman, B. J. (1988). The effects of apparel on compliance. *Personality and Social Psychology Bulletin, 14,* 459–467.

33. Deluga, R. J. (2003). Kissing up to the boss: What it is and what to do about it. *Business Forum, 26* (3/4), 14–18; Jones, E. (1990). *Interpersonal perception.* New York: Freeman; Michener, H., Plazewski, J., and Vaske, J. (1979). Ingratiation tactics channeled by target values and threat capability. *Journal of Personality, 47,* 35–56.

34. DeVries, M.F.R. (2001). *The leadership mystique,* p. 94. London: Financial Times/Prentice Hall.

35. Hegarty, W. (1974). Using subordinate ratings to elicit behavioral changes in supervisors. *Journal of Applied Psychology, 59,* 764–766; Tourish, D., and Robson, P. (2003). Critical upward feedback in organizations: Processes, problems, and implications for communication management. *Journal of Communication Management,* 8 (2), 150–167.

36. Nutt, P. (1999). Surprising but true: Half the decisions in organizations fail. *Academy of Management Executive,* 13, 75–90.

37. Atwater, L., Waldman, D., Atwater, D., and Carrier, P. (2000). An upward feedback field experiment: Supervisors' cynicism, reactions, and commitment to subordinates. *Personnel Psychology, 53,* 275–297.

38. Drucker, P. (1954). *The Practice of Management.* New York: Harper Collins.

39. Drucker, P. F. (1967). *The effective executive.* New York: Harper Collins.

40. Becerra, M., and Gupta, A. K. (2003). Perceived trustworthiness within the organization: The moderating impact of communication frequency on trustor and trustee effects. *Organization Science, 14,* 32–44.

41. Corman, S., and Poole, M. (2000). The need for common ground. In S. Corman and M. Poole (Eds.), *Perspectives on organizational communication: Finding common ground* (pp. 3–16). New York: Guilford Press.

42. Cable, D. M., and Judge, T. A. (2003). Managers' upward influence tactic strategies: The role of personality and supervisor leadership style. *Journal of Organizational Behavior, 24,* 197–210. Pater, R. (2005). High-level persuasion: Influencing up, down, and sideways. *Occupational Health & Safety, 74* (1) (January), 24–30.

43. Krone, K. (1992). A comparison of organizational, structural, and relationship effects on subordinates' upward influence choices. *Communication Quarterly, 40,* 1–15.

44. McCall, M. W., and Lombardo, M. M. (1983). *Off the track: Why and how successful executives get derailed. Technical Report 21.* Greensboro, NC: Center for Creative Leadership; Leslie, J., and Van Velsor, E. (1996). *A look at derailment today: North America and Europe. CCL No. 169.* Greensboro, NC: Center for Creative Leadership.

45. Ibid.

46. Cross, R., and Parker, A. (2004). *The hidden power of social networks.* Boston: Harvard Business School Press.

47. Cross, R., Davenport, T., and Cantrell, S. (2003). *Rising above the crowd: High performing knowledge workers differentiate themselves.* Accenture Institute for Strategic Change working paper.

48. Ibid.

Chapter 9

1. Bass, B. M. (1990). *Bass and Stogdill's handbook of leadership: Theory, research, and managerial applications.* New York: The Free Press.

2. Zhang, Z., Ilies, R., and Arvey, R. D. (2009). Beyond genetic explanations for leadership. The moderating role of the social environment. *Organizational Behavior and Human Decision Processes,* 110, 118–128.

3. Dierdorff, E. C., Rubin, R. S., and Morgeson, F. P. (2009). The milieu of managerial work: An integrative framework linking work context to role requirements. *Journal of Applied Psychology, 94,* 972–988.

4. Podsakoff, P. M., Bommer, W. H., Podsakoff, N. P., and MacKenzie, S. B. (2006). Relationships between leader reward and punishment behavior and subordinate attitudes, perceptions and behaviors: A meta-analytic review of existing and new research. *Organizational Behavior and Human Decision Processes,* 99, 113–142; Judge, T. A., and Piccolo, R. F. (2004). Transformational and transactional leadership: A meta-analytic test of their relative weights. *Journal of Applied Psychology, 89,* 75–768.

5. Pfeffer, J. (1996). *Competitive advantage through people.* Cambridge, MA: Harvard Press.

6. Amazon search conducted in September 2011. www.amazon.com.

7. Hogan, R., and Hogan, J. (2001). Assessing leadership: A view from the dark side. *International Journal of Selection and Assessment,* 9, 40–51.

8. Avolio, B. J. (1999). *Full leadership development: Building the vital forces in organizations.* Thousand Oaks, CA: Sage Publications.

9. Bass, B. M. (1990). *Bass and Stogdill's handbook of leadership.*

10. Hughes, R. L., Ginnett, R. C., and Curphy, G. J. (1993). *Leadership: Enhancing the lessons of experience.* Burr Ridge, IL: Richard D. Irwin, Inc.

11. Allison, S. T., and Eylon, D. (2005). The demise of leadership: Death positivity biases in posthumous impressions of leaders. In D. Messick and R. Kramer (Eds.), *The psychology of leadership: Some new approaches.* New York: Erlbaum.

12. Kouzes, J., and Posner, B. (1997). *The leadership challenge.* San Francisco: Jossey-Bass.

13. Fleishman, E. A. (1973). Twenty years of consideration and structure. In E. A. Fleishman and J. G. Hunt (Eds.), *Current developments in the study of leadership.* Carbondale, IL: Southern Illinois University Press.

14. Dansereau, F., Jr., Graen, G., and Haga, W. J. (1975). A vertical dyad linkage approach to leadership within formal organizations: A longitudinal investigation of the role-making process. *Organizational Behavior and Human Performance*, 13, 46–78.

15. Wayne, S. J., Shore, L. M., and Liden, R. C. (1997). Perceived organizational support and leader-member exchange: A social exchange perspective. *Academy of Management Journal*, 40, 82–111. Liden, R. C., Sparrowe, R. T., and Wayne, S. J. (1997). Leader-member exchange theory: The past and potential for the future. In G. Ferris (Ed.), *Research in personnel and human resources management* (pp. 47–119). Greenwich, CT: JAI Press.

16. Gerstner, C. R., and Day, D. V. (1997). Meta-analytic review of leader-member exchange theory: Correlates and construct issues. *Journal of Applied Psychology*, 82, 827–844.

17. Gouldner, A. W. (1960). The norm of reciprocity: A preliminary statement. *American Sociological Review*, 25, 161–177; Liden, R. C., Sparrowe, R. T., and Wayne, S. J. (1997). Leader-member exchange theory: The past and potential for the future. In G. R. Ferris (Ed.), *Research in personnel and human resources management* (Vol. 15, pp. 47–119). Greenwich, CT: JAI Press.

18. Podsakoff, P. M., Bommer, W. H., Podsakoff, N. P., and MacKenzie, S. B. (2006). Relationships between leader reward and punishment behavior and subordinate attitudes, perceptions, and behaviors.

19. Ibid.

20. Rubin, R. S., Bommer, W. H., and Bachrach, D. G. (2010). Operant leadership and employee citizenship: A question of trust? *The Leadership Quarterly*, 21, 400–408.

21. Bass, B. M. (1990). *Bass and Stogdill's handbook of leadership*, 14.

22. Podsakoff, P. M., MacKenzie, S. B., Moorman, R. H., and Fetter, R. (1990). Transformational leader behaviors and their effects on followers' trust in leader, satisfaction, and organizational citizenship behaviors. *Leadership Quarterly*, 1, 107–142.

23. Podsakoff, P. M., MacKenzie, S. B., and Bommer, W. H. (1996). Transformational leader behaviors and substitutes for leadership as determinants of employee satisfaction, commitment, trust, and organizational citizenship behaviors. *Journal of Management*, 22, 259–298.

24. Onnen, M. K. (1987). The relationship of clergy and leadership characteristics to growing or declining churches. Doctoral dissertation, University of Louisville, KY.

25. Barling, J., Weber, T., and Kelloway, E. K. (1996). Effects of transformational leadership training on attitudinal and financial outcomes: A field experiment. *Journal of Applied Psychology*, 81, 827–832.

26. Podsakoff, P. M., MacKenzie, S. B., and Bommer, W. H. (1996). Transformational leader behaviors and substitutes for leadership as determinants of employee satisfaction, commitment, trust, and organizational citizenship behaviors.

27. Jung, D., Wu, A., and Chow, C. W. (2008). Towards understanding the direct and indirect effects of CEOs' transformational leadership on firm innovation. *The Leadership Quarterly*, 19, 582–594.

28. Nemanich, L. A. and Keller, R. T. (2007). Transformational leadership in an acquisition: A field study of employees. *The Leadership Quarterly*, 18, 49–68.

29. Geyer, A.L.J., and Steyrer, J. M. (1998). Transformational leadership and objective performance in banks. *Applied Psychology: An International Review*, 47, 397–420.

30. MacKenzie, S. B., Podsakoff, P. M., and Rich, G. A. (2001). Transformational and transactional leadership and salesperson performance. *Journal of Academy of Marketing Science*, 29 (2), 115–134.

31. Williams, H. M., Parker, S. K., and Turner, N. (2010). Proactively performing teams: The role of work design, transformational leadership, and team composition. *Journal of Occupational and Organizational Psychology*, 83, 301–324.

32. Frese, M., Beimel, S., and Schoenborn, S. (2003). Action training for charismatic leadership: Two evaluations of studies of a commercial training module on inspirational communication of a vision. *Personnel Psychology*, 56, 671–699.

33. Kouzes, J., and Posner, B. (1997). *The leadership challenge*. San Francisco: Jossey-Bass.

34. Rosenthal, R., and Rubin, D. B. (1971). Pygmalion reaffirmed. In J. D. Elashoff and R. E. Snow (Eds.), *Pygmalion Reconsidered* (pp. 139–155). Worthington, OH: Jones Publishing.

35. Tannenbaum, S. I. (1998). Enhancing continuous learning: Diagnostic findings from multiple companies. *Human Resource Management*, 36, 437–452.

36. Examples in this section were taken verbatim from McCauley, Moxley, and Van Veslor (1998). *The Center for Creative Leadership handbook of leadership development*. San Francisco, CA: Jossey-Bass.

Chapter 10

1. Katzenbach, J. R., and Smith, D. (1993). *The wisdom of teams*. Cambridge, MA: Harvard Business School Press.

2. Freiberg, K., and Freiberg, J. (1998). *Nuts! Southwest Airlines' crazy recipe for business and personal success*. New York: Bantam Paperbacks.

3. Dumaine, B. (1993). The trouble with teams. *Fortune*, September 5, 86–92.

4. Adapted from Thompson, L. L. (2004). *Making the team: A guide for managers*. Upper Saddle River, NJ: Pearson Prentice Hall.

5. Maier, N.R.G. (1967). Assets and liabilities of group problem solving: The need for an integrative function. *Psychological Review*, 74, 239–249. Leavitt, H. (1975). Suppose we took groups seriously. In E. L. Cass and F. G. Zimmer (Eds.), *Man and work in society*. New York: Van Nostrand Reinhold.

6. Katzenbach, J. R., and Smith, D. (1993). *The wisdom of teams*. Cambridge, MA: Harvard Business School Press.

7. Hackman, J. R. (1990). *Groups that work and those that don't*. San Francisco, CA: Jossey-Bass.

8. Katzenbach, J. R., and Smith, D. (2001). *The discipline of teams*. New York: Wiley; Cohen, S. G., and Bailey, D. E. (1997). What makes teams work: Group effectiveness research from the shop floor to the executive suite. *Journal of Management, 23*, 239–290; Guzzo, R. A., and Dickson, M. W. (1996). Teams in organizations: Recent research on performance and effectiveness. *Annual Review of Psychology, 47*, 307–338; Campion, M. A., Papper, E. M., and Medsker, G. J. (1996). Relations between work team characteristics and effectiveness: A replication and extension. *Personnel Psychology, 49*, 429–452.

9. Katzenbach, J. R., and Smith, D. (1993). *The wisdom of teams*. Cambridge, MA: Harvard Business School Press.

10. Wicker, A. W., Kermeyer, S. L., Hanson, L., and Alexander, D. (1976). Effects of manning levels on subjective experiences, performance and verbal interaction in groups. *Organizational Behavior and Human Performance, 17*, 251–274; McGrath, J. E. (1990). *Groups: Interaction and performance*. Upper Saddle River, NJ: Prentice Hall.

11. Deutschman, A. (2004). Inside the mind of Jeff Bezos and his plans for Amazon. *Fast Company*, August, 52–58.

12. Stevens, M. A., and Campion, M. J. (1994). The knowledge, skill and ability requirements for teamwork: Implications for human resource management. *Journal of Management, 20*, 503–530.

13. Stevens, M. J., and Campion, M. A. (1999). Staffing work teams: Development and validation of a selection test for teamwork settings. *Journal of Management, 25* (2), 207–228.

14. Chen, G., Donahue, L. M., and Klimoski, R. J. (2004). Training undergraduates to work in organizational teams. *Academy of Management Learning and Education, 3* (1), 27–40. Stevens, M. J., and Campion, M. A. (1999). Staffing work teams: Development and validation of a selection test for teamwork settings. *Journal of Management, 25* (2), 207–228.

15. Neuman, G. A., and Wright, J. (1999). Team effectiveness: Beyond skills and cognitive ability. *Journal of Applied Psychology, 84*, 376–389.

16. Katzenbach, J. R., and Smith, D. (1993). *The wisdom of teams*. Cambridge, MA: Harvard Business School Press.

17. Ibid.

18. Pritchard, R. D., Jones, S. D., Roth, P. L., Stuebing, J., and Ekeberg, S. E. (1988). Effects of group feedback, goal setting and incentives on organizational productivity. *Journal of Applied Psychology, 73*, 337–58.

19. Anderson, D. C., Crowell, C. R., Doman, M., and Howard, G. S. (1988). Performance posting, goal setting and activity-contingent praise as applied to a college hockey team. *Journal of Applied Psychology, 73*, 87–95.

20. Zander, A., and Newcomb, T. (1967). Group level of aspiration in United Way Fund campaigns. *Journal of Personality and Social Psychology, 6*, 157–162.

21. Ibid.

22. Tuckman, B. W. (1965). Developmental sequence in small groups. *Psychological Bulletin, 63*, 384–399; Tuckman, B., and Jensen, M. (1977). Stages of small group development. *Group and Organizational Studies, 2*, 419–427.

23. Argote, L. (1989). Agreement about norms and work-unit effectiveness: Evidence from the field. *Basic and Applied Social Psychology, 10* (2), 131–140.

24. Miller, L. K., and Hamblin, R. L. (1963). Interdependence, differential rewarding, and productivity. *American Sociological Review, 28*, 768–778; Wageman, R. (1995). Interdependence and group effectiveness. *Administrative Science Quarterly, 40*, 145–180. Fan, E. T., and Gruenfeld, D. H. (1998). When needs outweigh desires: The effects of resource interdependence and reward interdependence on group problem solving. *Basic and Applied Social Psychology, 20* (1), 45–56. Thompson, L. L. (2004). *Making the team: A guide for managers*. Upper Saddle River, NJ: Pearson Prentice Hall.

25. Adapted from Parker, G., McAdams, J., and Zielinski, D. (2000). *Rewarding teams: Lessons from the trenches*. San Francisco: Jossey-Bass.

26. Ibid.

27. Ibid.

28. Lencioni, P. (2002). *The five dysfunctions of a team: A leadership fable*. San Francisco: Jossey-Bass.

29. Steiner, I. (1972). *Group process and productivity*. New York: Academic Press.

30. Adapted from Thompson, L. L. (2004). *Making the team: A guide for managers*. Upper Saddle River, NJ: Pearson Prentice Hall.

31. Baumeister, R. F. (1984). Choking under pressure: Self-consciousness and paradoxical effects of incentives on skillful performance. *Journal of Personality and Social Psychology, 46*, 610–620.

32. Staw, B. H. (1976). Knee-deep in the big muddy: A study of escalating commitment to a chosen course of action. *Organizational Behavior and Human Decision Processes, 16* (1), 27–44.

33. Milgram, S. (1974). *Obedience to authority: An experimental view*. New York: Harper Collins.

34. Keysar, B., and Henly, A. (2002). Speakers' overestimation of their effectiveness. *Psychological Science, 13* (3), 207–212.

35. Ibid.

36. Gigone, D., and Hastie, R. (1993). The common knowledge effect: Information sharing and group judgment. *Journal of Personality and Social Psychology, 65* (5), 959–974.

37. Shaw, M. E. (1981). *Group dynamics: The psychology of small group behavior*. (3rd ed.). New York: McGraw-Hill; Stasser, G., Stewart, D. D., and Wittenbaum, G. M. (1995). Expert roles and information exchange during discussion: The importance of knowing who knows what. *Journal of Experimental Social Psychology, 31*, 244–265.

38. Kravitz, D. A., and Martin, B. (1986). Ringelmann rediscovered: The original article. *Journal of Personality and Social Psychology, 50* (5), 936–941.

39. Ringelmann's research as cited in Forsyth, D. (1990). *Group dynamics*. Pacific Grove, CA: Brooks/Cole.

40. Williams, K., Harkins, S., and Latane, B. (1981). Identifiability as a deterrent to social loafing: Two cheering experiments. *Journal of Personality and Social Psychology, 40*, 303–311.

41. Mulvey, P. W., Veiga, J. F., and Elsass, P. M. (1996). When teammates raise a white flag. *Academy of Management Executive, 10* (1), 40–49.

42. Asch, S. E. (1951). Effects of group pressure upon the modification and distortion of judgments. In Guetzkow, H. (Ed.), *Groups, Leadership, and Men* (pp. 177–190). Pittsburgh: Carnegie Press.

43. Janis, I. L. (1982). *Groupthink: Psychological studies of policy decisions and fiascoes*. (2nd ed.) Boston: Houghton Mifflin.

44. Adapted from Parker, G., McAdams, J., and Zielinski, D. (2000). *Rewarding teams: Lessons from the trenches*. San Francisco: Jossey-Bass.

45. Harvey, J. (1974). The Abilene paradox: The management of agreement. *Organizational Dynamics, 3* (1), 63–80.

46. Ibid.

47. Benn, K. D., and Sheats, P. (1948). Functional roles of group members. *Journal of Social Issues, 4*, 41–49.

48. Mullen, B., and Cooper, C. (1994). The relation between group cohesiveness and performance: An integration. *Psychological Bulletin, 115*, 210–227; Berkowitz, L. (1954). Group standards, cohesiveness and productivity. *Human Relations, 7*, 509–519.

49. Brawley, L. R., Carron, A. V., and Widmeyer, W. N. (1988). Exploring the relationship between cohesion and group resistance to disruption. *Journal of Sport and Exercise Psychology, 10* (2), 199–213.

50. Mullen, B., and Cooper, C. (1994). The relation between group cohesiveness and performance: An integration. *Psychological Bulletin, 115*, 210–227. Berkowitz, L. (1954). Group standards, cohesiveness and productivity. *Human Relations, 7*, 509–519.

51. Heath, D., and Heath, C. (2008). Get back in the box: How constraints can free your team's thinking. *Fast Company*, January, 74–75.

52. Ibid.

53. Cascio, W. F. (2000). Managing a virtual workforce. *Academy of Management Executive, 14* (3), 81–90.

54. Haywood, M. (1998). *Managing virtual teams: Practical techniques for high technology managers*. Boston: Artech House. Henry, J. E., and Hartzler, M. (1998). *Tools for virtual teams: A team fitness companion*. Milwaukee, WI: ASQ Press.

55. Coutu, D. (1998). Trust in virtual teams. *Harvard Business Review, 76* (3) (May–June), 20–21.

56. Dennis, A., and Reinicke, B. (2004). Beta vs. VHS and the acceptance of electronic brainstorming technology. *MIS Quarterly, 28* (1), 1–20.

57. Adapted from Parker, G., McAdams, J., and Zielinski, D. (2000). *Rewarding teams: Lessons from the trenches*. San Francisco: Jossey-Bass.

58. Adapted from Kiger, P. J. (2006). Small groups big ideas. *Workforce Management, 85* (4), 22–27.

Chapter 11

1. Lax, D. A., and Sebenius, J. K. (1986). *Manager as negotiator*. New York: The Free Press.

2. Jehn, K. (1994). Enhancing effectiveness: An investigation of advantages and disadvantages of value-based intragroup conflict. *International Journal of Conflict Management, 5*, 223–238.

3. Amason, A. (1996). Distinguishing the effects of functional and dysfunctional conflict on strategic decision-making: Resolving a paradox for top management teams. *Academy of Management Journal, 39* (1), 123–148.

4. Ibid.

5. De Dreu, C.K.W. (2006). When too little or too much hurts: Evidence for a curvilinear relationship between task conflict and innovation in teams. *Journal of Management, 32*, 83–107.

6. De Wit, F.R.C., Greer, L. L., and Jehn, K. A. (in press). The paradox of intragroup conflict: A meta-analysis. *Journal of Applied Psychology*.

7. De Dreu, C.K.W., and Weingart, L. R. (2003). Task versus relationship conflict and team effectiveness: A meta-analysis. *Journal of Applied Psychology, 88*, 741–749; Jehn, K. A., and Mannix, E. (2001). The dynamic nature of conflict: A longitudinal study of intragroup conflict and group performance. *Academy of Management Journal, 44*, 238–251.

8. Simons, T. (1995). Top management team consensus, heterogeneity, and debate as contingent predictors of company performance: The complementarity of group structure and process. *Academy of Management Best Proceedings*, 62–66.

9. De Dreu, C.K.W., and Weingart, L. R. (2003). Task versus relationship conflict and team effectiveness.

10. Jehn, K. A., and Mannix, E. (2001). The dynamic nature of conflict.

11. Jainism and Buddhism. *Udana*, 68–69.

12. Hottes, J. H., and Kahn, A. (1974). Sex differences in a mixed-motive conflict situation. *Journal of Personality, 42*, 260–275.

13. Bergmann, T. J., and Volkema, R. J. (1994). Issues, behavioral responses, and consequences in interpersonal conflicts. *Journal of Organizational Behavior, 15* (5), 467–471.

14. Ibid.

15. Sherif, M., Harvey, O. J., White, B. J., Hood, W. R., and Sherif, C. W. (1954). *Experimental study of positive and negative intergroup attitudes between experimentally produced groups. Robbers Cave Study*. Norman, OK: University of Oklahoma Press.

16. Fisher, R., and Ury, W. (1981). *Getting to yes: Negotiating agreement without giving in*. New York: Penguin Books.

17. Lee, K. N. (1982). Defining success in environmental dispute resolution. *Resolve*, Spring, 1–6.

18. Bazerman, M. A., and Neale, M. H. (1991). *Negotiating rationally*. New York: Free Press.

19. Adapted from Yourdon, E. (2004). *Death march*. Upper Saddle River, NJ: Prentice Hall.

20. Lewicki, R., Barry, B., Saunders, D., and Minton, J. (2003). *Essentials of negotiation*. Burr Ridge, IL: McGraw-Hill.

21. General Electric Co., 150 NLRB 192, 57 LRRM 1491 (1964), *enf'd sub nom*, NLRB v. General Electric Co., 418 F.2d 736, 72 LRRM 2530 (2d Cir. 1969), *cert. denied*, 397 U.S. 965, 73 LRRM 2600 (1970).

22. Rackham, N. (1999). The behaviour of successful negotiators. In Lewicki, Saunders, and Minton (Eds.), *Negotiation readings, exercises and cases*. Burr Ridge, IL: McGraw-Hill, pp. 341–353.

23. Colosi, T. (1983). Negotiating in the public and private sectors. *American Behavioral Scientist*, 27 (November–December), 229–253.

24. Ibid.

Chapter 12

1. Pfeffer, J. (1996). *Competitive advantage through people: Unleashing the power of the work force*. Watertown, MA: Harvard Business Press.

2. Combs, J., Liu, Y., Hall, A., and Ketchen, D. (2006). How much do high-performance work practices matter? A meta-analysis of their effects on organizational performance. *Personnel Psychology*, 59, 501–528.

3. Rynes, S. L., Brown, K. G., and Colbert, A. E. (2002). Seven misconceptions about human resource practices: Research findings versus practitioner beliefs. *Academy of Management Executive*, 16 (3), 92–103. Terpstra, D. E. (1996). The search for effective methods. *HRFocus*, 73, 16–17.

4. Dougherty, T. W., Tuban, D. B., and Callender, J. C. (1994). Confirming first impressions in the employment interview: A field study of interviewer behavior. *Journal of Applied Psychology*, 79, 659–665. Dipboye, R. L., and Gaugler, B. B. (1993). Cognitive and behavioral processes in the selection interview. In N. Schmitt and W. Borman (Eds.), *Personnel selection in organizations* (pp. 135–170). San Francisco: Jossey-Bass.

5. Anderson, C. W. (1960). The relation between speaking times and decisions in the employment interview. *Journal of Applied Psychology*, 44, 267–268.

6. Klenmuntz, B. (1990). Why we still use our heads instead of formulas: Toward an integrative approach. *Psychological Bulletin*, 107, 296–310; Meehl, P. (1954). *Clinical versus statistical prediction*. Minneapolis, MN: University of Minnesota Press.

7. O'Reilly, C. A., Chatman, J. A., and Caldwell, D. F. (1991). People and organizational culture: A profile comparison approach to person–organization fit. *Academy of Management Journal*, 34 (3), 487–516. Kristof, A. L. (1996). Person–organization fit: An integrative review of its conceptualizations, measurement, and implications. *Personnel Psychology*, 49, 1–49.

8. Ledeen, M. (2002). The real Bobby Knight. *American Enterprise*, 7, 24–27.

9. Breaugh, J. A., and Starke, M. (2000). Research on employee recruitment: So many studies, so many remaining questions. *Journal of Management*, 26 (3), 405–434.

10. Ibid.

11. Ibid.

12. Combs, J., Liu, Y., Hall, A., and Ketchen, D. (2006). How much do high-performance work practices matter? A meta-analysis of their effects on organizational performance. *Personnel Psychology*, 59, 501–528.

13. Zottoli, M. A., and Wanous, J. P. (2000). Recruitment source research: Current status and future directions. *Human Resource Management Review*, 10, 353–382.

14. Breaugh, J. A., and Starke, M. (2000). Research on employee recruitment: So many studies, so many remaining questions. *Journal of Management*, 26 (3), 405–434.

15. Martinez, M. H. (2001). The headhunter within. *HR Magazine*, 46, 48–56.

16. Allen, D., Mahto, R., and Otondo, R. (2007). Web-based recruitment: Effects of information, organizational brand, and attitudes toward a web site on applicant attraction. *Journal of Applied Psychology*, 92, 1696–1708.

17. Van Hoye, G., and Lievens, F. (2007). Investigating web-based recruitment sources: Employee testimonials versus word-of-mouse. *International Journal of Selection and Assessment*, 15, 372–382.

18. Roth, P. L., et al. (1996). Meta-analyzing the relationship between grades and job performance. *Journal of Applied Psychology*, 81, 548–556.

19. McKinney, A. P., et al. (2003). Recruiters use of GPA in initial screening decisions. Higher GPAs don't always make the cut. *Personnel Psychology*, 56, 823–845.

20. Ployhart, R. E., Schneider, B., and Schmitt, N. (2006). *Staffing organizations: Contemporary practice and research*. Mahwah, NJ: Lawrence Erlbaum Associates.

21. Avery, D. R., and McKay, P. F. (2006). Target practice: An organizational impression management approach to attracting minority and female job applicants. *Personnel Psychology*, 59, 157–187.

22. Barber, A. E. (1998). *Recruiting employees: Individual and organizational perspectives*. Thousand Oaks, CA: Sage Publications.

23. Brown, B. K., and Campion, M. A. (1994). Biodata phenomenology: Recruiters' perceptions and use of biographical information in resume screening. *Journal of Applied Psychology*, 79, 897–808.

24. Rynes, S. L, Trank, C. Q., Lawson, A. M., and Ilies, R. (2003). Behavioral coursework in business education: Growing evidence of a legitimacy crisis. *Academy of Management Learning & Education*, 2, 269–283.

25. Phillips, J. M. (1998). Effects of realistic job previews on multiple organizational outcomes: A meta-analysis. *Academy of Management Journal*, 41 (6), 673–690.

26. Meglino, B. M., Ravlin, E. C., and DeNisi, A. S. (2000). A meta-analytic examination of realistic job preview effectiveness: A test of three counterintuitive propositions. *Human Resource Management Review*, 10 (4), 407–434.

27. Rynes, S. L., Brown, K. G., and Colbert, A. E. (2002). Seven misconceptions about human resource practices: Research findings versus practitioner beliefs. *Academy of Management Executive*, 16 (3), 92–103. Terpstra, D. E. (1996). The search for effective methods. *HRFocus*, 73, 16–19.

28. Schmidt, F., and Hunter, J. E. (1998). The validity and utility of selection methods in personnel psychology: Practical and theoretical implications of 85 years of research findings. *Psychological Bulletin*, 124 (2), 262–274. Hurtz, G. M., and Donovan, J. J. (2000). Personality and job performance: The big five revisited. *Journal of Applied Psychology*, 85 (6), 869–879.

29. Judge, T. A., Higgins, C. A., and Cable, D. M. (2000). The employment interview: A review of recent research and recommendations for future research. *Human Resource Management Review*, 4, 383–406.

30. Harris, M. M. (1989). Reconsidering the employment interview: A review of recent literature and suggestions for future research. *Personnel Psychology*, 42, 691–726. Judge, T. A., Higgins, C. A., and Cable, D. M. (2000). The employment interview: A review of recent research and recommendations for future research. *Human Resource Management Review*, 4, 383–406.

31. Schmidt, F. L., and Zimmerman, R. D. (2004). A counterintuitive hypothesis about employment interview validity and some supporting evidence. *Journal of Applied Psychology*, 89 (3), 535–561.

32. Van der Zee, K. I., Bakker, A. B., and Bakker, P. (2002). Why are structured interviews so rarely used in personnel selection? *Journal of Applied Psychology*, 87 (1), 176–184.

33. Campion, M. A., Palmer, D. K., and Campion, J. E. (1997). A review of structure in the selection interview. *Personnel Psychology*, 50, 655–702.

34. For grounding in the situational interview, see Latham, G. P., and Saari, L. M. (1984). Do people do what they say? Further studies of the situational interview. *Journal of Applied Psychology*, 69, 569–573. For theory regarding the behavioral interview, see Janz, T. (1989). The patterned behavior description interview: The best prophet of the future is the past. In R. W. Eder and G. R. Ferris (Eds.), *The employment interview: Theory, research and practice* (pp. 158–168). Newberry Park, CA: Sage.

35. Huffcutt, A. I., Weekley, J. A., Wiesner, W. H., and Degroot, T. G. (2001). Comparison of situational and behavior description interview questions for higher-level positions. *Personnel Psychology*, 54, 619–644.

36. Example adapted from Sacco, J. M., Scheu, C. R., Ryan, A. M., and Schmitt, N. (2003). An investigation of race and sex similarity effects in interviews: A multilevel approach to relationship demography. *Journal of Applied Psychology*, 88 (5), 852–865.

37. McDaniel, M. A., Whetzel, D. L., Schmidt, F. L., and Maurer, S. D. (1994). The validity of employment interviews. A comprehensive review and meta-analysis. *Journal of Applied Psychology*, 79, 599–616.

38. Strauss, S. G., Miles, J. A., and Levesque, L. L. (2001). The effects of videoconference, telephone, and face-to-face media on interviewer and applicant judgments in employment interviews. *Journal of Management*, 27, 363–381.

39. Ibid.

40. Rowe, P. M. (1985). Unfavorable information and interview decisions. In R. W. Eder and G. R. Ferris (Eds.), *The employment interview: Theory, research and practice* (pp. 77–89). Newberry Park, CA: Sage.

41. Heilmann, M., and Saruwatari, L. (1979). When beauty is beastly: The effects of appearance and sex on evaluation of job applicants for managerial and nonmanagerial jobs. *Organizational Behavior and Human Performance*, 23, 360–370. Huffcutt, A. I., and Roth, P. (1998). Racial group differences in employment interview evaluations. *Journal of Applied Psychology*, 83 (2), 179–189. Degroot, T., and Motowidlo, S. J. (1999). Why visual and vocal interview cues can affect interviewers' judgments and predicted job performance. *Journal of Applied Psychology*, 84 (6), 968–984.

42. Waldman, D. A., and Kobar, T. (2004). Student assessment center performance in the prediction of early career success. *Academy of Management Learning & Education*, 3 (2), 151–167.

43. Schmidt, F. L., and Hunter, J. (2004). General mental ability in the world of work: Occupational attainment and job performance. *Journal of Personality and Social Psychology*, 86, 162–174.

44. Sackett, P. R., and Ostgaard, D. J. (1994). Job-specific applicant pools and national norms for cognitive ability tests: Implications for range restriction corrections in validation research. *Journal of Applied Psychology*, 79 (5), 680–684.

45. Ryan, A. M., and Ployhart, R. E. (2000). Applicants' perceptions of selection procedures and decisions: A critical review and agenda for the future. *Journal of Management*, 26 (3), 565–606.

46. Rynes, S. L., Brown, K. G., and Colbert, A. E. (2002). Seven common misconceptions about human resources practices: Research findings versus practitioner beliefs. *Academy of Management Executive*, 16 (3), 92–103.

47. Adapted from www.wonderlic.com/promotion/nfl_article.asp.

48. Lyons, B. D., Hoffman, B., and Michel, J. (2009). Not much more than g? An examination of the impact of intelligence on NFL performance. *Human Performance*, 22, 225–245.

49. Ones, D. S., Viswesvaran, C., and Schmidt, F. L. (1993). Comprehensive meta-analysis of integrity test validities: Findings and implications for personnel selection and theories of job performance. *Journal of Applied Psychology*, 78 (4), 679–703.

50. Hurtz, G. M., and Donovan, J. J. (2000). Personality and job performance: The big five revisited. *Journal of Applied Psychology*, 85 (6), 869–879.

51. Morgeson, F. P., Campion, M. A., Dipboye, R. L., Hollenbeck, J. R., Murphy, K., and Schmitt, N. (2007).

Reconsidering the use of personality tests in personnel selection contexts. *Personnel Psychology, 60*, 683–729; Morgeson, F. P., Campion, M. A., Dipboye, R. L., Hollenbeck, J. R., Murphy, K., and Schmitt N. (2007). Are we getting fooled again? Coming to terms with the limitations in the use of personality tests for personnel selection. *Personnel Psychology, 60*, 1029–1049.

52. For MBTI review, see Hess, A. K. (2001). Myers-Briggs Type Indicator Step II (Form Q). *Mental Measurements Yearbook, 15*. For review of the DiSC, see Conoley, C. W., and Castillo, L. (2001). DiSC Classic. *Mental Measurements Yearbook, 16*.

53. Steel, R. P., Griffeth, R. W., and Horn, P. W. (2002). Practical retention policy for the practical manager. *Academy of Management Executive, 16* (2), 149–162.

54. Harrison, D., Virick, M., and Williams, S. (1996). Working without a net: Time, performance, and turnover under maximally contingent rewards. *Journal of Applied Psychology, 81*, 331–345. Trevor, C. O., Gerhart, B., and Boudreau, J. W. (1997). Voluntary turnover and job performance: Curvilinearity and the moderating influences of salary growth and promotions. *Journal of Applied Psychology, 82*, 44–61.

55. Williams, M. L., McDaniel, M. A., and Nguyen, N. T. (2006). A meta-analysis of the antecedents and consequences of pay level satisfaction. *Journal of Applied Psychology, 91*, 392–413.

56. Adapted from Ruiz, G. (2006). UnitedHealth Group. *Workforce Management, 85*, 30. Retrieved from EBSCOhost.

Chapter 13

1. Schein, E. H. (1988). *Process consultation.* Reading, MA: Addison-Wesley.

2. Trice, H. M., and Beyer, J. M. (1984). Studying organizational cultures through rites and ceremonies. *Academy of Management Review, 9*, 653–669; Trice, H., and Beyer, J. M. (1993). *The culture of work organizations.* Englewood Cliffs, NJ: Prentice-Hall.

3. See Quinn, R. E. (1984). Applying the competing values approach to leadership: Toward an integrative framework. In J. G. Hunt, D. M. Hosking, C. A. Schriesheim, and R. Stewart (Eds.), *Leaders and managers: International perspectives on managerial behavior and leadership* (pp. 10–27). New York: Pergamon; Quinn, R. E. (1988). *Beyond rational management: Mastering the paradoxes and competing demands of high performance.* San Francisco: Jossey-Bass; Quinn, R. E., Faerman, S. R., Thompson, M. P., and McGrath, M. R. (1996). *Becoming a master manager: A competency framework.* New York: John Wiley; Quinn, R. E., and Rohrbaugh, J. (1983). A spatial model of effectiveness criteria: Towards a competing values approach to organizational analysis. *Management Science, 29*, 363–377.

4. This Tool Kit is taken from Morgan, S., and Dennehy, R. F. (1997). The power of organizational storytelling: A management development perspective. *Journal of Management Development, 16*, 494–501.

5. Skinner, B. F. (1974). *About behaviorism.* New York: Knopf.

6. Kerr, J., and Slocum, J. W. (1987). Managing corporate culture through reward systems. *Academy of Management Executive, 1*, 99–108.

7. Kerr, J., and Slocum, J. W. (1987). Managing corporate culture through reward systems.

8. Trice, H., and Beyer, J. M. (1993). *The culture of work organizations.* Englewood Cliffs, NJ: Prentice-Hall; O'Reilly, C., and Chatman, J. (1986). Organizational commitment and psychological attachment: The effects of compliance, identification and internalization on prosocial behavior. *Journal of Applied Psychology, 71*, 492–499.

9. Haney, C., Banks, W. C., and Zimbardo, P. G. (1973). Study of prisoners and guards in a simulated prison. *Naval Research Reviews, 9*, 1–17.

10. Schneider, B. (1987). People make the place. *Personnel Psychology, 40*, 437–453.

11. Kristof-Brown, A. L., and Guay, R. P. (2011). Person-environment fit. In S. Zedeck (Ed.), *APA handbook of industrial and organizational psychology* (pp. 3–50). Washington, DC: American Psychological Association.

12. Bauer, T. N., and Erdogan, B. (2011) Organization socialization: The effective onboarding of new employees. In S. Zedeck (Ed.), *APA handbook of industrial and organizational psychology, 51–64.* Washington, DC: American Psychological Association.

13. Hambrick, D. C., Davison, S. C., Snell, S. A., and Snow, C. C. (1998). When groups consist of multiple nationalities: Toward an understanding of the implications. *Organization Studies, 19*, 181–205.

14. Table representation adapted from Geert Hofstede's website: http://www.geerthofstede.nl/index.aspx, as well as http://www.mindtools.com/pages/article/newLDR_66.htm.

15. Adapted from www.articlesbase.com/ethics-articles/creating-an-inclusive-corporate-culture-2355644.html#ixzz0ulJXOCDQ.

16. Grossman, R. J. (2000). Is diversity working? *HR Magazine,* March, 47–50.

17. Ibid.

18. Cox, T., Jr., and Beale, R. (1997). *Developing competency to manage diversity.* San Francisco: Berrett-Koehler Publishers, Inc.

19. Colvin, G. (1999). The 50 best companies for Asians, Blacks, and Hispanics. *Fortune,* July 19, 53–57.

20. Dubrin, A. J. (2001). *Leadership: Research findings, practice, and skills.* Boston: Houghton Mifflin.

21. Hayles, R. V., and Russell, A. M. (1997). *The diversity directive: Why some initiatives fail & what to do about it.* Madison, WI: American Society for Training & Development.

22. Sandlund, C. (1999). There's a new face to America. *Success,* April, 38–45.

23. Colvin, p. 56.

24. Leonard, B. (2001). Diverse workforce tends to attract more female and minority job applicants. *HR Magazine,* April, 27.

25. Colvin, p. 56.
26. Wiethoff, C., and Roberson, Q. (2001). Diversity initiatives and job choice: The mediating role of recruits' perceptions of organizational justice. Working paper, Indiana University–Bloomington.
27. Caldwell, D. F., and Ancona, D. G. (1992). Demography and design: Predictors of new product team performance. *Organization Science*, 3, 321–341; Randel, A. S., and Jaussi, K. S. (2003). Functional background identity, diversity, and individual performance in cross-functional teams. *Academy of Management Journal*, 46, 763–774; van Knippenberg, D., De Dreu, C.K.W., and Homan, A. C. (2004). Work group diversity and group performance: An integrative model and research agenda. *Journal of Applied Psychology*, 89, 1008–1022.
28. Watson, W. E., Kumar, K., and Michaelson, L. K. (1993). Cultural diversity's impact on interaction process and performance: Comparing homogenous and diverse task groups. *Academy of Management Journal*, 36 (3), 590–602.
29. Jehn, K. A., Northcraft, G. B., and Neale, M. A. (1999). Why differences make a difference: A field study of diversity, conflict and performance in workgroups. *Administrative Science Quarterly*, 44, 741–763.
30. Harrison, D. A., Price, K. H., and Bell, M. P. (1998). Beyond relational demography: Time and the effects of surface- and deep-level diversity on work group cohesion. *Academy of Management Journal*, 41 (1), 96–107.
31. Raines, C. (2003). *Connecting generations: The sourcebook for a new generation.* New York: Crisp Publications.
32. Tannen, D. (1990). *You just don't understand: Women and men in conversation.* New York: William Morrow.
33. Boiney, L. G. (2001). Gender impacts virtual work teams. *Graziado School of Business Report, Pepperdine University*, 1 (4).
34. Kraiger, K., and Ford, J. K. (1985). A meta-analysis of race effects in performance ratings. *Journal of Applied Psychology*, 70, 56–65.
35. Pfeffer, J. (1998). *The human equation: Building profits by putting people first.* Boston: Harvard Business School Press.
36. Ibid.
37. Buckingham, M., and Coffman, C. (1999). *First, break all the rules: What the world's greatest managers do differently.* New York: Simon & Schuster.
38. Ibid.
39. Delery, J. E., and Shaw, J. D. (2001). The strategic management of people in work organizations: Review, synthesis, and extension. In G. R. Ferris (Ed.), *Research in personnel and human resources management.* Stamford, CT: JAI Press, 165–197; Evans, W. R., and Davis, W. D. (2005). High-performance work systems and organizational performance: The mediating role of internal social structure. *Journal of Management*, 31, 758–775.
40. Combs, J., Liu, Y., Hall, A., and Ketchen, D. (2006). How much do high-performance work practices matter? A meta-analysis of their effects on organizational performance. *Personnel Psychology*, 59, 501–528.
41. Pfeffer, J. (1998). *The human equation: Building profits by putting people first.* Boston: Harvard Business School Press.
42. Pfeffer, J. (1998). The real keys to high performance. *Leader to Leader*, Spring (8), 23–29.
43. Goldfield, B. (2010). Time for a company culture audit. Retrieved March 1, 2011, from www.entrepreneur.com/humanresources/humanresourceburtongoldfield/article207232.html.

Chapter 14

1. Deutschman, A. (2005). Change or die. *Fast Company*, May, 54–62.
2. Porras, J., and Berg, P. (1978). The impact of organization development. *Academy of Management Review*, 3, 249–266.
3. Katzell, R. A., and Guzzo, R. A. (1983). Psychological approaches to productivity improvement. *American Psychologist*, 38 (4), 468–472.
4. Golembiewski, R., Proehl, C., and Sink, D. (1982). Estimating success of OD applications. *Training and Development Journal*, 72, 86–95.
5. Lewin, K. (1951). *Field theory in social science; selected theoretical papers.* (D. Cartwright, Ed.). New York: Harper & Row.
6. Jick, T. D. (1995). Accelerating change for competitive advantage. *Organizational Dynamics*, 24 (1), 77–82.
7. Kanter, R., Stein, B, and Jick, T. (1992). *The challenge of organizational change: How companies experience it and leaders guide it.* New York: The Free Press.
8. Hannan, M. T., and Freeman, J. (1977). The population ecology of organizations. *American Journal of Sociology*, 82 (5), 929–964.; Romanelli, E., and Tushman, M. (1994). Organizational transformation as punctuated equilibrium: An empirical test. *Academy of Management Journal*, 37 (5), 1141–1166.; Tushman, M., and Anderson, P. (1986). Technological discontinuities and organizational environments. *Administrative Science Quarterly*, 31 (3), 439–465.
9. Bridges, W. (1980). *Transitions: Making sense of life's changes.* New York: Perseus Books.
10. Bridges, W. (2004). *Managing Transitions: Making the Most of Change, 2E.* Reprinted by permission of Da Capo Press, a member of the Perseus Books Group.
11. Kotter, J. (1996). *Leading change.* Boston: Harvard Business School Press.
12. Kotter, J., and Cohen, D. (2002). *The heart of change.* Boston: Harvard Business School Press.
13. Kanter, R., Stein, B. A., and Jick, T. (1994). *The challenge of organizational change.* New York: Free Press.
14. Block, P. (2002). *Flawless consulting: A guide to getting your expertise used.* San Francisco: Jossey-Bass/Pfeiffer.
15. Kanter, R., Stein, B, and Jick, T. (1992). *The challenge of organizational change: How companies experience it and leaders guide it.* New York: The Free Press.

16. Hammonds, K. H. (2001). Leaders for the long haul. *Fast Company,* July, 56–60.

17. Vaill, P. B. (1996). *Learning as a way of being: Strategies for survival in a world of permanent white water.* San Francisco: Jossey-Bass, Inc.

18. Schaffer, R. H. (2002). *High-impact consulting: How clients and consultants can work together to achieve extraordinary results.* San Francisco: Jossey-Bass.

19. Kaplan, R. S. (2005). Add a customer profitability metric to your balanced scorecard. *Balanced Scorecard Report,* 7 (4) (July–August).

20. Golembiewki, R., Proehl, C., and Sink, D. (1982). Estimating success of OD applications. *Training and Development Journal,* 72, 86–95.

21. Schein, E. H. (1999). *Process consultation revisited: Building the helping relationship.* Reading, MA: Addison-Wesley.

22. Cooperrider, D., and Srivasta, S. (1987). Appreciative inquiry in organizational life. In R. Woodman and W. Pasmore (Eds.), *Research in organizational change and development, vol. 1* (pp. 129–169). Greenwich, CT: JAI Press.

23. Ibid.

24. Schwartz, R. (2002). *The skilled facilitator.* San Francisco: Jossey-Bass.

25. Nadler, D. (1977). *Feedback and organization development. Using data-based methods.* Reading, MA: Addison-Wesley.

26. Block, P. (2002). *Flawless consulting: A guide to getting your expertise used.* San Francisco: Jossey-Bass/Pfeiffer.

27. Schaffer, R. H. (2002). *High-impact consulting: How clients and consultants can work together to achieve extraordinary results.* San Francisco: Jossey-Bass.

28. Dalton, C. C., and Gottlieb, L. N. (2003). The concept of readiness to change. *Journal of Advanced Nursing,* 42 (2), 108–117.

29. Cummings, T. G., and Worley, C. G. (1997). *Organization development & change.* (6th ed.). Cincinnati, OH: Southwestern Publishing.

30. Bolman, L., and Deal, T. (1991). *Reframing organizations. Artistry, choice, and leadership.* San Francisco: Jossey-Bass.

31. Cheng, Y. C. (1994). Principal's leadership as a critical indicator of school performance: Evidence from multi-levels of primary schools. *School Effectiveness and School Improvement: An International Journal of Research, Policy, and Practice,* 5 (3), 299–317. Wimpelberg, R. K. (1987). Managerial images and school effectiveness. *Administrators' Notebook,* 32, 1–4.

32. Bolman, L., and Deal, T. (1991). *Reframing organizations. Artistry, choice, and leadership.* San Francisco: Jossey-Bass.

33. Kotter, J. (1996). *Leading change.* Boston: Harvard Business School Press.

34. Kotter, J. P., and Schlesinger, L. A. (1979). Choosing strategies for change. *Harvard Business Review,* 57 (2) (March–April), 106–114.

35. Rubin, R. S., Dierdorff, E. C., Bommer, W. H., and Baldwin, T. T. (2009). Do leaders reap what they sow? Leader and employee outcomes of leader organizational cynicism about change. *The Leadership Quarterly,* 20, 680–688.

36. McClough, A. C., Rogelberg, S. G., Fisher, G. G., and Bachiochi, P. D. (1998). Cynicism and the quality of an individual's contribution to an organizational diagnostic survey. *Organization Development Journal,* 16, 31–41.

37. Block, P. (2002). *Flawless consulting: A guide to getting your expertise used.* San Francisco: Jossey-Bass/Pfeiffer.

38. Katzenbach, J. R., and RCL Team. (1995). *Real change leaders.* New York: Random House.

GLOSSARY

A

ABC method   Prioritization method used to rank job tasks in terms of their importance and urgency.

Abilene Paradox   Paradox through which a particular situation forces a group of people to act in a way that is counter to their actual preferences. It represents the mismanagement of agreement.

Ability   A capacity to successfully perform job tasks.

Absolute subjective assessment   Involves comparing an employee's performance to that of a model or set performance standard.

Accommodation   Conflict style in which individuals neglect their own concerns to satisfy the concerns of others.

Active listening   Communication technique in which an individual confirms his/her understanding of content and feelings of the person speaking.

Activity-based goals   Describe solely the activities by which success will be determined.

Adhocracy   Cultural orientation that values flexibility and an external focus outside of the company.

Adjourning stage   Stage of group development that involves completing a task and disbanding the team.

Adverse impact   Legal term referring to normally unintentional discrimination caused by the use of certain types of selection tests.

Affective commitment   Attitude representing one's emotional attachment to the organization.

After action review   Technique used to learn from a group's successes and failures by thoroughly reviewing the process and outcomes of an exercise or project.

Altruism   Form of organizational citizenship behavior that has the effect of helping a specific other person with an organizationally relevant task or problem.

Analogies   A well-tested technique for improving creative problem solving by helping make the strange familiar or the familiar strange.

Anchoring and adjustment bias   Tendency to use a number or value as a starting point and then adjust future judgments based upon the initial value.

Appraisal support   Feedback that builds one's self-esteem.

Appreciative inquiry   An approach that seeks to identify the unique qualities and special strengths of an organization.

Articulating a vision   Behavior that allows the leader to identify new opportunities for his or her group and talk positively about what that means for them.

Artifacts   Organizational attributes that can be observed, felt, and heard as an individual enters a new culture.

Assertive communication   Clearly and respectfully expressing one's needs to others.

Assessment center   Method for assessing and developing managerial capabilities consisting of a series of behavioral exercises.

Attention   First component of Bandura's observational learning requiring one to focus personal resources on learning.

Attitudes   Appraisals or evaluations of people, objects, or events.

Attraction-selection-attrition (ASA) framework   A framework for understanding how individuals and organizations are attracted to each other based on similar values and goals.

Authority   The rights inherent in a managerial position.

Autonomy   The decisional freedom to select how and when particular tasks are performed.

Availability bias   The tendency for people to base their judgments on information that is readily available or easy to bring to mind.

Avoidance   Conflict style in which individuals circumvent their own concerns or those of the other person.

B

Balanced scorecard   A method for tracking business results across a number of critical areas including financial, customer, internal process, and employee factors.

BATNA (best alternative to a negotiated agreement)   The alternative a person will be left with if he or she cannot reach a negotiated agreement with another party.

Behavioral intentions   The motivation and thoughts that are immediate precursors of a person's actual behavior.

Behavioral interviews   Interview technique that requires candidates to recount actual instances from their past work or relevant experiences relative to the job at hand.

Behaviorally anchored rating scale (BARS)   Performance evaluation technique that compares job behaviors with specific performance statements on a scale from poor to outstanding.

Benchmarking   Technique used to compare one organization's practices with another, usually successful organization's practices.

Best alternative to a negotiated agreement *See* **BATNA.**

Big E evidence   Generalizable knowledge regarding cause-and-effect connections derived from scientific methods.

Big Five   The five basic dimensions of personality, which include extraversion, agreeableness, conscientiousness, emotional stability, and openness to experience. Also known as "Five Factor Model."

Black or white fallacy   The tendency to assume that a solution to a problem is limited to two distinct possibilities.

Boomers   Born between the mid-1940s and early 1960s, Baby Boomers were named as a result of a large increase in the birth rate during this time period—some 4.3 million births per year at the trend's peak.

Bounded rationality   Limiting decision making to simplified solutions that do not represent the full complexity of the problem.

Brainwriting   Technique used to generate solutions to a problem which allows participants time to generate ideas on their own, record them, and then share with the group.

Burnout   A syndrome of emotional exhaustion, depersonalization, and reduced personal accomplishment that employees may experience after prolonged stress.

C

Career orientation   A preference for a specific type of occupation and work context.

Categorical imperative   Kant's central ideal that each person should act on only those principles that she or he would identify as universal laws to be applied to everyone.

Change agent   An individual who possesses knowledge and power to guide and facilitate an organizational change effort.

Choking   Slang term used to describe the observed performance decrements under pressure circumstances.

Civic virtue   Form of organizational citizenship behavior that includes responsible participation in the political life of the organization.

Clan   Cultural orientation that values flexibility and an internal focus of the organization.

Coercive power   Power base that draws upon an individual's ability to control the distribution of undesirable outcomes.

Cognitive ability   The capacity to learn and process cognitive information such as reading comprehension, mathematical patterns, and spatial patterns.

Collaboration   Conflict style in which individuals work to find an alternative that meets all parties' concerns.

Collectivism   Country cultural characteristic that places value on group harmony, cohesiveness, and consensus.

Competition   Conflict style in which individuals pursue their own concerns relatively aggressively, often at the expense of other people's concerns.

Competitive team rewards   Situation in which a team is rewarded based upon each individual's contribution and each member's reward varies according to his individual performance.

Compromise   Conflict style in which individuals pursue a mutually acceptable solution that partially satisfies everyone involved.

Conceptual competencies   Managerial work role requirements that are associated with cognitive processes.

Confirmation bias   Tendency to seek information that verifies past or current beliefs while ignoring information that contradicts past or current beliefs.

Conflict   The process in which one party perceives that its interests are being opposed or negatively affected by another party.

Conformity   Loyal adherence by individuals or group members to group or societal norms.

Conscientiousness   Form of organizational citizenship behavior that includes going well beyond the organization's role requirements, in the areas of attendance, taking breaks, and obeying organizational policies.

Conservation of resources (COR) theory   Theory that stress results from three possible threats to personal resources: (1) the threat of losing a personal resource; (2) the actual net loss of a personal resource; or (3) the lack of resource gain following investment of other personal resources.

Consultative coaching   Approach to employee development that helps an employee develop or solve problems by exploring alternatives and challenging the employee's thinking through asking questions.

Contextual performance   Employee behaviors that contribute to the overall effectiveness of the organization but are not formally required or considered part of an employee's core job tasks.

Contingent punishment   Leader behavior that administers a negative outcome to a subordinate based upon the performance of the subordinate.

Contingent reward behavior   Leader behavior that provides a positive outcome to a subordinate based upon the performance of the subordinate.

Continuance commitment   Attitude representing a decision to remain with an organization because the costs of leaving outweigh the benefits of remaining.

Contracting   A process in which a change agent establishes a relationship with key stakeholders and agrees to the process for change.

Control   The amount of personal discretion and autonomy the person has in doing a job.

Convergent thinking   Group problem solving which is oriented toward deriving the single best answer to a clearly defined question.

Cooperative team rewards   Situation in which a team is rewarded as a group for its successful performance, and each member receives exactly the same reward.

Core job dimensions   The key characteristics of any job: skill variety, task identity, task significance, autonomy, and feedback.

Courtesy   Form of organizational citizenship behavior that includes touching base with those parties whose work would be affected by one's decisions or commitments.

Cultural audit   A tool to evaluate a company's values and practices to ensure they are aligned with their corporate strategy.

D

Daily hassles   Frequent minor annoyances or events that contribute to an individual's overall stress level.

Daily uplifts   Frequent unexpected positive events which can reduce an individual's overall stress level.

Deductive argument   Based on a structure which moves from the general assertion to the specific evidence supporting the assertion.

Deep acting   Coping strategy for emotional labor whereby employees actually try to feel a certain way that is consistent with the emotions that are supposed to be expressed.

Deep-level diversity   Differences among people reflected in underlying attitudes, beliefs, knowledge, skills, and values.

Demands   Physical, intellectual, and emotional requirements of a job.

Deontological   Category of ethical theory that determines the ethics of an act by looking to the process of the decision (the means).

Departmentation   The grouping of resources (including people and technology) into work units.

Dependence   The power attributed to one individual in a relationship when he/she possesses something that another individual desires.

Depersonalization   Emotional component of burnout that results in feeling cynical, psychologically detached, and indifferent to one's work.

Devil's advocate   A person who advocates an opposing or unpopular cause to expose it to a thorough examination.

Diffusion of responsibility   A condition whereby team members feel their personal responsibility is limited because others will step up and act.

Disparate treatment   Legal term referring to intentional discrimination caused by the selection preferences or practices of a manager or organization.

Distributive justice   Perceived fairness of a particular outcome.

Divergent thinking   Involves producing multiple or alternative answers from available information. It requires making unexpected combinations, recognizing links among remotely associated issues, and transforming information into unexpected forms.

Diversity distance   A measure of the cultural heterogeneity of the people in a group.

Doctor–patient consulting model   Approach to consulting whereby the consultant provides both the diagnosis of a problem and the recommended treatment.

Downsizing   Terminating large numbers of employees to recapture losses or gain some form of competitive advantage.

E

Effectiveness   The quality of the results an employee achieves.

Efficiency   Amount of resources dedicated to attaining results.

80/20 rule   This principle states that for many phenomena, 80% of the consequences stem from 20% of the causes.

Emoticons   An evolving set of symbols for expressing emotions in e-mail communications.

Emotional exhaustion   Emotional component of burnout that results in feeling psychologically "drained" or "used up" by the job.

Emotional intelligence   The ability to accurately detect and manage emotional information in oneself and others.

Emotional labor   The process of regulating both feelings and expressions for the benefit of organizational goals.

Emotional support   Support offered via sympathy, listening, and caring for others.

Employee socialization   The process of helping employees quickly adjust to and reinforce the central values the organization espouses.

Equality rule   Process by which resources and rewards are distributed so that each employee gets the same outcome regardless of contributions.

Equifinality   A condition in which different initial conditions lead to similar effects.

Equity   Calculation by employees as to whether their efforts and outcomes are commensurate with others' efforts and outcomes.

Equity rule   Process by which resources and rewards are distributed to employees with respect to their abilities or contributions.

Equity sensitivity   Those high in equity sensitivity are more outcome-oriented and want more than others for the same level of inputs. Those low in equity sensitivity pay more attention to their inputs and are less sensitive to equity issues.

Equity theory   Refers to an individual's perceptions of the fairness of outcomes he/she receives on the job.

ERG theory   Motivational need theory based upon three primary needs: existence, relatedness, and growth.

Escalation of commitment   The phenomenon where people increase their investment in a decision despite new evidence suggesting that the decision was probably wrong. Such investment may include money (known informally as "throwing good money after bad"), time, or other resources.

Ethical commitment   Level of dedication or desire to do what is right even in the face of potentially harmful personal repercussions.

Ethical competency   Skillful consideration of ethics in each stage of the problem-solving process.

Ethical consciousness   The ability to understand the ramifications of choosing less ethical courses of action.

Ethics   The principles, norms, and standards of conduct governing an individual or group.

Ethos   Greek term used to describe the acceptance of a communicator's arguments on the basis of the communicator's perceived competence, ethics, or professional character.

Eustress   Positive, desirable form of stress.

Evidence-based management (EBM)   Process of translating principles based on the best available scientific evidence into organizational practices and making decisions through the conscientious, explicit, and judicious use of such evidence.

Expectancy   The understanding of what performance is desired and the belief that effort will lead to a desired level of performance.

Expectancy theory   The level of an individual's motivation depends on the strength of his/her expectation that work behavior will be valued by others and followed by an outcome that is attractive to the individual.

Expert coaching   Approach to employee development that helps an employee develop or solve problems by dispensing advice, instructing, or prescribing recommendations.

Expert power   Power base that draws upon an individual's special skills or knowledge.

Extinction   The gradual disappearance of a behavior that occurs after the termination of any reinforcement of such behavior.

Extraversion   A personality dimension that characterizes people who tend to be outgoing, talkative, sociable, and assertive.

Extrinsic outcomes   Outcomes obtained from sources external to the individual, including pay and benefits.

F

Face validity   The degree to which a selection method or test is perceived to measure what it intends to measure.

Fairness   When used in a selection context, fairness refers to the degree to which a selection method avoids adverse impact (discrimination).

Family interference with work (FIW)   Experienced when in fulfilling a family role, a work role is neglected.

Feasibility   When used in a selection context, feasibility refers to the degree to which a selection method can reasonably be employed in different situations, and its overall cost.

Feedback   Degree to which individuals receive knowledge of their results from the job itself.

Feminine orientation   Country cultural characteristic that places value on quality of life, warm and personal relationships, and service and care for the weak.

Filter   Selectively listening to some content from a communicator and not to others.

Five S's   A simple, five-step process that can guide an individual preparing a persuasive presentation. The five S's are strategy, structure, support, style, and supplement.

Force field analysis   Lewin's model of systemwide change that helps change agents diagnose the forces that drive and restrain proposed organizational change.

Forced distribution   Evaluation technique that assesses employees based on predetermined evaluation categories and forces employees into these categories to form a desired and fixed distribution.

Forming stage   In this stage of group development, a primary concern is the initial entry of members into a group. Individuals ask questions as they begin to identify with other group members and with the group itself.

Fostering the acceptance of group goals   Behavior on the part of the leader aimed at promoting cooperation among employees and getting them to work together toward a common goal.

Four frames model   An approach to change suggesting that four frames exist in organizations of every kind: structural, human resource, political, and symbolic. The four frames can be respectively likened to factories, families, jungles, and theaters or temples.

Full range of leadership   An approach to leadership using transactional leader behaviors to establish a good relationship and then utilizing transformational leader behaviors to get "performance beyond expectations."

Fundamental attribution error   The tendency of a decision maker to underestimate or largely ignore external factors and overestimate internal factors.

G

Gap analysis   Tool used to evaluate the relationship between an organization's current practices and its desired future practices.

Generation X   Members of Generation X (known as Xers) were born during the mid-1960s through about 1980.

Graphic rating scale   Performance evaluation technique in which managers rate a particular employee behavior on a predetermined graduated scale.

Groupthink   A pattern of faulty decision making that occurs in groups where members seek agreement at the expense of decision quality.

Growth need strength   The need to want to grow or develop in one's job.

H

Half-truths   Practices or concepts that may be true some of the time under some circumstances.

Hasty generalization fallacy   Tendency to draw an inappropriate general conclusion from a single specific case.

Hearing   The physical reality of receiving sounds; it is a passive act that happens even when we are asleep.

Height of an organization   The number of hierarchical levels in an organization.

Hierarchy   Culture that places value on stability and control with an internal focus.

High-performance expectations   Leader behavior that communicates expectations for excellence, quality, and high performance on the part of followers.

High-performance work practices   Management practices associated with sustained performance that exceeds that of its competitors.

Histogram   A graphic bar-chart display of data (on the X axis) tracked against some important standard (on the Y axis).

Hygiene factors   Factors in the work environment that lead to dissatisfaction in one's job.

Hypothetical   A theoretical suggestion or comment that lets you explore creative possibilities with less pressure and helps both parties think through issues they may have not previously considered.

I

Identifiability   A strategy for reducing social loafing by making member contribution to a task explicit.

Individualism   Country cultural characteristic that places value on individual achievement, freedom, and competition.

Inductive argument   Based on a structure which moves from specific evidence to a general assertion supported by the evidence.

Influence   The use of power to affect others.

Influence tactic   Behavior that attempts to alter another individual's attitude or behavior.

Information richness   The potential information-carrying capacity of a communication channel, and the extent to which it facilitates developing a common understanding between people.

Informational support   Support offered in the form of expertise to solve a problem.

Innocent bystander effect   When a person sees others are present, he or she will be more likely not to get involved, assuming that others will take care of the problem. This is the effect caused by a diffusion of responsibility.

Inquiry skills   Skills used to surface others' assumptions by asking questions about a problem.

Instrumental support   Support that is tangible and practical in nature and a direct means of helping someone.

Instrumentality   An individual's subjective belief about the likelihood that performing a behavior will result in a particular outcome.

Integrity   The adherence to an ethical code or standard.

Integrity tests   Tests designed to predict applicant deviant behaviors on the job.

Intellectual stimulation   Leader behavior that challenges followers to reexamine assumptions about their work and rethink how it can be performed.

Interactional justice   Perceived fairness of interpersonal treatment and informational adequacy.

Interpersonal competencies   Managerial work role requirements that are associated with interacting, influencing, and leading others.

Intrinsic outcomes   Outcomes that stem from sources internal to the individual, including a sense of accomplishment and satisfaction.

Introversion   A personality dimension that characterizes people who tend to be quiet and solitary.

Intuition   A sense of something not evident or deducible; an impression or gut feeling.

Involuntary turnover   Separation that is initiated by an organization.

J

Jargon   Technical language and acronyms as well as recognized words with specialized meaning in specific organizations or groups.

Job analysis   The process of collecting information about the tasks, knowledge, skills, and abilities required for a job.

Job characteristics model (JCM)   Description of the potential motivation level inherent in various jobs.

Job performance   Degree to which the enactment of one's work role contributes to a group or organization achieving its desired outcomes.

Job satisfaction   Appraisal of how one feels about all aspects of a particular job.

K

Kotter's change model   An eight-step framework that is a useful way to think about the critical elements necessary to create successful change interventions. (Increase urgency, create a guiding coalition, get the vision right, communicate for buy-in, empower action, create short-term wins, consolidate gains and don't let up, anchor change in your culture.)

L

Ladder of inference   A common mental pathway in which people observe events or information and ultimately form misguided beliefs based upon their perception of the events or information.

Lag measures   Provide information about performance that has already occurred; most financial measures are lag measures.

Lead measures   Do not guarantee future profitability, but these measures are used to predict success in the future.

Leader-member exchange (LMX)   Refers to the quality of the relationship between a manager and his or her subordinate.

Leadership   The ability to influence people to set aside their personal concerns and support a larger agenda.

Leadership emergence   The perception of leadership accorded to individuals, usually in group settings where no formal leader has been appointed.

Legitimate power   Power base that relies on a position in the formal hierarchy of an organization.

Listening   An active process that means a conscious effort to hear and understand. To listen, we must not only hear but also pay attention, understand, and assimilate.

Little e evidence   Context-specific knowledge based on local data collection efforts to inform a specific decision.

Locus of control   Extent to which we believe we control our own environments and lives.

Logos   Greek term for logical arguments presented by a speaker, including facts, figures, and other forms of persuasion.

Long-term orientation (LTO)   Derives from values that include saving and persistence in achieving goals.

M

Market   Culture that places value on control and stability, with a focus outside of the organization.

Masculine orientation   Cultural orientation that values assertiveness, performance, success, and competition, and is results-oriented.

Maslow's hierarchy of needs   Depiction of five basic needs that motivate behavior arranged in a hierarchy from lower order (physiological) to highest order (self-actualization).

Mental models   The broad worldviews that people rely on to guide their perceptions and behaviors.

Mentor   A more experienced person who provides assistance and guidance as part of a long-term relationship.

Mentoring   An intense, long-term relationship between a more experienced individual (mentor) and a less experienced individual (protégé).

Millennials   Born in the early 1980s through the turn of the century, Millennials are the first generation to be truly surrounded by technology and a media-driven world.

Mixed-motive situation   Situation in which an individual is motivated to both compete and cooperate.

Model of transitions   A change model that depicts individuals experiencing three stages of transition while undergoing change: endings, neutral zones, and beginnings.

Modeling   Learning by imitating the behavior of others.

Moral imagination   Ability to cognitively remove oneself from a problem and see the possible ethical problems present, imagine other possibilities and alternatives, and evaluate new possibilities.

Moral intensity   The degree to which an issue demands the application of ethical principles.

Motivating force   In expectancy theory, the total drive toward action that a person experiences. Consists of the multiplicative product of expectancy, instrumentality, and valence. Generally represented by the formula MF = E × I × V.

Motivation   Psychological factors that determine the direction of an individual's behavior, effort, and persistence.

Motivation factors   Factors in the work environment that lead to satisfaction in one's job.

Motivation potential score (MPS)   Predictive index suggesting the motivating potential in a job, derived from the job characteristics model.

Multisource feedback   Feedback provided by many sources other than one's self, such as from a boss, co-worker, customer, or subordinate.

N

Need for achievement   Degree to which an individual has a desire to achieve, in relation to a set of standards and will to succeed.

Need for affiliation   Degree to which an individual has a desire for friendly and close interpersonal relationships.

Need for power   Degree to which an individual has a desire to influence or control other people.

Need rule   Process by which resources and rewards are distributed to an employee or employees who need them most.

Negative reinforcement   Eliminating an undesirable outcome when an individual performs a desired behavior.

Normative commitment   Attitude representing the degree to which an employee desires to stay with the organization out of feelings of obligation.

Norming stage   The point at which the group begins to come together as a coordinated unit.

Norms   The informal rules and expectations that groups establish to regulate the behavior of their members.

O

Objective assessment   Evaluation technique based on results or impartial performance outcomes that are easily identifiable, representing employee output that is visible and/or countable.

Operant conditioning   The process of learning that links desired consequences to desired behaviors.

Organization culture   A shared way of being, acting, and interpreting life in the company.

Organizational behavior (OB)   Social science that attempts to describe, explain, and predict human behavior in an organizational context.

Organizational behavior modification   An application of reinforcement theory to increasing an individual's motivation and performance.

Organizational citizenship behavior (OCB)   Discretionary behaviors beneficial to the organization but that are not explicitly recognized by the formal reward system.

Organizational commitment   Extent to which an employee identifies with his organization and desires to remain a member of the organization.

Organizational cynicism   A feeling of distrust toward an organization. Usually associated with prior misdeeds by the organization whereby the trust of the employees has been undermined.

Organizational development   A systemwide strategy intended to change the beliefs, attitudes, values, and structure of organizations so that they can better adapt to new technologies, markets, and challenges.

Organizational structure   The work roles and authority relationships in an organization.

Outcome-based goals   Describe the specific results by which success will be determined.

Overconfidence bias   Tendency to be overly optimistic or confident in one's decisions.

P

PADIL   Acronym to describe the five key steps in the problem-solving process: problem, alternatives, decide, implement, and learn.

Pair of hands consulting model   Approach to consulting whereby the consultant is given the diagnoses and solution to a problem and is hired to implement the solution.

Pareto efficient   Represents an outcome in which no other possible agreement results in both parties being better off.

Pathos   Greek term for appeals that rely on emotion to persuade.

Performance management cycle (PMC)   The key steps involved in managing employee performance: selecting, assessing, and managing performance.

Performance tests   Employment tests designed specifically to measure hands-on skills that are highly predictive of future job performance.

Performing stage   The emergence of a mature, organized, and well-functioning team.

Personality   Set of characteristics possessed by an individual that may have unique influence on one's cognition, motivation, and/or behavior.

Personality assessments   Category of tests used to gauge various aspects of an individual's personality (see personality).

Personality preferences   Choices we make, mostly unconsciously, to navigate the world.

Person–organization fit   The extent to which a person's values, personality, and work needs are aligned with an organization's culture.

Platinum rule   Variant of the golden rule: treat others how *they* wish to be treated.

Political skills   Skills associated with the effective influence of others to act in ways that enhance one's personal and/or organizational objectives.

Positive reinforcement   Providing a desirable outcome for an individual who performs a desired behavior.

Positive self-talk   A self-management tool intended to create a frame of mind that energizes your self-confidence and gets you beyond self-defeating and negative feelings that can accompany learning difficult tasks.

Power   The capacity of a person, team, or organization to influence others.

Power bases   The sources of power an individual may rely upon for influence including, but not limited to, reward, legitimate, referent, expert, and coercive power.

Power distance   The worldview that values economic and social differences in wealth, status, and well-being as natural and normal.

Procedural justice   Perceived fairness of a particular process.

Process consultation consulting model   Approach to consulting whereby the consultant serves as a facilitator of the problem-solving process.

Professionalism   A level of behavior that is consistent with the current standards and practices of individuals in organizations.

Progressive discipline   Process of using increasingly stringent measures when an employee fails to correct a problem after being given a reasonable opportunity to do so.

Protégé   A junior, less experienced person in an organization that forms a relationship with a mentor.

Providing an appropriate model   Behavior on the part of the leader that sets an example for employees to follow that is consistent with the values the leader or the organization espouses.

Providing individualized support   Behavior that indicates the leader respects followers and is concerned about their personal feelings and needs.

Prudence   The practical wisdom to make the right choice at the right time.

Psychological hardiness   The ability to remain psychologically stable and healthy in the face of significant stress.

Psychological reactance   Phenomenon that when a person's choice is limited or threatened, the need to retain freedom makes the person want that option more than if the choice had not been limited or threatened in the first place.

Psychological states   The personal states experienced by an individual that are employed in the job characteristics model.

Punishment   Providing an undesirable outcome for an individual who performs an undesired behavior.

Pygmalion effect   Based on the premise that we form expectations of others and then communicate those expectations through our behavior, and as a result people tend to respond to our behavior by adjusting their behavior to match our expectations. This is also called a self-fulfilling prophecy.

R

Ranking   A relative standards evaluation technique involving a simple listing of employees from best to worst.

Realistic job preview (RJP)   Presentation to applicant regarding both the positive and negative aspects of a job.

Reciprocal determinism   In Bandura's social learning theory any new behavior is the result of three main factors—the person, the environment, and the behavior—and they all influence each other.

Reduced personal accomplishment   Feeling that one's work doesn't really matter.

Referent power   Power base that relies on the possession by an individual of desirable resources or personal traits.

Reframing   To explore organizational issues through multiple lenses or frames and to use those frames to uncover new opportunities and options in confusing or ambiguous situations.

Reinforcement theory   Set of principles based on the notion that behavior is a function of its consequences.

Relationship conflict   Conflict that arises from incompatible or strained personal interactions.

Relative subjective assessment   Performance evaluation technique that compares an employee's performance against another employee's performance.

Representative bias   Tendency to classify something or someone according to how similar it is to a typical case or to previous situations in the past.

Reproduction   Component of Bandura's observational learning requiring one to practice or rehearse observed behavior.

Reversing the problem   In problem solving, this refers to the process of turning a problem around to try to come up with creative solutions. An example would be rather than looking at why some people are getting ill, look at why most people are staying healthy.

Reward   A thing given in recognition of service, effort, or achievement.

Reward power   Power base that relies on the ability to distribute rewards that others view as valuable.

Ringelmann effect   Describes the situation in which some people do not work as hard in groups as they do individually.

Risky shift   Phenomenon that groups tend to make riskier decisions than the average of each group member's risk propensity would suggest.

Role ambiguity   Uncertainty about what the organization expects from an employee in terms of the central job requirements.

Role clarity   The degree to which employees understand their job requirements.

Role conflict   An employee's recognition that the demands of the job are incompatible or contradictory.

Role theory   Perspective that individuals create their own unique role in accomplishing work requirements.

S

Satisficing   Settling for the first alternative that meets some minimum level of acceptability.

Self-efficacy   Individual's assessment of how well one can execute courses of action required to deal with prospective situations.

Self-limiting behavior   Behavior in which a team member chooses to limit his or her involvement in the team's work.

Self-management   The ability to manage one's own, behavior, cognitions, emotions, and impulses.

Self-observation   The ability to determine when, why, and under what conditions an individual should engage in certain behaviors.

Self-serving bias   Tendency of an individual to attribute favorable outcomes to his/her internal factors and failures to his/her external factors.

Short-term orientation (STO)   Reflects values such as a concern for happiness or stability and living for the present.

Situational interview   Interview technique that requires candidates indicate how they would respond to various hypothetical job scenarios.

Skill variety   Range in number of skills used to complete the job tasks.

Small wins   Small but meaningful milestones in order to build self-confidence in completing a large task.

SMART goals   Effective goals whose key characteristics are represented by the acronym SMART: specific, measurable, attainable, relevant, and time-bound.

Social conformity   Involves social pressures to conform to the perceived wishes of the group.

Social contracting   A strategy for trying to actively reduce loafing by addressing the issue before it happens. Before a goal gets set, a task assigned, or work divided, the team might discuss and agree upon the consequences for members who do not pull their own weight.

Social facilitation   The process of individual motivation and performance being enhanced by the presence of others.

Social influence   The ability to influence others without formal authority.

Social influence weapons   Set of influence tactics described by Cialdini which include friendship/liking, commitment and consistency, scarcity, reciprocity, social proof, and appeals to authority.

Social learning theory   Perspective that people learn the best through direct observation and experience.

Social loafing   A situation in which people exert less effort when working in groups than when working alone.

Social network   An extended group of people with similar concerns who rely on each other for advice and support and share resources that benefit those involved.

Span of control   The number of people that report directly to a single manager.

Sportsmanship   Form of organizational citizenship behavior that includes an individual's willingness to tolerate less-than-ideal situations by not filing petty grievances or complaining about minor issues.

Stakeholders   Shareholders, customers, suppliers, governments, and any other groups with a vested interest in the organization or problem.

Storming stage   This is a period of high emotion and tension among the members while the group is still in its relatively early stages of development. Hostility and infighting between members may occur, and the group typically experiences some changes.

Strains   Physical and psychological outcomes of stress.

Stress   An individual's response to a situation that is perceived as challenging or threatening to the person's well-being.

Strong culture   A culture where there is relatively little variance in the way people think and behave within the organization.

Strong ties   Direct personal connections between people.

Structured interview   Interview technique in which interviewers ask the same set of predetermined questions to all job applicants.

Subdivision   The process of breaking things, such as problems, products, or services, into their smallest component parts or attributes.

Subjective assessment   Performance evaluation methods that involve human judgments of performance.

Suboptimization   The pursuit of goals that ignores other important objectives (not formally covered by goals) and that may do things outside the spirit of the goals, even unethical behavior, to achieve the goals.

Superordinate goal   A common objective that transcends individuals' needs and can serve as a unifying purpose.

Surface acting   Coping strategy for emotional labor whereby employees actively manage observable expressions.

Surface-level diversity   Differences among people that are easily seen and generally verifiable via a quick assessment of physical characteristics, including gender, age, race, and national origin/ethnicity.

Swiss Cheese Method   Refers to poking small holes in important projects. In this way, work is being accomplished toward the larger objective and progress is being made.

System   A perceived whole whose elements hang together because they continually affect each other over time and operate toward a common purpose.

Systemic structure   A pattern of interrelationships among the system components that sustains behavior.

T

Task conflict   Conflict that arises from disagreements of ideas or project content.

Task identity   Degree to which the job requires completion of a whole or identifiable piece of work.

Task performance   Performance outcomes related to the core substantive or technical tasks that are essential to any job.

Task significance   Degree to which the job has a direct effect on the work or lives of other people.

Team   A group of two or more people who have a high degree of interaction and interdependence and are mutually accountable for achieving common objectives.

Technical/administrative competencies   Managerial work role requirements that are associated with the traditional functions of business.

Teleological   Category of ethical theory that determines the ethics of an act by looking to the probable outcome or consequences of the decision (the ends).

Topgrading   *See* **Forced distribution.**

Traditionalists   Born between 1922 and 1943, the Traditionalists entered the workforce in the mid-1940s and 1950s. Often referred to as "the greatest generation" because of their survival and ingenuity during the years of the Depression and World War II, these workers tend to embrace strong work-ethic values.

Transactional leadership   Leadership behaviors based on exchange that motivate followers to achieve by rewarding them for good performance and reprimanding them for poor performance.

Transactional theory   Theory which suggests that the negative effects of stress on a person are a function of the *interaction* between the person and his or her environment.

Transformational leadership   Leadership behaviors based on appealing to higher-level needs that motivate followers to achieve beyond expectations by inspiring them to transcend personal interests.

Type A behavior   Individuals who experience a chronic struggle to obtain an unlimited number of things from their environment in the shortest period of time and, if necessary, against the opposing effects of other things or persons in this same environment.

U

Uncertainty avoidance   Country cultural characteristic that places little value in risk taking.

Underlying assumptions   Phenomena that remain unexplained when insiders are asked about the values of the organizational culture.

Unfreeze-change-refreeze model   Unfreezing is the first part of the change process whereby the change agent produces disequilibrium between the driving and restraining forces. Change refers to when the change intervention is started and ongoing. Refreezing is the latter part of the change process in which systems and conditions are introduced that reinforce and maintain the desired behaviors.

Universalism   Ethical theory that directs us to make decisions based upon the consideration of whether the decision would be acceptable if everyone in every situation made the same decision.

Unstructured interview   Interview technique in which the interviewer and applicant have an unscripted conversation.

Utilitarianism   Ethical theory that directs us to make decisions based upon the greatest "good" for the greatest number.

V

Valence   The value an individual places on received outcomes.

Validity   The statistical relationship between a predictor and criterion.

Value system   An individual's values arranged in a hierarchy of preferences.

Values   In cultural terms, these are espoused goals, ideals, norms, standards, and moral principles, and are usually the level that is measured through survey questionnaires

Virtual teams   Teams with members who do not meet in face-to-face settings and are typically geographically dispersed.

Virtue ethics Ethical theory that directs us to make decisions based upon an individual's core principles or motivations.

Voluntary turnover Separation that is initiated by an employee.

W

Weak culture A culture where there is a great deal of variance in the way people think and behave within the organization.

Weak ties Indirect personal connections between people. An example would be a "friend of a friend."

Whistle-blowing The act of exposing unethical or illegal activities to the public.

Win–lose negotiation Negotiation approach in which an individual seeks to win the negotiation, thereby causing the other party to lose.

Win–win negotiation Negotiation approach in which an individual works to seek a mutually acceptable solution to the conflict.

Withdrawal behaviors Set of behaviors involving avoiding or leaving the work situation altogether.

Work–family conflict A form of inter-role conflict in which the role pressures from the work and family domains are mutually incompatible in some respect.

Work interference with family (WIF) Occurs when in fulfilling their work roles, people are unable to fulfill their family roles in the way that they want.

Work sample Employment test whereby an applicant performs an actual component of the job for which he/she has applied.

Z

Zero-sum game Describes a situation in which a person's gain or loss is exactly balanced by the losses or gains of the other people. It is so named because when the total gains of the people are added up, and the total losses are subtracted, they will sum to zero.

NAME INDEX

SUBJECT INDEX